LEGO® HEAVY WEAPONS

LEGO® HEAVY WEAPONS

Build Working Replicas of Four of the World's Most Impressive Guns

jack streat

LEGO® Heavy Weapons.

First printing

16 15 14 13 12 1 2 3 4 5 6 7 8 9

ISBN-10: 1-59327-412-2
ISBN-13: 978-1-59327-412-2

Publisher: William Pollock
Cover Design: Eric Leisy
Cover Renders: Eric "Blakbird" Albrecht
Production Editor: Riley Hoffman
Developmental Editor: Tyler Ortman
Technical Reviewer: Mark Bassett
Copyeditor: Serena Yang
Compositor: Susan Glinert Stevens
Proofreaders: Serena Yang and Riley Hoffman

For information on book distributors or translations, please contact No Starch Press, Inc. directly:
No Starch Press, Inc.
38 Ringold Street, San Francisco, CA 94103
phone: 415.863.9900; fax: 415.863.9950; info@nostarch.com; www.nostarch.com

Library of Congress Cataloging-in-Publication Data

Streat, Jack.
LEGO heavy weapons : build working replicas of four of the world's most impressive guns / by Jack Streat.
p. cm.
ISBN-13: 978-1-59327-412-2
ISBN-10: 1-59327-412-2
1. Firearms--Models. 2. LEGO toys. 3. Toy guns. 4. War toys. I. Title.
UD380.S78 2012
623.4022'8--dc23

2012012644

WARNING

These models are not suitable for children under the age of 12, and adult supervision is required. Most of these guns really shoot bricks. When building or firing them, always wear eye protection.

For maximum safety when carrying these models, the hammer and bolt should both be forward and the chamber empty. The replicas may fire when dropped or hit.

Be particularly careful when handling these models in public because they have been mistaken for real weapons. If you take your LEGO gun out in public, add a bright orange tip to the muzzle as a way of saying that it's not the real thing.

ACKNOWLEDGMENTS

Although a lot of hard work went into making this book, it was by no means mine alone. In fact, I think I may well have done less actual "work" than everyone else involved. I mostly did just the fun bits: building the models in real life and then rebuilding them on the computer.

First of all, thanks to my parents, who bought me LEGO sets on my birthdays and kept up my enthusiasm for it all, and to my sister for putting up with the endless mealtime conversations about it. Thanks to MOCpages and YouTube for allowing me to post my creations and receive feedback from all over the world. The revenue service provided by YouTube also helped provide funds for *even more* LEGO pieces, because you can never have enough.

More thanks to anyone and everyone who watched my videos and read through the rambling descriptions. I would have never gained the attention of No Starch Press without their interest and support. The community of enthusiasts who created the LDraw platform and all its related programs deserve a huge round of applause as well.

I am very much indebted to The LEGO Group, of course, and I am extremely grateful to No Starch Press and my test builders, who saved me from the most irritating predicament of all: having sets of garbled building instructions useful only to myself.

BRIEF CONTENTS

CONTENTS IN DETAIL

INTRODUCTION

LEGO bricks are one of the most popular toys on the market today, and for good reason. While many toys restrict their use to a particular kind of play, LEGO allows almost infinite freedom. The best part of playing with LEGO pieces is creation itself: anticipating what the final result will look like, how it's going to work, and even *whether* it will work. And although a completed LEGO model is similar to a fixed-role toy, it can be redesigned at any time.

The range of things that can be built with LEGO pieces is boundless. A quick search on the Internet will find incredible creations of all shapes, sizes, colors, and themes. Builders and communities specialize in spacecraft, cars, abstract art, vignettes, dioramas, architecture . . . the list goes on. Many models aren't actually meant to be toys, either. A huge community of adult builders create masterpieces that are more like works of art than toys, and they probably wouldn't let a child near their models for fear of it all ending in little bits all over the floor.

This book explores the possibility of replicating real, existing weaponry. Some might question whether such a peaceful toy should be associated with violence, but in reality there are so many children who have already managed to do so without my help that it's sort of a moot point.

I'll be the first to admit that these guns are not perfect replicas, but building a working gun from LEGO pieces requires some sacrifices in terms of aesthetics. Obviously, designers of real weapons don't have to take into account the strength and structural rigidity of LEGO pieces when creating guns, but I had to make sure that the mechanism would fit inside the gun and that the gun wouldn't fall apart at the drop of a hat. My modifications may make a model less realistic, but now it won't smash apart if you accidentally bang it against a wall during a commando roll through the kitchen. Not that you would do that, of course. Kitchens aren't really the place for that sort of thing.

MY DESIGN METHODS

My general method of building a gun is to finish the magazine first (and I usually make two of them) and then build the rest of the gun around it.

And really, much of the time spent "building" is spent sitting on a floor littered with bricks and thinking, or simply crawling all over the place trying to find that one piece I saw fifteen times when I didn't need it. I'd estimate that the time spent thinking about a model versus the time spent actually connecting bricks is about 1 to 1.

NOTE: *Different people design using different methods, so don't think you're doing things wrong if you want to do it your own way. As long as your final creation does what you want it to, there's no* wrong *way to design.*

PRINT A REFERENCE

One of the easiest ways to build an accurate model is to work from a scaled picture of it. Because my main goal was to create replicas that worked and actually looked like their real counterparts, I always used a scale of 1:1.

Creating printouts is very simple. Find a profile picture of the weapon in question and research its exact length. Make sure this is the measurement you want. (Which generation of the gun is this measurement from? Is the stock folded or unfolded?) Scale your image so it'll print life-size. If necessary, crop it into sections, print them out separately, and then tape them together. Now you have the correct silhouette of the gun and a guide to its components.

MODULAR BUILDING

When I first started building weapons, I built them in the same way you might build a house: with strong joins and as one big unit. However, while you're unlikely to want to dismantle a house, LEGO guns in the design stage require regular disassembly, modification, and reassembly.

I found this out the hard way while designing a Heckler and Koch MP5 replica, a rubber band gun designed to change between semi- and fully automatic depending on how far the trigger was pulled. The mechanism seemed perfectly functional when I visualized it in my head, but after I finished and tested the model, there were several things I wanted to change, including the gear ratio inside the gun (to speed up the firing rate). But because I'd built the gun so solidly, the only way to get inside the gun to fix it was to break apart the whole thing!

The moral of the story is to use a *modular* building technique: Design the model so that you can dismantle it quickly and easily into its main components, almost like field stripping a real weapon. You can, for example, independently remove all the modules of the Jungle Carbine (stock, barrel, bolt, trigger mechanism, and hammer) by removing a few locking plate modules and then taking off one of the frame walls.

WHICH BRICKS TO USE?

Different LEGO pieces are suitable for different purposes. Take, for example, the barrel module of any of the guns in this book. Even though I could have built the walls from studded bricks, I chose to use studless beams instead because they're more versatile than bricks and also slightly slimmer. You'd still describe them as being 1 stud wide, but using a beam instead of a brick can be the difference between a bullet smoothly gliding down the barrel and a bullet getting jammed halfway because the barrel walls were slightly too close together.

These simplified barrel designs show how beams are ever-so-slightly thinner than bricks, allowing for the travel of a 1×4 bullet.

Aesthetics can also play a major role in the success of a model, and to get that sturdy look, you need solid bricks. When building weapons I suggest using classic LEGO studded bricks to form the frame and beams to create the internal modules. Integrate a few Technic bricks (the ones with the pin holes in the side) into the frame, and then you can connect the frame to the internal modules with Technic pins. To make your frame truly solid, you can also use beams as vertical reinforcements in order to clamp the studded bricks together.

Vertical reinforcing beams can dramatically increase the structural integrity of a model.

LEGO CAD SOFTWARE

If it weren't for all the hardworking programmers who created a set of completely free CAD (computer-aided design) programs for LEGO enthusiasts, this book would have been almost impossible to make. The LDraw platform and its related programs (MLCad, LPub, and LDView) were utterly indispensable in creating the instructions you're about to read. The LEGO Group also released its own CAD software (called LEGO Digital Designer, or LDD), but the two programs work in slightly different ways.

Essentially, when you add a part in LDD, its position is relatively determined by the connections made between pieces. The downfall of LDD, though, is that many model builders (myself included) slightly stress some pieces and joints in order to get them to fit together. I have found this technique especially useful when, for example, attaching pistol grips to frames, as the extra stress creates a more solid, inflexible joint. The problem is that if a joint is stressed, it's *technically* not a joint, so LDD can't recognize it—at all.

In contrast, MLCad (the main CAD program for the LDraw platform) simply remembers the position of each piece by a set of 3D coordinates and a few rotation values, which not only makes the program much faster to run, but also allows for stressed joints. The program doesn't even complain when you make pieces overlap each other. MLCad also has a much larger library of pieces, allows the addition of nontraditional pieces like rubber bands, and uses, in my opinion, a more precise way of viewing the model as you're creating it: three orthographic views plus a fourth, non-perspective 3D view, as opposed to the single, perspective 3D view used by LDD.

The quid pro quo for the benefits of MLCad is that there's a lot more work involved in creating instructions. LDD has a simple button that will automatically generate instructions totally from scratch, whereas in MLCad you essentially have to plan the instructions

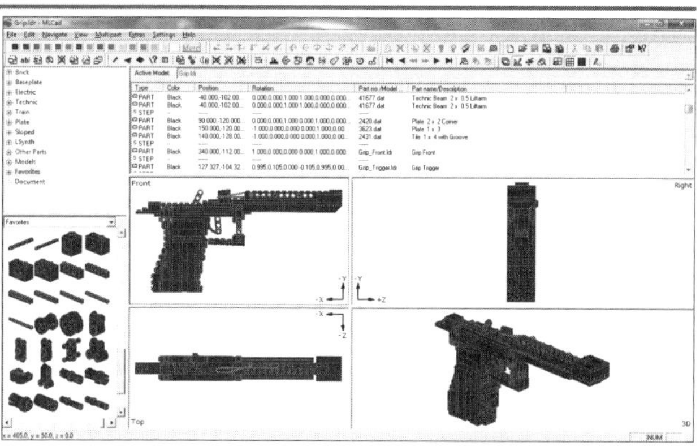

Step 1: Model your creation in MLCad (include step instructions and improve the general flow by using submodels).

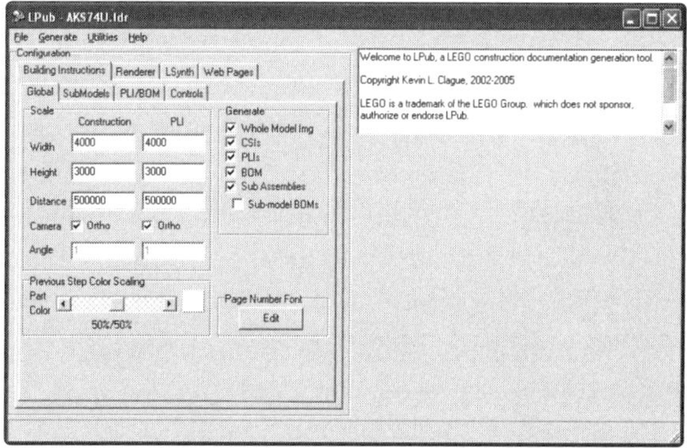

Step 2: Open the files in LPub and choose the settings you need. (I used a very high-quality setting so the instructions would look good in print.)

Step 3: Wait for POV-Ray to generate your instructions (here, it's rendering one of the AKS-74U images). This may take a while depending on your quality settings, but once the instructions are done, you have a set of easily understandable, professional instructions that could have come straight out of an official LEGO set!

out in your head and tell the computer which pieces are added in which steps.

To create the instructions for this book, I needed to build the physical model first and then separate it into its individual modules. After modeling each module in its own MLCad file (which included the information used to work out which pieces were added in which step), I created a final MLCad file in which the "pieces" in the file were the modules themselves. Modular building helped me out yet again, since it allowed me to model in discrete chunks, which made it easier to work out the order of each step. I often had modules made of other modules! I added rubber bands using an add-on called LSynth and then used LDView to get a slightly more realistic real-time view of the model as I worked, in order to check that everything fit together properly.

Once the files were finished, I imported the main file (along with all the subfiles) into LPub, a program that takes the step order information in the files to create separate 3D models of each step. It automatically exported these to a program called POV-Ray (Persistence of Vision Raytracer), which then rendered each instruction image, the parts lists for each step, and a final Bill of Materials (BOM) for the whole model. It turned out that some of the instruction files were too complicated for the BOM-generating part of the software (for example, the stock section of the AKS-74U, which had a lot of steps that involved moving pieces instead of adding them), so I had to write a program of my own that would generate a separate BOM once POV-Ray had finished. From here, the models went to the page design program of my publisher (Adobe InDesign).

This sounds complicated, but once I got into the rhythm of it all, it turned out to be quite simple, though time consuming. If you're looking to create your own instructions, there's a lot of helpful material on the Internet. Some of the particular lines of code that can be implemented in MLCad files (buffer exchanges, rotation steps, etc.) need a bit of thinking and experimentation before they work perfectly, but once you get the hang of it, you'll find yourself with an incredibly powerful array of programs at your fingertips, just waiting to be explored.

BUYING BRICKS

As you may have noticed, LEGO bricks can be a fairly expensive commodity. They are even more expensive when bought from the LEGO Group directly, because when you buy a LEGO set, you're not just buying pieces, but also a lot of hard work that went into creating the model. Consequently, LEGO builders have created their own, less expensive system of buying bricks: BrickLink (*http://bricklink.com/*). Essentially an online marketplace specifically for LEGO bricks, it's very useful when you know the exact pieces you need, how many of them, and in which color.

I obtained most of my LEGO pieces either in sets or in bulk, but I also acquired random lots of pieces on eBay and used BrickLink a few times. I found BrickLink a lot easier (and certainly cheaper) than the other methods and wholeheartedly recommend it.

Each model in this book lists its BOM before the building instructions begin. It gives the part name of each piece (e.g., 2780), its color, and the number needed in the model. In the Desert Eagle, there are a couple of pieces that need to be modified; I recommend doing this with a sharp, nonserrated knife.

USING THE INSTRUCTIONS

The first thing to know is that these are *very complex builds*. You're going to need a lot of pieces, a lot of spare time, and a decent amount of building experience to get these models working properly.

Remember, nobody expects you to sit down one morning, have an entirely problem-free build, and then reappear that night with a finished, beautiful model, whether you're designing it yourself or building from instructions. Experience counts for a lot, as does the ability to visualize how moving parts are going to relate to each other.

As long as you follow the instructions correctly, your models will function perfectly. But you will need to change the rubber bands every now and then when they wear out. There are also a few things I'd like to point out before we begin.

COLOR SCALING

I've used color scaling throughout the instructions. Essentially, all new pieces are rendered in their correct colors, while any pieces added in previous steps are rendered with all their colors 50 percent lighter. This makes the new pieces much easier to locate.

Color scaling highlights the bricks that are added in the current step (an inverted slope brick and two plates), while greying out the bricks that were added in previous steps.

There is, however, one slight hiccup, involving grey pieces. Color scaling makes an old black piece look grey. It also makes an old grey piece look grey and a *new* grey piece look grey. This can lead to some confusion.

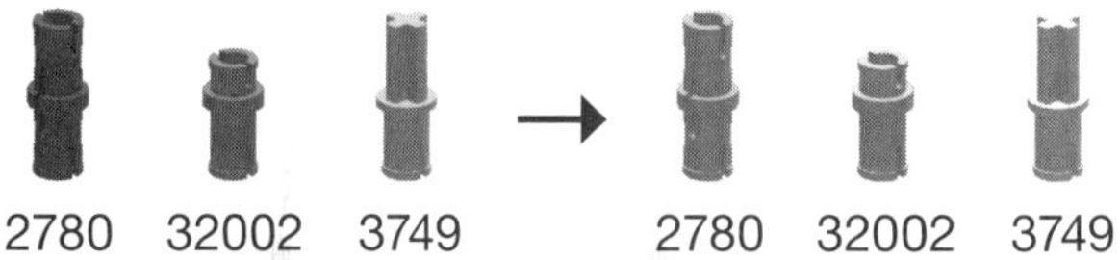

Color scaling can cause some confusion.

On the left side of the above figure are three pieces in their normal colors (black, dark grey, and light grey). On the right are the same three pieces rendered 50 percent lighter, as though they were added in a previous step. The color of the Technic axle pin (#3749) *before* scaling is very similar to that of the Technic pin with friction (#2780) *after* scaling. So, as you can see, a new grey piece can be difficult to find if it's surrounded by a lot of old black pieces that have been turned grey by the scaling.

In the more ambiguous steps, the new grey pieces are circled to make them stand out. As long as you take extra care whenever you see a grey piece in a step's parts list, I think you'll find the color scaling very useful.

STUD VS. MODULE

When talking about LEGO pieces, the words *stud* and *module* mean the same thing: a distance of 8 mm, or the length and width of a 1×1 brick. However, as we're using modular building, I'll use the word *stud* when referring to a distance, and *module* when referring to a main component of a model.

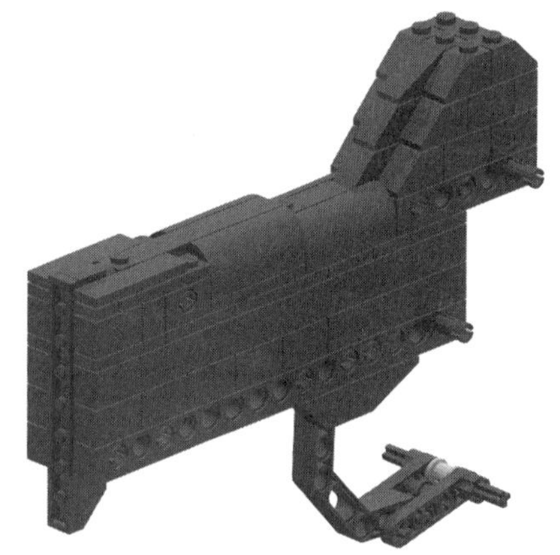

A module (the Pistol Grip module from the SPAS 12)

RUBBER BANDS

You can use many different sizes of rubber bands in these models. I made all the guns with one size of rubber band by simply looping the rubber band over itself when it was too big. In the case of the

SPAS 12's magazine, I looped two bands together to make an extra long band. Otherwise I would have ended up with a rubber band that was stretched so far it was nearly at its elastic limit and didn't do its job properly.

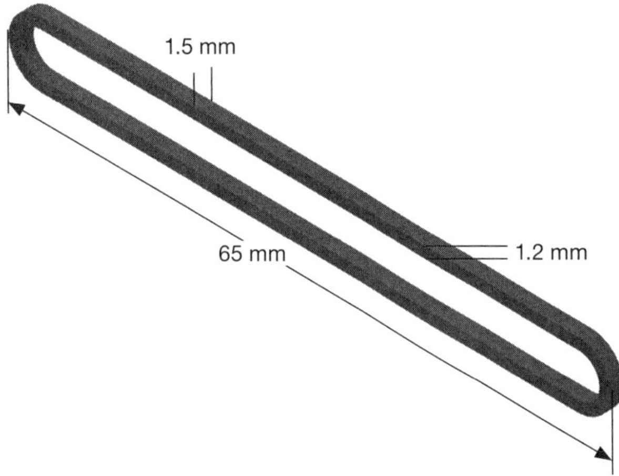

This is the rubber band I used in my models.

PINS AND FRICTION

Some LEGO Technic pins are designed to create a smooth, almost frictionless joint with the hole they're plugged into. Generally, they're colored light grey (*lt grey* in the BOMs). Other pins have ridges that form what's known as an *interference fit* with the hole. Essentially the pin is slightly too big to fit, creating friction, which prevents it from spinning freely. These pins are generally colored black.

As all of the models in this book have mechanisms and moving parts in them, it's essential that you use the right pin in the right place, or the mechanism might not work correctly.

NOW GO BUILD!

Words of warning aside, there's a lot of fun to be had in creating and tweaking LEGO models, and I hope you enjoy building these guns as much as I enjoyed designing them. Good luck!

ABOUT ME

It may sound cheesy, but I've been building with LEGO bricks for as long as I can remember.

When I was eight or nine, my room, the hallway, and the stairs down to the ground floor were usually littered with small bricks of various shapes and sizes. Back then most of my models were minifig-scale jets, racecars, or robots. And with the help of friends, I created great action sequences with these vehicles and their drivers. As I got more creative with the design of these vehicles, I started including ejector seats, detachable missiles, and the like.

These greatly improved our stories, which usually ended with the vehicles, robots, and pretty much everything else getting blown up, falling off huge "cliffs" (i.e., the stairs), or being dismantled for parts. After we concluded our story we'd gather up all the stray pieces and rebuild the models, usually with improvements in mind. ("The rubber band in that ejector seat was too powerful. We can replace that, but I've no idea what we're going to do about that mark on the ceiling. . . . ")

The general theme of the models I created back then spurred me to create one of my first motor-driven designs: a machine gun. While it looked nothing like any design in existence, I thought it was brilliant because it actually worked. When the trigger was pulled, a motor made the barrel reciprocate and it made a great clicking noise. I used this principle of function over form later on when designing my working replicas. If nothing else, a gun *must* work.

Moving away from weapons for a while, I experimented with the LEGO MINDSTORMS kits, using the RCX and NXT intelligent bricks. With these I gained even more experience making mechanisms, but with only three motor outputs per brick, I felt limited in what I could build. Nevertheless, the Technic pieces that come with the MINDSTORMS sets turned out to be incredibly useful when I moved on to building working replicas.

My first proper working replica was the Desert Eagle. This features a blowback mechanism: When the trigger is pulled, the slide moves backward and forward to mimic a round being fired. Previously, I'd created a studless blowback pistol entirely from Technic beams, but the Desert Eagle was my first attempt at mirroring the aesthetics of an existing weapon. For a long while, it was my most prized creation, and I kept it assembled for well over a year before scrapping it for pieces.

Not long after I designed the Desert Eagle, I came across MOCpages, a popular site where users can post pictures and descriptions of their own creations (*MOC* stands for *My Own Creation*). There were only a few weapon models posted to the site, a few of which were popular, and I was driven to become one of those great builders. I posted the Desert Eagle to the site, where it was a reasonable success, and I was overjoyed that it got any attention at all.

I tried a few studless guns after the Desert Eagle as well as some guns using standard bricks, and I found that people didn't really care if a model was incredibly powerful if it didn't look good. The skeletal structure of studless creations turned out to be unpopular, and I decided that if I was going to build guns, why not make them accurate replicas? This actually made it easier to decide what to do next (even if the actual building was more difficult), because all I had to do was pick an existing gun.

After designing several more guns, I decided to start making videos. My success on MOCpages kick-started me into YouTube popularity, and many weapons enthusiasts and builders noticed my work. Things settled down for a while, but then I got featured on various geek blogs and on Wired.co.uk. My view counts rocketed, doubling over and over again, and I found articles about my creations all over the Internet. But I was running out of guns to replicate and inspiration to build them.

By this time I'd taught myself how to use such programs as LDraw and LPub to create building instructions for the guns, and I wondered what to do with some of the finished sets of instructions I had lying around. By happy coincidence, I got an email from No Starch Press asking if I'd like to have a go at writing a book of instructions. And after a year of hard work, the result is what you're holding in your hands now!

DESERT

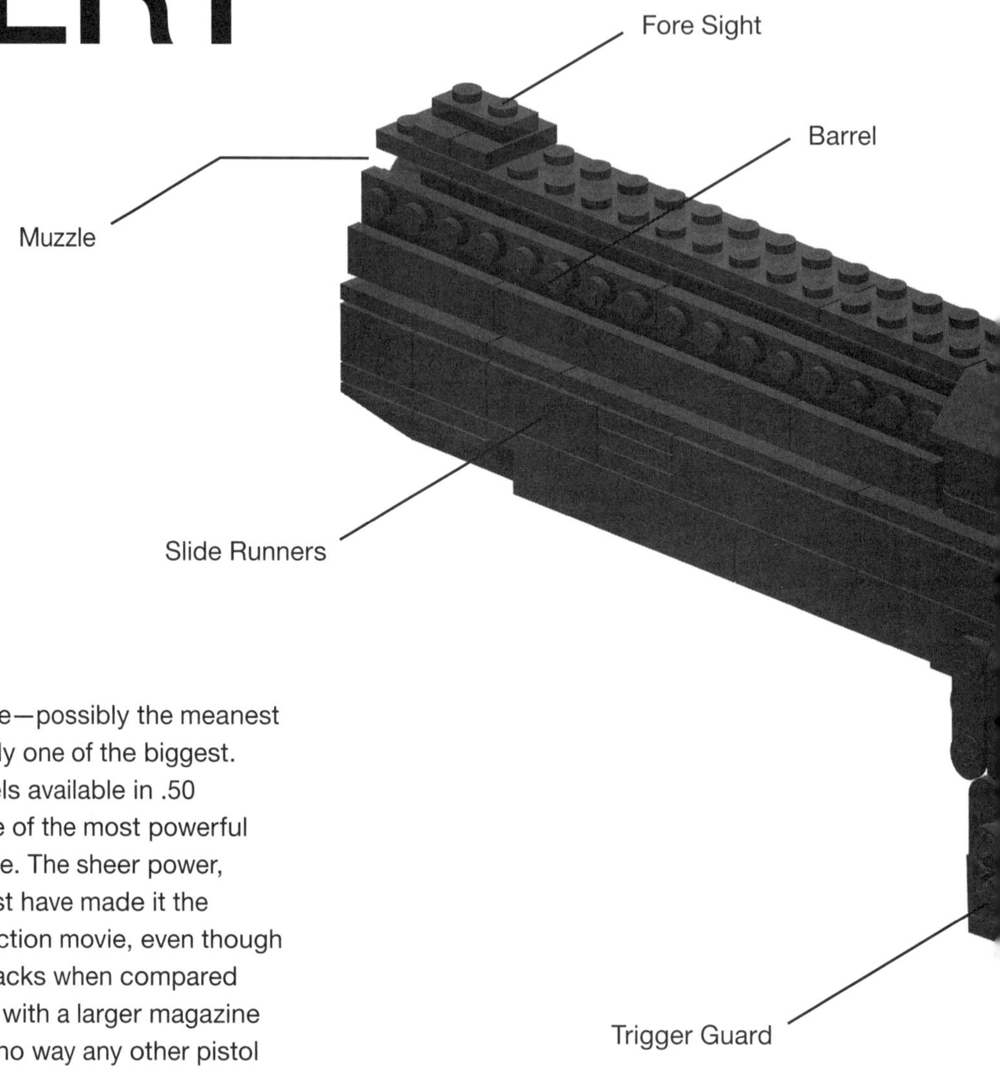

Fore Sight

Barrel

Muzzle

Slide Runners

Trigger Guard

Say hello to the Desert Eagle—possibly the meanest of all handguns and definitely one of the biggest. With Mark VII and XIX models available in .50 Action Express, it's also one of the most powerful production handguns to date. The sheer power, size, and weight of this beast have made it the director's pick in many an action movie, even though it has some inherent drawbacks when compared to a smaller, lighter weapon with a larger magazine capacity. That said, there's no way any other pistol comes close on a scale of sheer awesomeness.

The Desert Eagle is a gas-operated, semiautomatic pistol. Gas operation (where the expanding gasses from the fired round push a piston, which operates the action to chamber a new round) for a pistol is unusual, as normally a pistol's action is cycled simply by recoil. The gun can be chambered for a variety of rounds, including the previously mentioned .50 Action Express and the .44 Magnum. It feeds from a detachable box magazine, which holds nine, eight, or seven rounds (single stack), depending on the caliber being used.

EAGLE

LENGTH: *34 studs*
WIDTH: *4.5 studs*
HEIGHT: *21 studs*
PIECES: *382*
MAGAZINE TYPE: *Detachable box magazine with first round visible*

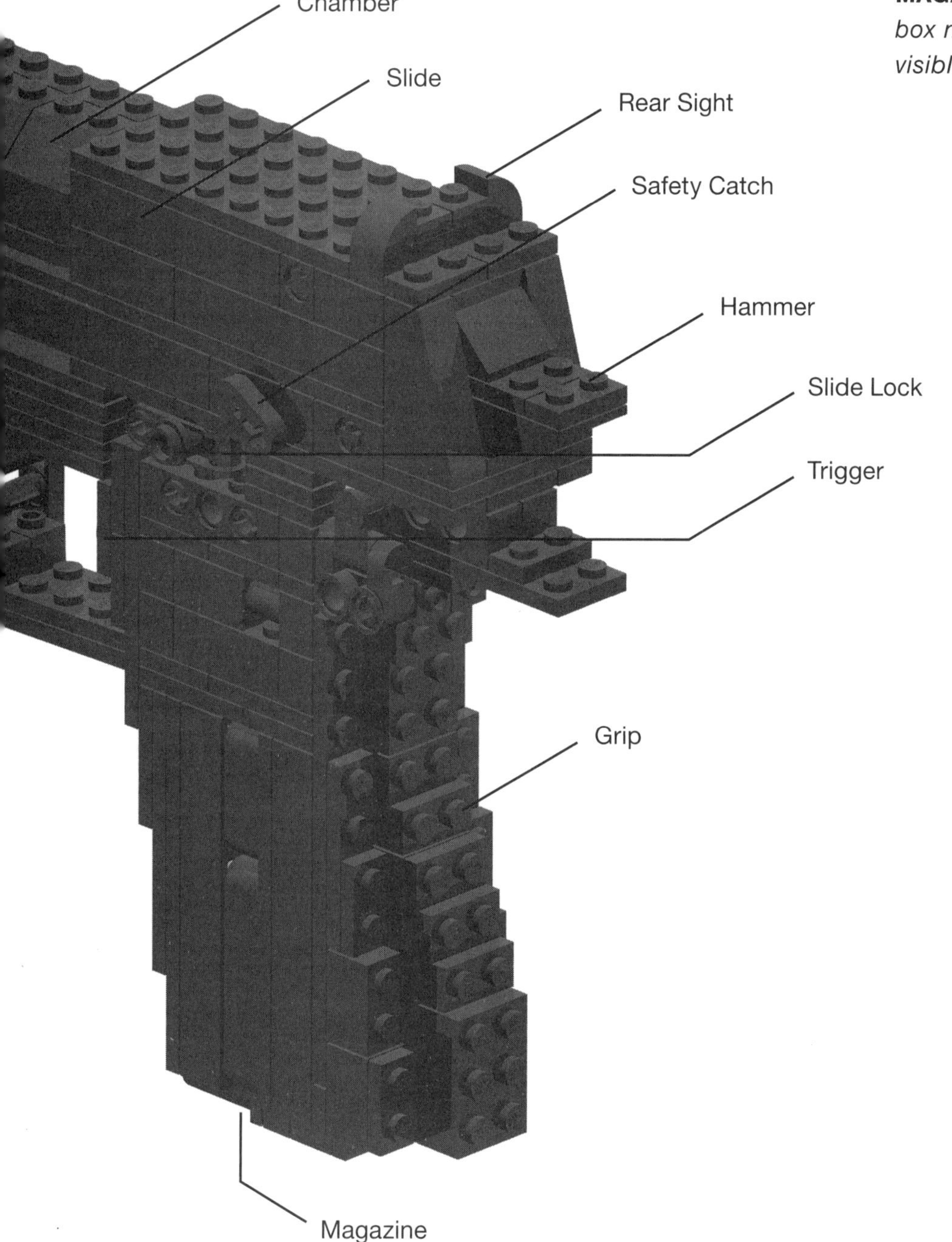

DESIGN HISTORY

Back when I was around 13 years old and experimenting with rubber band guns, I decided to build a replica of a pistol with an authentic blowback action mechanism. This probably came from watching too many films that featured slow-motion action sequences in which the protagonist flew through the air, guns blazing, while empty casings dropped in his wake. What 13-year-old kid could resist?

As I began designing this pistol, it soon became obvious that I would need to use of a lot of studded bricks (I'd previously been working with the LEGO MINDSTORMS NXT system, where studless beams were the norm) and that I'd need a big gun to fit the mechanism in. Compared to, say, a Glock 17, the Desert Eagle is huge, so it was the perfect choice for this project. But it was still a challenge to fit the firing mechanism inside the body of the weapon while keeping it true to size.

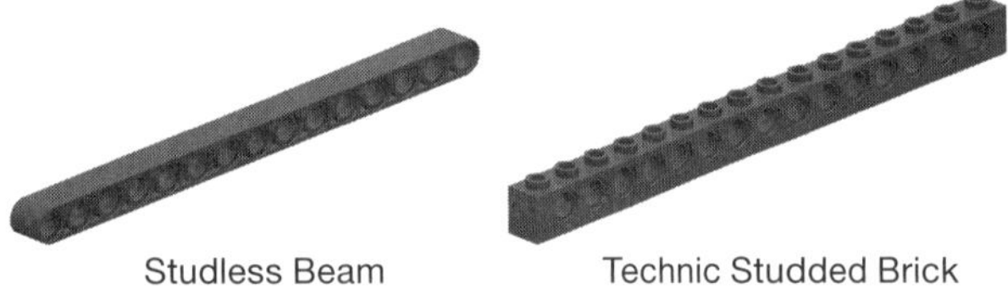

Studless Beam   Technic Studded Brick

As with most of my LEGO projects, the problem was not devising a working mechanism but transferring the concept into LEGO bricks and working within all the constraints that came with that. While I'd found a gun that could accommodate the mechanism in its side-on profile, I was still restricted in terms of width: I was aiming for a total gun width of four studs, so the mechanism could be only two studs wide, as the rest of the width would be taken up by the walls of the slide.

With that in mind, I realized I was going to have to modify some LEGO pieces to make it all fit. Fortunately it was only a few pins and axles—nothing too drastic. This went against most of my building principles, but in the end I decided to give it a go. Luckily, I was able to modify some already mangled pieces

This view of the grip shows how the parts of the mechanism that protrude from the top will fit in between the rails of the slide. With so little space to spare, every last gap has been utilized.

from my collection, so I avoided having to sacrifice any pristine pieces. To this day, I still hate the idea of modifying pieces but know that sometimes it's the only possible solution. Besides, if *nobody* ever modified a piece, we'd have only 4×2 bricks and the occasional sloped roof brick.

The Desert Eagle was the first serious weapon model that I put on the Internet (I had previously uploaded mechanical creations to the LEGO Group's NXTlog), so I'd yet to cotton on to some of the main methods and principles of replica building, such as using a 1:1 picture reference for accuracy or using solid, "ordinary" LEGO bricks. Because of this, my first design was not only pitted with holes from using Technic bricks but also the wrong shape and color in some places. It took several redesigns to fix these problems, but looking at the bigger picture, none of that really mattered. The selling point was that the gun worked: pulling the trigger moved the slide back and forth, the magazine was removable, the slide lock allowed a realistic imitation of the "out of ammo" situation, and the safety catch worked. I had accomplished my main goals, so the aesthetics weren't a big deal.

In fact, I loved this gun so much that I decided to keep it around, even while I built other guns. This severely limited the number of pieces I could use for my other guns, but it allowed me to constantly tinker with my flagship model. Eventually, after more than a year (during which I posted more than 30 different weapons to MOCpages), I decided to break it up.

Breaking the gun down was actually one of the best decisions I've made. When I started working toward this book in 2010, I rebuilt the gun completely from scratch. The only thing I kept the same was the basic idea of how the mechanism worked; if any two pieces are actually arranged in the same way as in the old version, it's purely by chance. Redesigning the gun meant that I could get rid of all the old design's inherent flaws, like the stiff mechanism, uncomfortable grip, long trigger pull (which required an oversized trigger guard), and so on. The old model's list of problems is a long one.

When building the new model, I was able to use all the skills I'd developed since that first version, including how to create a more efficient mechanism, using a 1:1 printout to make the gun actually look right, and a much better understanding of all the different ways LEGO pieces can fit together. I'm particularly proud of the almost seamless transition of upward- to sideways-facing studs in the grip. And the fact that the space for the slide's runners is now a fraction bigger than the runners themselves makes the action much smoother and faster. Looking at all the versions of this model shows me just how far it's come.

The first-ever version of my Desert Eagle (1) was never posted publicly on the Internet. It was functional but had some major aesthetic flaws—such as not really looking like a Desert Eagle at all! Through subsequent modifications and redesigns the model became more and more refined until the final, most lifelike of them all: the version in this book (4).

HOW IT WORKS

Understanding what makes this gun tick is an invaluable way of improving its reliability. As with most of the guns in this book, there's definitely a knack to making the mechanism work smoothly and consistently. I'd advise pulling the Trigger firmly and quickly, making sure not to bend it. Don't release the pressure on the Trigger until the Slide is moving forward again; otherwise it may get a bit stuck. In the worst-case scenario, improper use can break the mechanism.

MAIN MECHANISM

1

The gun is at rest and ready to be "fired."

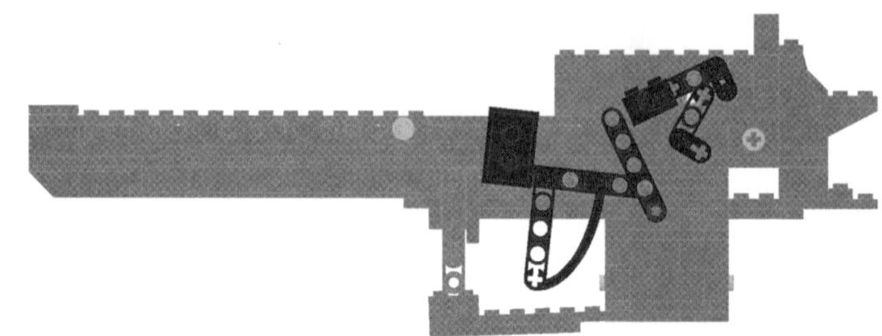

2

Pulling the Trigger pushes the trigger lever against the Slide Mechanism so that the whole Slide is pushed back.

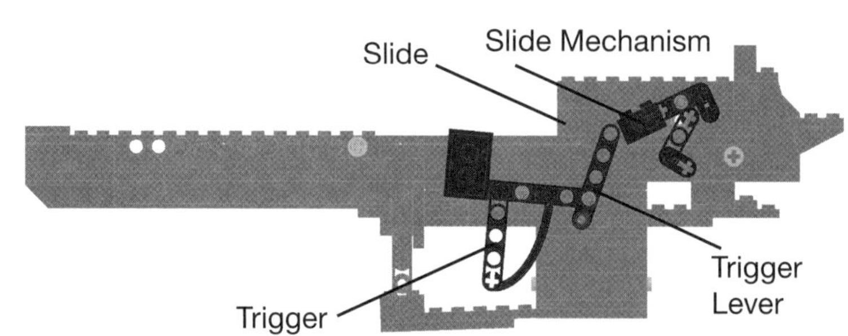

3

The trigger lever continues to rotate until it's lower than the Slide Mechanism. This is as far back as the Slide goes.

4

Now the Slide moves forward again, even though the Trigger is still fully depressed. (In this illustration, the safety catch seems to be on top of the Trigger, but in reality, there's a gap between the two that can't be shown in a 2D drawing.)

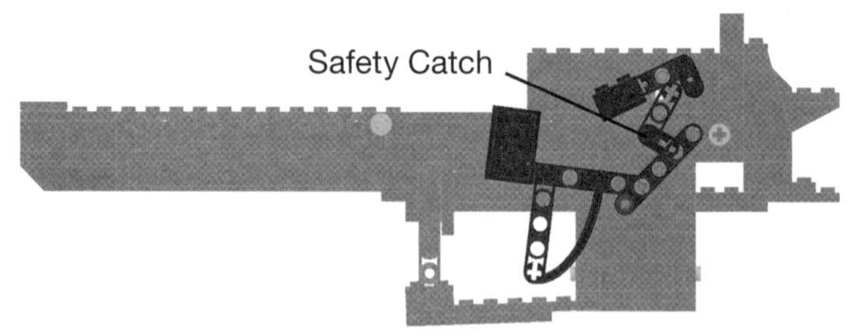

5

Begin to release the Trigger. The Slide Mechanism rotates clockwise to allow the trigger lever to pass by, and the safety catch also moves slightly.

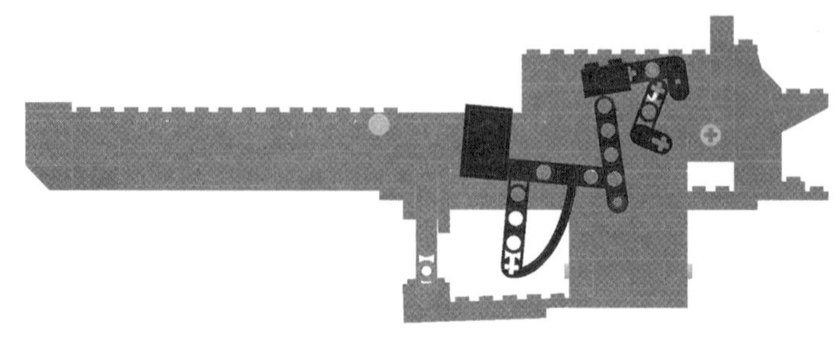

6

When the Trigger is fully released, the gun returns to its original state.

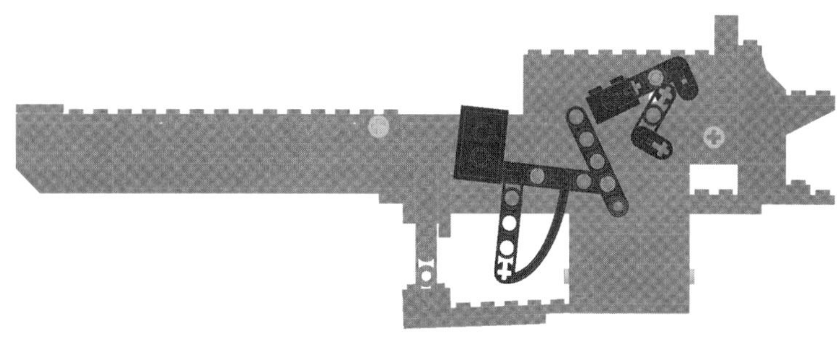

SAFETY CATCH

1

The safety catch is not engaged.

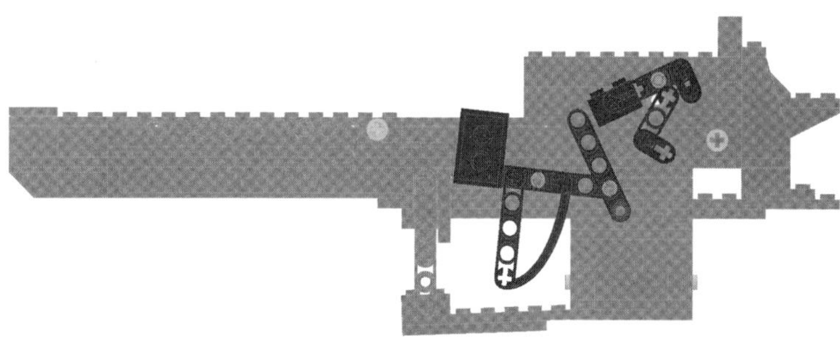

2

When the safety catch is engaged, the gun is in "safe" mode. Note how the safety catch rotates the Slide Mechanism clockwise and upward.

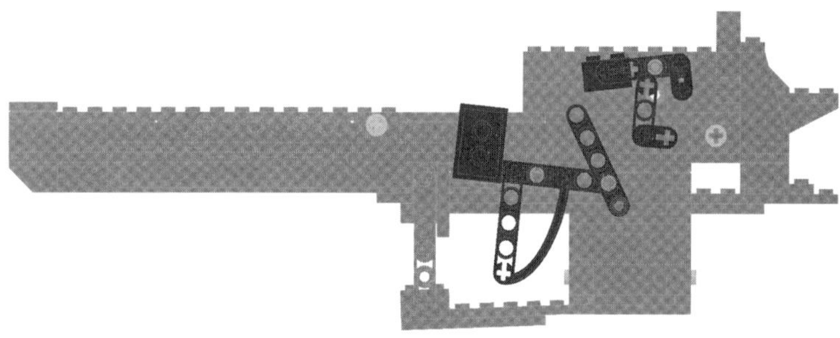

3

With the safety catch applied, the Slide Mechanism is locked in this upward position. Pulling the Trigger rotates the trigger lever, but it's not going to come into contact with the Slide Mechanism, so it can't push the Slide back and the gun will not "fire."

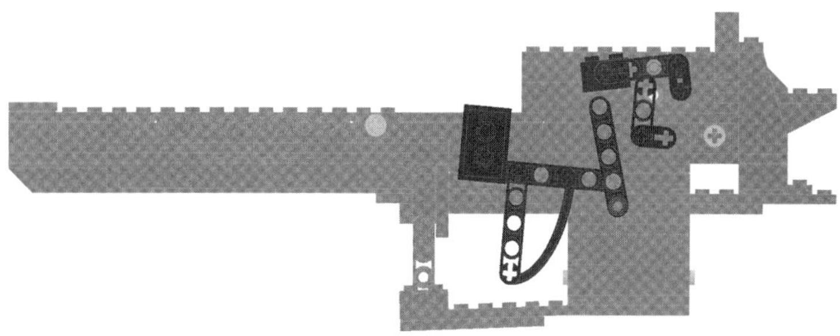

BILL OF MATERIALS

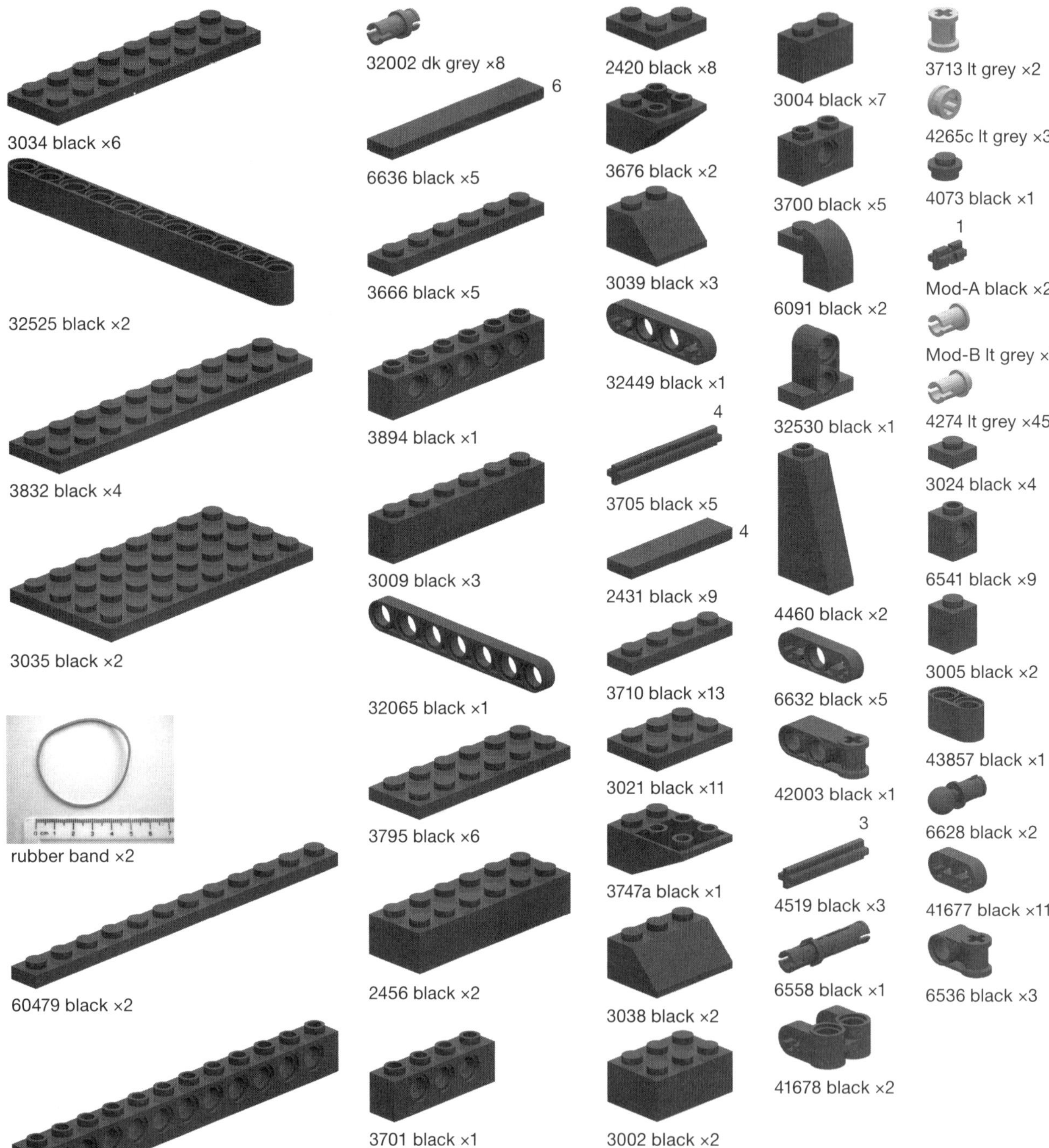

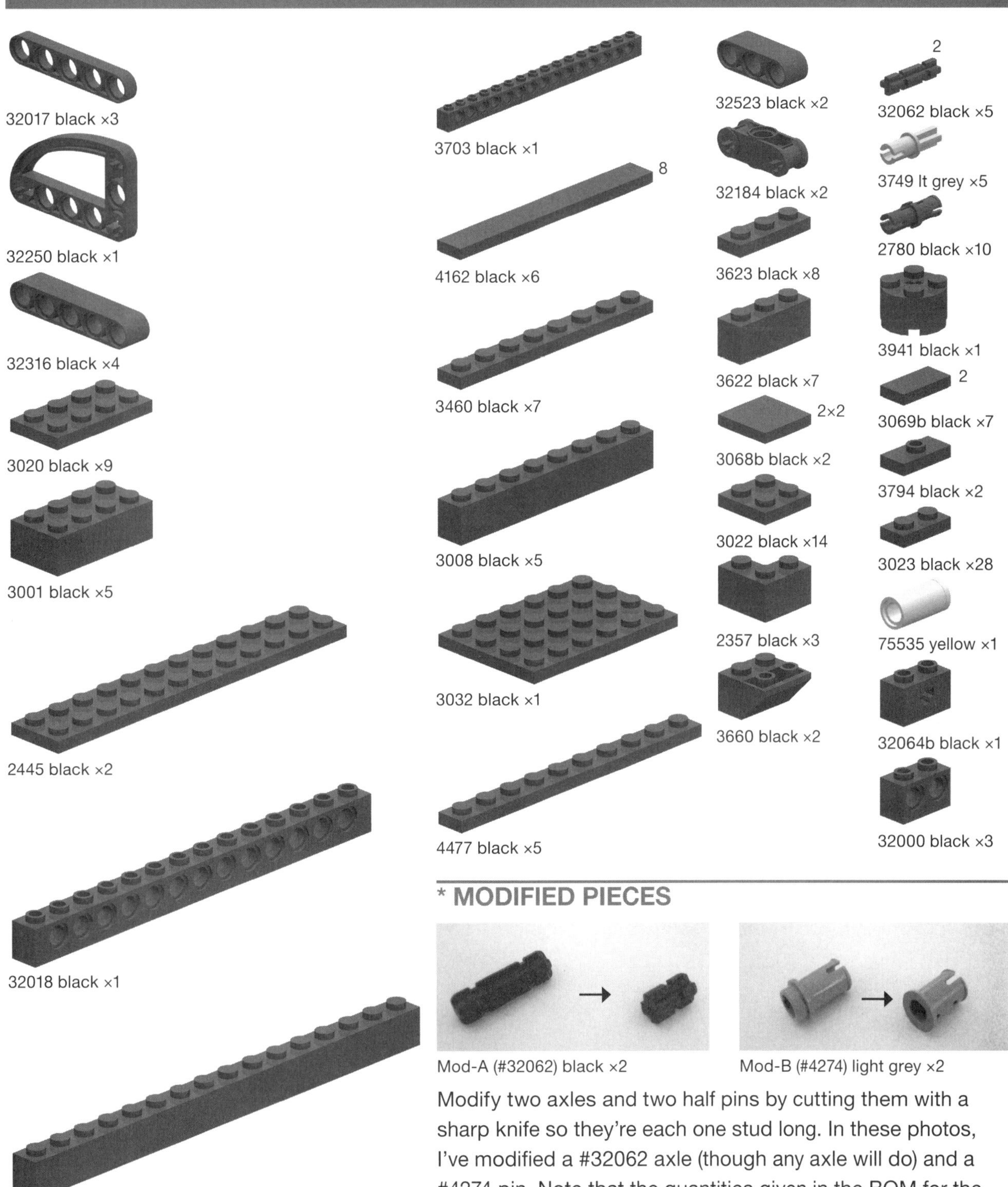

* MODIFIED PIECES

Mod-A (#32062) black ×2

Mod-B (#4274) light grey ×2

Modify two axles and two half pins by cutting them with a sharp knife so they're each one stud long. In these photos, I've modified a #32062 axle (though any axle will do) and a #4274 pin. Note that the quantities given in the BOM for the #32062 axle (×5) and the #4274 pin (×45) don't include the modified pieces—you'll need two more of each to make a total of four modified pieces.

GRIP FRONT

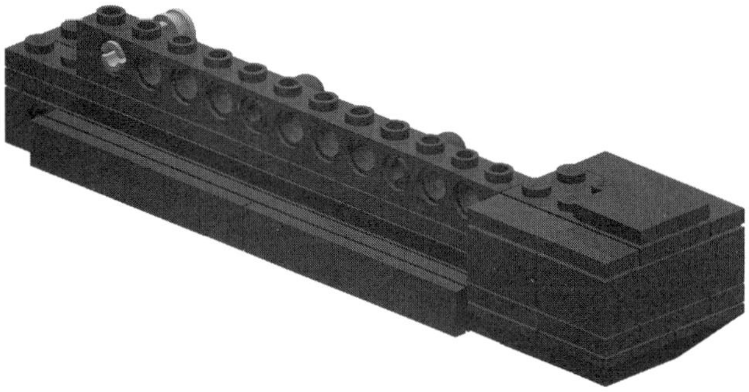

1

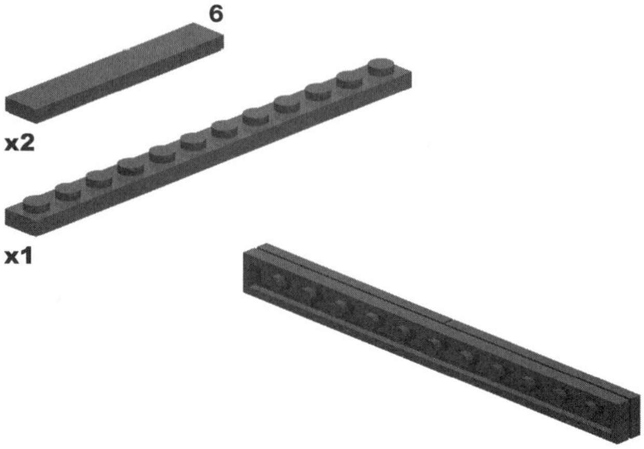

6

x2

x1

2

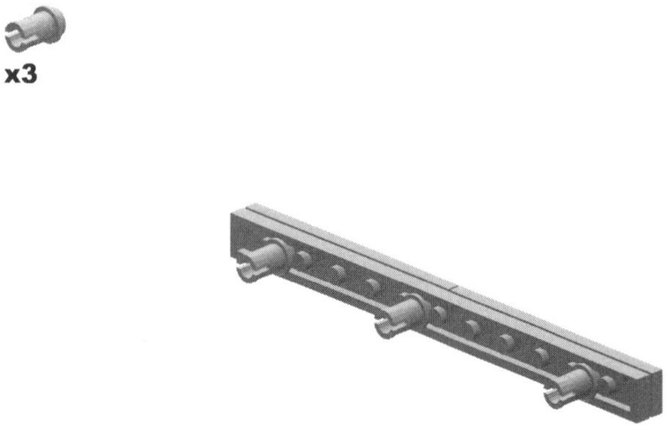

x3

3

x2

x1

4

x3

x1

5

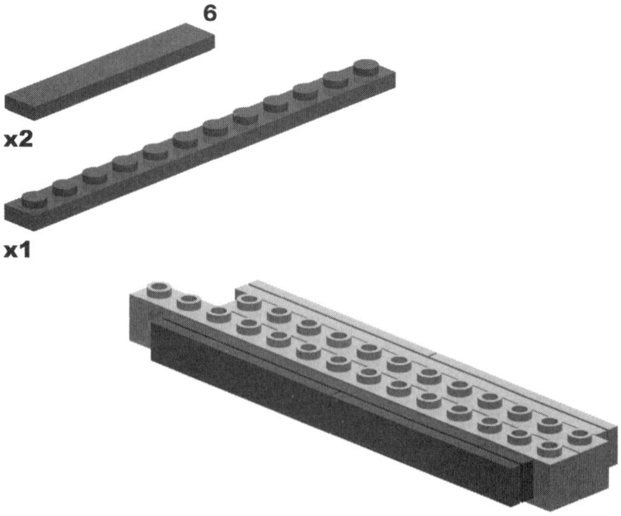

6

x2

x1

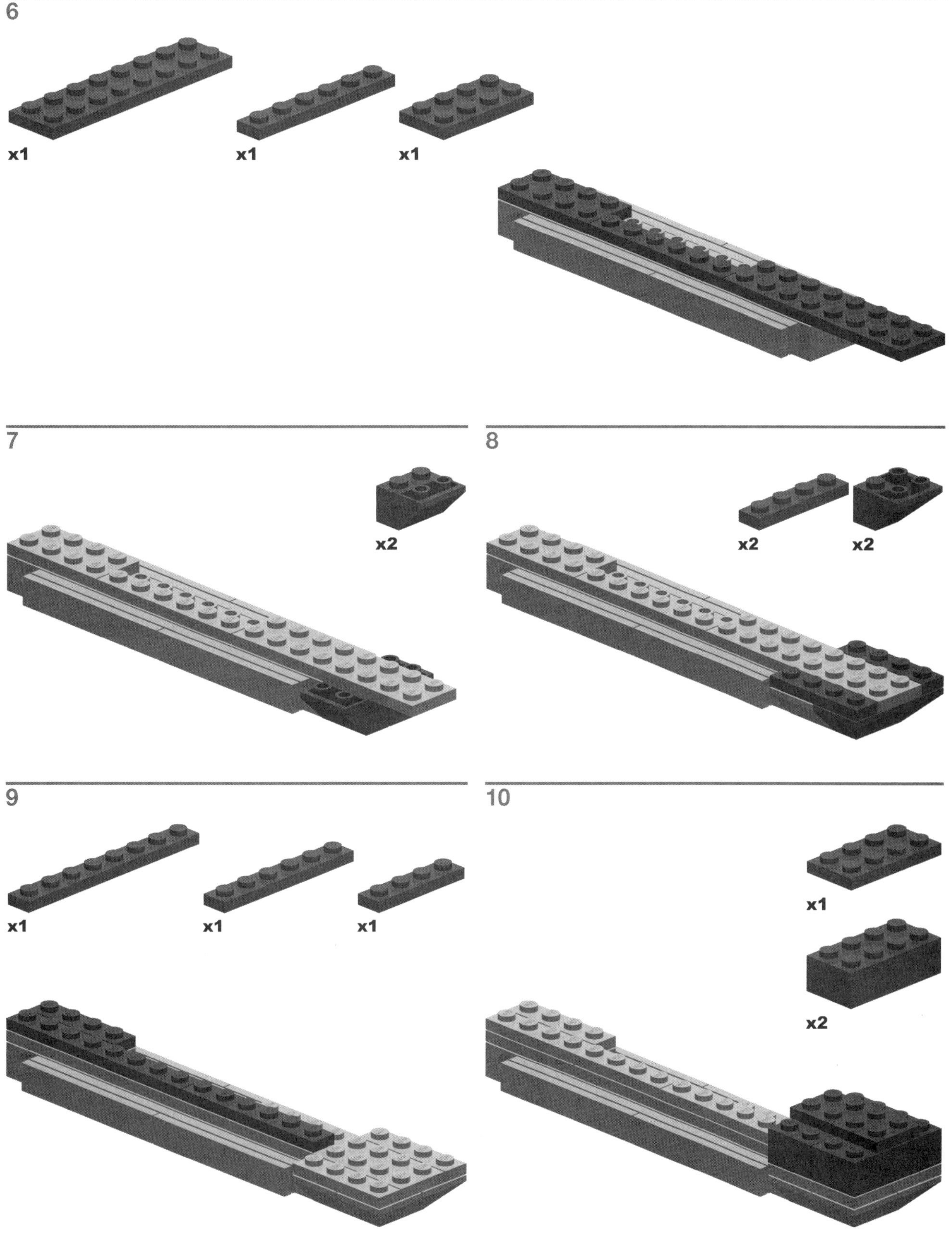
6
x1
x1
x1
7
x2
8
x2
x2
9
x1
x1
x1
10
x1
x2

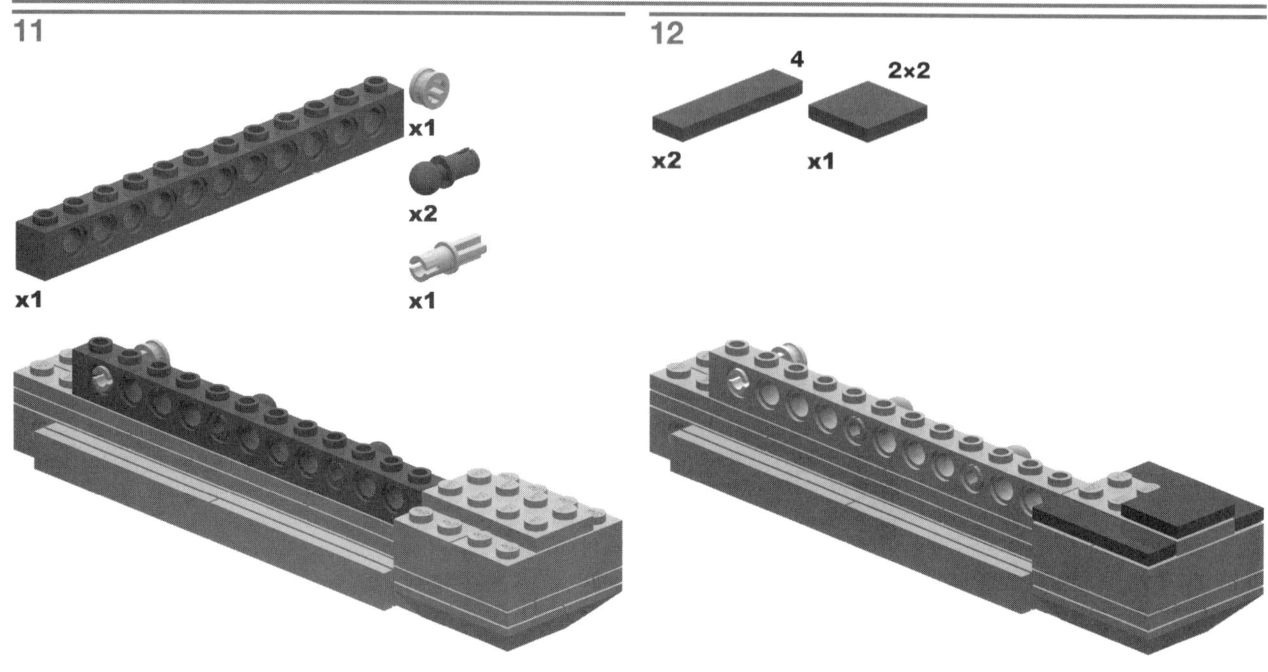

TRIGGER

1

2

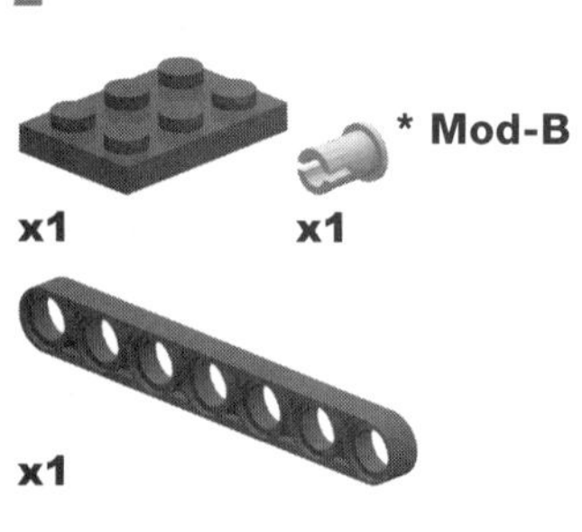

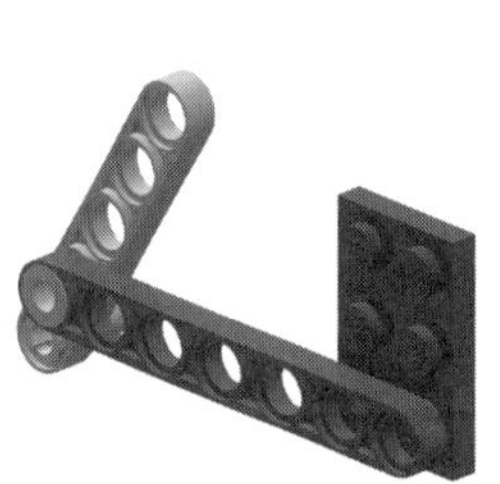

3

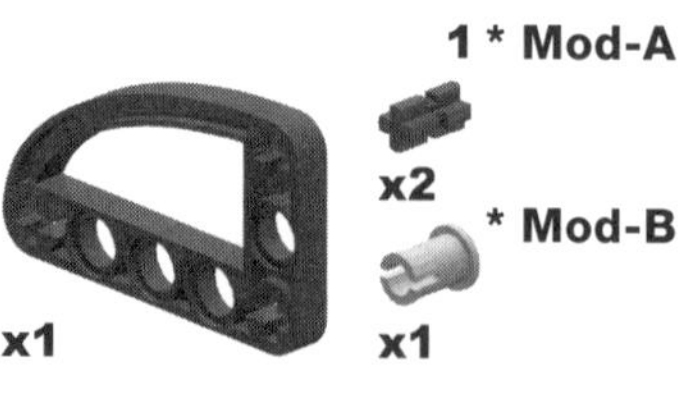

GRIP UNDERSIDE

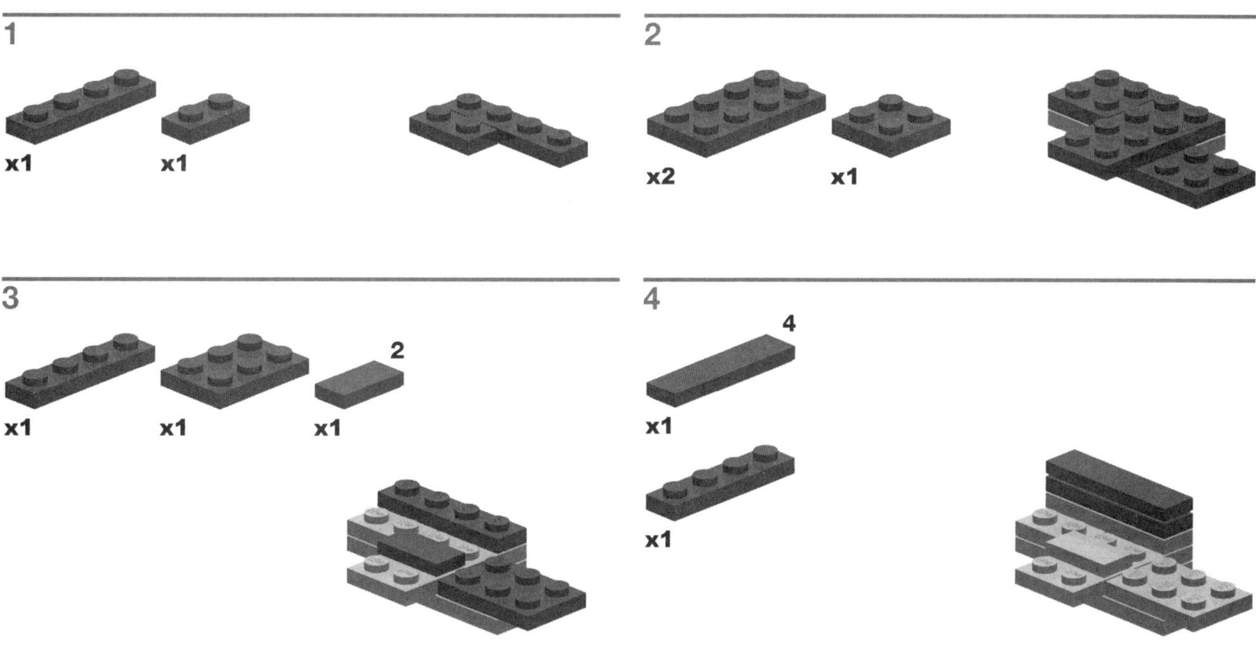

TRIGGER GUARD

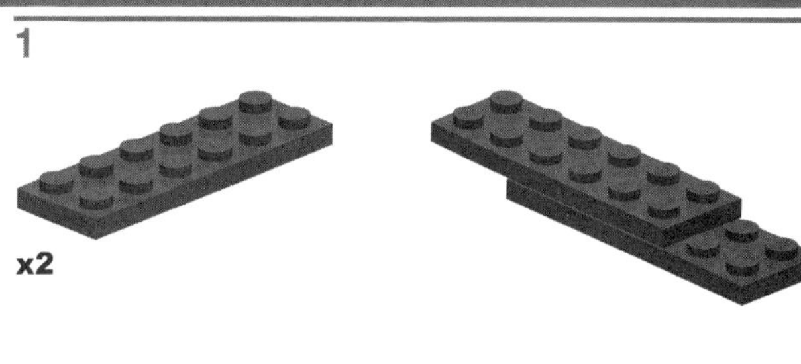

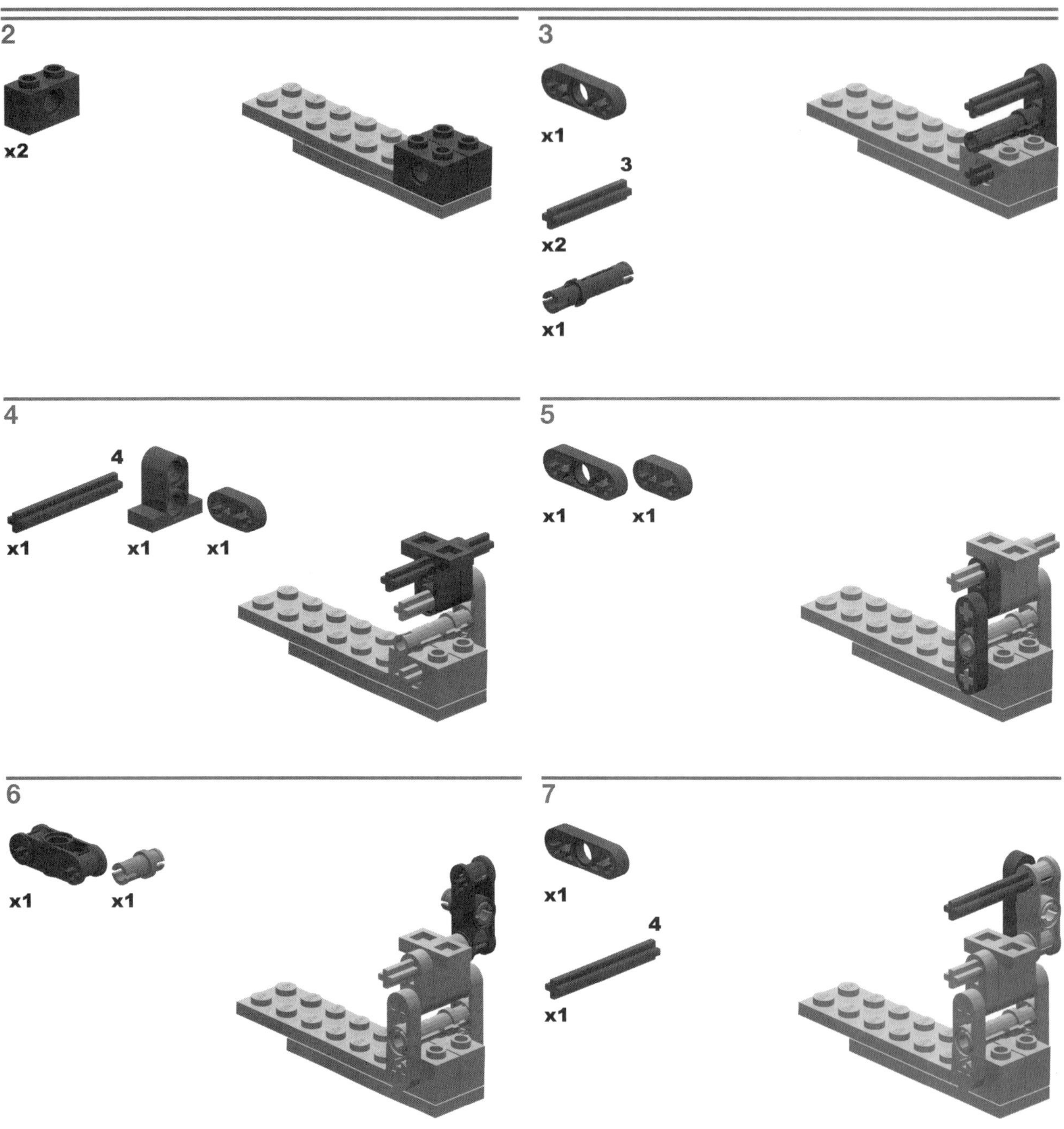
2
x2
3
x1
3
x2
x1
4
4
x1
x1
x1
5
x1
x1
6
x1
x1
7
x1
4
x1

GRIP HANDLE BACK

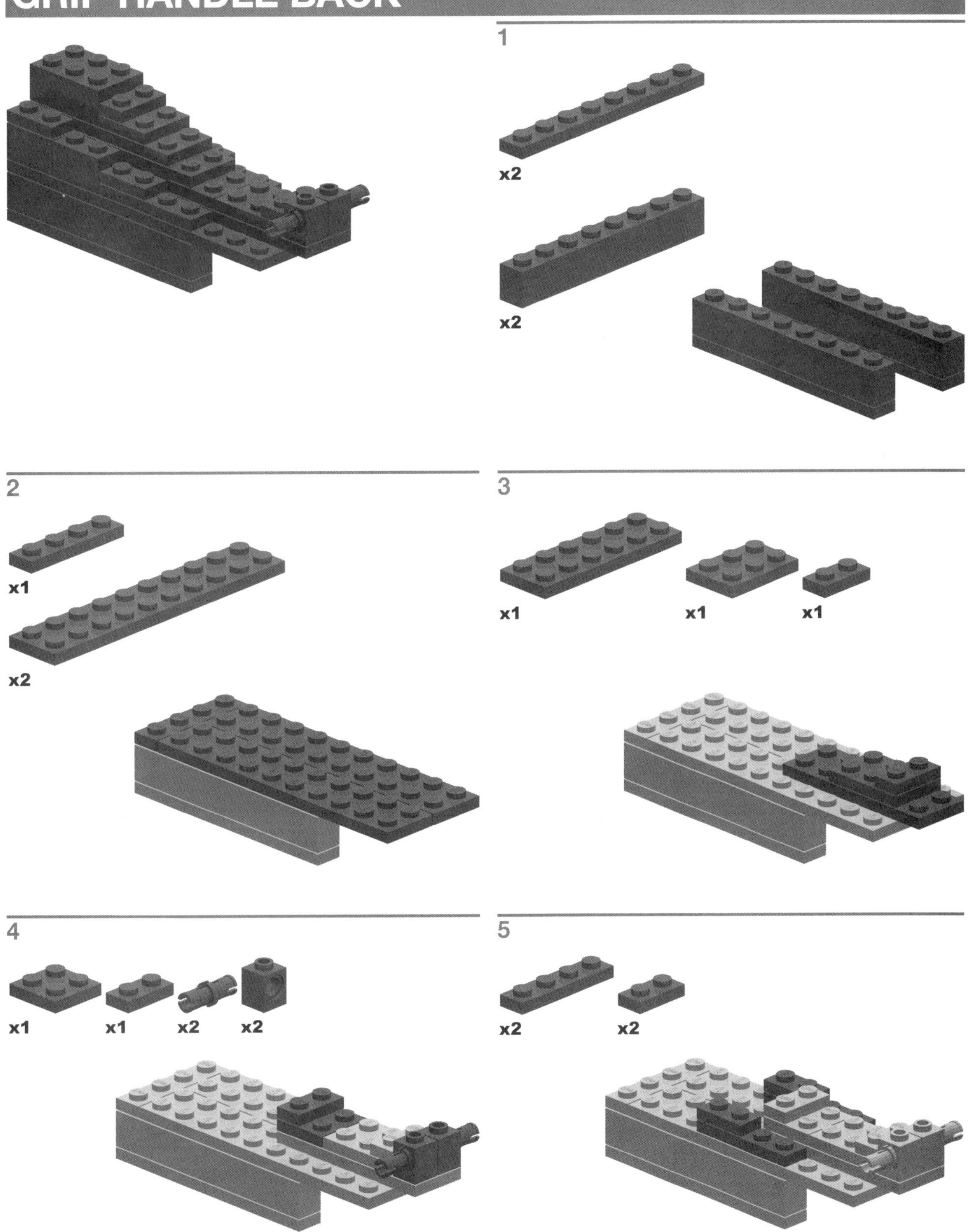

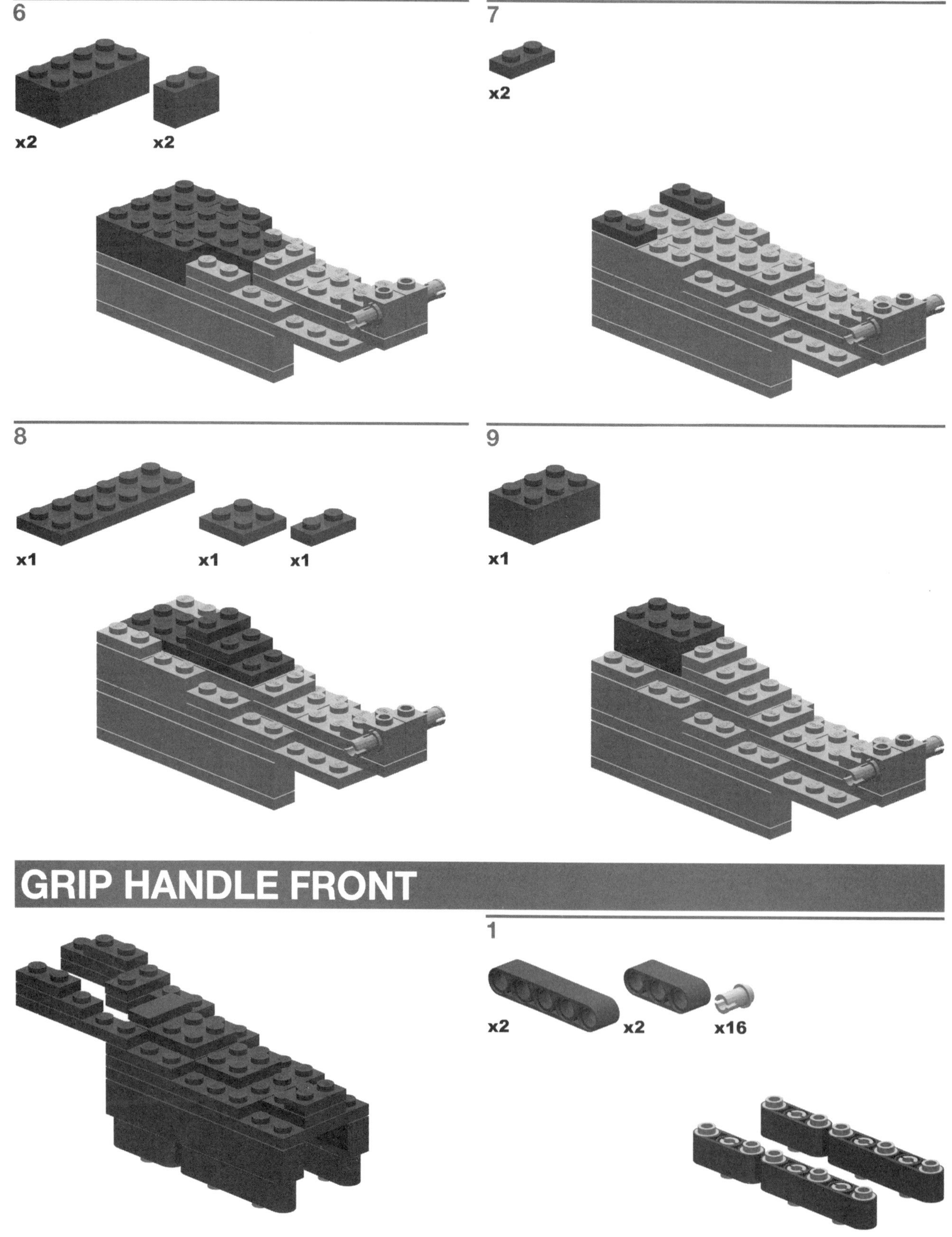

GRIP HANDLE FRONT

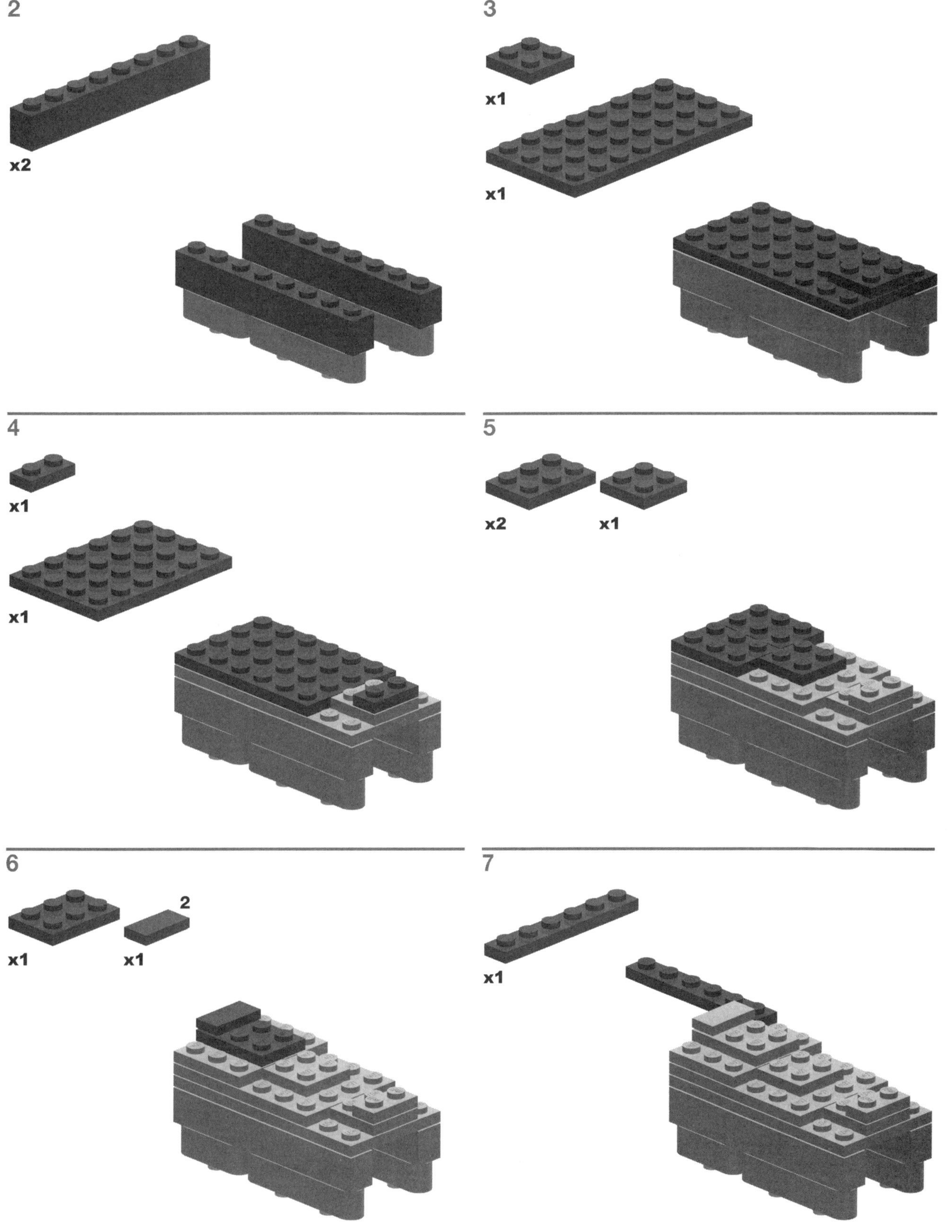
2
x2
3
x1
x1
4
x1
x1
5
x2
x1
6
x1
2
x1
7
x1

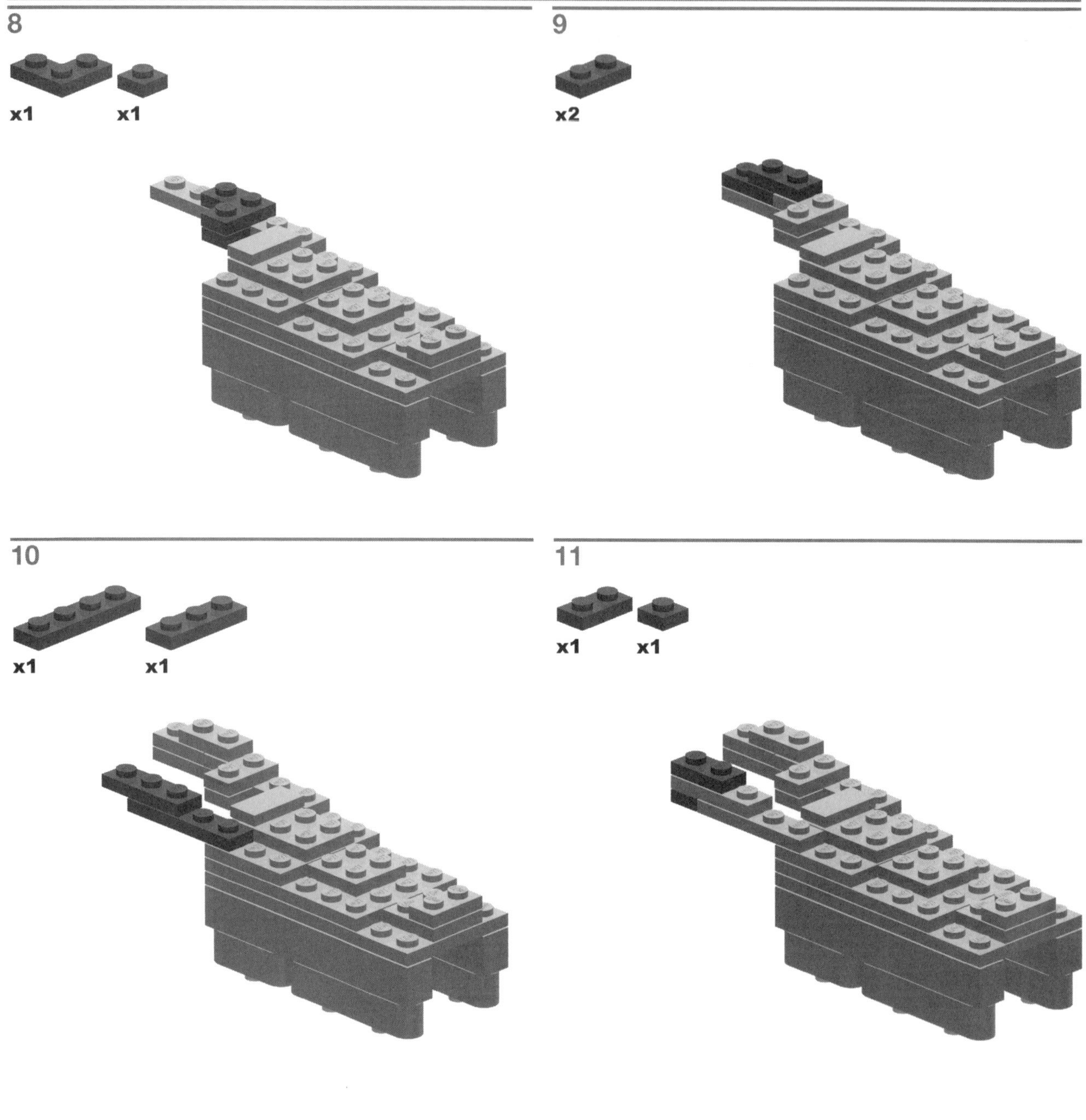
8
x1
x1
9
x2
10
x1
x1
11
x1
x1

GRIP ASSEMBLY

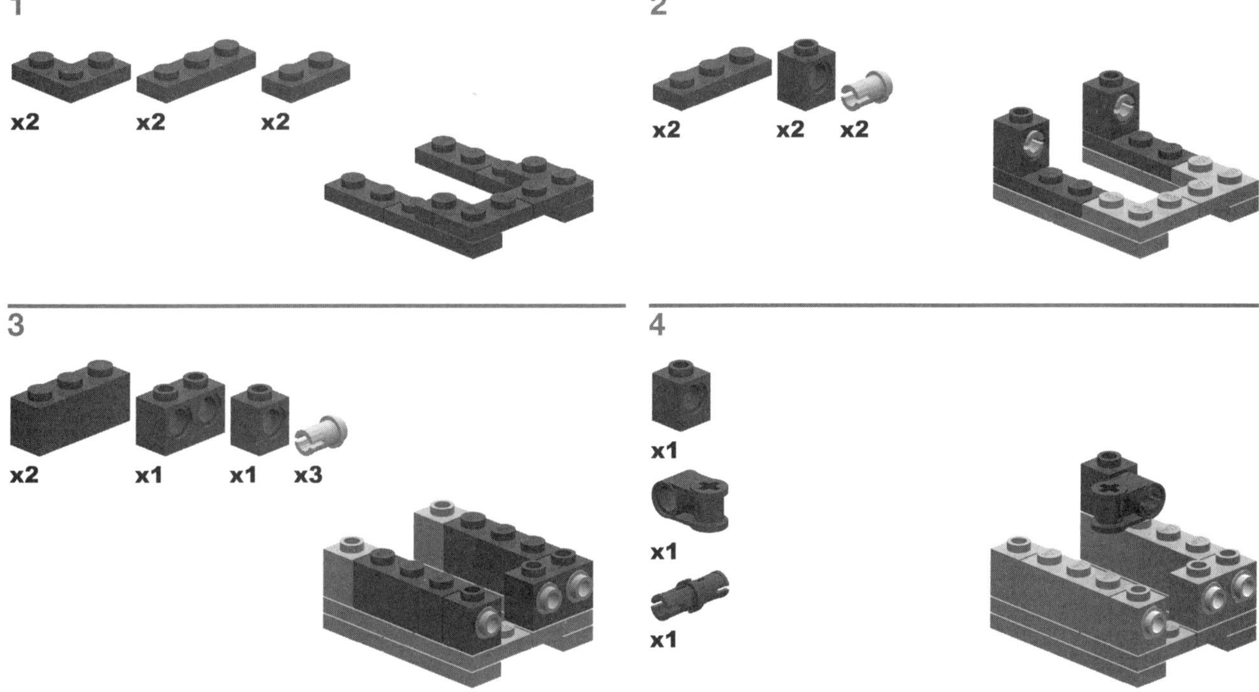

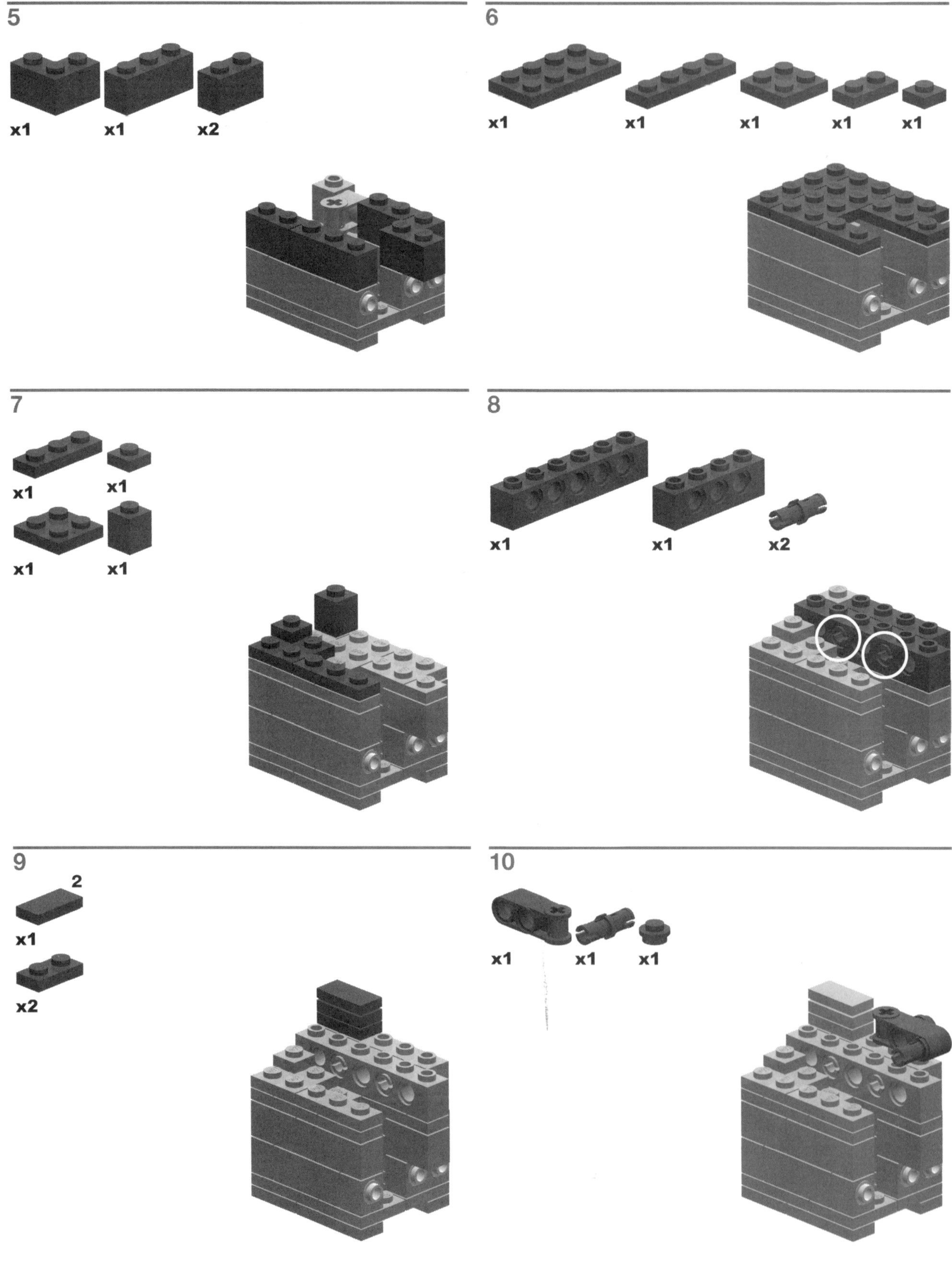
5
x1
x1
x2
6
x1
x1
x1
x1
x1
7
x1
x1
x1
x1
8
x1
x1
x2
9
2
x1
x2
10
x1
x1
x1

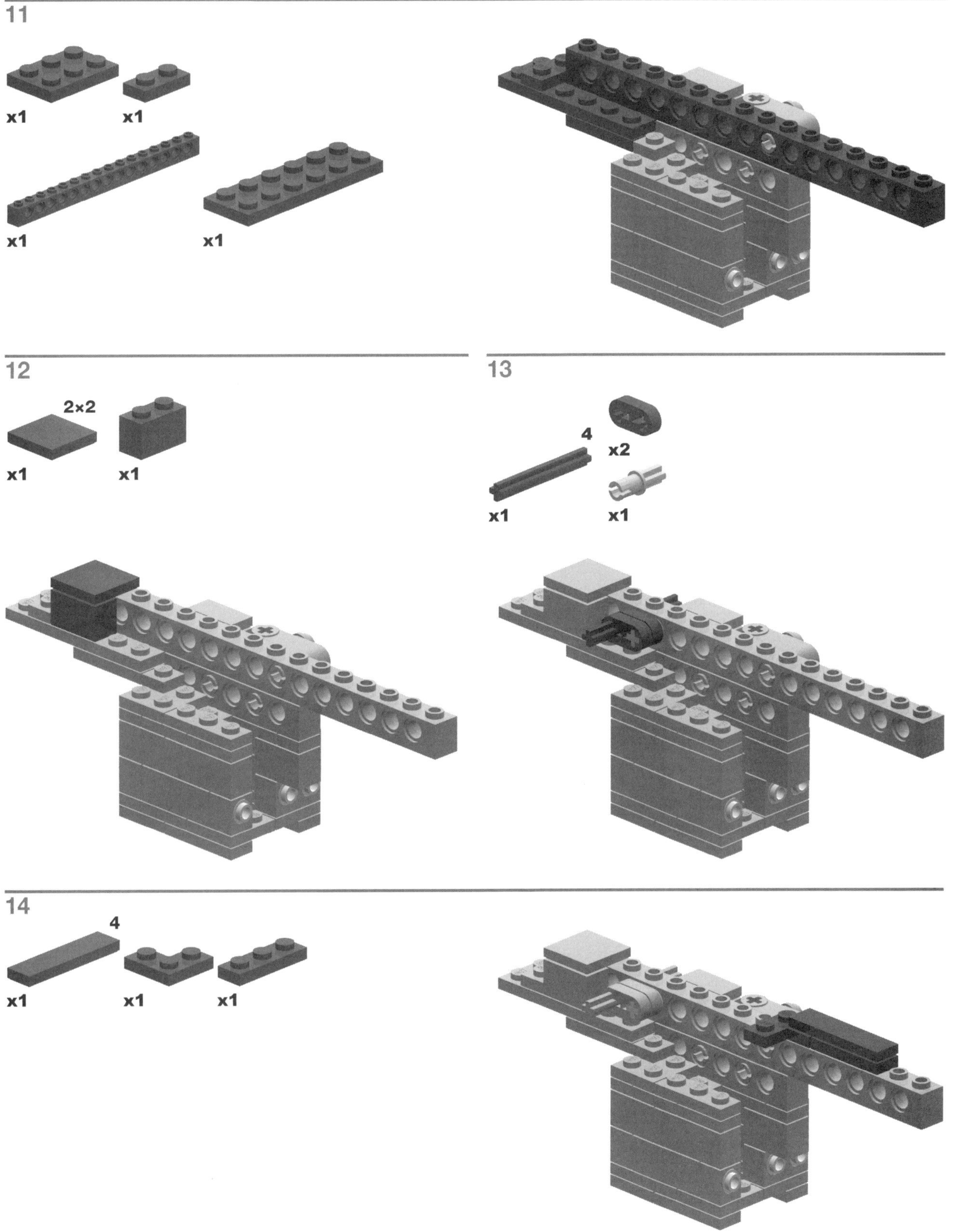
11
x1
x1
x1
x1
12
2×2
x1
x1
13
4
x2
x1
x1
14
4
x1
x1
x1

15

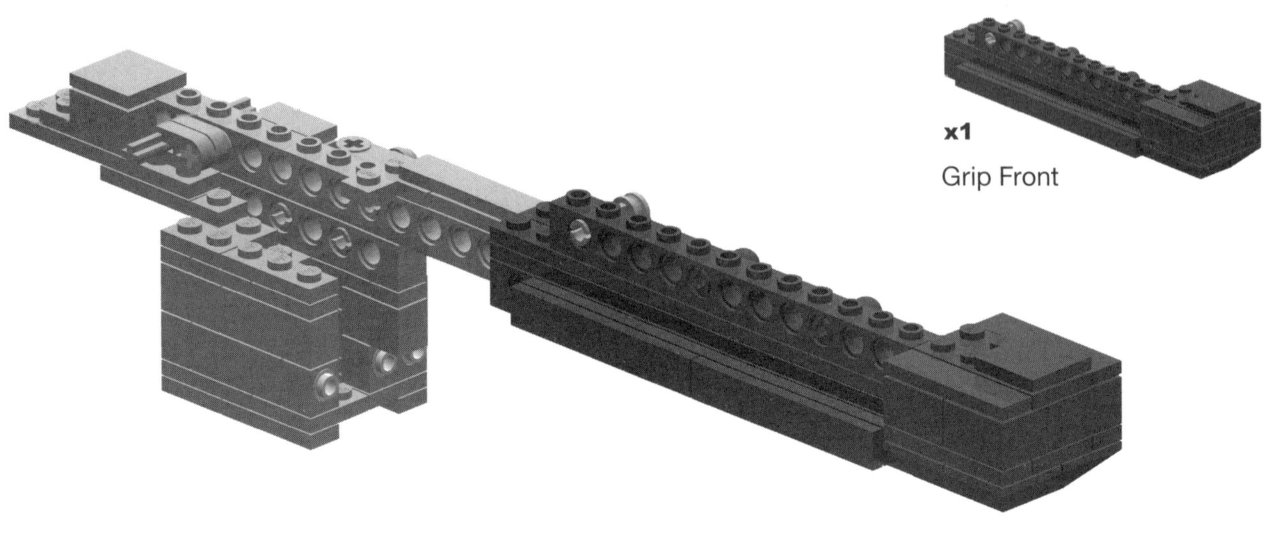

16

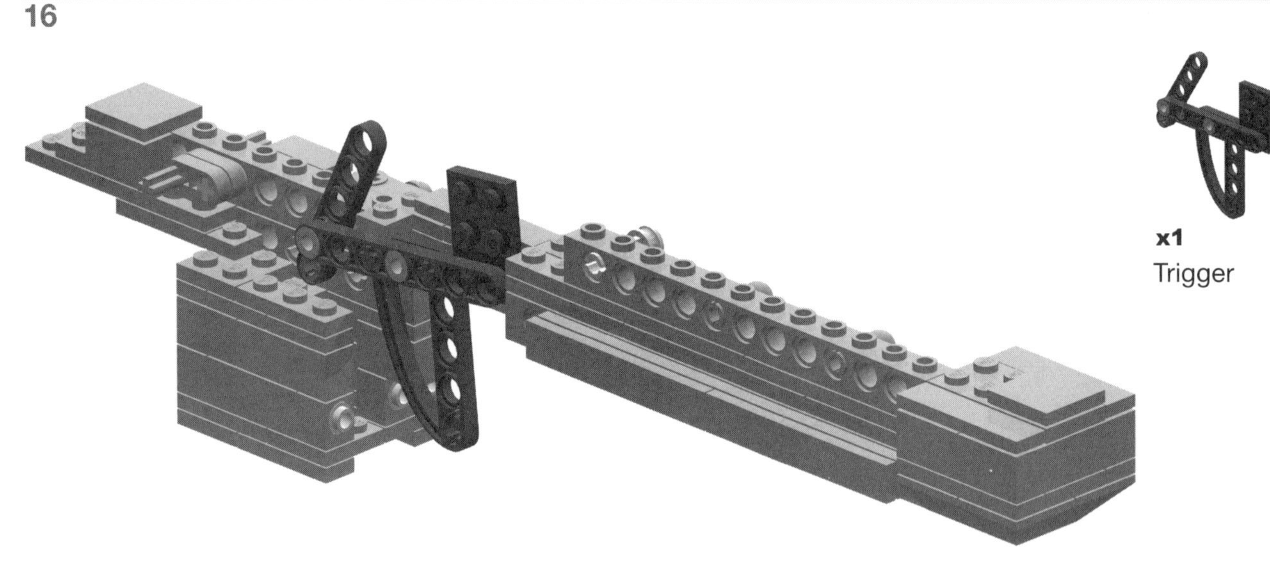

17

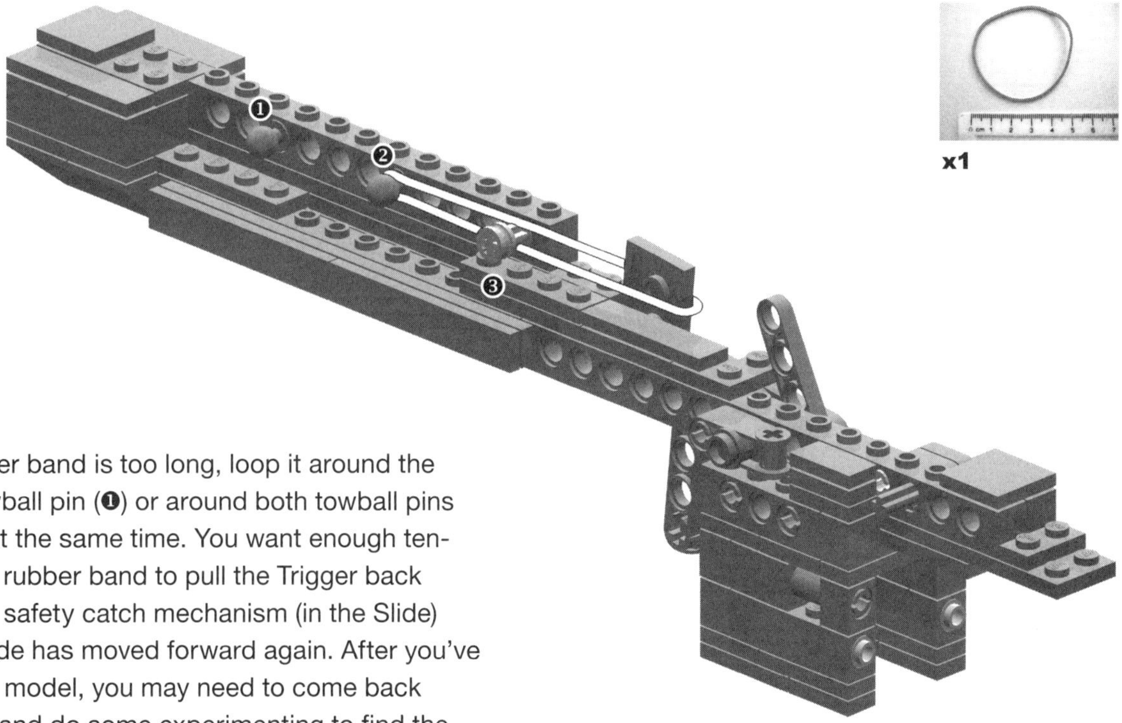

x1

If your rubber band is too long, loop it around the farthest towball pin (❶) or around both towball pins (❶ and ❷) at the same time. You want enough tension in your rubber band to pull the Trigger back through the safety catch mechanism (in the Slide) after the Slide has moved forward again. After you've finished the model, you may need to come back to this step and do some experimenting to find the optimal amount of tension.

Make sure the rubber band fits between the 12-stud Technic brick and the 1/2-stud bushing as shown at ❸—this will stop interference between this rubber band and the one that powers the Slide.

18

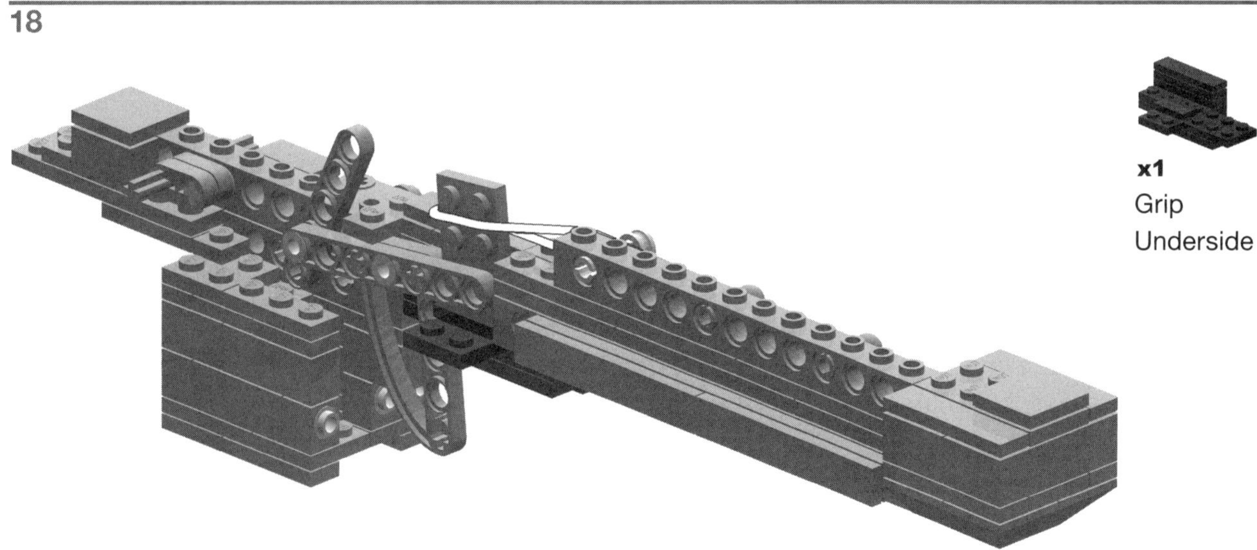

x1
Grip Underside

19

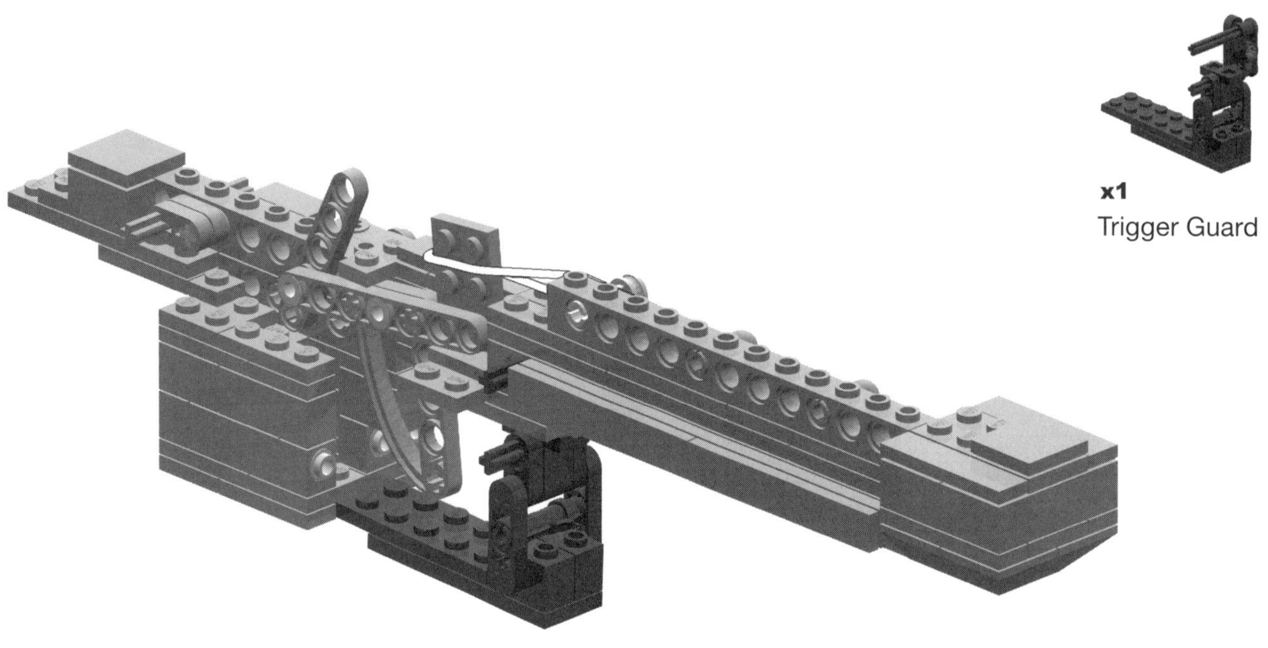

20

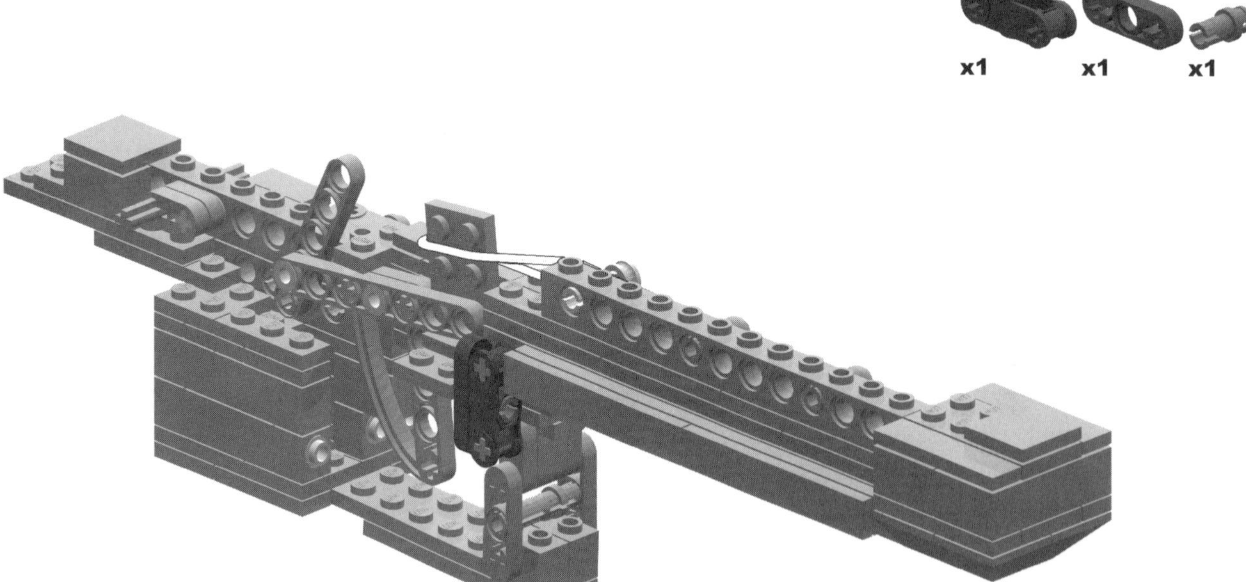

21

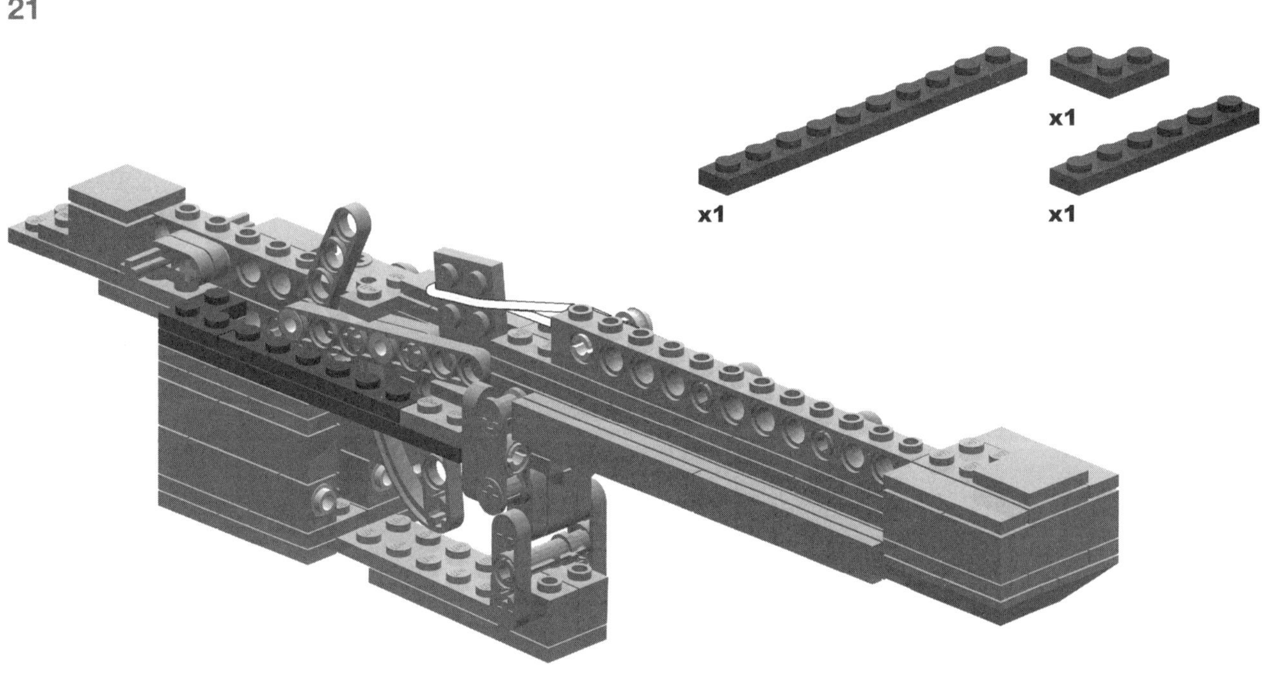

22

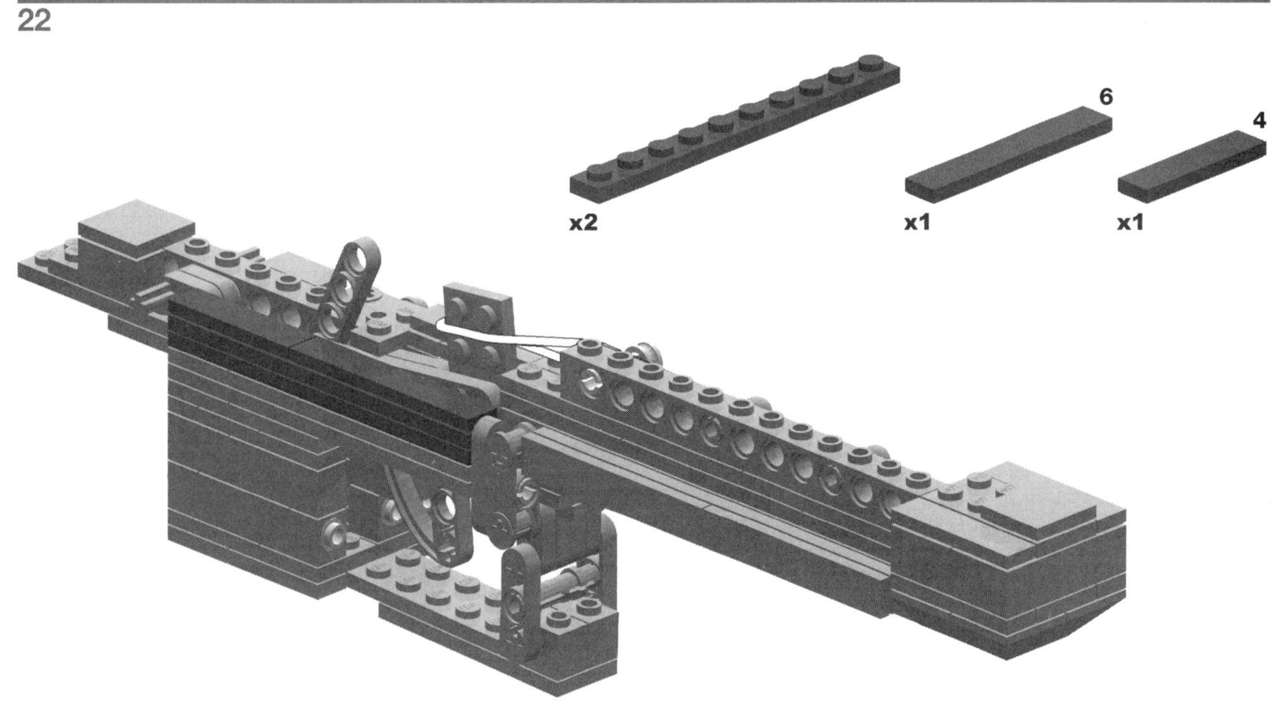

23

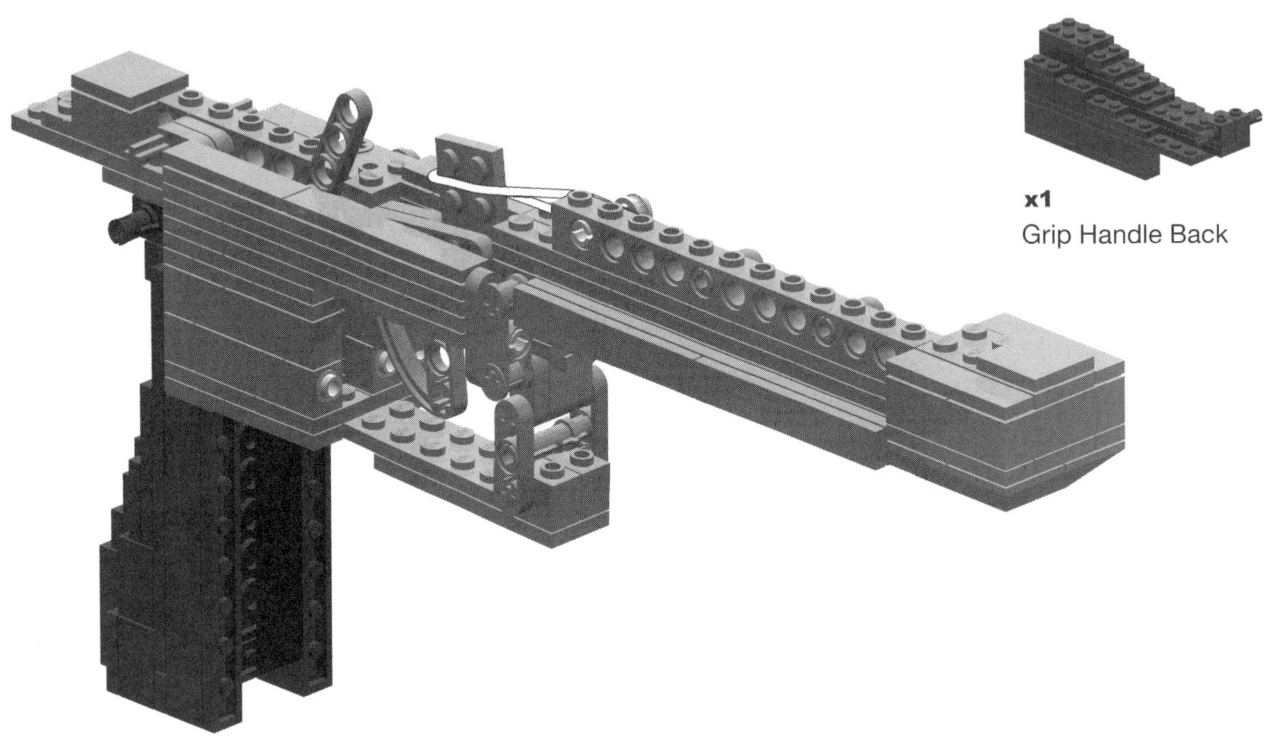

24

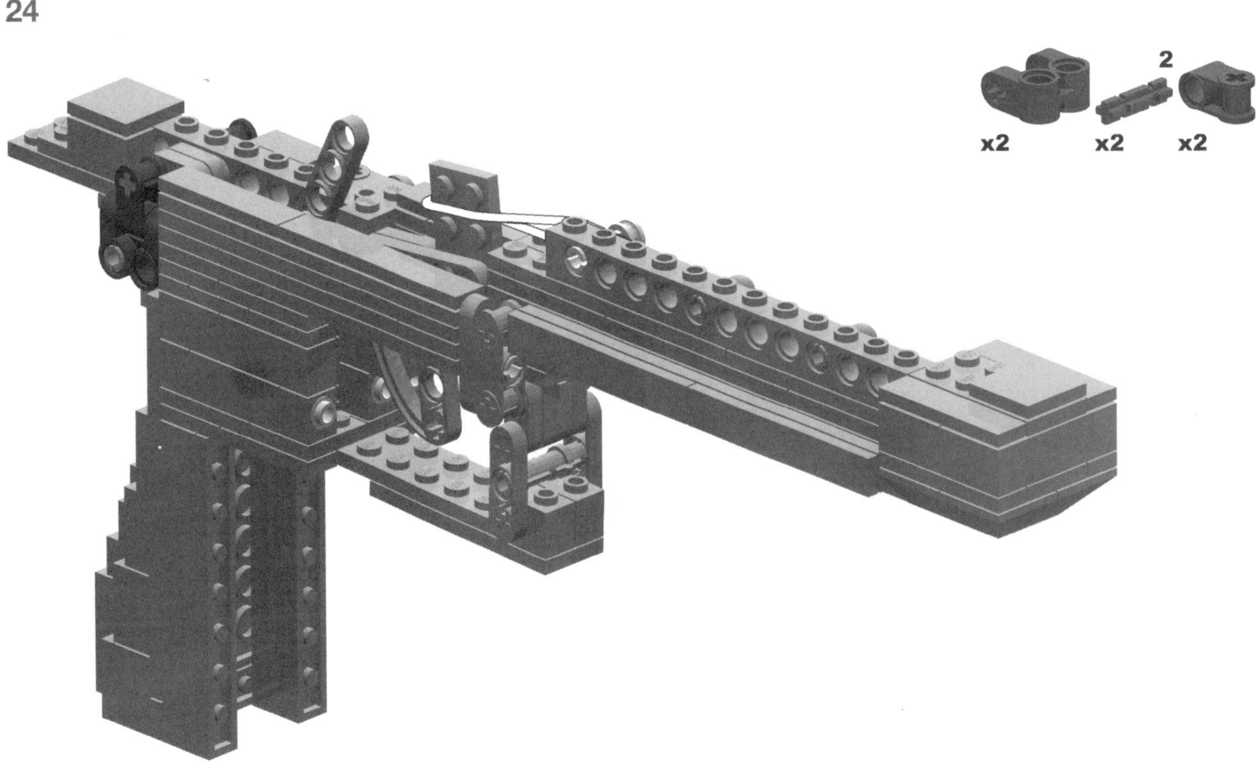

25

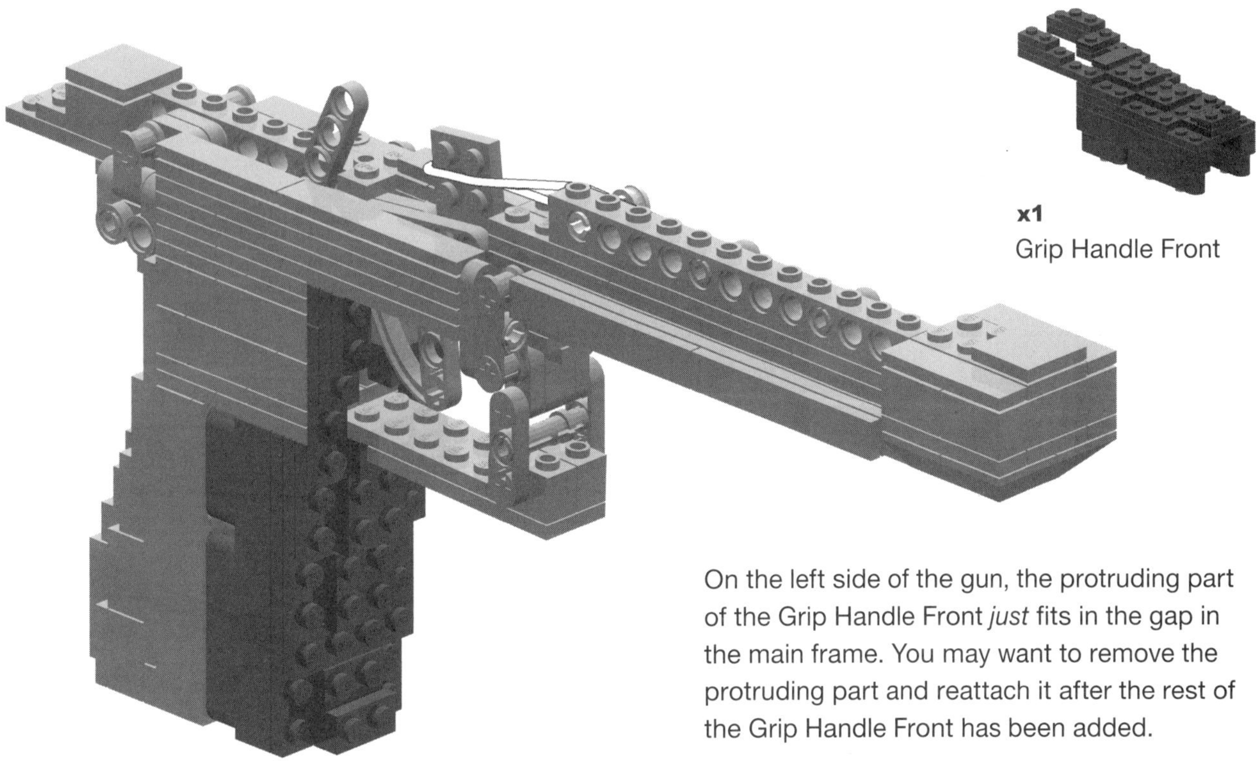

On the left side of the gun, the protruding part of the Grip Handle Front *just* fits in the gap in the main frame. You may want to remove the protruding part and reattach it after the rest of the Grip Handle Front has been added.

SLIDE RIGHT

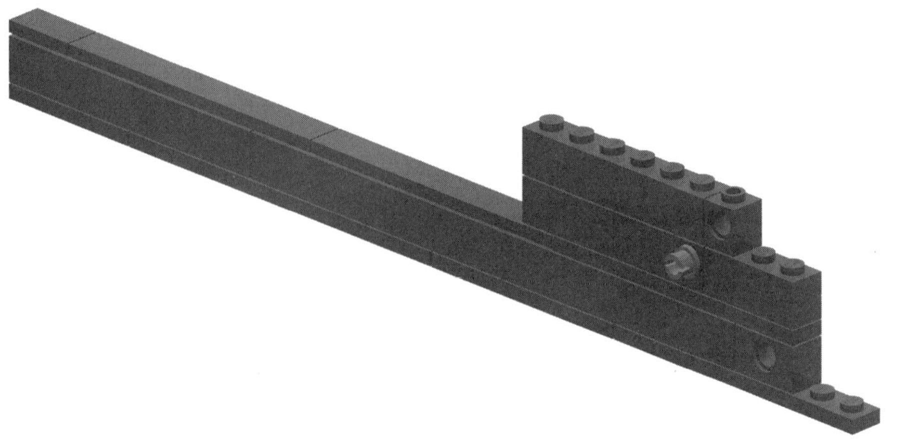

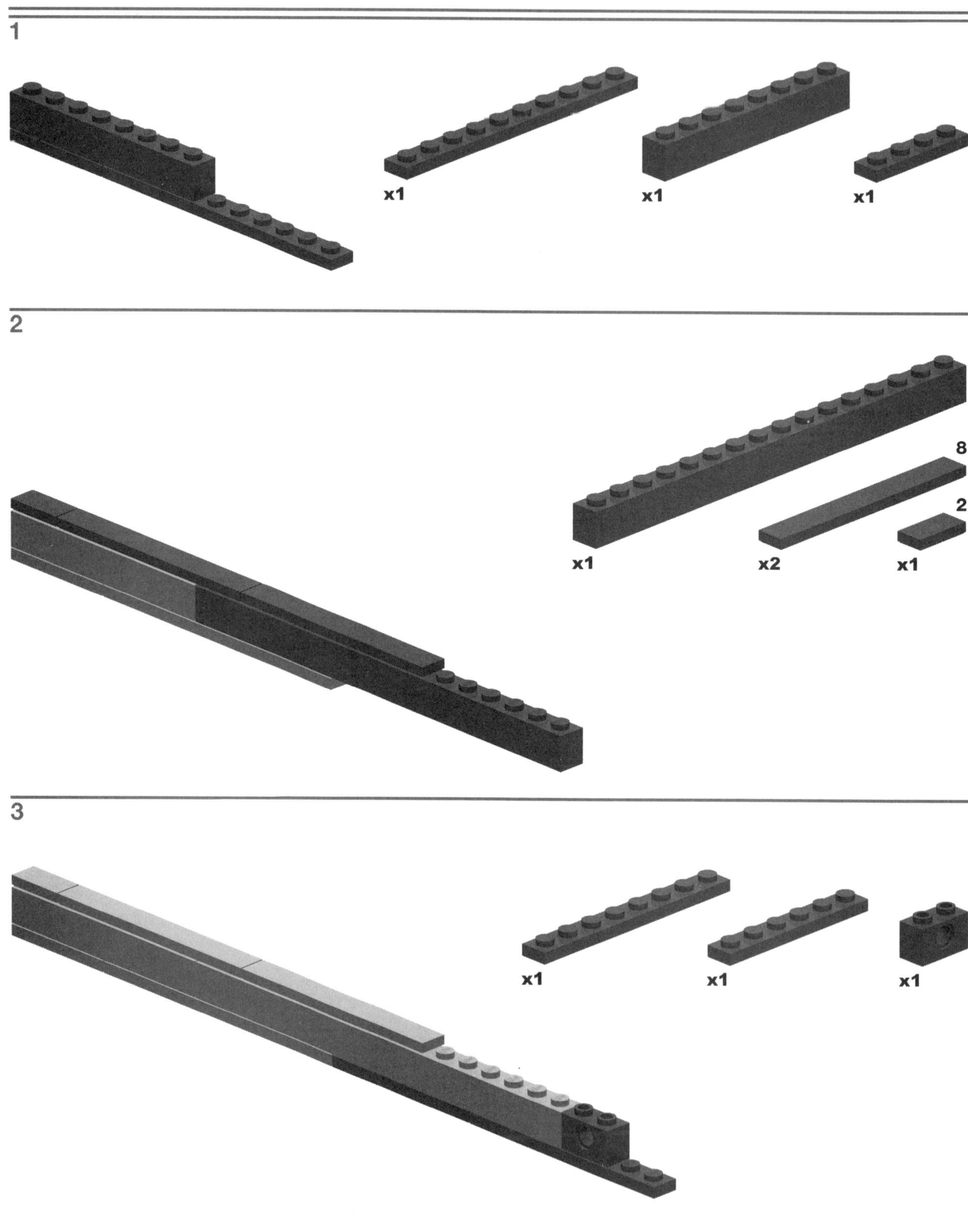
1
x1
x1
x1
2
8
2
x1
x2
x1
3
x1
x1
x1

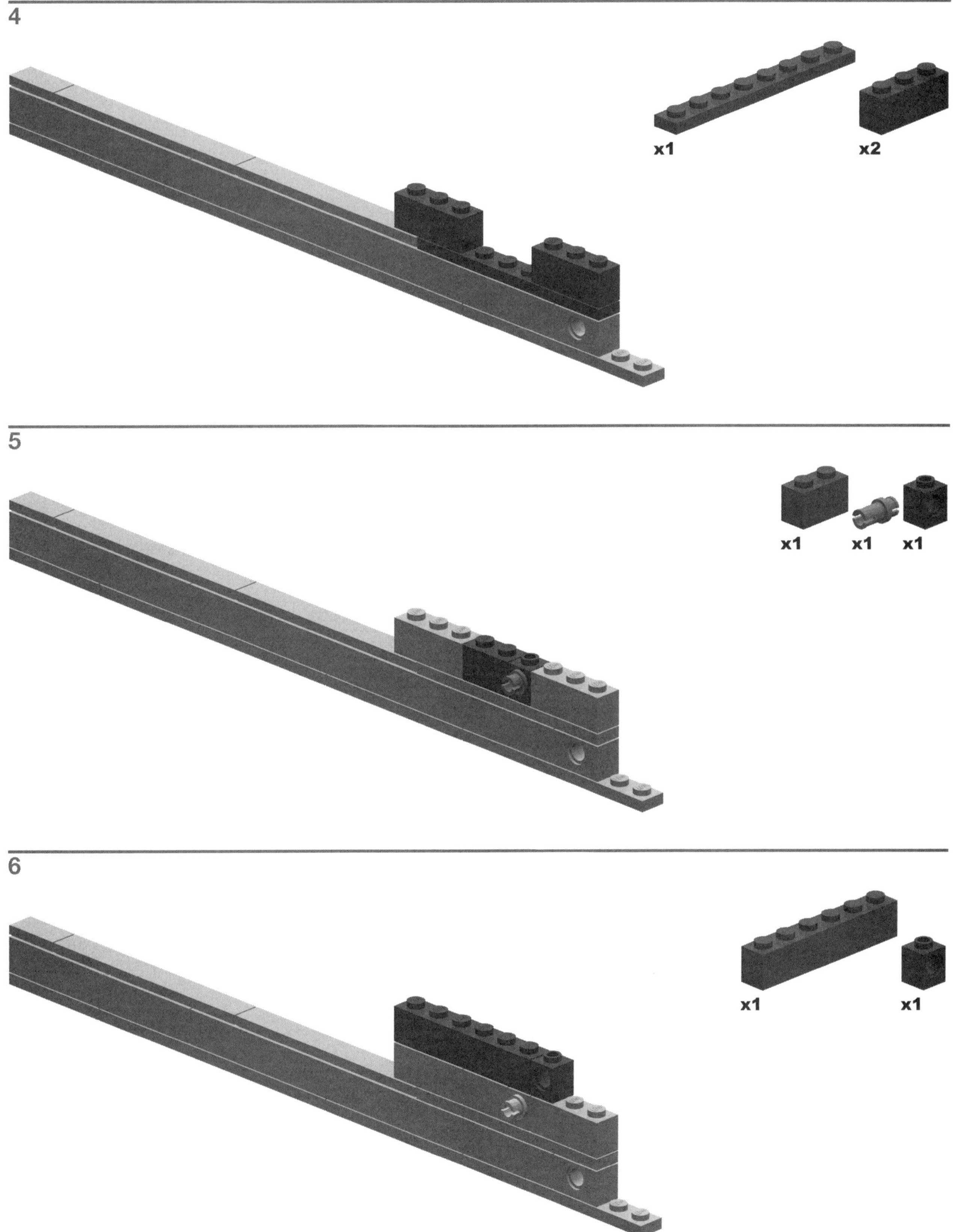
4
x1
x2
5
x1
x1
x1
6
x1
x1

SLIDE MECHANISM

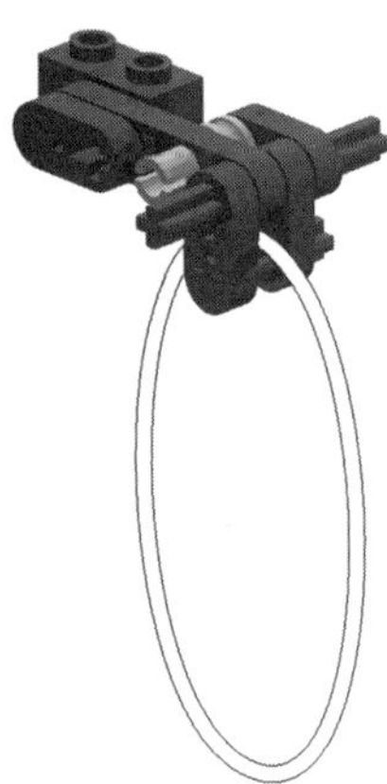

1

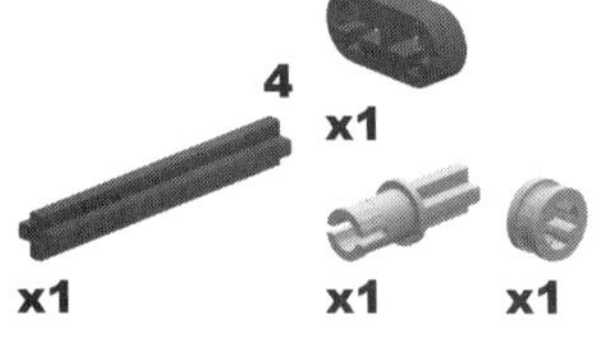

4

x1

x1 x1 x1

2

x1 x1

3

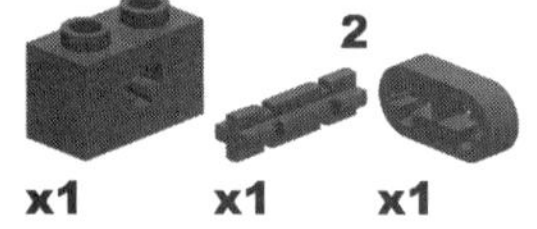

2

x1 x1 x1

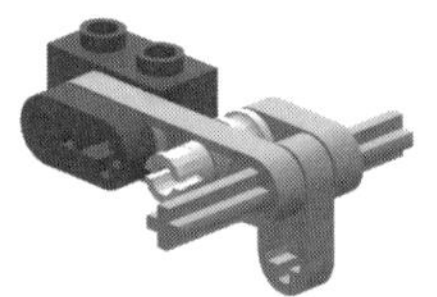

4

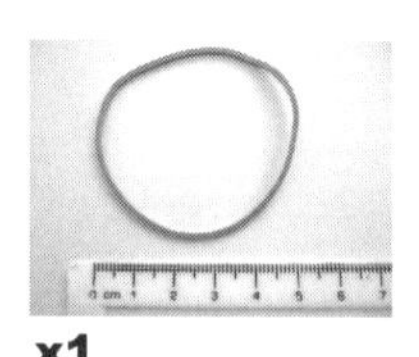

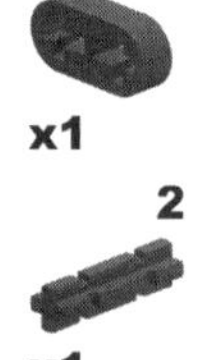

x1

2

x1 x1

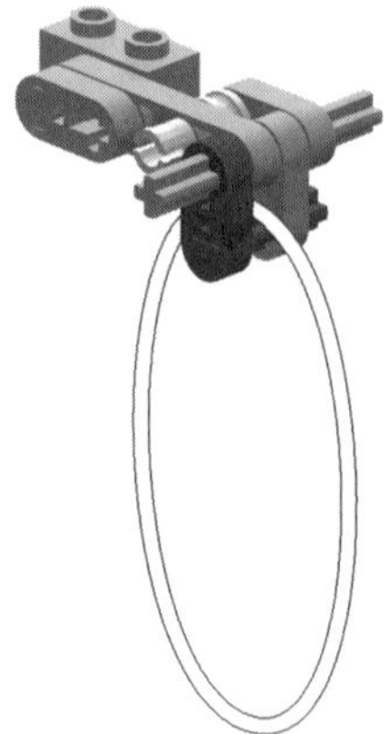

SLIDE LEFT

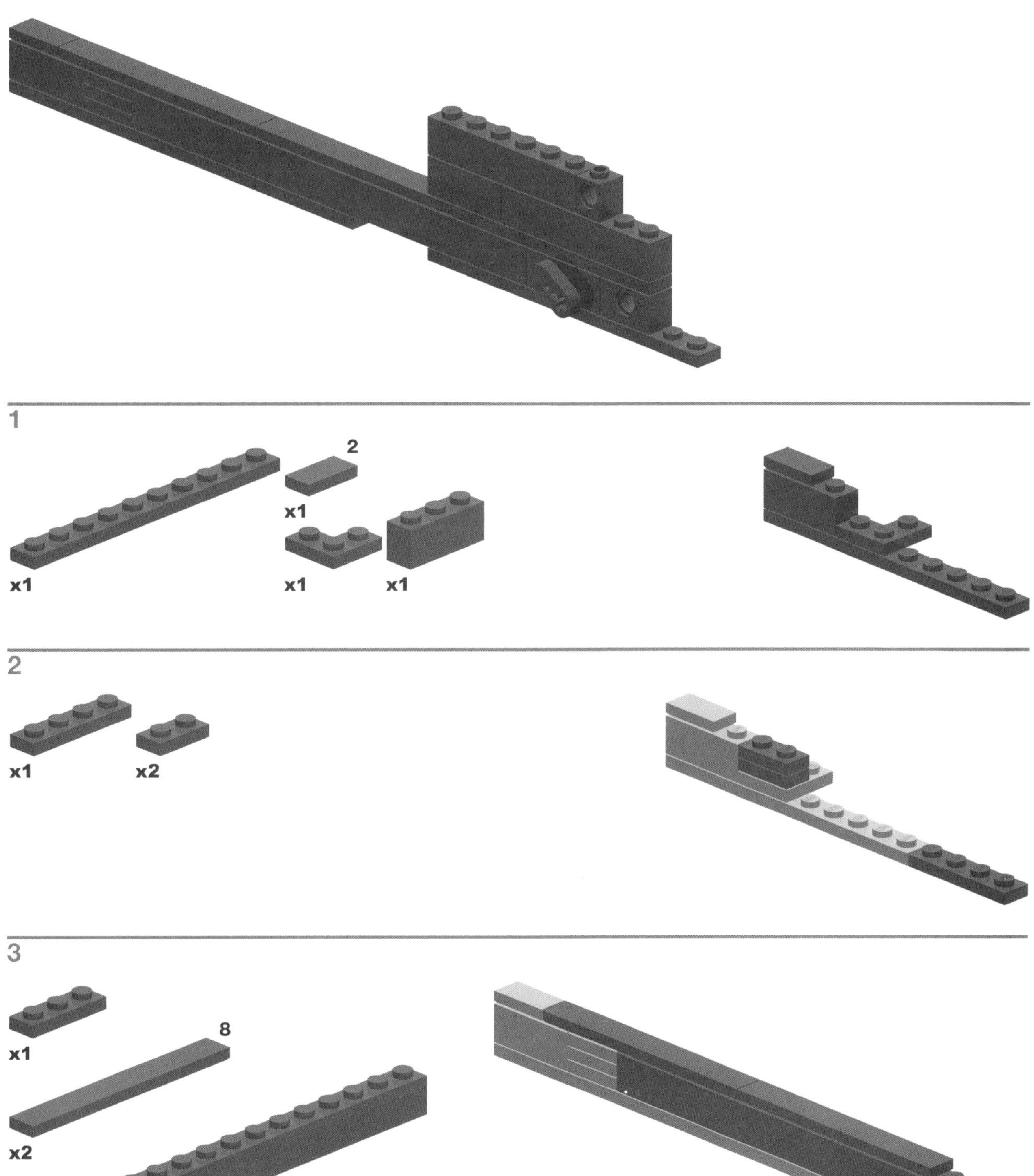

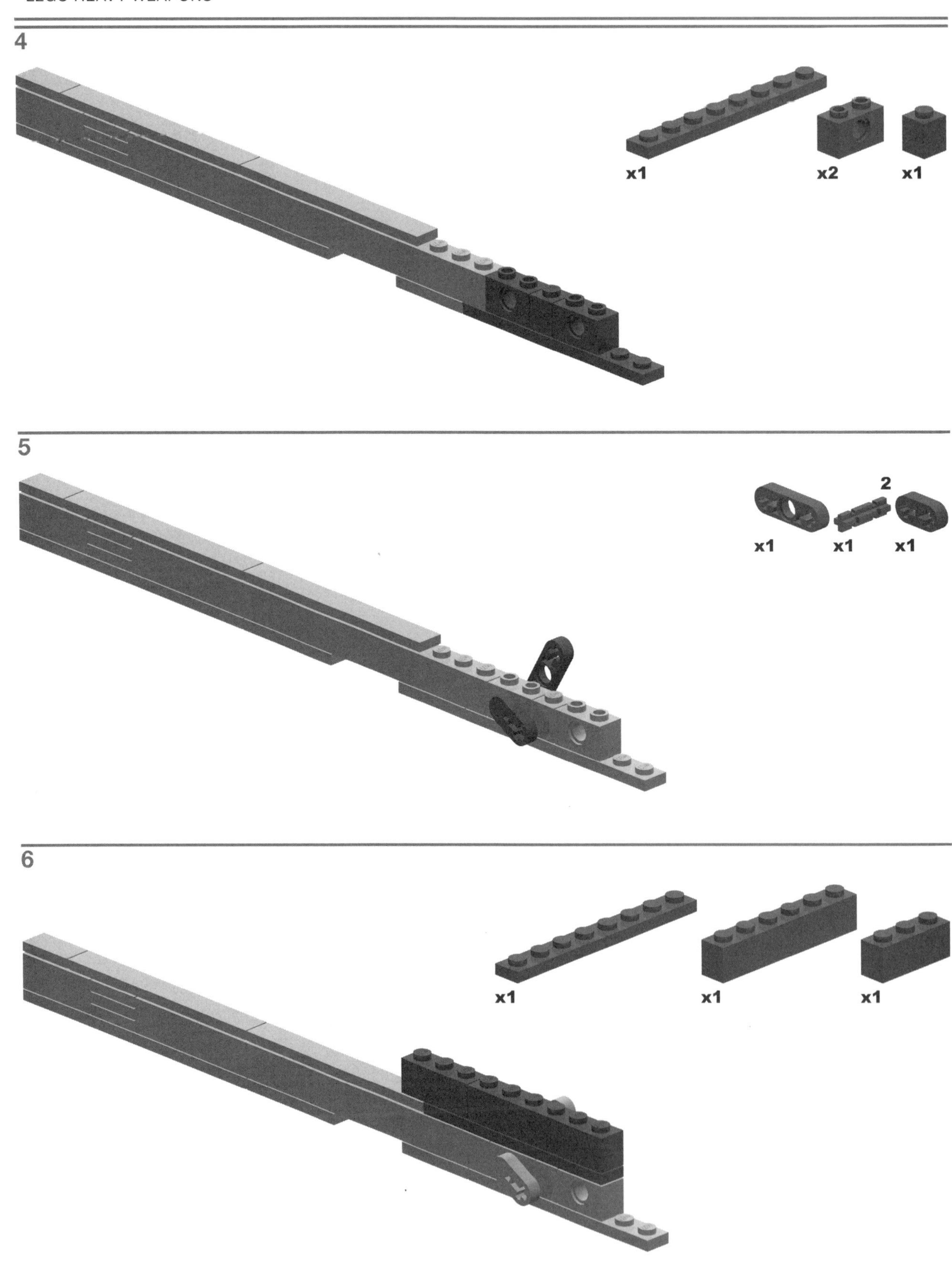
4
x1
x2
x1
5
2
x1
x1
x1
6
x1
x1
x1

7

x1 x1

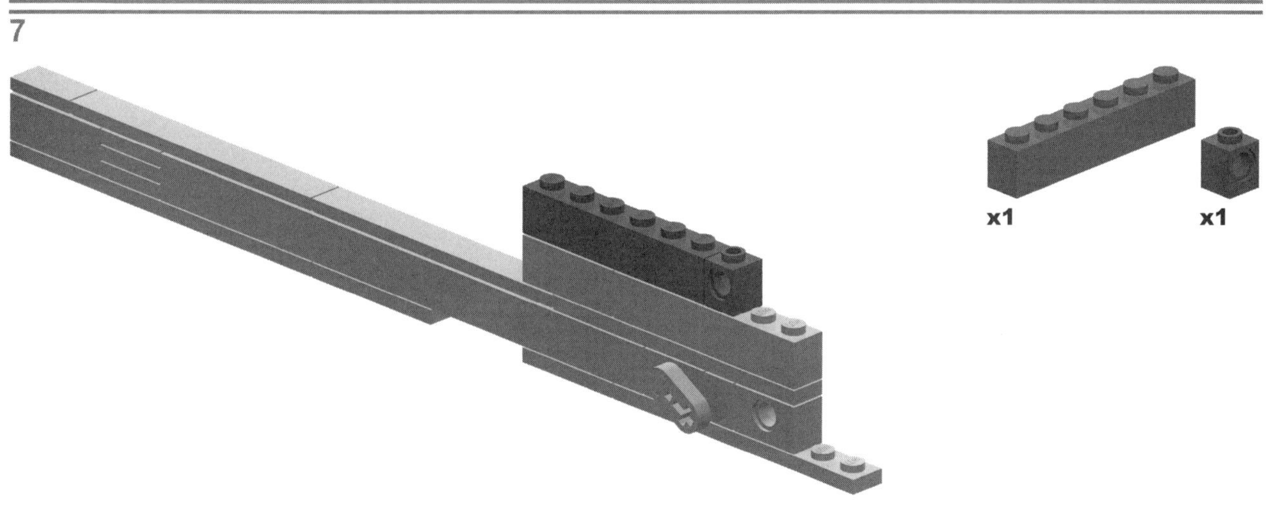

SLIDE BACK

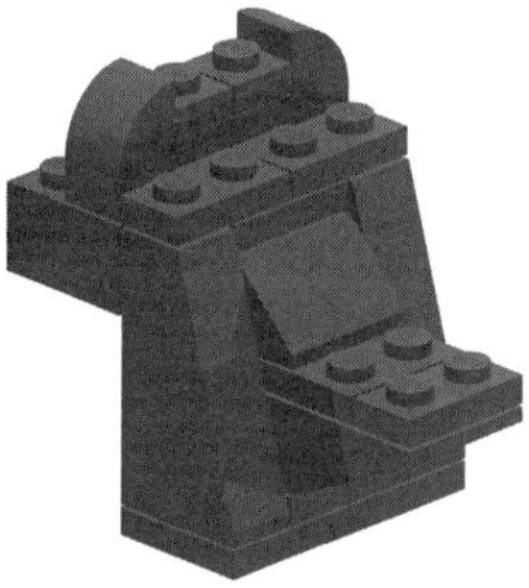

1

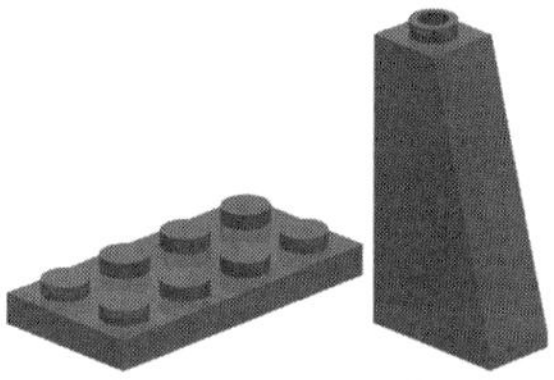

x1 x1

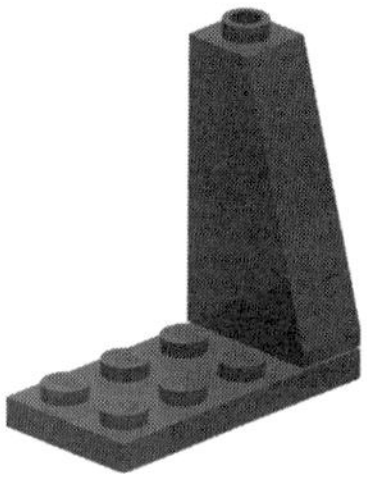

2

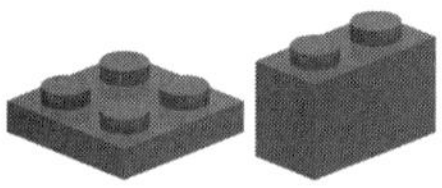

x1 x1

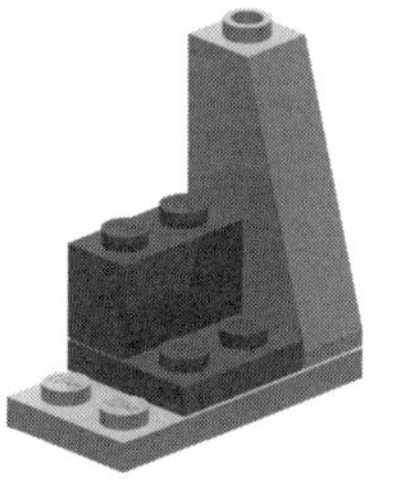

3

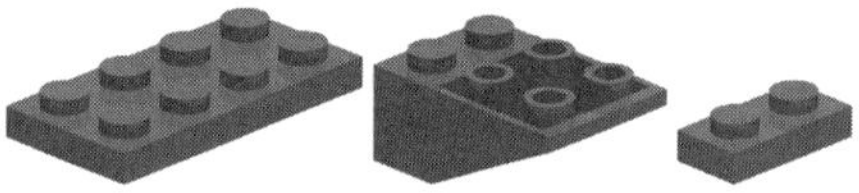

x1 x1 x1

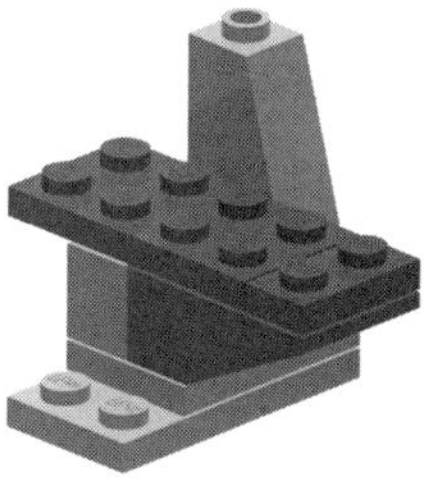

4

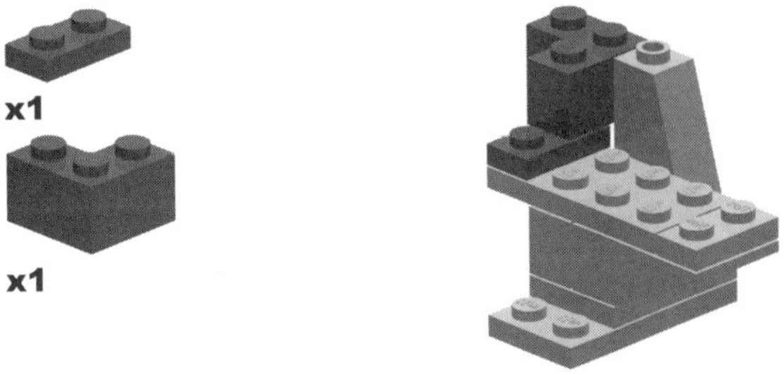

x1

x1

5

x1

x1

x1

6

x1

x2

7

x1

x2

SLIDE ASSEMBLY

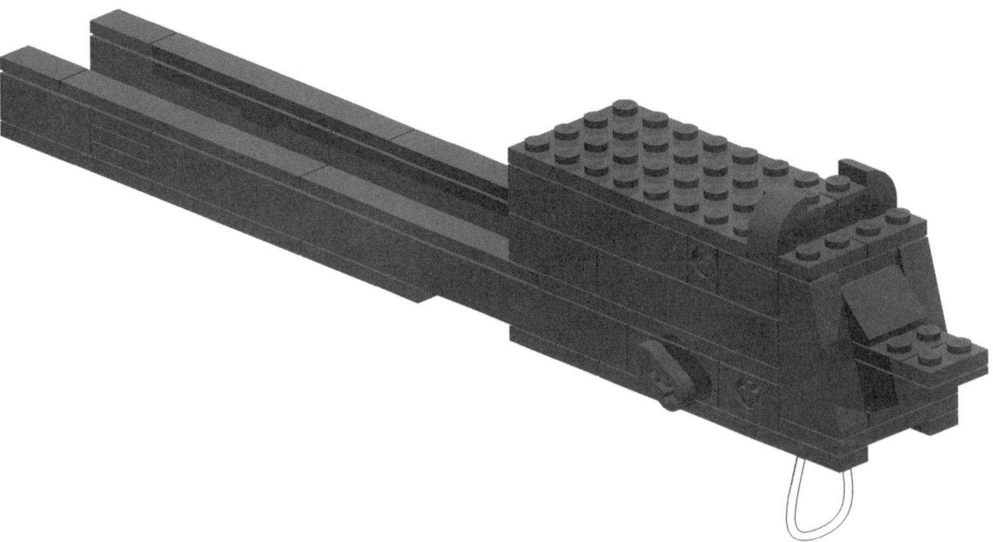

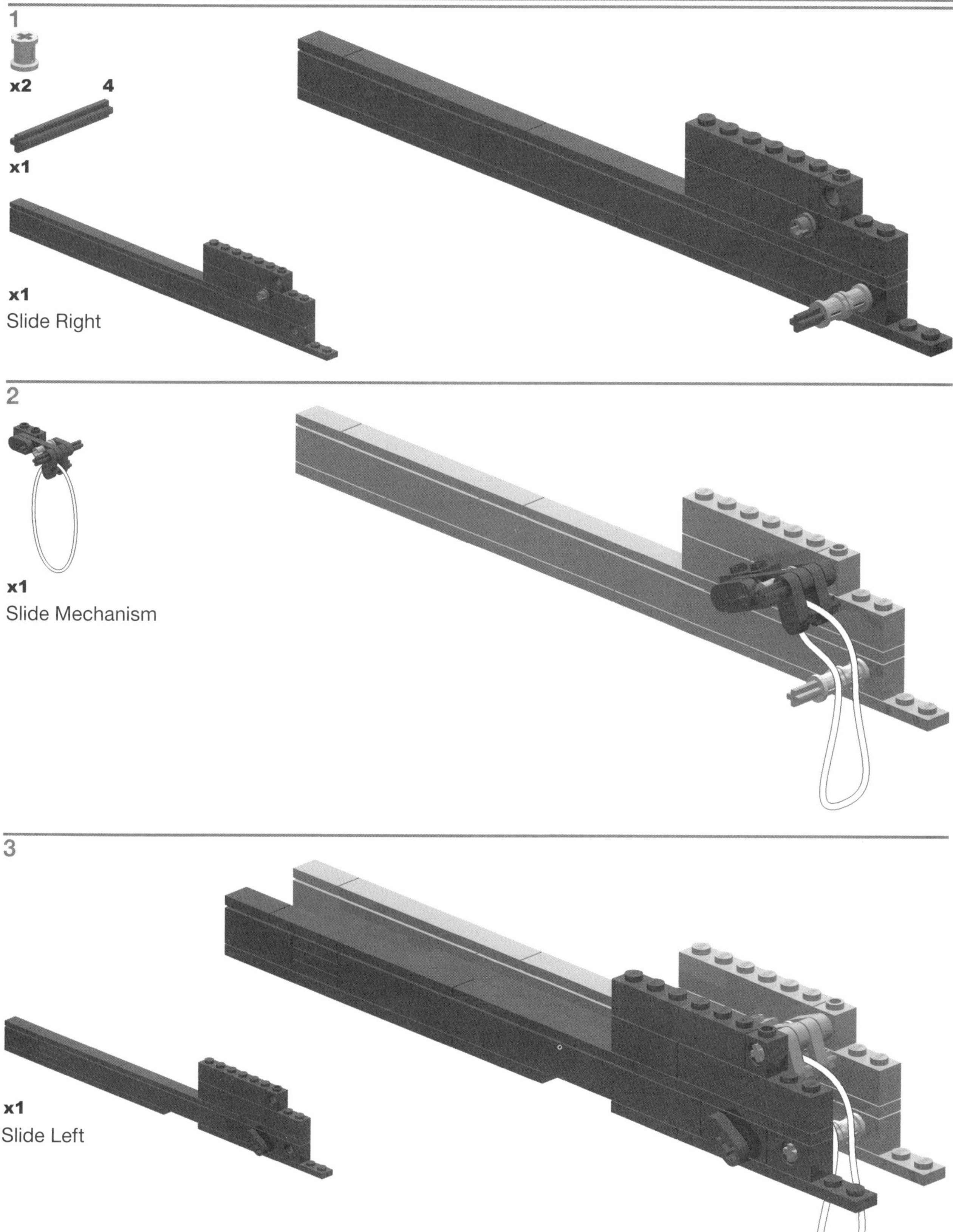
1
x2
4
x1
x1
Slide Right
2
x1
Slide Mechanism
3
x1
Slide Left

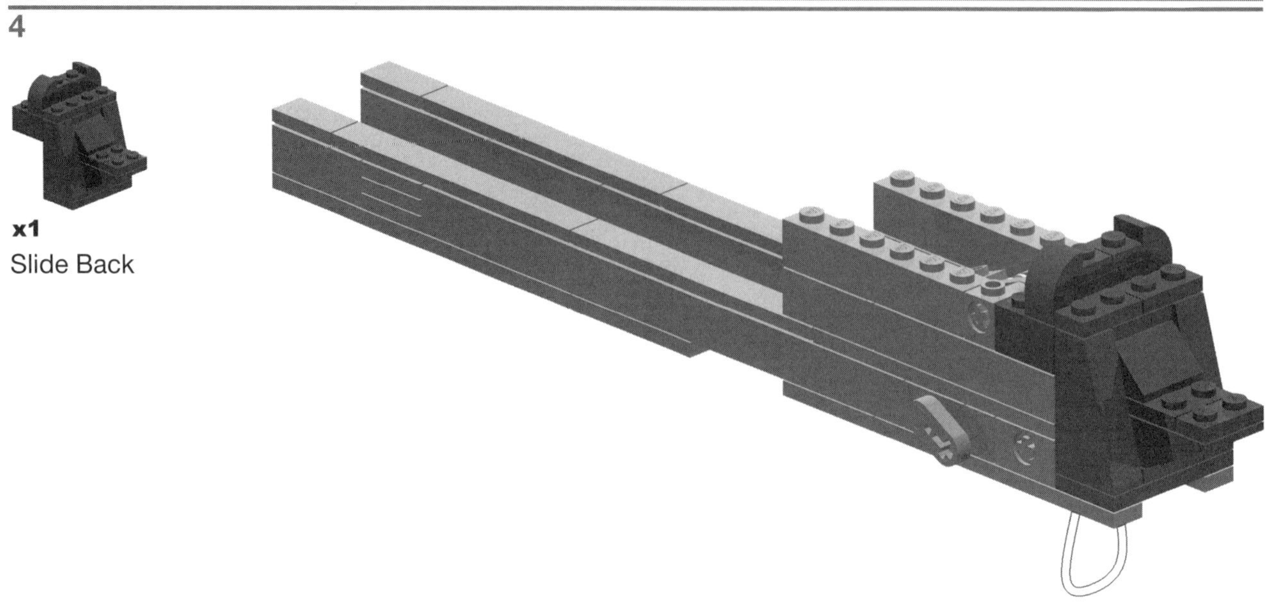

5

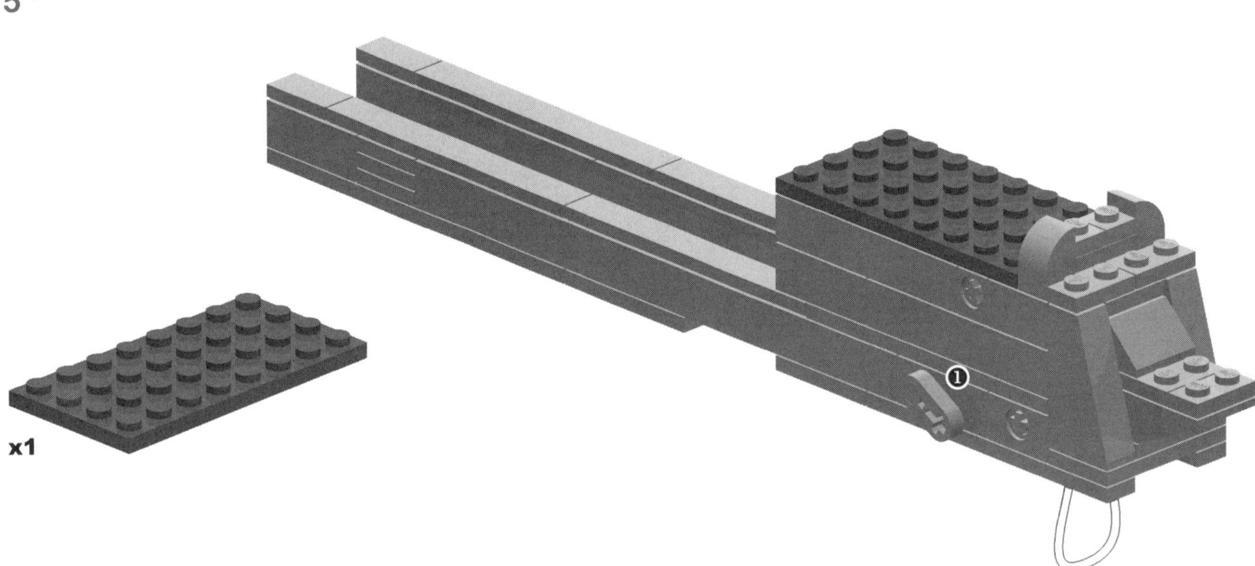

To check whether the safety catch is working properly, flick the back of the safety catch (the 1×2×0.5 liftarm ➊) upward while pulling on the end of the rubber band (pulling it *away* from the frame and increasing tension). The safety catch should click into a position roughly horizontal in relation to the rest of the Slide, but it shouldn't be able to move any farther counterclockwise. To disengage the safety catch, just flick it downward (clockwise). It should now be pointing at about 4 o'clock and be unable to move any farther clockwise.

If your safety catch isn't working, you may have misaligned its mechanism with the Slide Mechanism. Refer to "Safety Catch" on page 13 to see how the safety catch fits with the Slide Mechanism.

CHAMBER

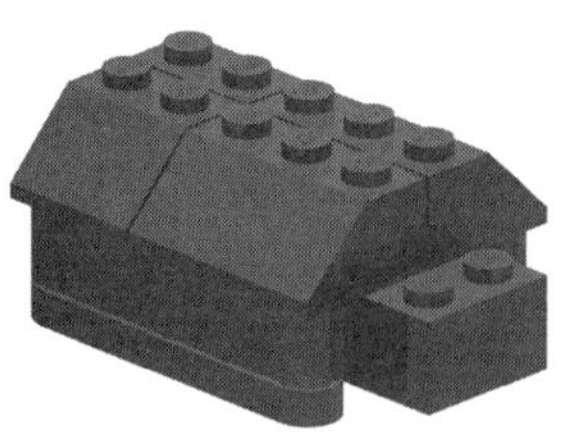

1

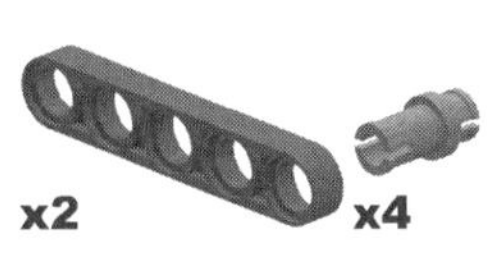

2

3

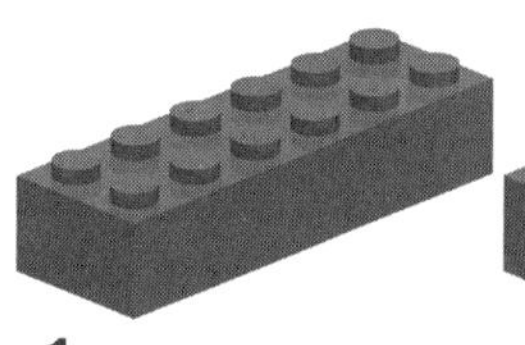

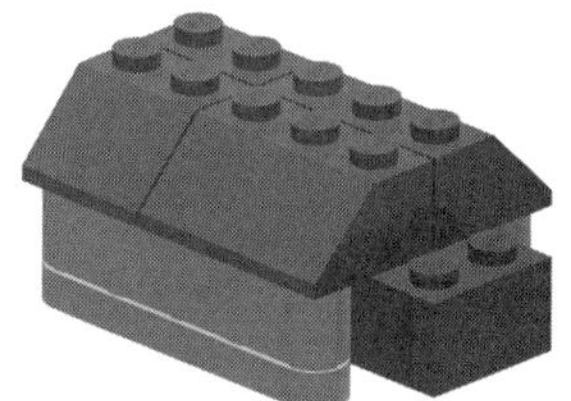

BARREL

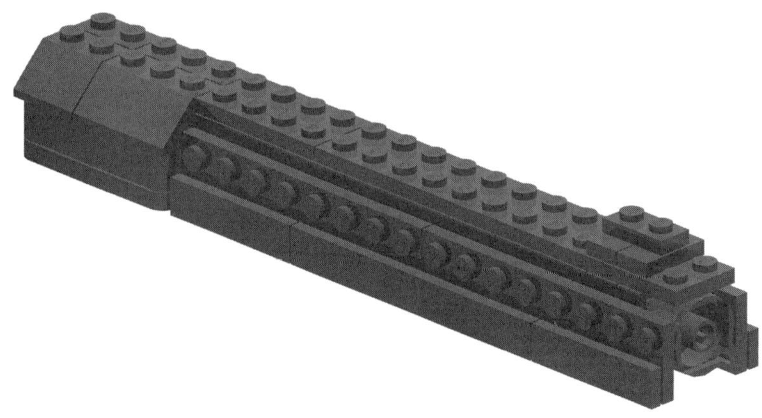

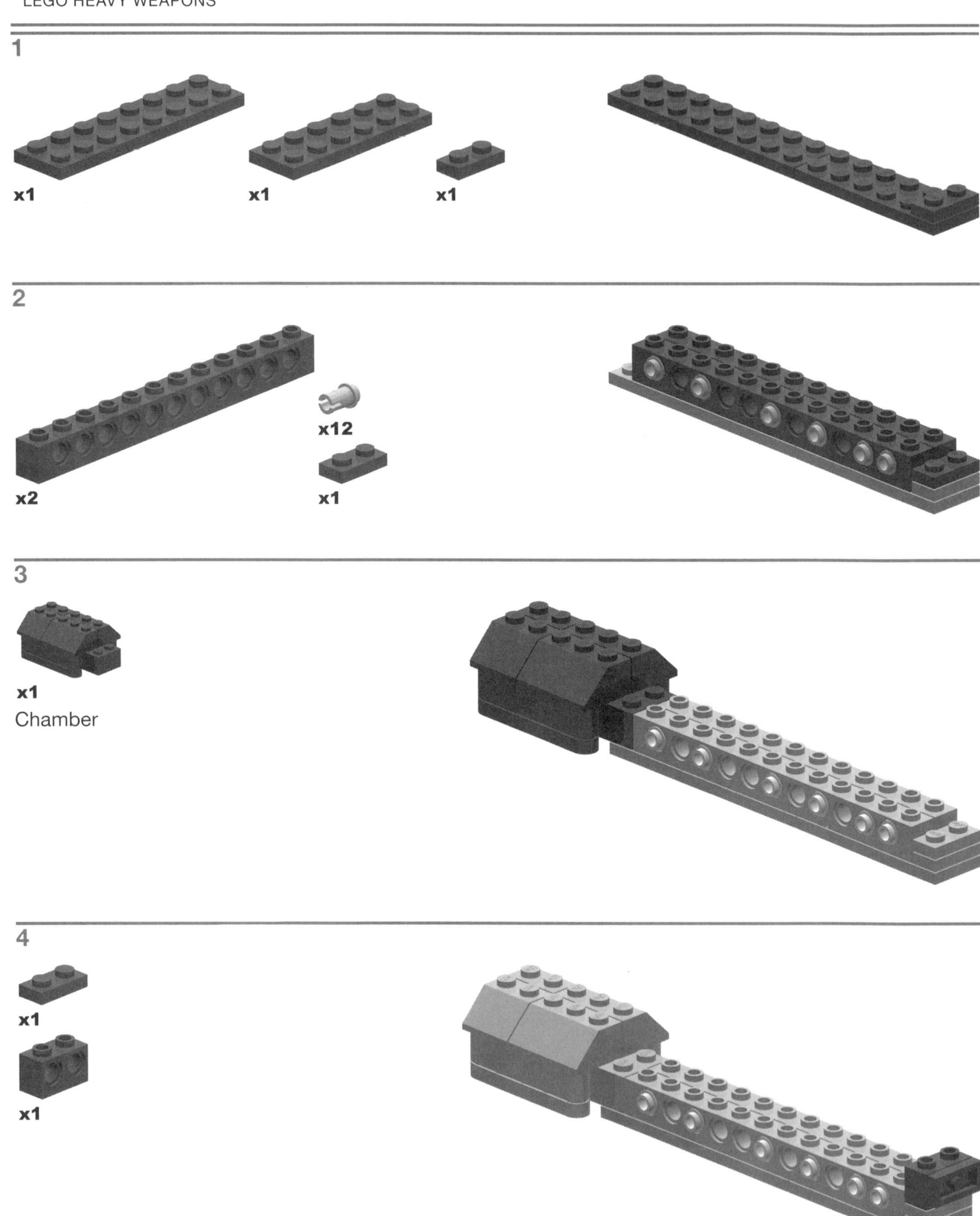
1
x1
x1
x1
2
x12
x2
x1
3
x1
Chamber
4
x1
x1

5

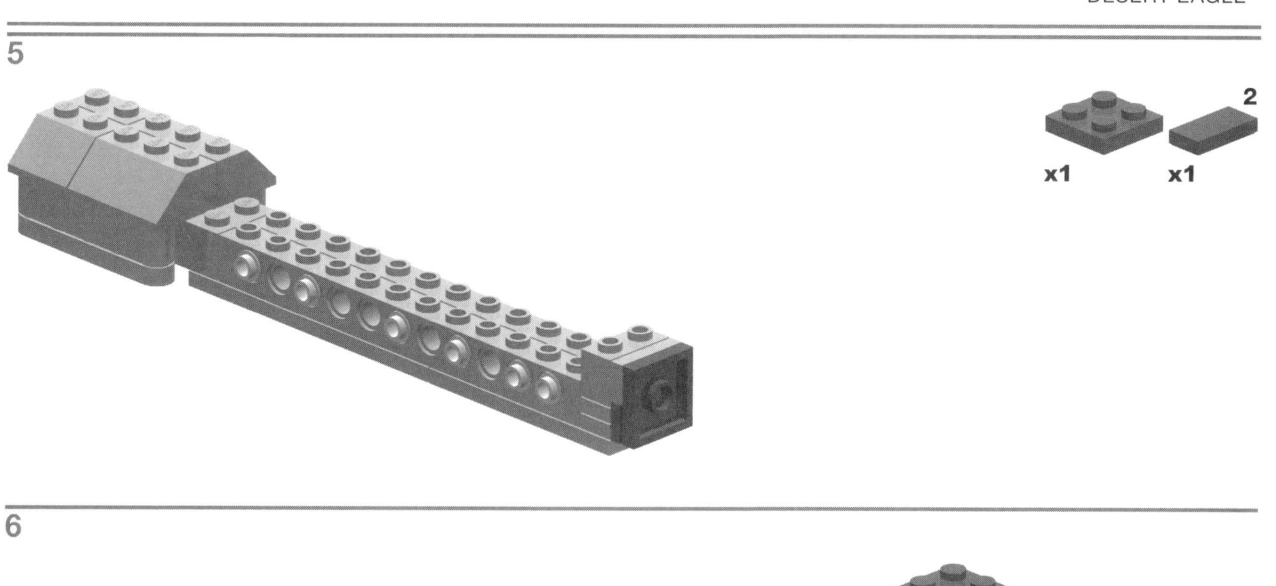

6

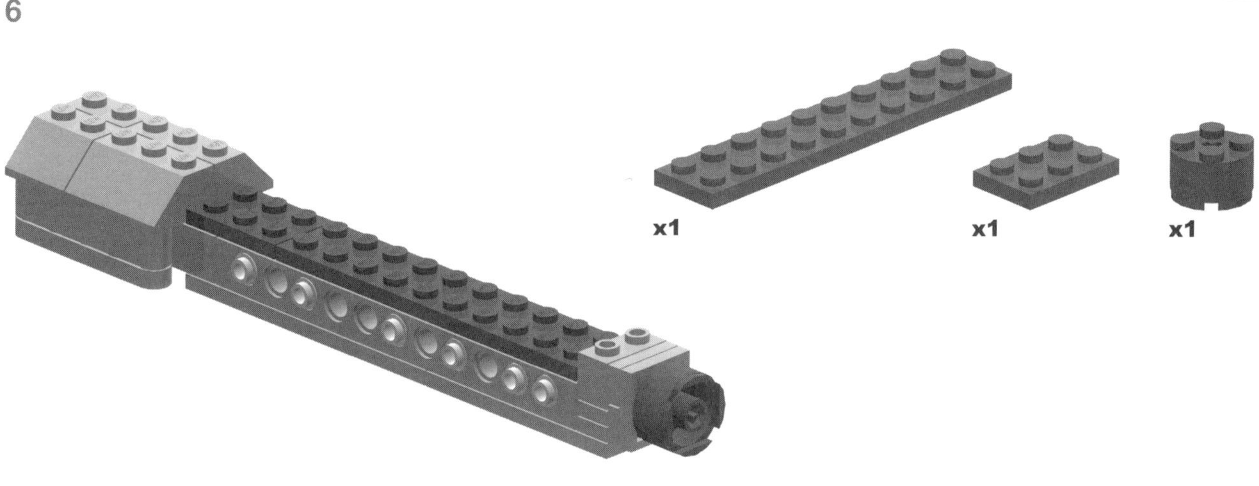

7

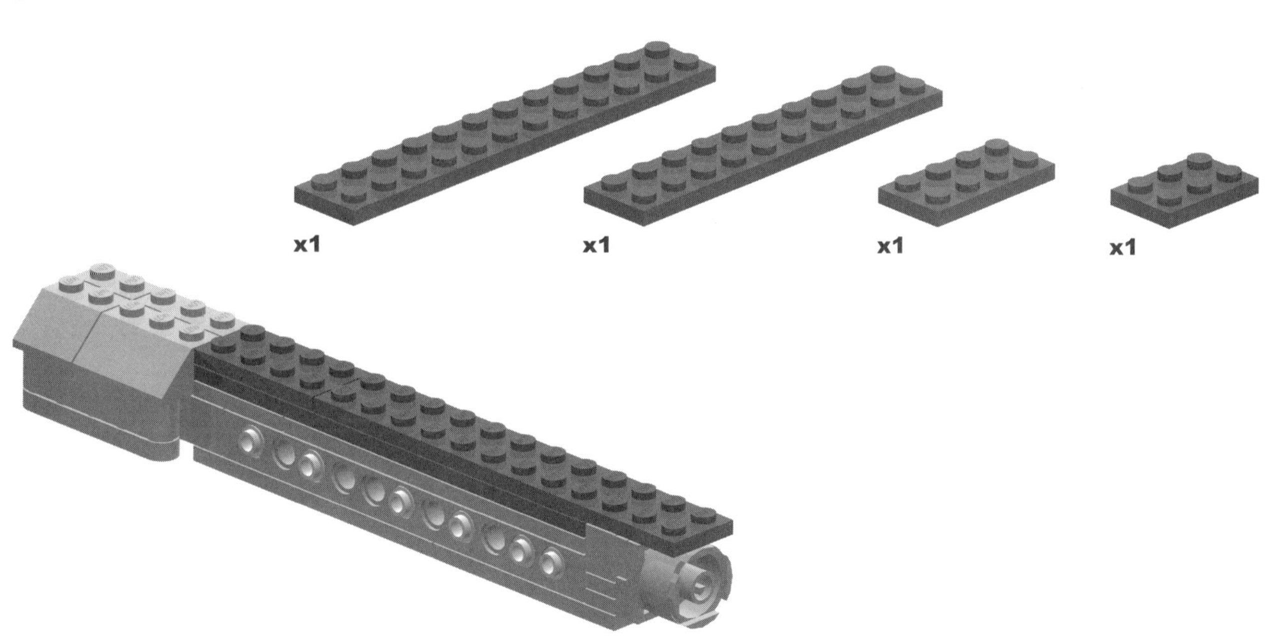

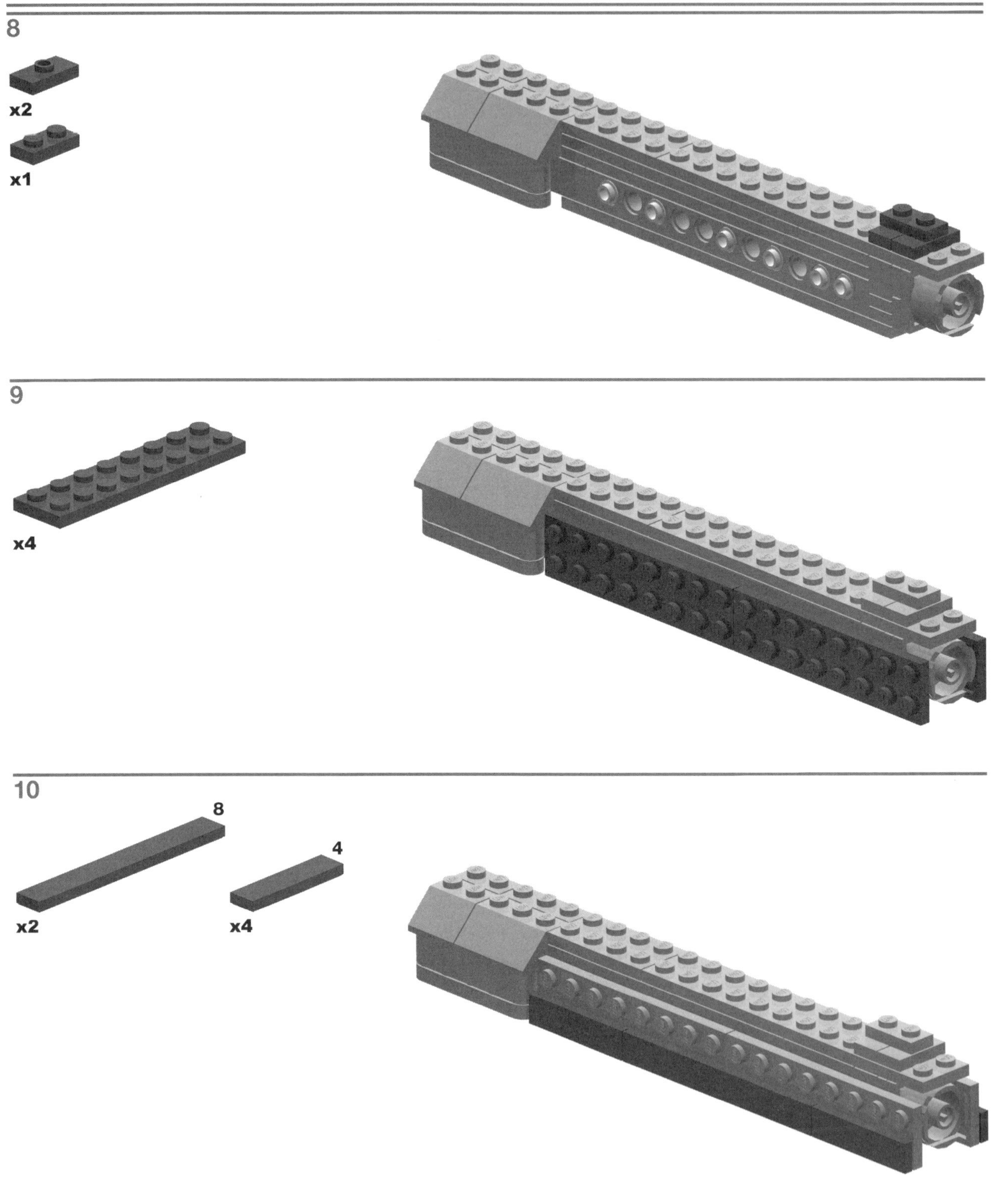
8
x2
x1
9
x4
10
8
4
x2
x4

MAGAZINE

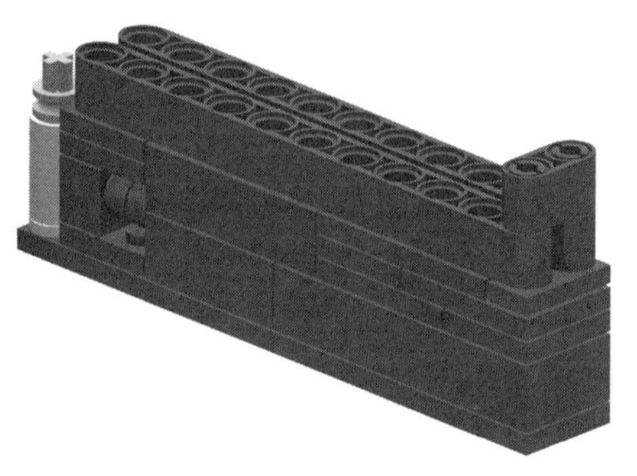

1

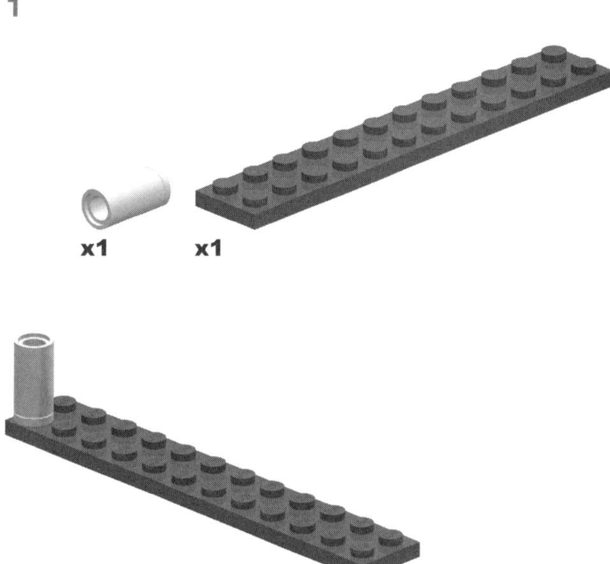

2

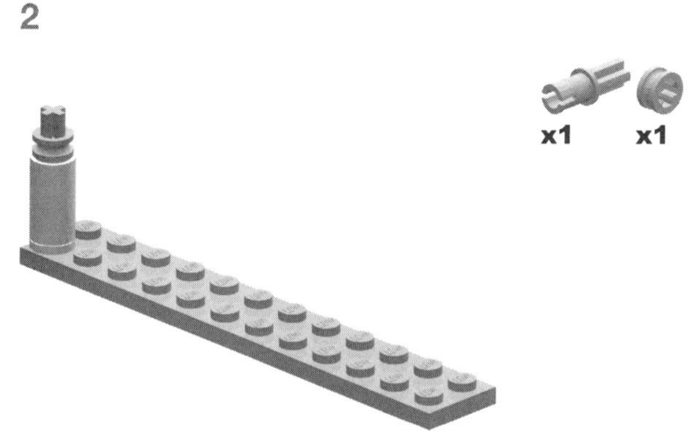

3

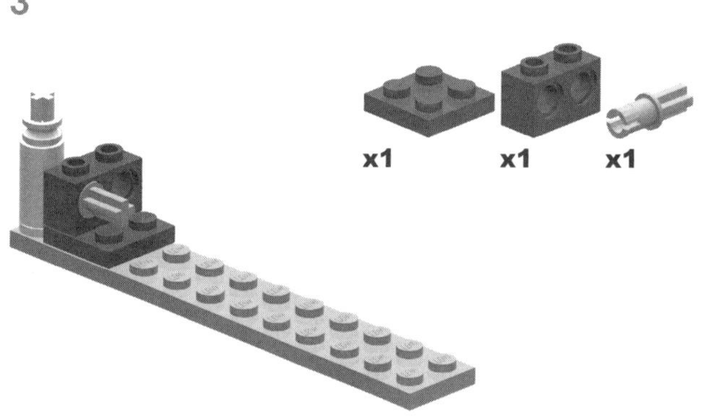

4

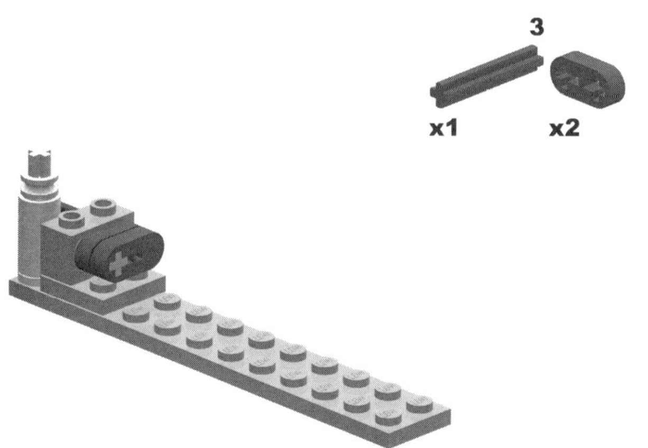

5

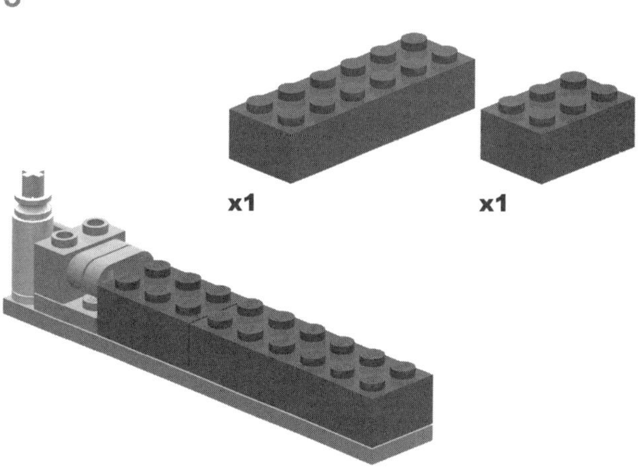

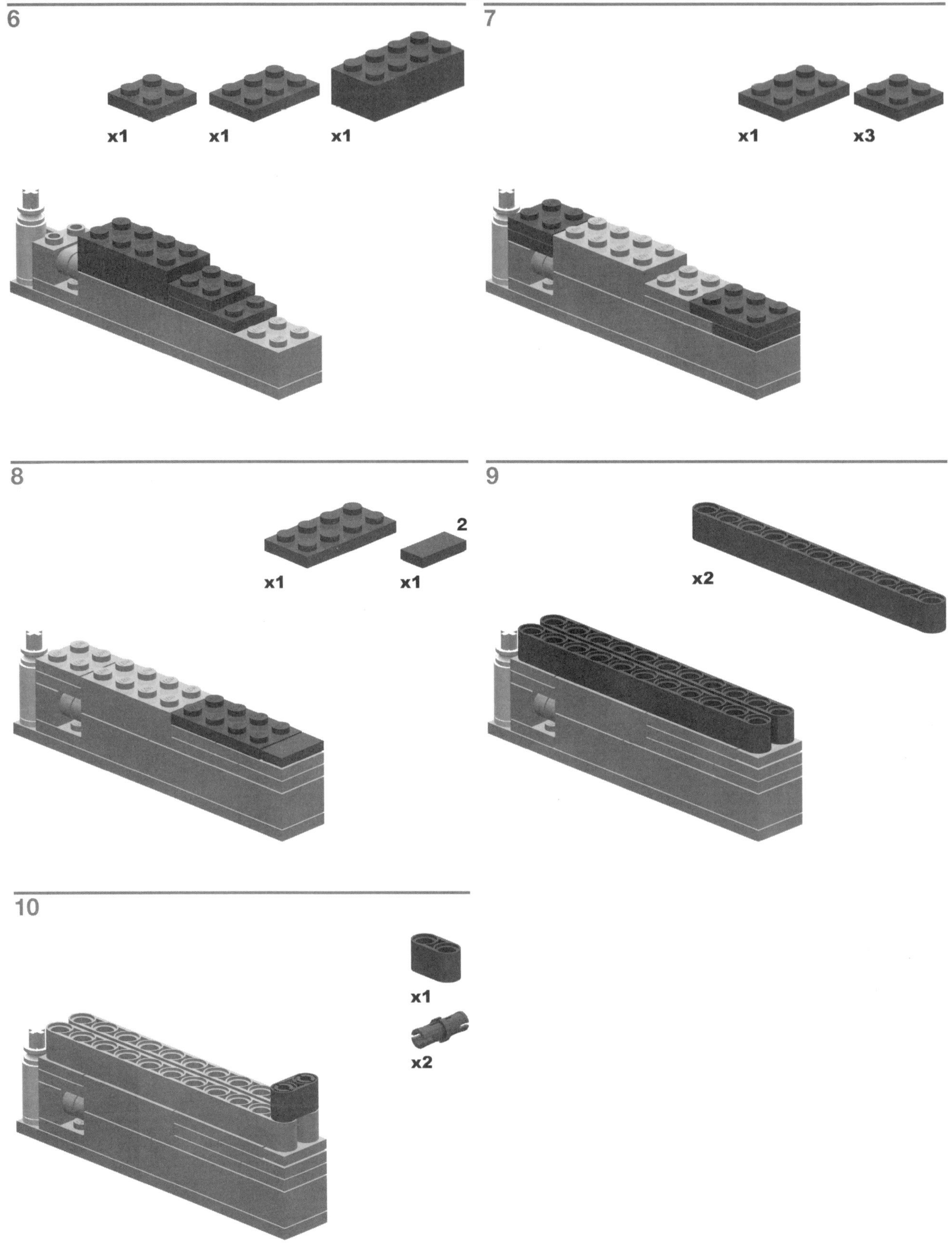
6
x1
x1
x1
7
x1
x3
8
2
x1
x1
9
x2
10
x1
x2

MAIN ASSEMBLY

1

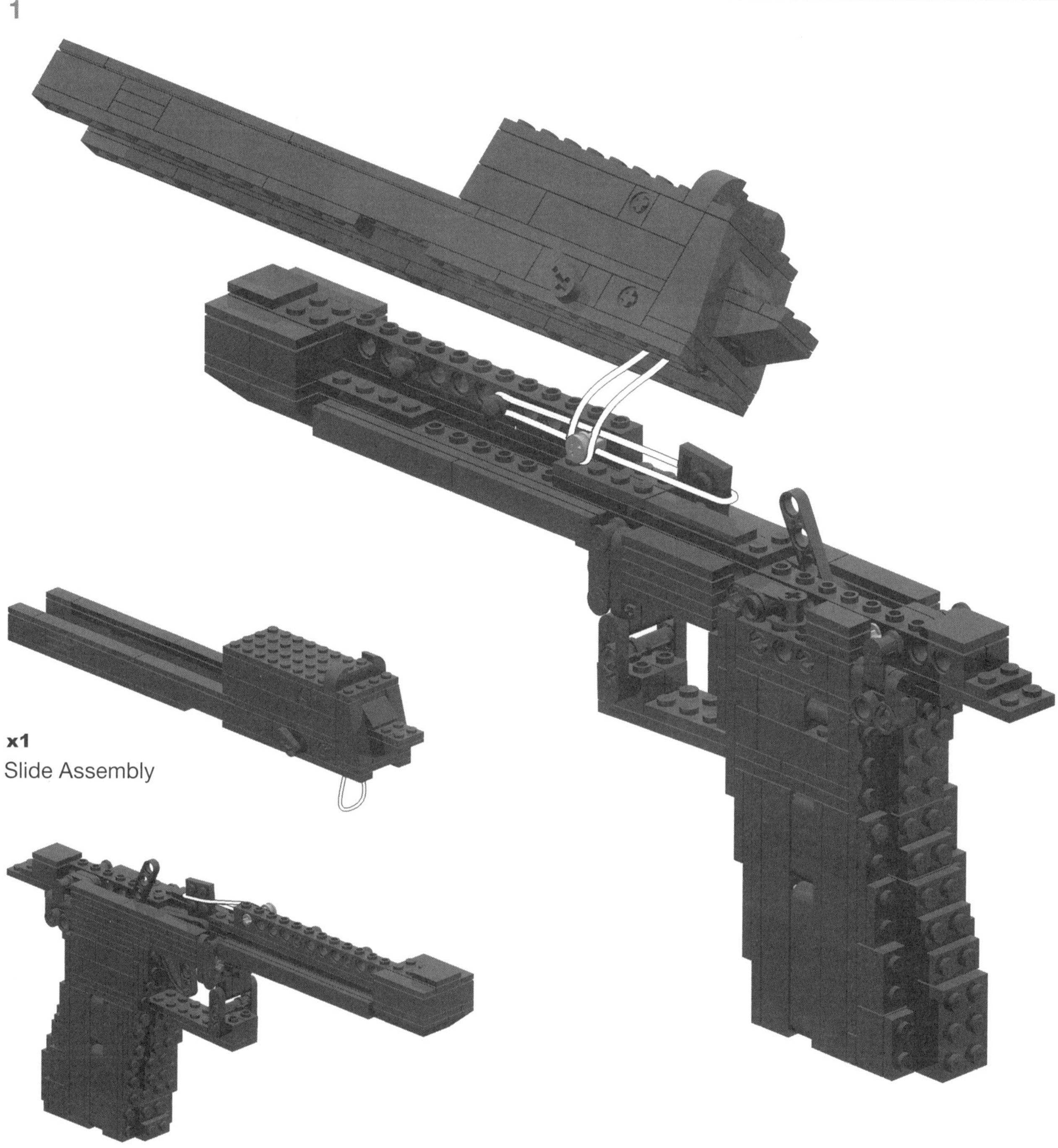

x1
Slide Assembly

x1
Grip Assembly

Fit the rubber band from the Slide onto the bushing as shown. This will keep it away from the rubber band that operates the trigger mechanism.

2

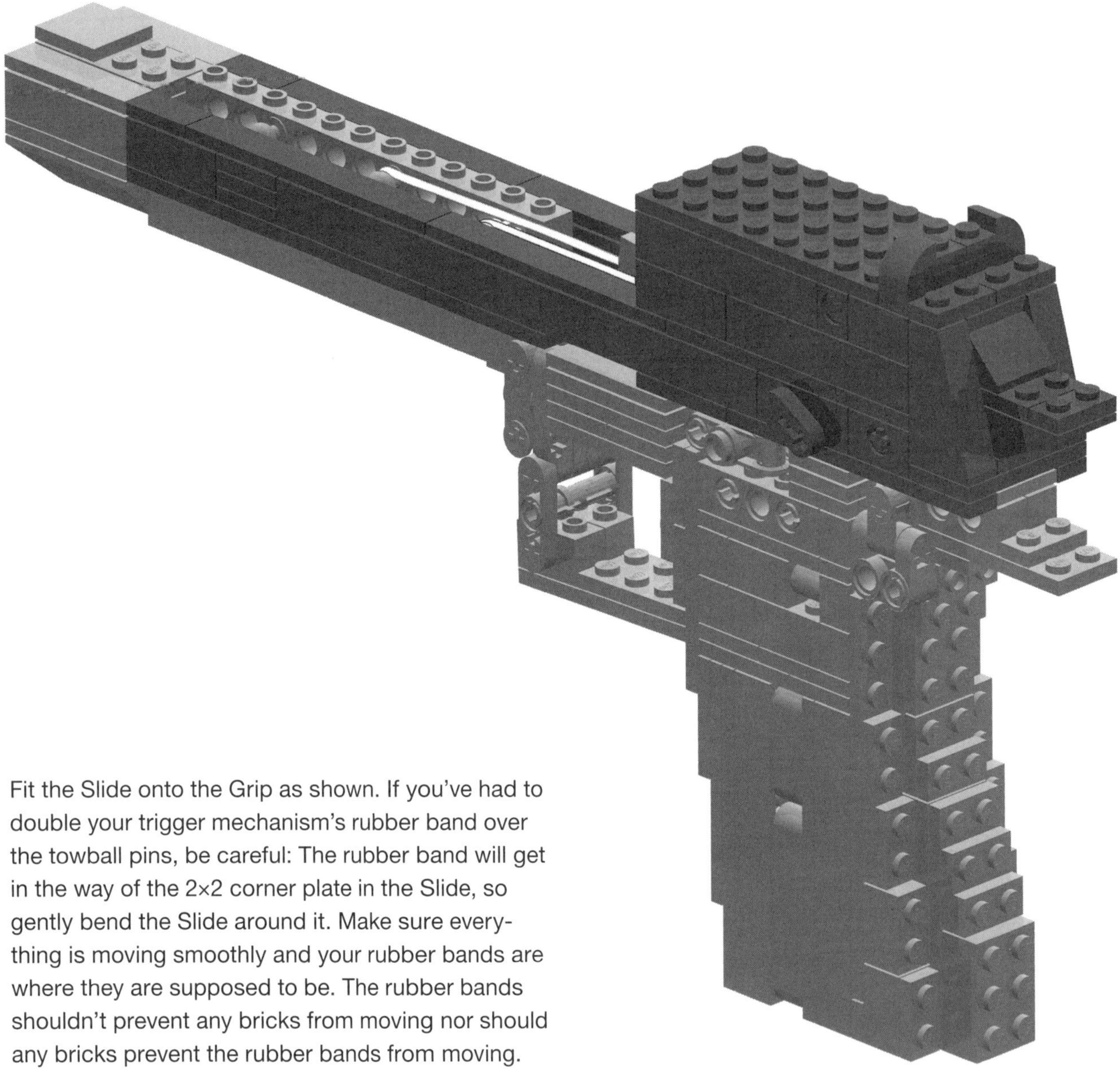

Fit the Slide onto the Grip as shown. If you've had to double your trigger mechanism's rubber band over the towball pins, be careful: The rubber band will get in the way of the 2×2 corner plate in the Slide, so gently bend the Slide around it. Make sure everything is moving smoothly and your rubber bands are where they are supposed to be. The rubber bands shouldn't prevent any bricks from moving nor should any bricks prevent the rubber bands from moving.

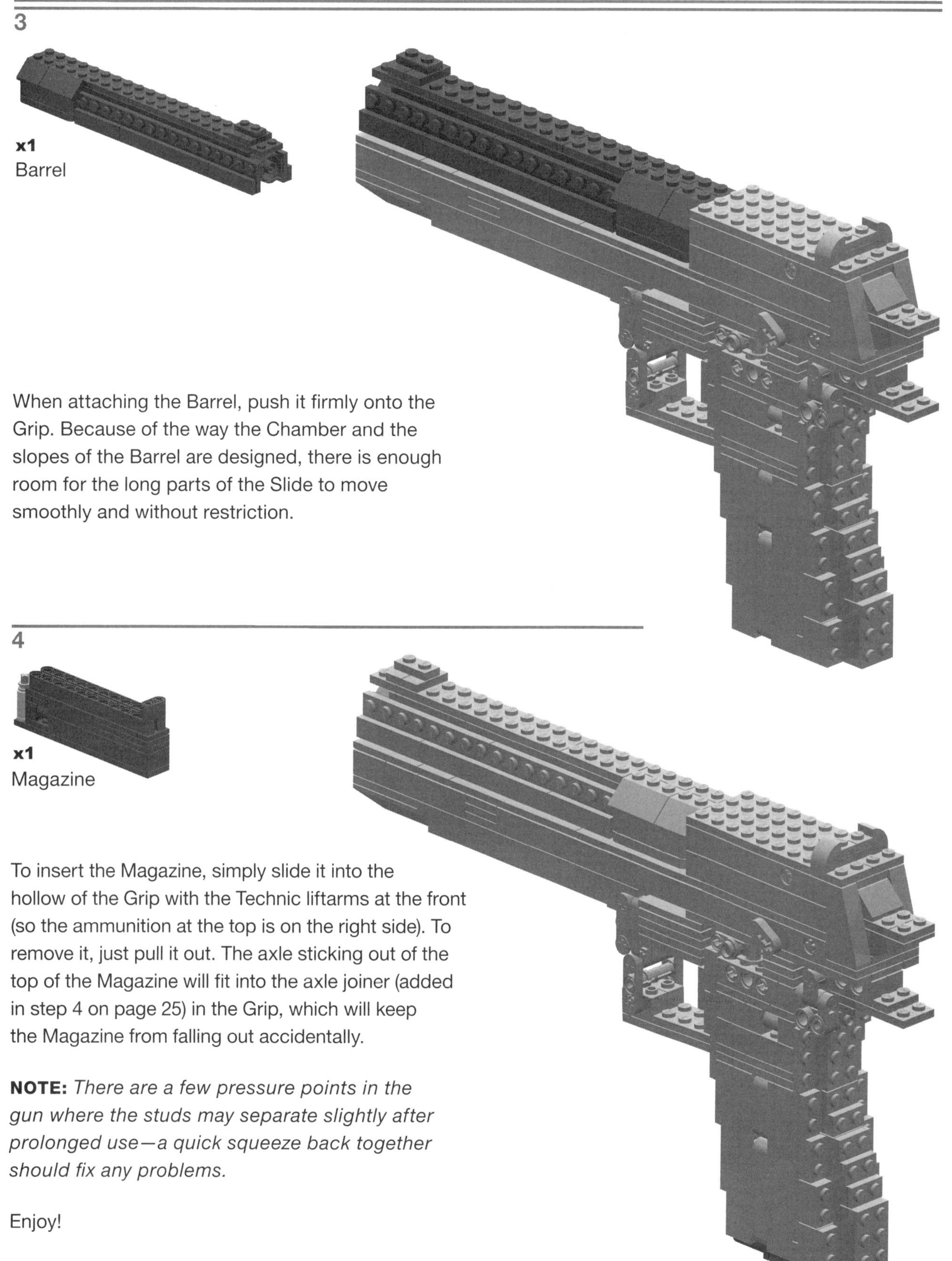

3

x1
Barrel

When attaching the Barrel, push it firmly onto the Grip. Because of the way the Chamber and the slopes of the Barrel are designed, there is enough room for the long parts of the Slide to move smoothly and without restriction.

4

x1
Magazine

To insert the Magazine, simply slide it into the hollow of the Grip with the Technic liftarms at the front (so the ammunition at the top is on the right side). To remove it, just pull it out. The axle sticking out of the top of the Magazine will fit into the axle joiner (added in step 4 on page 25) in the Grip, which will keep the Magazine from falling out accidentally.

NOTE: *There are a few pressure points in the gun where the studs may separate slightly after prolonged use—a quick squeeze back together should fix any problems.*

Enjoy!

AKS-74U

LENGTH: *83.5 studs*
WIDTH: *9 studs*
HEIGHT: *32 studs*
PIECES: *792*
MAGAZINE TYPE: *Detachable box magazine*
MAGAZINE CAPACITY: *Thirteen 1×4 bricks*

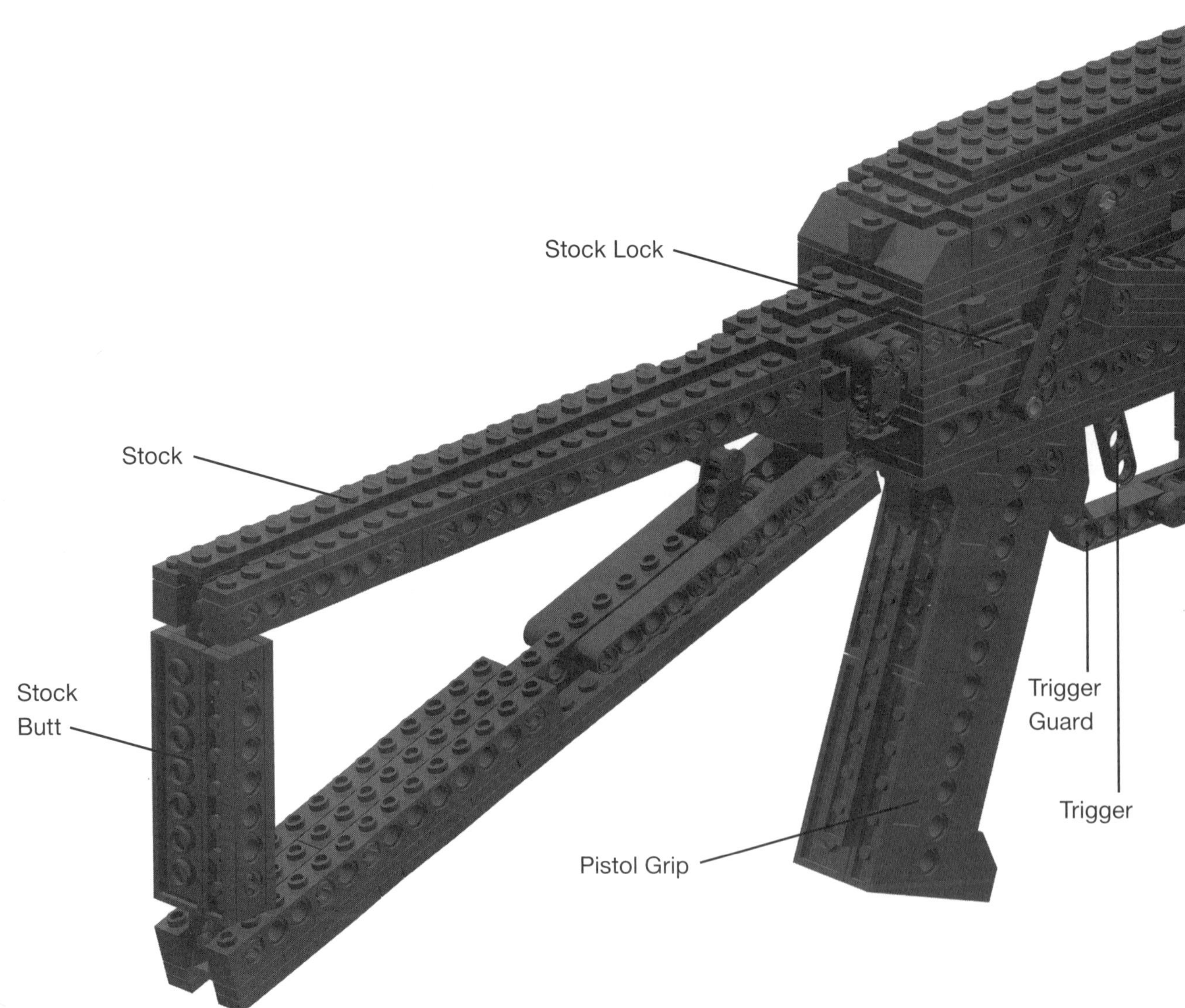

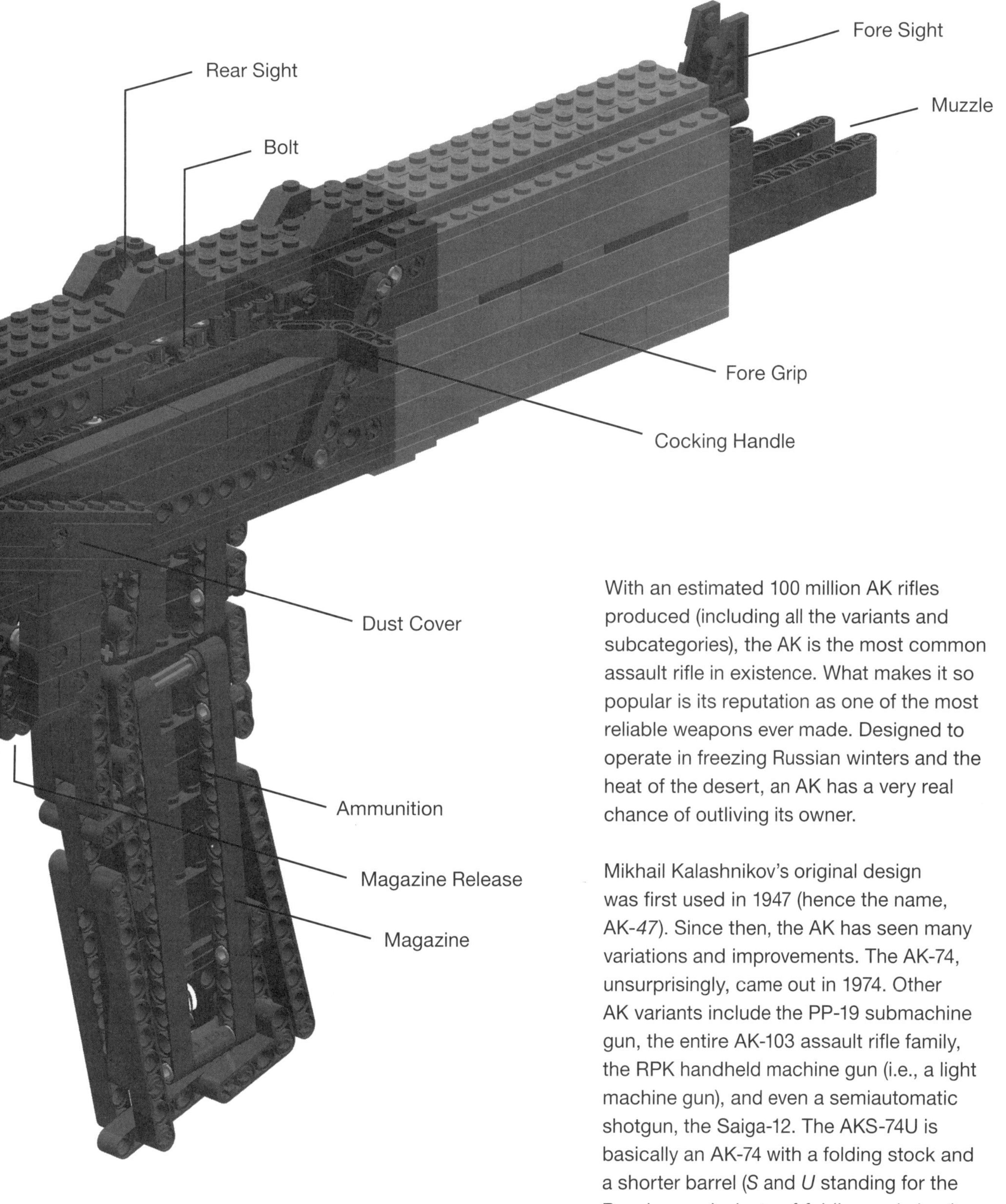

With an estimated 100 million AK rifles produced (including all the variants and subcategories), the AK is the most common assault rifle in existence. What makes it so popular is its reputation as one of the most reliable weapons ever made. Designed to operate in freezing Russian winters and the heat of the desert, an AK has a very real chance of outliving its owner.

Mikhail Kalashnikov's original design was first used in 1947 (hence the name, AK-*47*). Since then, the AK has seen many variations and improvements. The AK-74, unsurprisingly, came out in 1974. Other AK variants include the PP-19 submachine gun, the entire AK-103 assault rifle family, the RPK handheld machine gun (i.e., a light machine gun), and even a semiautomatic shotgun, the Saiga-12. The AKS-74U is basically an AK-74 with a folding stock and a shorter barrel (*S* and *U* standing for the Russian equivalents of *folding* and *short*).

DESIGN HISTORY

I was going to make a full size AK-47 replica for this book, but then I decided on a wider range of guns—I wanted to include a gun that was smaller than the SPAS 12 and the Lee Enfield but still packed a decent punch. Of course, I wanted to include a Kalashnikov of some sort. I decided on the AKS-74U, an assault rifle small enough to occasionally be referred to as a submachine gun!

The AKS-74U is a bit more "tweakable" than the other guns in this book as its fore grip allows for some interpretation when it comes to the color scheme. When I built the gun, I used red bricks to mimic the wooden elements. However, you can see from the black-and-white images in this book that the gun doesn't look too bad with a grey grip either. More modern AKS-74Us also have plastic fore grips, some with built-in rail integration systems (for attaching aiming aids and other gadgets), so there's some room for scope customization too. Add your own scopes, laser sights, or even a bayonet, and mod this beast!

My very first AK was a stockless AKS-74U (left), which utilized the same type of firing mechanism that my original Lee Enfield did. As a result, I had to expand the receiver to contain the mechanism, which ultimately led to a very ugly-looking gun, and I never uploaded the design to the Internet.

When I finally got around to designing a new firing mechanism, the AK-47 was one of the first weapons I built with it. If you're looking for a simple, effective mechanism to use in your own designs, this is a good one to start from.

HOW IT WORKS

A common problem with this model is the Bolt. Due to the alignment of the cocking handle and the part of the Bolt that the rubber bands are attached to, it's sometimes easier to cock this gun by using your index finger and thumb to firmly grip the cocking handle, instead of just ripping the Bolt back with a hooked finger like some sort of special forces operative. Remember we have the structural rigidity of LEGO bricks to consider here! This alternative cocking method allows you to make sure the handle piece doesn't bend as you pull it back.

I also have to mention the Stock. It really is strong enough to take the entire force of the rubber bands when you're cocking the gun. This means you can use your left hand on the Fore Grip to steady the gun and let your shoulder provide the bracing force needed to prevent the entire gun from moving back when you cock it.

FIRING MECHANISM

1

To begin loading the Magazine, insert it into the gun and hook it over the Magazine Ramp.

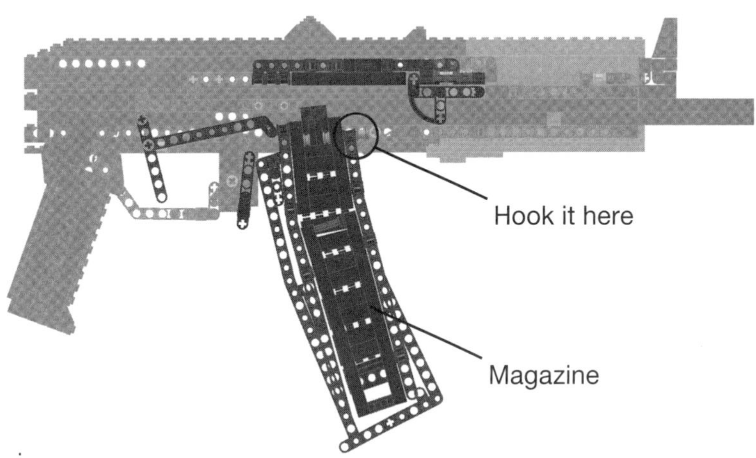

2

Swivel the Magazine in, allowing the magazine release to lock it in place. The Magazine is now loaded.

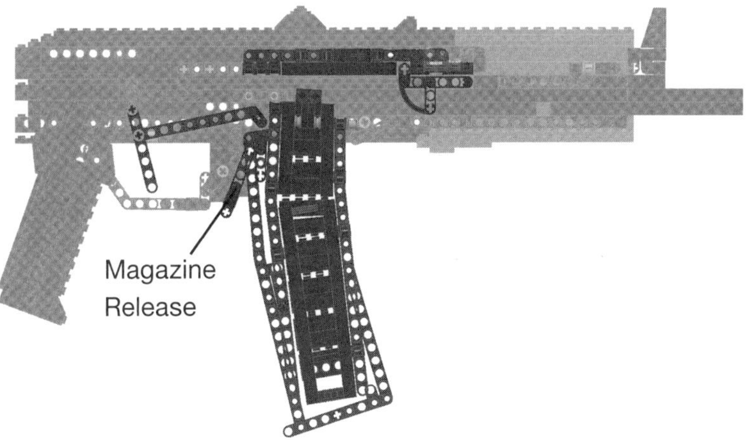

3

Begin pulling the Bolt backward, which brings the Hammer with it and stretches the rubber bands. As the Hammer passes over the Magazine, its sloped bottom gently presses against the bricks in the Magazine.

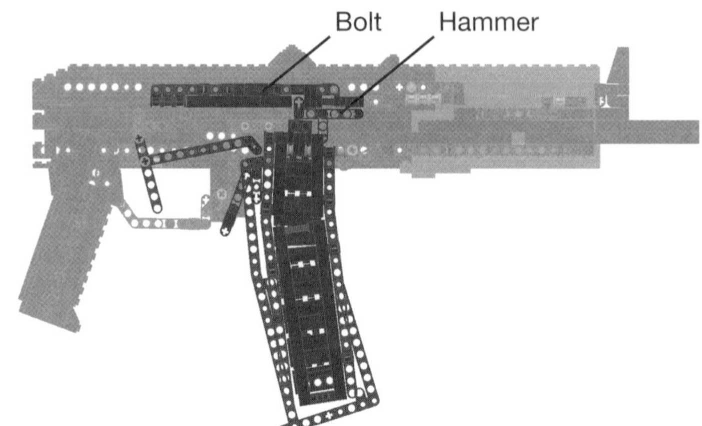

4

Continue pulling the Bolt backward. As the Hammer clears the Magazine, the bricks spring up again. In order to keep moving backward, the Hammer depresses part of the trigger mechanism.

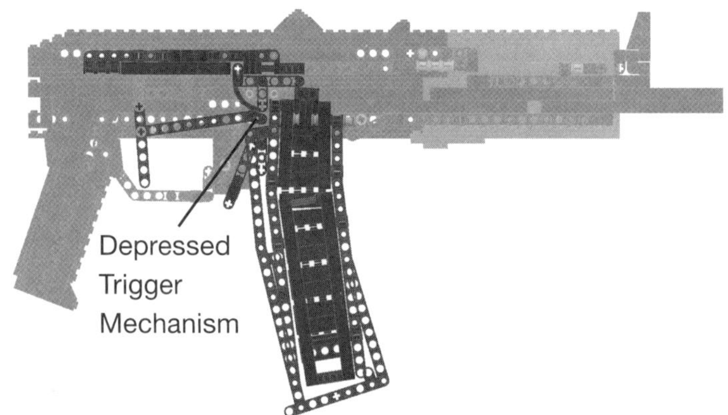

5

Once the Bolt is pulled all the way back, the Hammer is locked behind the Trigger, which has also returned to its original position.

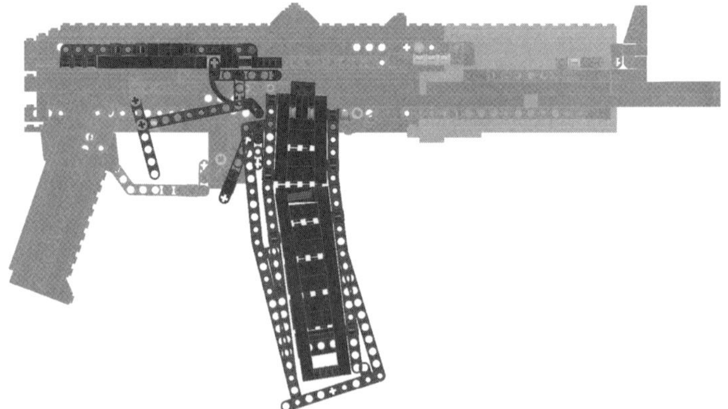

6

Release the Bolt. The rubber band it's attached to pulls it back to its original position, but the Hammer is left behind.

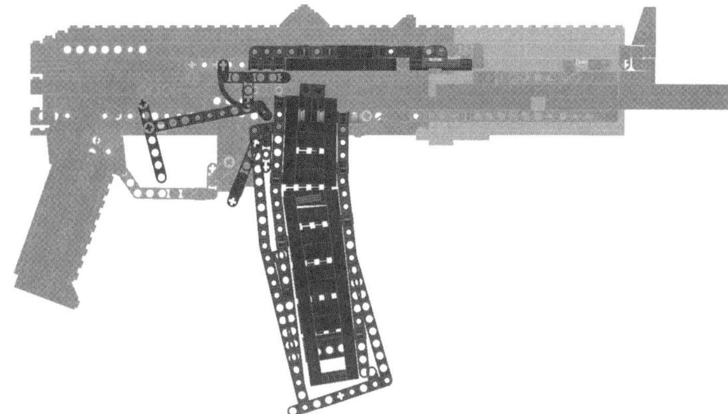

7

Pulling the Trigger allows the Hammer to start moving forward.

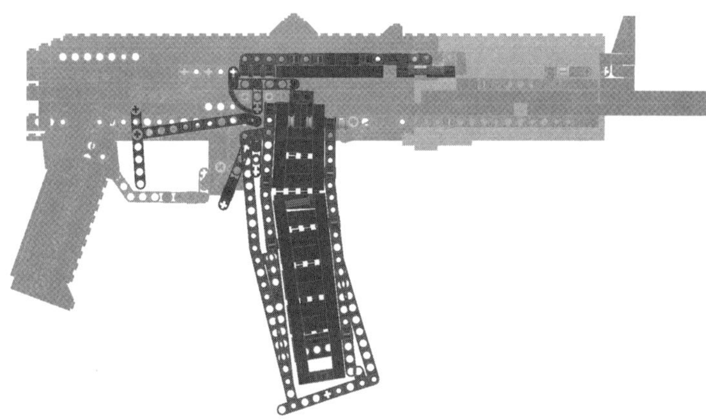

8

As the Hammer passes over the Magazine, it picks up the top brick, pushing it up and out.

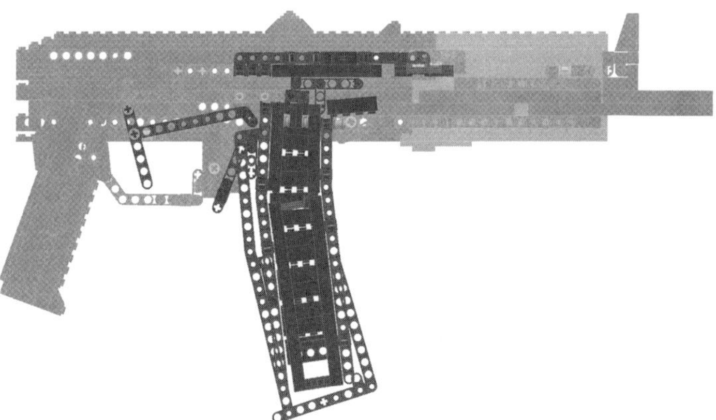

9

The Hammer continues to move forward, and the brick is now out of the Magazine and entirely in the barrel. The remaining bricks in the Magazine spring upward to take its place.

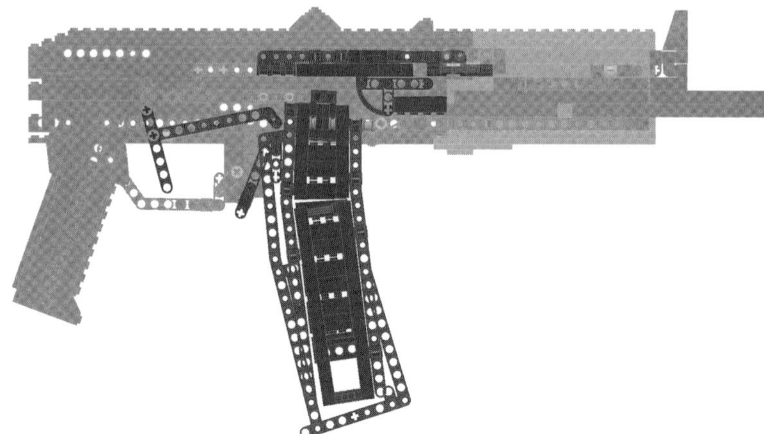

10

When the Hammer reaches the Bolt, it comes to a stop, but the brick is free to continue down the barrel and out the end. Pow!

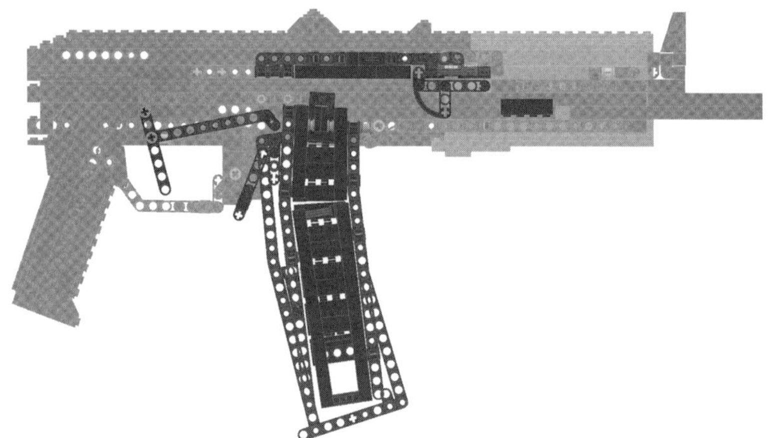

FOLDING STOCK

One of my favorite parts of this gun is the Stock. Building a stock out of LEGO pieces can be tricky. The stock of a real SPAS 12, for example, attaches at the sides of the gun and swivels 180 degrees to fold and unfold. The exact way in which it does this makes it very difficult to re-create in LEGO bricks, which is why the Stock on my SPAS 12 is for aesthetic purposes only. On the other hand, the stock of an AKS-74U folds differently, so I was able to build one strong enough to take the full force of all the rubber bands when the user cocks the gun, which is exactly what the stock is for.

The SPAS 12's stock unfolds in a way that is very difficult to mimic in LEGO: It's hardly attached to the weapon, and it rotates in a rather annoying way in which the connecting arm is not at a helpful angle (i.e., vertical or horizontal). The entire stock's structure is weakened by the kink halfway down the arms, and it's also very dense at the butt end, putting even more force on the joints.

In contrast, the AKS-74U's Stock is attached along the solid edge of the Frame Wall Left, where there's constant stock-to-frame contact for a strong connection. The horizontal top beam on the Stock also helps keep it sturdy. The Stock's locking mechanism, however, was a huge challenge, as the Pistol Grip made an unhelpful intrusion into the space behind the Trigger. The fact that I managed to get it all working makes this my favorite stock from all the guns I've ever made.

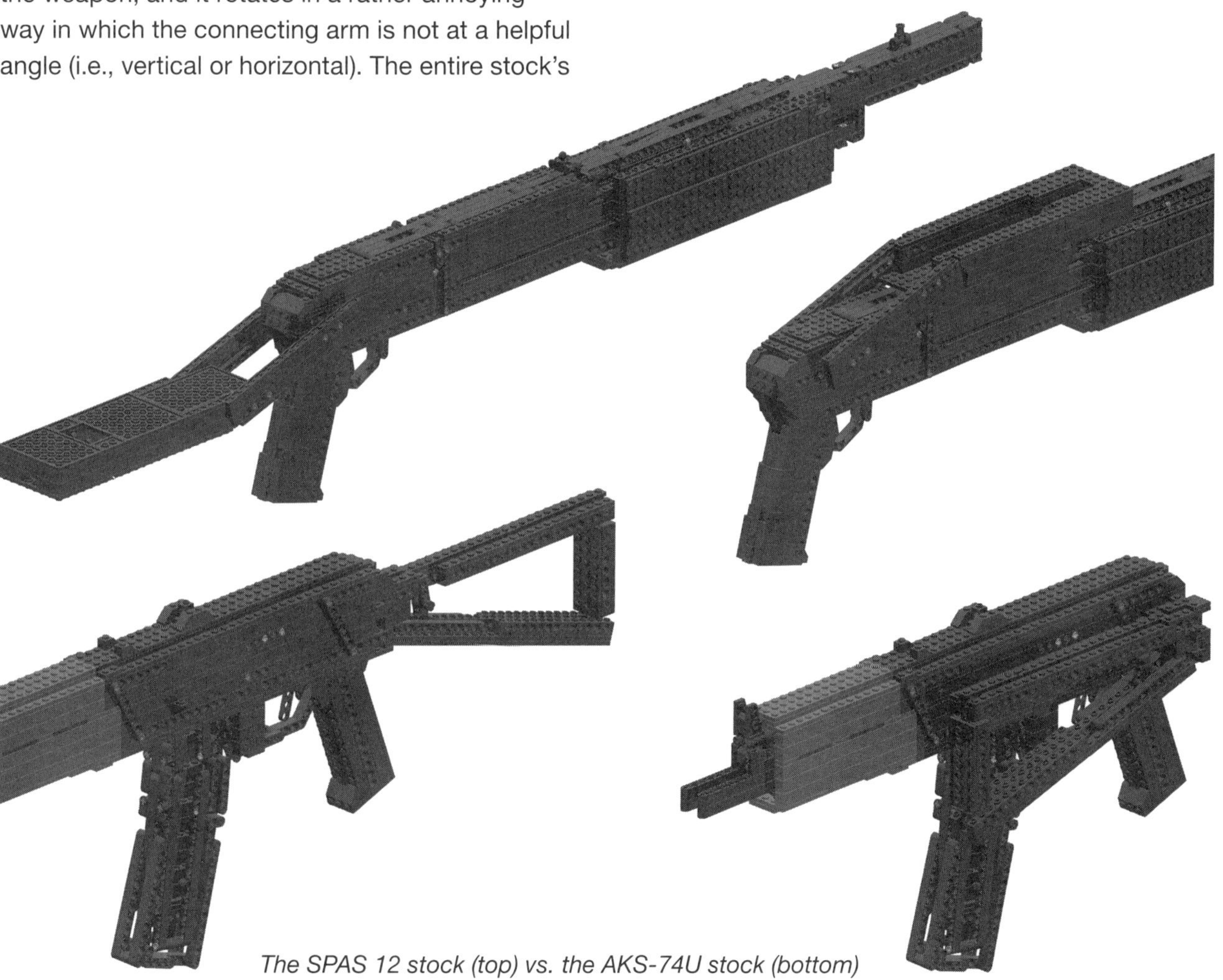

The SPAS 12 stock (top) vs. the AKS-74U stock (bottom)

1

Here is the gun at rest with the Stock fully extended.

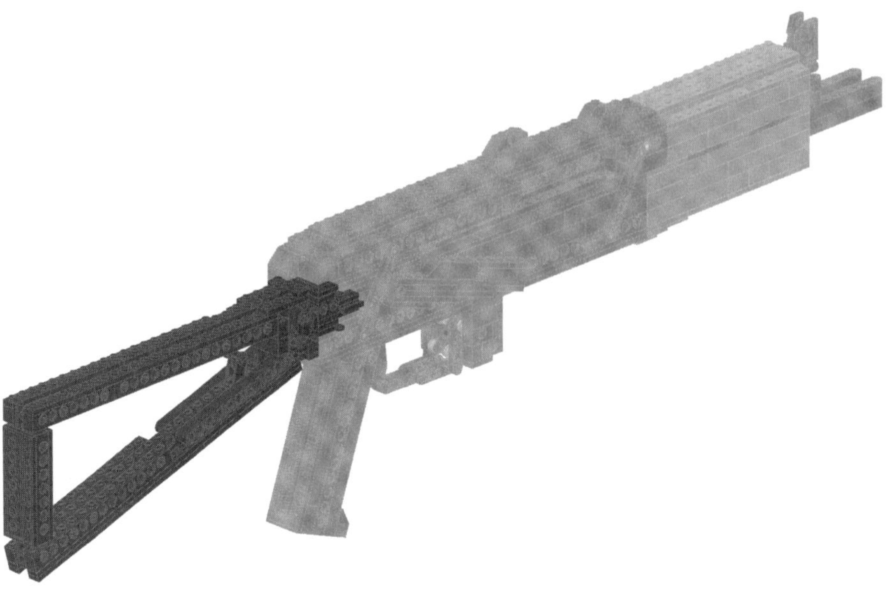

2

Depress the stock lock to unlock the Stock.

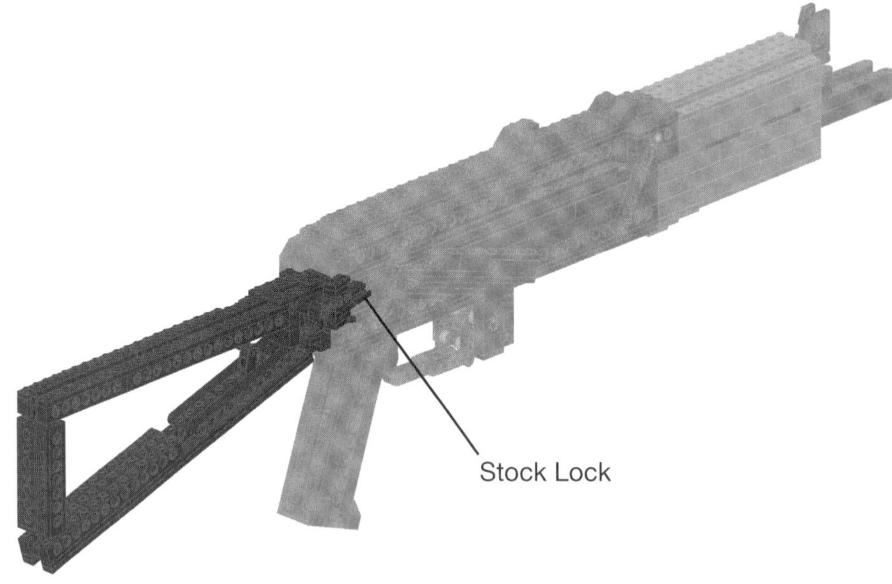

3

As the Stock starts to swivel to the left, the stock lock returns to its original position.

4

As the Stock completes its 180-degree turn, it flexes a little at the hinge so that it can slip over the 1×2 inverted slope piece added in step 3 on page 76. Don't worry—it's fine for the pieces do this, and it won't break them. Take a look at your own model to see why we need to add that 1×2 tile to the Stock Butt (in step 3 on page 66); if we used a 1×2 plate instead, the studs would get in the way and we wouldn't be able to rotate the Stock the entire 180 degrees.

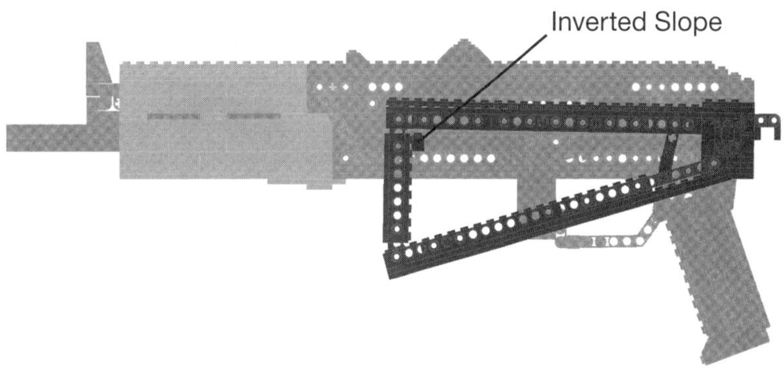

5

The Stock attaches to the stud of the 1×2 inverted slope piece, which locks it into place and relieves the stress on the hinge.

To unfold the Stock again, just unclip it from the stud and swivel it out. The stock lock will engage automatically, locking the Stock in place so it's ready for use.

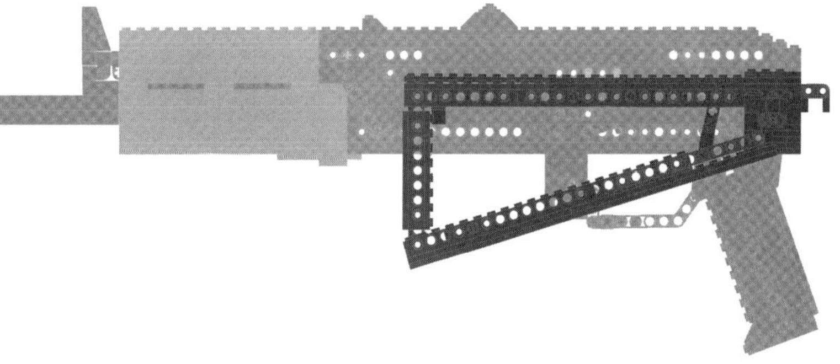

BILL OF MATERIALS

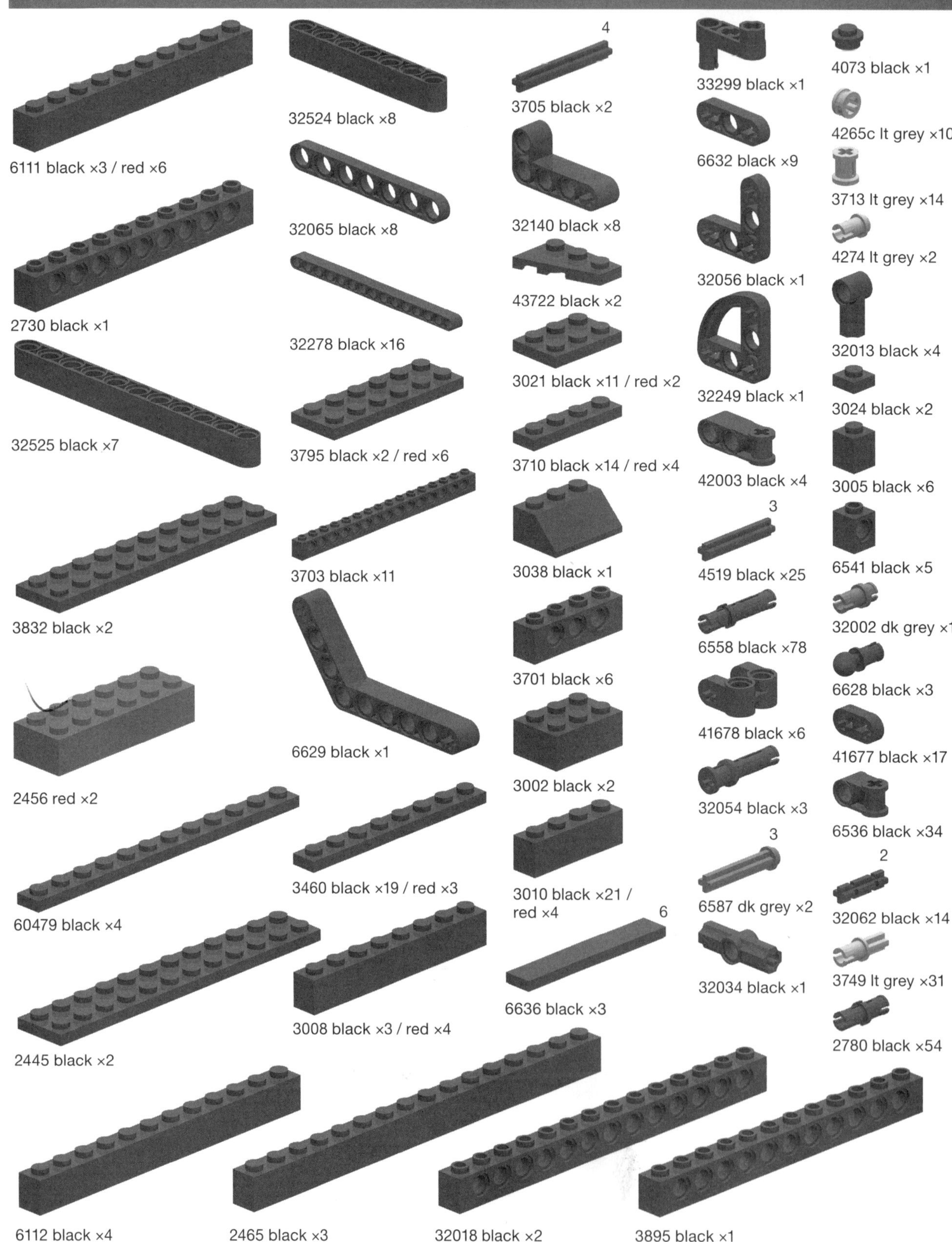

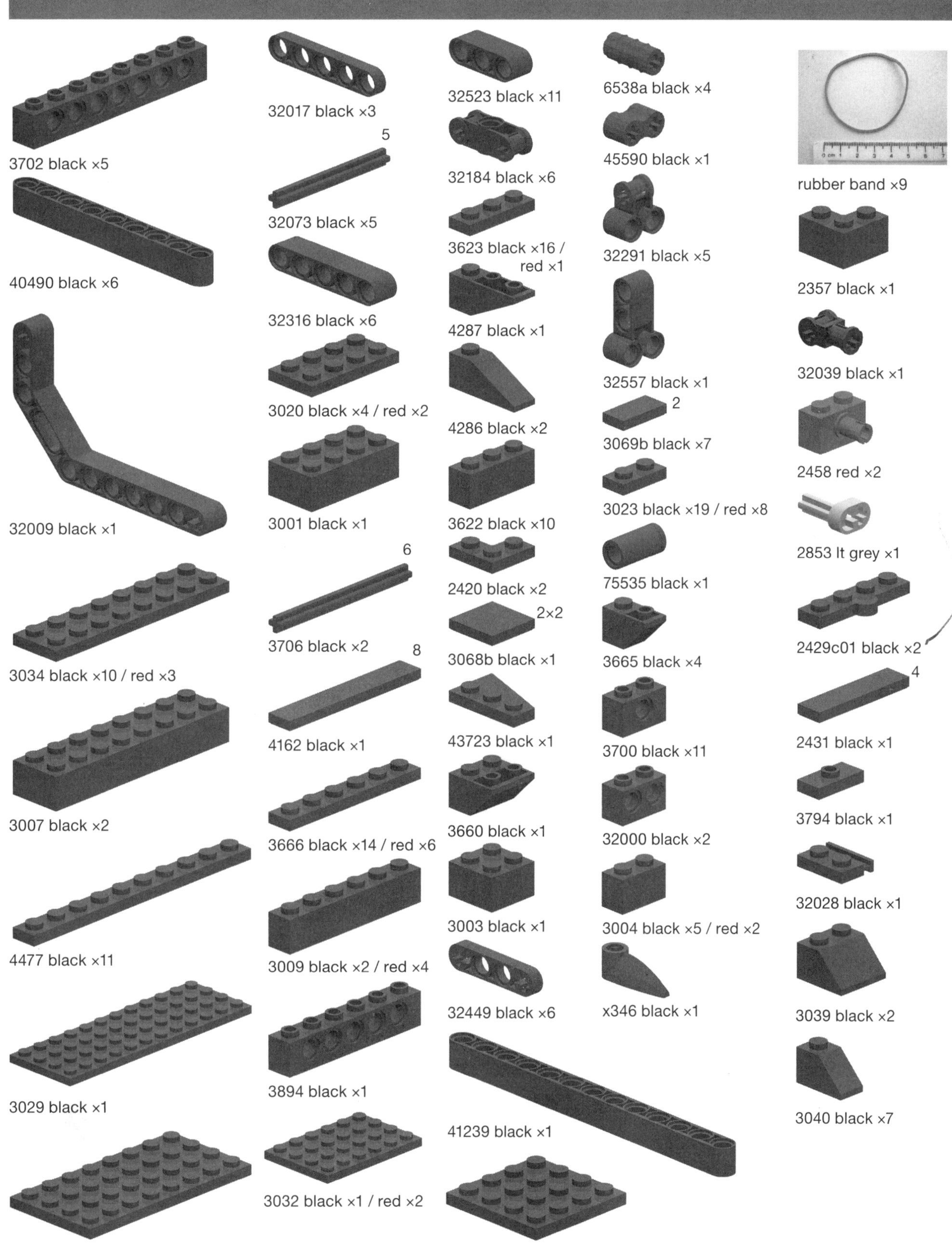
3702 black ×5
40490 black ×6
32009 black ×1
3034 black ×10 / red ×3
3007 black ×2
4477 black ×11
3029 black ×1
3035 black ×1
32017 black ×3
5
32073 black ×5
32316 black ×6
3020 black ×4 / red ×2
3001 black ×1
6
3706 black ×2
8
4162 black ×1
3666 black ×14 / red ×6
3009 black ×2 / red ×4
3894 black ×1
3032 black ×1 / red ×2
32523 black ×11
32184 black ×6
3623 black ×16 / red ×1
4287 black ×1
4286 black ×2
3622 black ×10
2420 black ×2
2×2
3068b black ×1
43723 black ×1
3660 black ×1
3003 black ×1
32449 black ×6
41239 black ×1
3031 black ×1 / red ×2
6538a black ×4
45590 black ×1
32291 black ×5
32557 black ×1
2
3069b black ×7
3023 black ×19 / red ×8
75535 black ×1
3665 black ×4
3700 black ×11
32000 black ×2
3004 black ×5 / red ×2
x346 black ×1
rubber band ×9
2357 black ×1
32039 black ×1
2458 red ×2
2853 lt grey ×1
2429c01 black ×2
4
2431 black ×1
3794 black ×1
32028 black ×1
3039 black ×2
3040 black ×7

STOCK LOWER FRONT

1

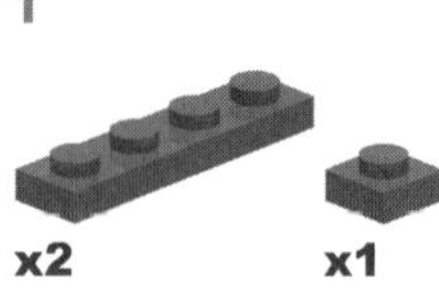

x2 x1

2

x2

3

x2

4

x1

x1

5

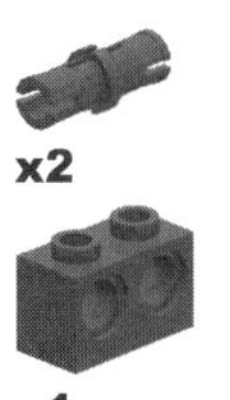

x2

x1

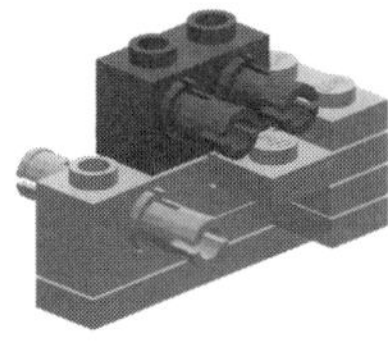

6

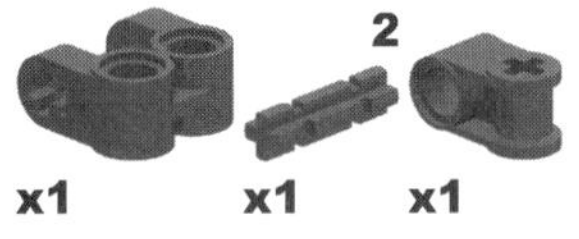

x1 x1 x1

7

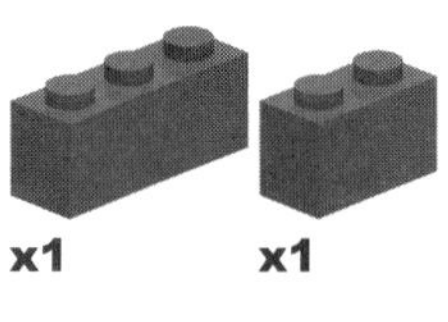

x1 x1

8

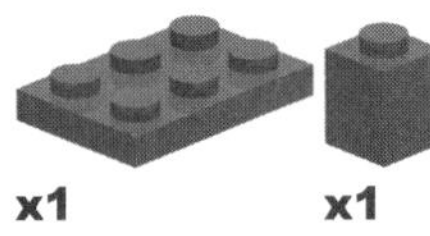

x1 x1

STOCK LOWER

1

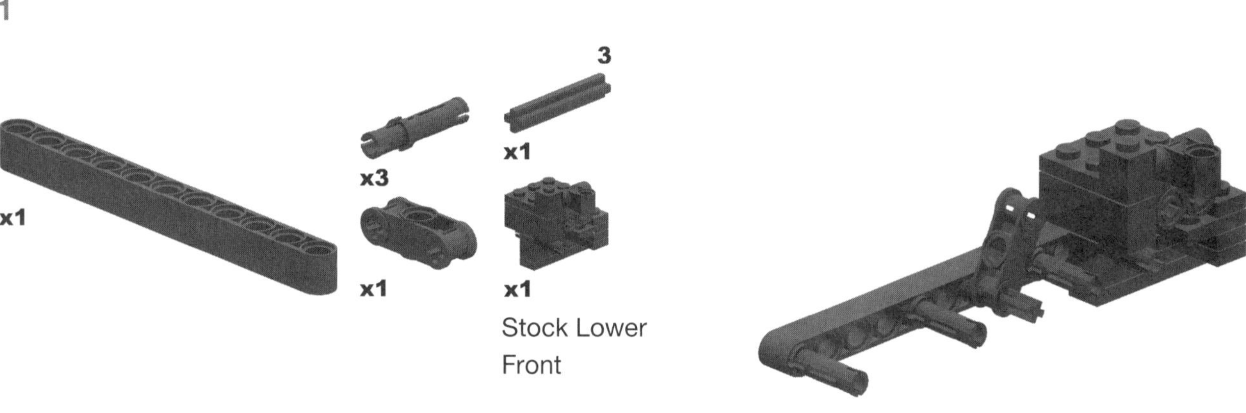

2

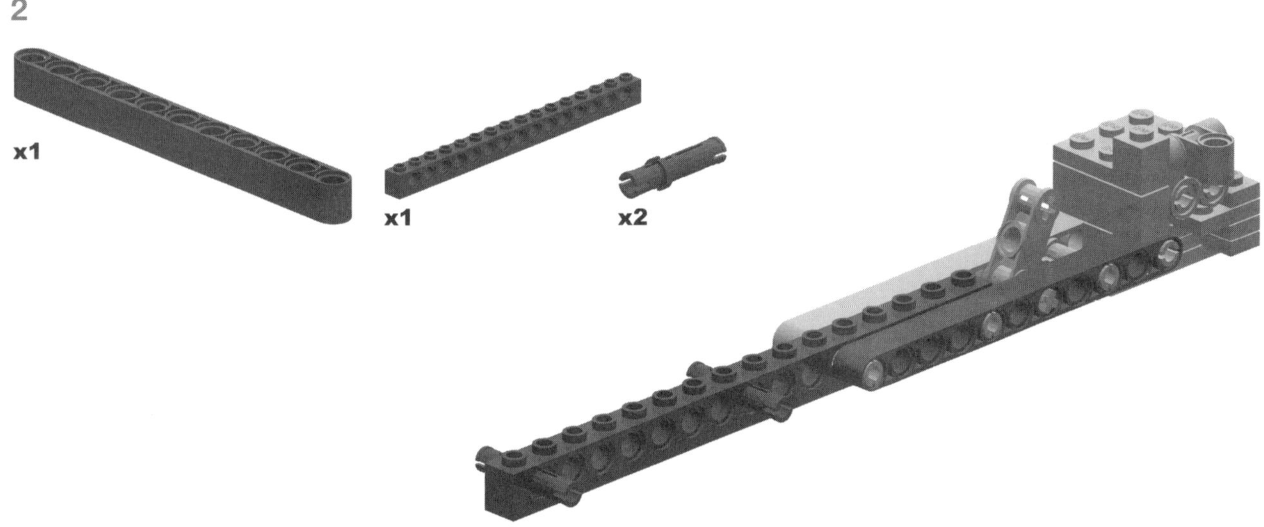

3

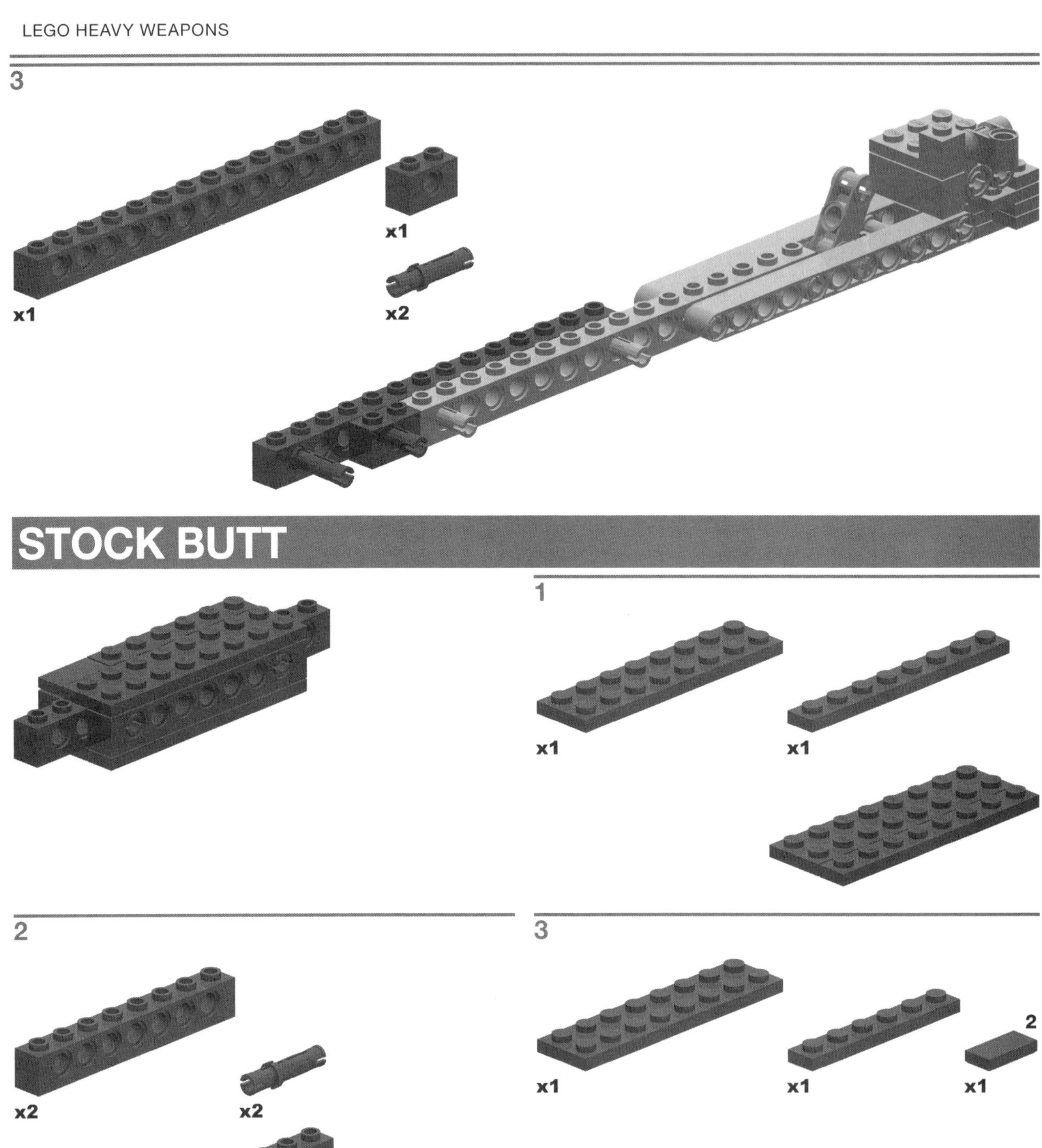

STOCK BUTT

1

x1

x1

2

x2

x2

x1

3

2

x1

x1

x1

STOCK LOWER PLATE

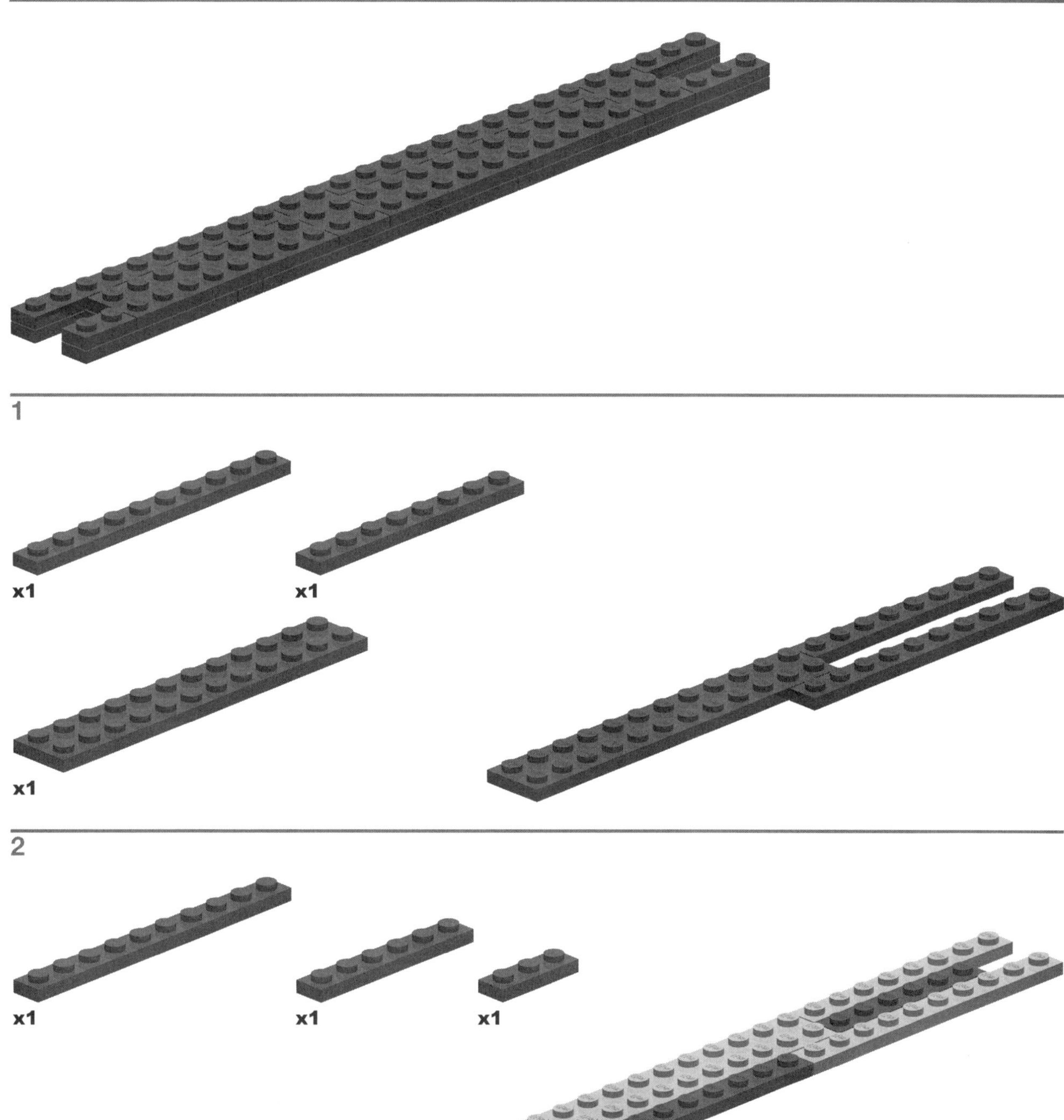

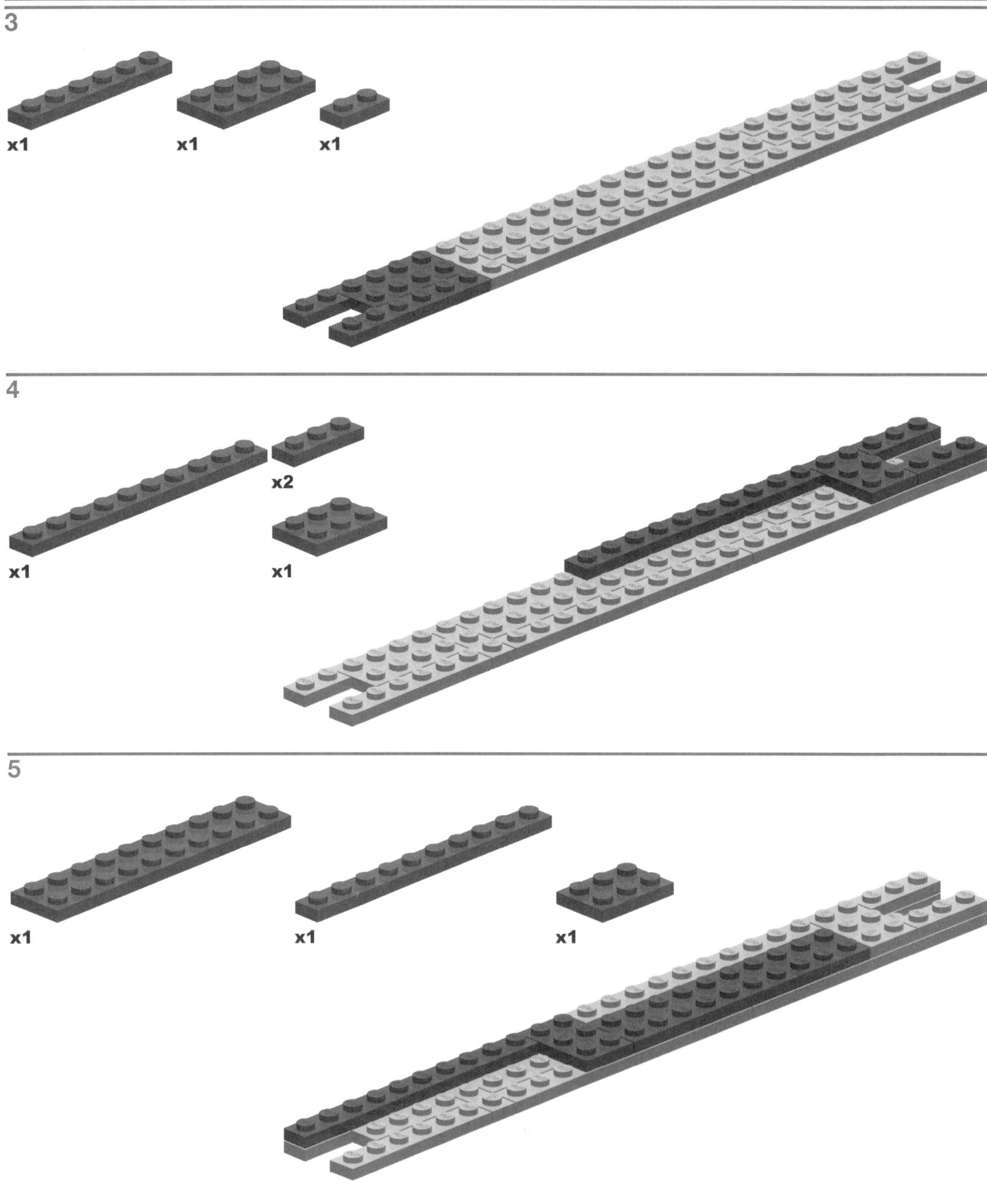
3
x1
x1
x1
4
x2
x1
x1
5
x1
x1
x1

6

x1

x1

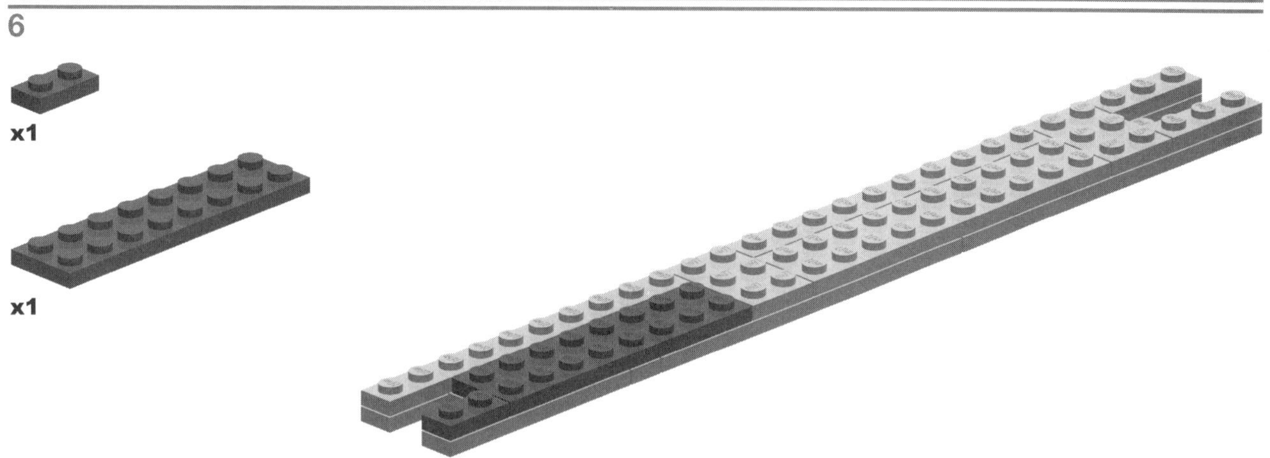

STOCK UPPER

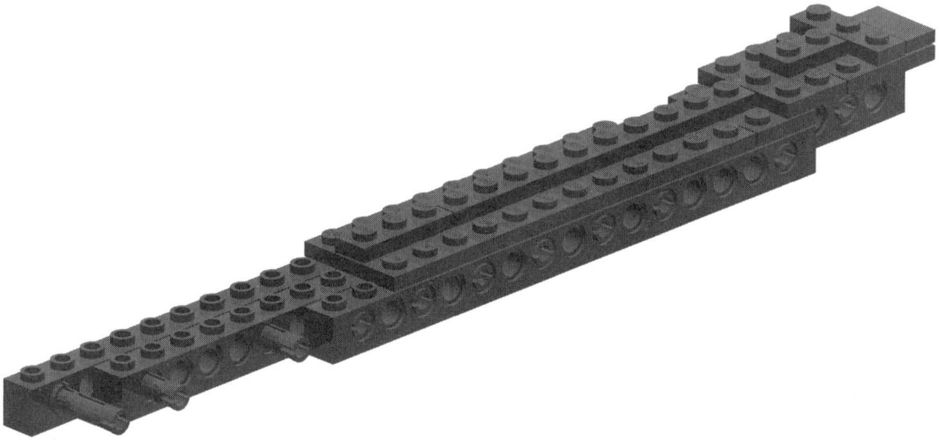

1

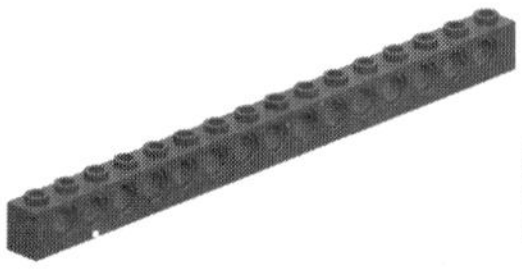

x1  x1  x2

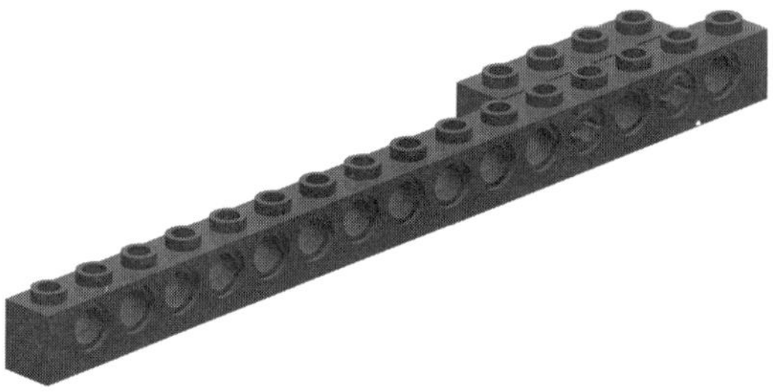

2

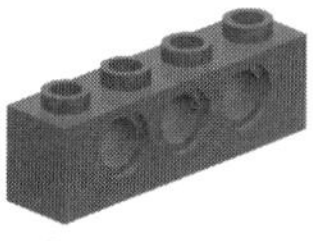

x1

x1  x4

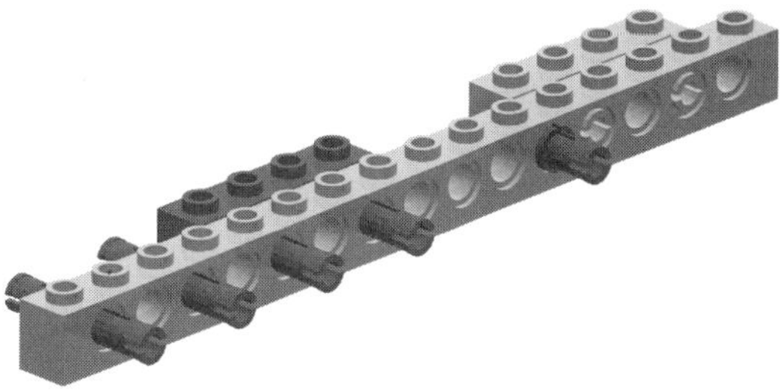

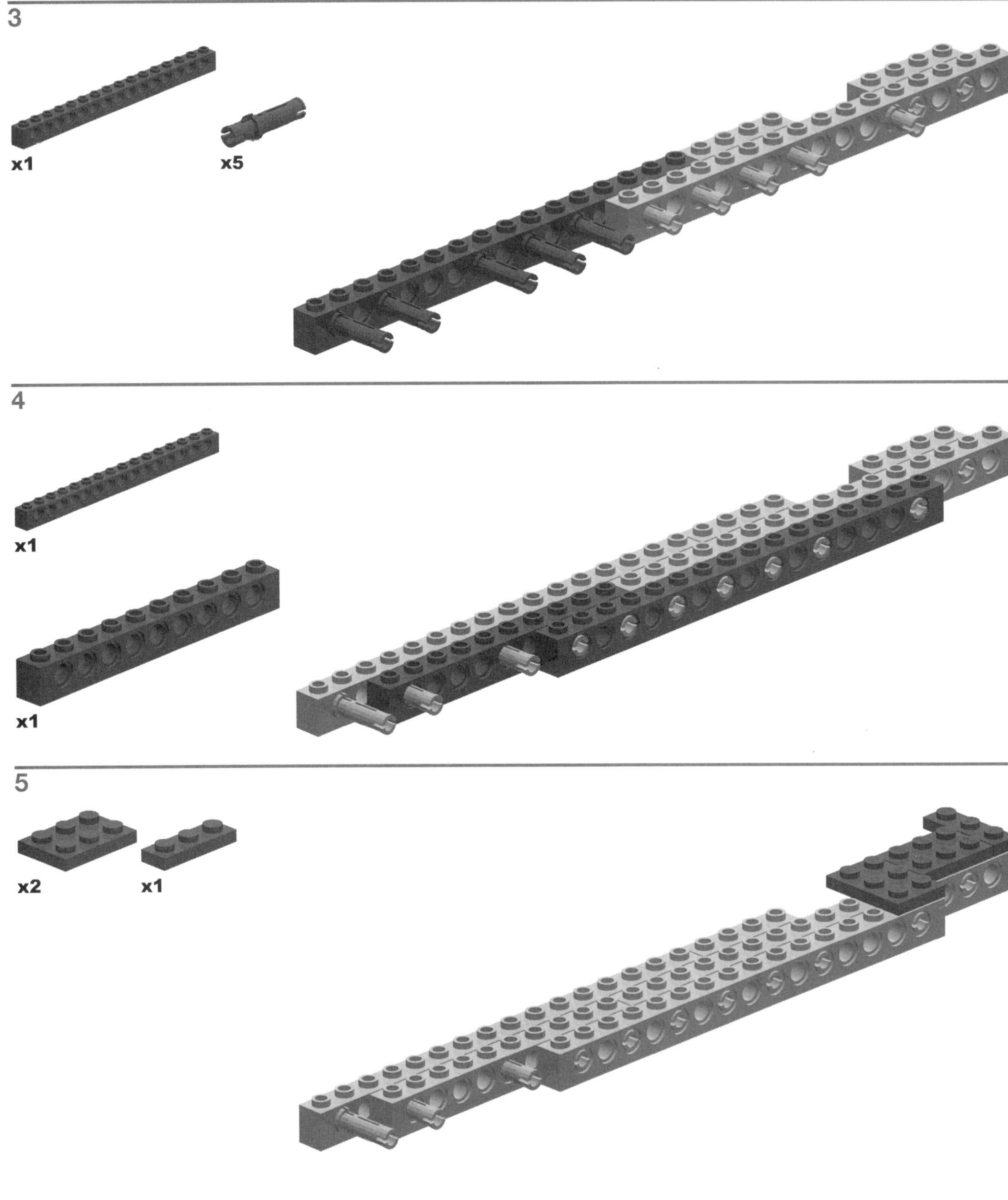
3
x1
x5
4
x1
x1
5
x2
x1

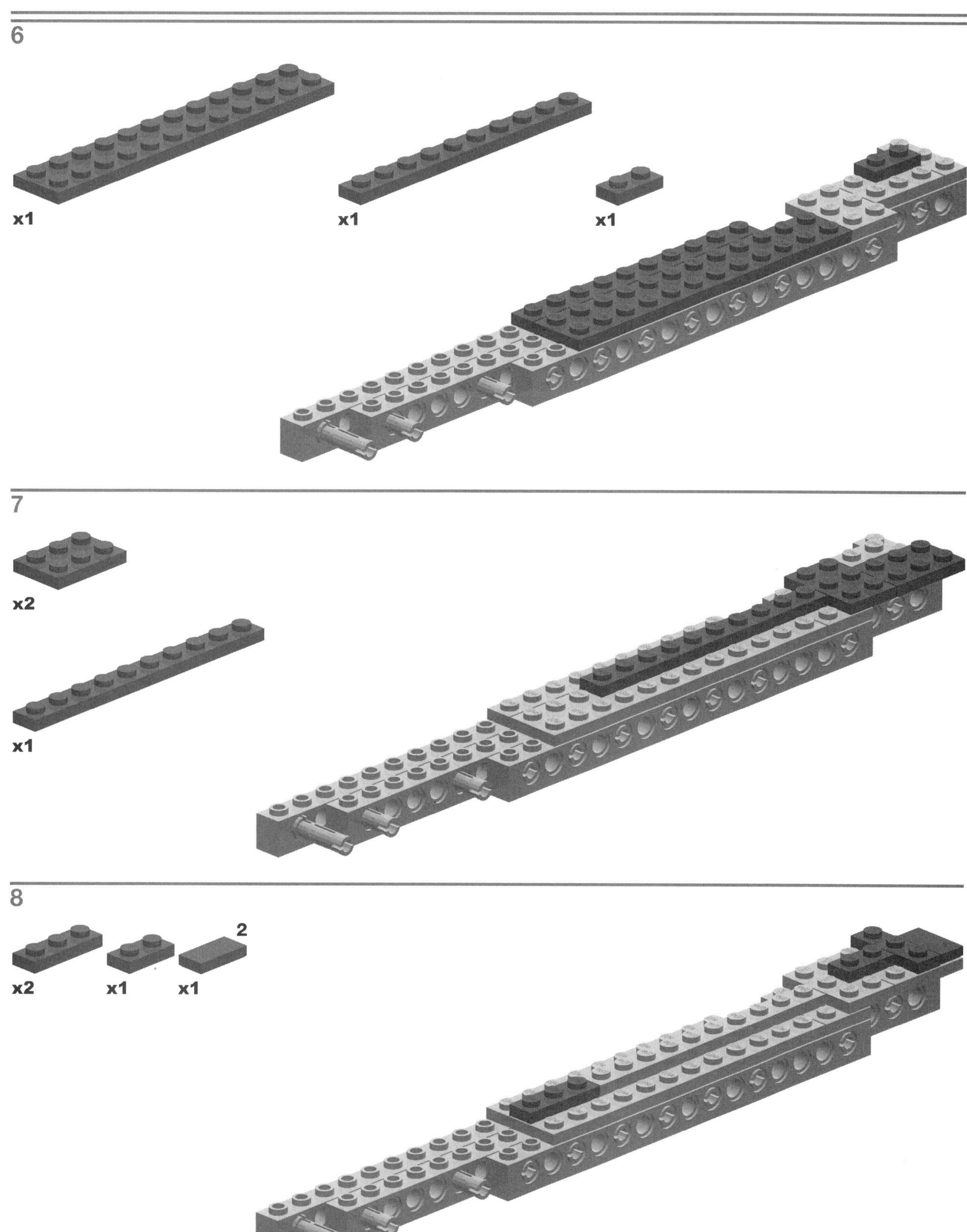
6
x1
x1
x1
7
x2
x1
8
2
x2
x1
x1

STOCK ASSEMBLY

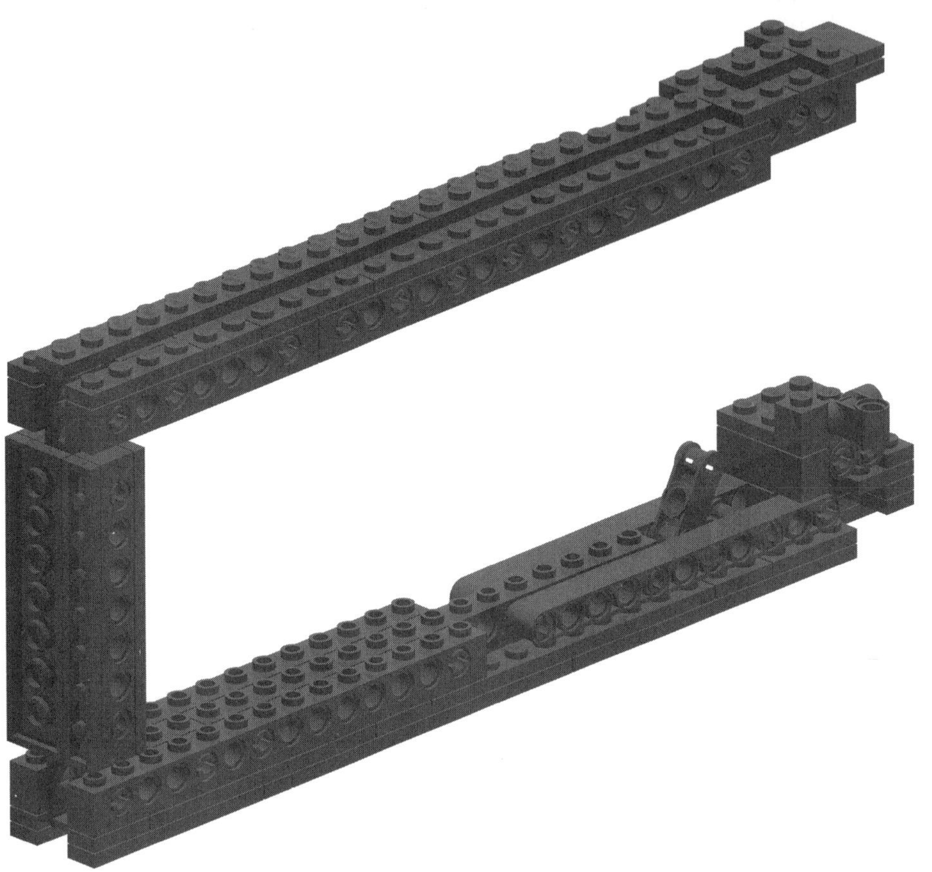

1

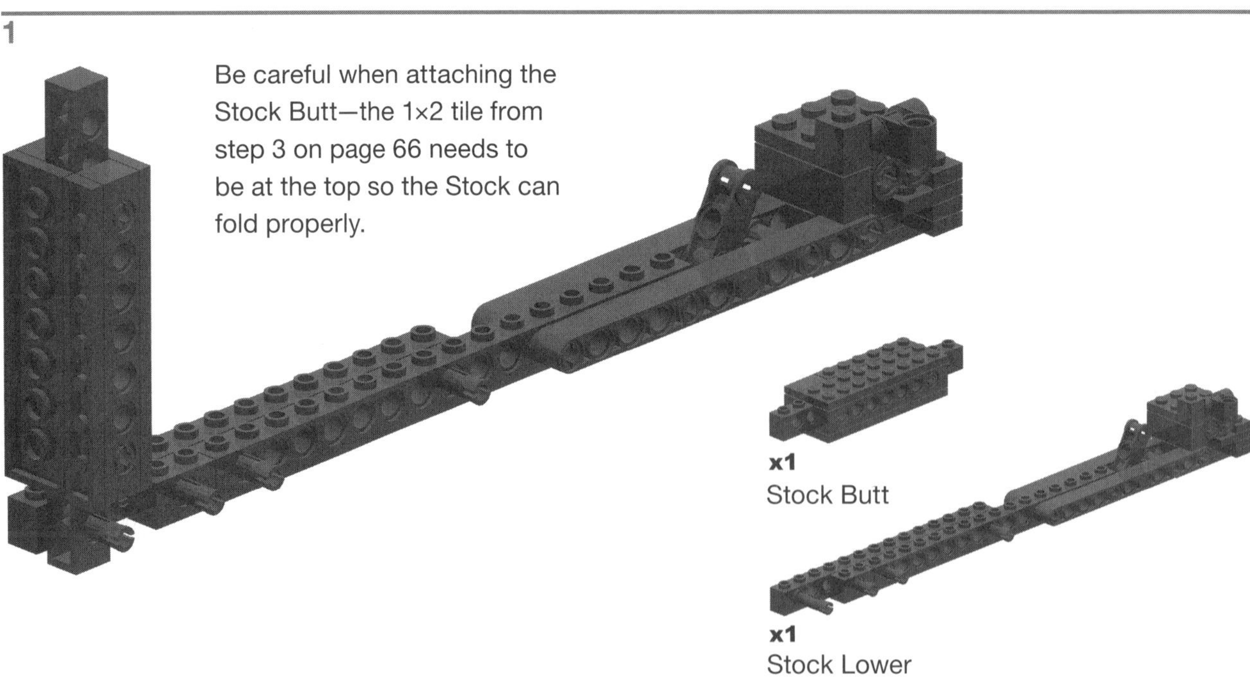

Be careful when attaching the Stock Butt—the 1×2 tile from step 3 on page 66 needs to be at the top so the Stock can fold properly.

2

Make sure the Stock Lower Plate is oriented as shown here, with the 1×3 plates under the Stock Lower Front and the 1×2 and 1×10 plates under the Stock Butt.

x1
Stock Lower Plate

x1

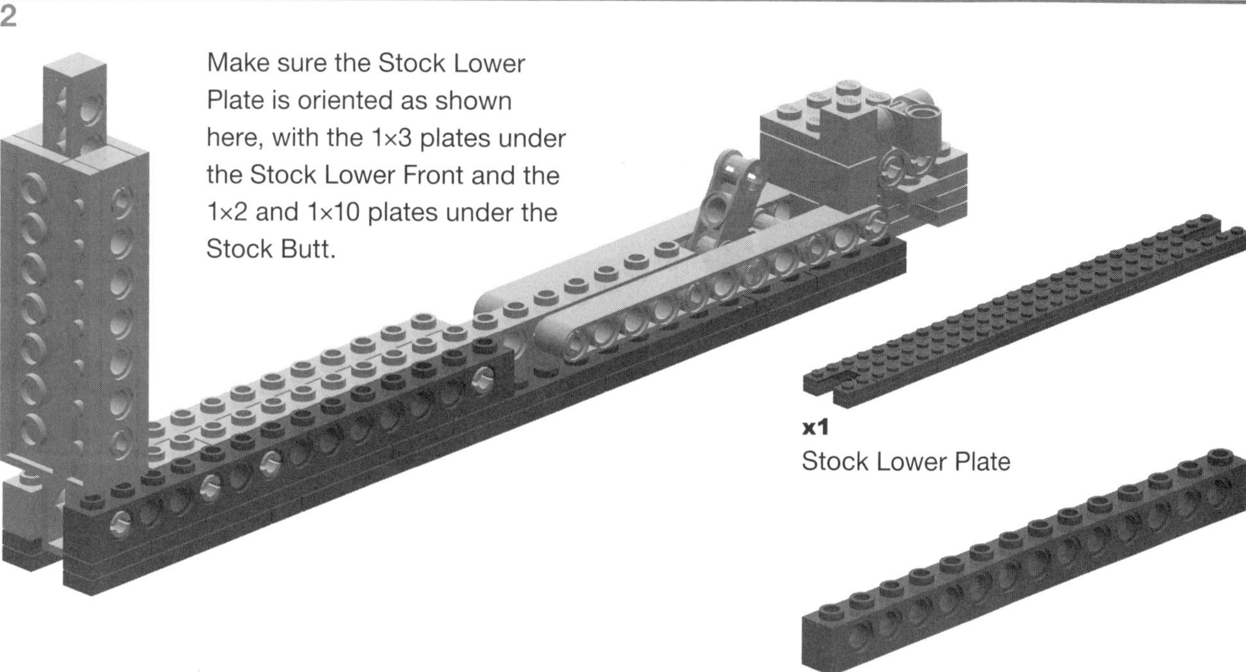

3

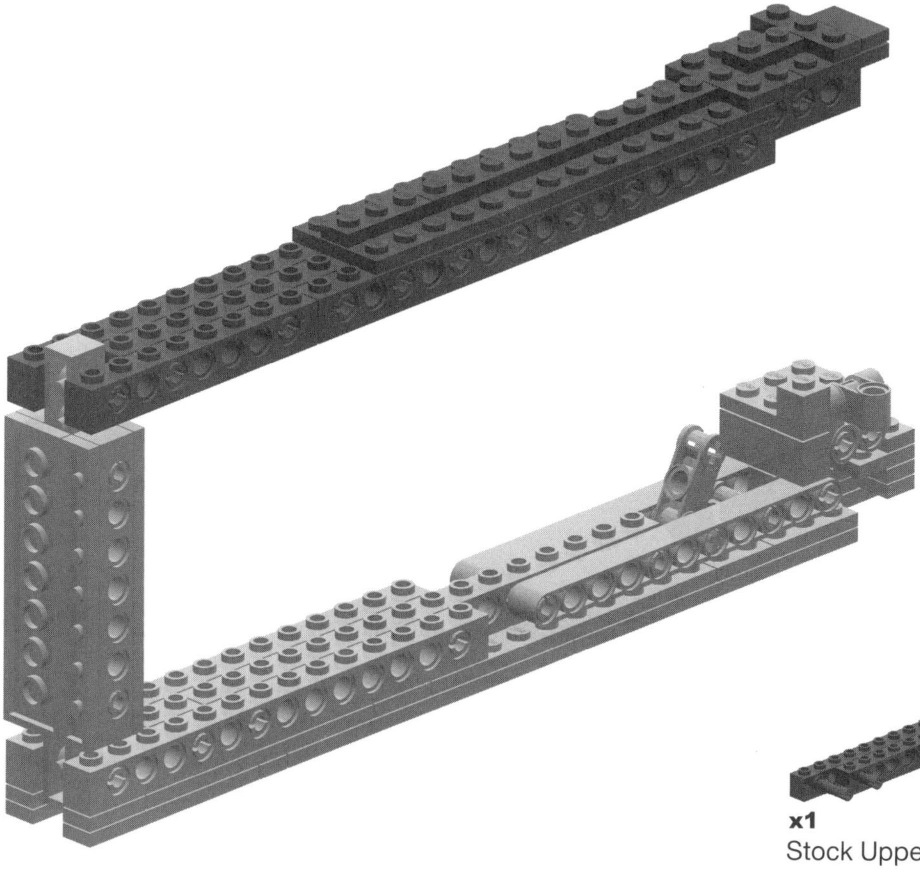

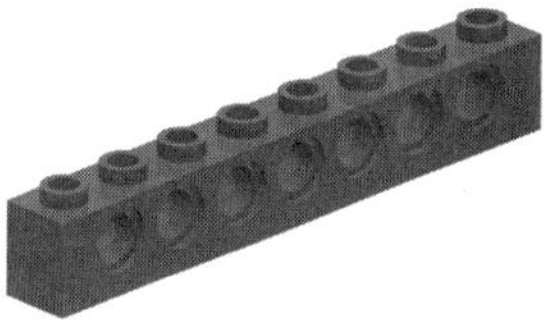

x1

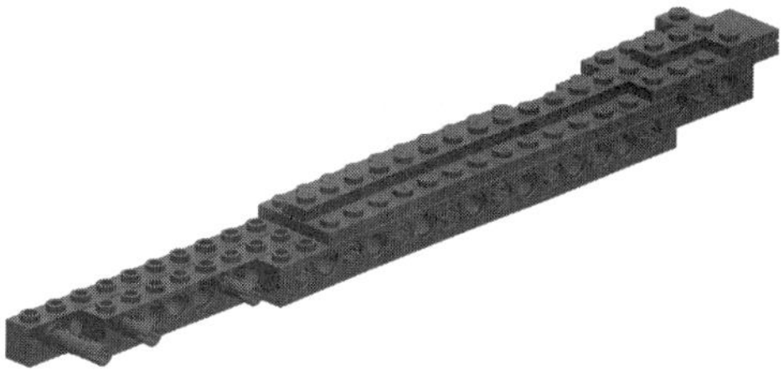

x1
Stock Upper

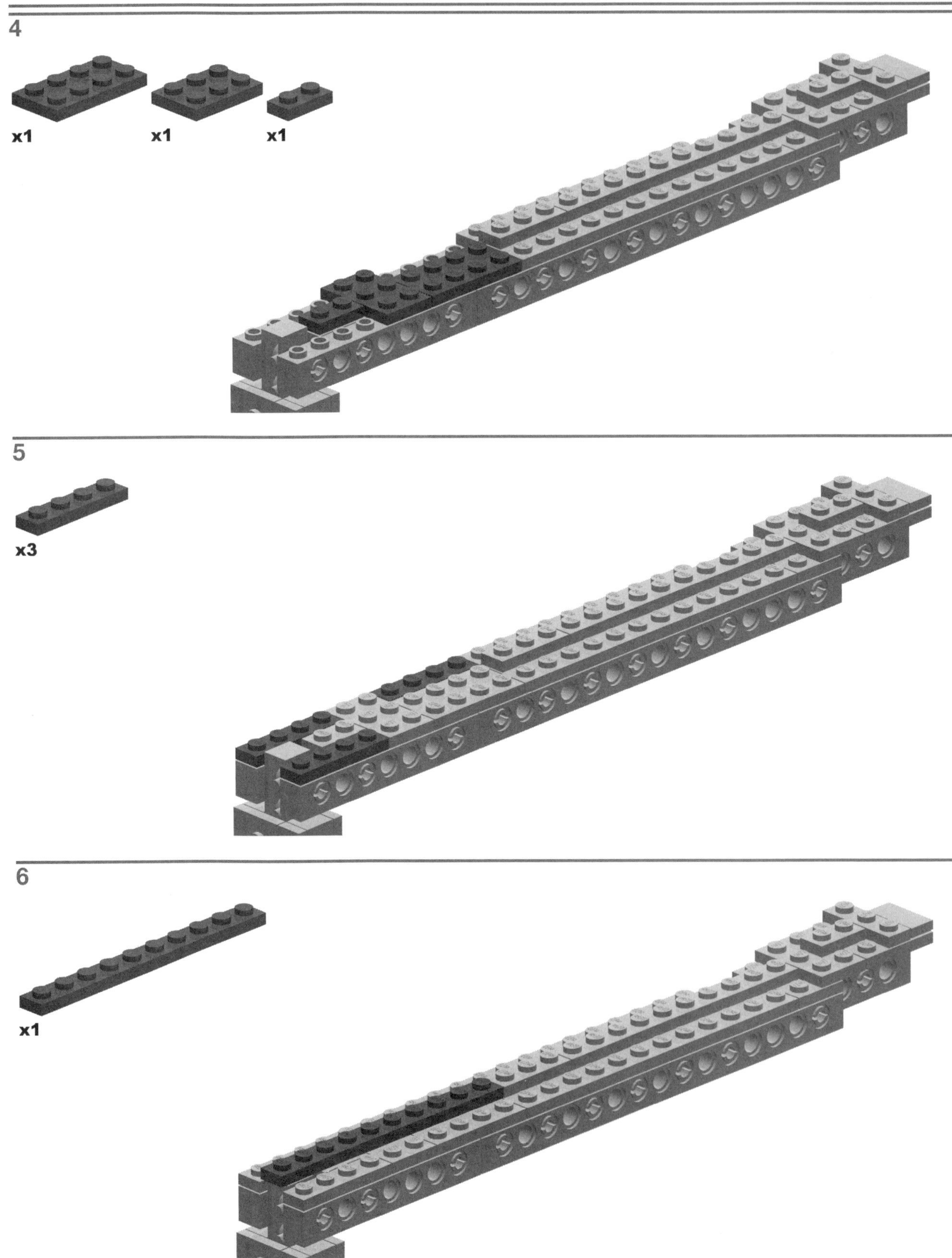
4
x1
x1
x1
5
x3
6
x1

FRAME WALL LEFT

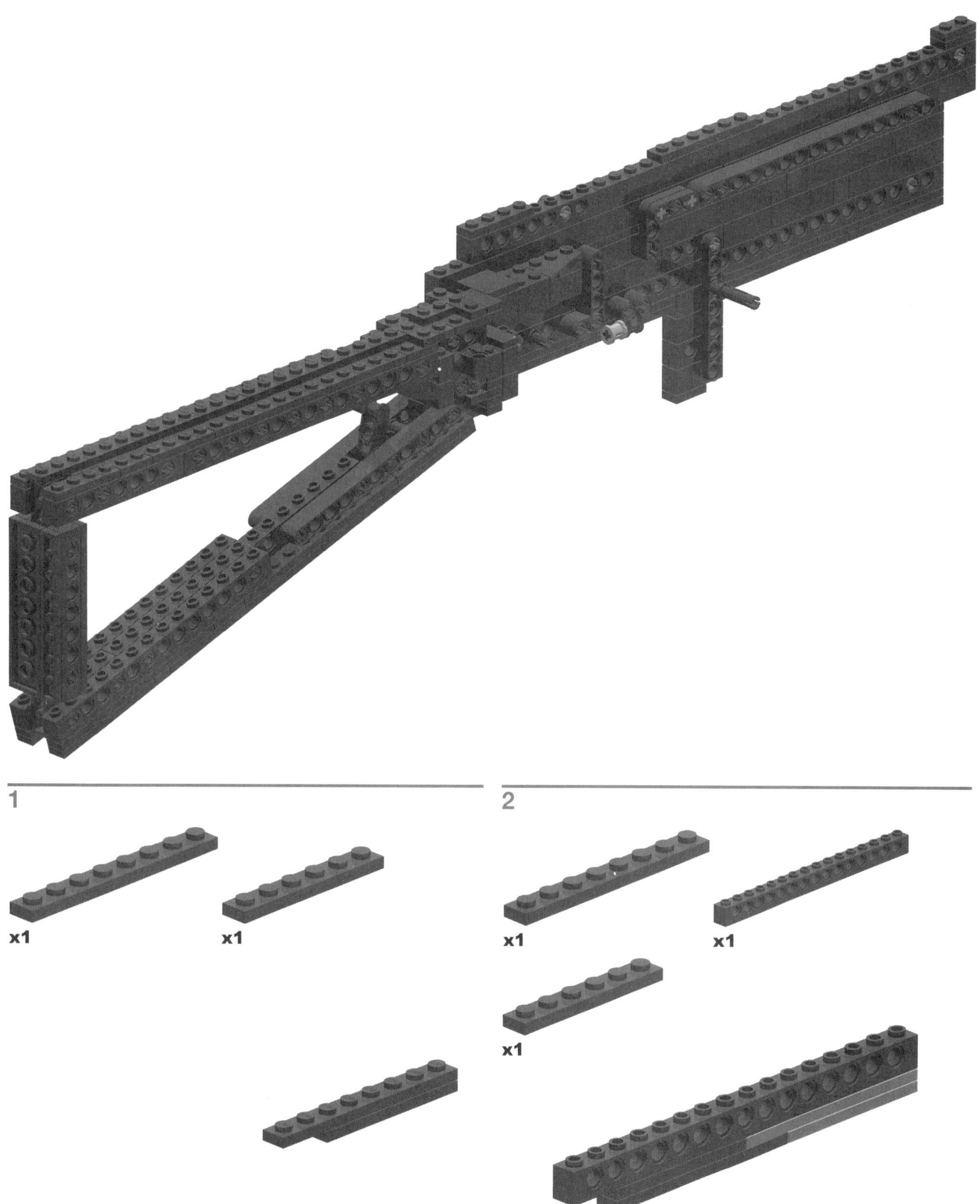

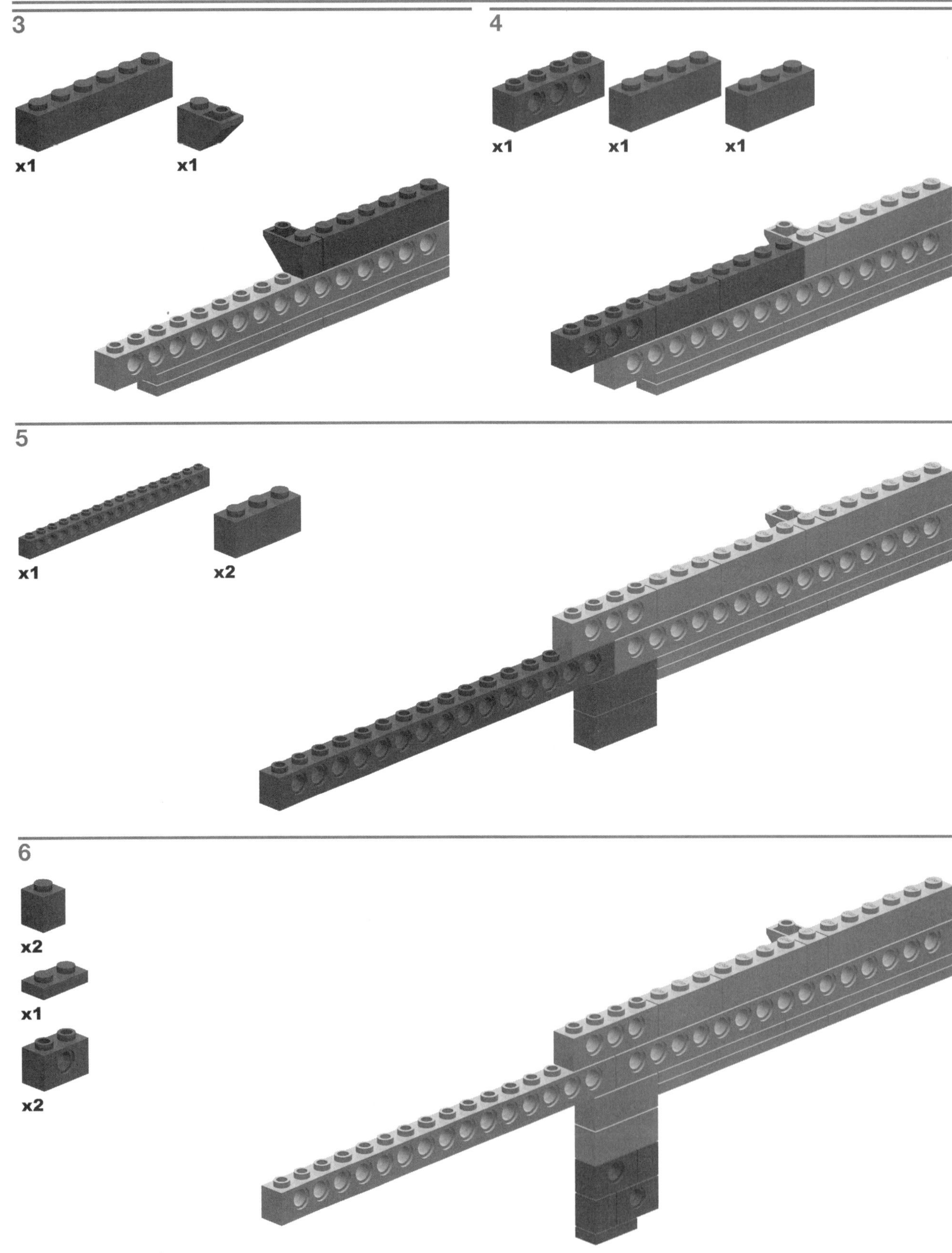
3
x1
x1
4
x1
x1
x1
5
x1
x2
6
x2
x1
x2

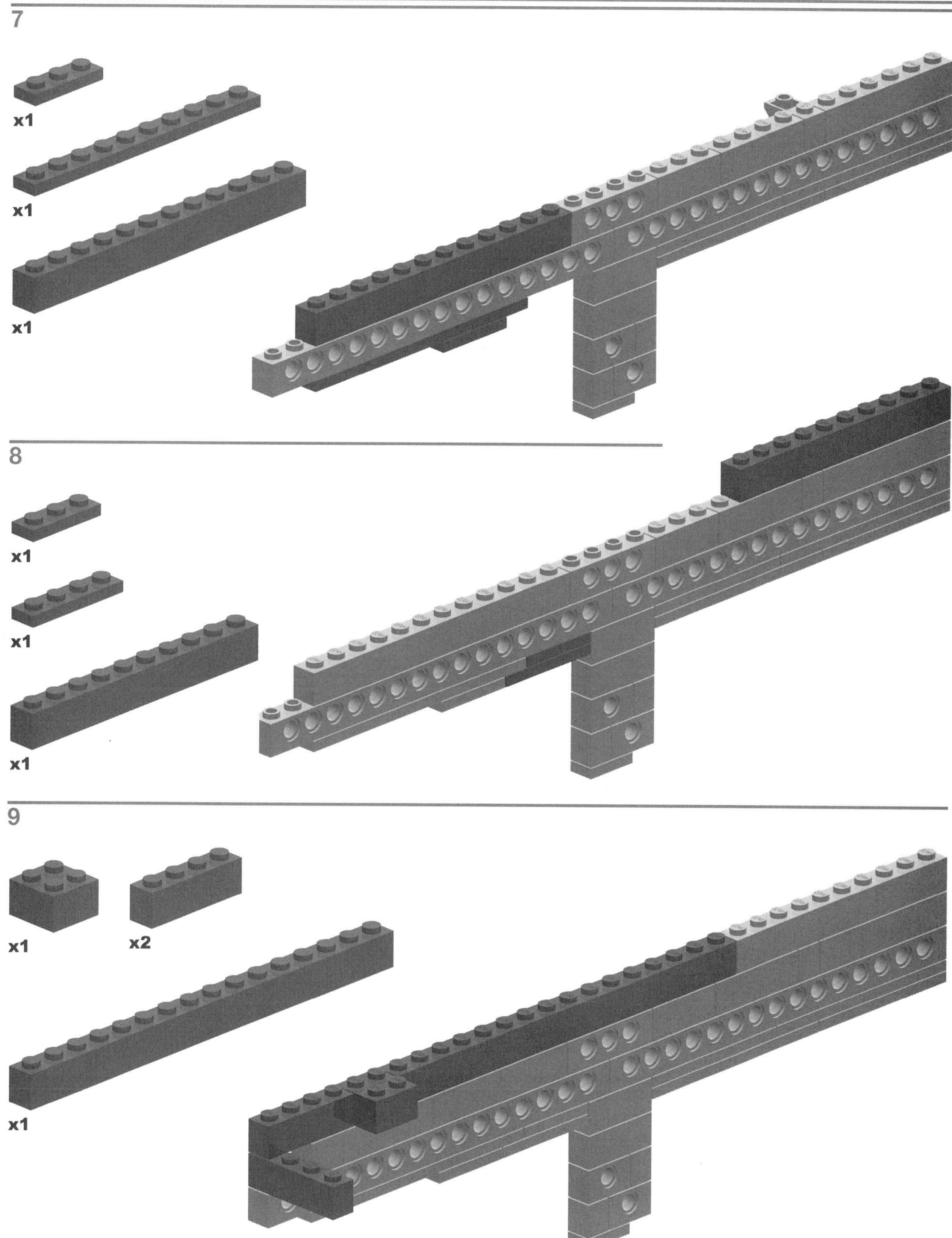
7
x1
x1
x1
8
x1
x1
x1
9
x1
x2
x1

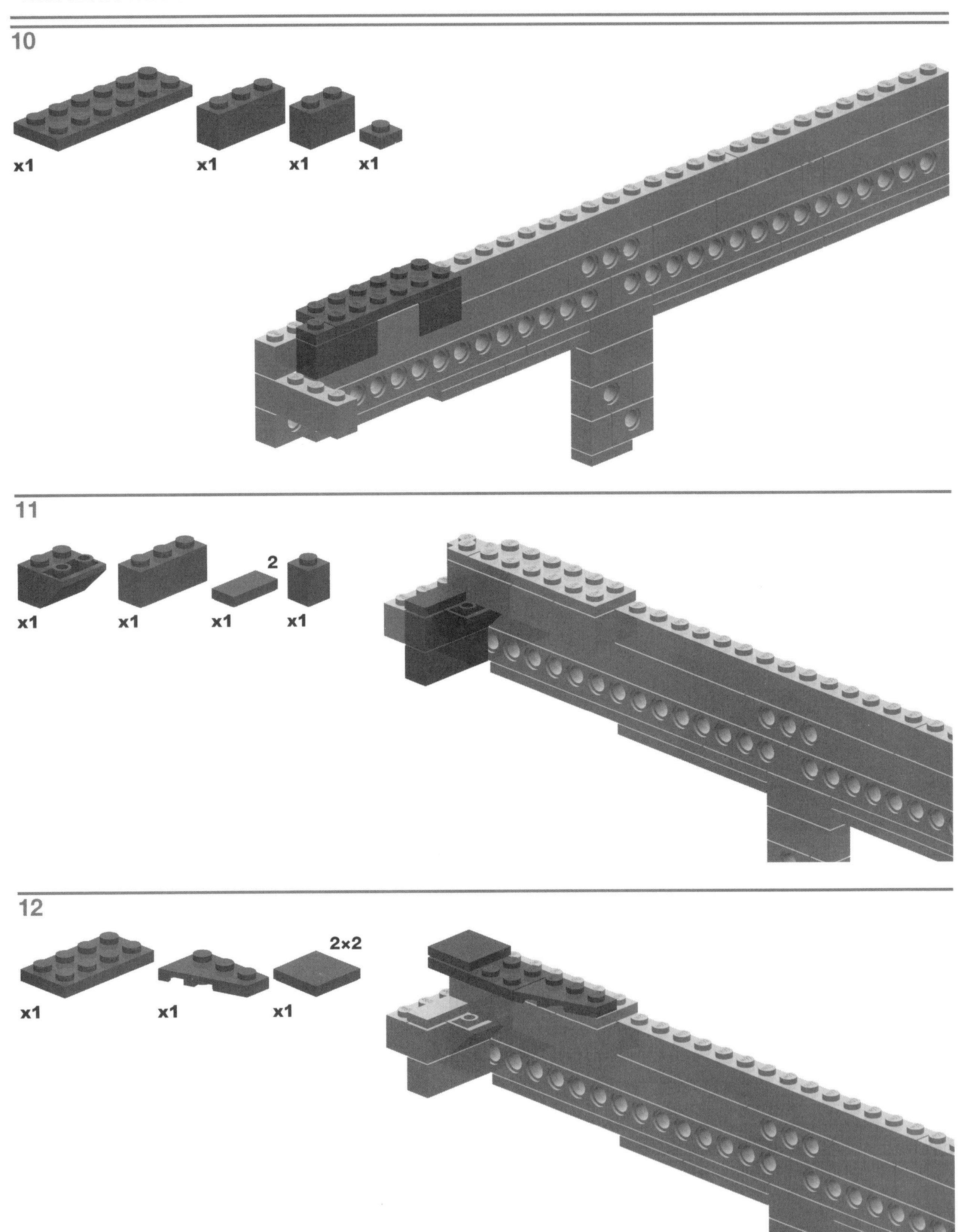
10
x1
x1
x1
x1
11
2
x1
x1
x1
x1
12
2×2
x1
x1
x1

13

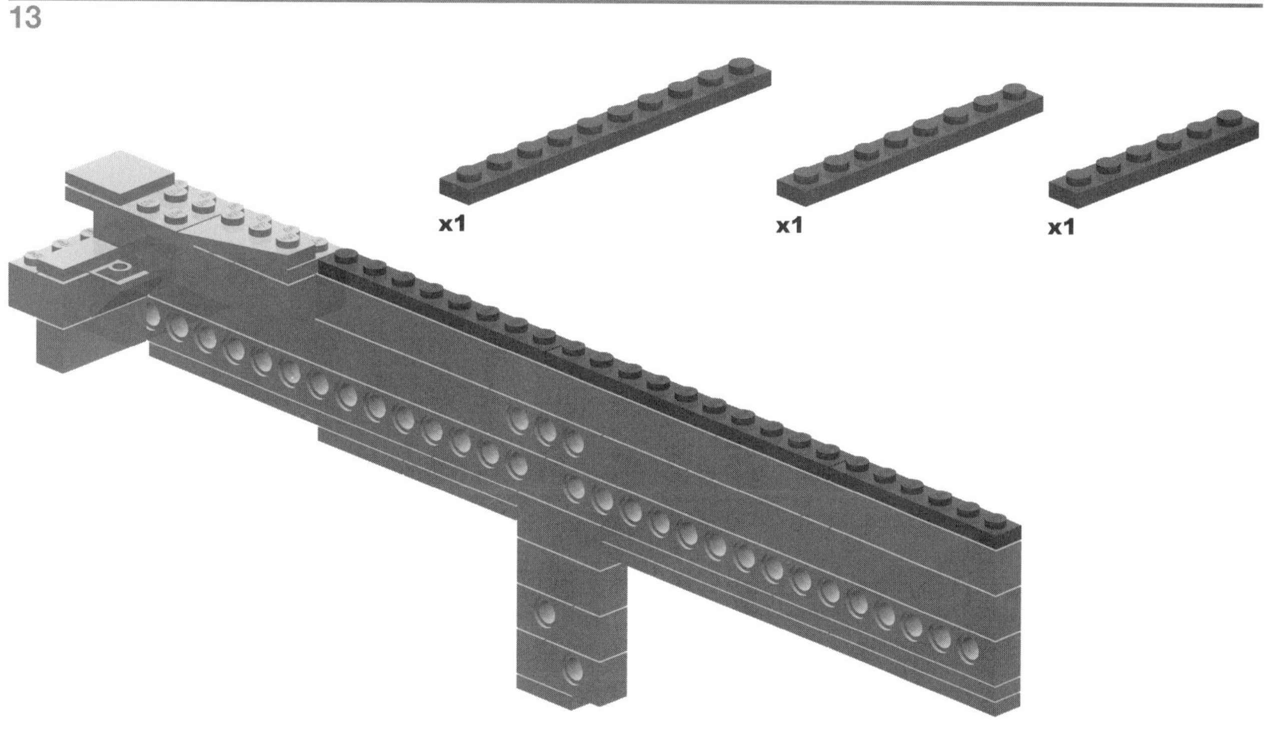

14

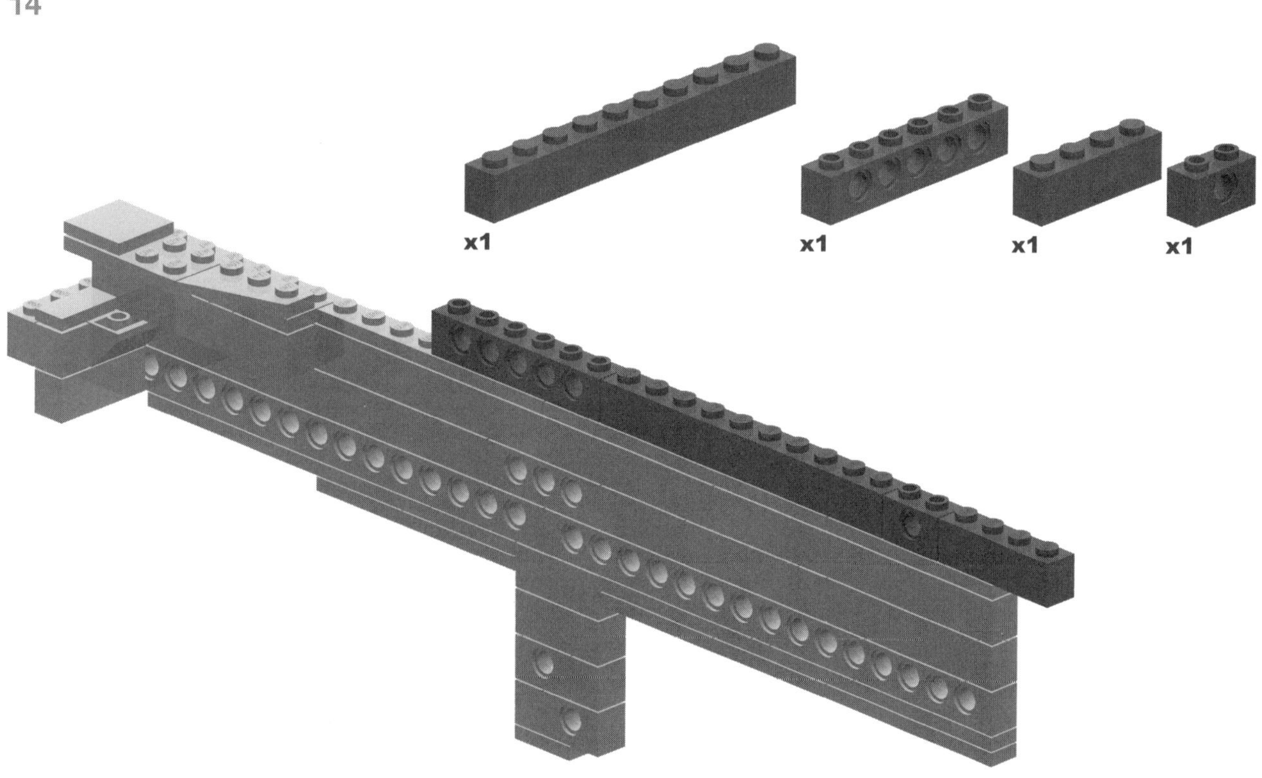

15

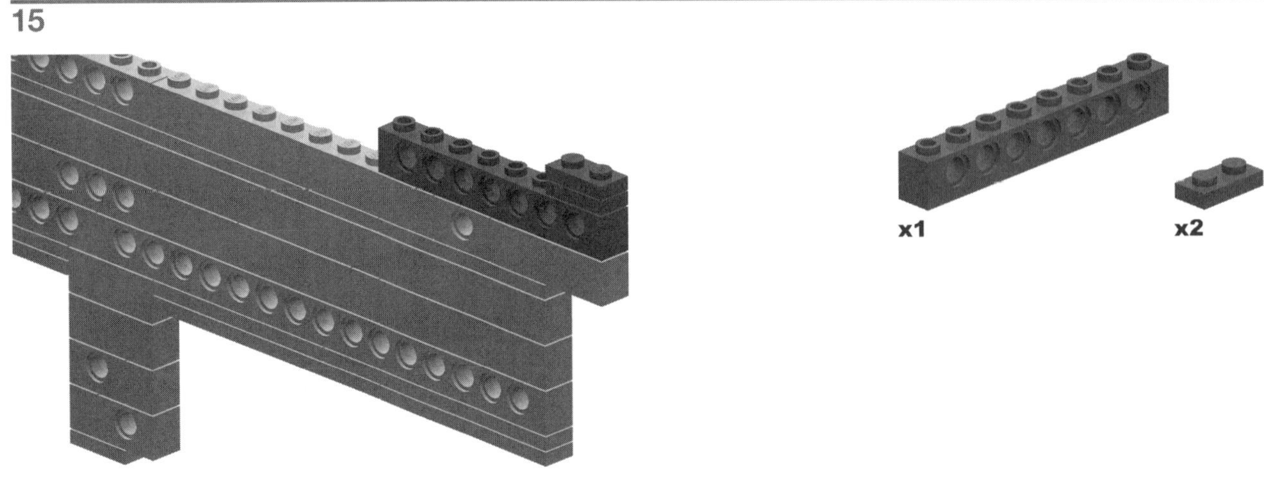

16

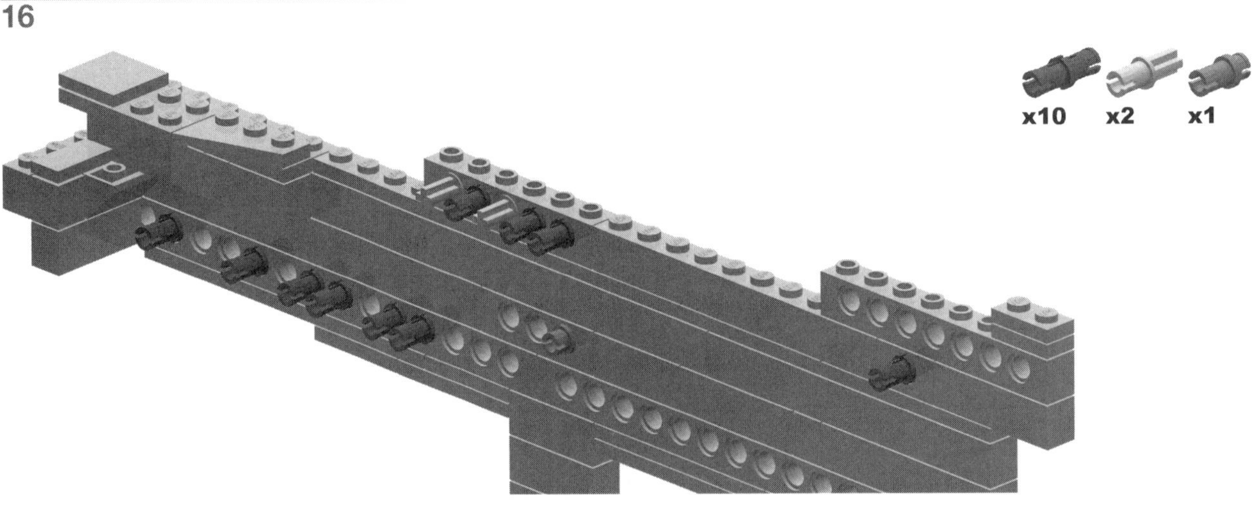

17

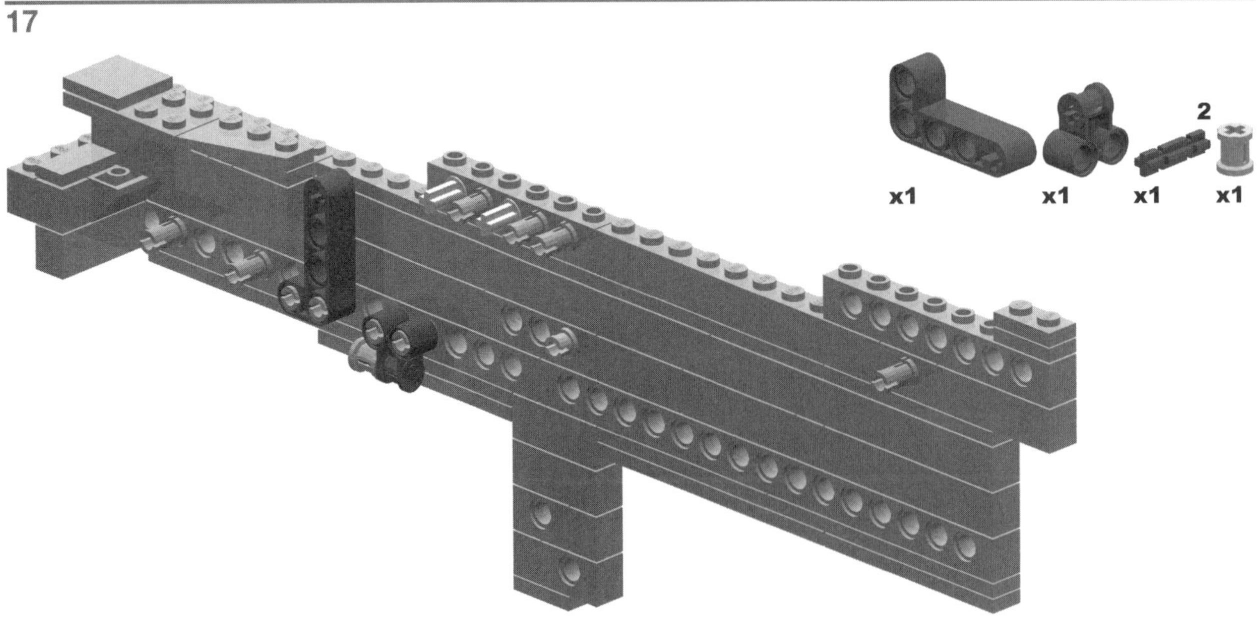

18

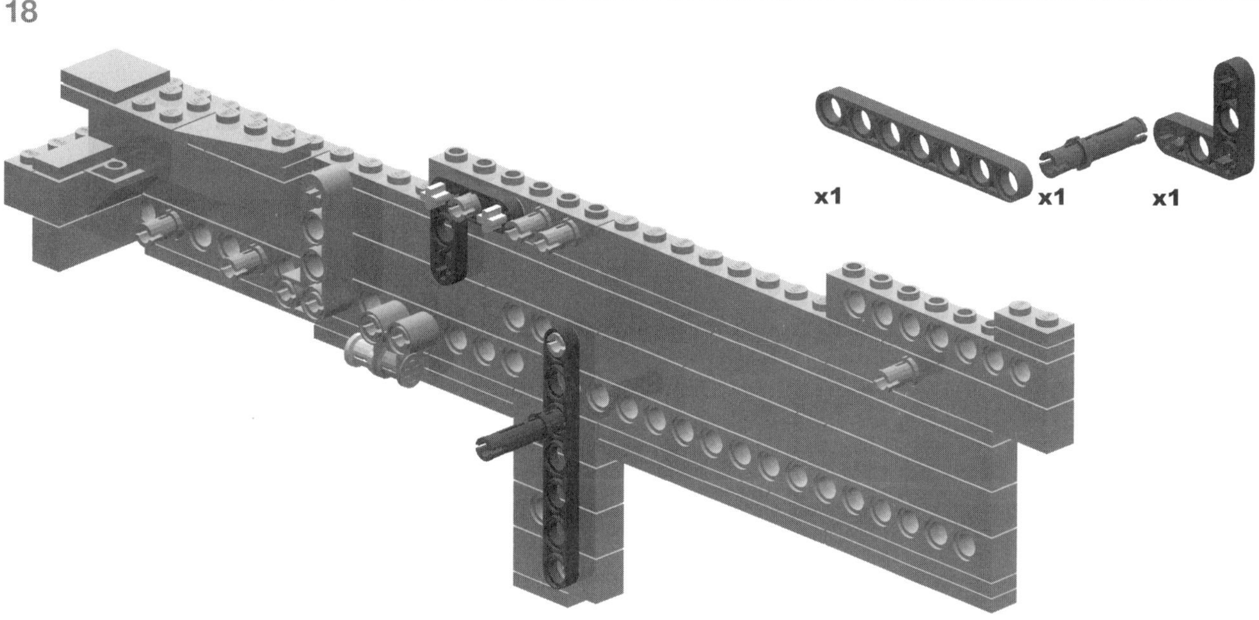

19

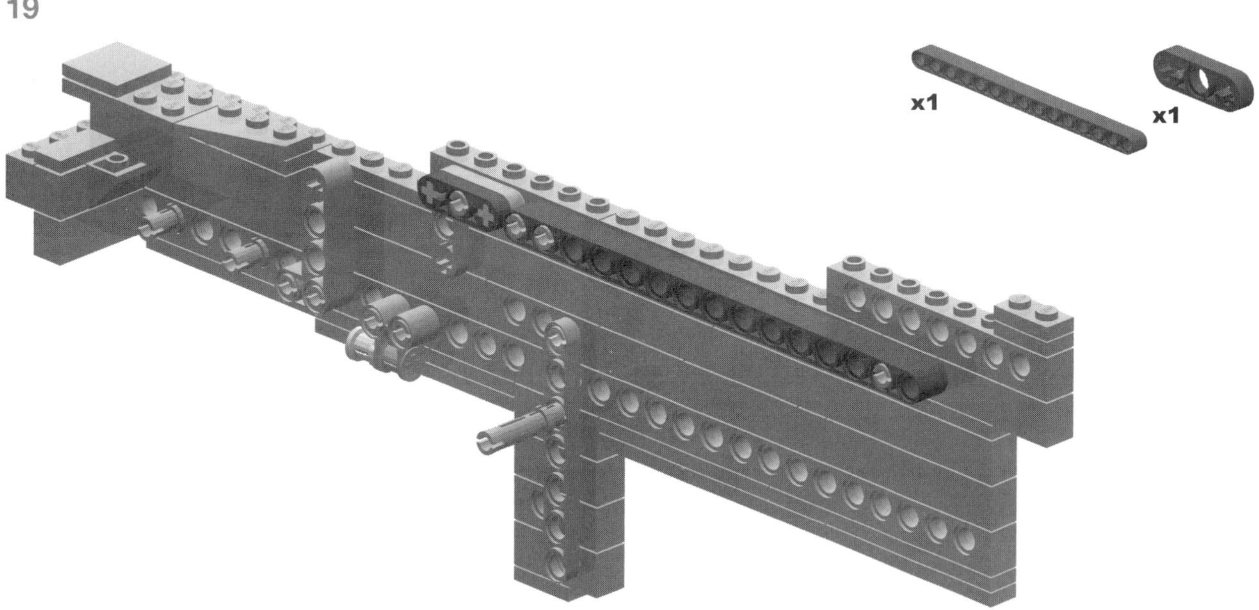

20

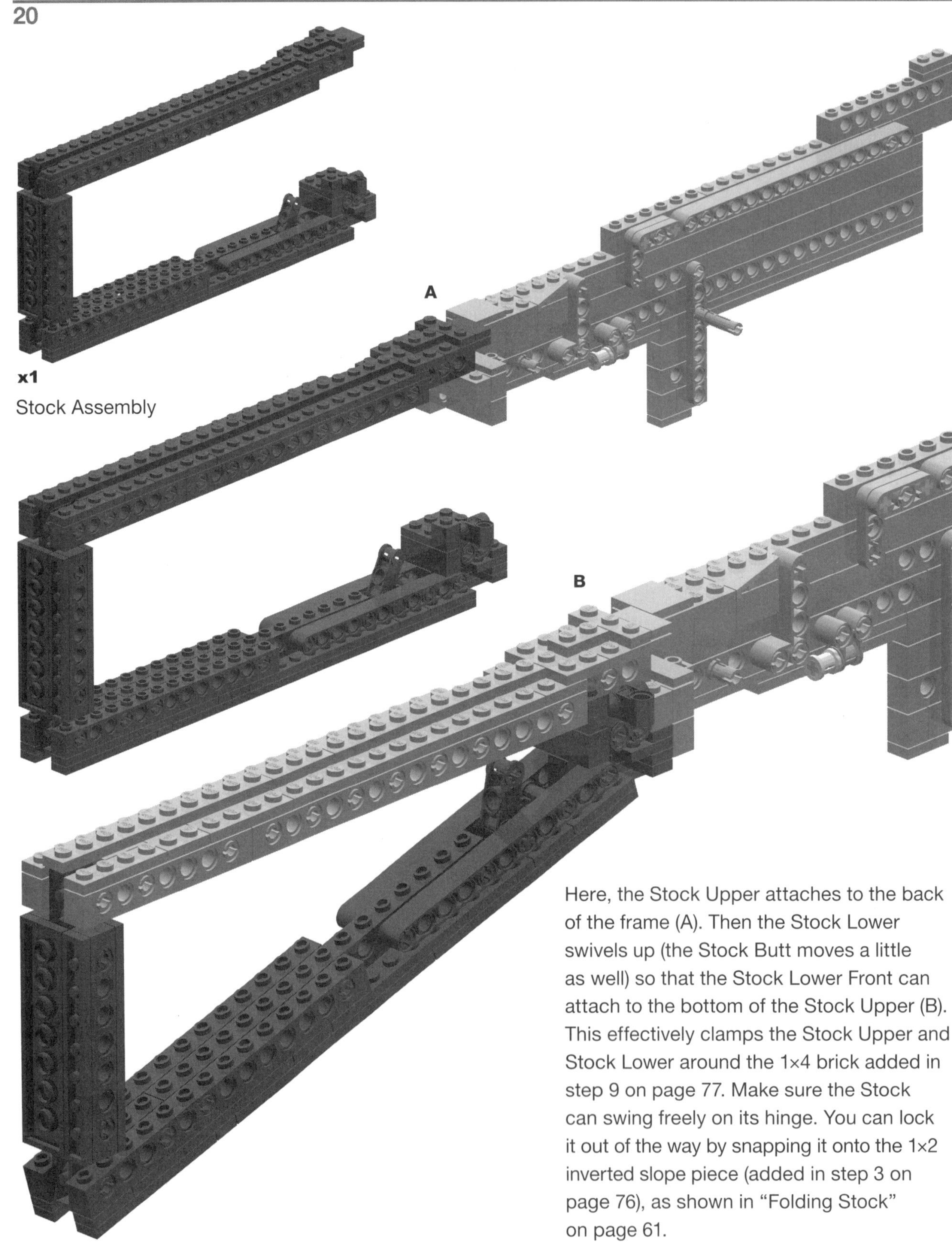

x1

Stock Assembly

Here, the Stock Upper attaches to the back of the frame (A). Then the Stock Lower swivels up (the Stock Butt moves a little as well) so that the Stock Lower Front can attach to the bottom of the Stock Upper (B). This effectively clamps the Stock Upper and Stock Lower around the 1×4 brick added in step 9 on page 77. Make sure the Stock can swing freely on its hinge. You can lock it out of the way by snapping it onto the 1×2 inverted slope piece (added in step 3 on page 76), as shown in "Folding Stock" on page 61.

21

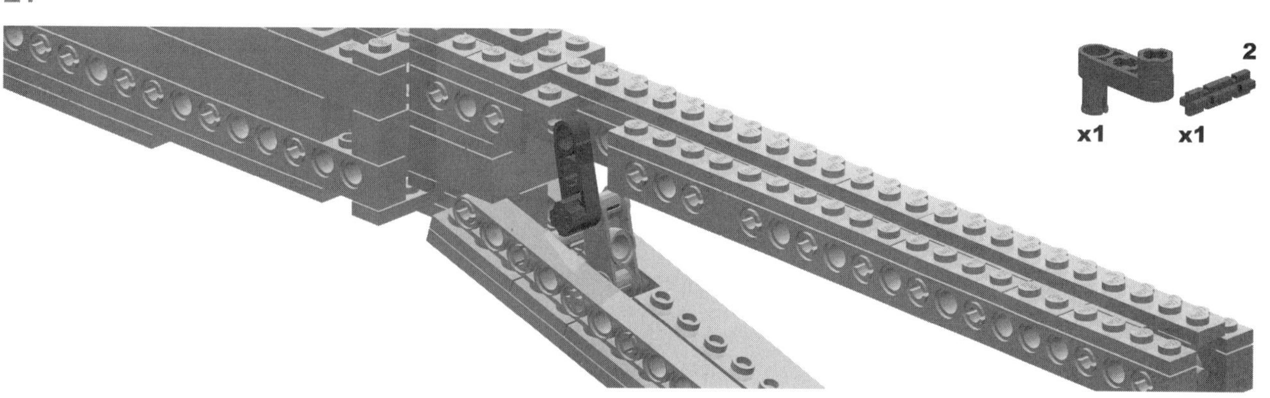

22

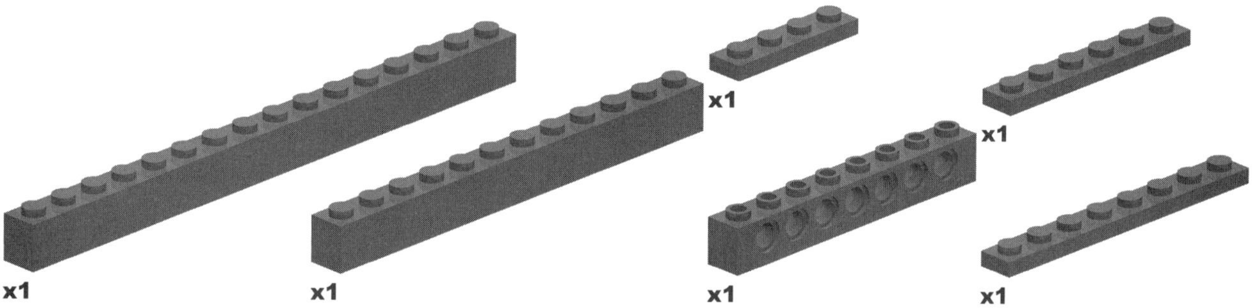

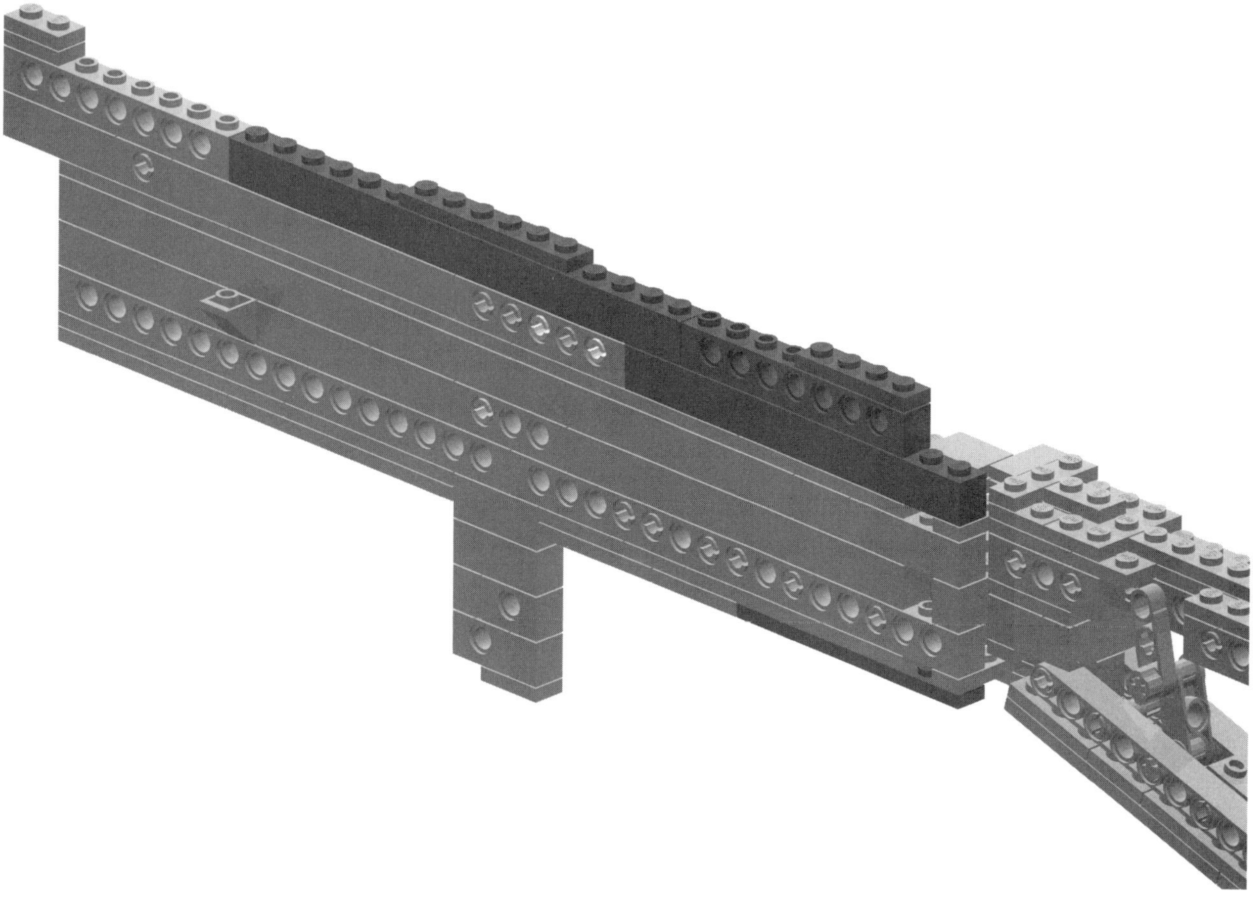

x1

x1

x1

x1

x1

x1

23

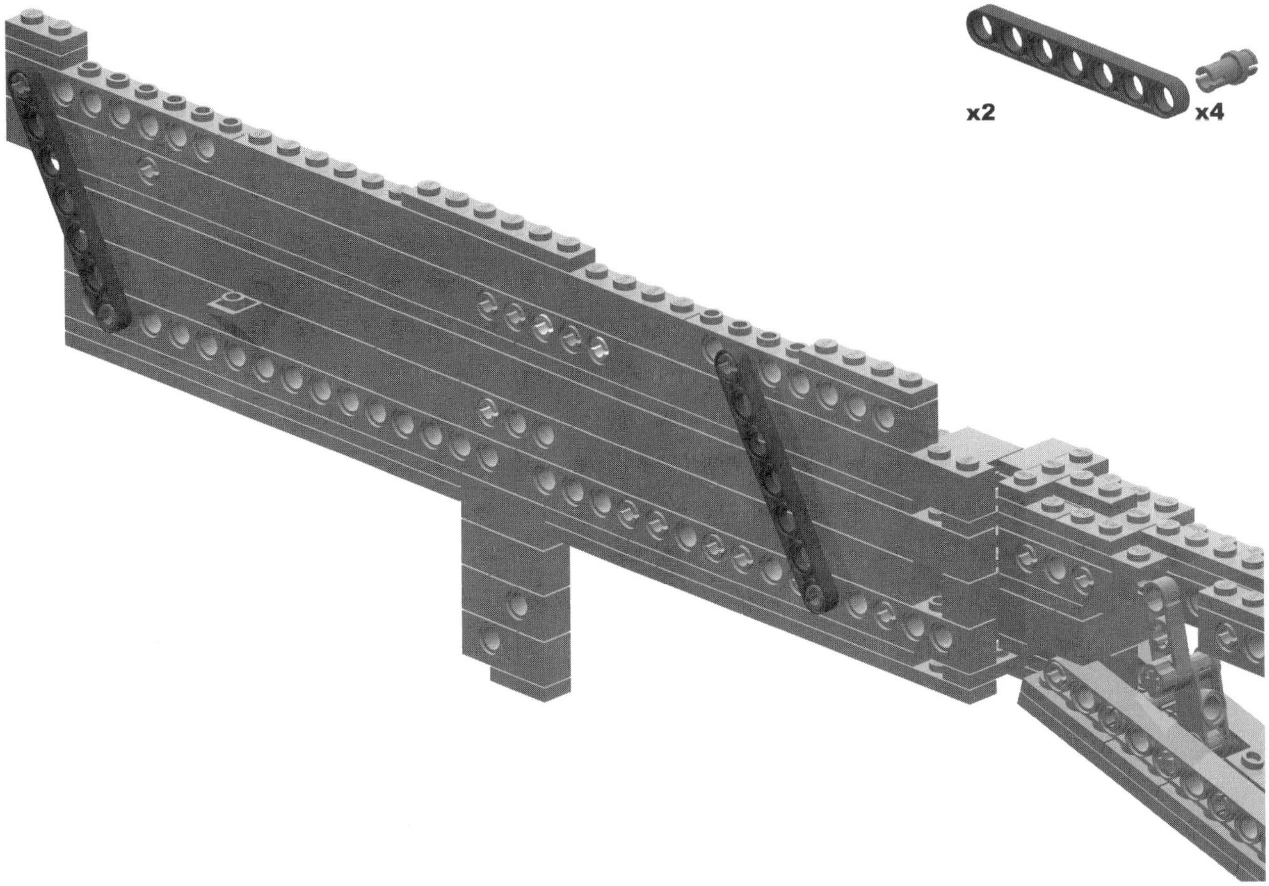

x2

x4

TRIGGER

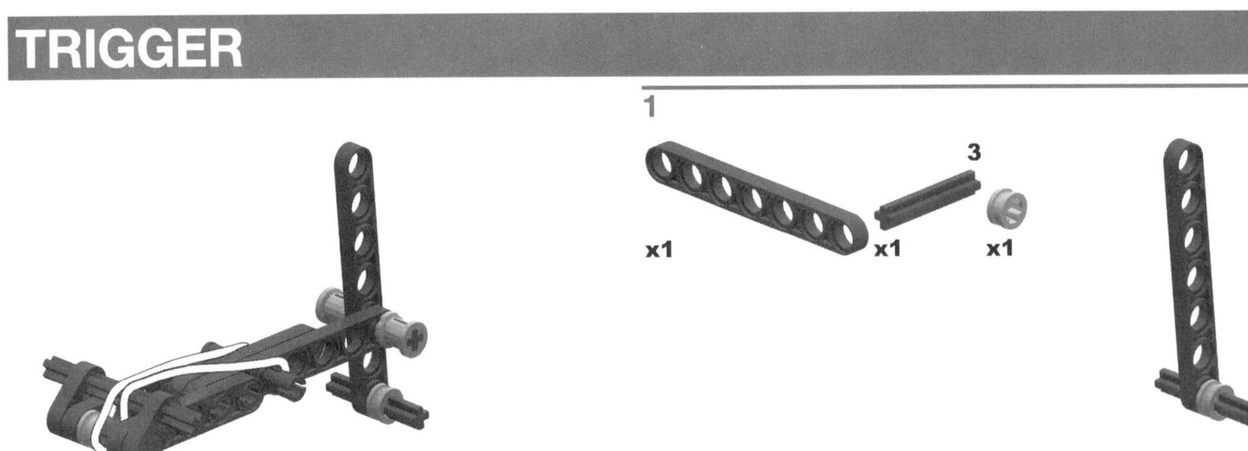

2

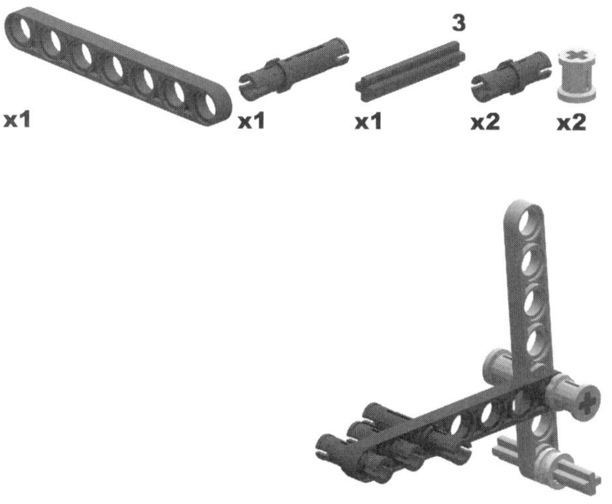

3 x1 x1 x1 x2 x2

3

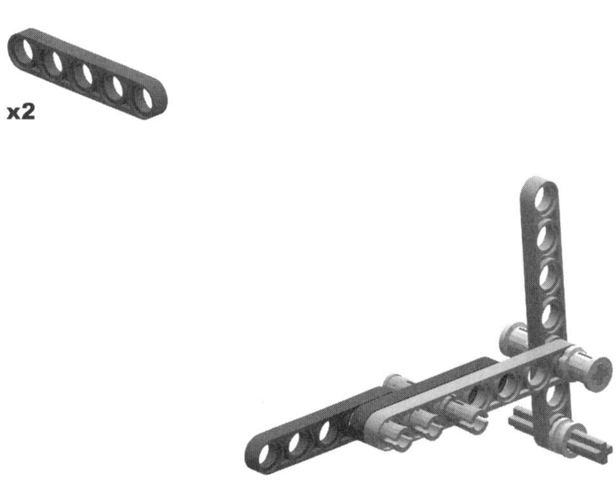

x2

4

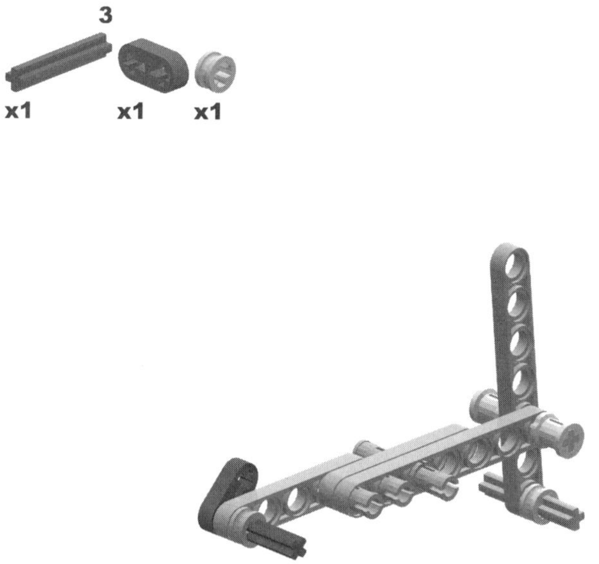

3 x1 x1 x1

5

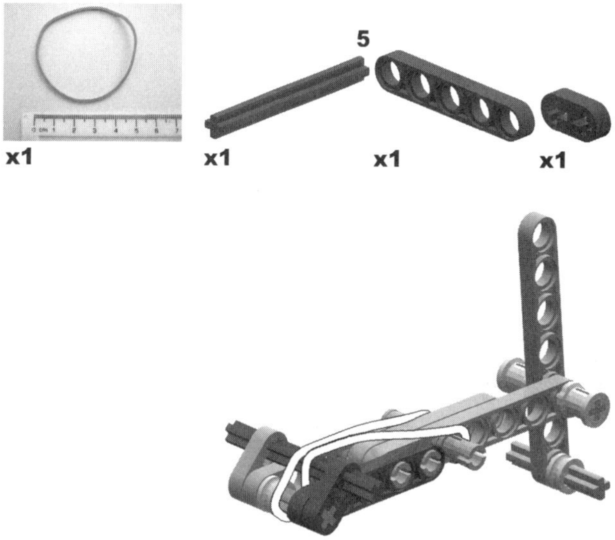

5 x1 x1 x1 x1

PISTOL GRIP UNDERSIDE

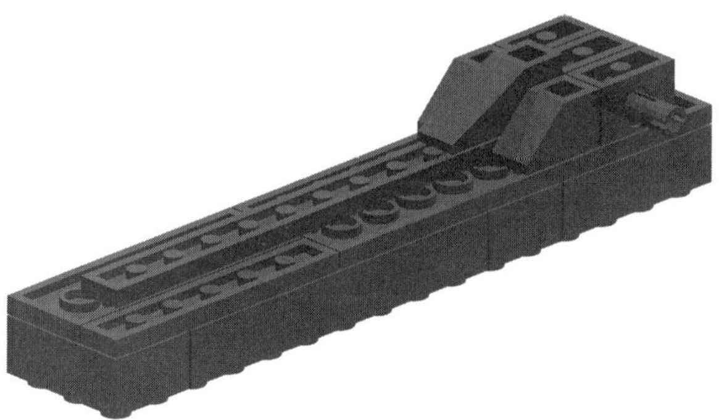

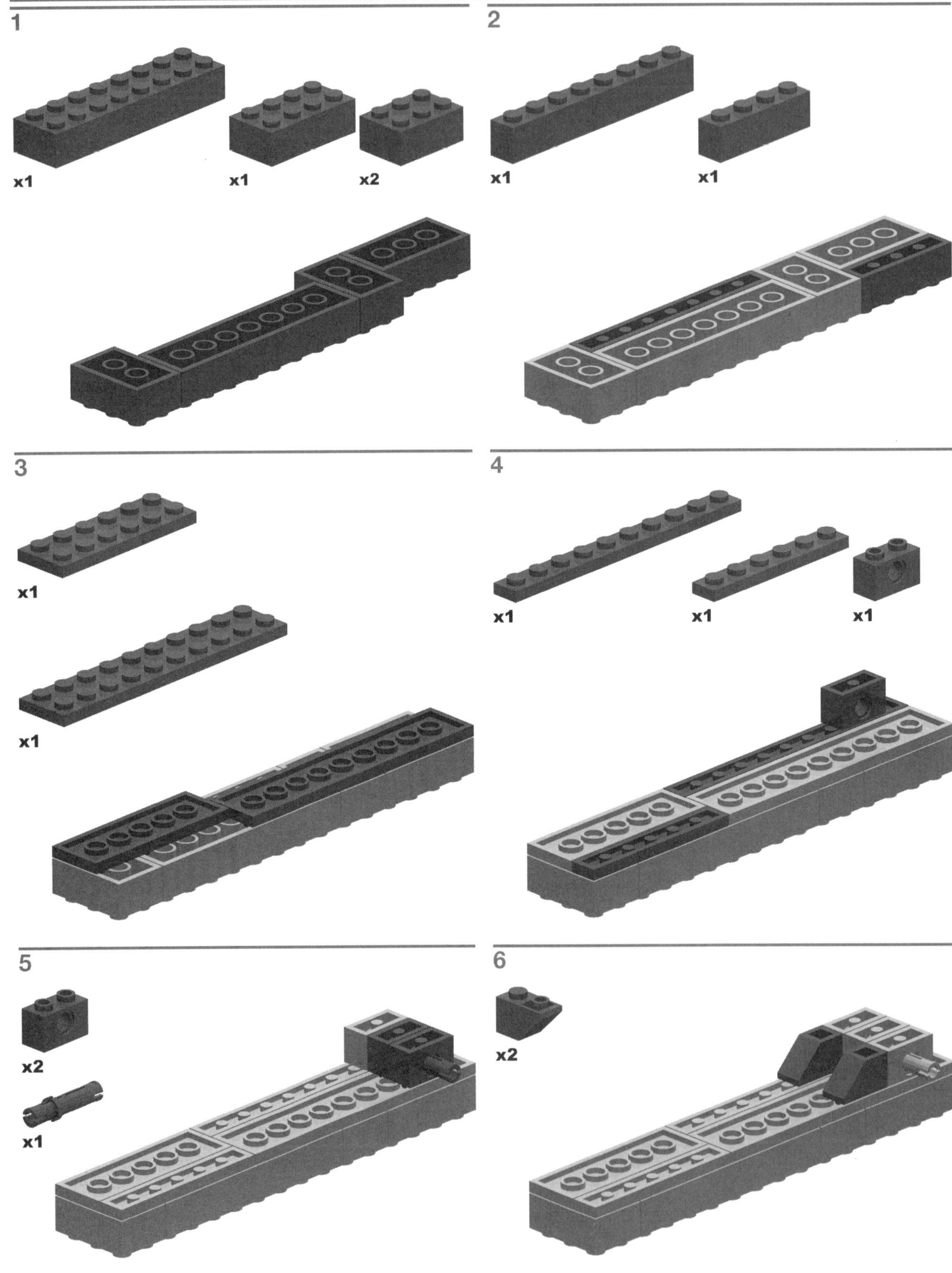
1
x1
x1
x2
2
x1
x1
3
x1
x1
4
x1
x1
x1
5
x2
x1
6
x2

7

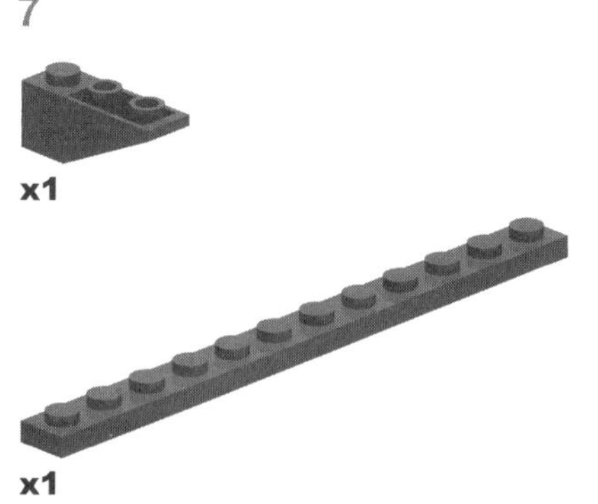

x1

x1

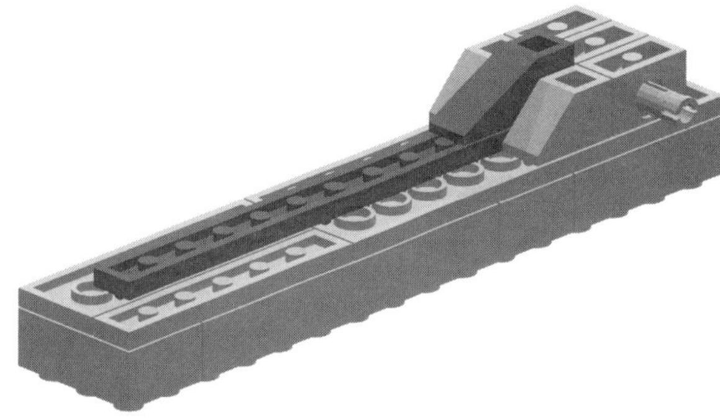

PISTOL GRIP ASSEMBLY

1

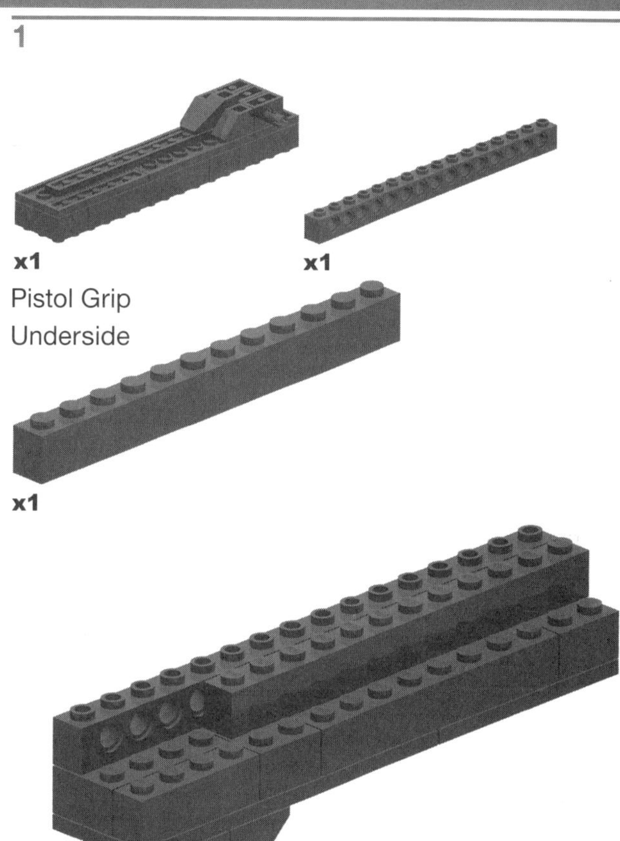

x1

x1

Pistol Grip
Underside

x1

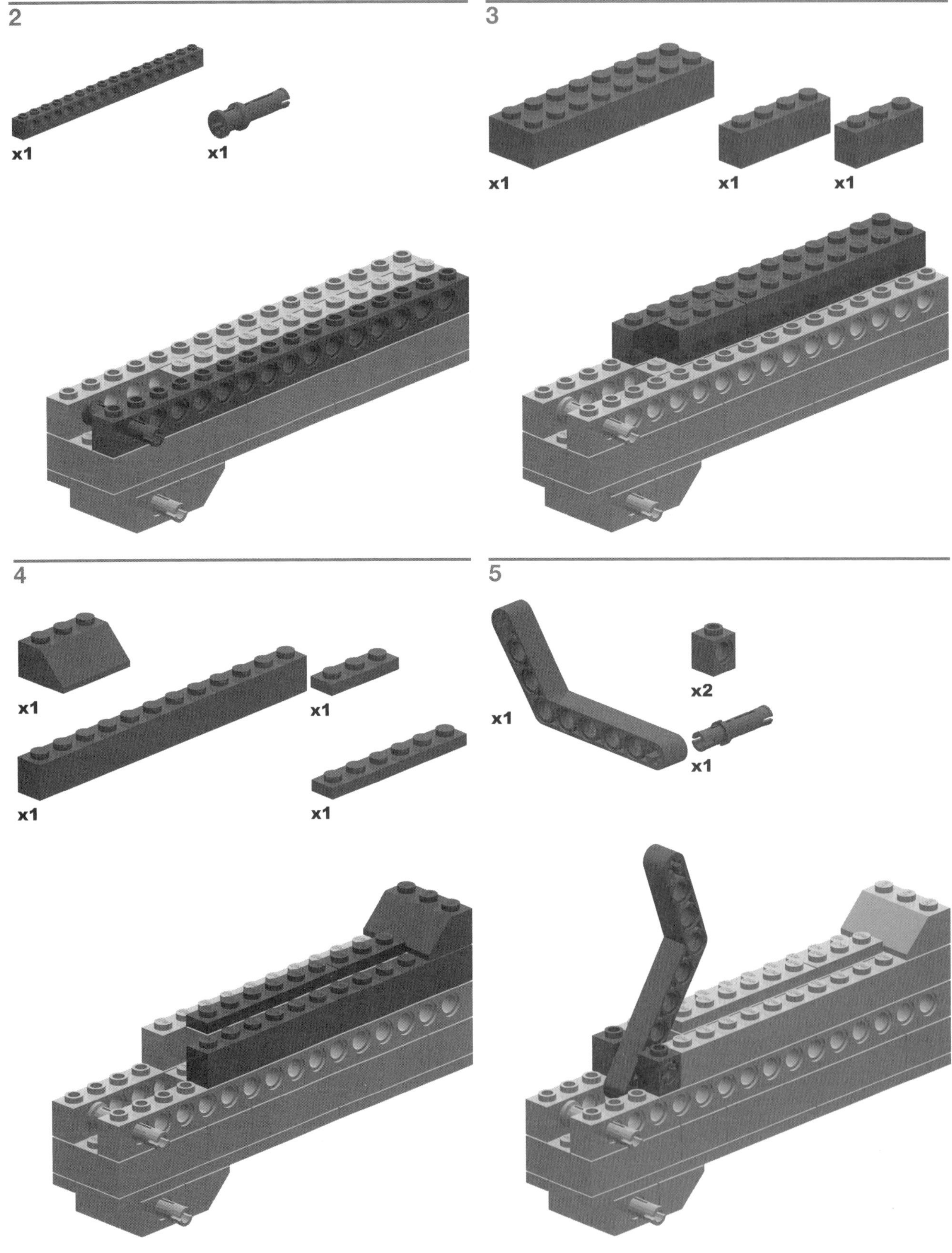
2
x1
x1
3
x1
x1
x1
4
x1
x1
x1
x1
5
x1
x2
x1

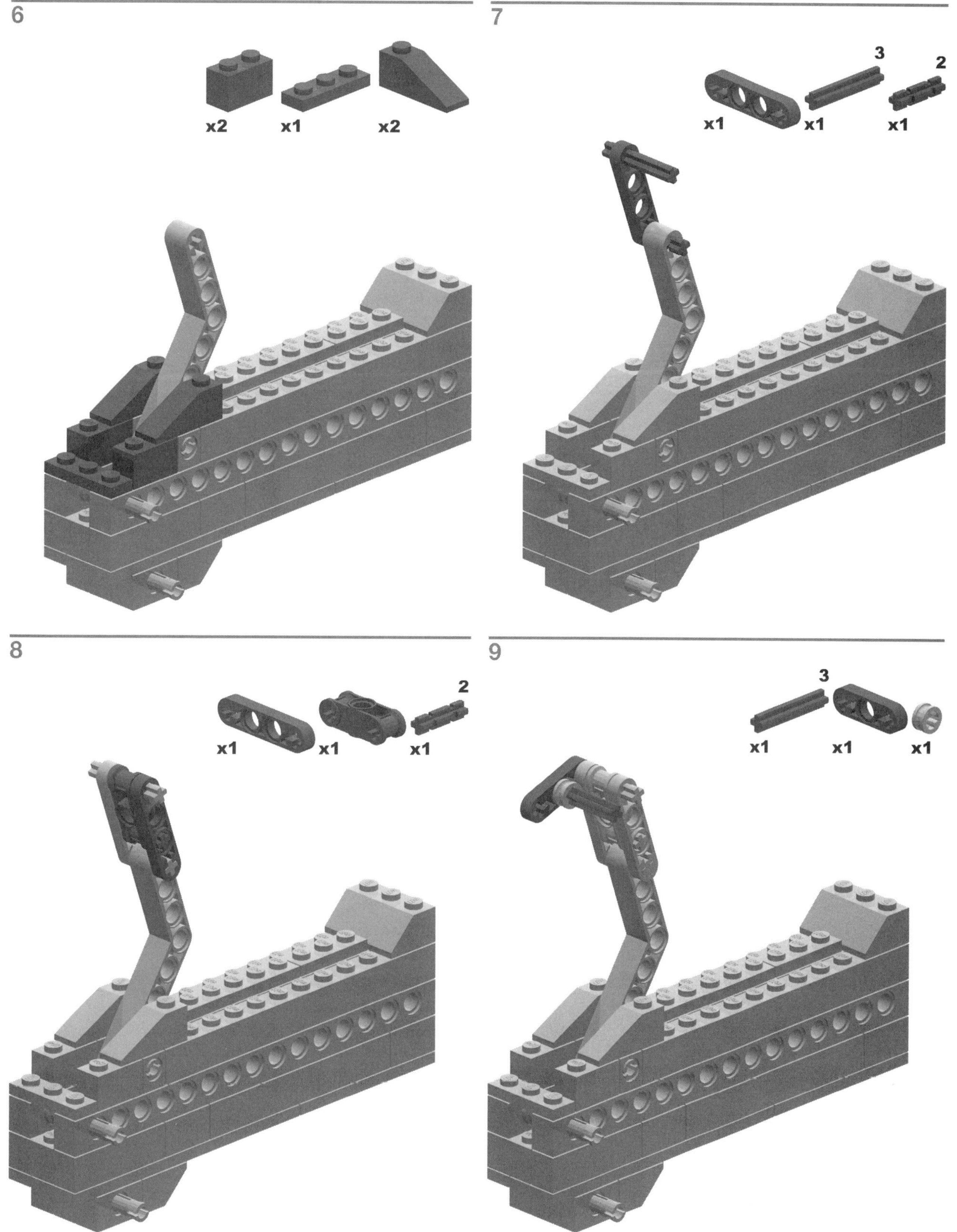
6
x2
x1
x2
7
3
2
x1
x1
x1
8
2
x1
x1
x1
9
3
x1
x1
x1

10

x1
x1
x1

11

5
x2
x1
x1

MAGAZINE RELEASE

1

x1
5
x1

2

x1
x1

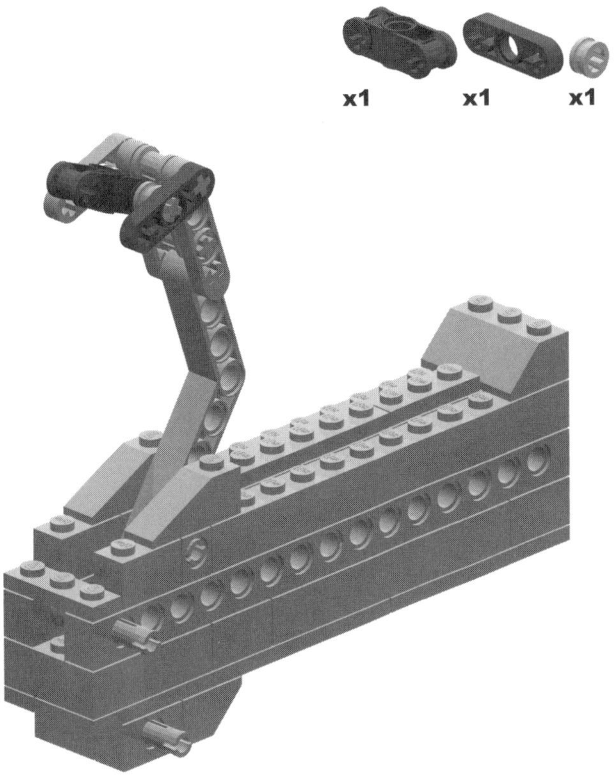

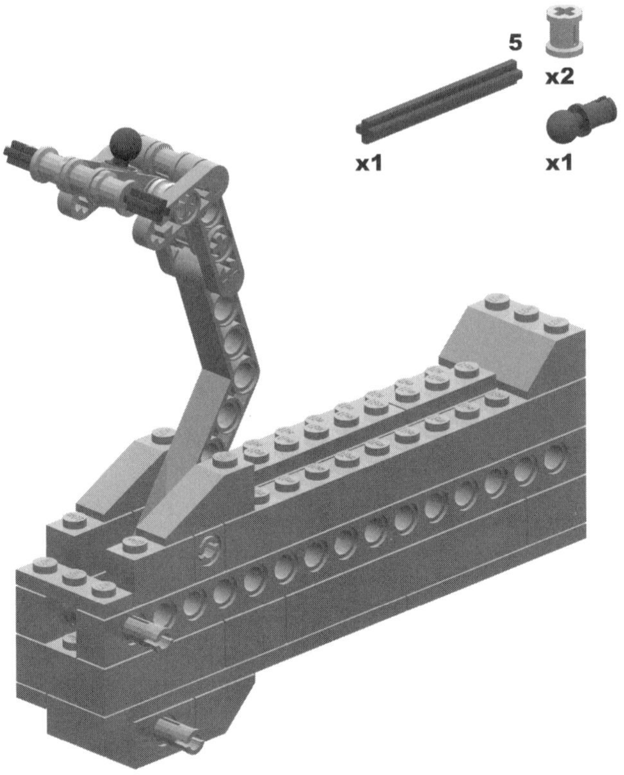

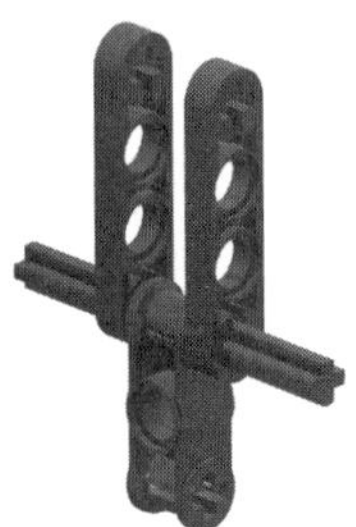

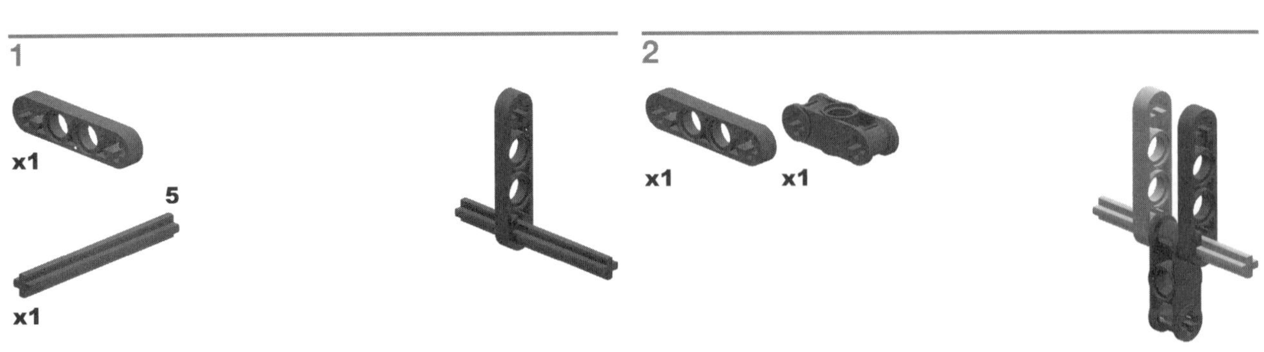

INTERNALS WALL LEFT

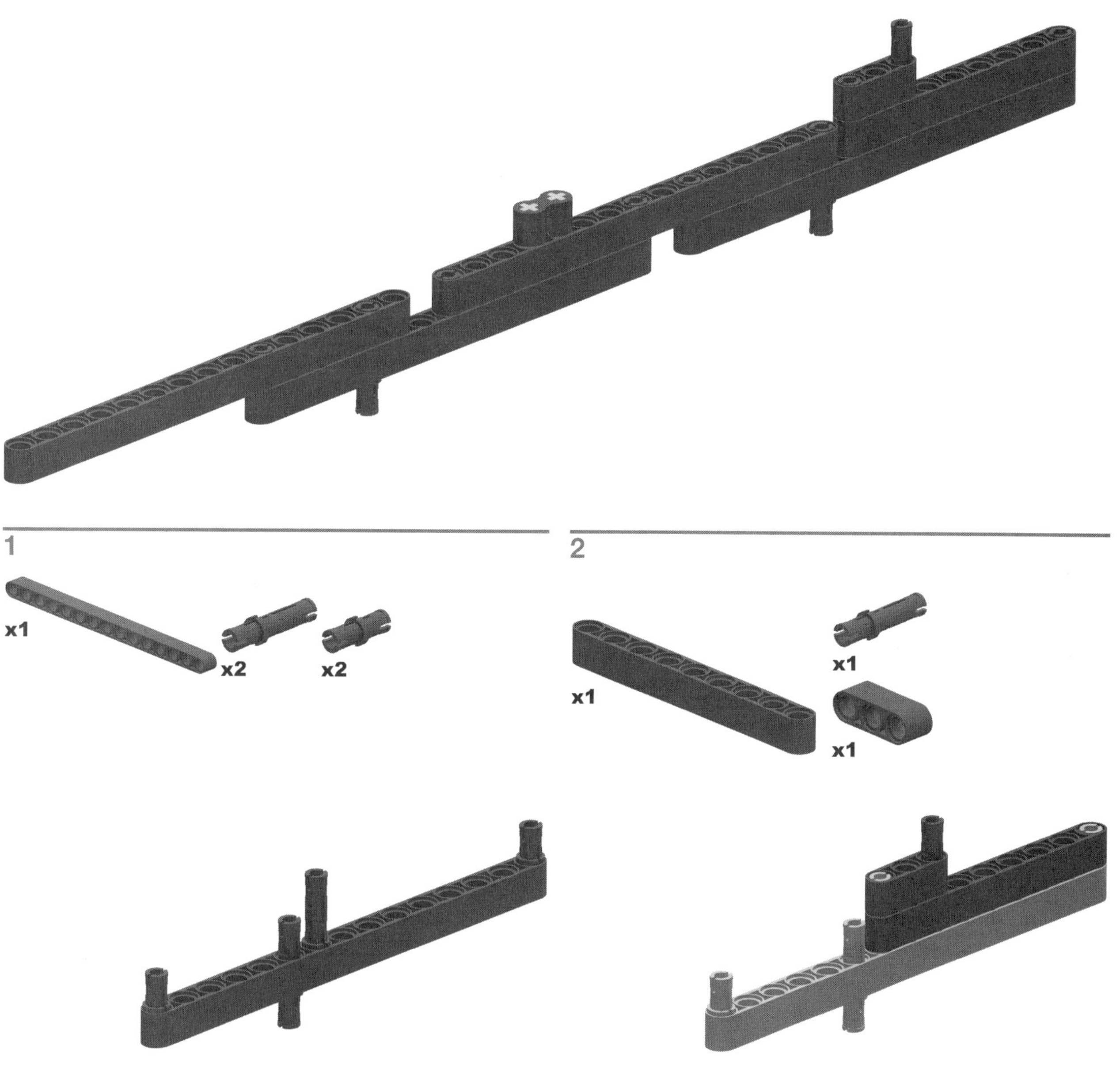

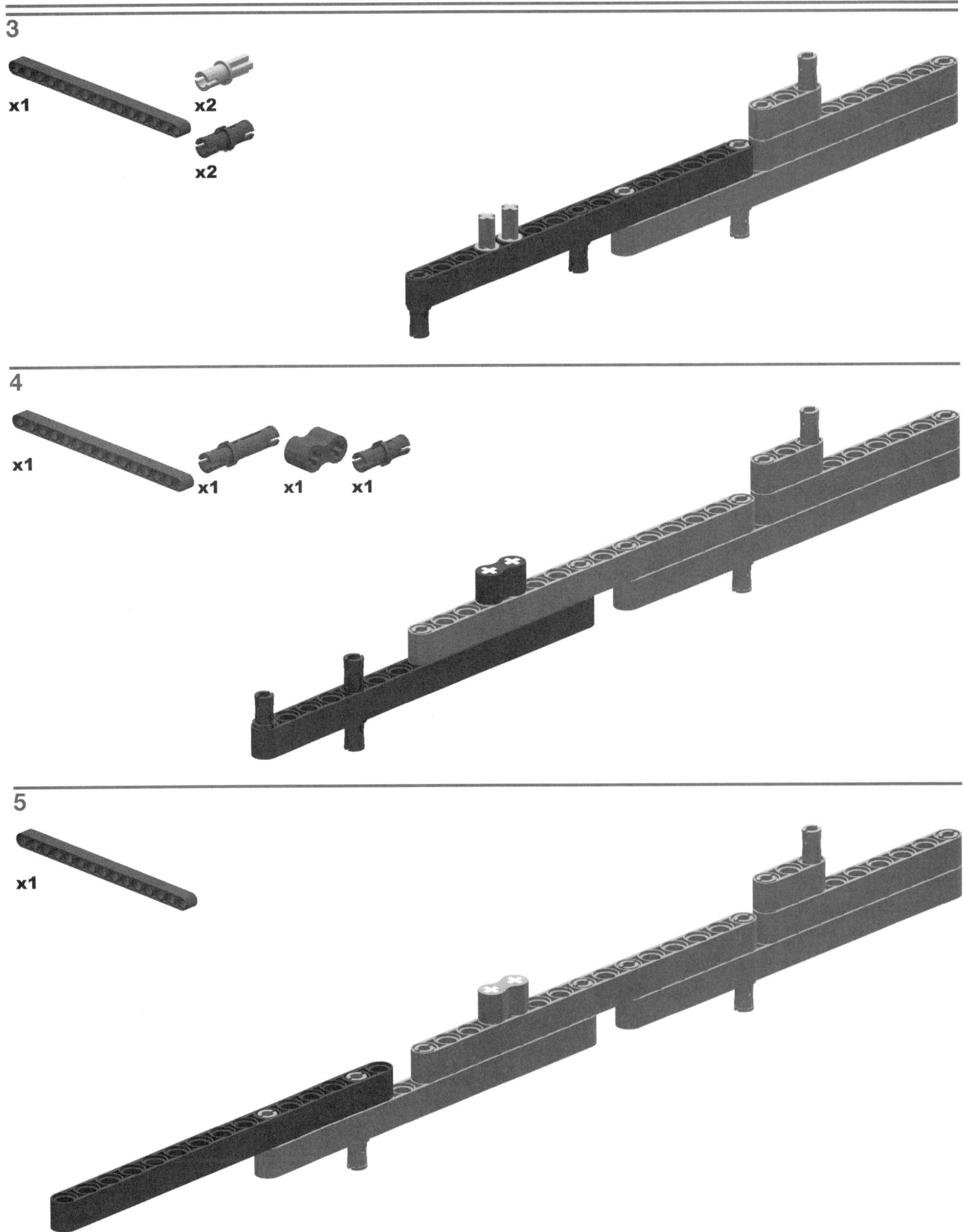
3
x1
x2
x2
4
x1
x1
x1
x1
5
x1

INTERNALS MAGAZINE RAMP

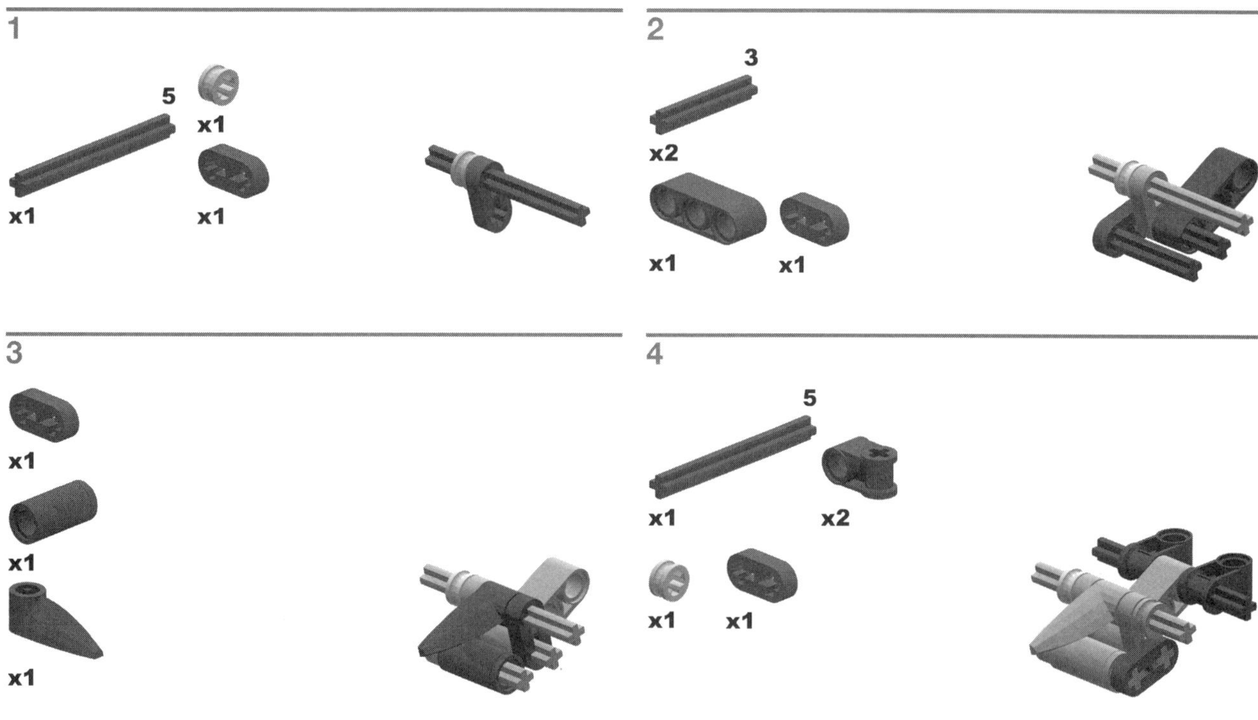

INTERNALS LOWER

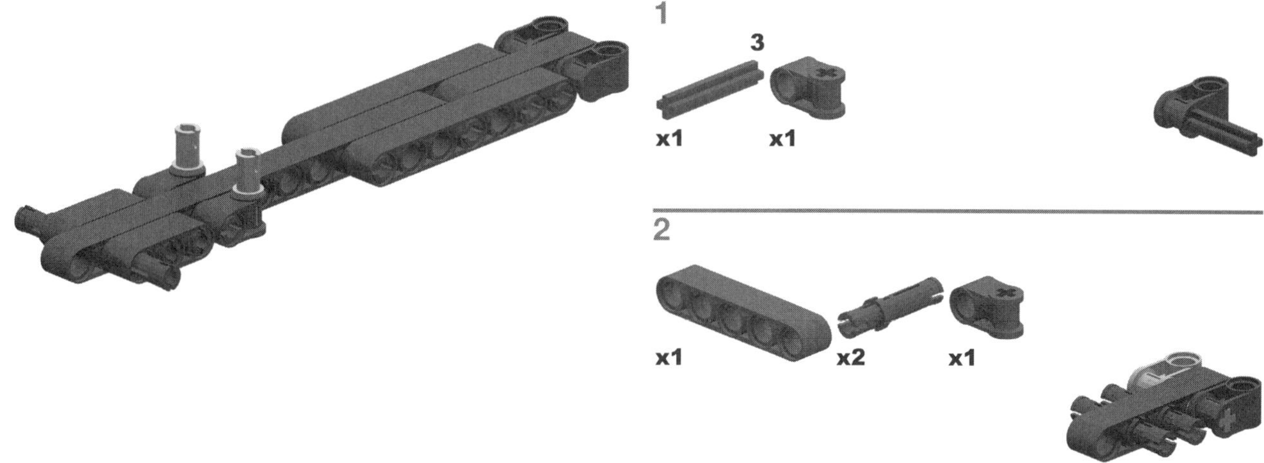

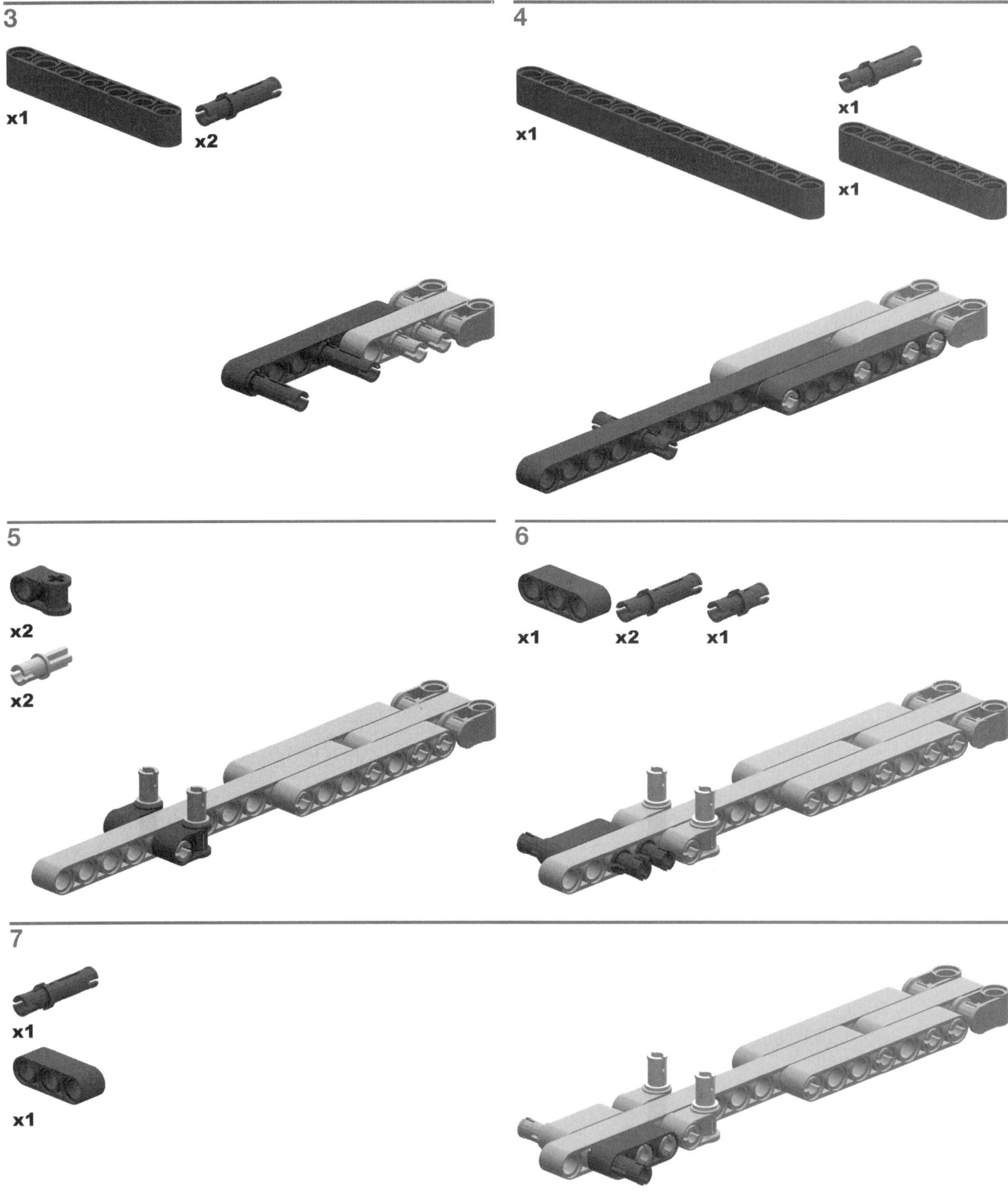
3
x1
x2
4
x1
x1
x1
5
x2
x2
6
x1
x2
x1
7
x1
x1

INTERNALS WALL RIGHT

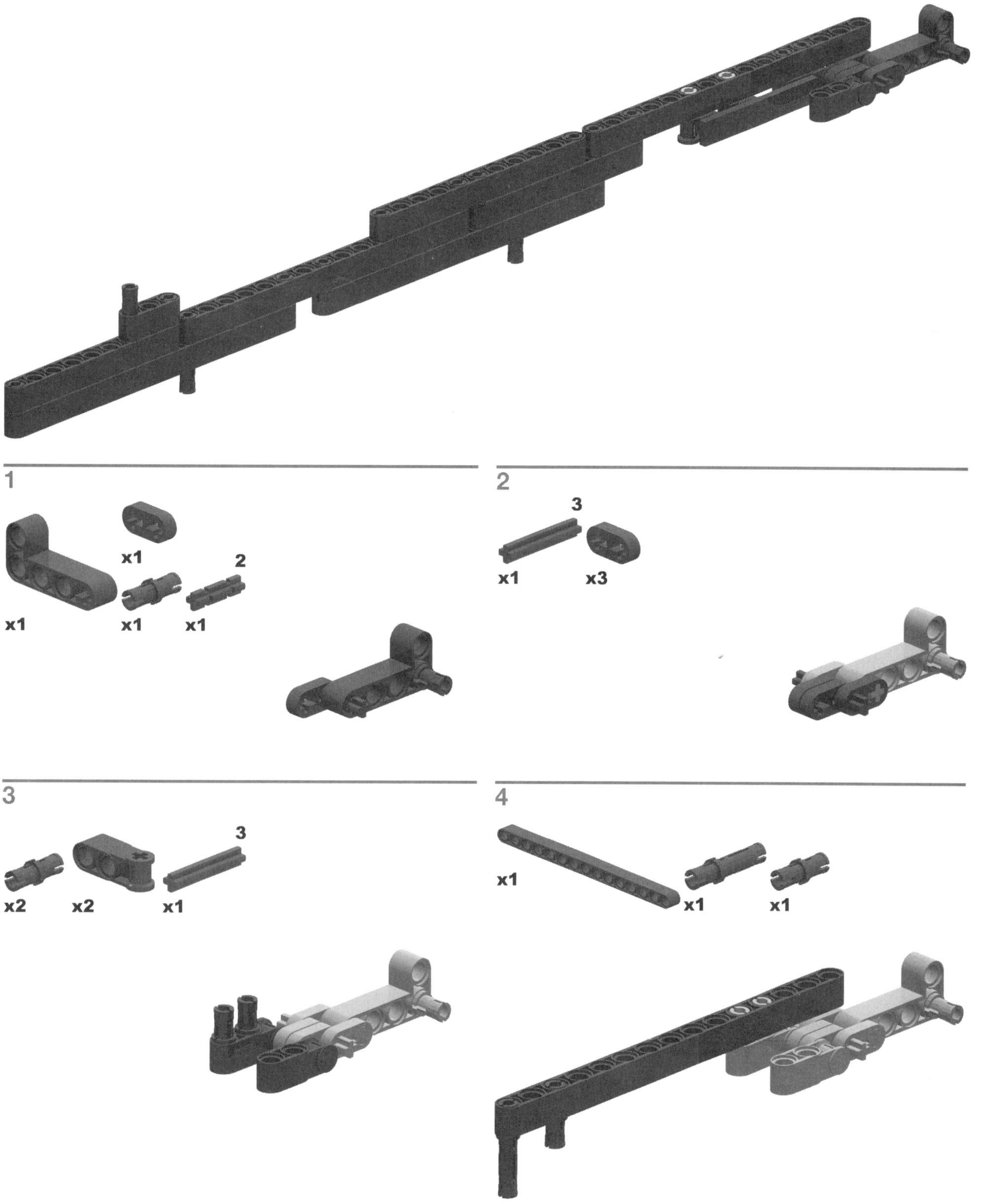

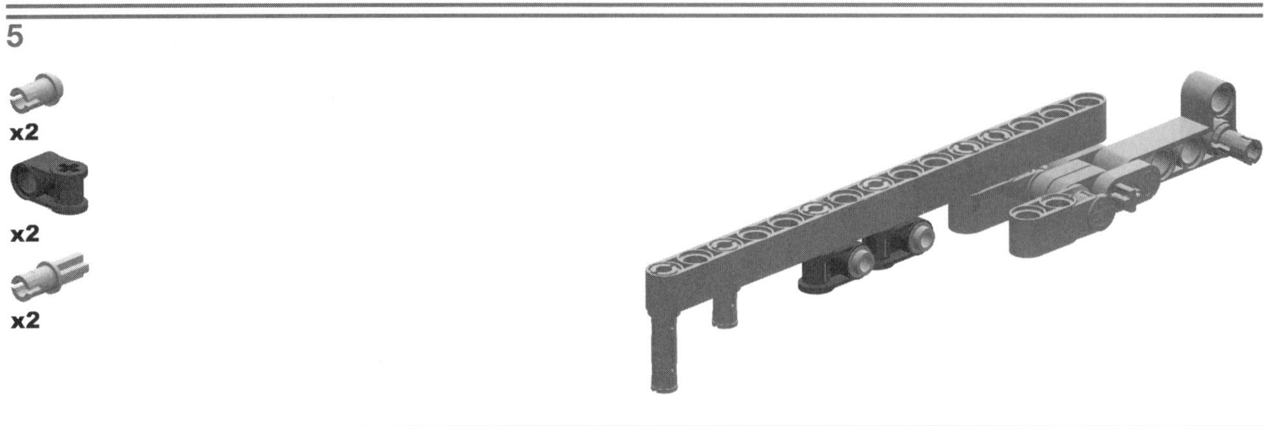

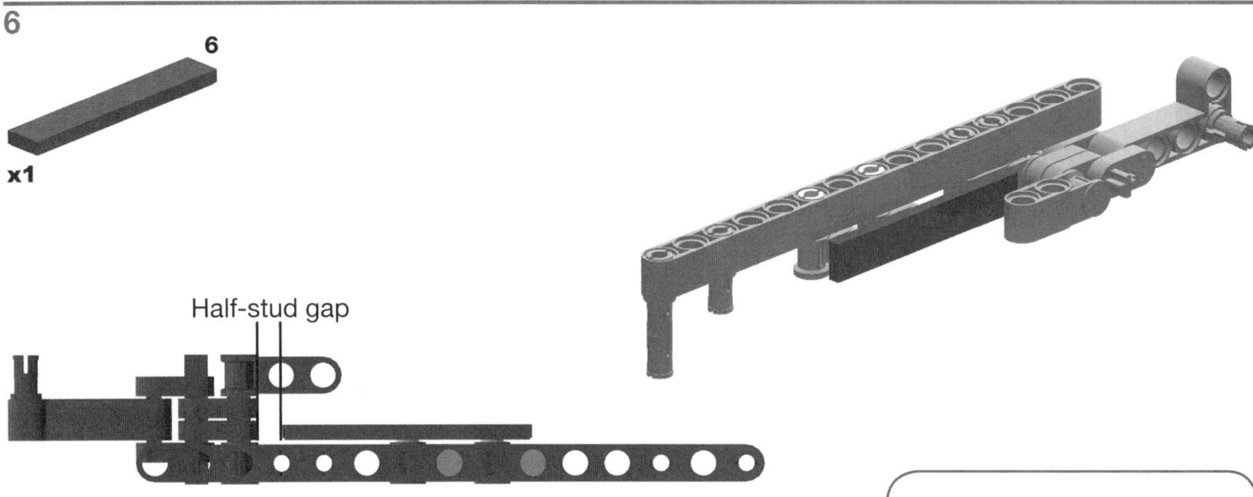

Note that the 1×6 plate does not perfectly line up with the rest of the pieces. As shown above, there should be a half-stud gap between the plate and the 1×2 liftarms (added in step 2 on page 95). The pins added in the previous step should fit over the dots on the underside of the 1×6 plate (shown at right), not between them.

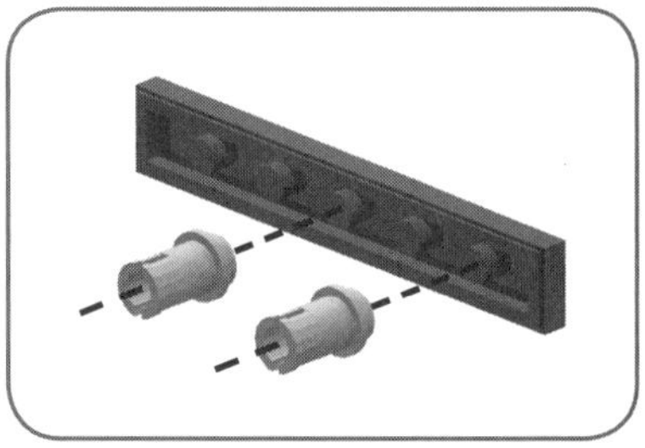

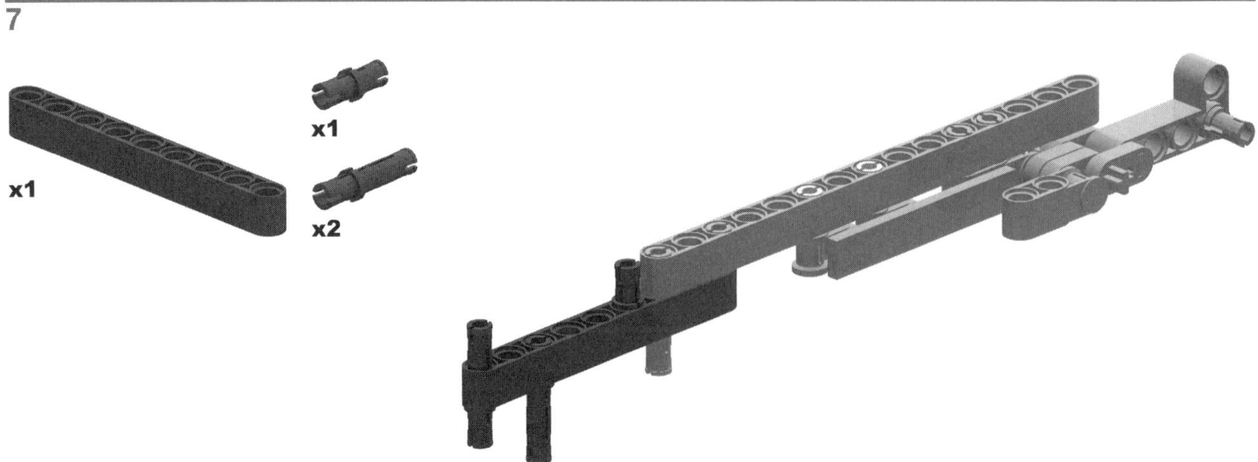

8

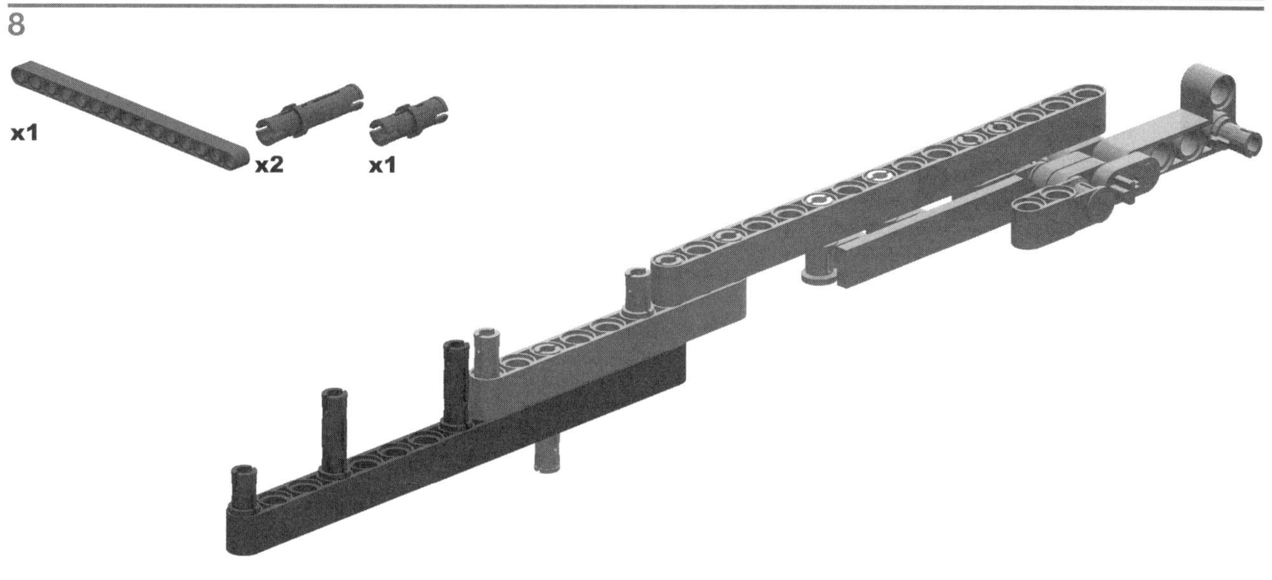

9

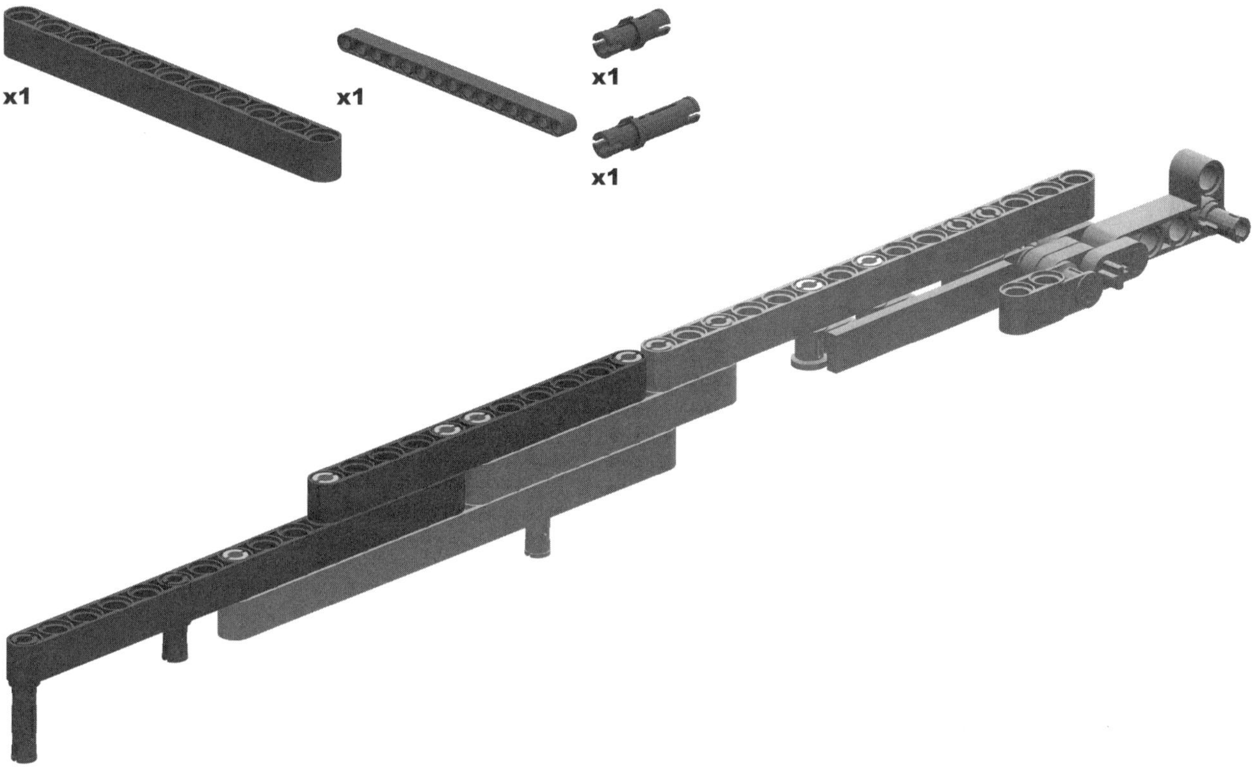

x1

x1

x1

x1

10

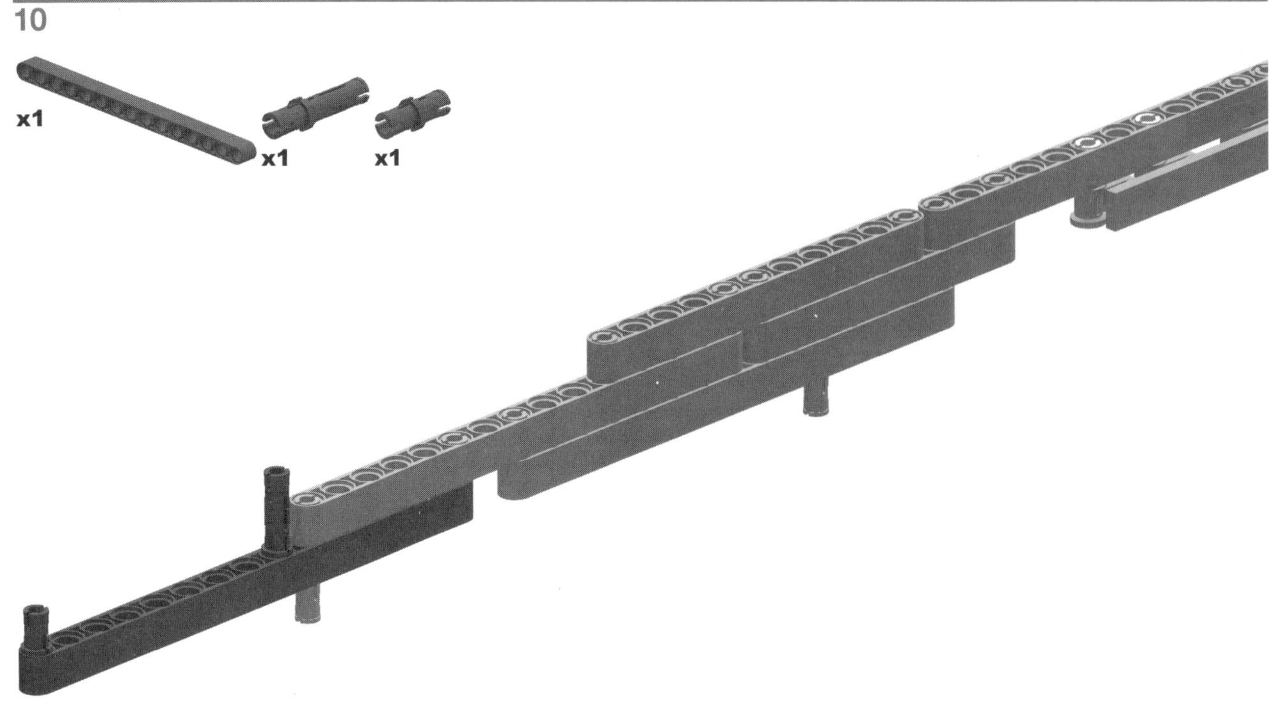

11

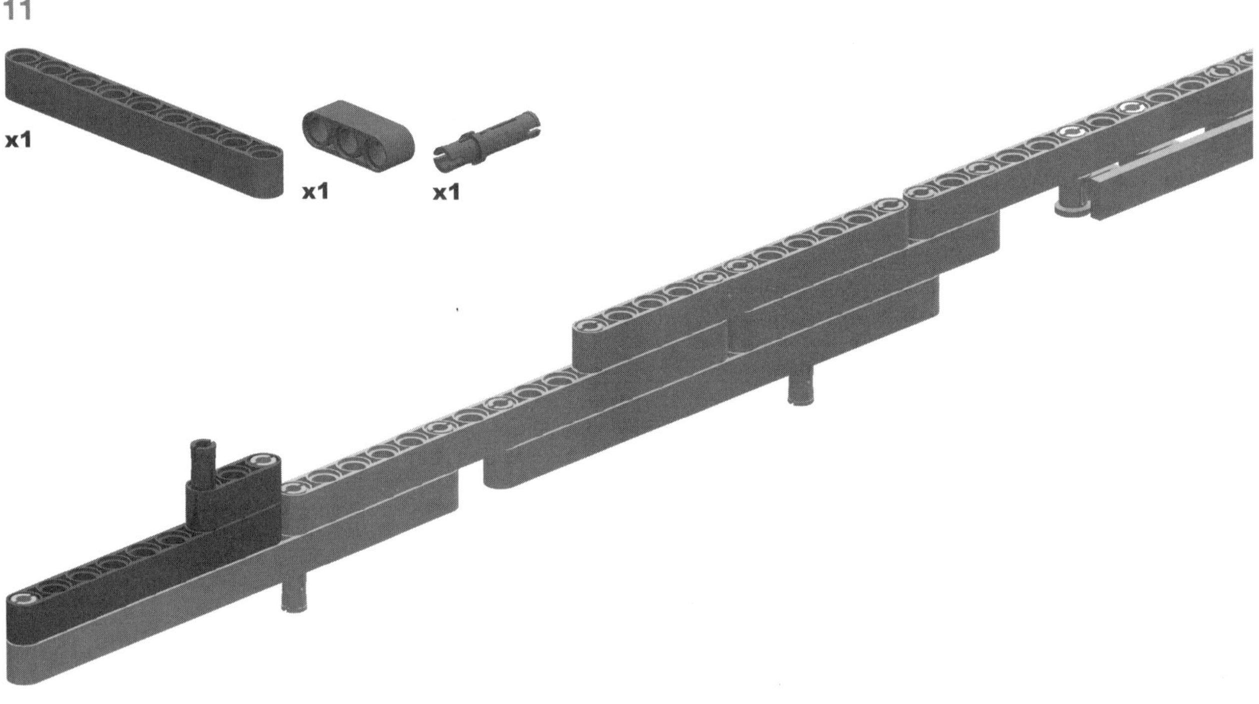

INTERNALS UPPER

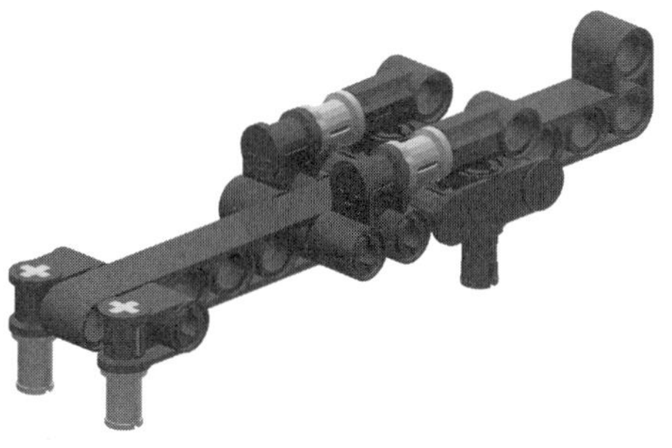

1

2

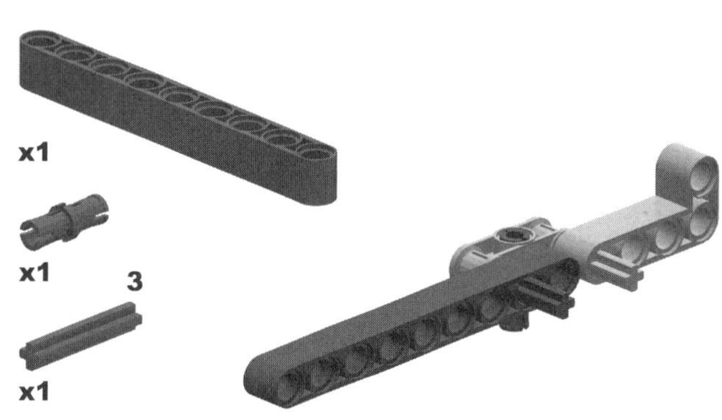

3

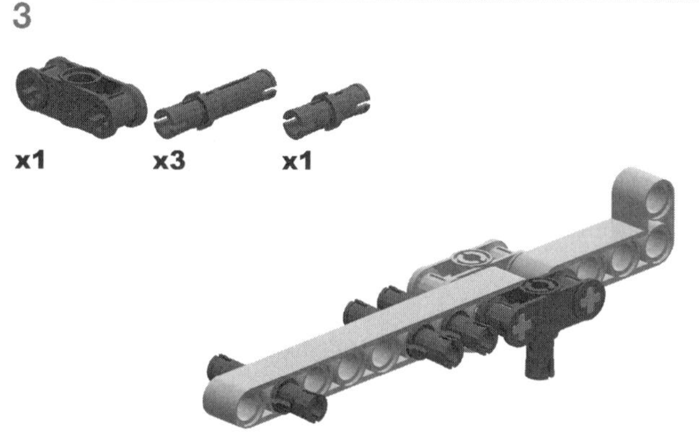

4

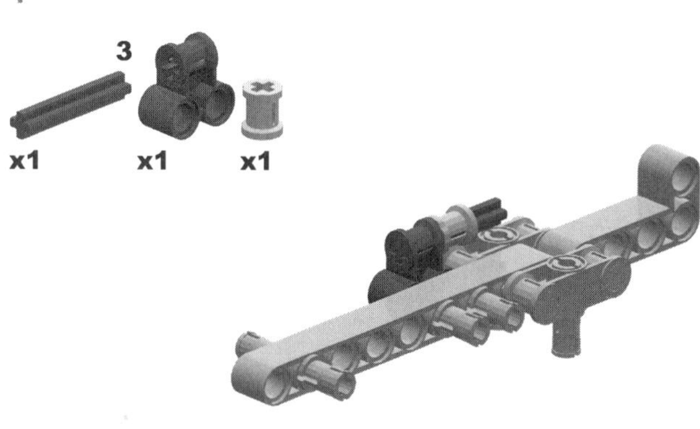

5

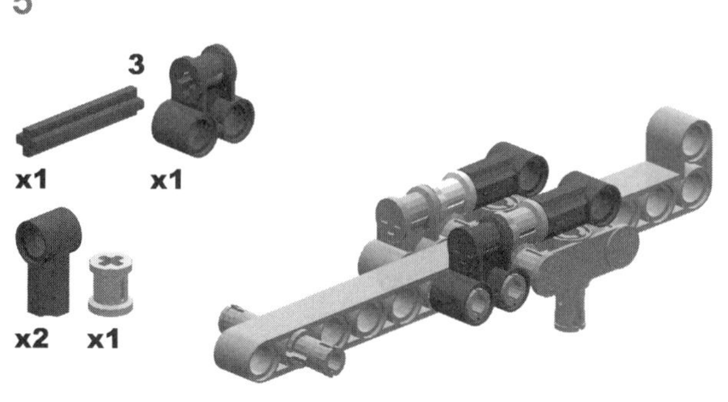

6

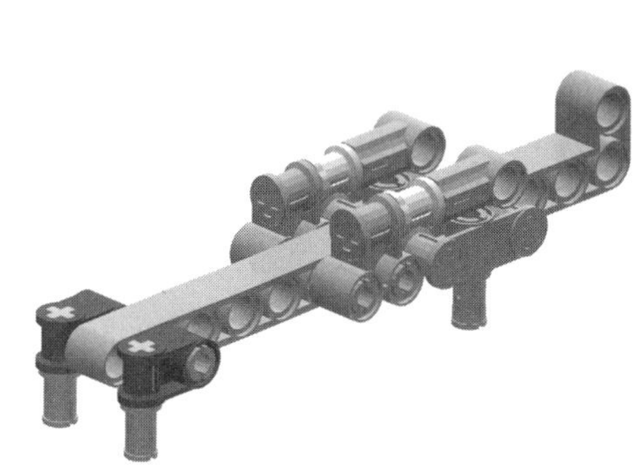

INTERNALS FORE SIGHT

1

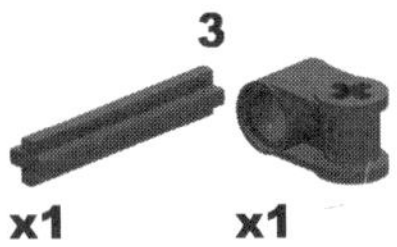

3

x1 x1

2

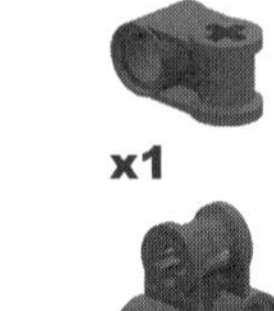

x1

x1

3

x1

x2

4

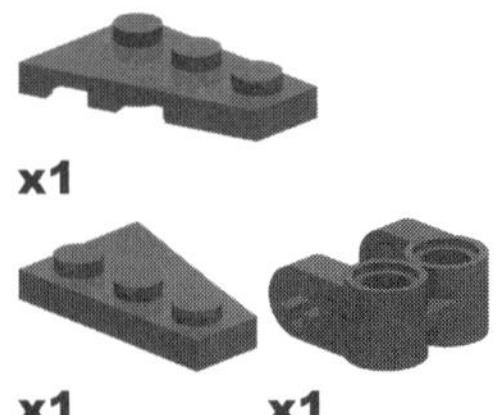

x1

x1 x1

INTERNALS HAMMER

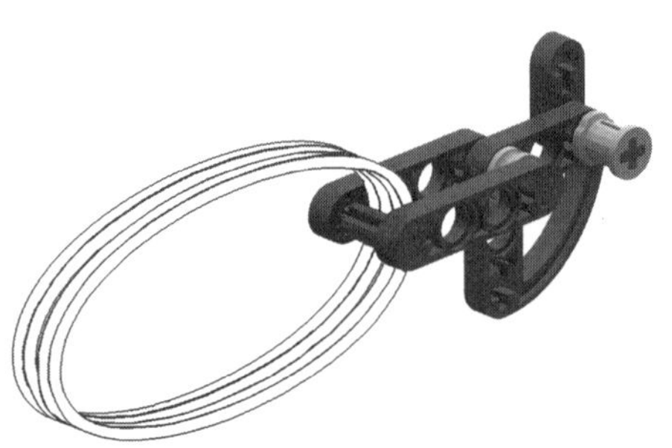

1

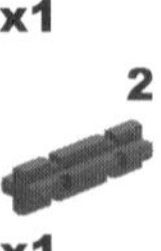

x1

2

x1

2

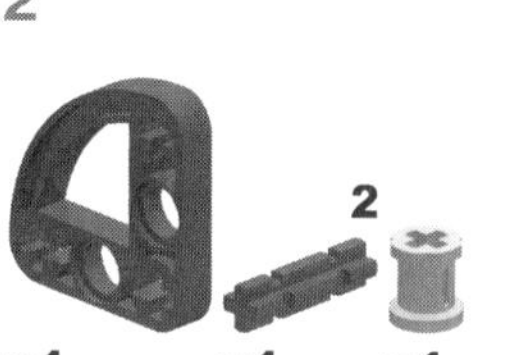

x1 x1 x1

3

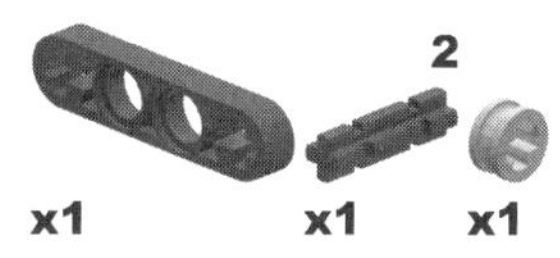

x1 x1 x1

4

x1

x4

These rubber bands power the firing mechanism, so use a reasonable number of them. Twisting multiple rubber bands together can be useful if your build is getting a little messy or if you want to increase the tension, but wait until the final assembly to do so. Flip ahead to page 143 to see a picture of how I twisted the bands together—even though I used six rubber bands, it was still very neat.

INTERNALS BOLT

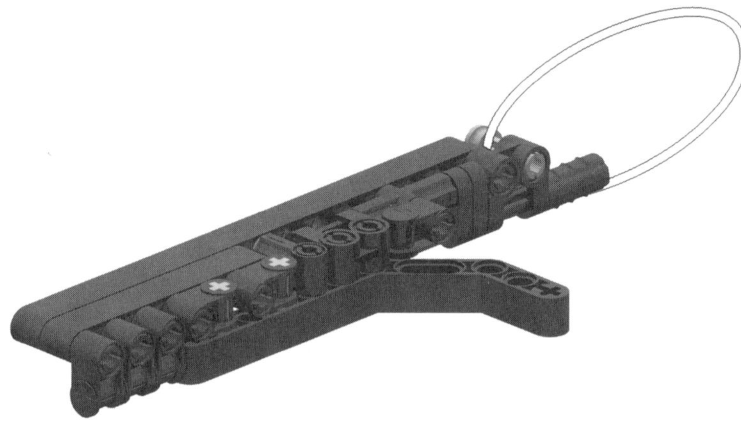

1

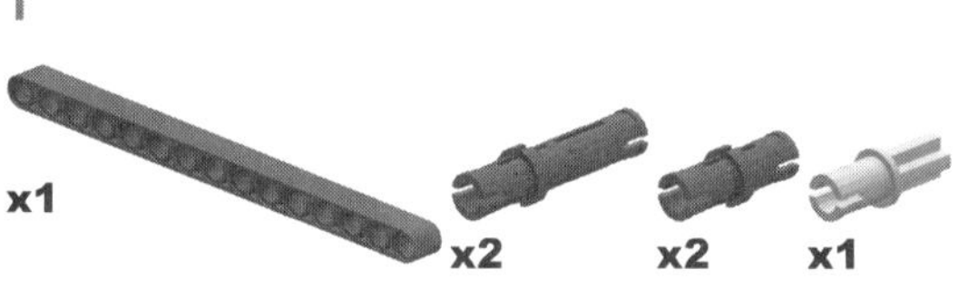

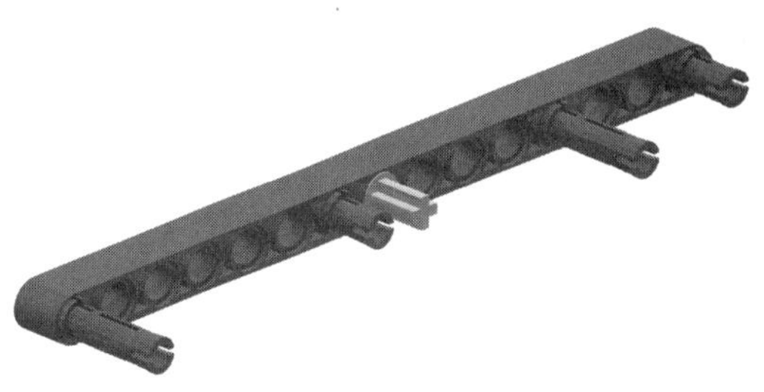

2

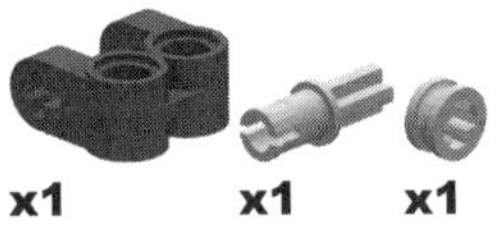

x1 x1 x1

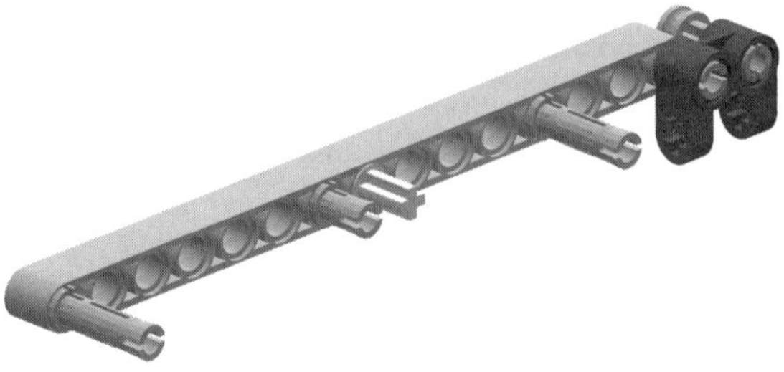

3

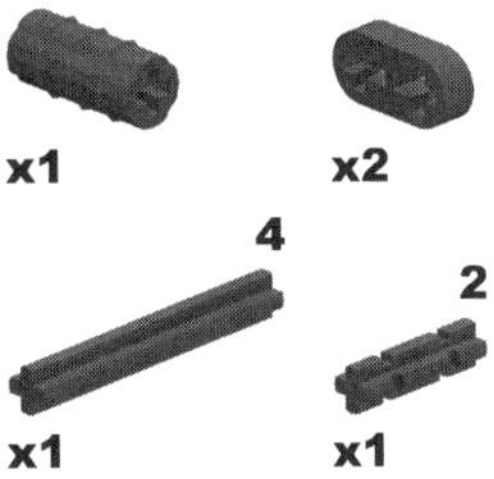

x1 x2

4 2

x1 x1

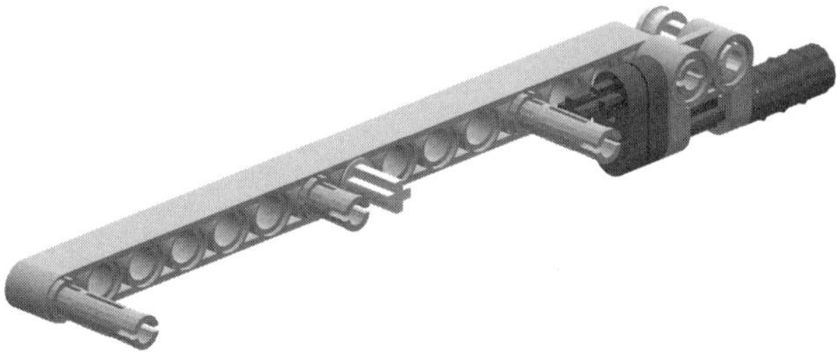

4

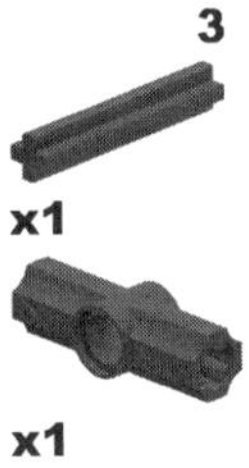

3

x1

x1

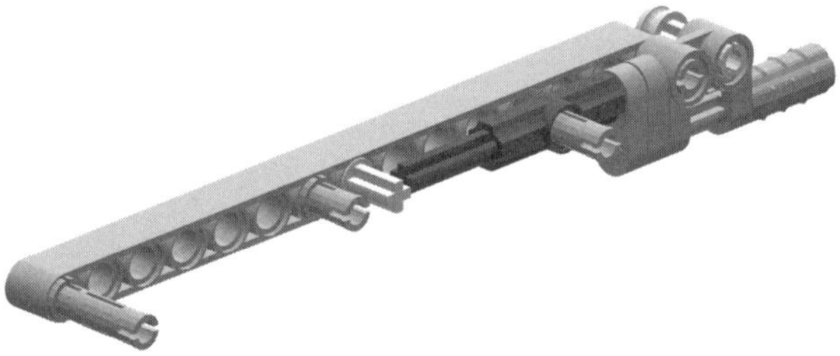

5

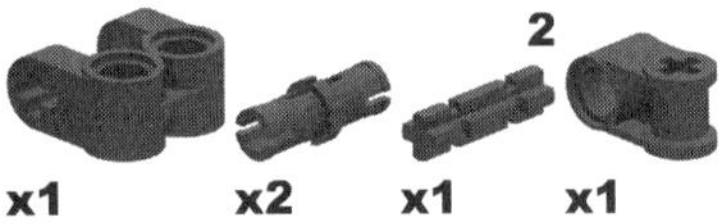

2

x1 x2 x1 x1

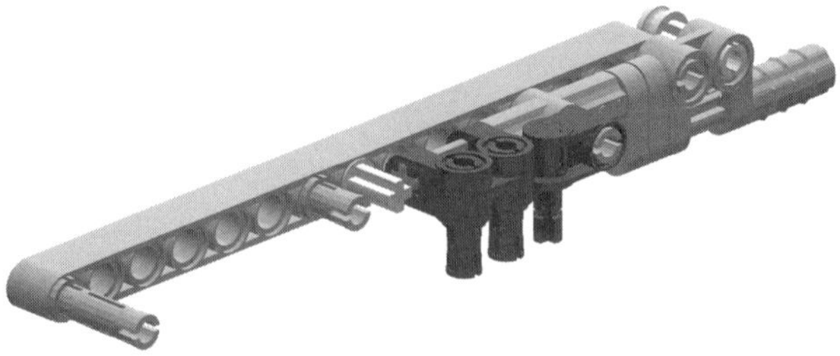

6

x1

x1

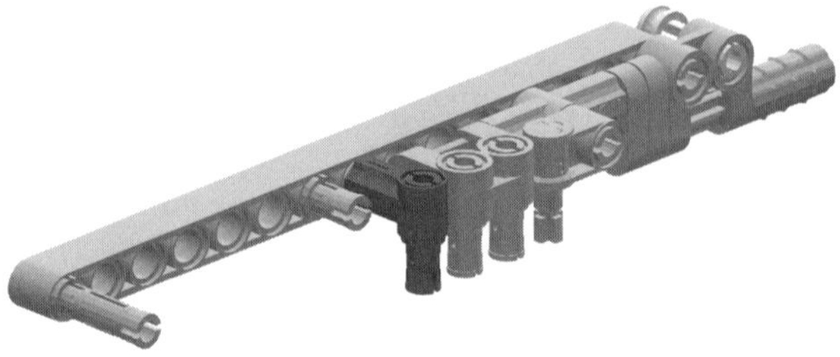

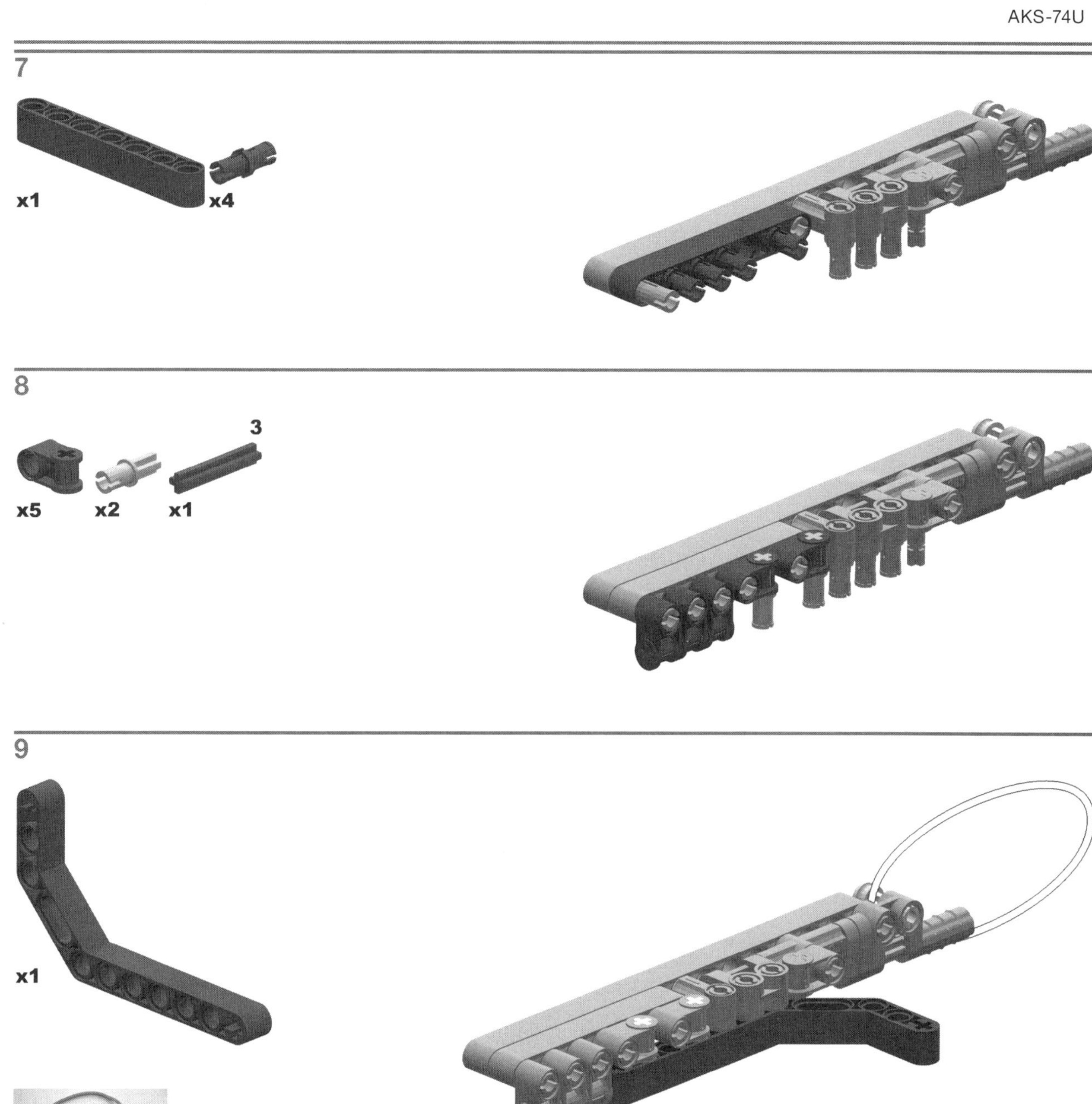
7
x1
x4
8
3
x5
x2
x1
9
x1
x1

INTERNALS ASSEMBLY

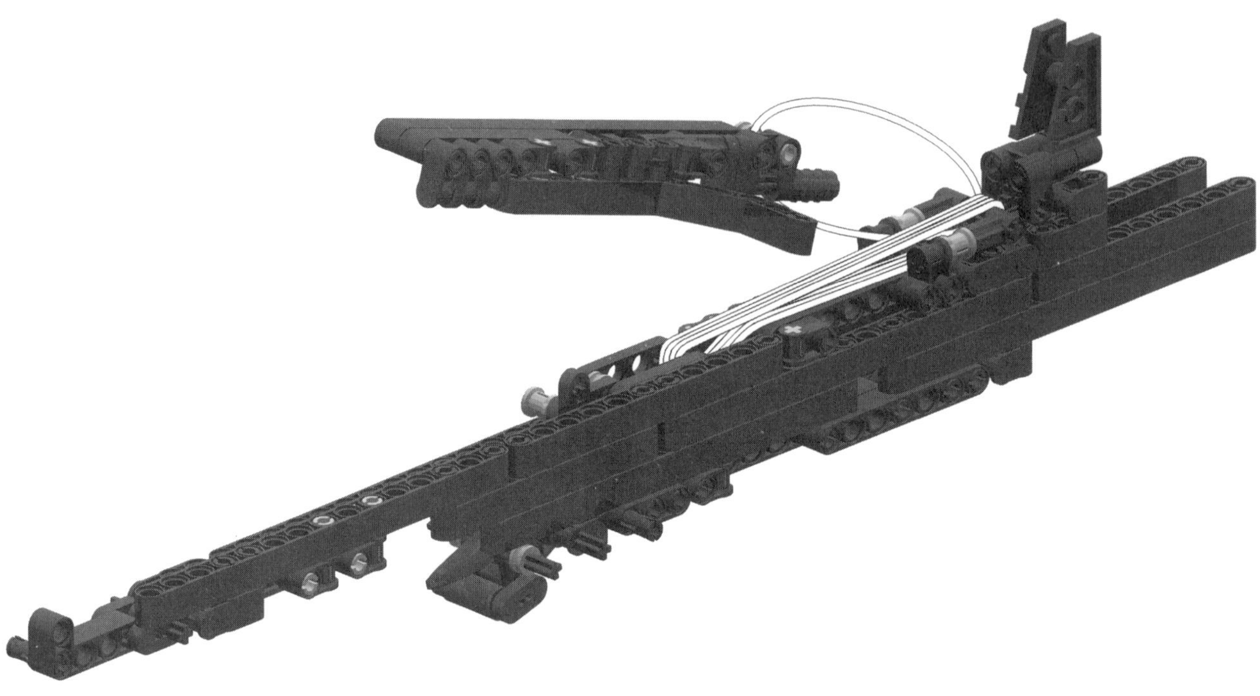

1

x1
Internals
Magazine Ramp

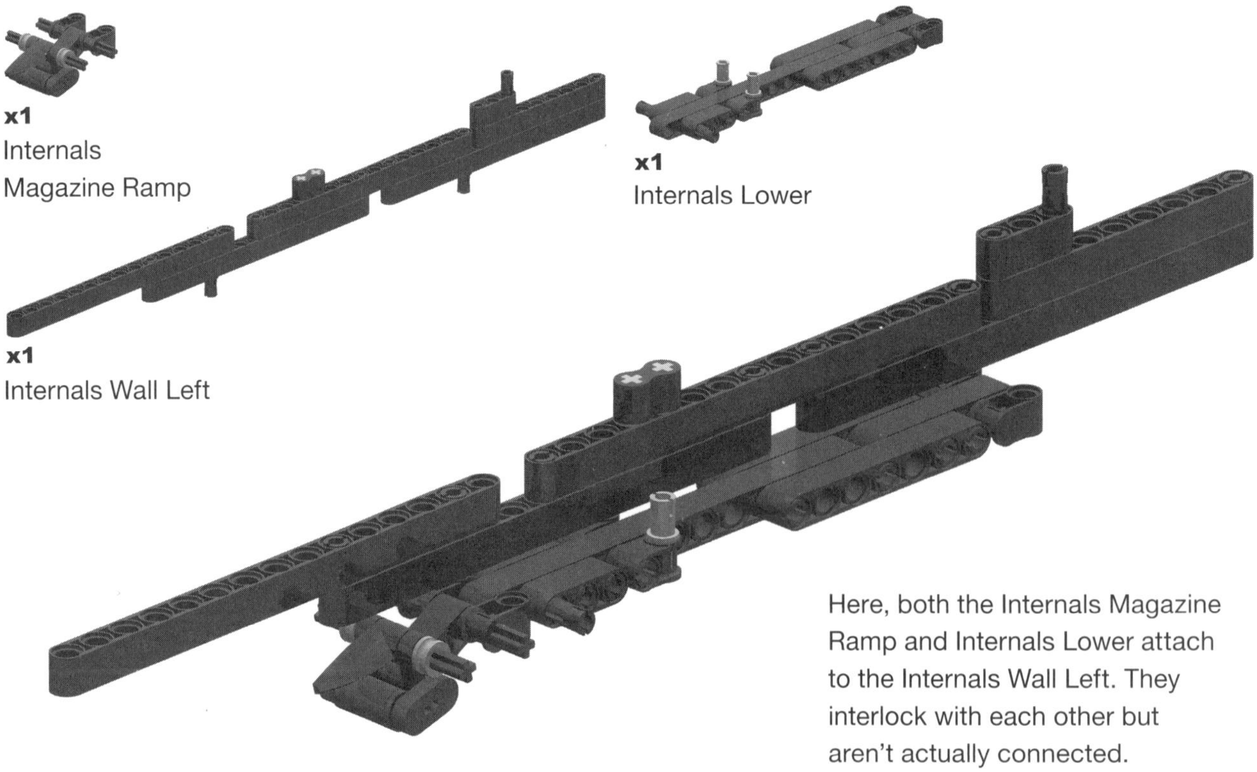

x1
Internals Lower

x1
Internals Wall Left

Here, both the Internals Magazine Ramp and Internals Lower attach to the Internals Wall Left. They interlock with each other but aren't actually connected.

2

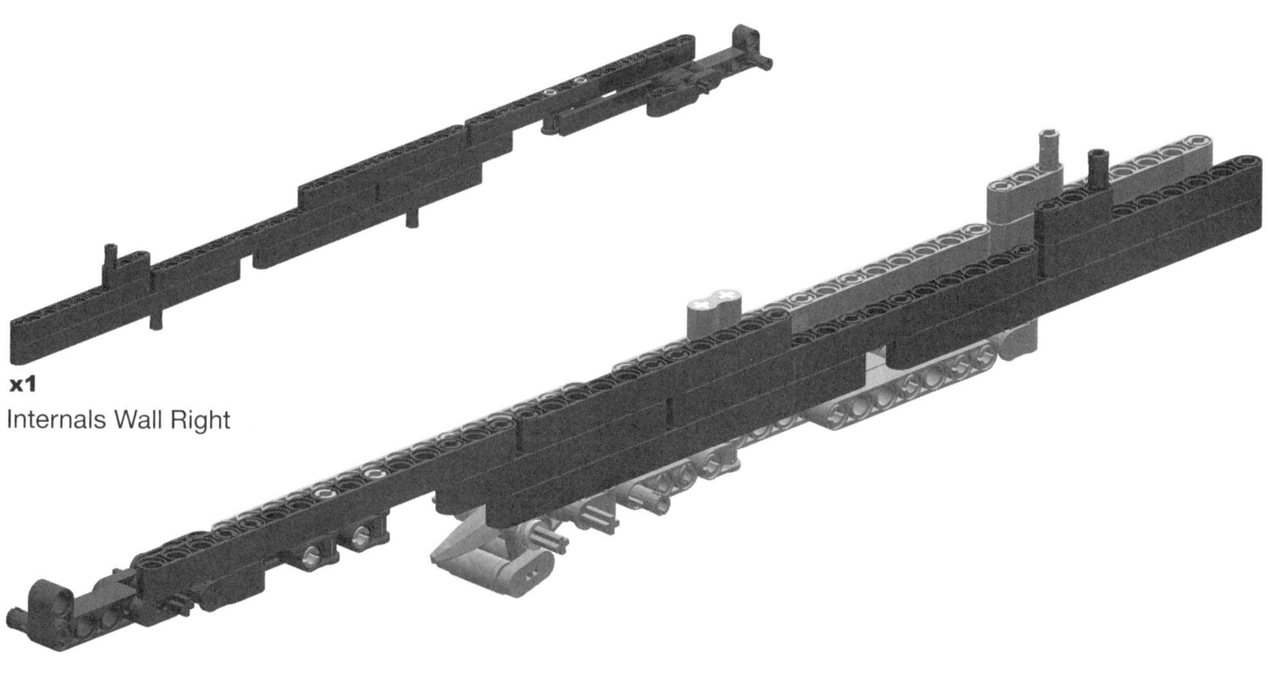

x1
Internals Wall Right

3

4

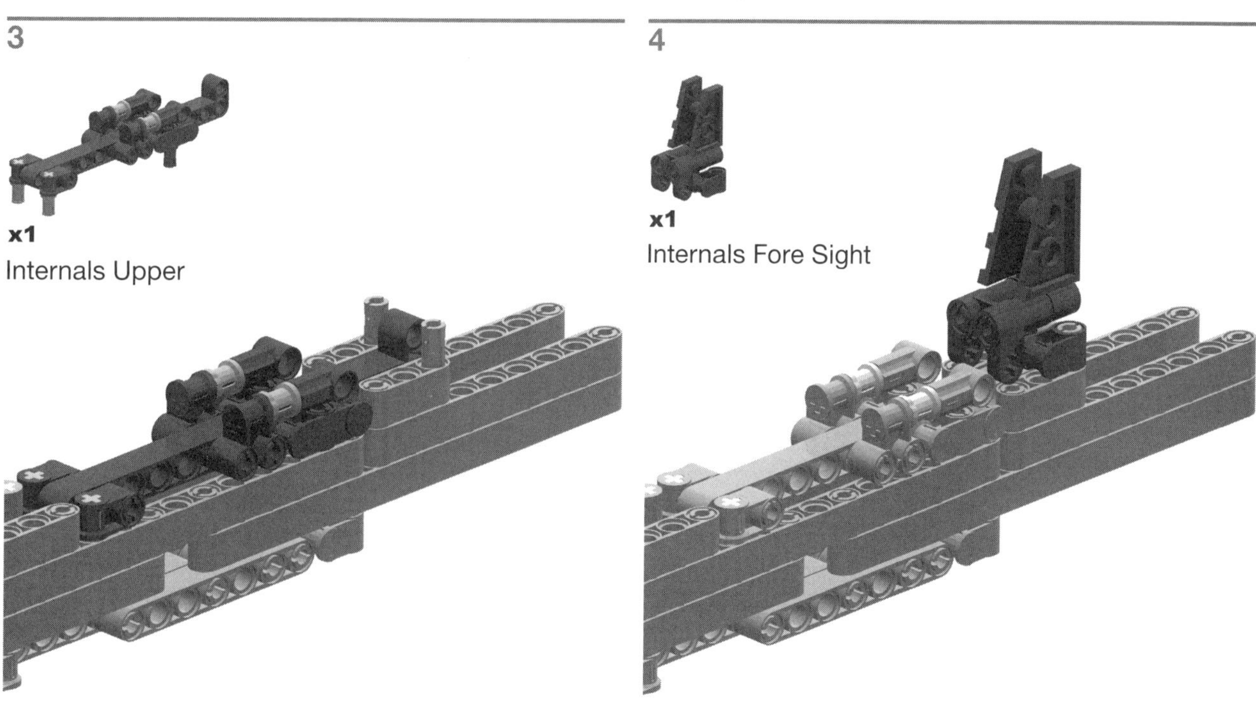

x1
Internals Upper

x1
Internals Fore Sight

5

x1
Internals Bolt

x1
Internals
Hammer

If you're lucky, the Hammer will fit snugly into position, and the tension from the rubber bands will keep it in place. However, it might just hang loosely like the Bolt, so remember to reposition it when you add the Internals to the final model in step 5 on page 142, where part of the Frame Wall Left will keep it from falling out.

3

x1

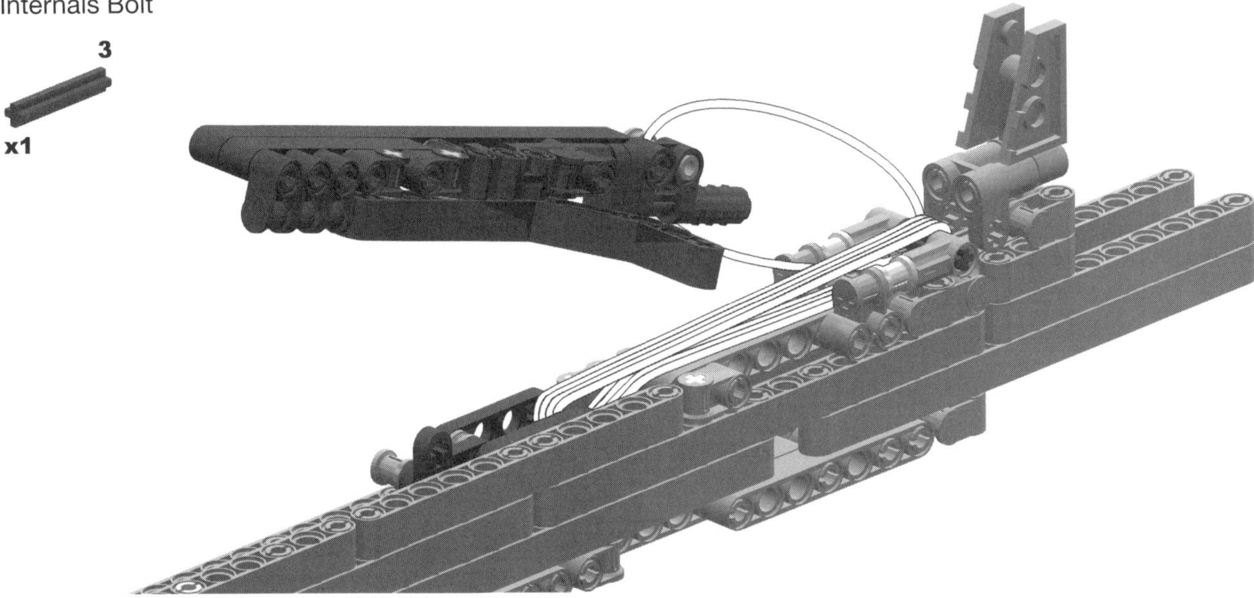

FRAME WALL RIGHT

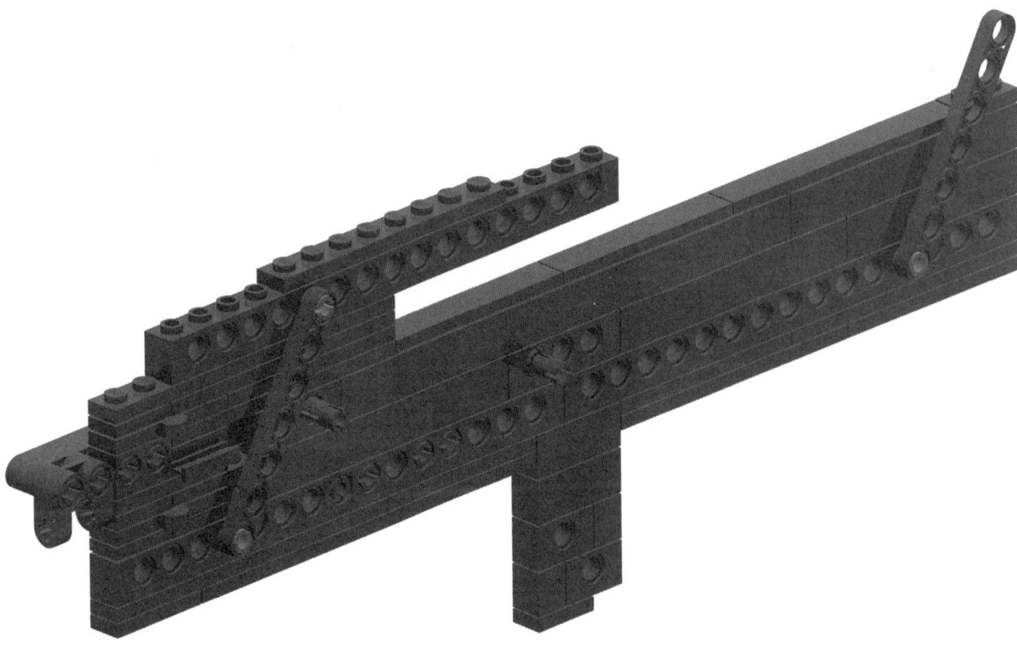

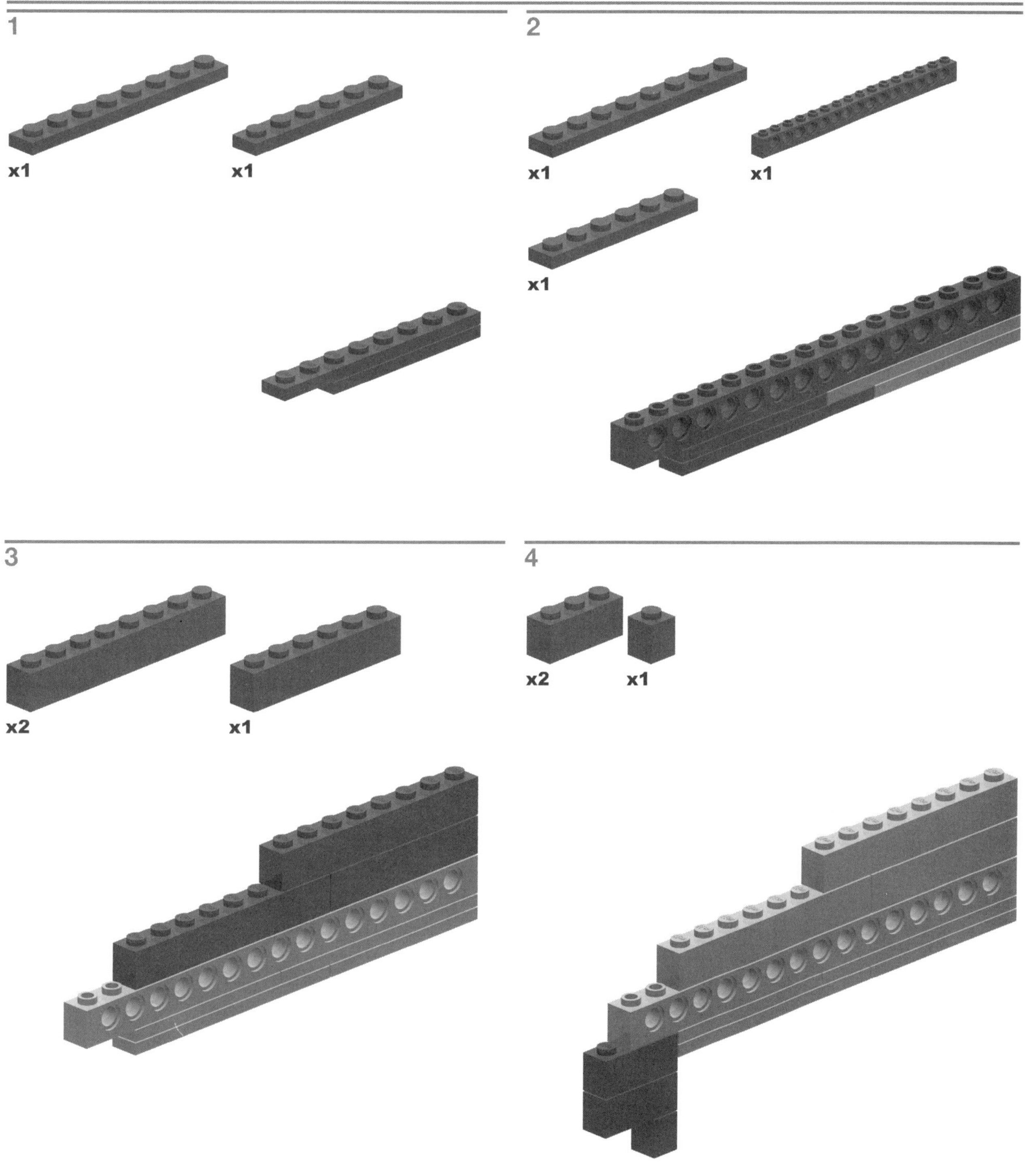
1
x1
x1
2
x1
x1
x1
3
x2
x1
4
x2
x1

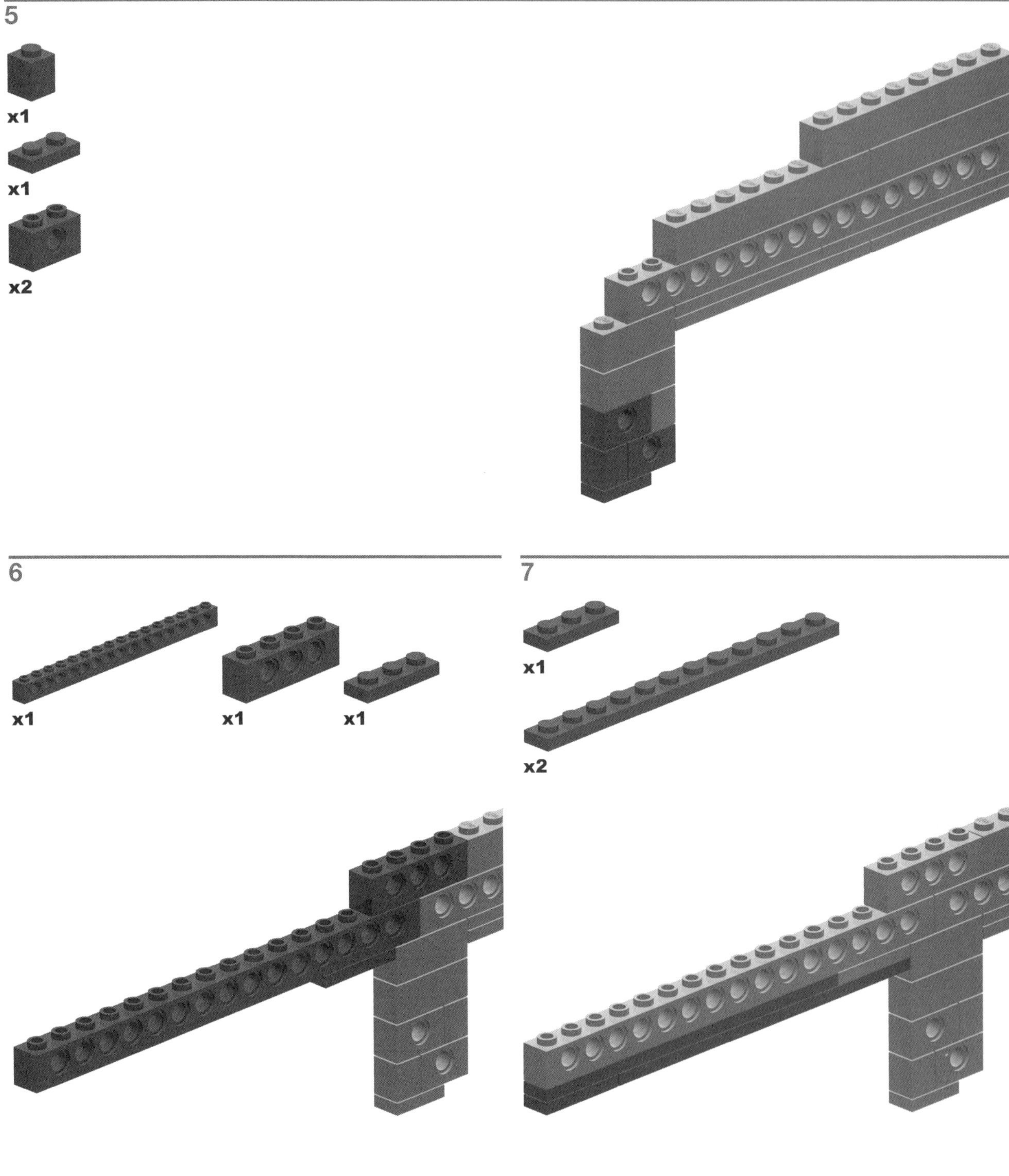
5
x1
x1
x2
6
x1
x1
x1
7
x1
x2

8

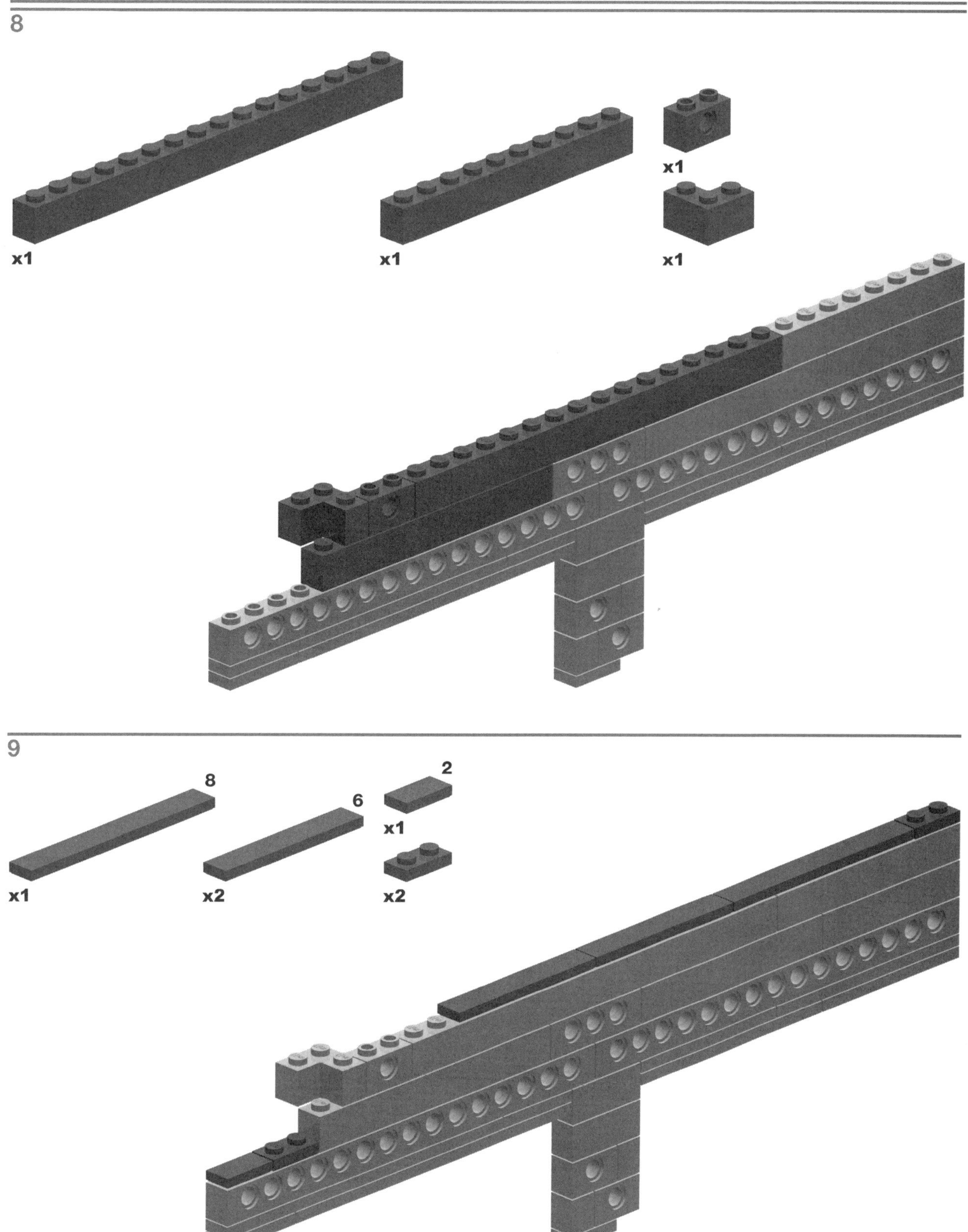

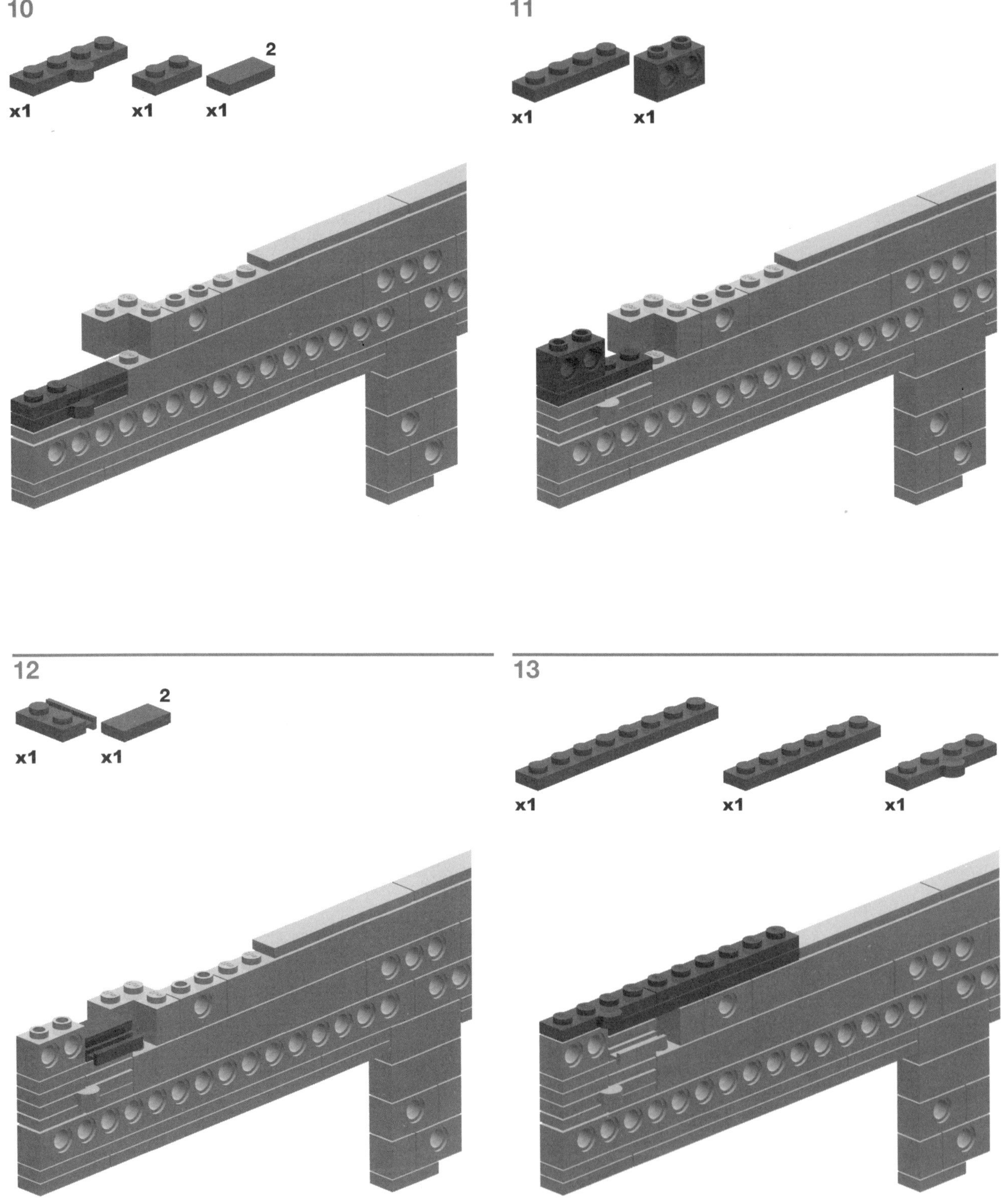
10
x1
x1
2
x1
11
x1
x1
12
x1
2
x1
13
x1
x1
x1

14

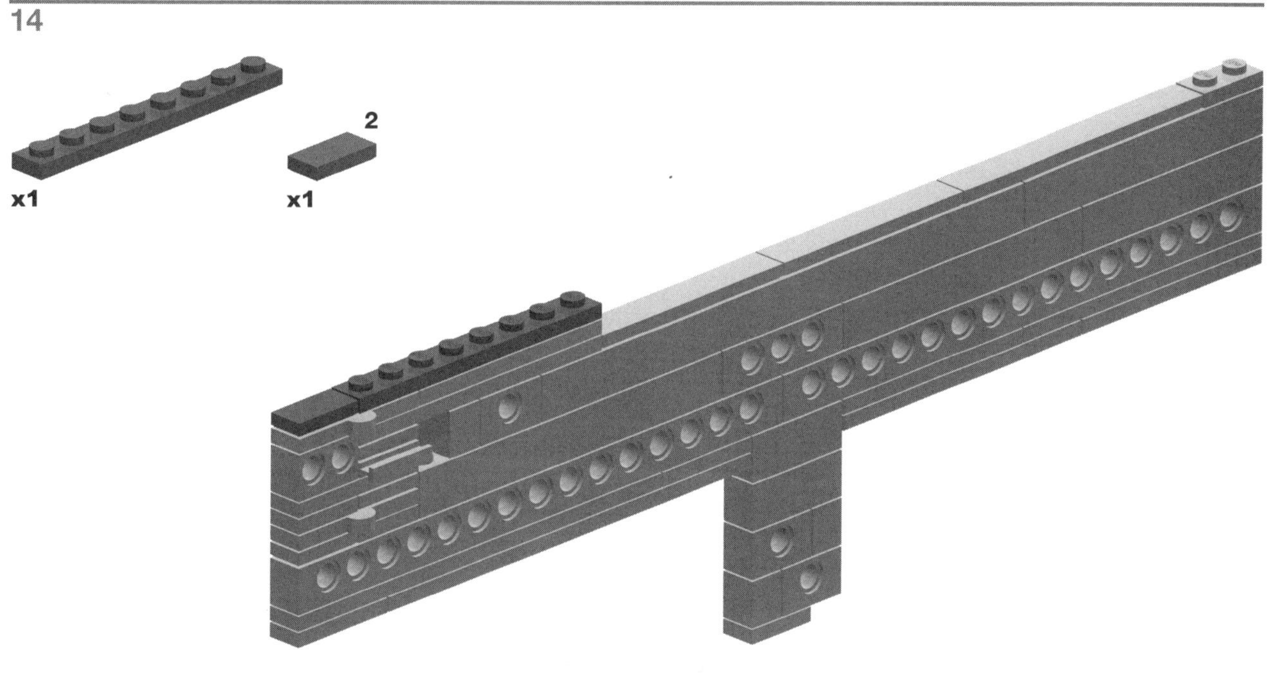

15

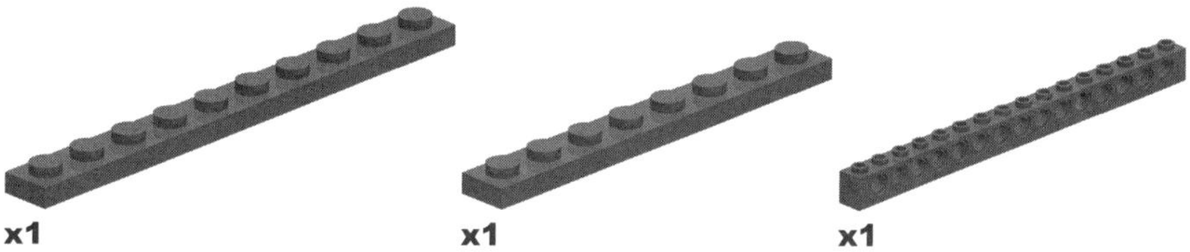

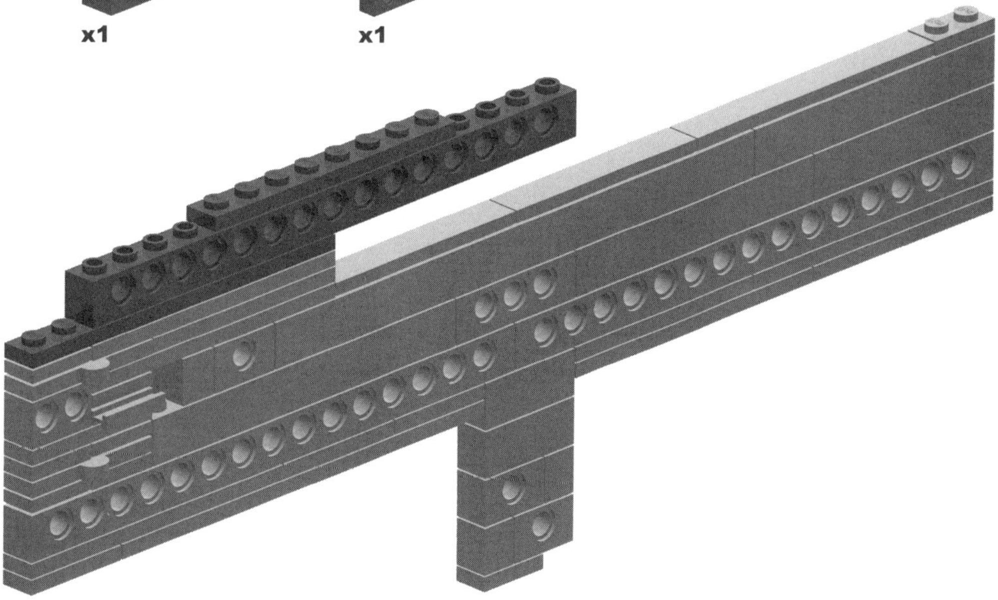

x1

x1

x1

16

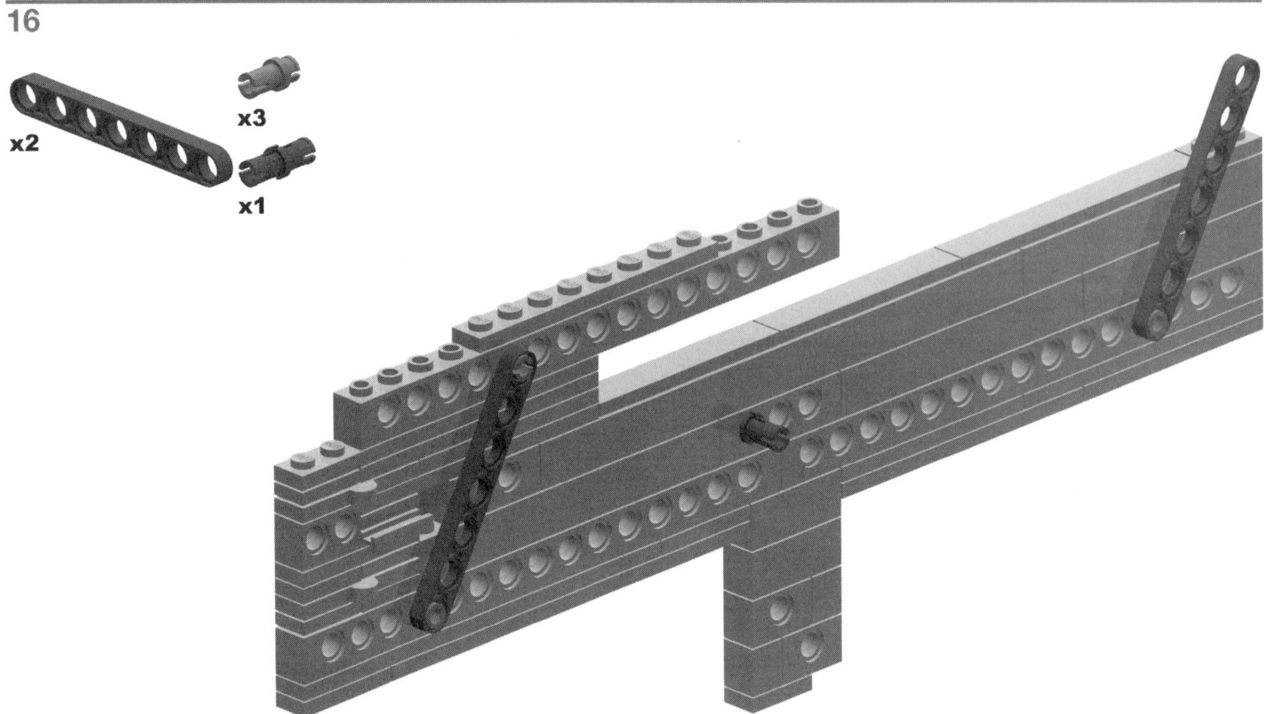

17

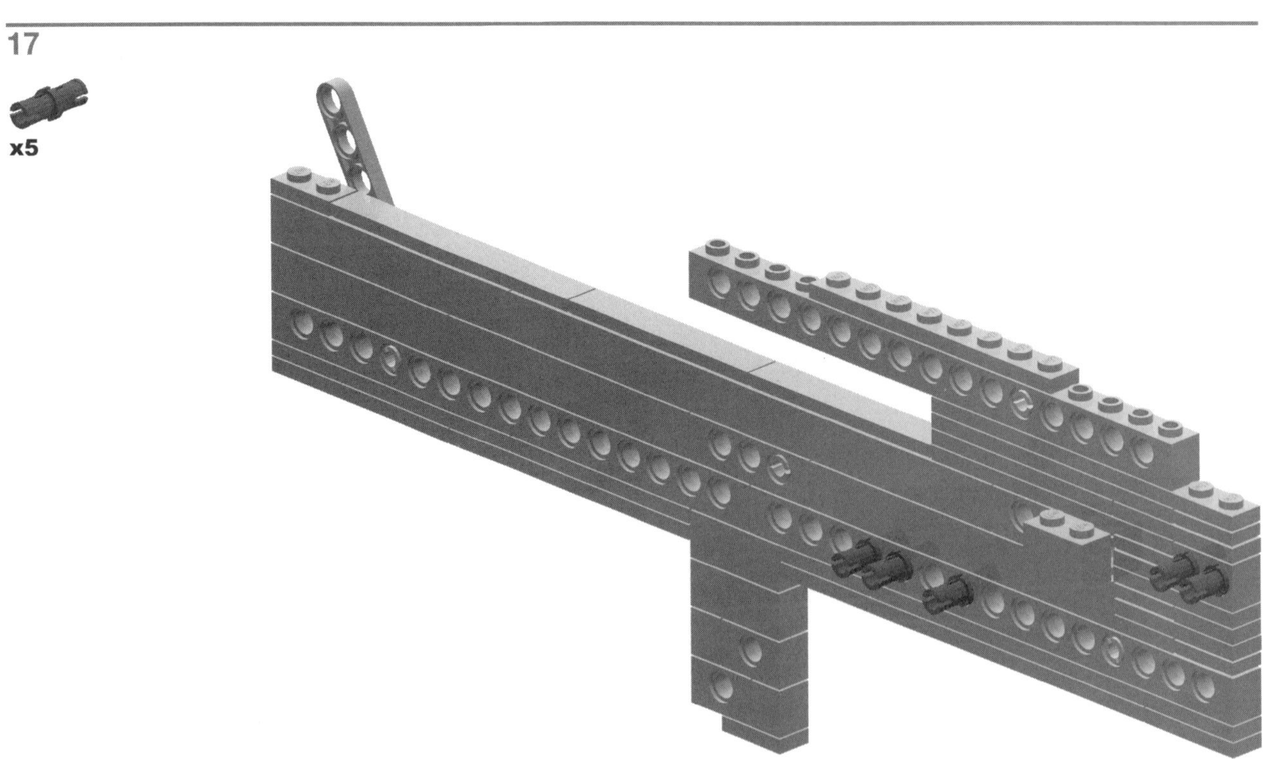

18

x2

x1

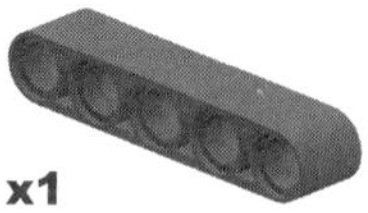

x1

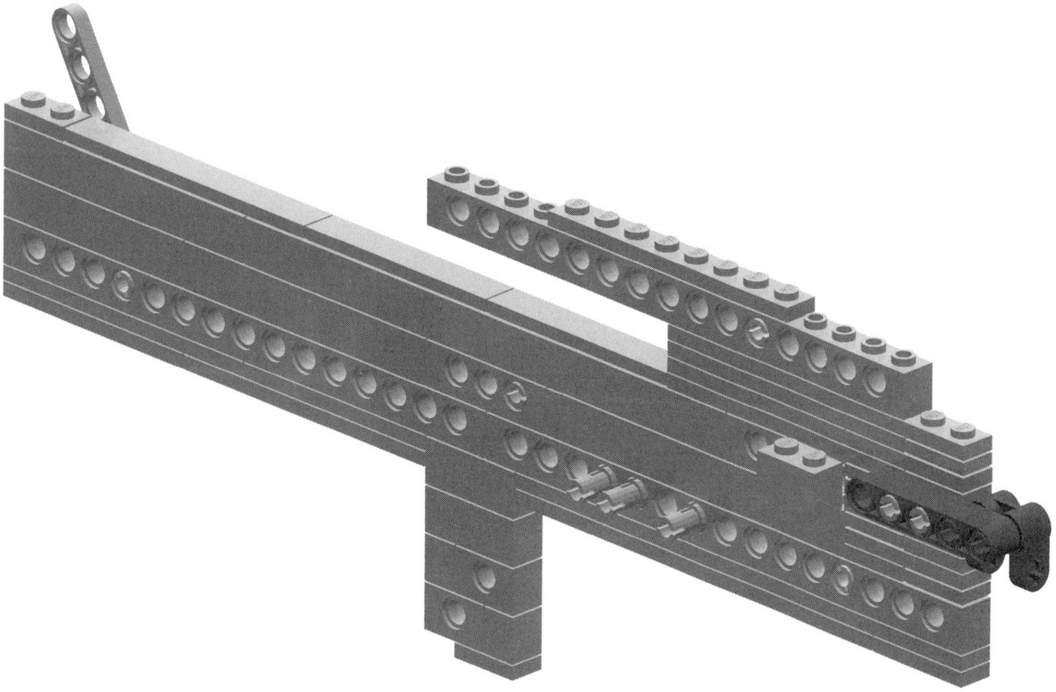

19

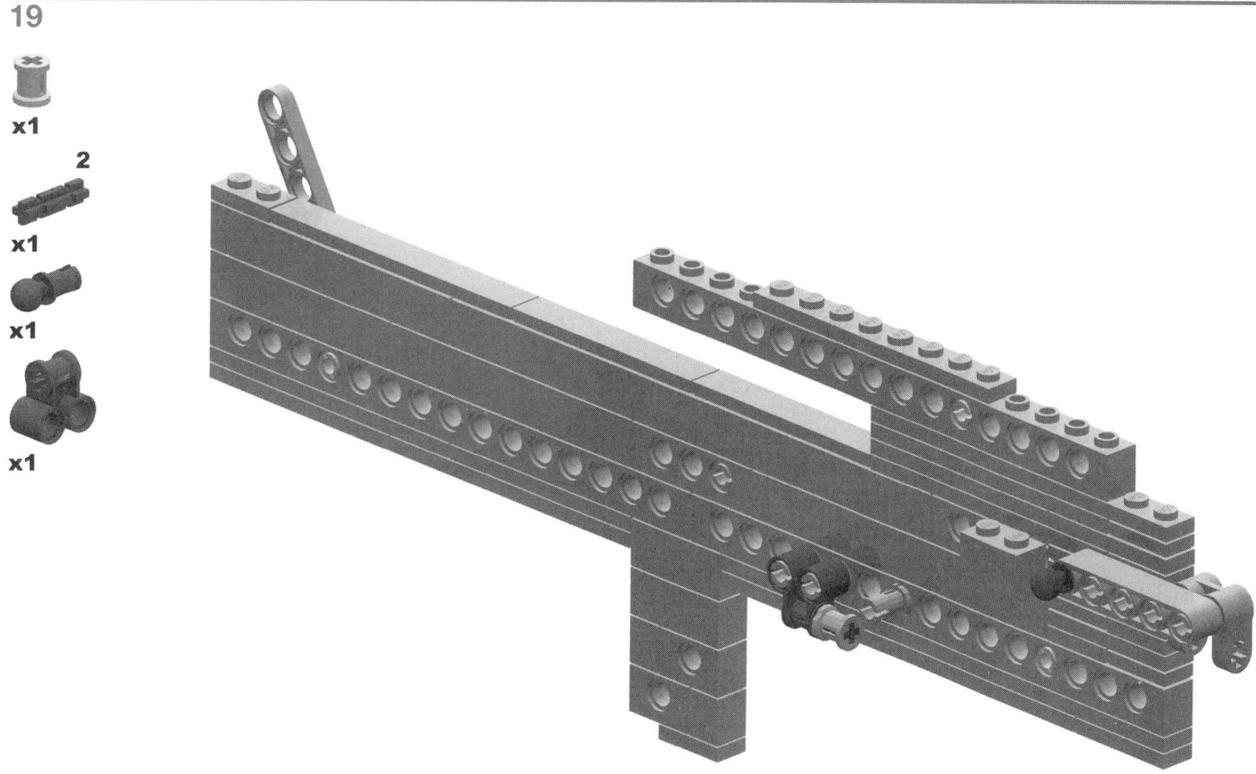

20

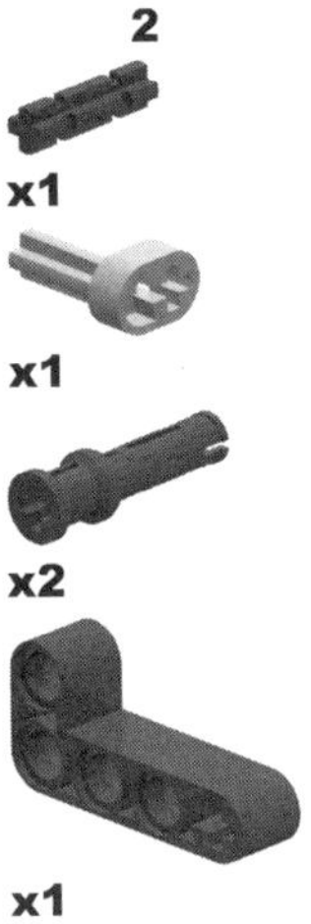

2

x1

x1

x2

x1

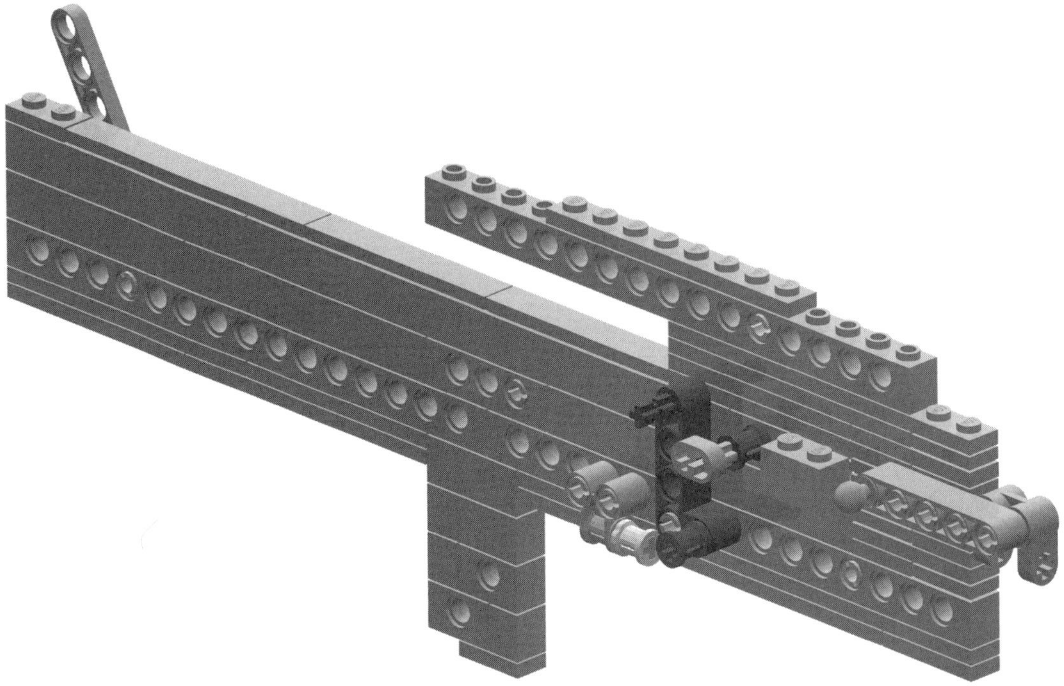

21

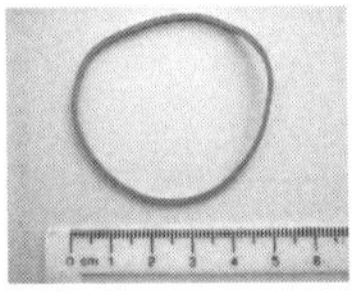

x1

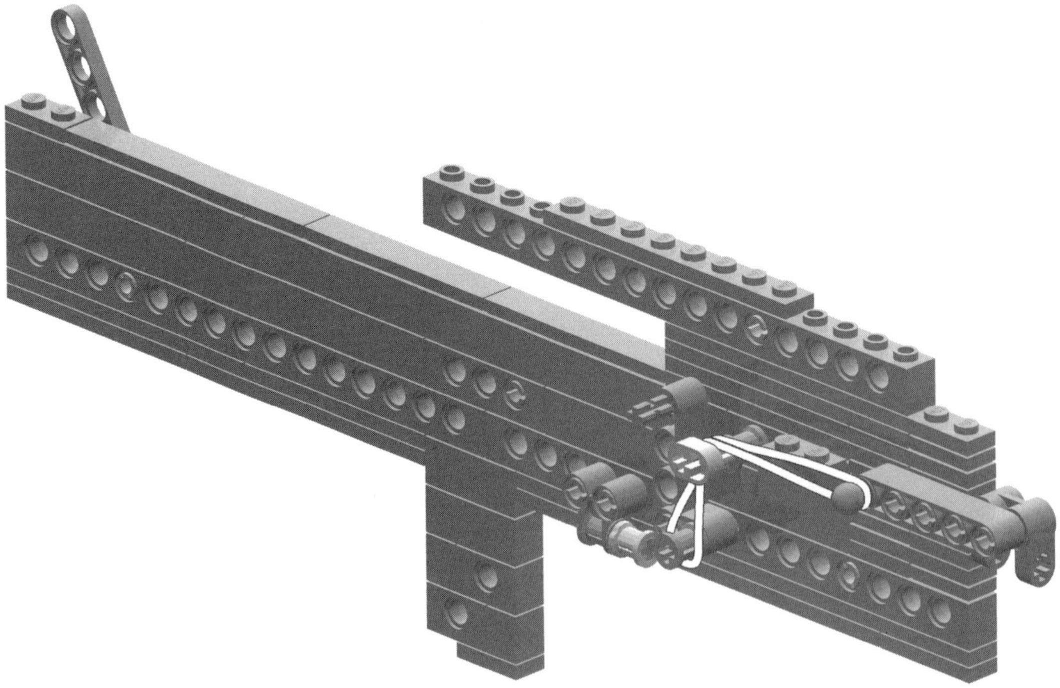

DUST COVER

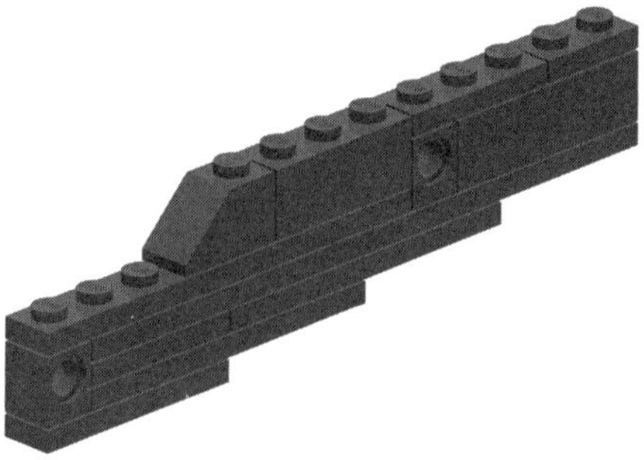

1

x1  x1

2

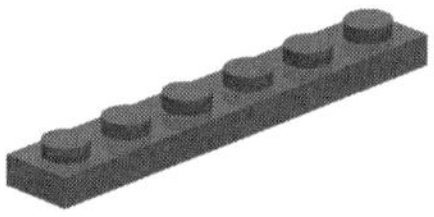

x2  x1

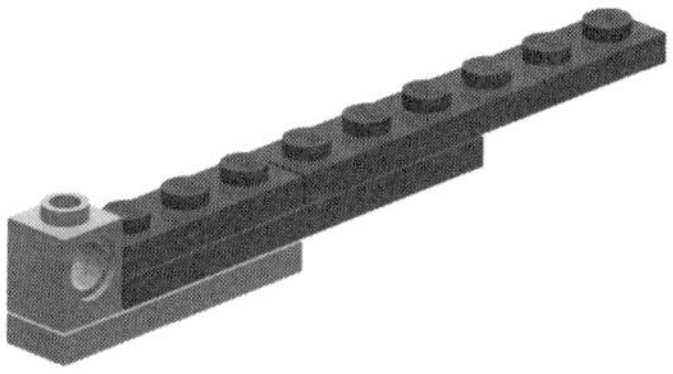

3

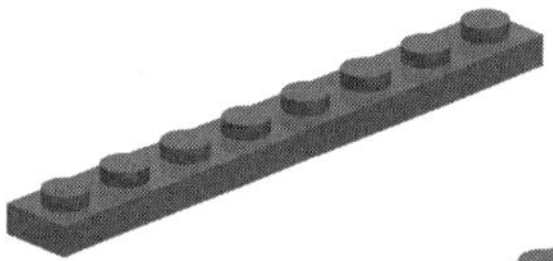

x1

x1

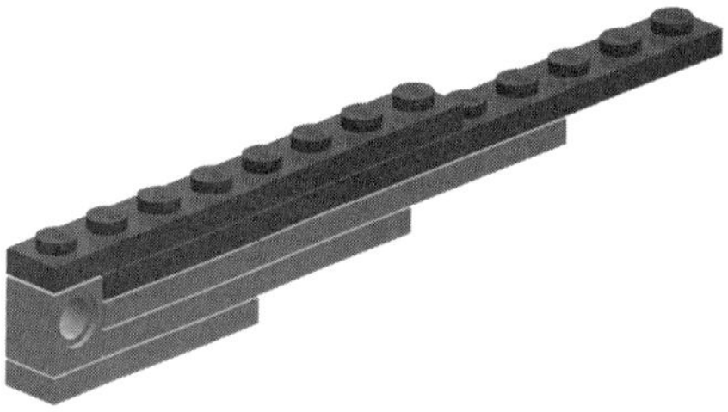

4

x1  x1  x1

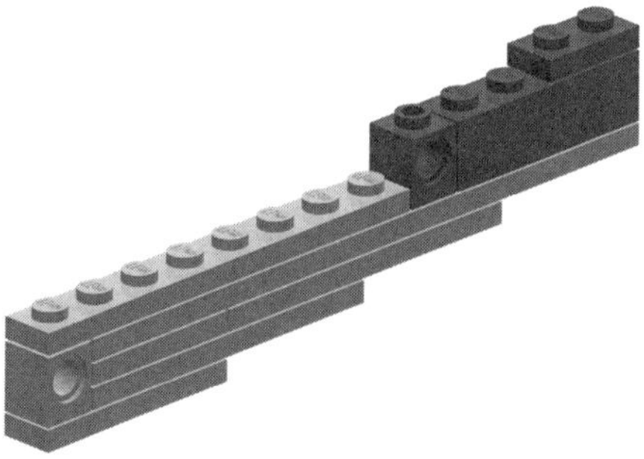

5

x1

x1

x1

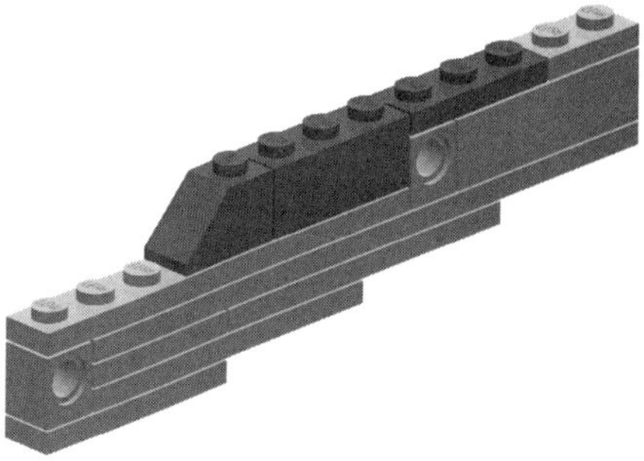

BOLT STOPPER

1

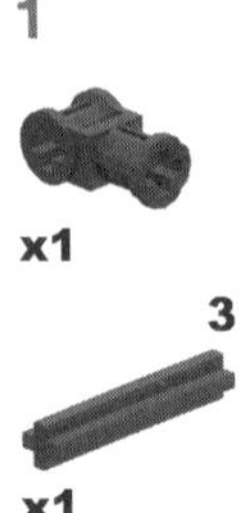

2

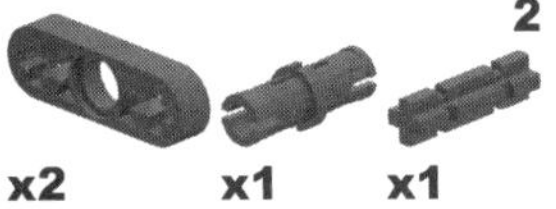

3

4

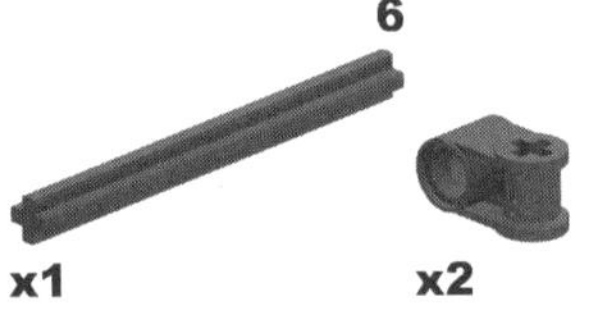

5

x1 x3

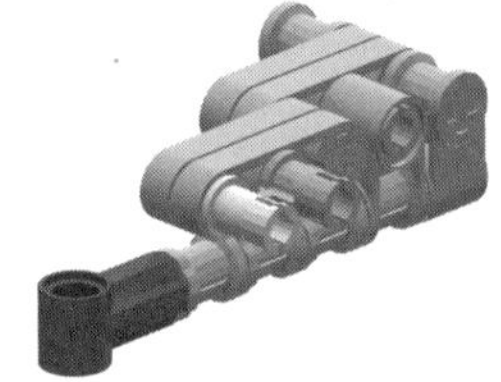

6

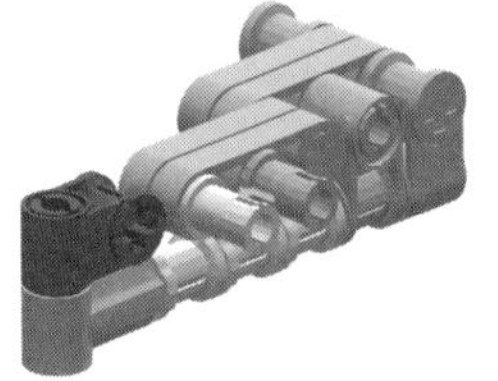

7

x1 x1

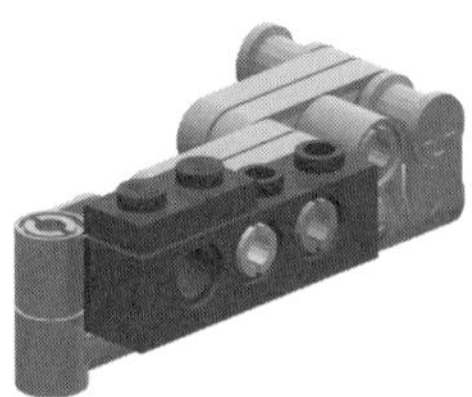

8

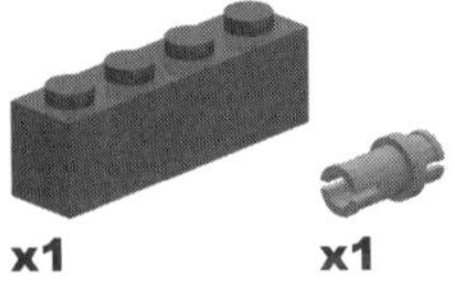

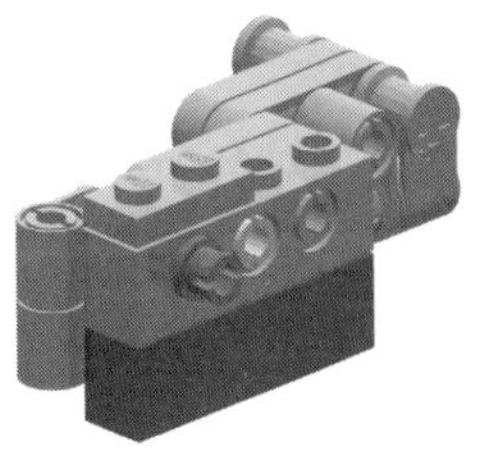

FORE GRIP WALL RIGHT

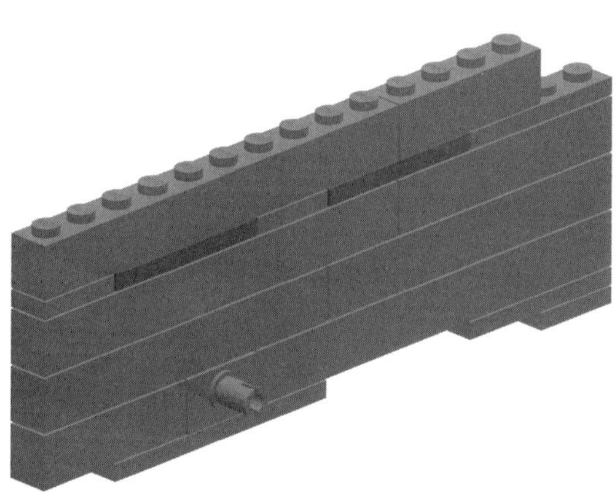

1

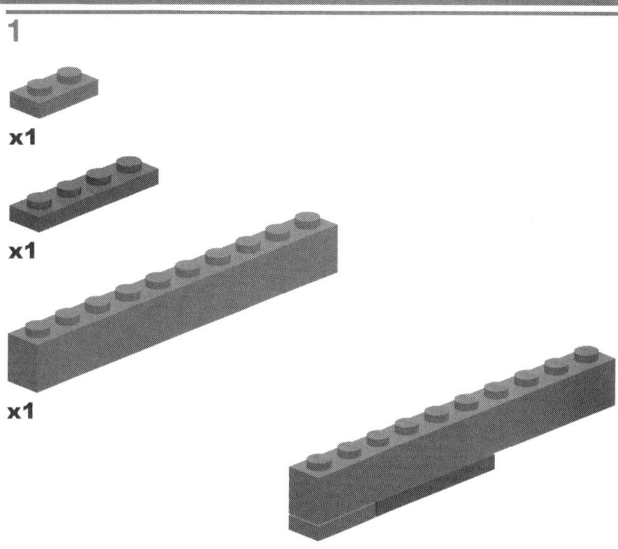

The Fore Grip Wall Right, Fore Grip Wall Left, Fore Grip Plate, and Roof Plate Front modules have red pieces (as shown on the cover), but because the book is in black and white, they appear dark grey. Feel free to make up your own color scheme, but if you want to follow this one, make sure you keep an eye on which pieces are black and which ones are red.

2

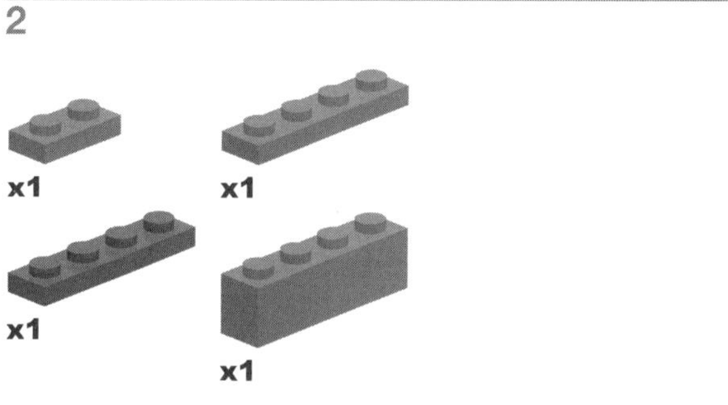

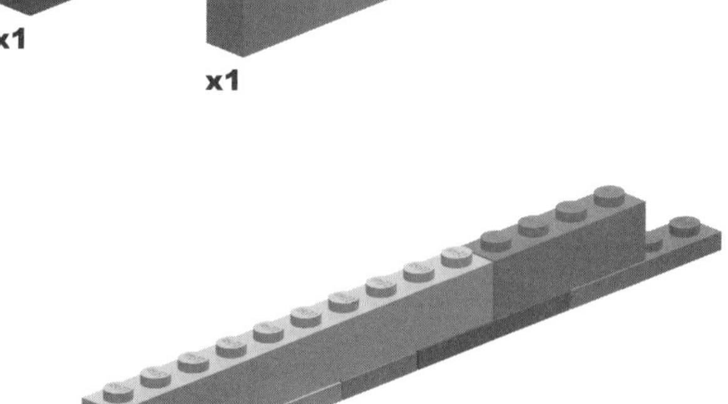

3

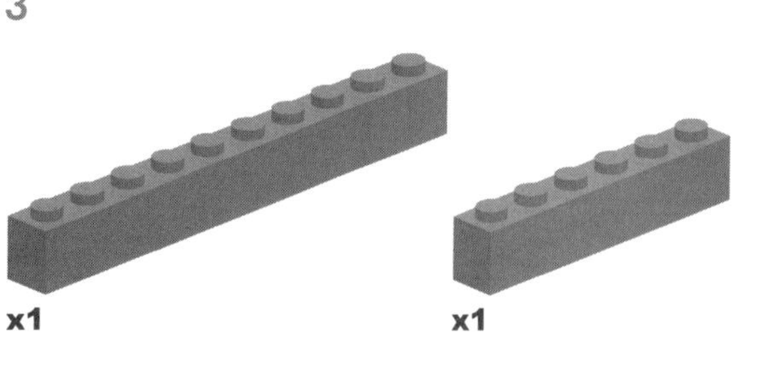

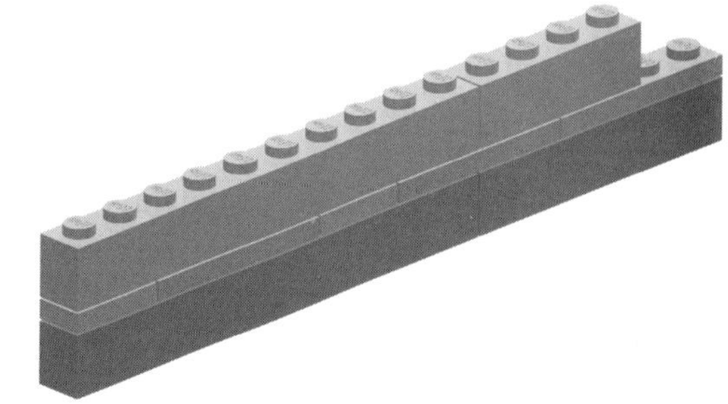

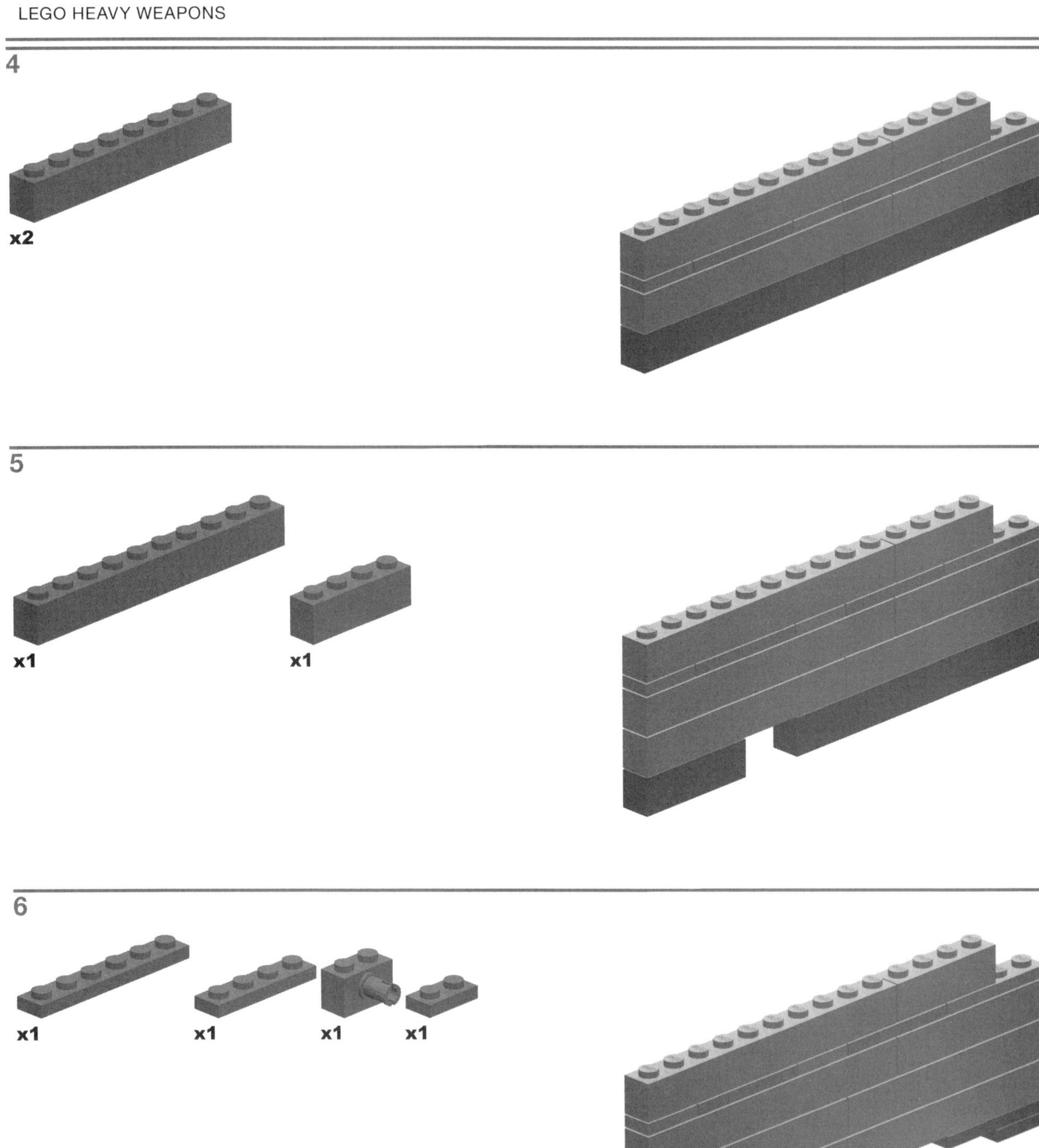
4
x2
5
x1
x1
6
x1
x1
x1
x1

FORE GRIP WALL LEFT

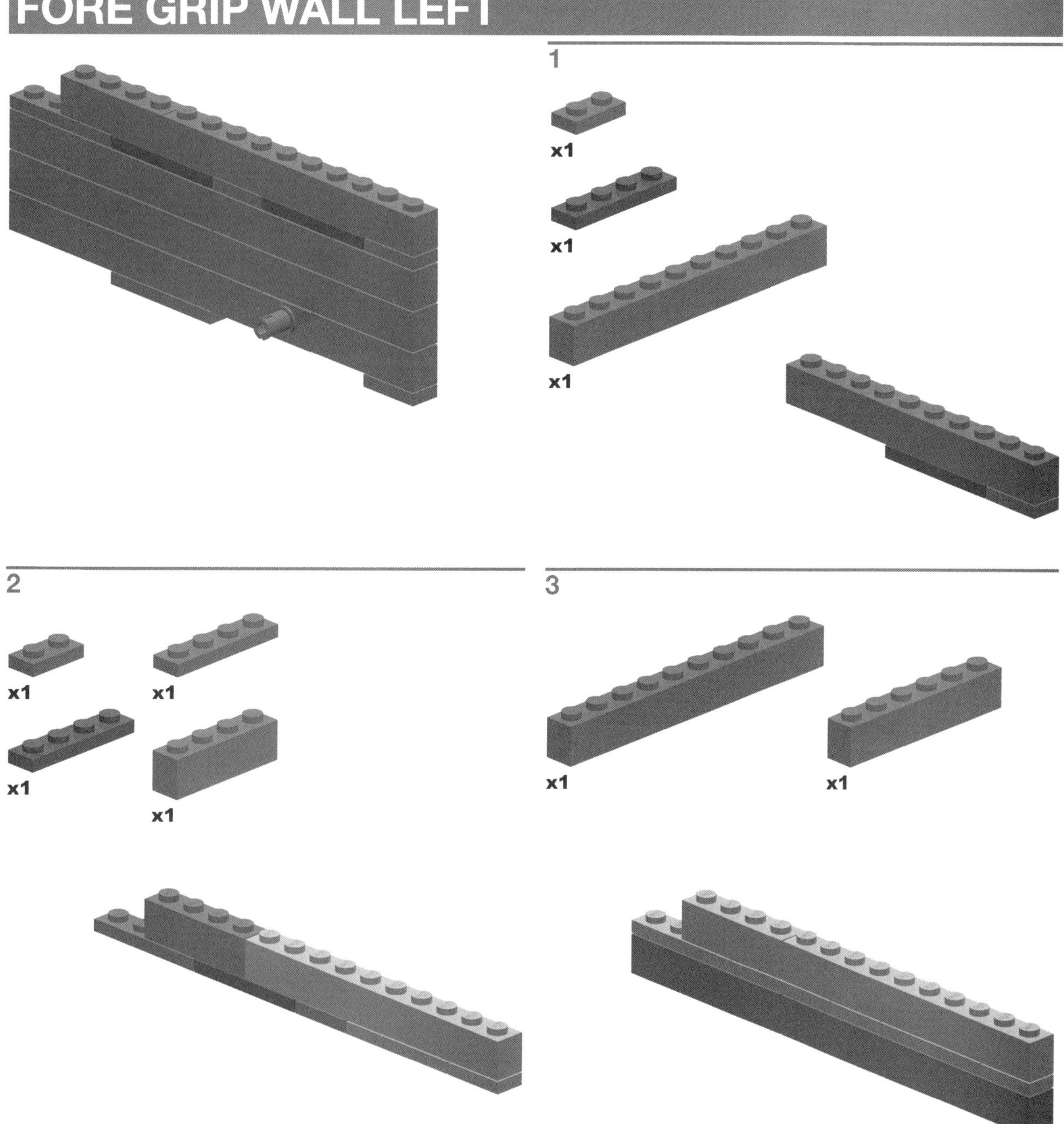

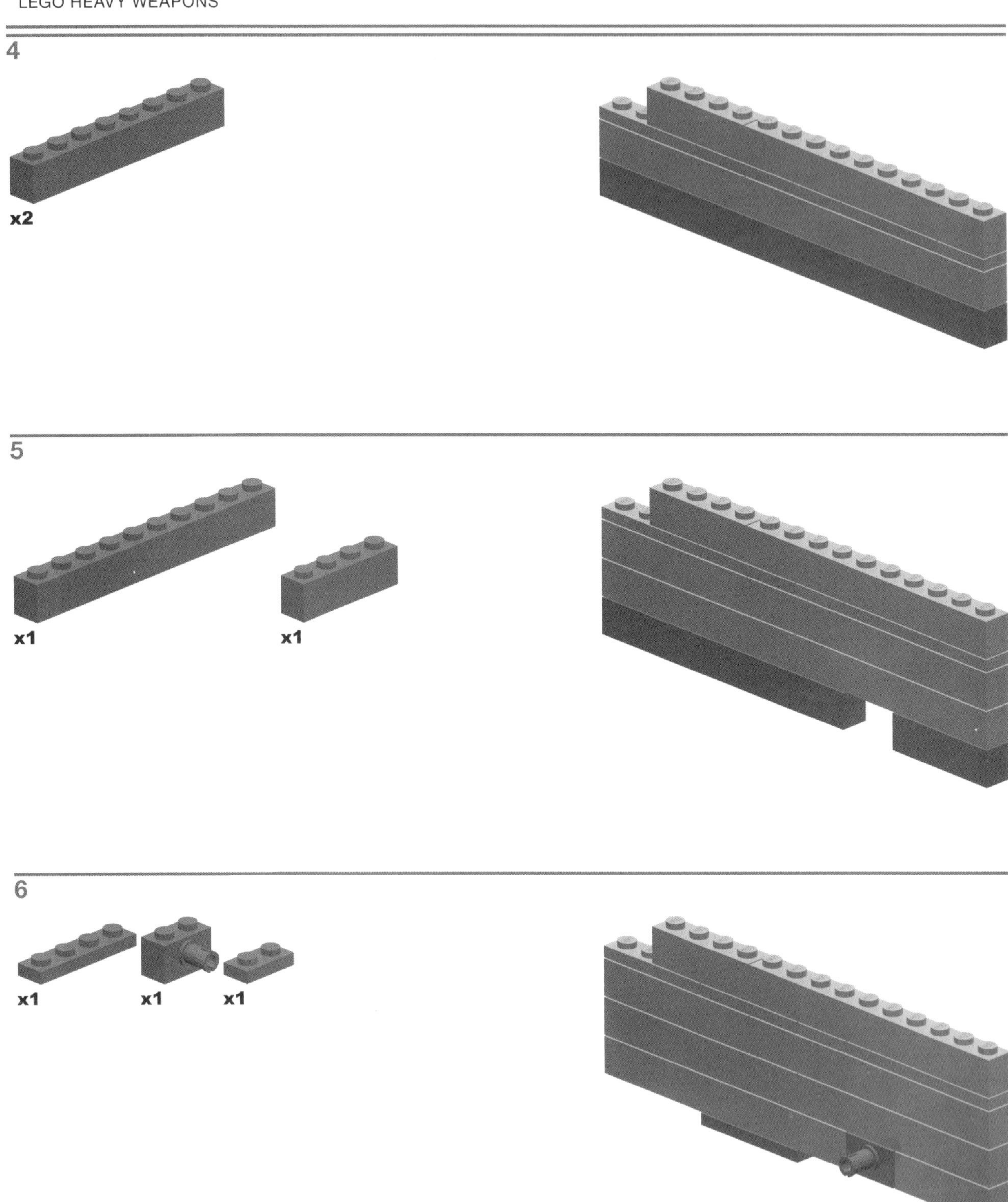
4
x2
5
x1
x1
6
x1
x1
x1

FORE GRIP PLATE

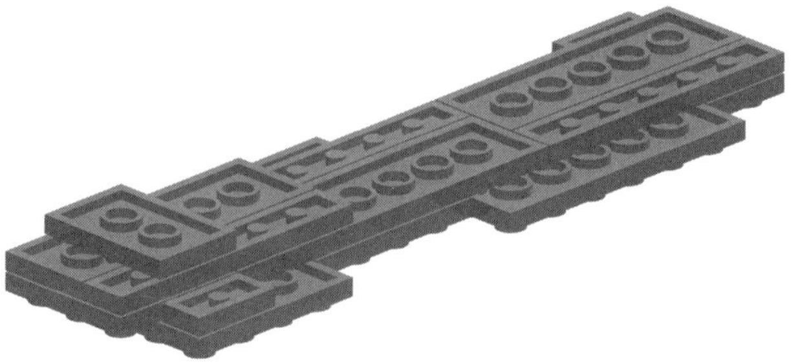

1

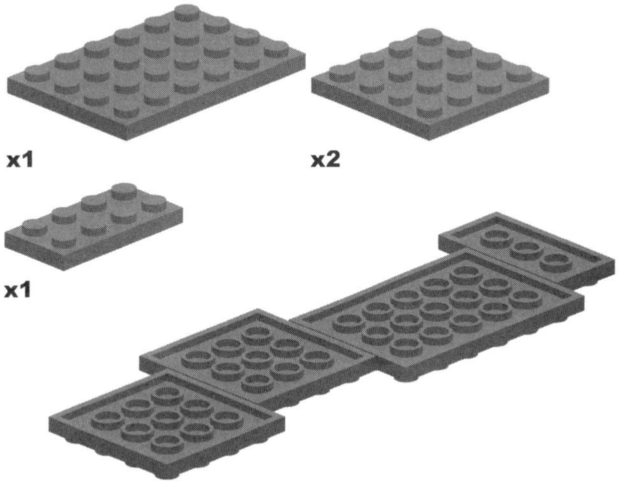

x1

x2

x1

2

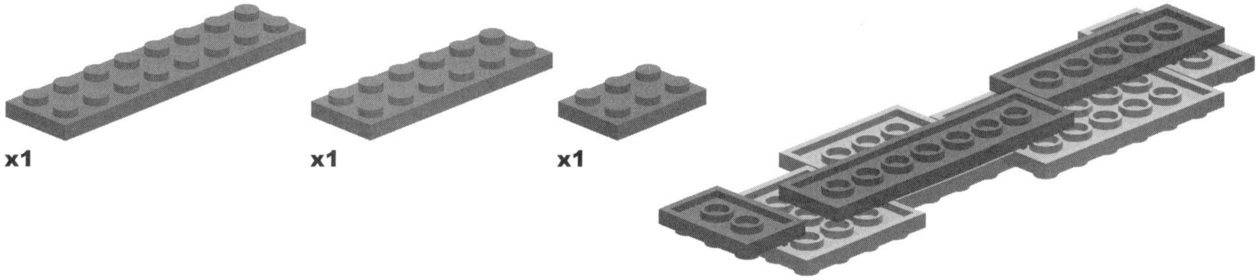

x1

x1

x1

3

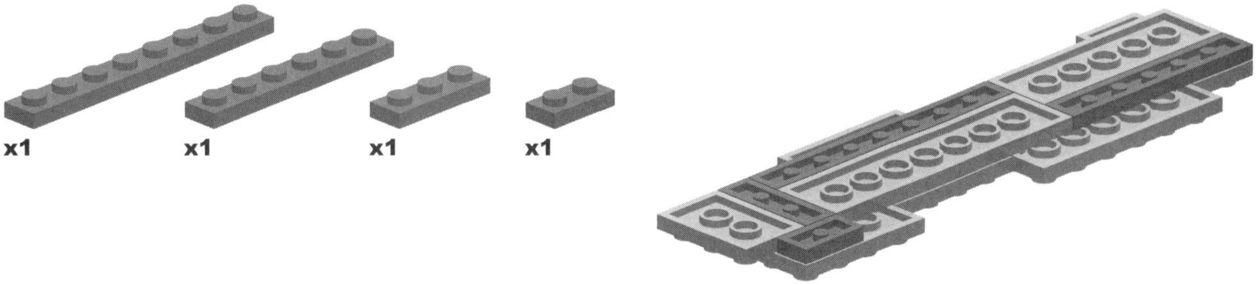

x1

x1

x1

x1

4

x1

x1

x1

ROOF PLATE FRONT

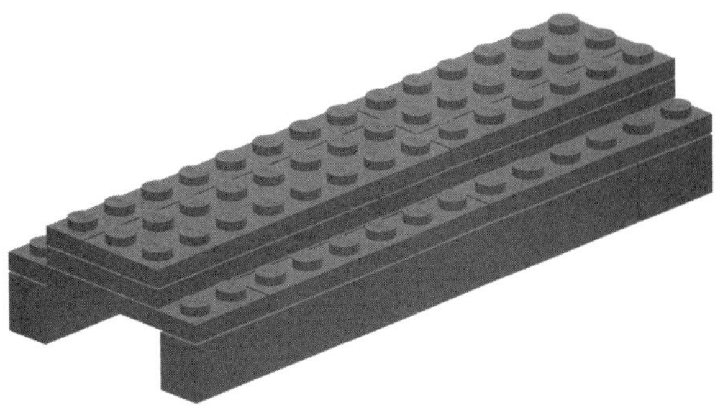

1

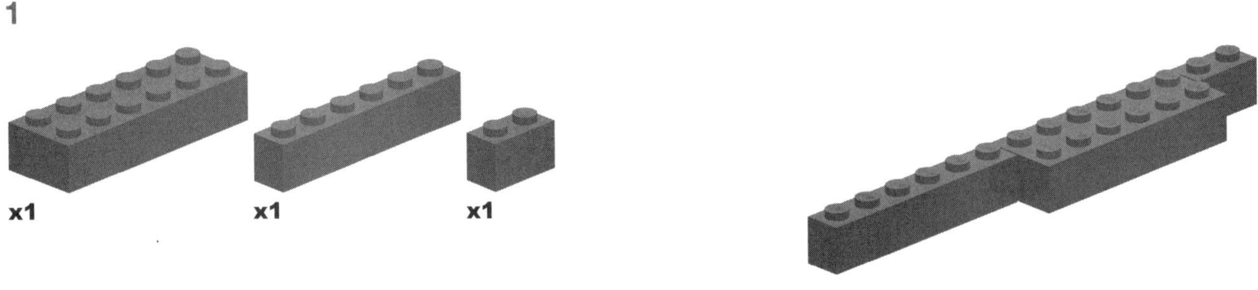

2

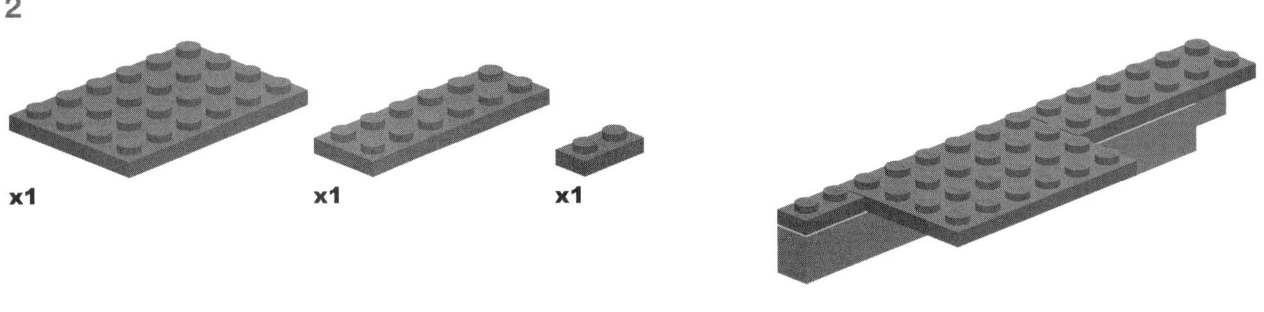

3

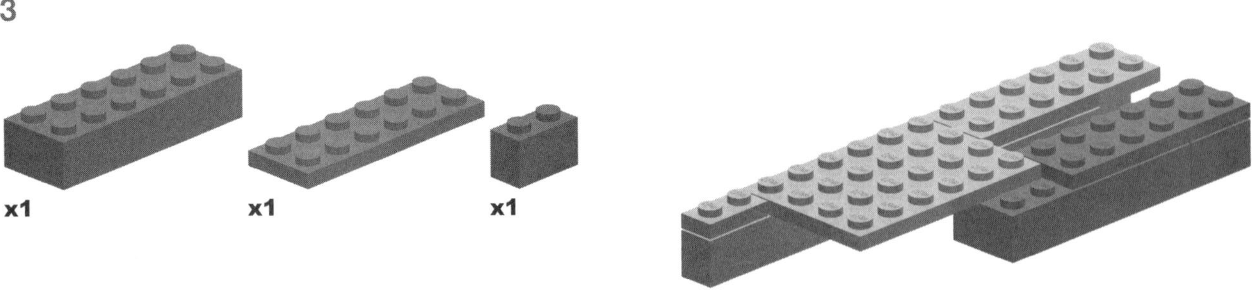

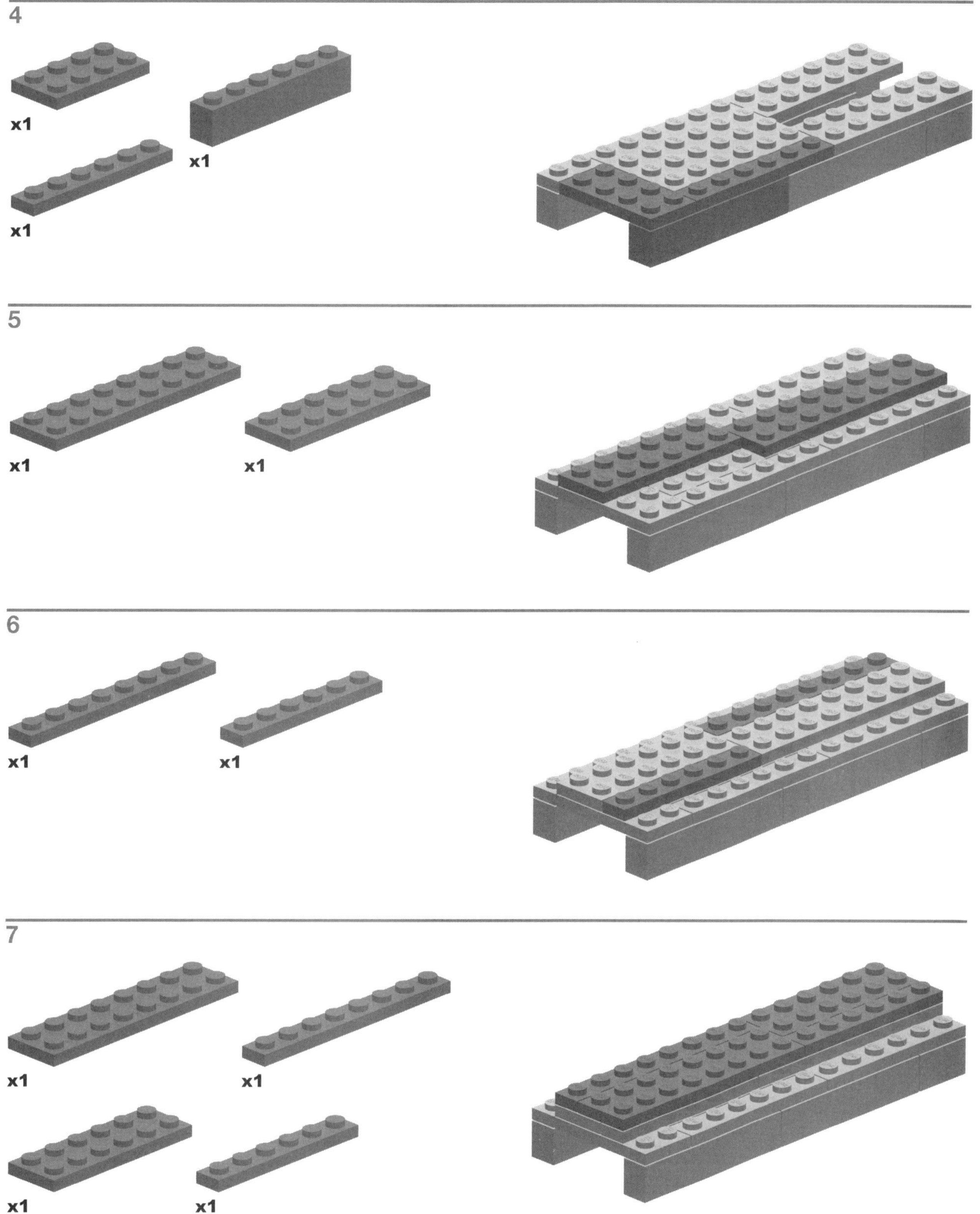
4
x1
x1
x1
5
x1
x1
6
x1
x1
7
x1
x1
x1
x1

BACK BLOCK

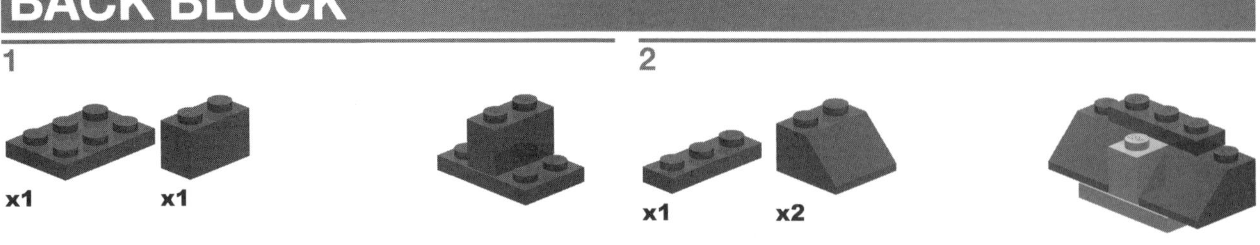

ROOF PLATE BACK

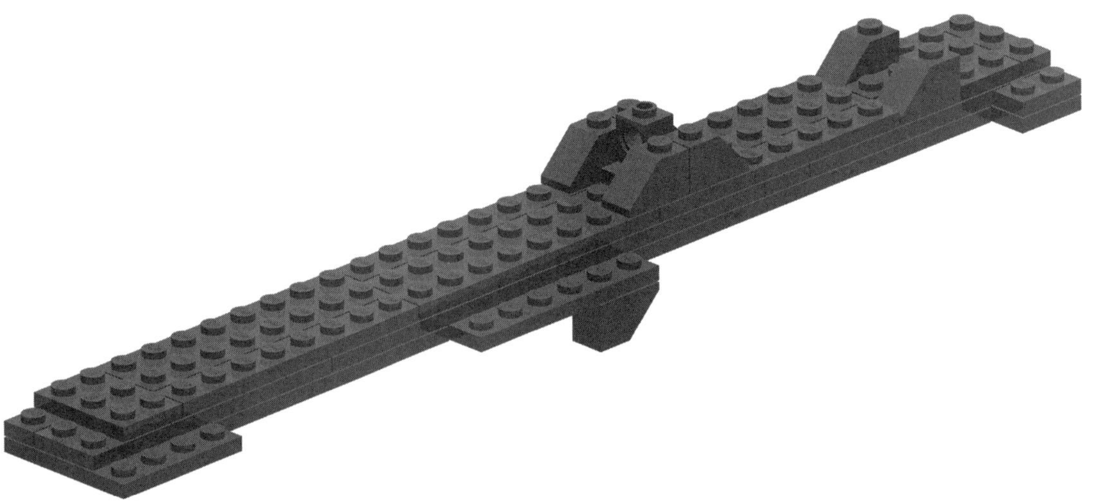

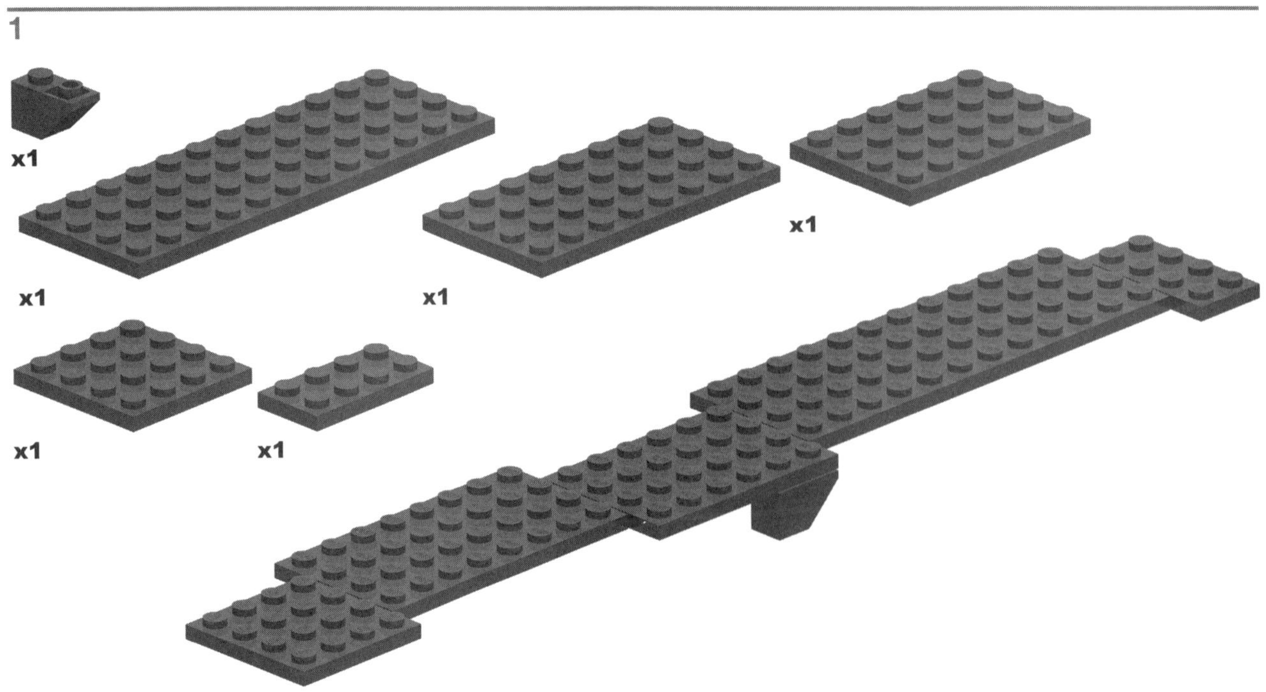

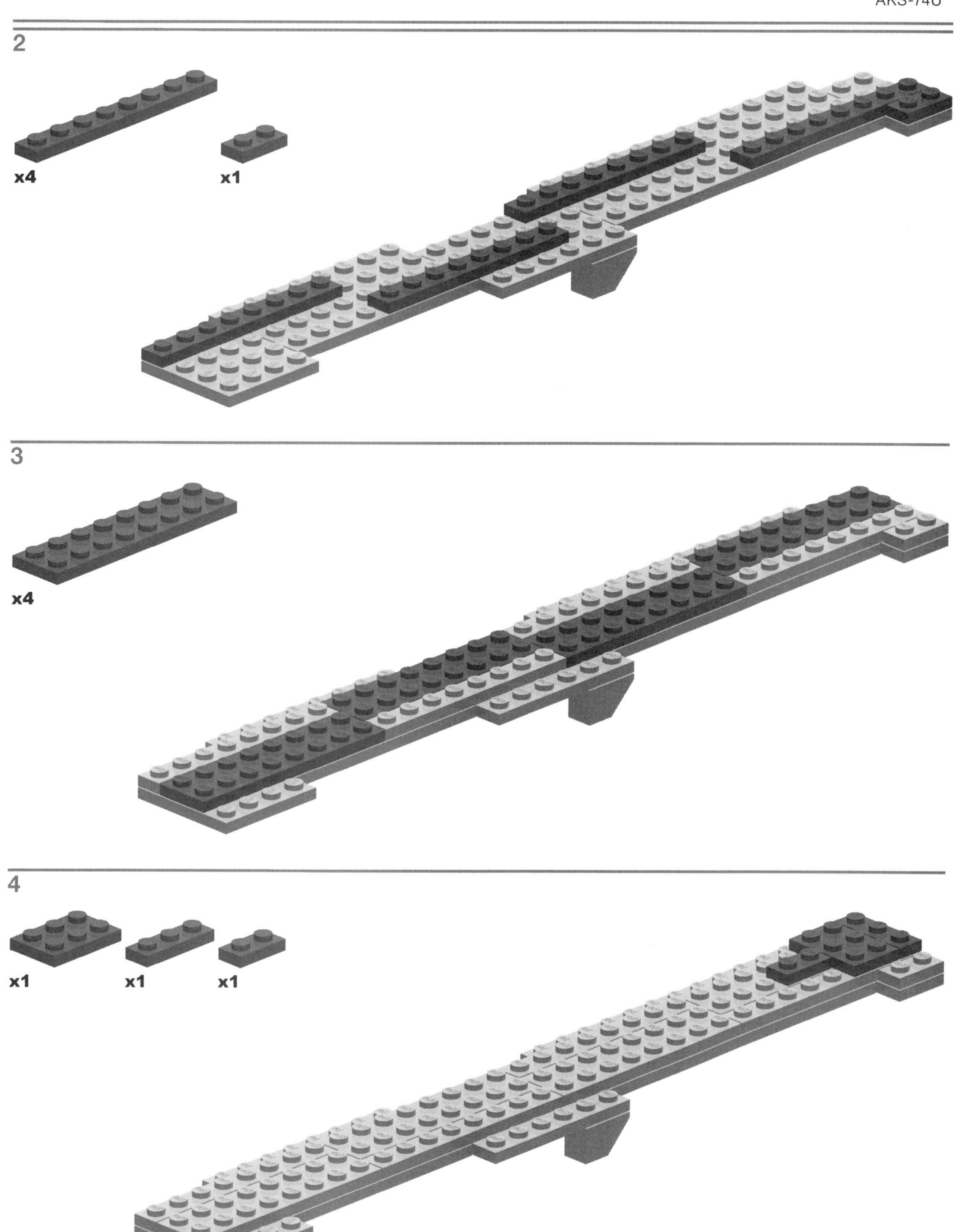
2
x4
x1
3
x4
4
x1
x1
x1

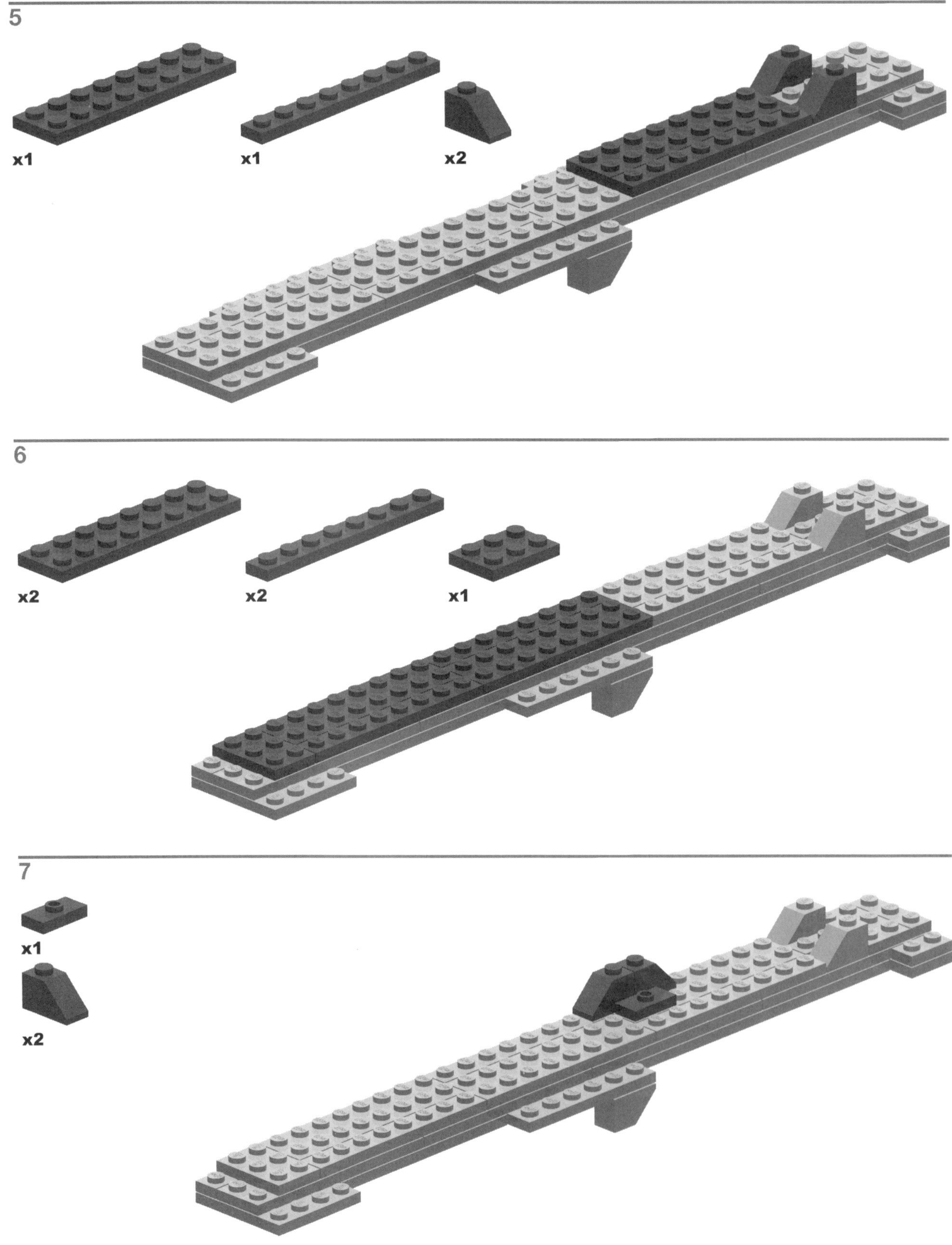
5
x1
x1
x2
6
x2
x2
x1
7
x1
x2

8

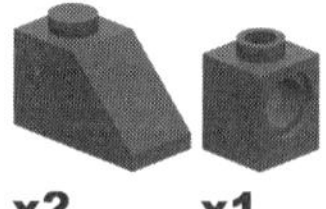

x2 x1

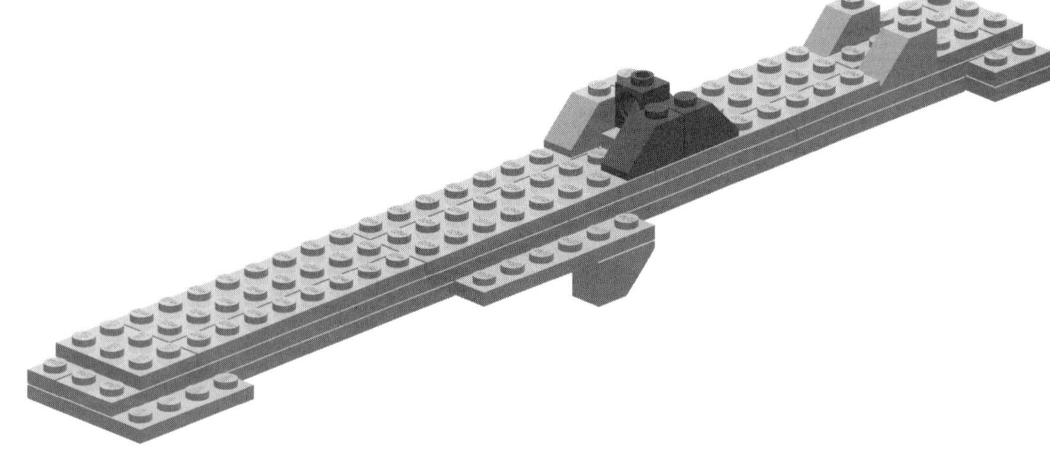

MAGAZINE SLIDE

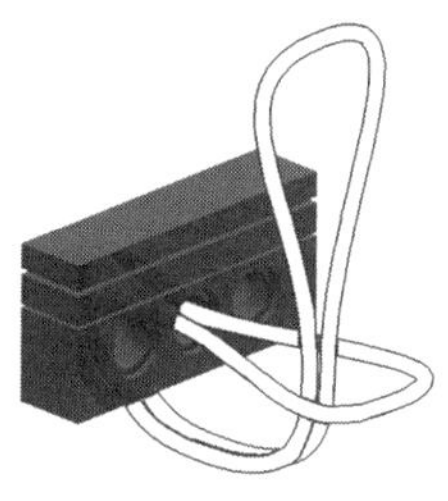

1

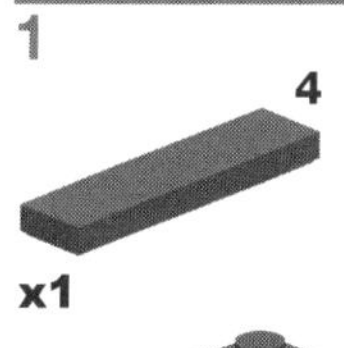

x1

x1

x1

2

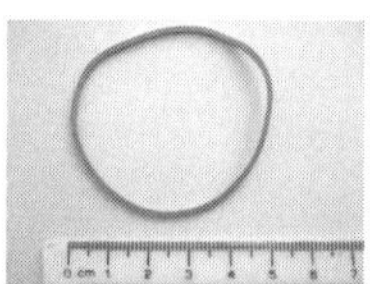

x1

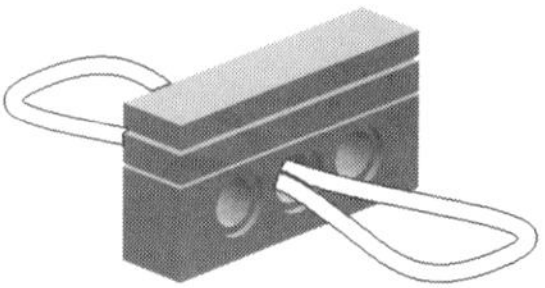

3

Pull one end of the rubber band under the brick and through the other end of the rubber band as shown.

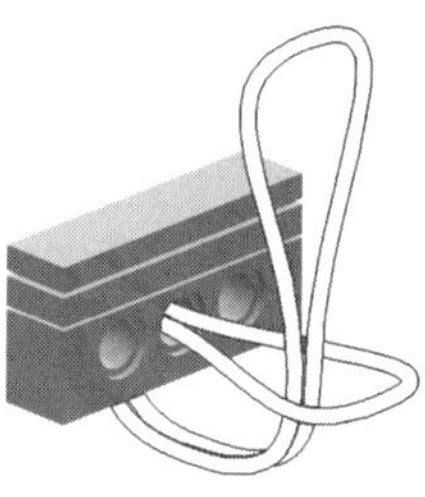

MAGAZINE ASSEMBLY

1

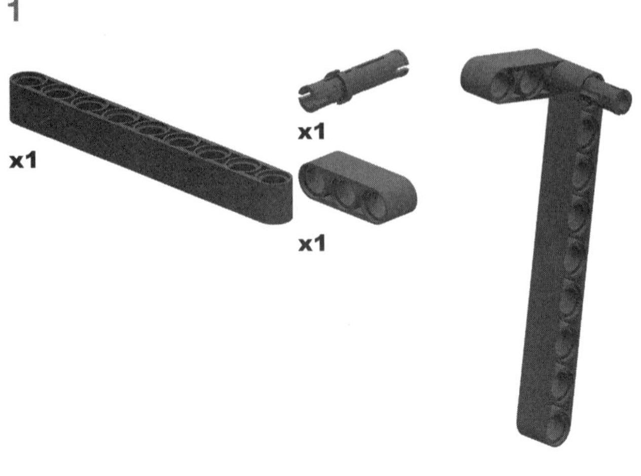

2

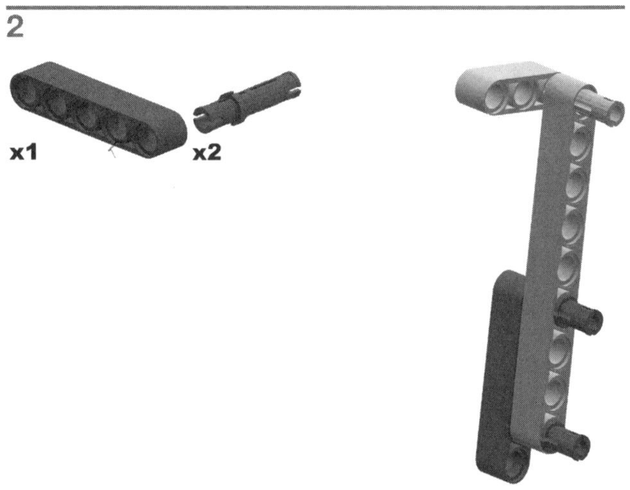

3

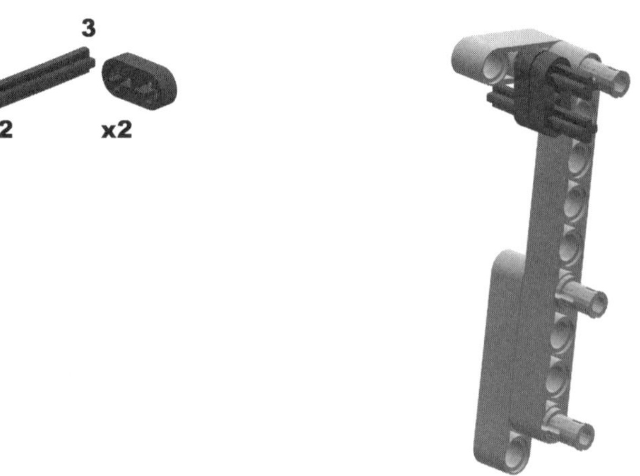

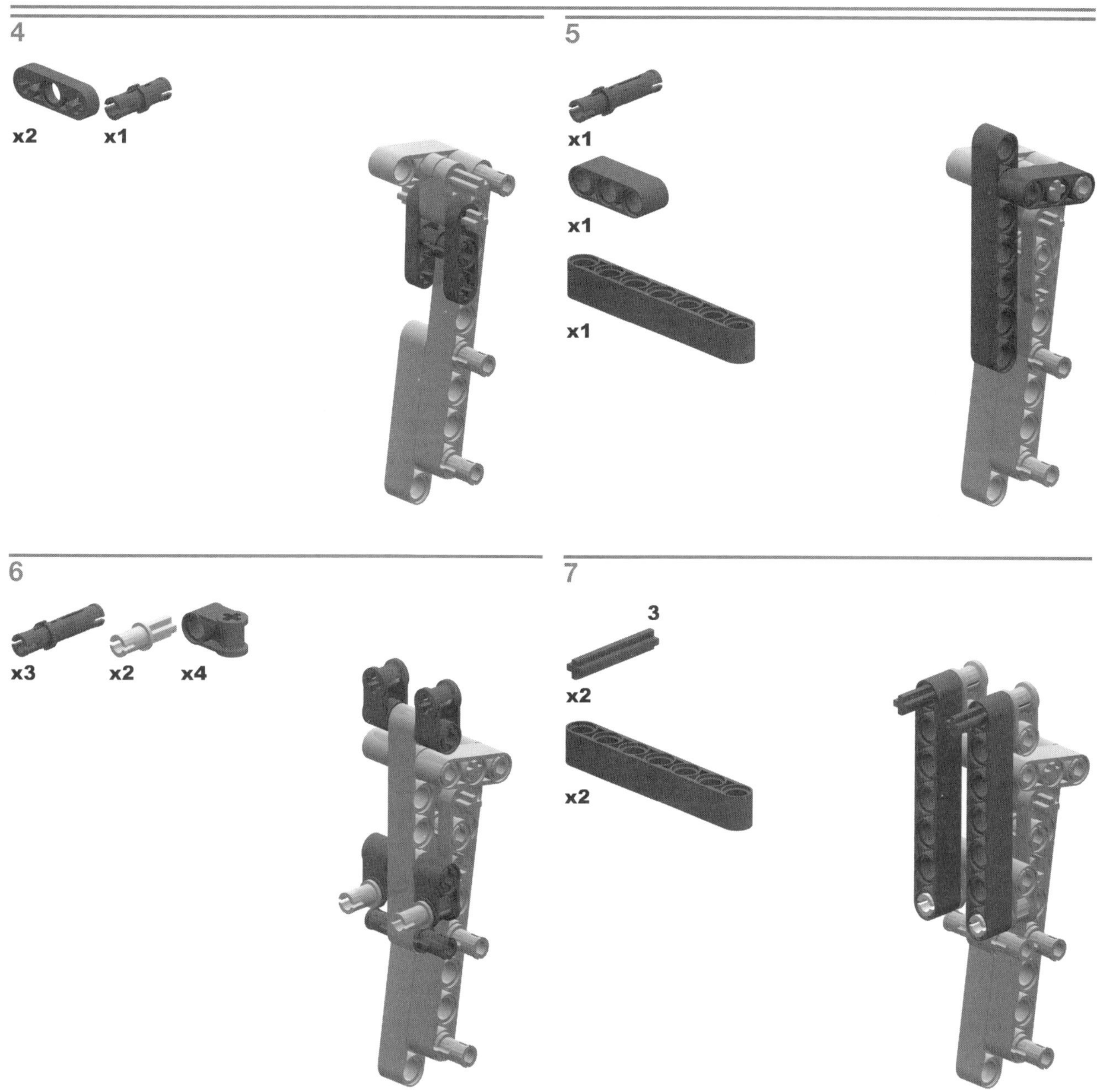
4
x2
x1
5
x1
x1
x1
6
x3
x2
x4
7
3
x2
x2

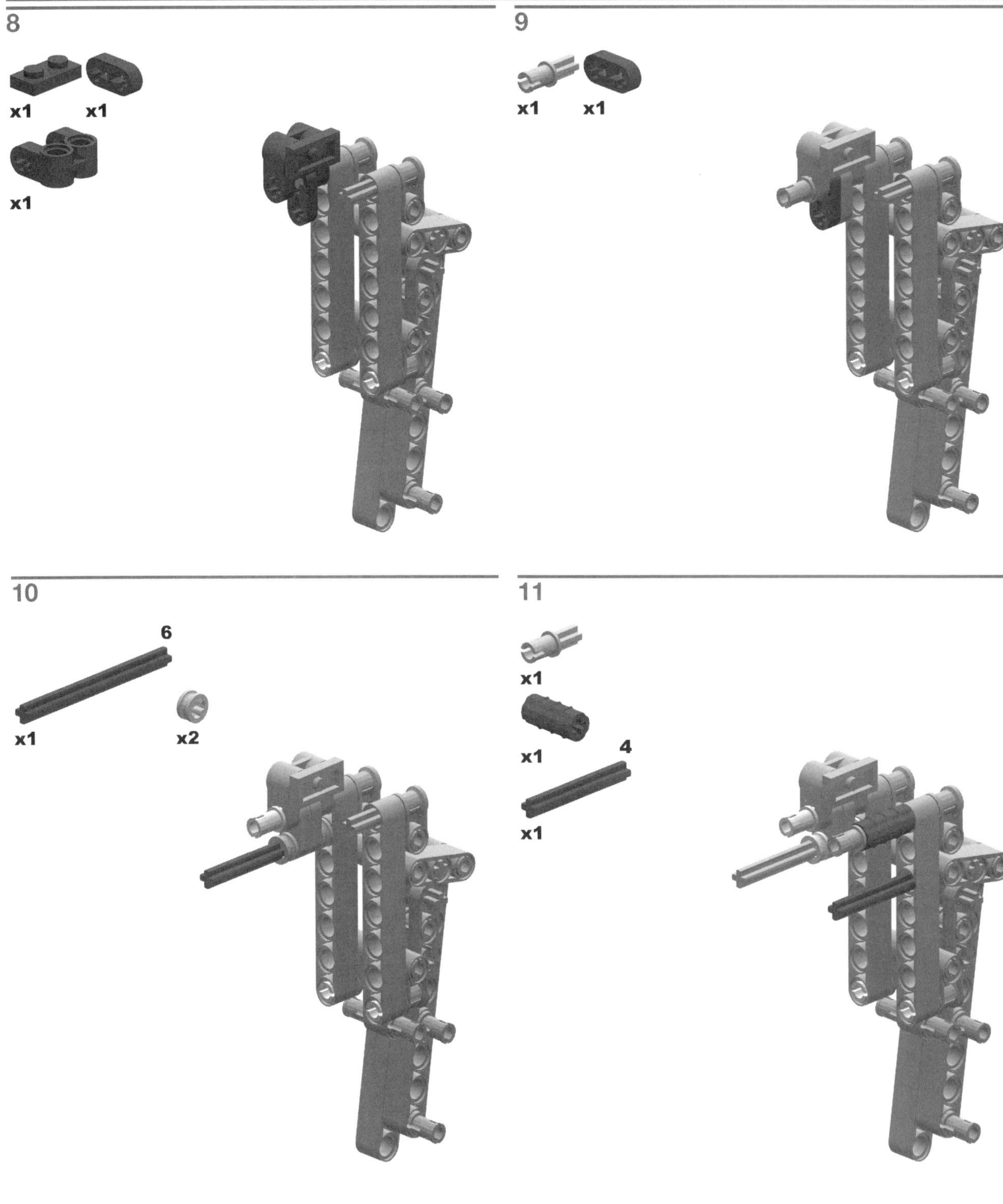
8
x1
x1
x1
9
x1
x1
10
6
x1
x2
11
x1
x1
4
x1

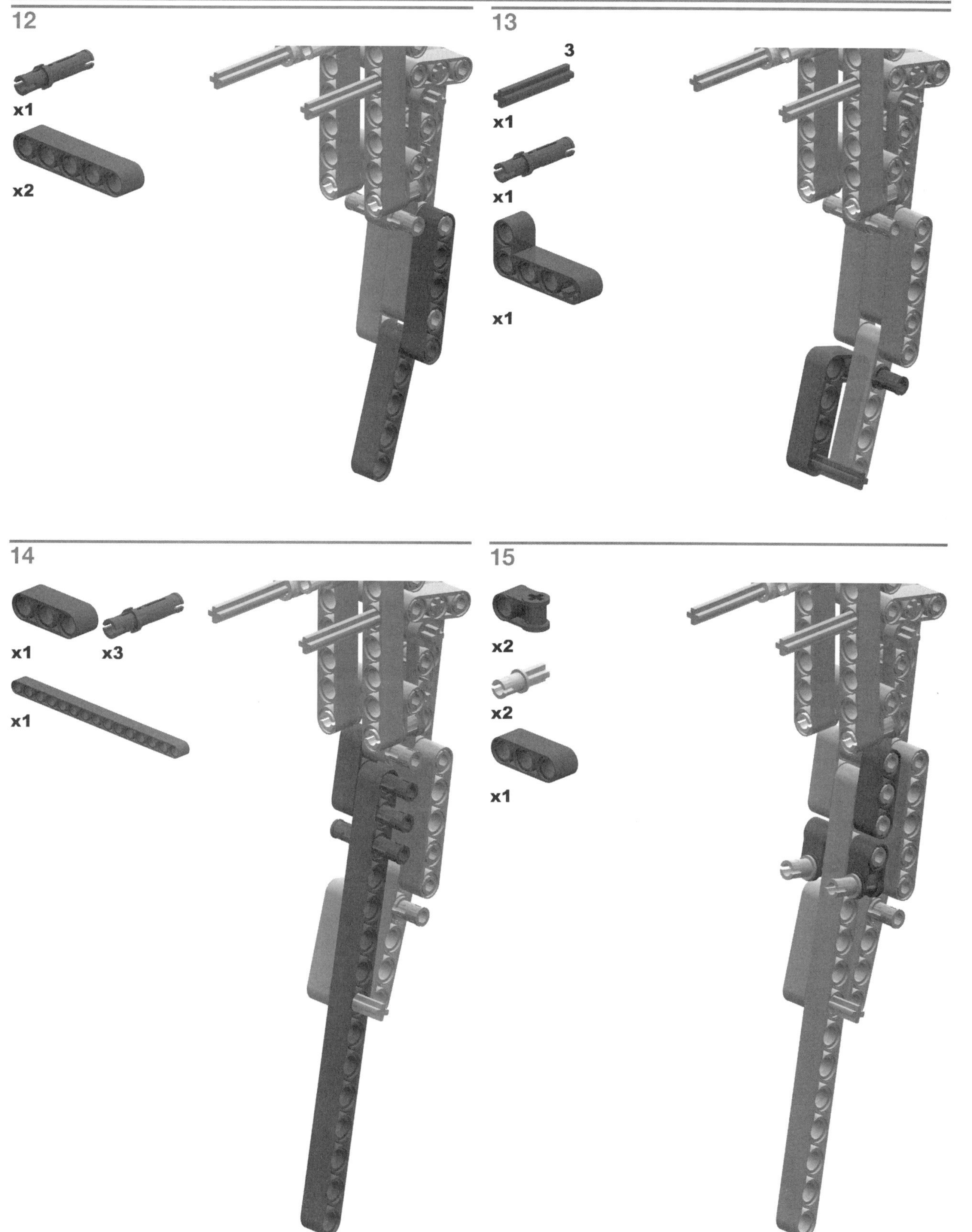
12
x1
x2
13
3
x1
x1
x1
14
x1
x3
x1
15
x2
x2
x1

16

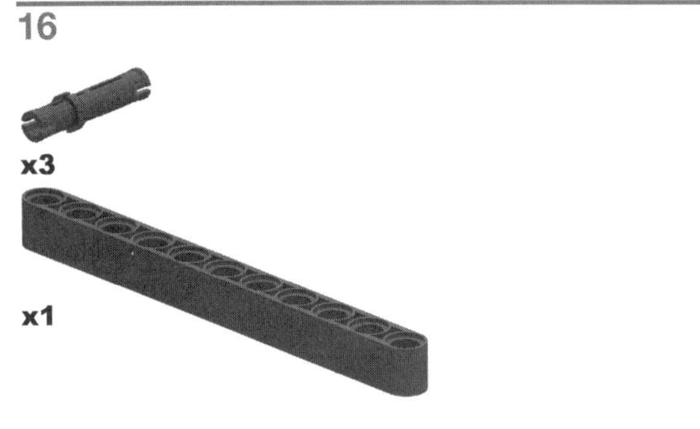

17

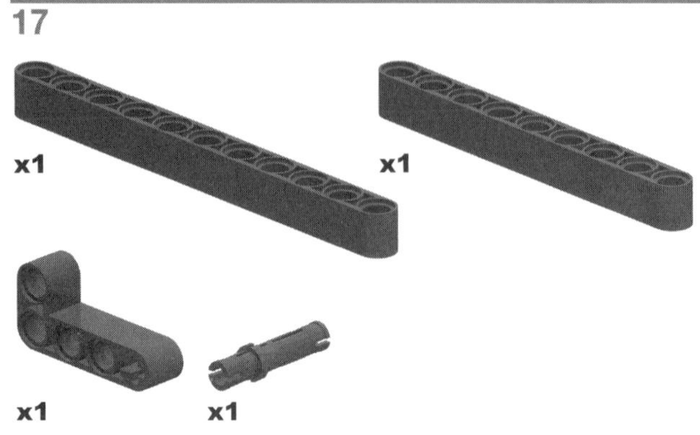

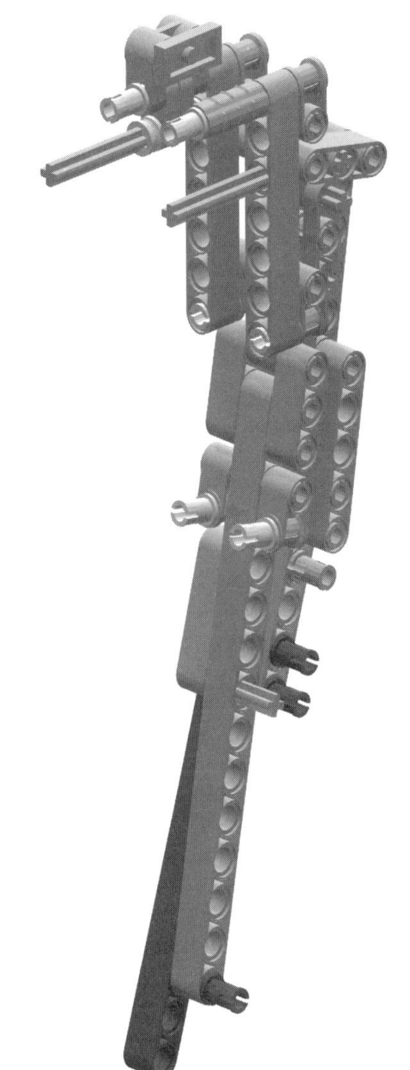

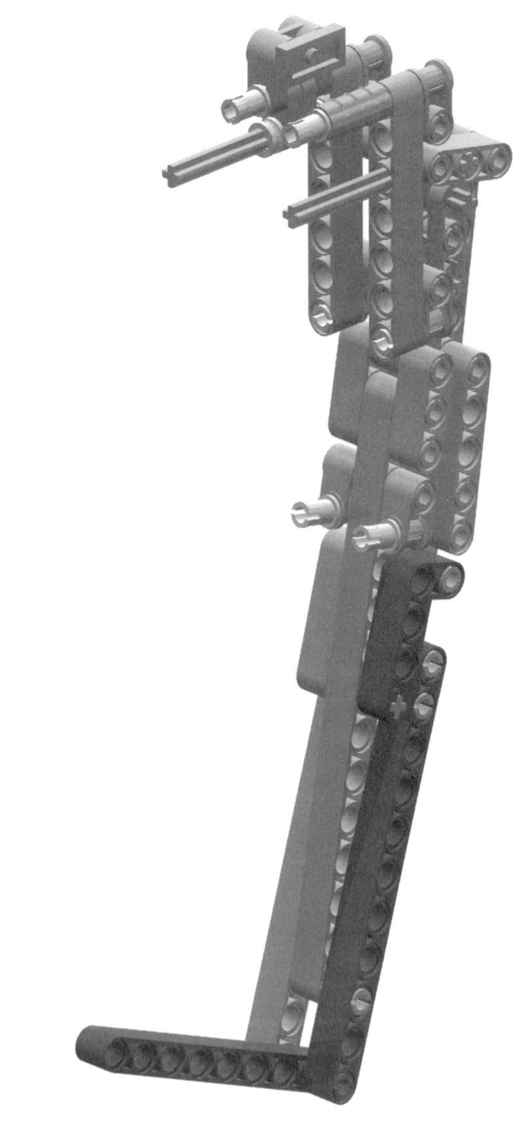

18

19

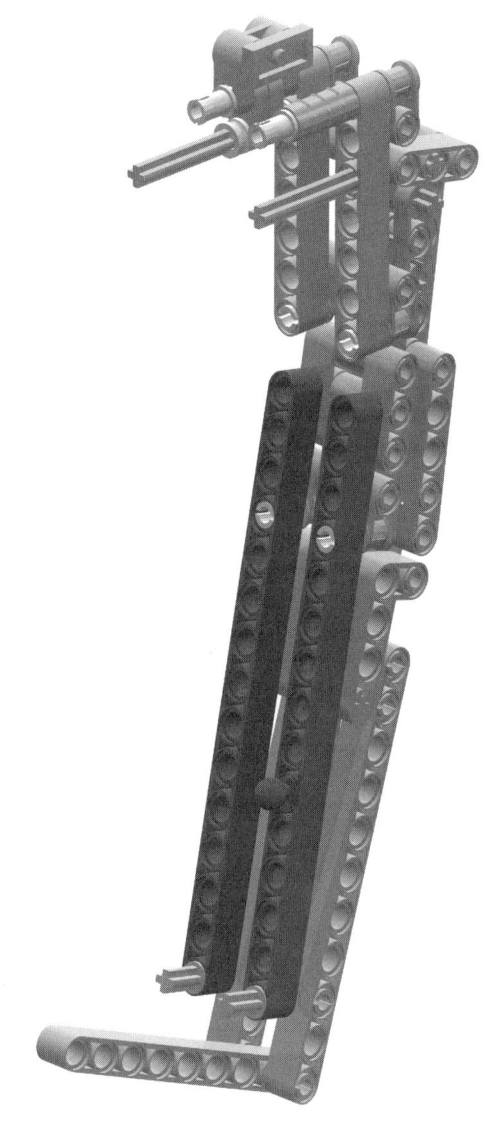

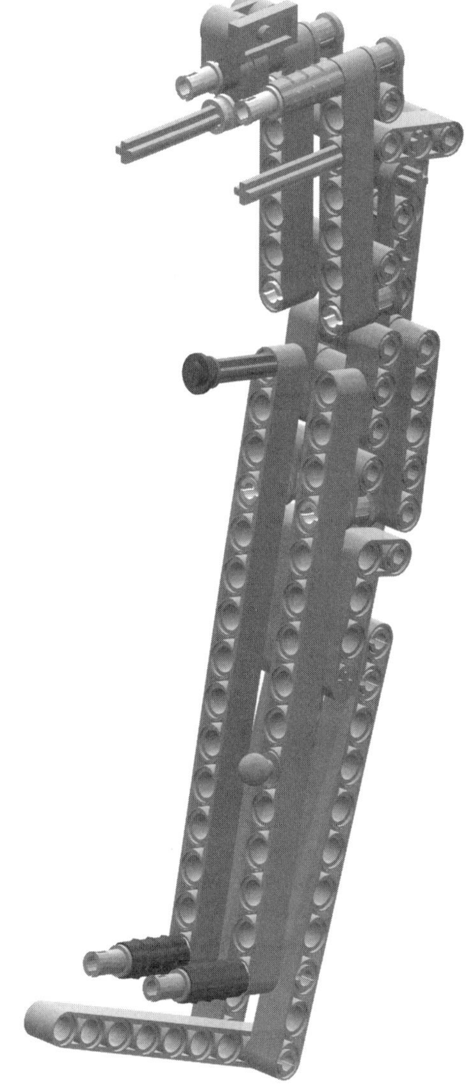

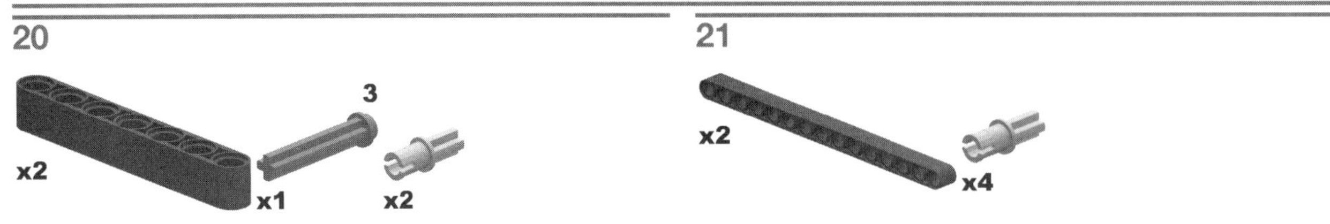
20
x2
3
x1
x2
21
x2
x4

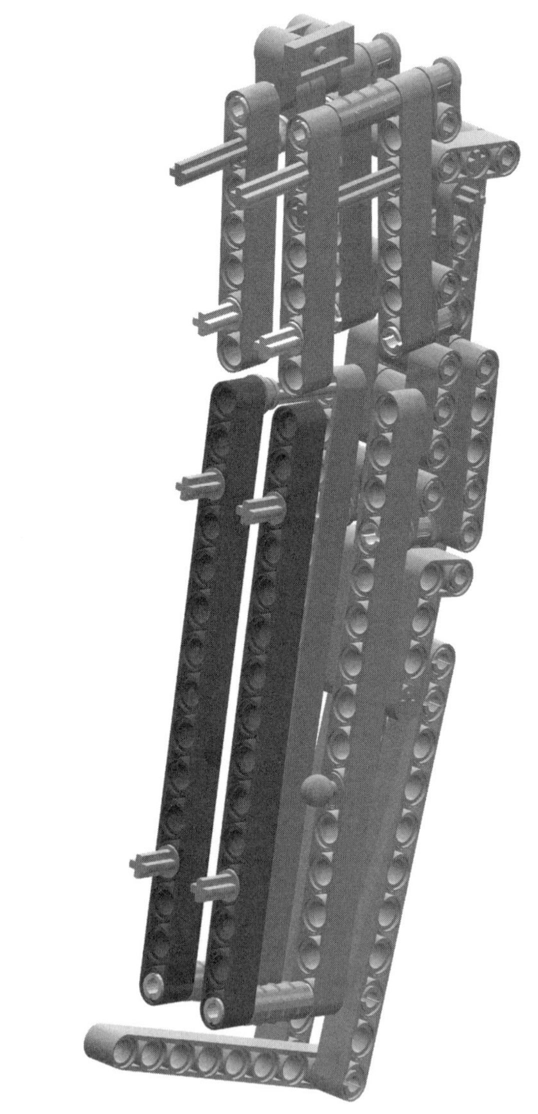

22

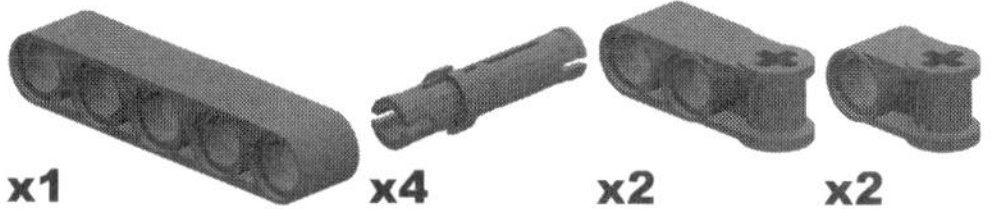

23

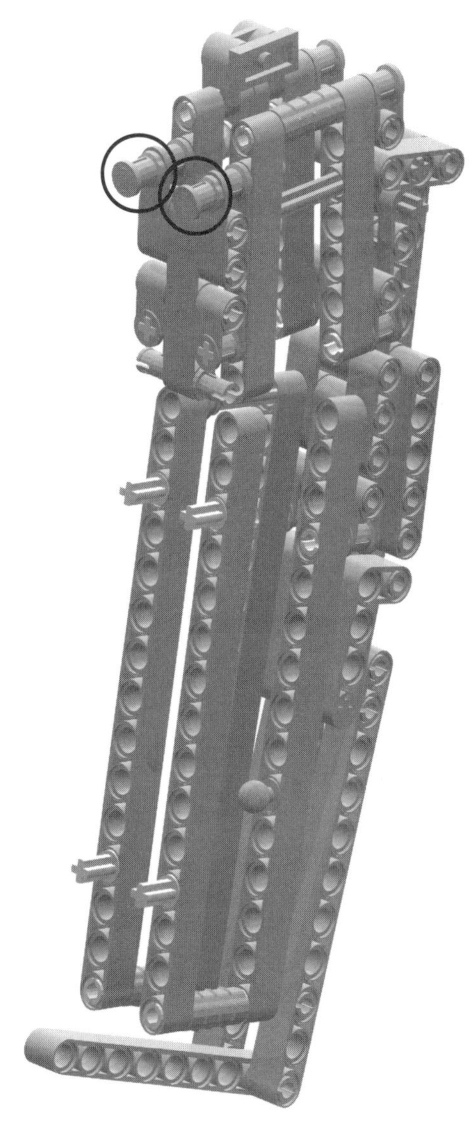

24

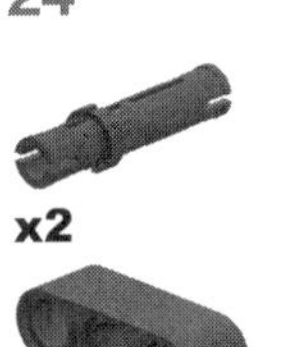

25

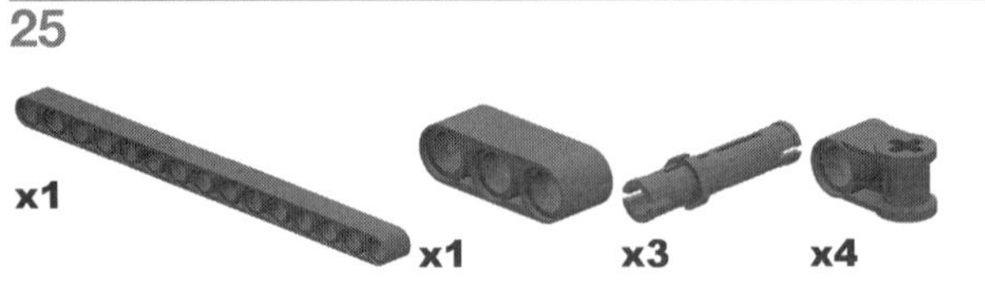

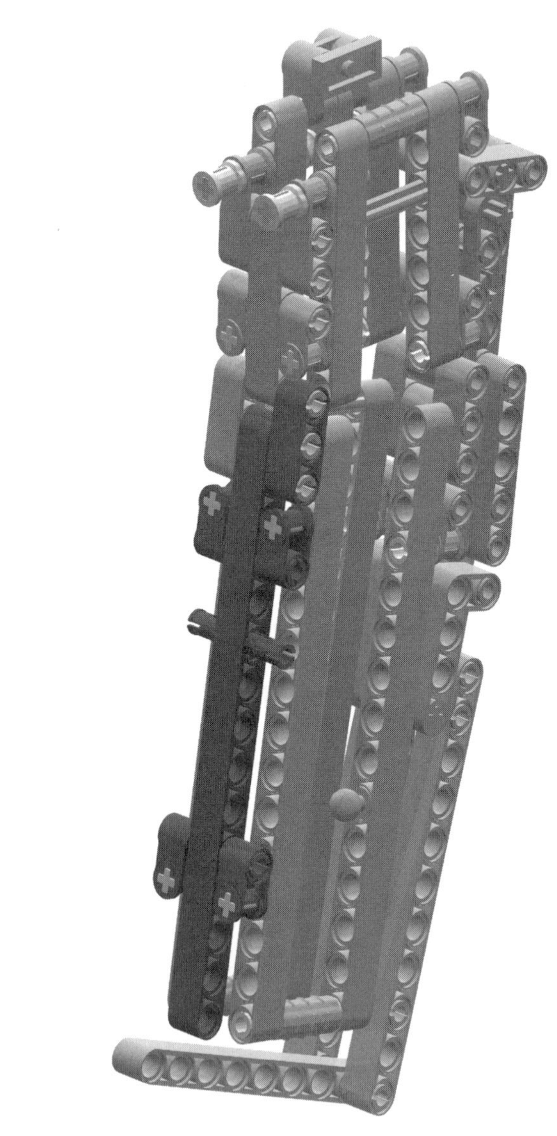

26

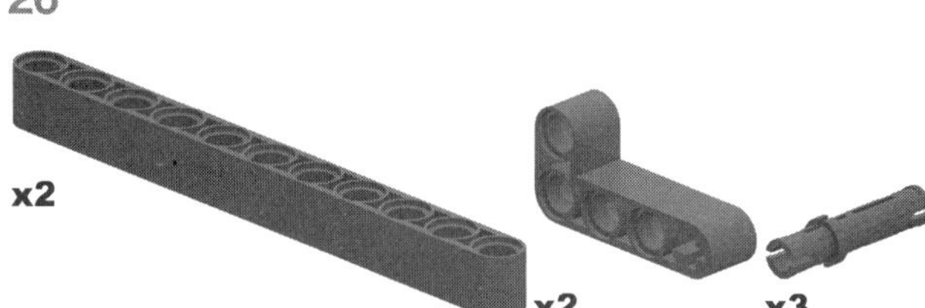

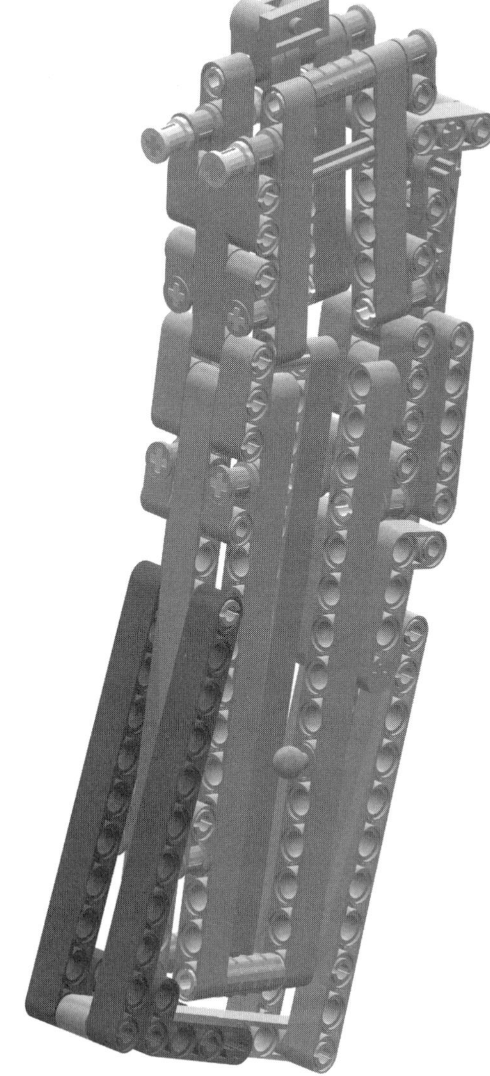

27

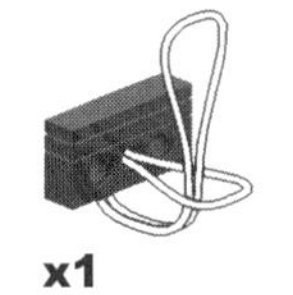

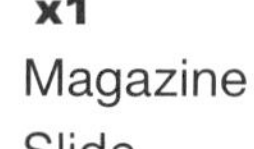

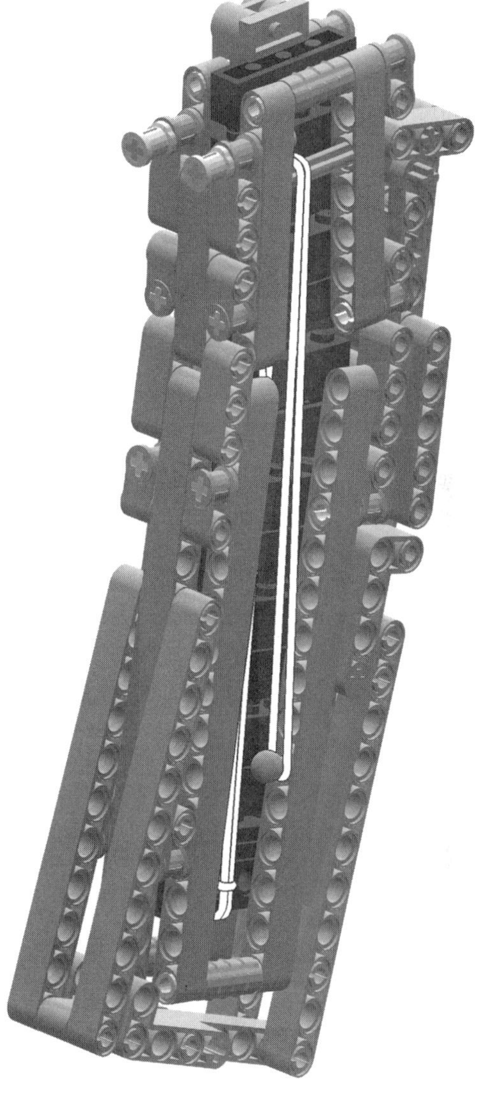

Insert the Magazine Slide into the hollow of the Magazine. Loop the rubber band over the 4-stud axle at the top, pull it down, and then slip it over the towball pin (added in step 18 on page 133). If necessary, you can adjust the tension in the rubber band by moving the towball pin to a different hole. Once you've added the Magazine Slide, load the 1×4 bricks one by one. Make sure to add them stud-to-stud and base-to-base so they don't accidentally snap together.

MAIN ASSEMBLY

TIP: *If you're unsure exactly which hole you should be attaching a module to, a quick look ahead to step 6 on page 142 will show where everything should go. But make sure you remember which step you're on before you skip ahead—each module needs to be added in the following order.*

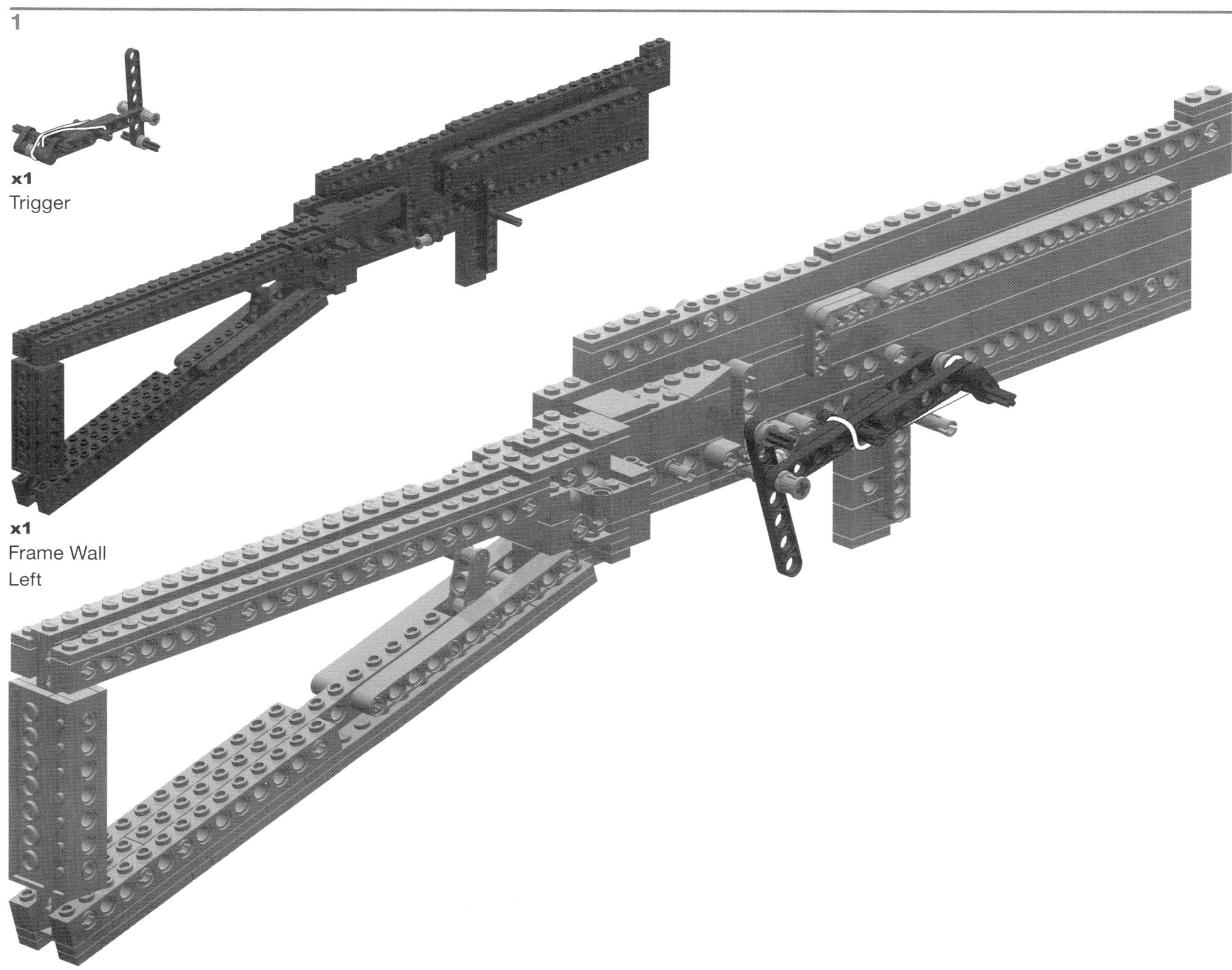
1
x1
Trigger
x1
Frame Wall
Left

2

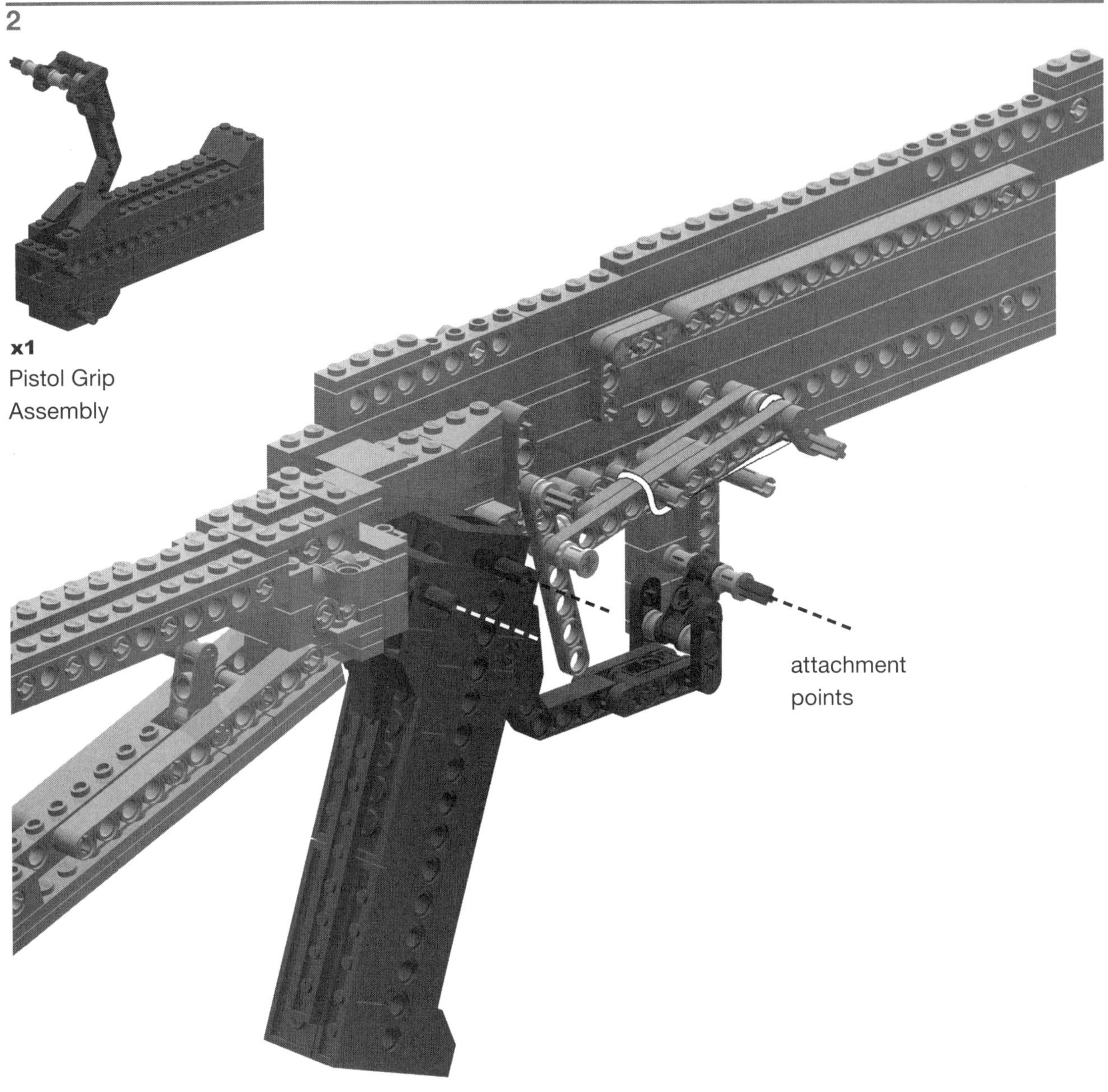

3

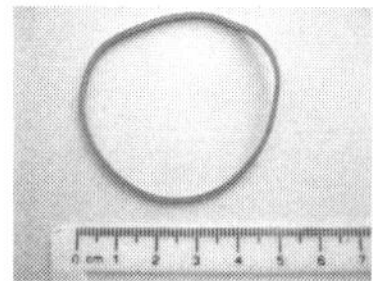

x1

x1
Magazine Release

The rubber band hooks under the 5-stud axle in the Magazine Release and then loops over the exposed 3-stud pin above. You may need to fold the rubber band over itself in order to increase the tension so that the Magazine Release works properly. You will attach the rest of that mechanism in the next step, so it's okay to give the rubber band enough tension to pull out the pin.

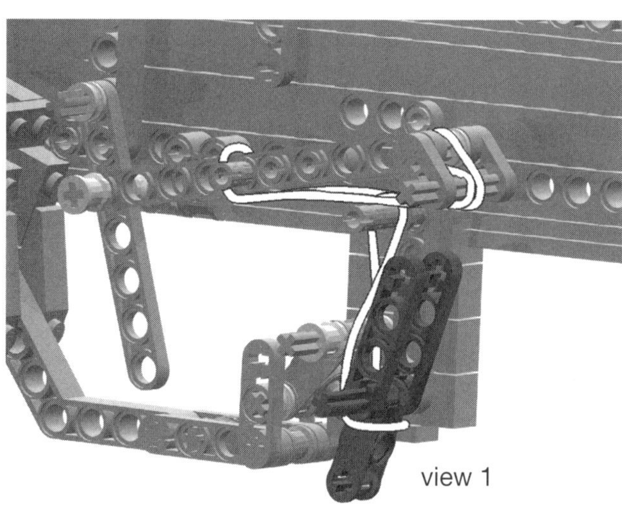

view 1

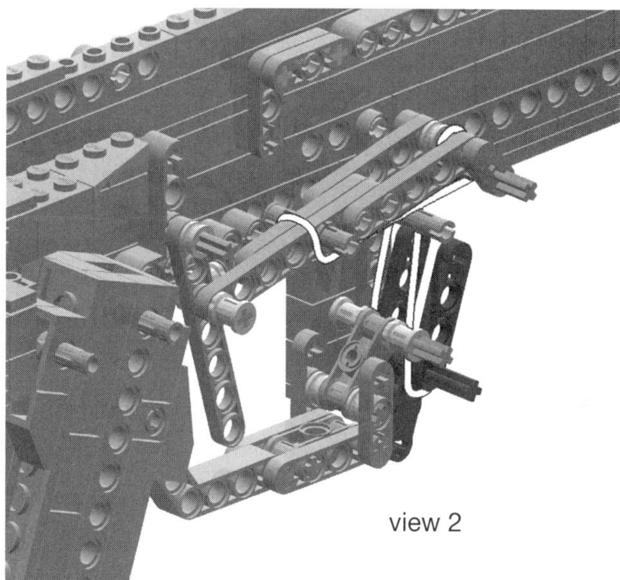

view 2

4

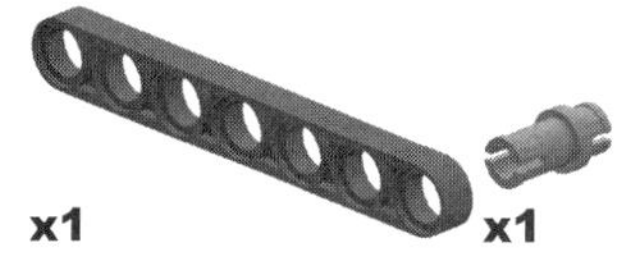

x1 x1

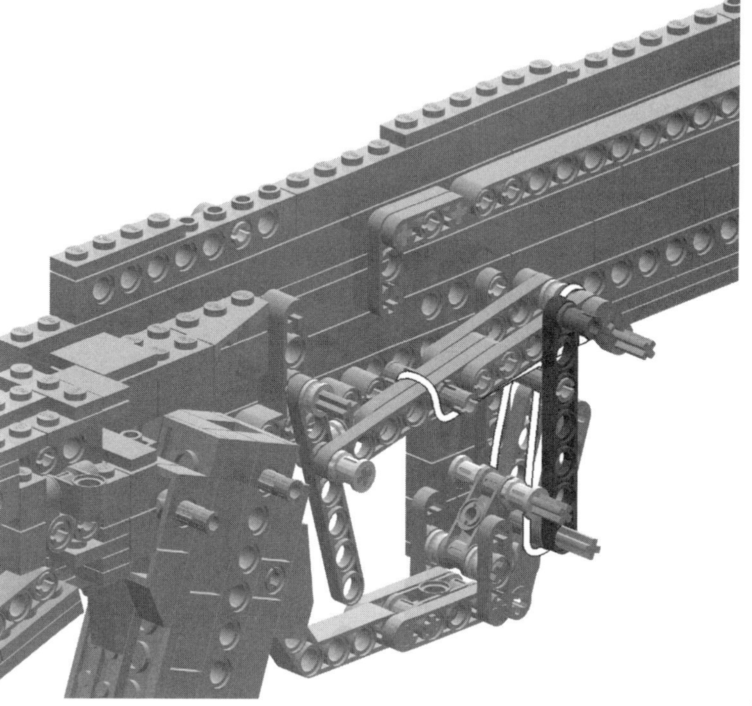

5

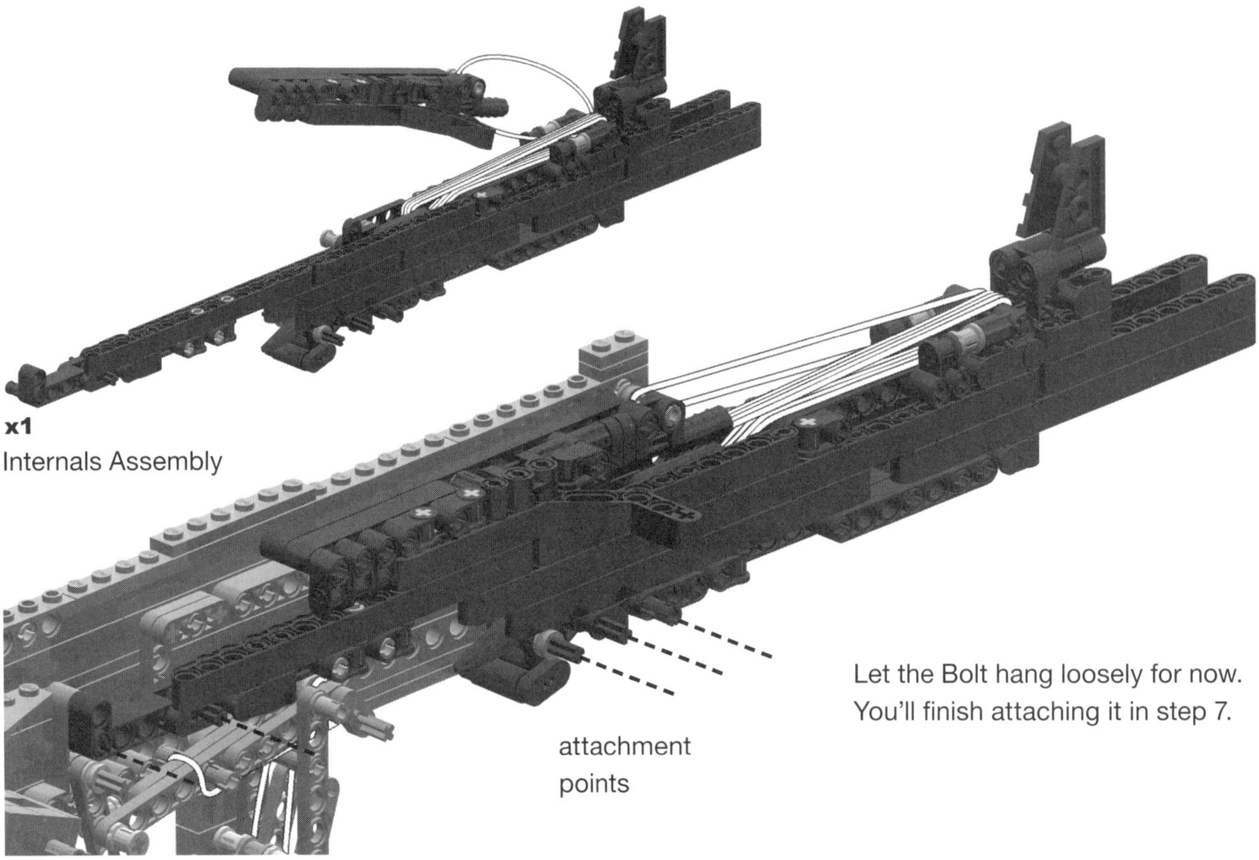

x1
Internals Assembly
Let the Bolt hang loosely for now.
You'll finish attaching it in step 7.
attachment
points

6

x1
Frame Wall Right

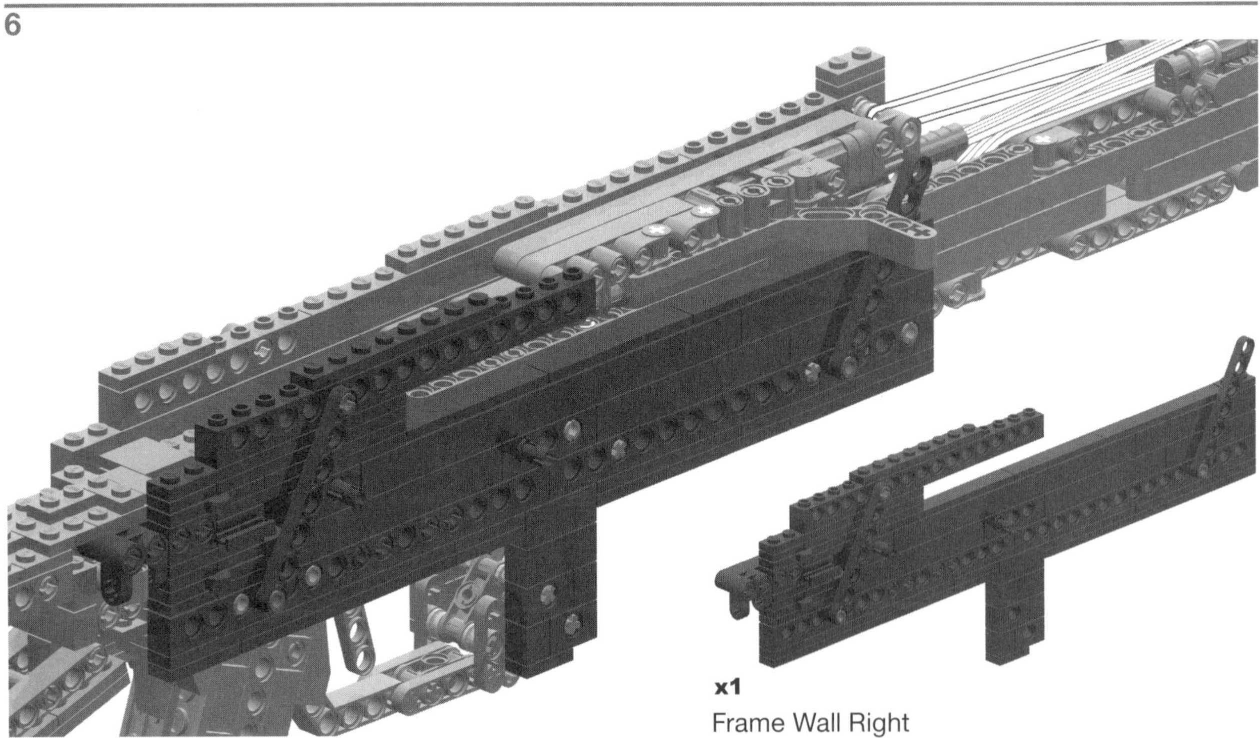

7

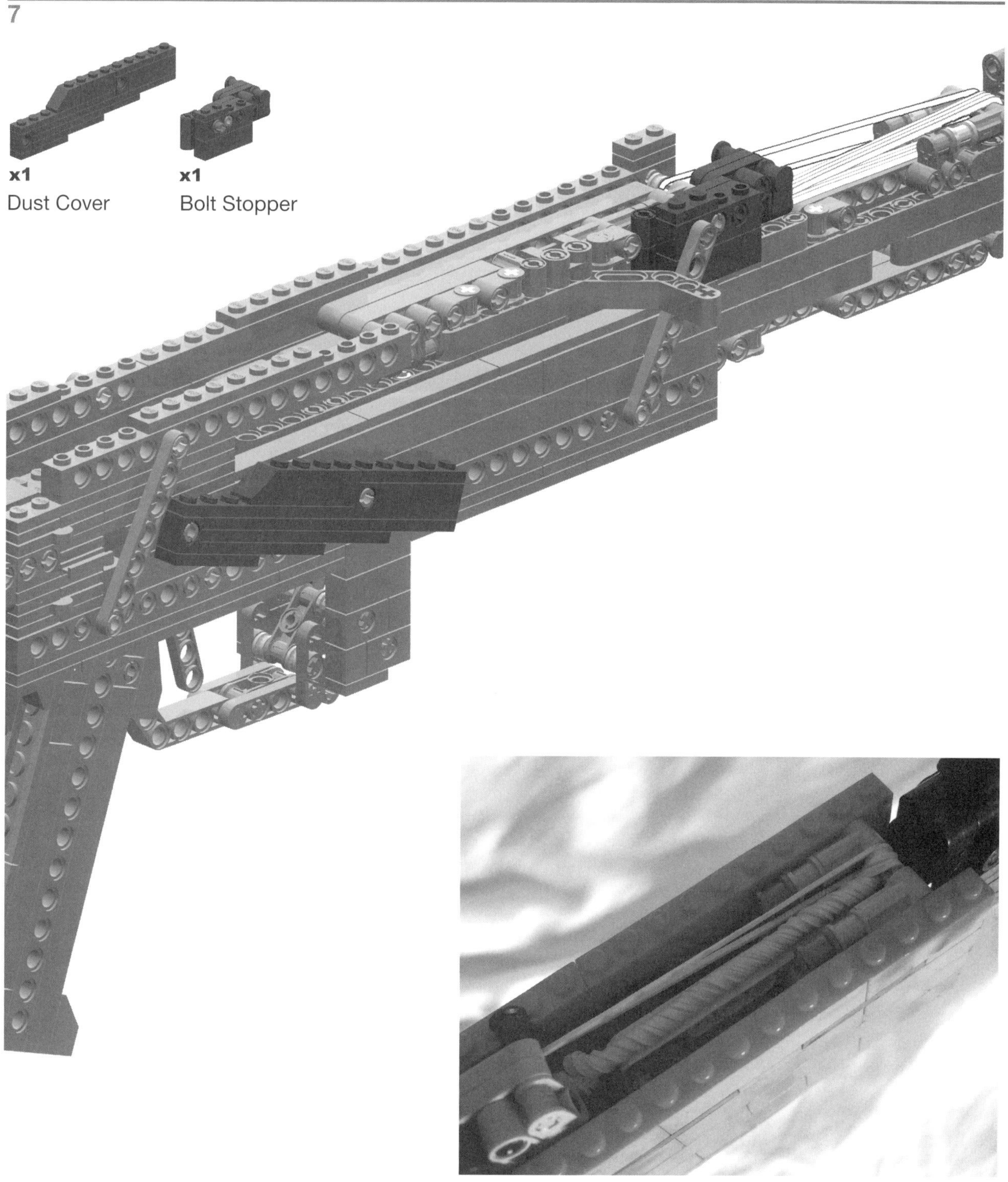

The Bolt Stopper attaches over all of the rubber bands here and keeps it all tidy. As I mentioned on page 101, twisting the Hammer's bands around each other can help tidy things up, as shown in the picture here.

8

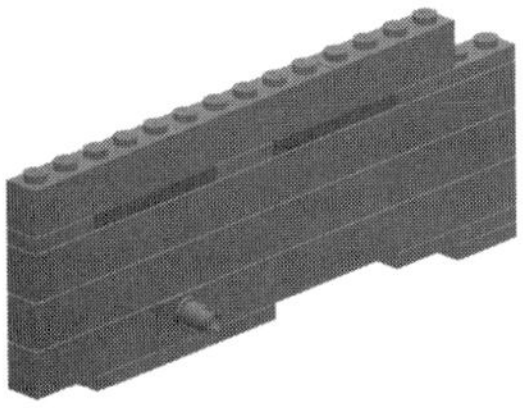

x1
Fore Grip Wall Right

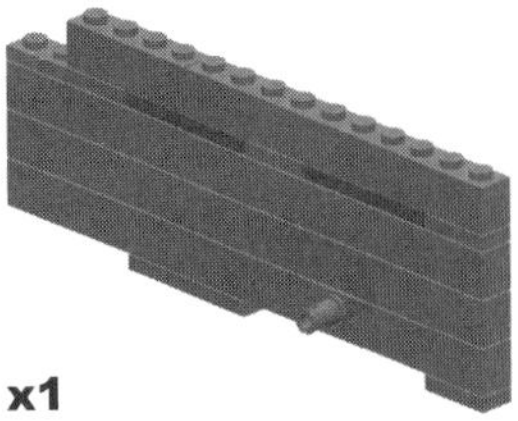

x1
Fore Grip Wall Left

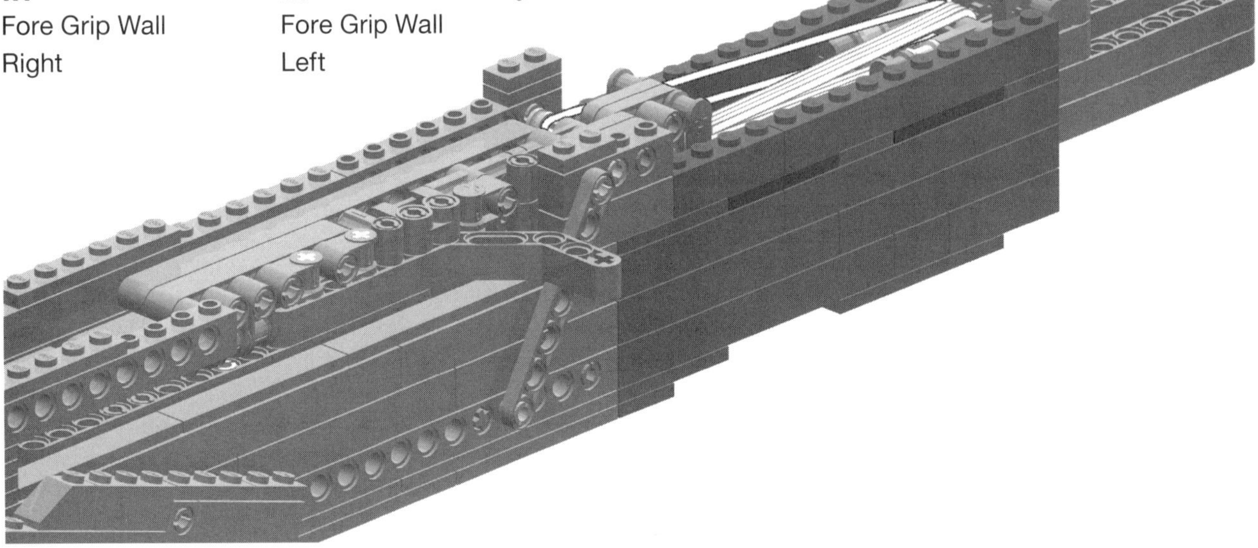

9

x1
Roof Plate Front

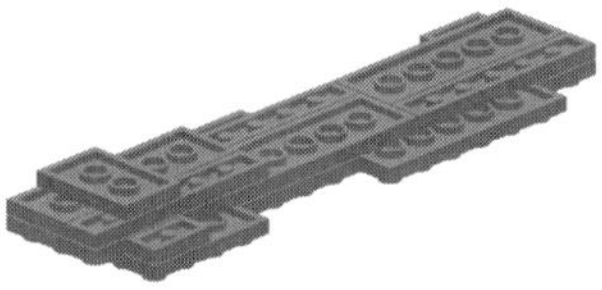

x1
Fore Grip Plate

10

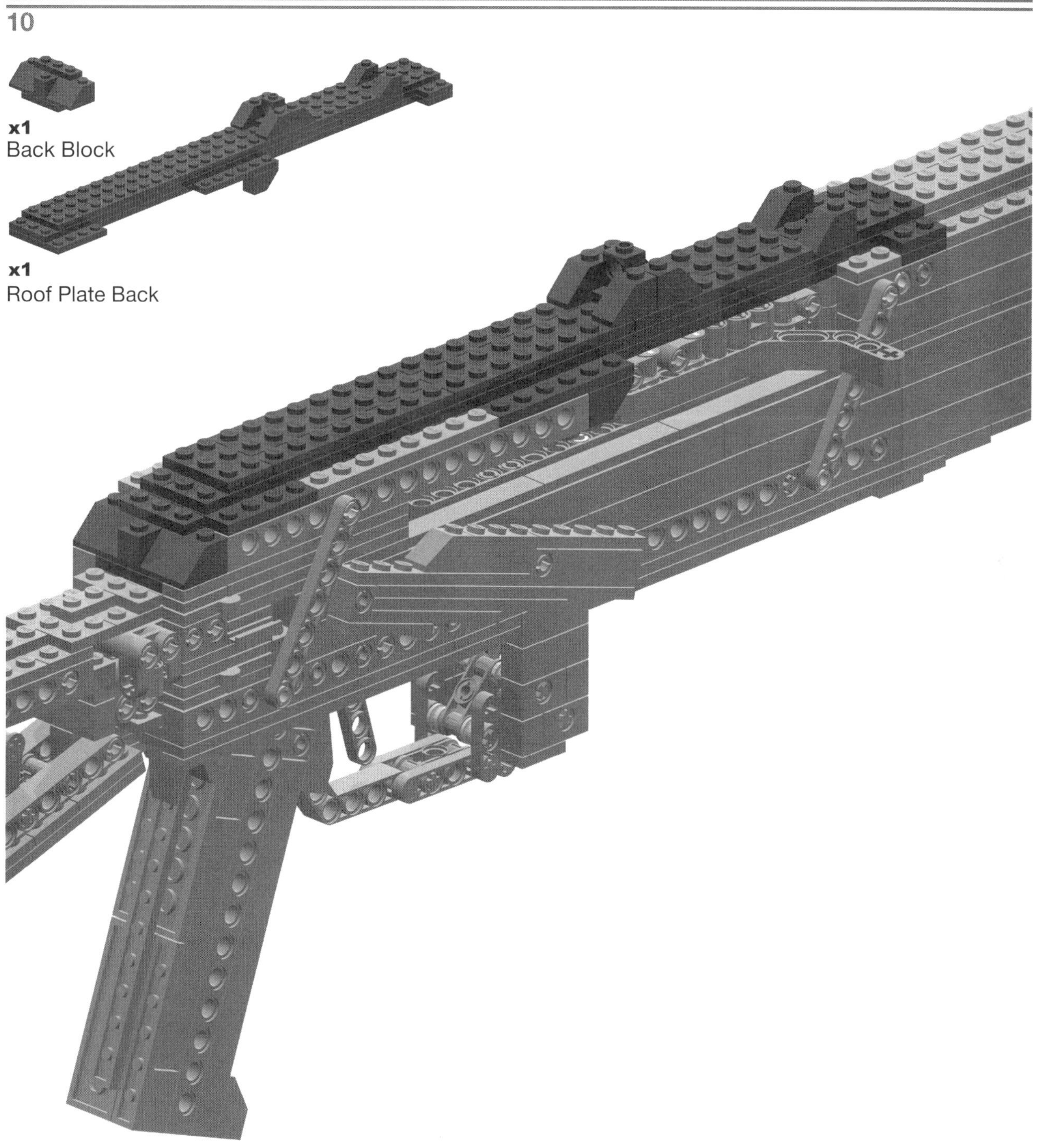

11

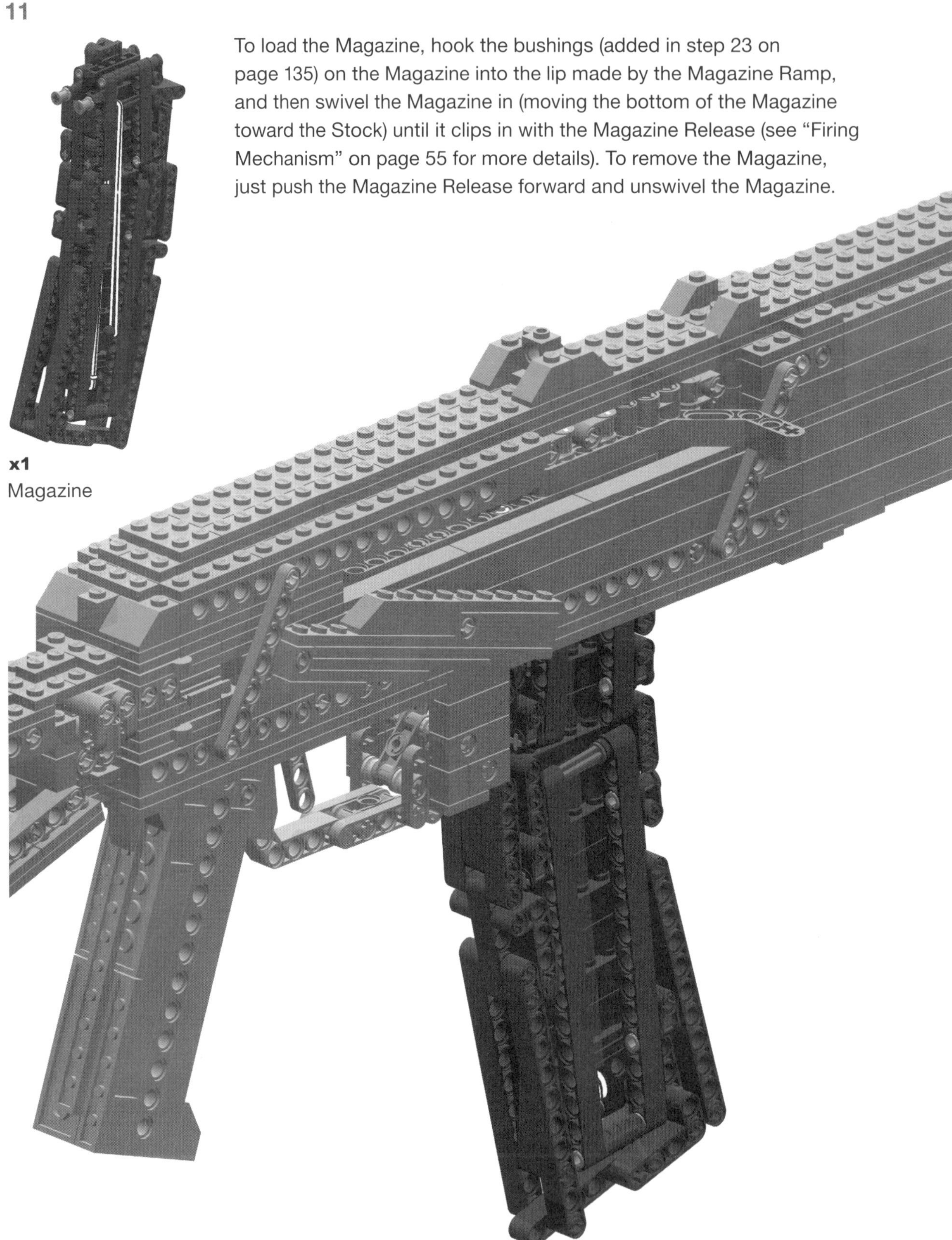

x1
Magazine

To load the Magazine, hook the bushings (added in step 23 on page 135) on the Magazine into the lip made by the Magazine Ramp, and then swivel the Magazine in (moving the bottom of the Magazine toward the Stock) until it clips in with the Magazine Release (see "Firing Mechanism" on page 55 for more details). To remove the Magazine, just push the Magazine Release forward and unswivel the Magazine.

MAGAZINE: OPTIONAL MODIFICATION

Sometimes, the force from the bricks in the Magazine is enough to push the little 1×2 plate off the top and let all the bricks fly free. For some people, this may happen often; others may never experience it. (The following suggestions are only for people who experience any problems with the plate—if you don't know what I'm talking about because you've never experienced it, then don't worry!)

A quick fix is to try using a different 1×2 plate—the one you were using may be worn, so there is not enough friction to hold it in place. However, if you've tried this and you find that you're still having this problem, try replacing the 1×2 plate with two #4274 pins, as shown on the right. While they don't stick out as much the plate does (so you may occasionally run into problems with a single brick popping out), there won't be the sort of explosive catastrophes like the ones you experienced with the 1×2 plate.

If you want to keep the plate and not resort to pins, there is a third possible option: Glue the 1×2 plate to the axle and pin connector. But I'm not a fan of gluing pieces together, so I wouldn't recommend it.

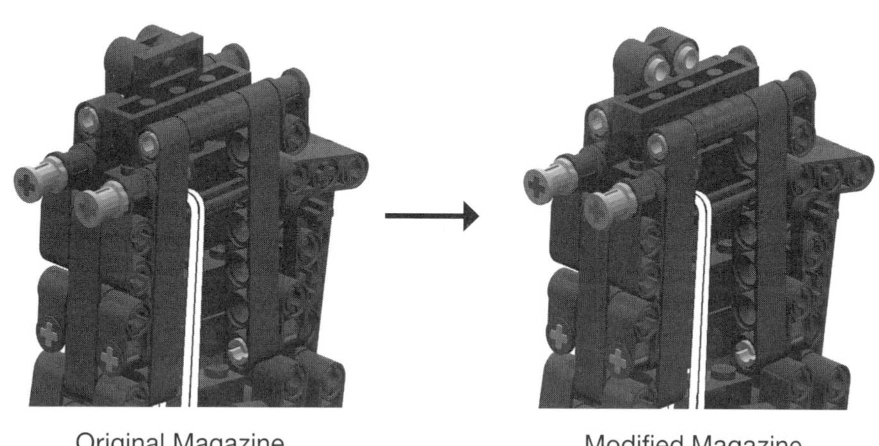

Original Magazine

Modified Magazine

JUNGLE

LENGTH: *120 studs*
WIDTH: *10.5 studs*
HEIGHT: *21 studs*
PIECES: *771*
MAGAZINE TYPE: *Detachable box magazine*
MAGAZINE CAPACITY: *Six 1×4 bricks*

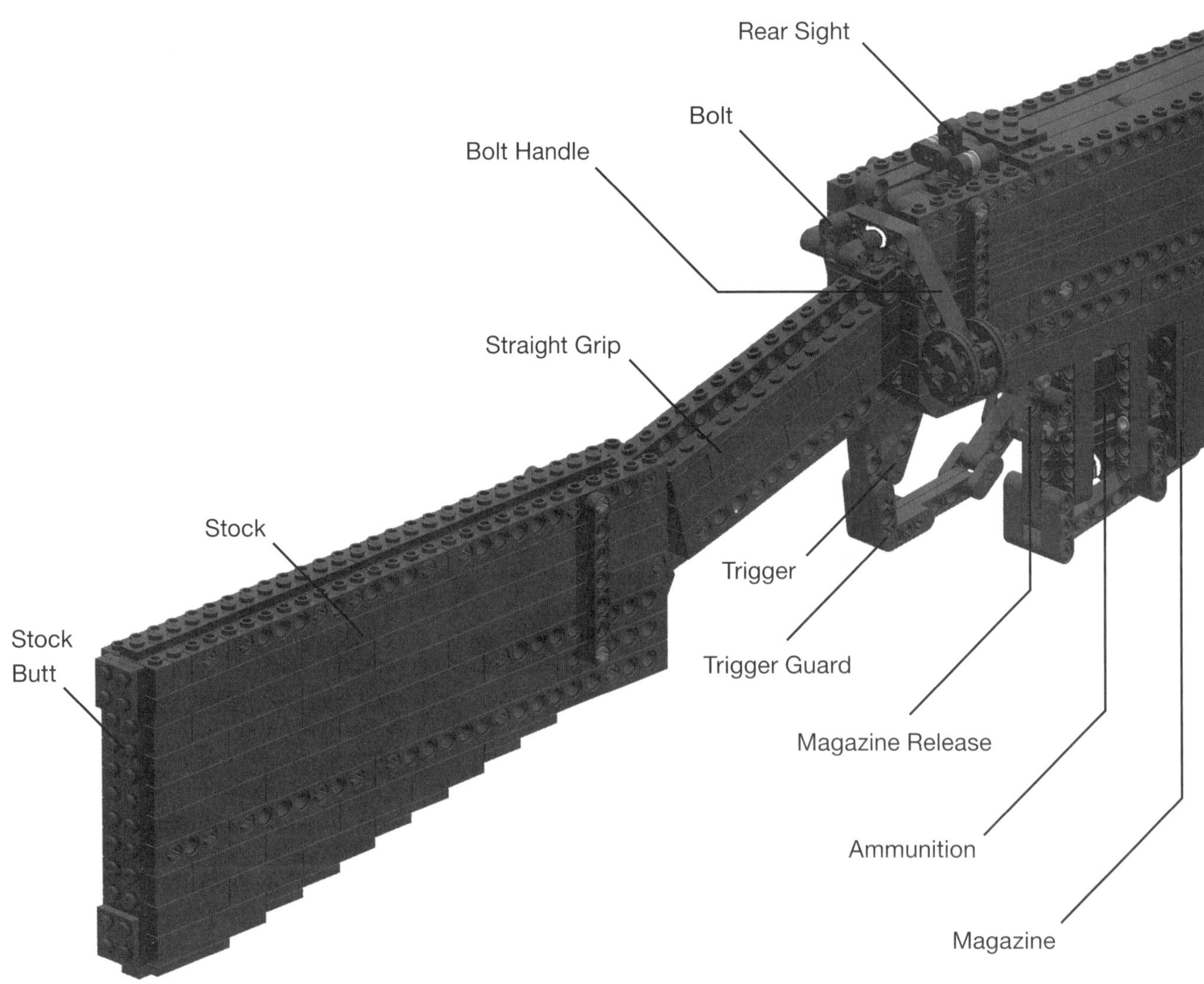

CARBINE

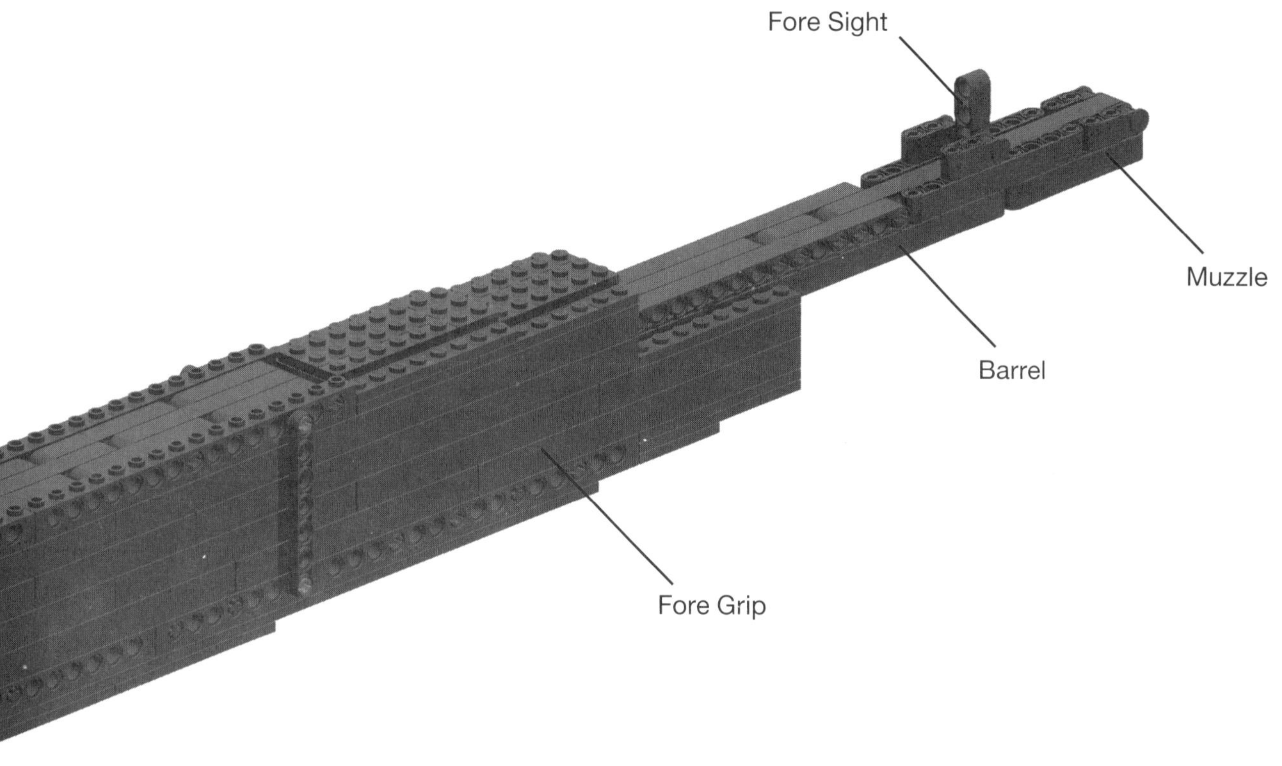

Also known as the Lee Enfield No. 5, the Jungle Carbine is a shorter, lighter version of the iconic Lee Enfield bolt-action rifle. The official standard-issue rifle for the British Army for more than 60 years, the Lee Enfield saw service in both world wars, and the total number produced is estimated at over 17 million rifles. While this is less than a fifth of the estimated AK rifles produced around the world, it's still a massive amount, especially considering the Lee Enfield was developed about 50 years earlier with inferior machinery.

With a classic rifle profile, the Lee Enfield looks fairly unremarkable, just another pointy-ended stick that goes "bang." However, it *was* better than most rifles at the time it was introduced, resulting in its widespread use in more than ten wars.

DESIGN HISTORY

The Lee Enfield was an important milestone for me, because it was my first reliable brick-shooting model that also vaguely looked the part. Until my first Lee Enfield design, I'd been fiddling around with various ways of powering firing mechanisms, some with bits of thread (which worked well but required regular maintenance), others that involved motors, and many that flat out didn't work.

In the early stages of developing the bolt-action firing mechanism (which I also used in several other models), I had little time for aesthetics. I just wanted to get the whole thing to work and fit inside a body that looked relatively gunlike. When my completed model looked suitably "pointy," I declared it a Lee Enfield . . . although in reality, the likeness left a lot to be desired.

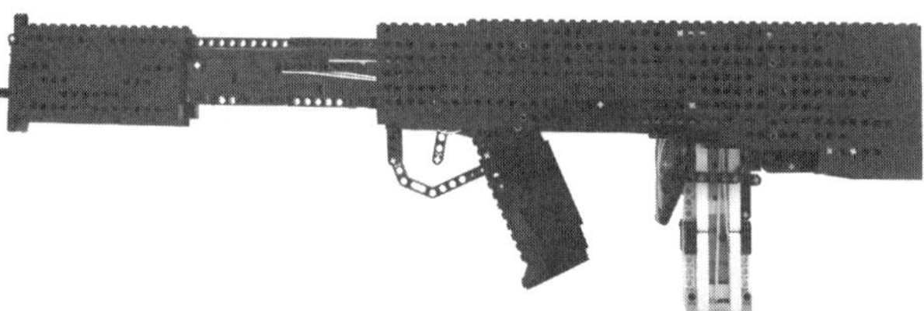

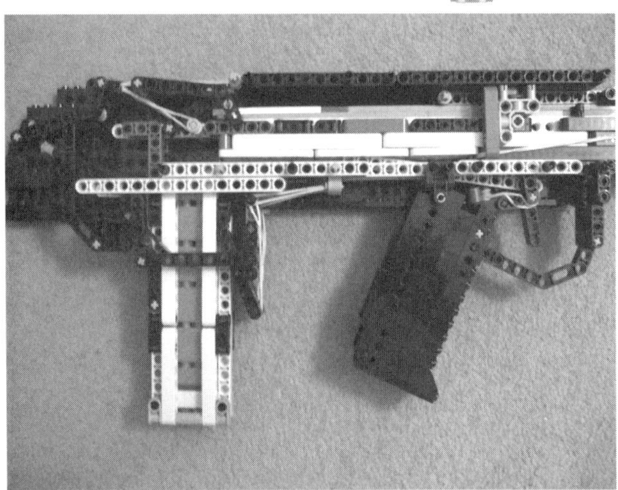

My Bullpup pump-action rifle was definitely a step in the right direction. Created less than a month before my original Lee Enfield model, the Bullpup was essentially the mechanism's first proper prototype.

The Lee Enfield turned out to be one of my most popular weapons. In June 2010, over a year after I first posted it online, a flurry of articles about it appeared on the Internet, drawing more attention to my other designs and even leading to the publication of this book. By then, I'd made about 20 new weapons, all of which were fairly popular. I remember thinking, "Why are people so interested in the Lee Enfield? Why not one of my more recent guns, like the AK-47 or L85?" But I have since realized that the writers of those articles really did pick the best gun to showcase. The original Lee Enfield was a breakthrough model; rather than half-heartedly firing bricks and vaguely resembling its namesake, it *does* fire and *does* look like it's supposed to.

About six months after these articles appeared, I began to think it was time to stop building. I believed that, with my design of the G36 family, I had gone as far as I was going to get, in terms of power, for bolt-action mechanisms. But then I had flash of inspiration. I realized that while I may well have maximized power for a gun whose rubber bands were stretched as the bolt was pulled *backward*, there was probably even more power available in a gun whose bands were stretched as the bolt was pushed *forward*.

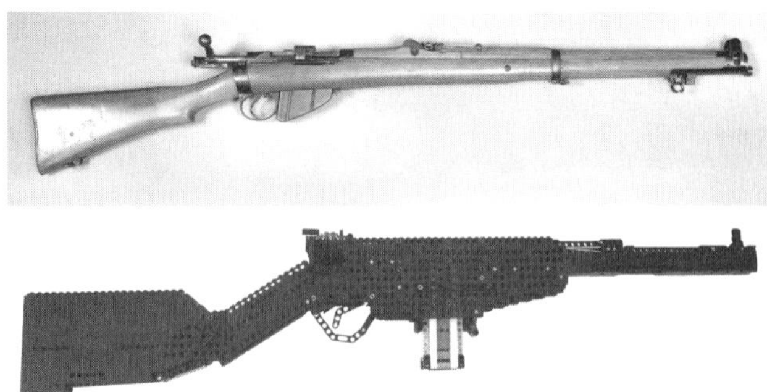

Built without any reference to the real thing, my first Lee Enfield bears hardly even a passing resemblance to its namesake, but I didn't really mind. It was hard enough just finding enough pieces to make it all black!

Most of the replicas I'd made were of automatic weapons, in which the mechanism is cycled with the rearward pull of the bolt, and this made them totally unsuitable for this new mechanism I had in mind. I needed a true bolt-action model, so I decided that it would be fitting for my final gun to be a remake of the most significant model I'd ever created, the Lee Enfield.

This time, I put more effort into the aesthetics and used a 1:1 printout. After some experimentation, I discovered I liked the look of the Jungle Carbine with its shorter barrel that was exposed before the end of the receiver. It gave the project a fresh face and made it more than just another revision. And although it *is* a little piece-heavy, it's definitely worth the effort and is easily the most powerful and most accurate LEGO gun I've ever made.

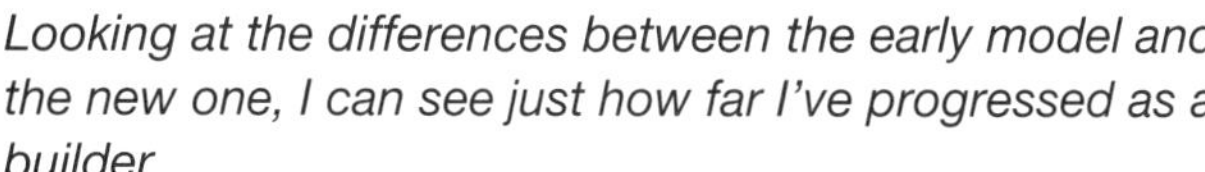

Looking at the differences between the early model and the new one, I can see just how far I've progressed as a builder.

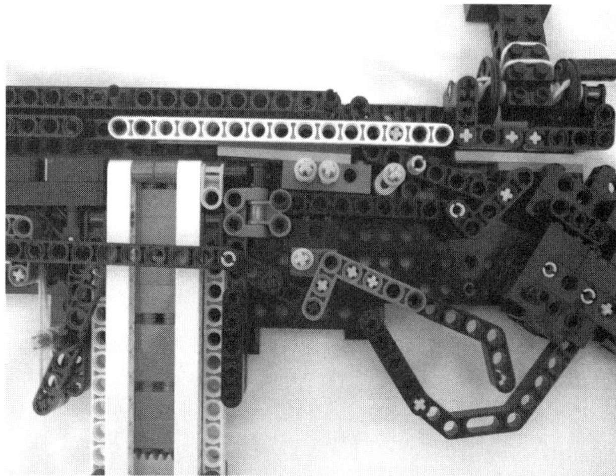

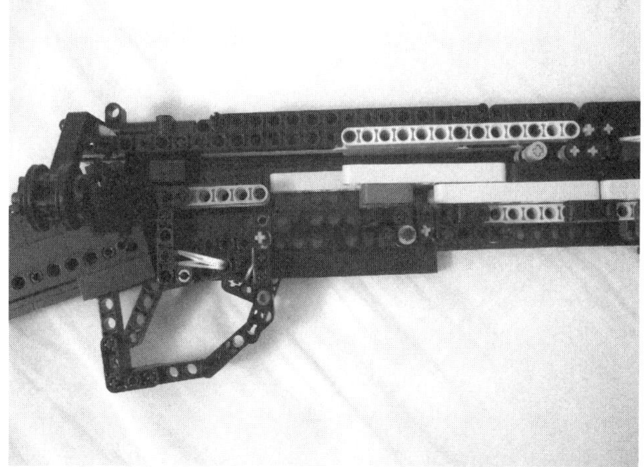

Although a complex mechanism can be mesmerizing to look at, the real winner is the design that is the simplest.

HOW IT WORKS

To cock the gun, it's best to flip the Bolt Handle up and then use the Bolt itself, not the ball-end of the Bolt Handle, to pull the Bolt back (see step 4). The same goes for pushing the Bolt back into the receiver—in fact it's more important here since the bands are being stretched: Press the back of the Bolt, not the actual Bolt Handle, forward with your thumb. I've added arrows to the relevant diagrams to demonstrate what I mean. Operating the weapon's action in this way makes it much smoother and easier, while also putting less stress on the pieces.

1

Insert the Magazine. Note that the magazine release has rotated out of the way.

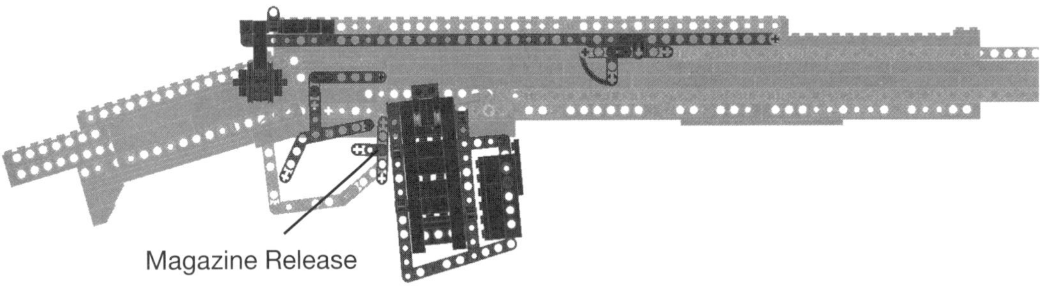

2

When the Magazine is fully inserted, the magazine release flicks back to its normal position, which locks the Magazine in place.

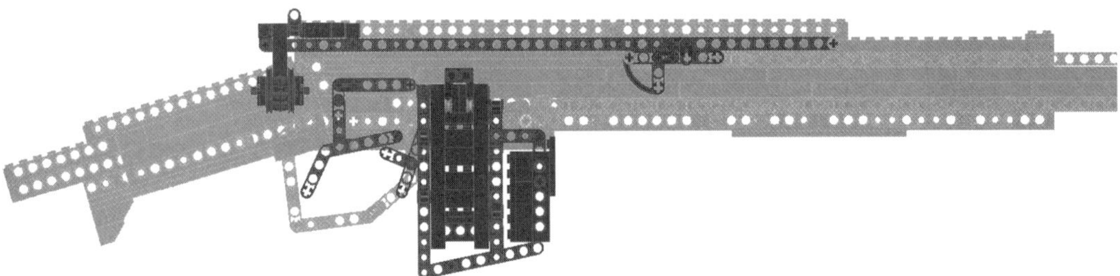

3

Flip the Bolt Handle up.

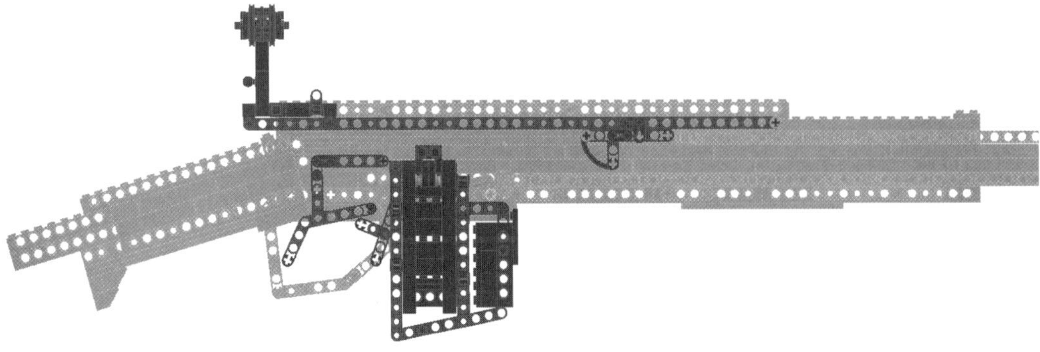

4

Begin pulling the Bolt backward. This also pulls the Hammer back. As the Hammer passes over the Magazine, the bricks inside are depressed.

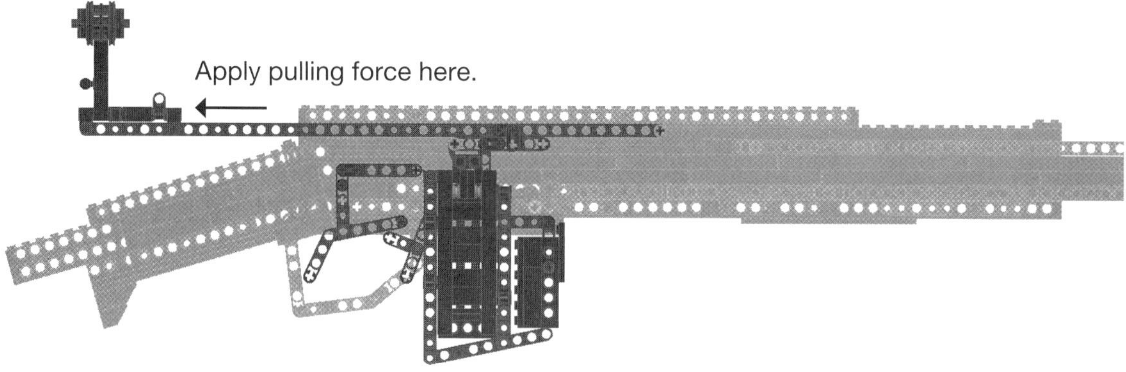

5

Continue pulling the Bolt backward. Once the Hammer has passed by the Magazine, the bricks can move back up to their normal position. Now, the Hammer presses down on the trigger mechanism.

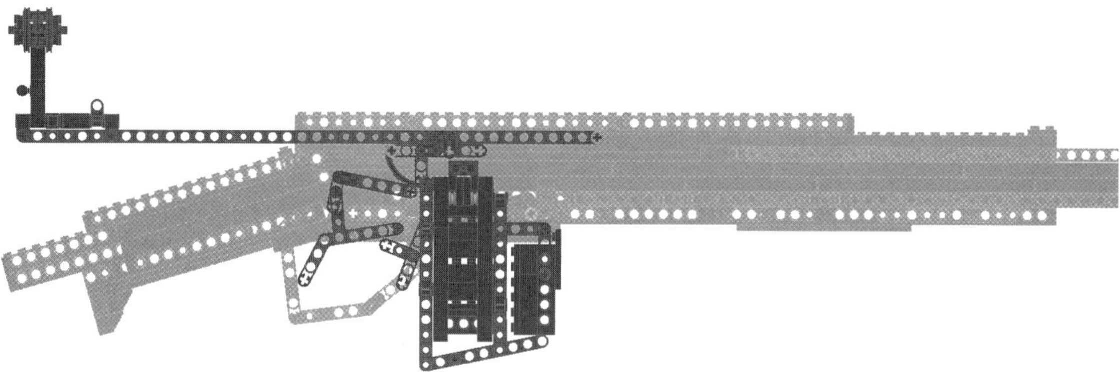

6

With the Bolt pulled out fully, the Hammer is locked inside the trigger mechanism.

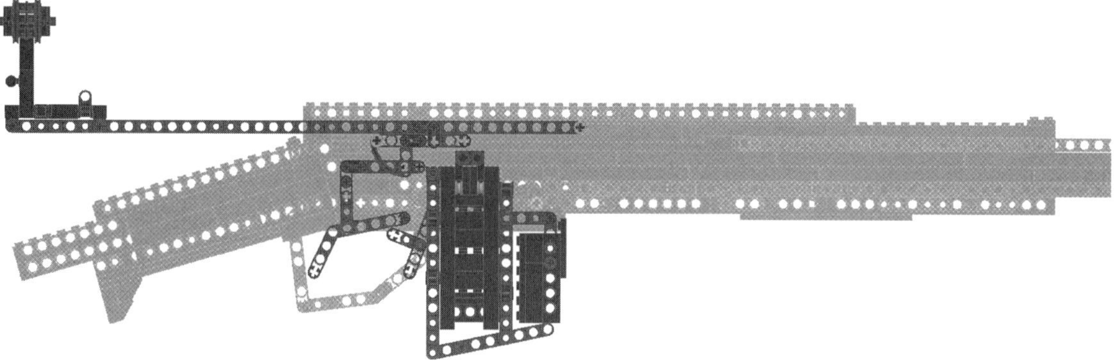

7

Pushing the Bolt back into the receiver stretches the rubber bands.

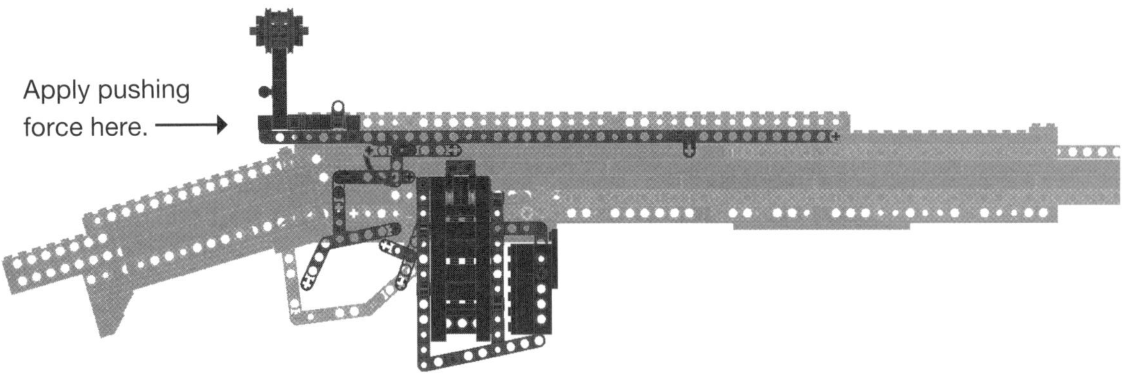

8

Flip down the Bolt Handle to lock the Bolt in the forward position. Now the tension from the rubber bands can't push it back out.

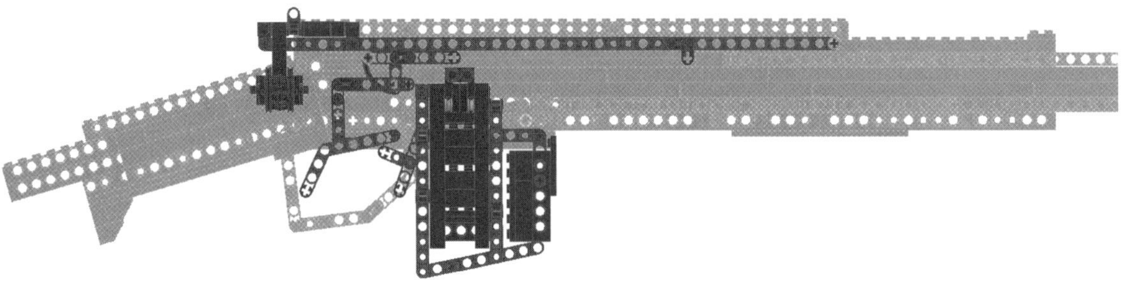

9

Pull the Trigger to release the Hammer.

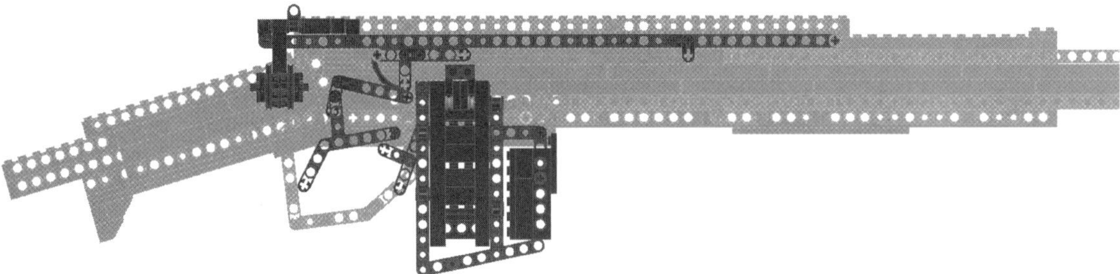

10

As the Hammer moves forward, it hits the back of the top brick in the Magazine, pushing it into the Barrel.

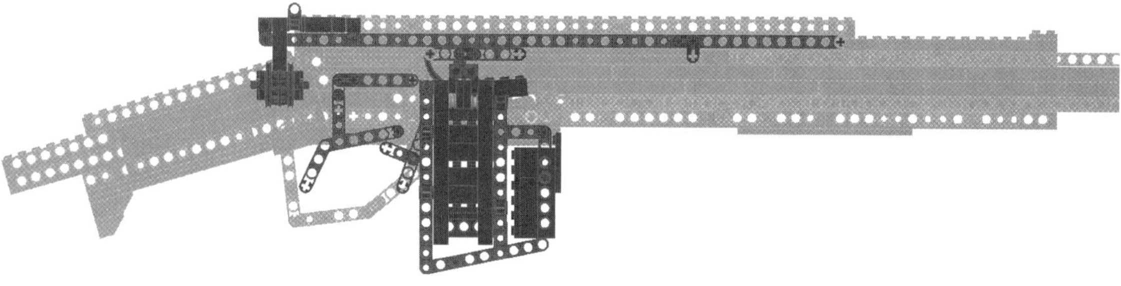

11

The Hammer and brick continue down the Barrel.

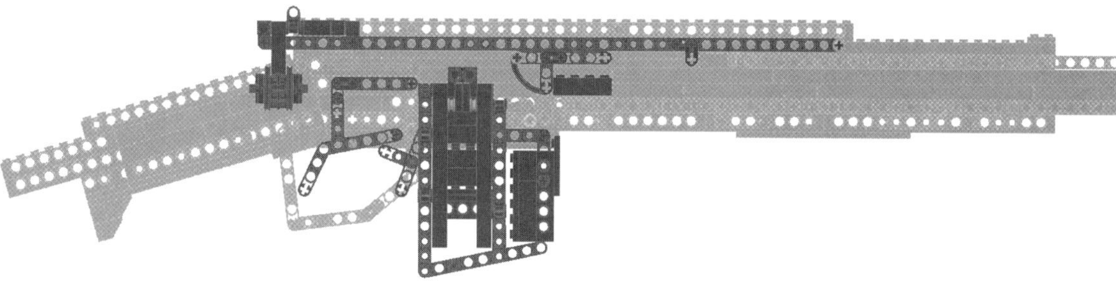

12

The Hammer stops moving forward once it hits the protruding part of the Bolt (it is now in its original position), but the brick continues down the Barrel and out the muzzle.

BILL OF MATERIALS

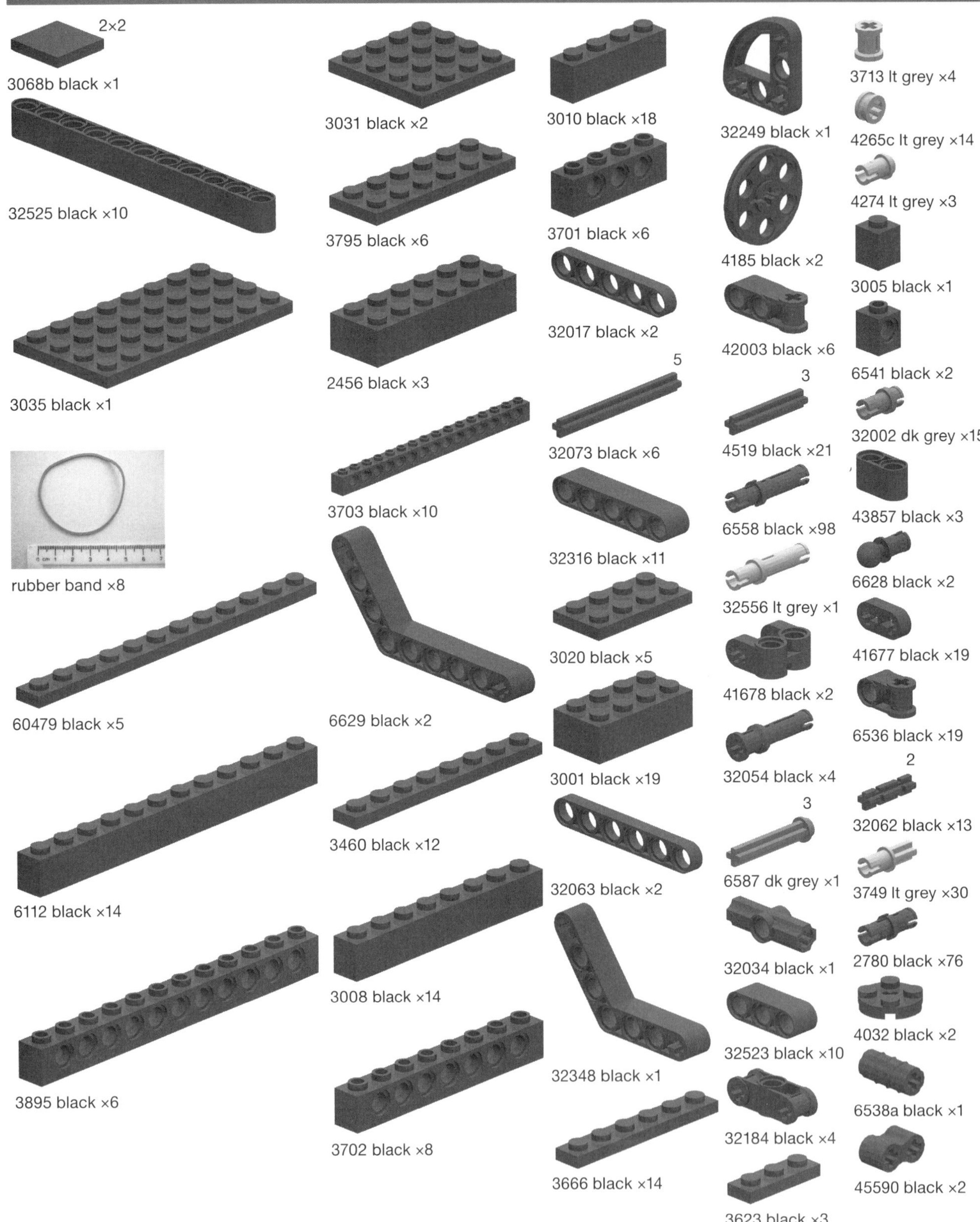

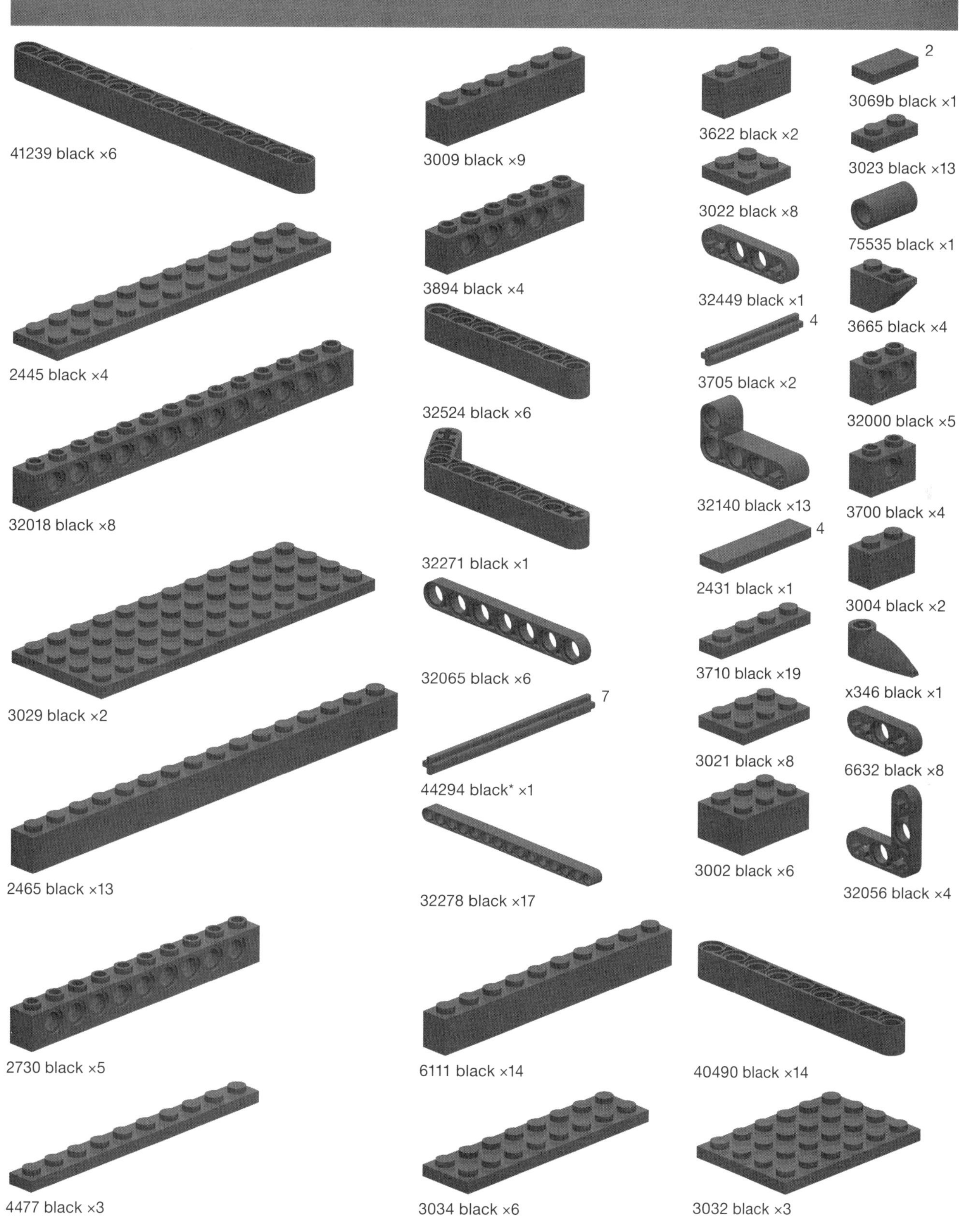

* Although this piece is available in black, you're far more likely to find it in light grey.

FRAME WALL LEFT

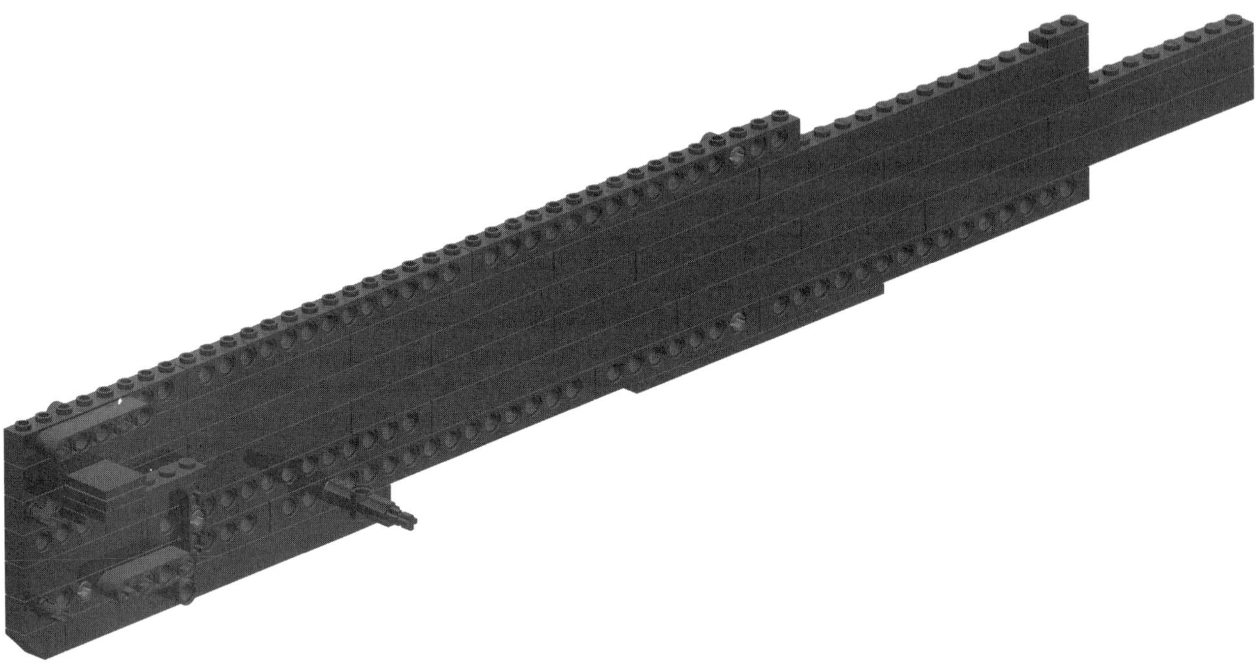

1

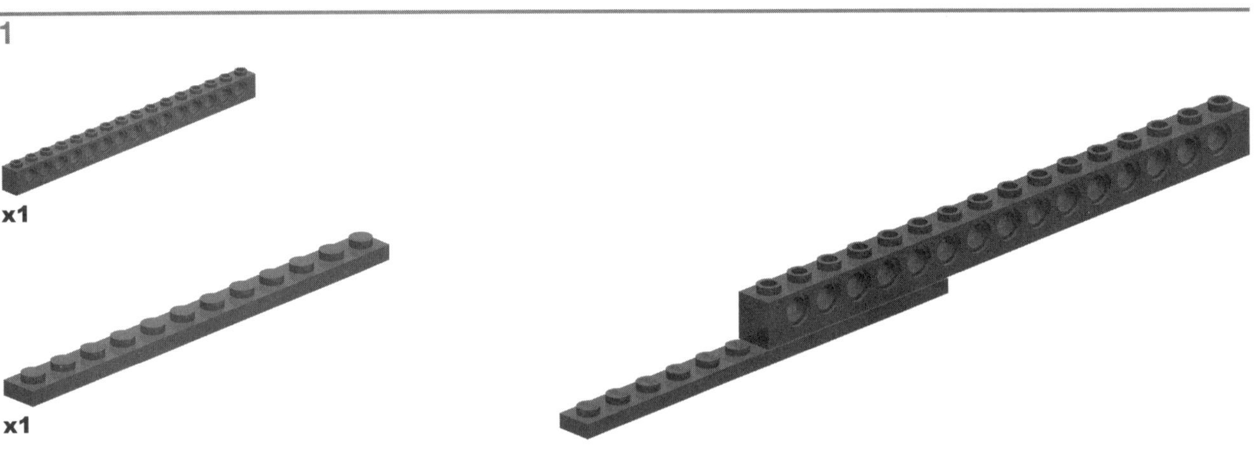

2

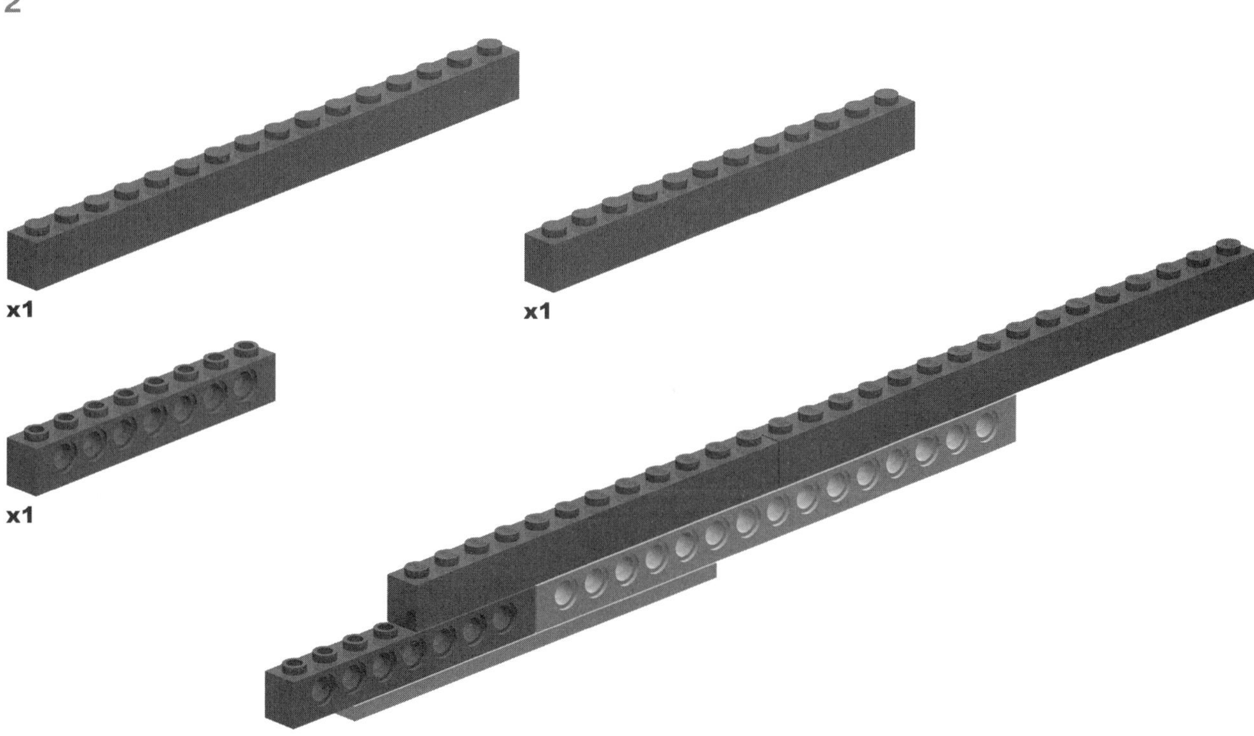

3

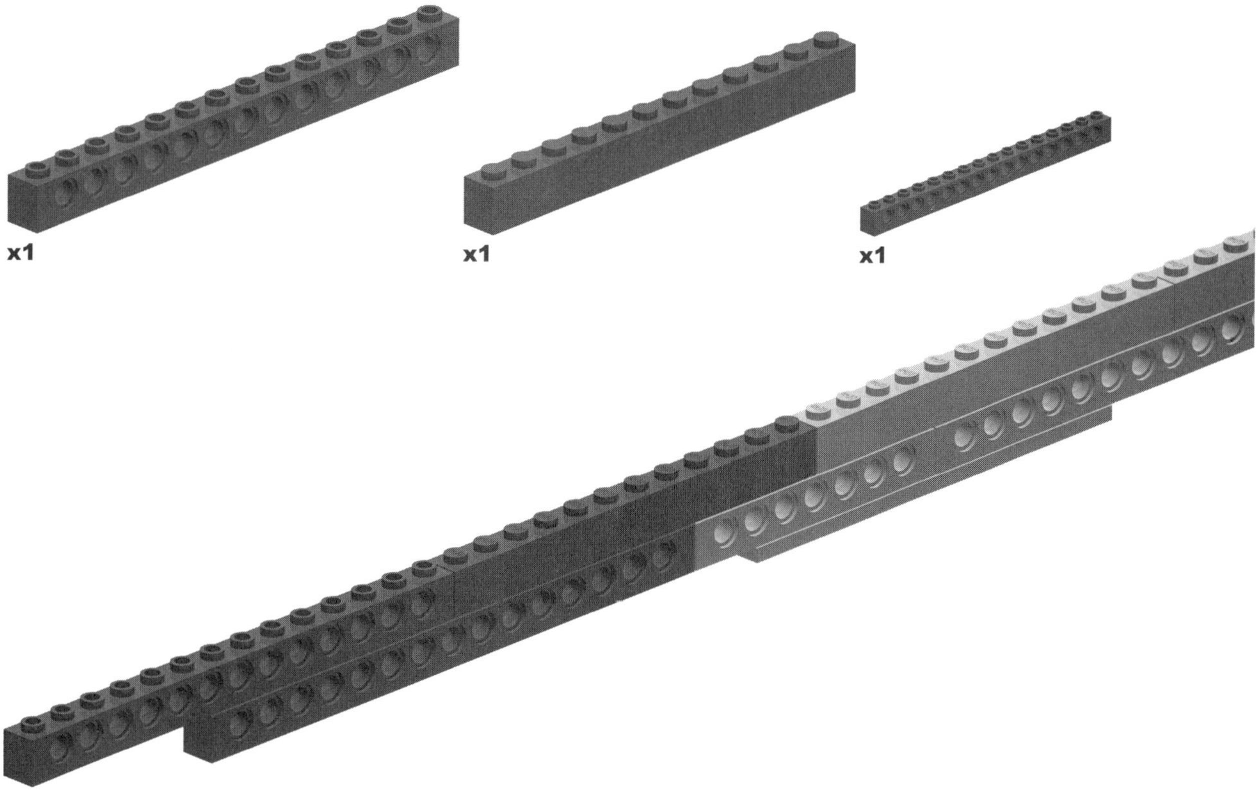

x1 x1 x1

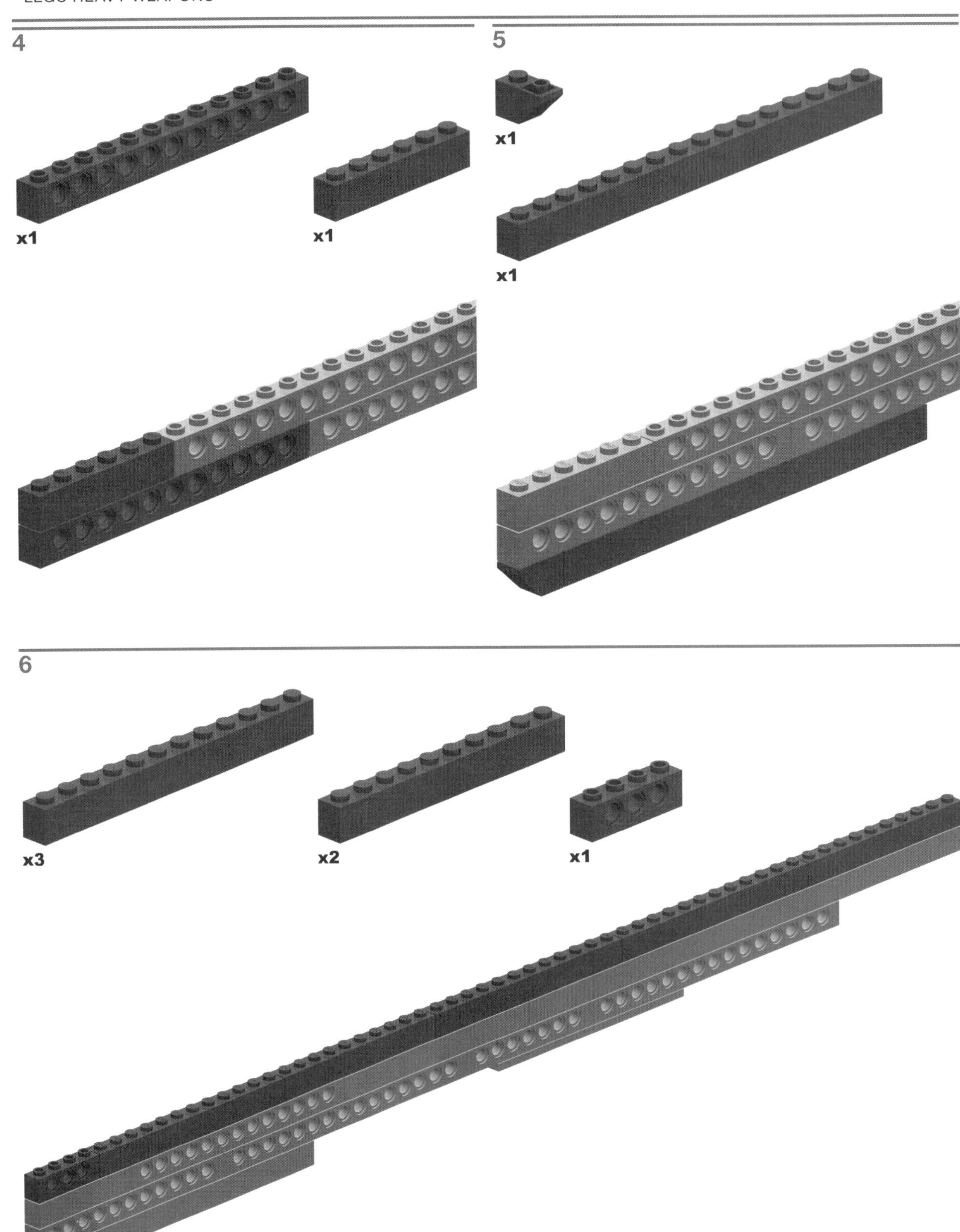
4
x1
x1
5
x1
x1
6
x3
x2
x1

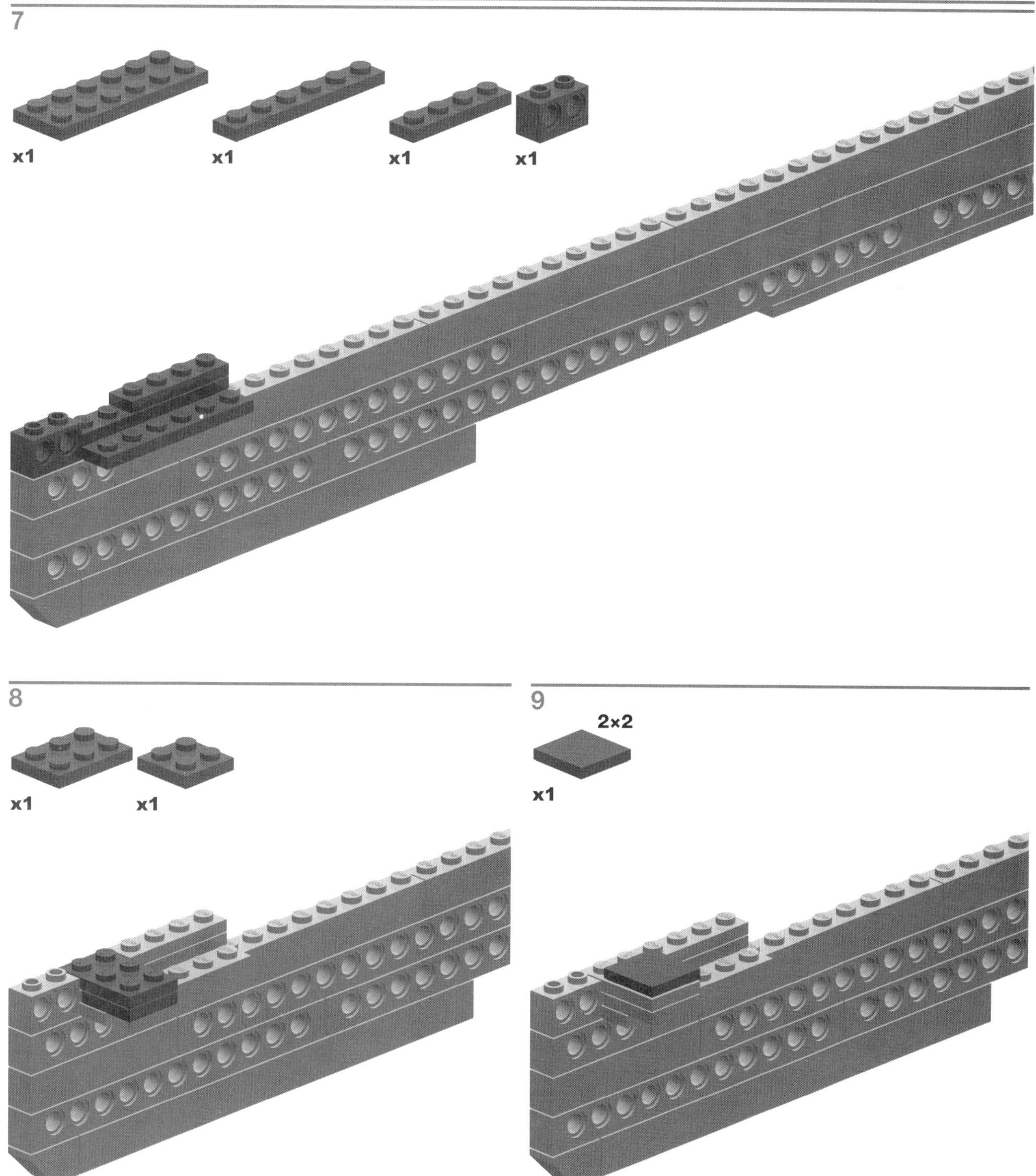
7
x1
x1
x1
x1
8
x1
x1
9
2×2
x1

10

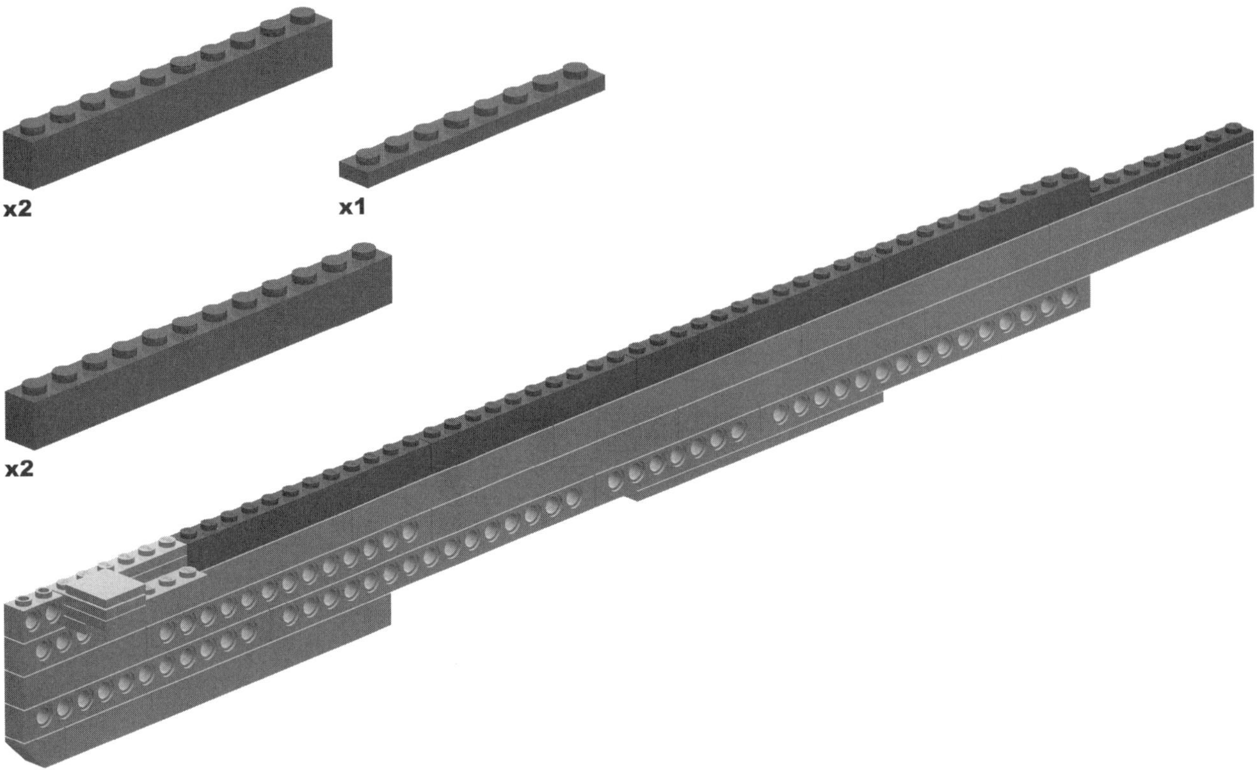

x2

x1

x2

11

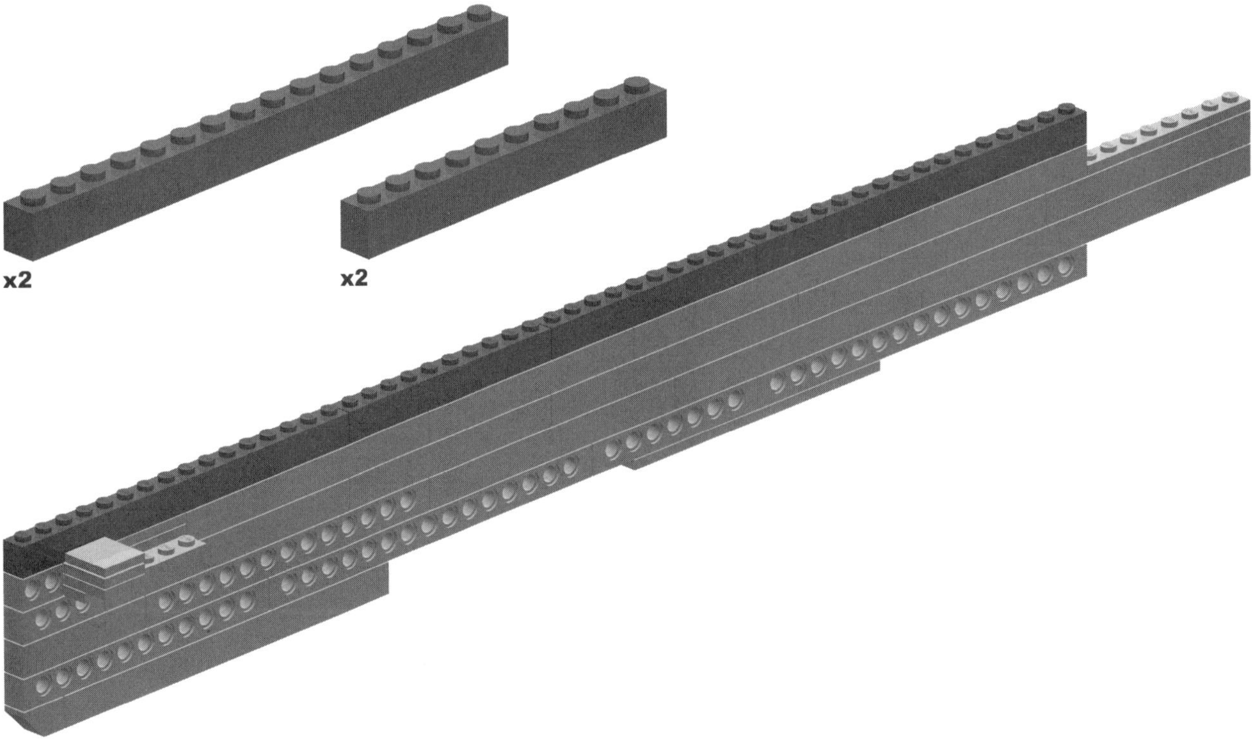

x2

x2

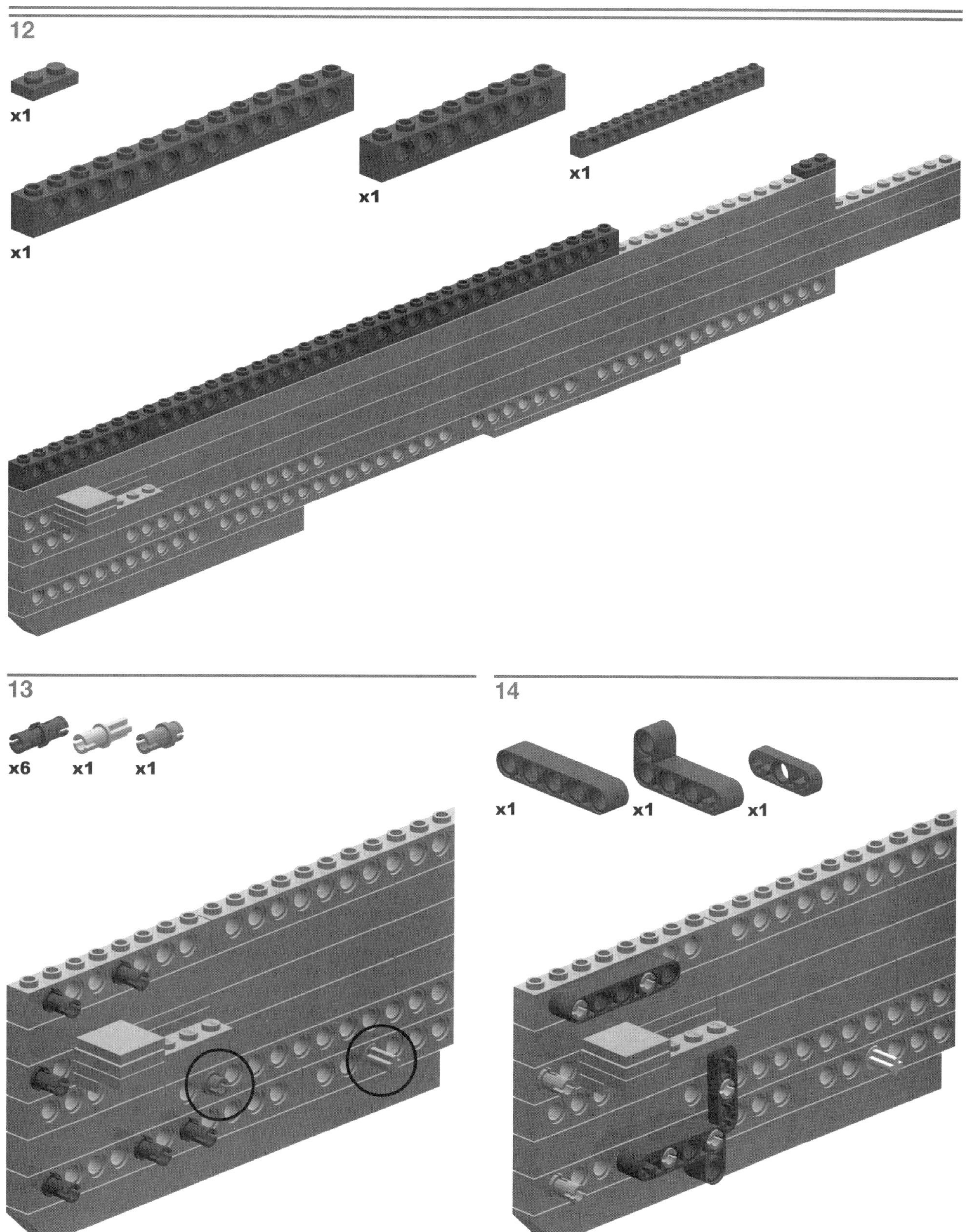
12
x1
x1
x1
x1
13
x6
x1
x1
14
x1
x1
x1

15

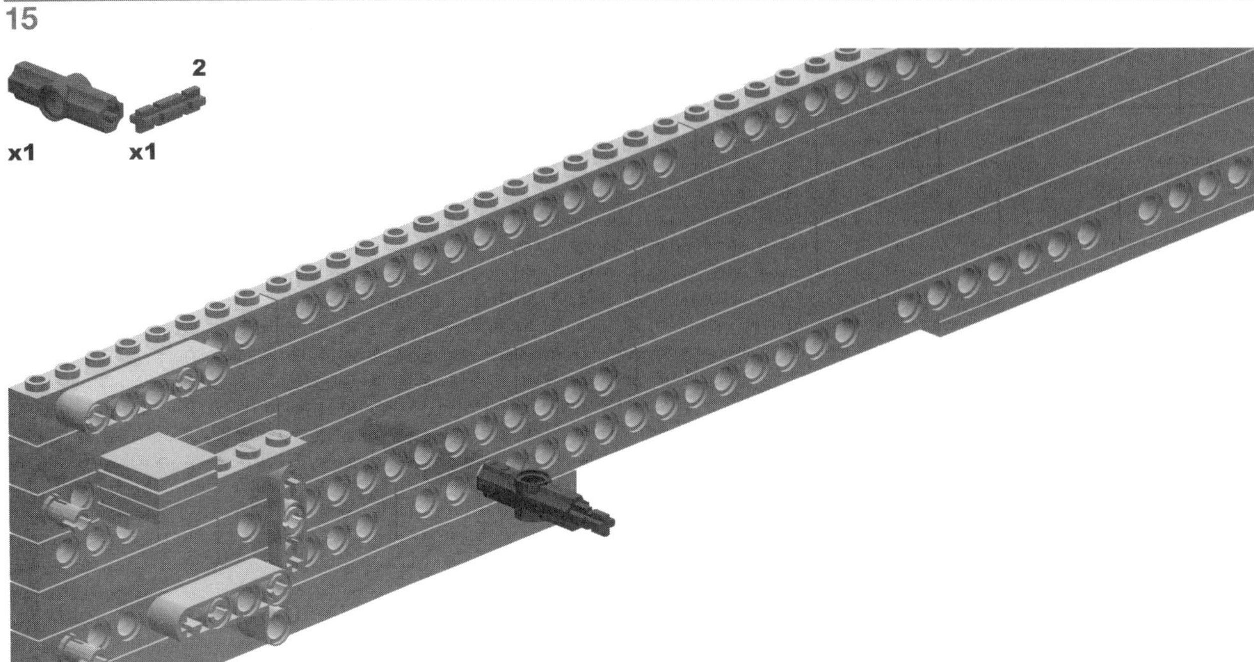

16

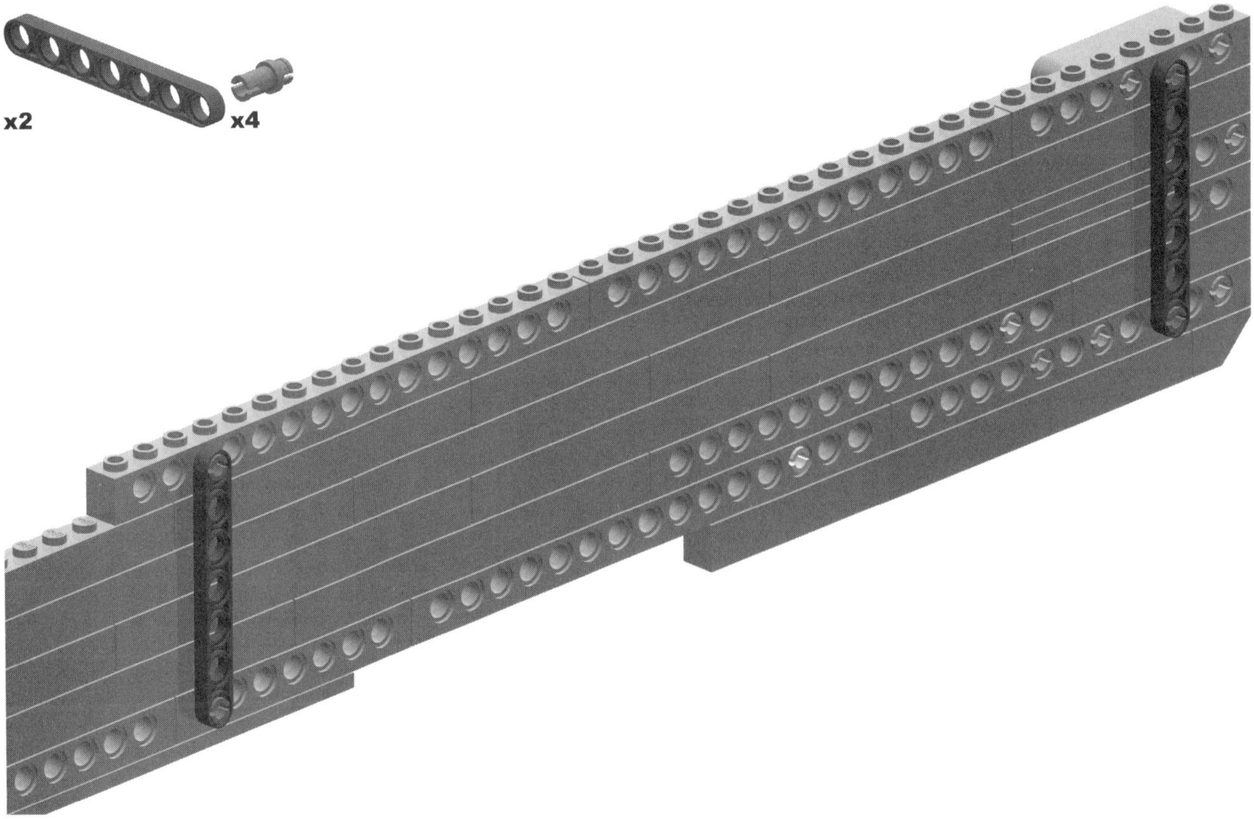

x2 x4

TRIGGER GUARD

1

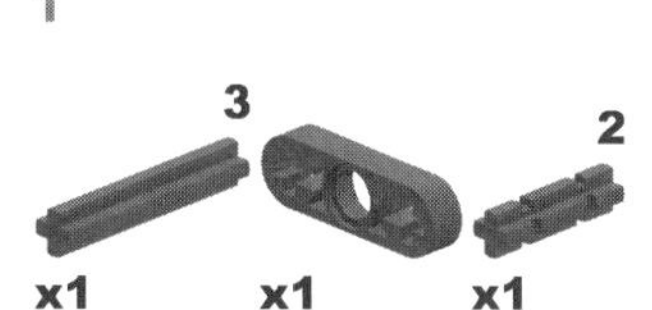

2

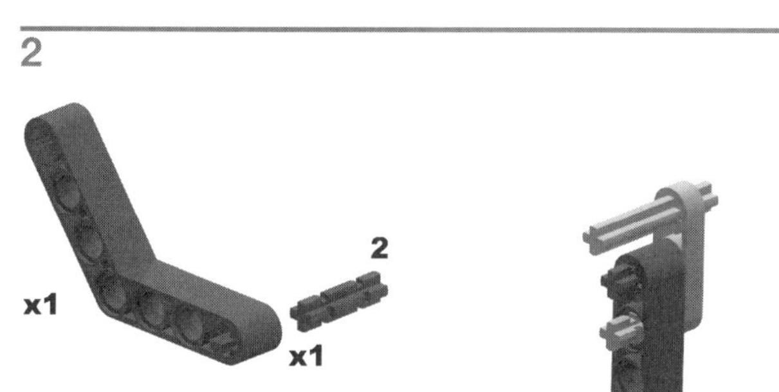

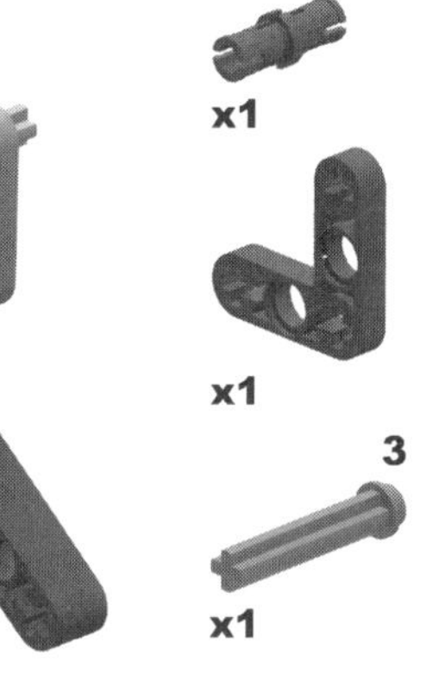

3

x1

x1

3

x1

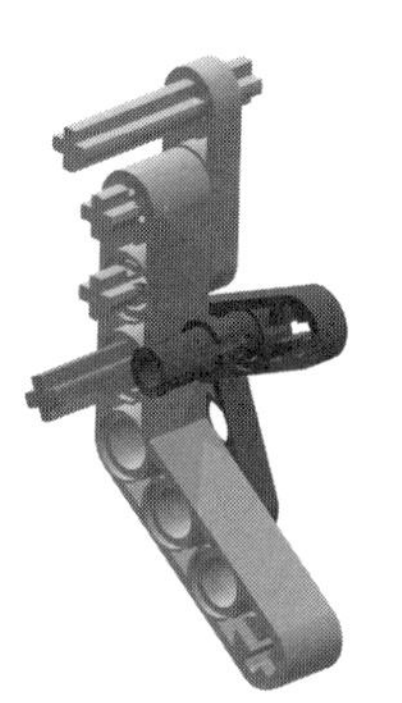

4

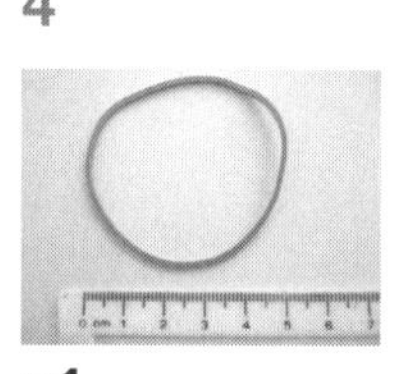

x1

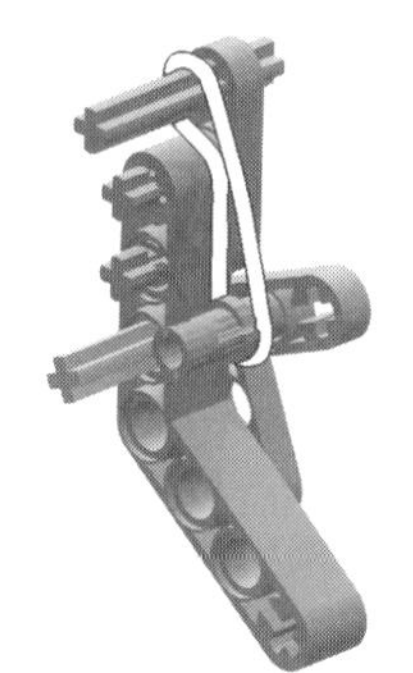

5

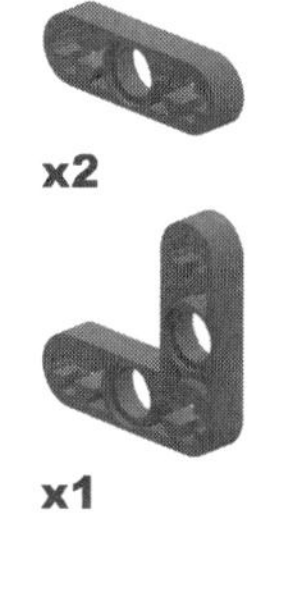

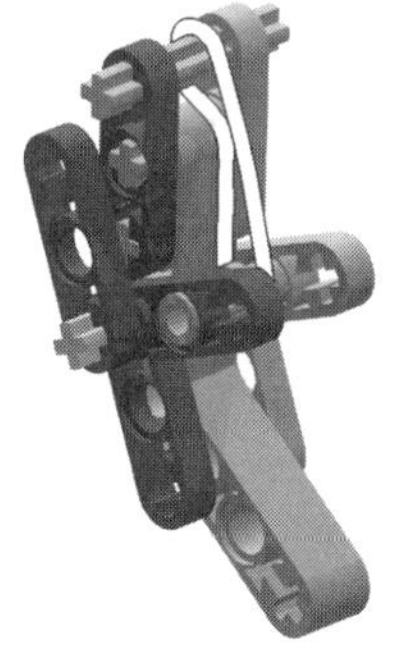

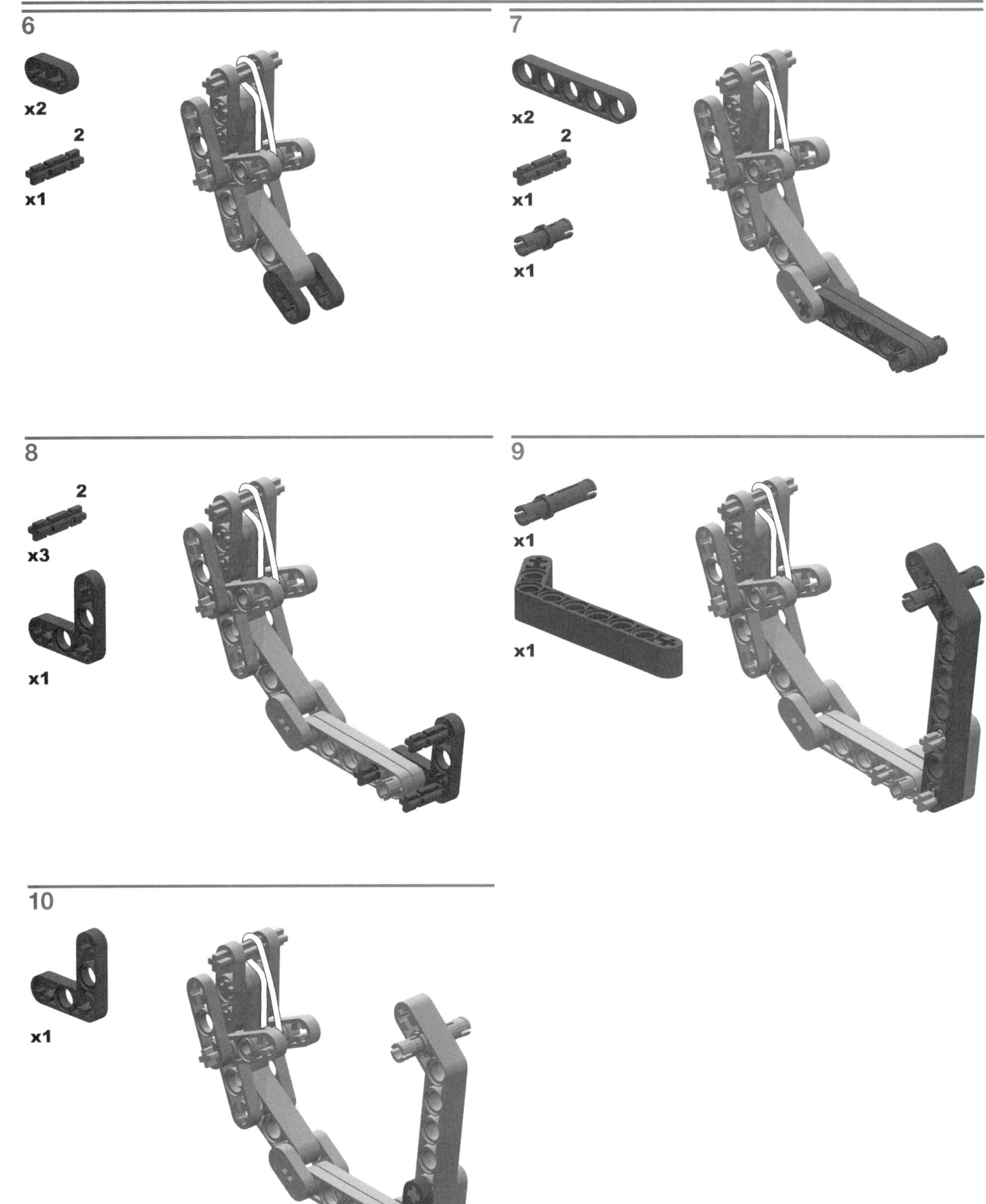
6
x2
2
x1
7
x2
2
x1
x1
8
2
x3
x1
9
x1
x1
10
x1

STOCK GRIP

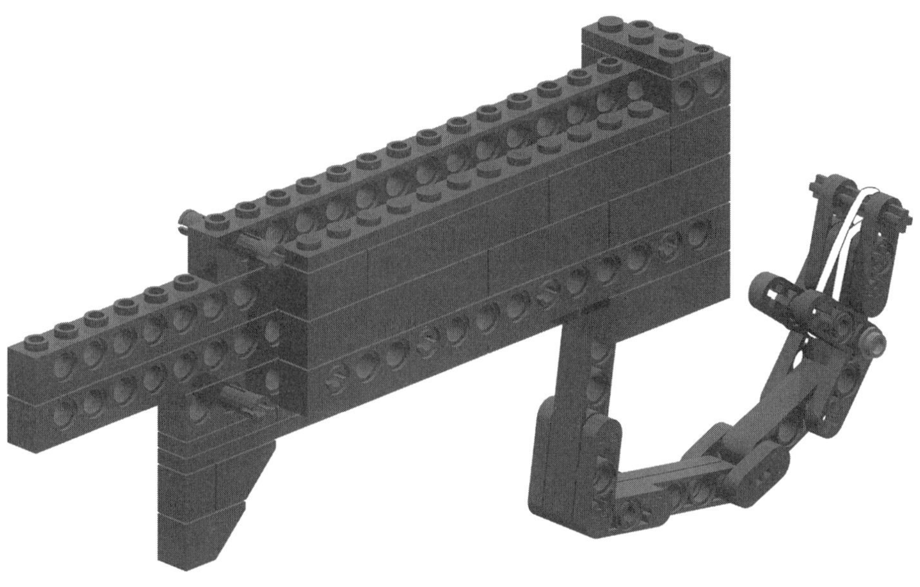

1

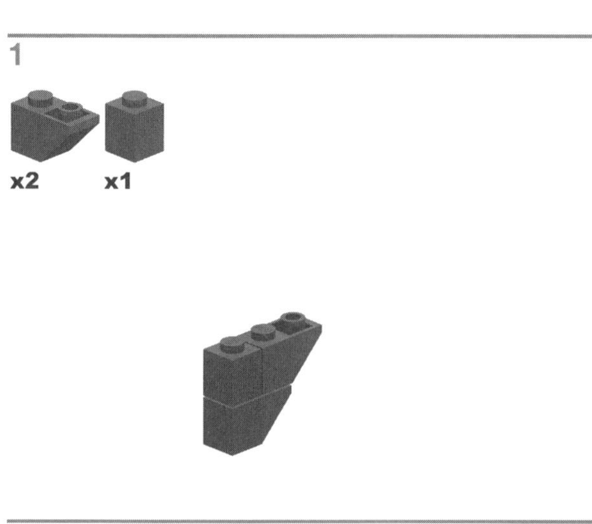

2

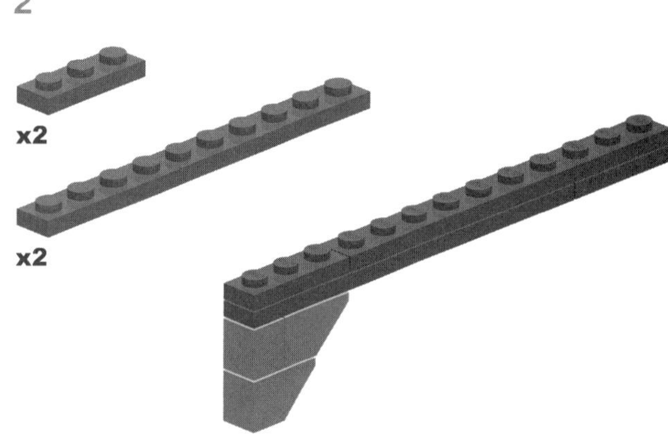

3

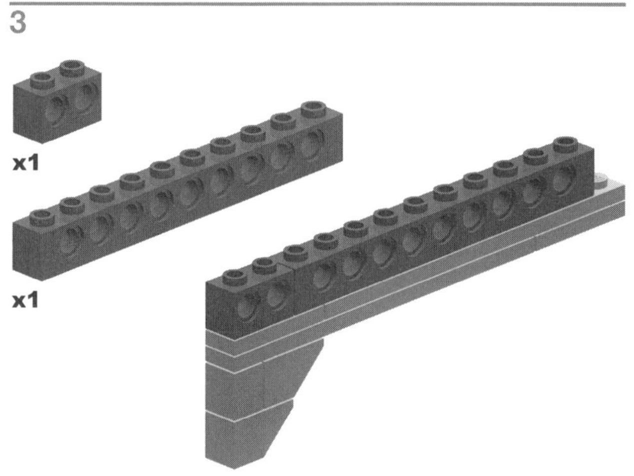

4

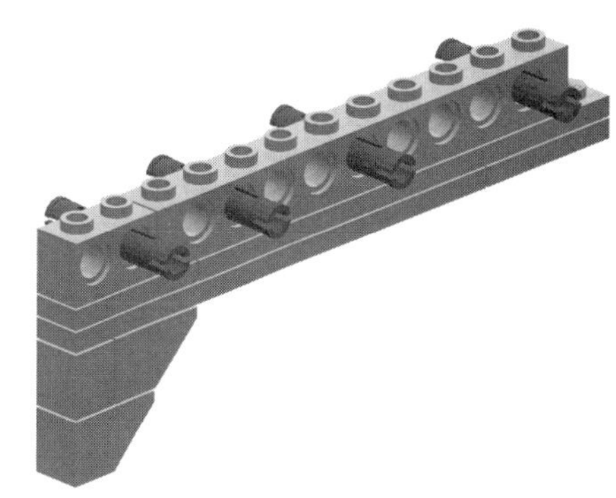

5

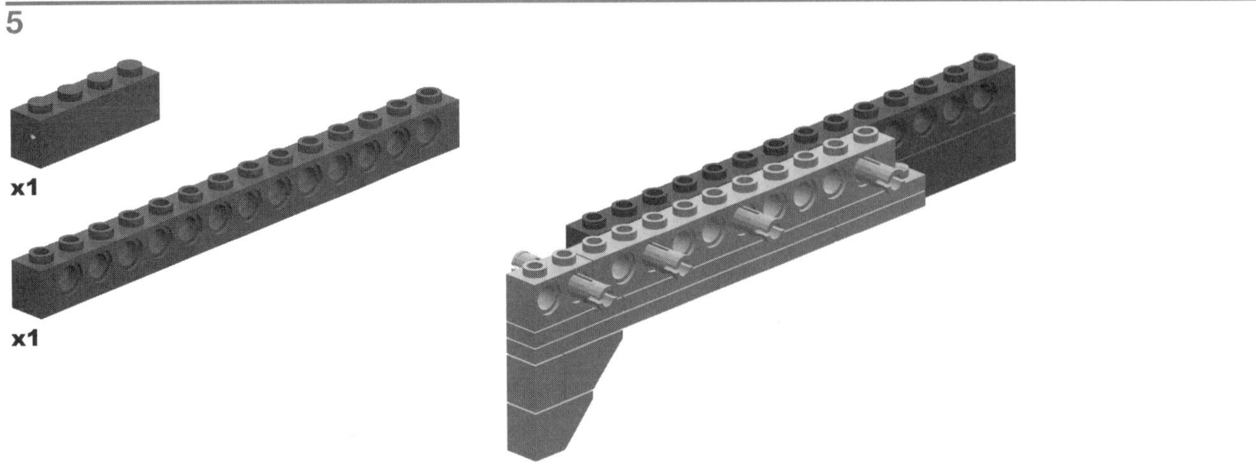

6

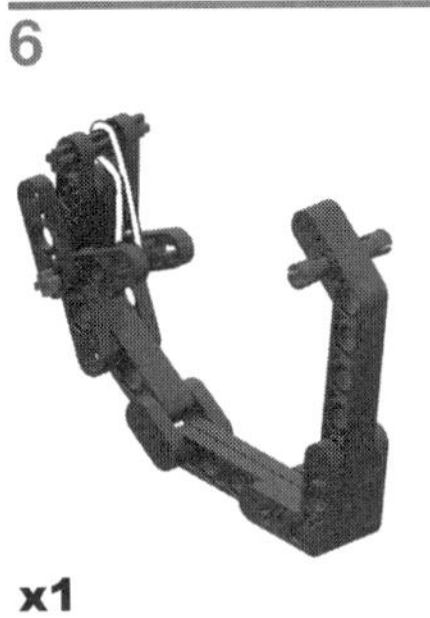

Trigger Guard

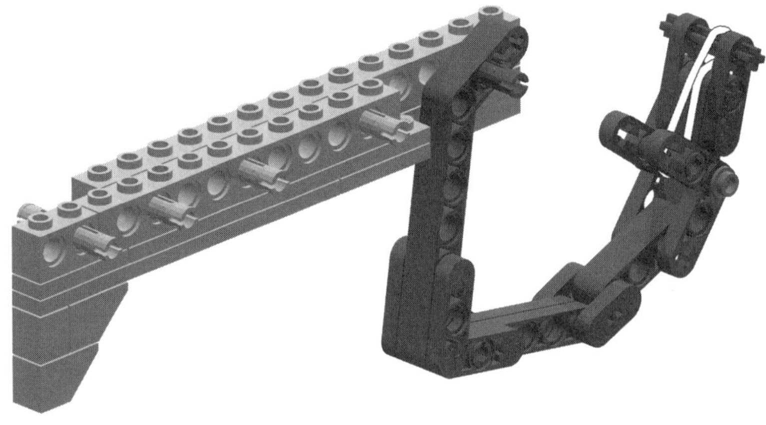

7

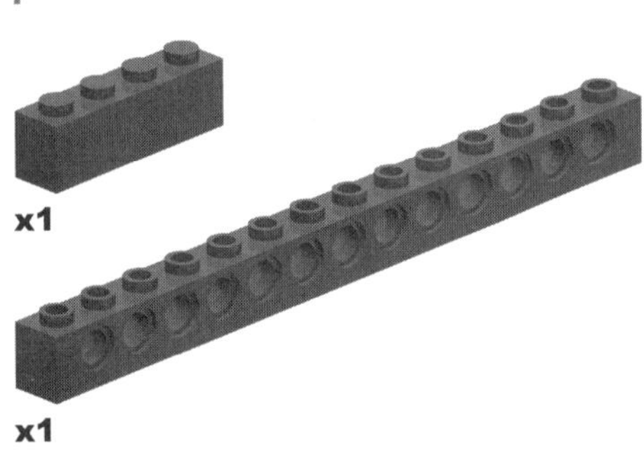

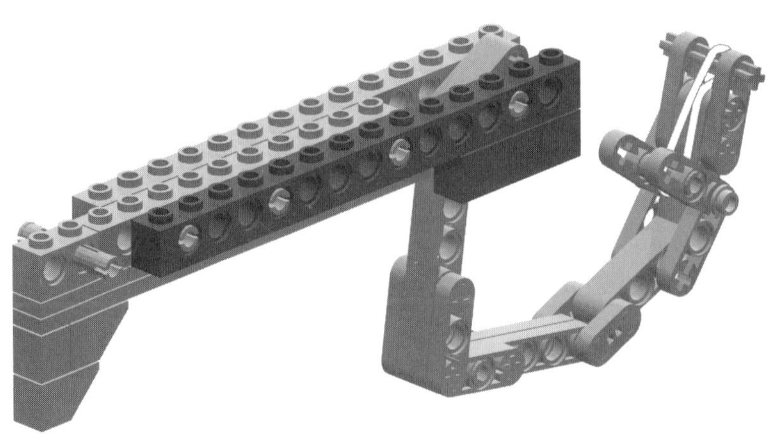

8

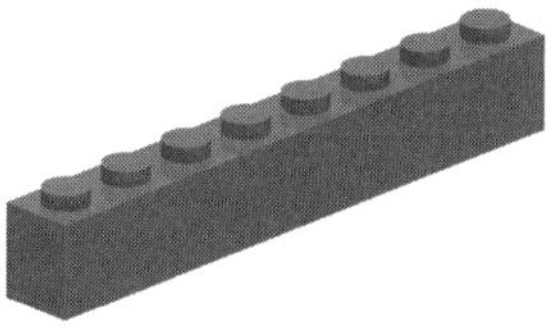

x1 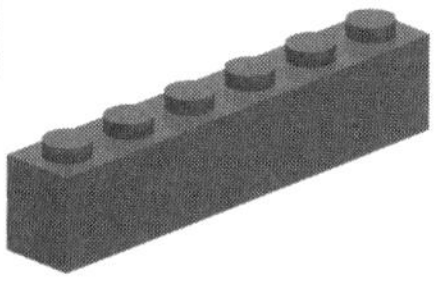 x1

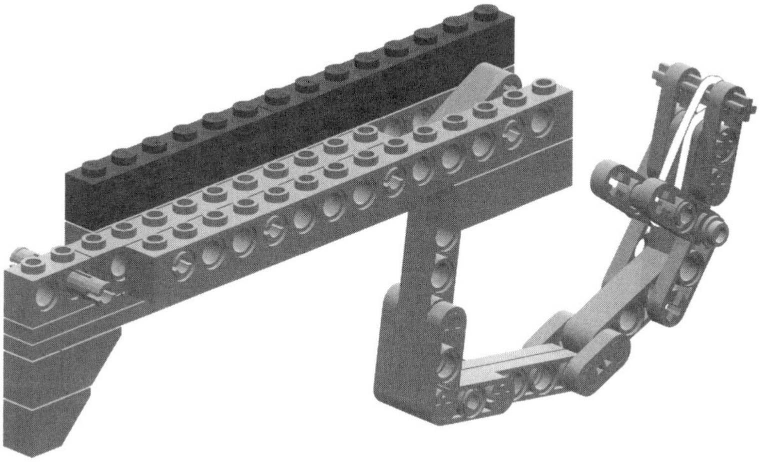

9

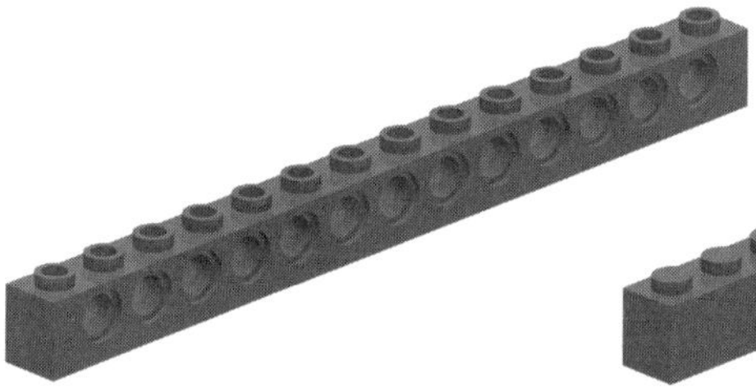

x1 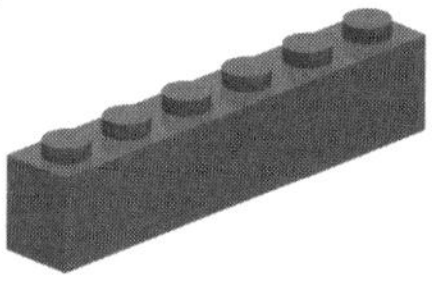 x1

x1 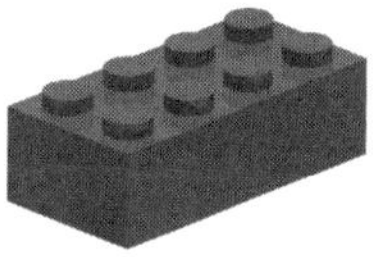 x1 x1

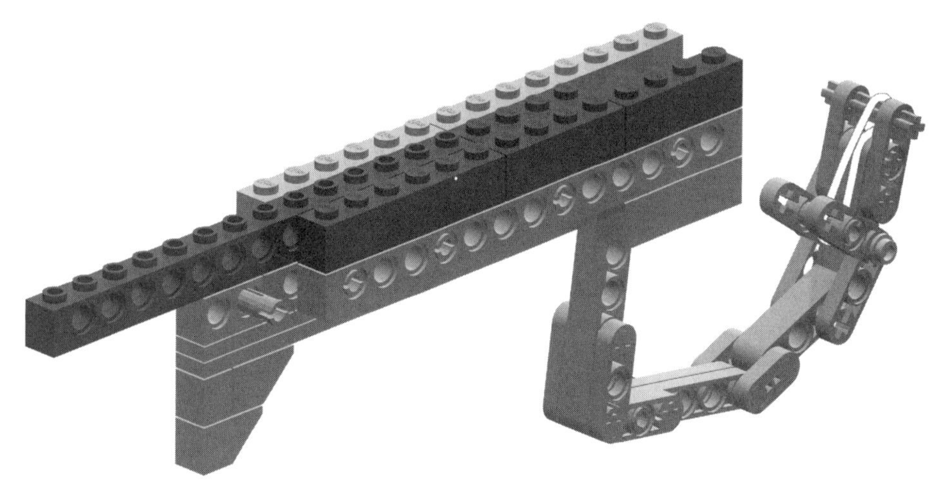

10

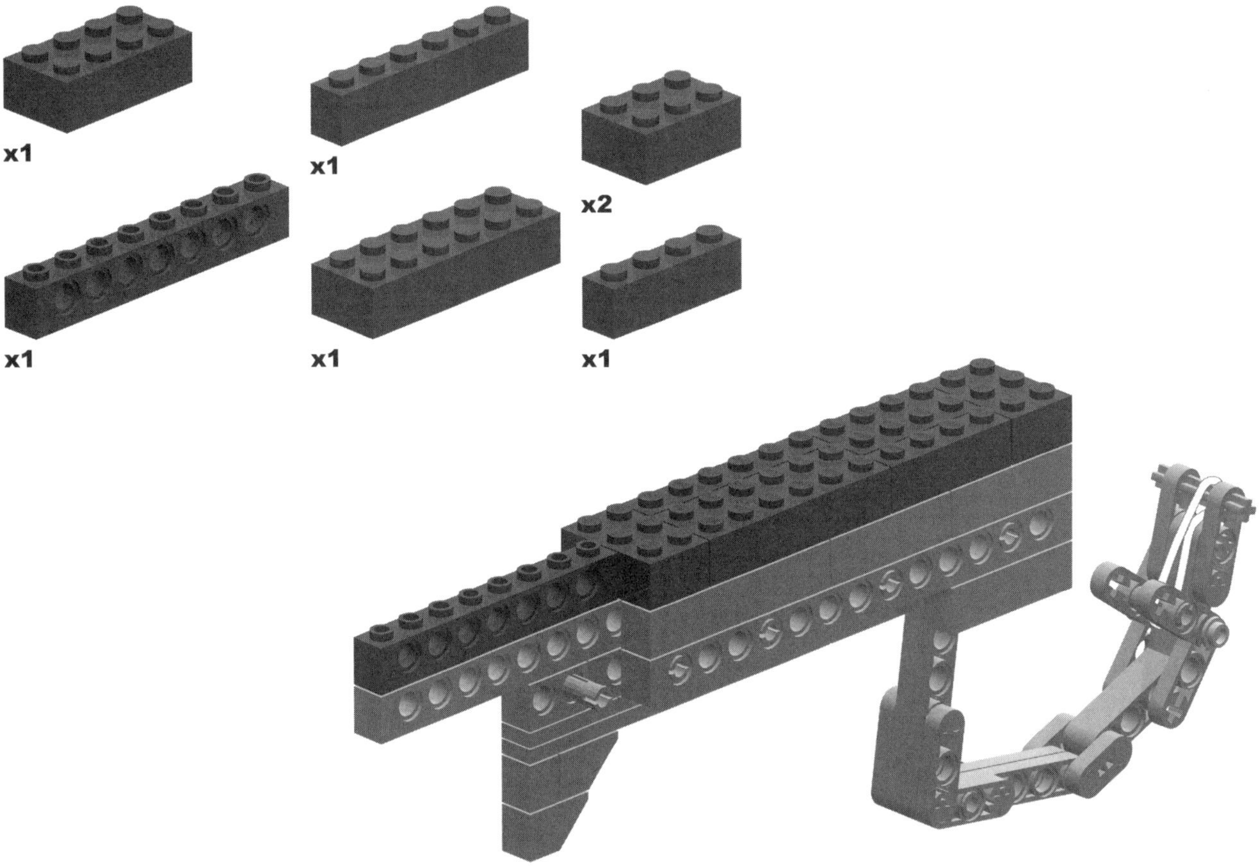

x1

x1

x2

x1

x1

x1

11

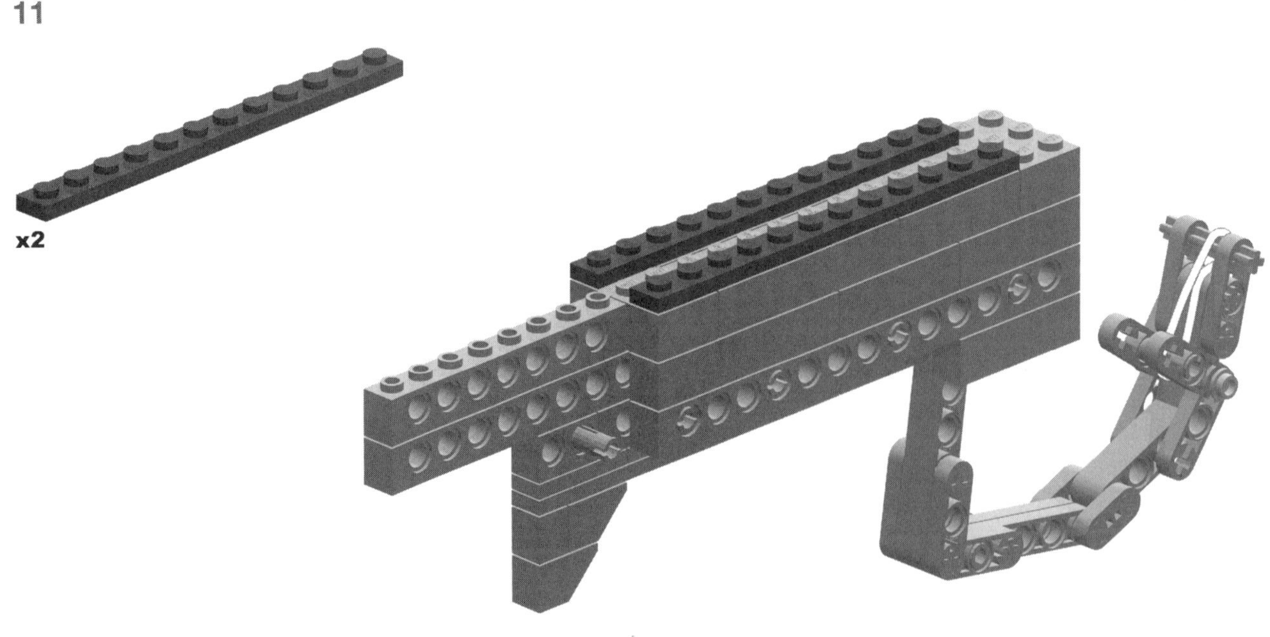

12

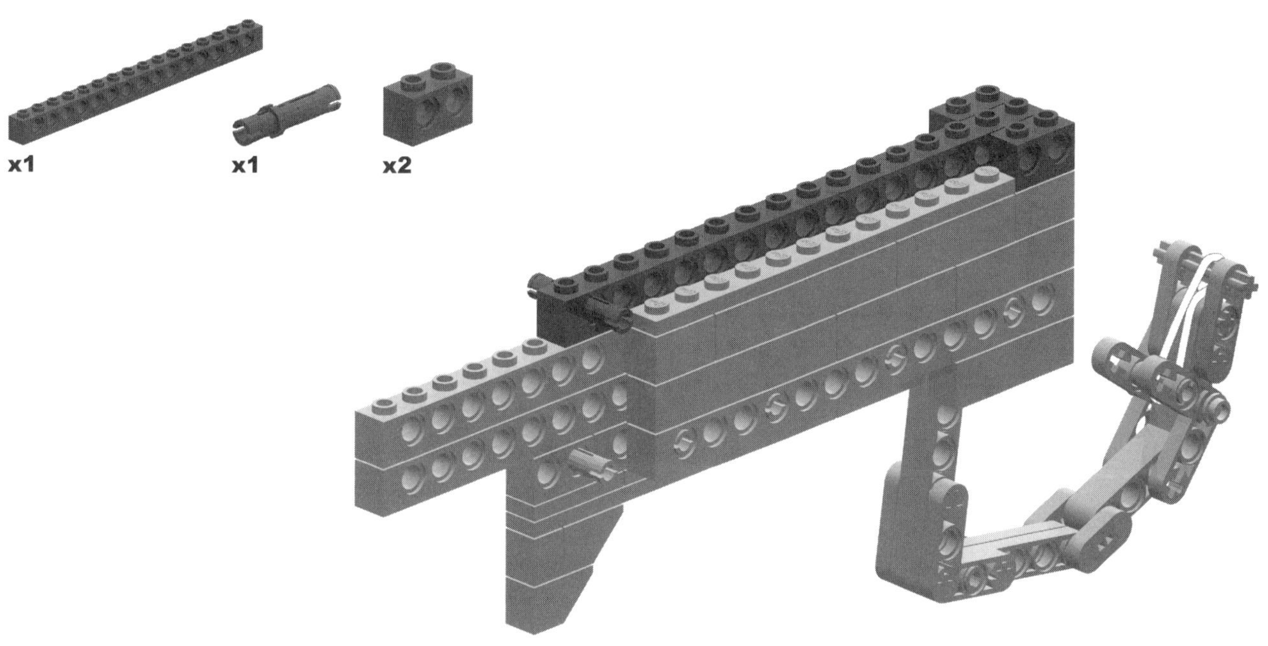

13

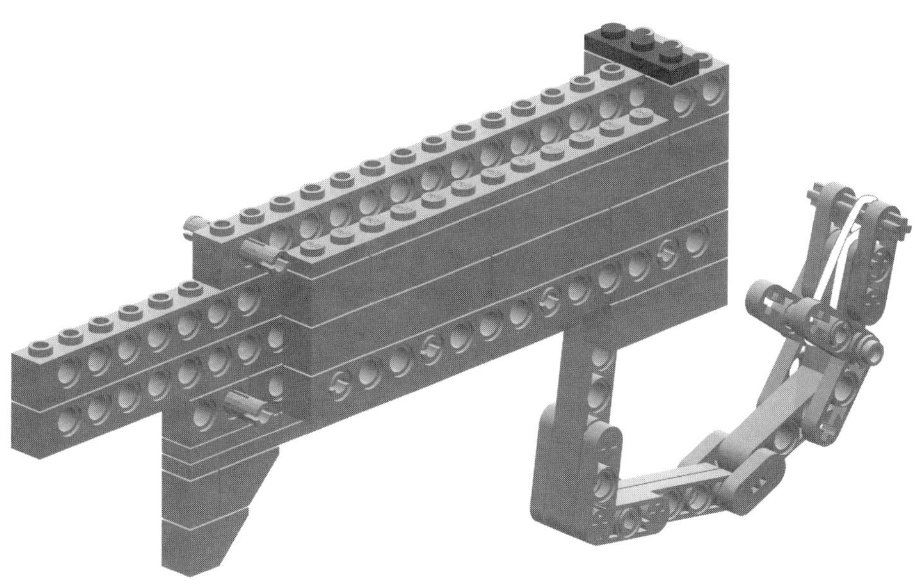

STOCK SLOPE

Make three Stock Slopes.

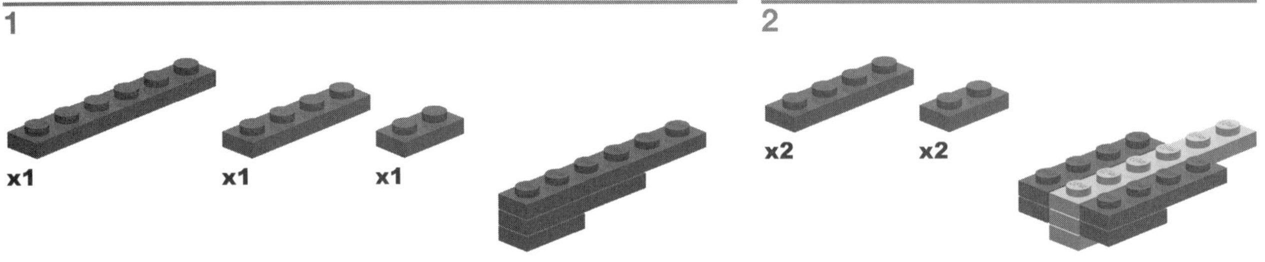

STOCK ASSEMBLY

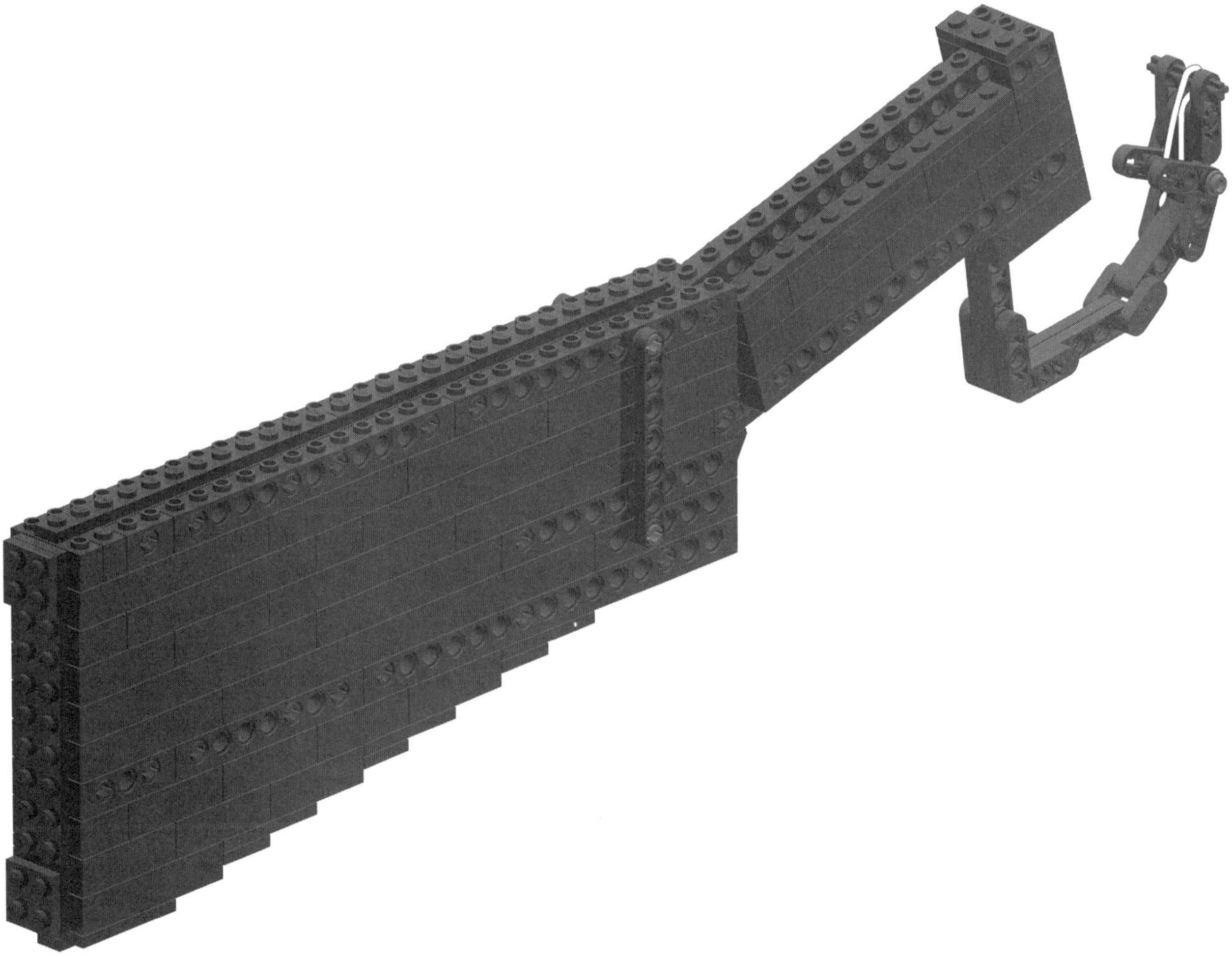

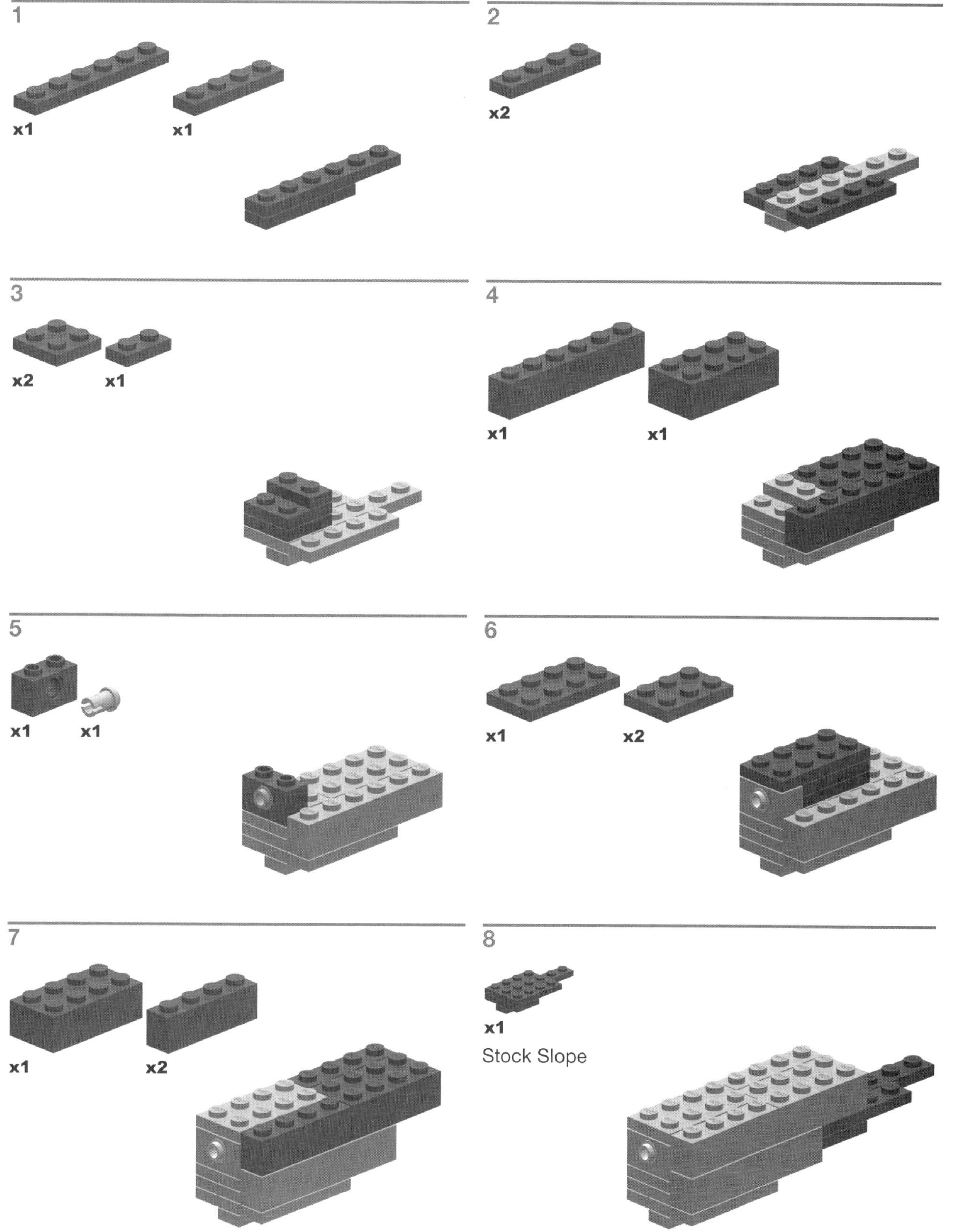
1
x1
x1
2
x2
3
x2
x1
4
x1
x1
5
x1
x1
6
x1
x2
7
x1
x2
8
x1
Stock Slope

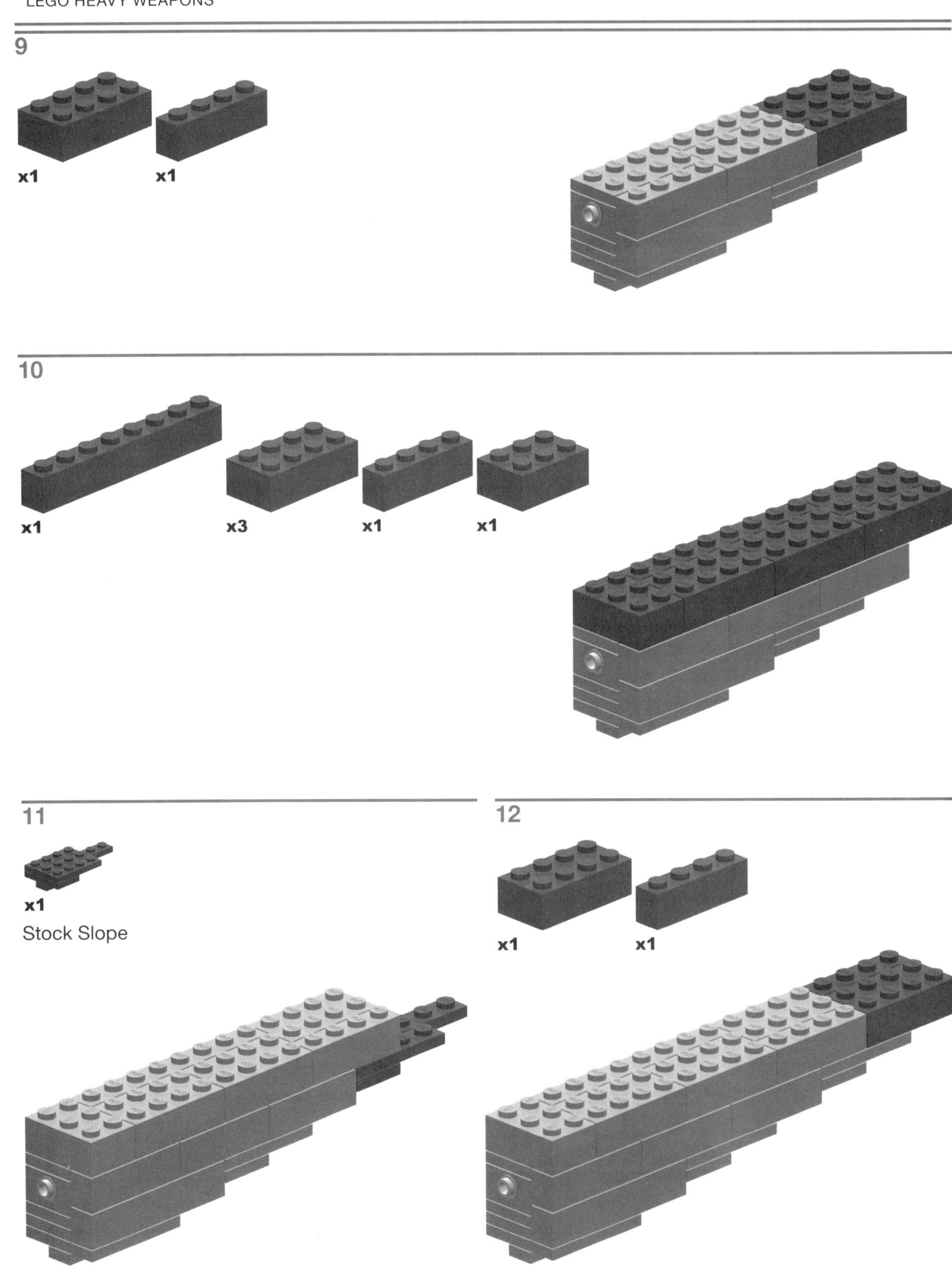
9
x1
x1
10
x1
x3
x1
x1
11
x1
Stock Slope
12
x1
x1

13

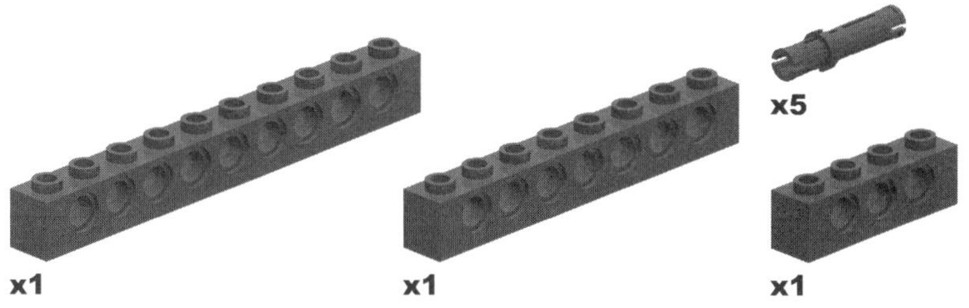
x5
x1
x1
x1

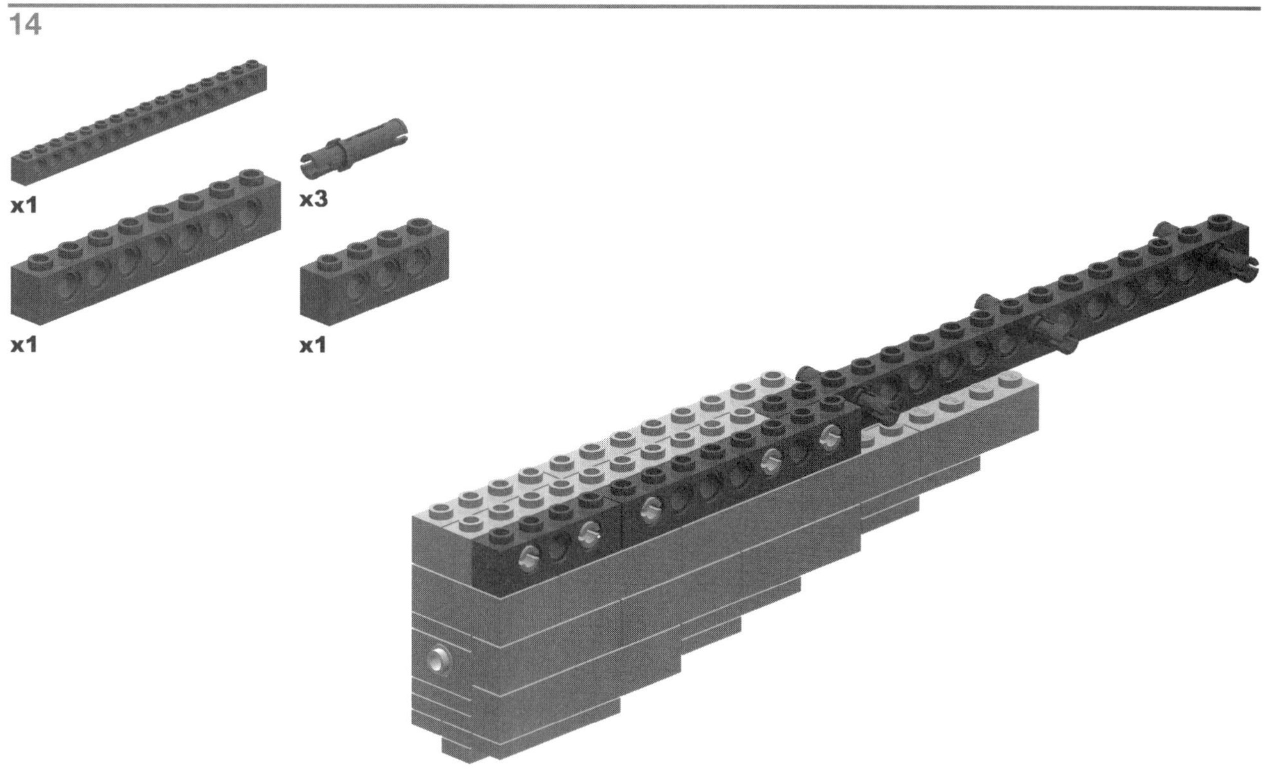
14
x1
x3
x1
x1

15

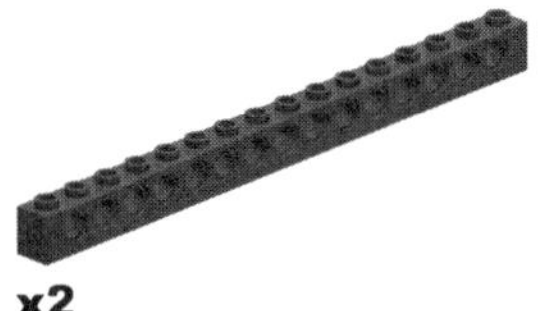

x2

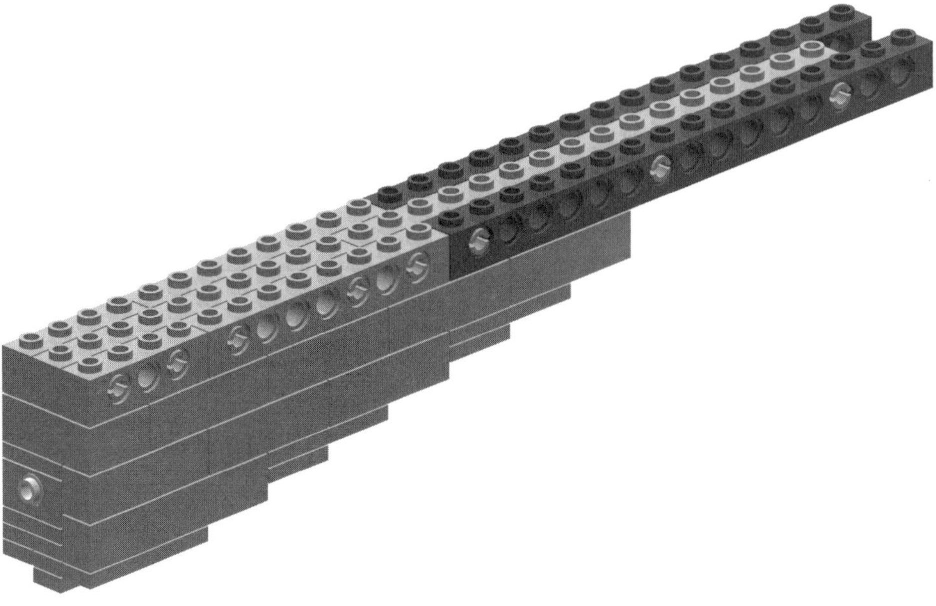

16

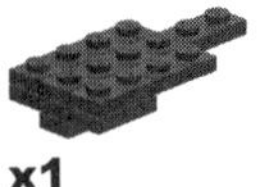

x1

Stock Slope

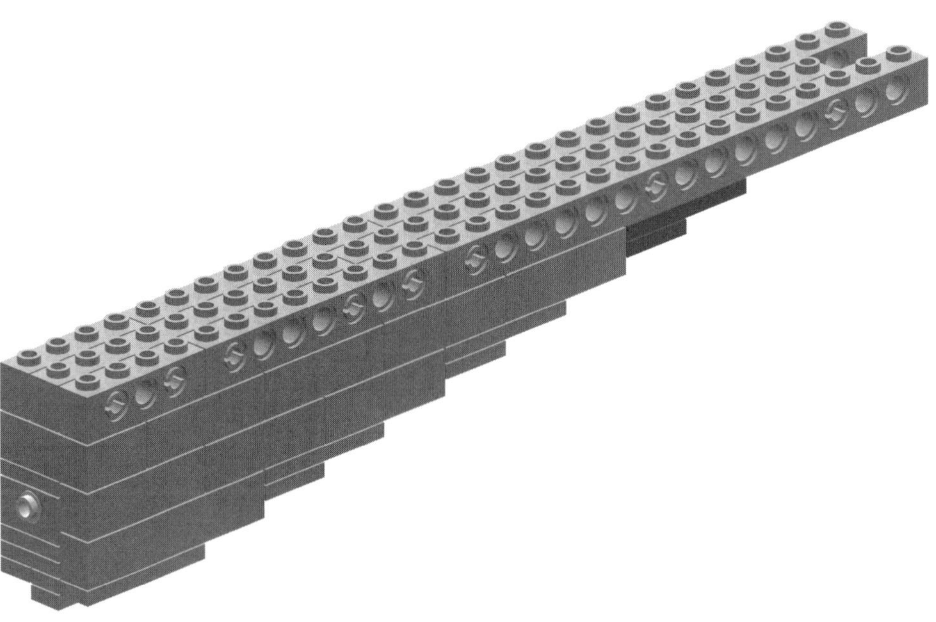

17

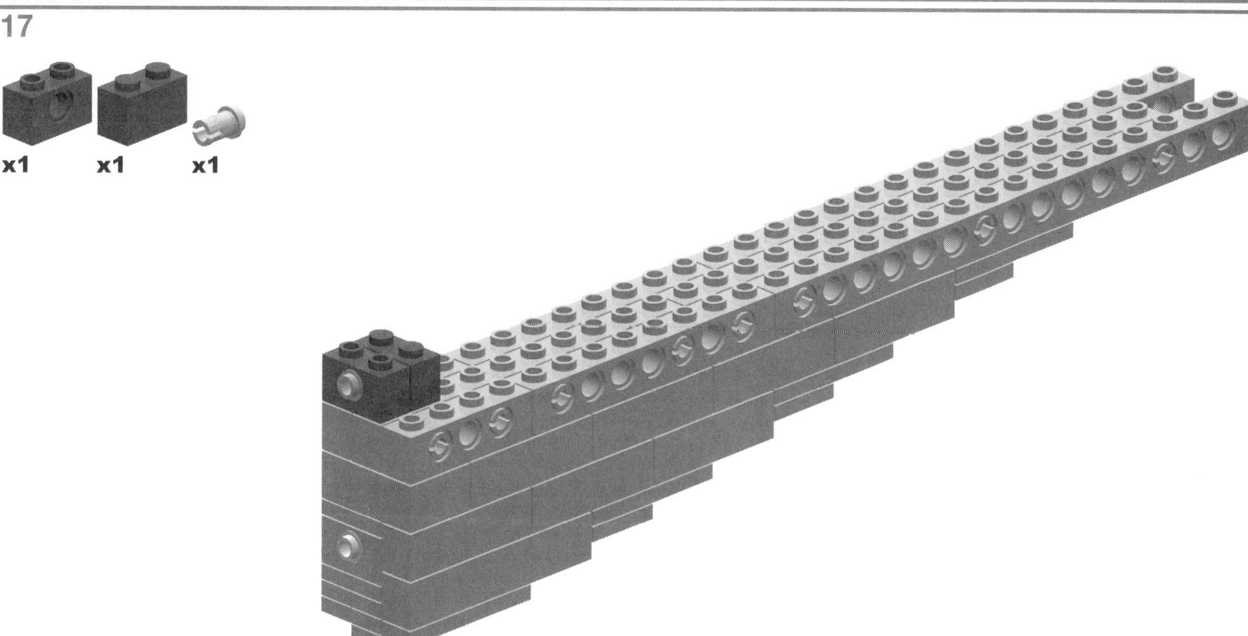

18

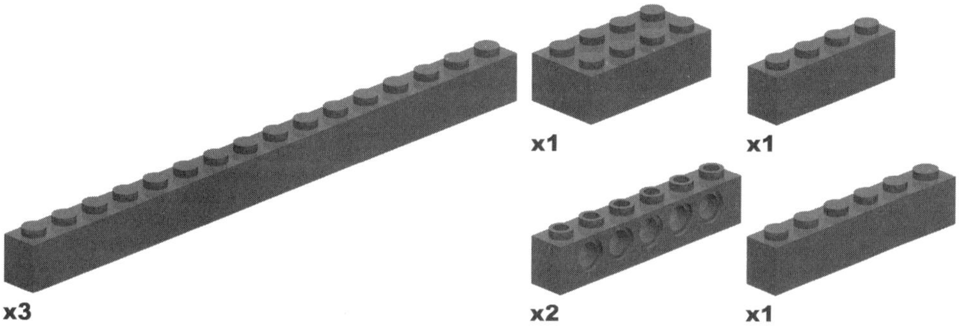

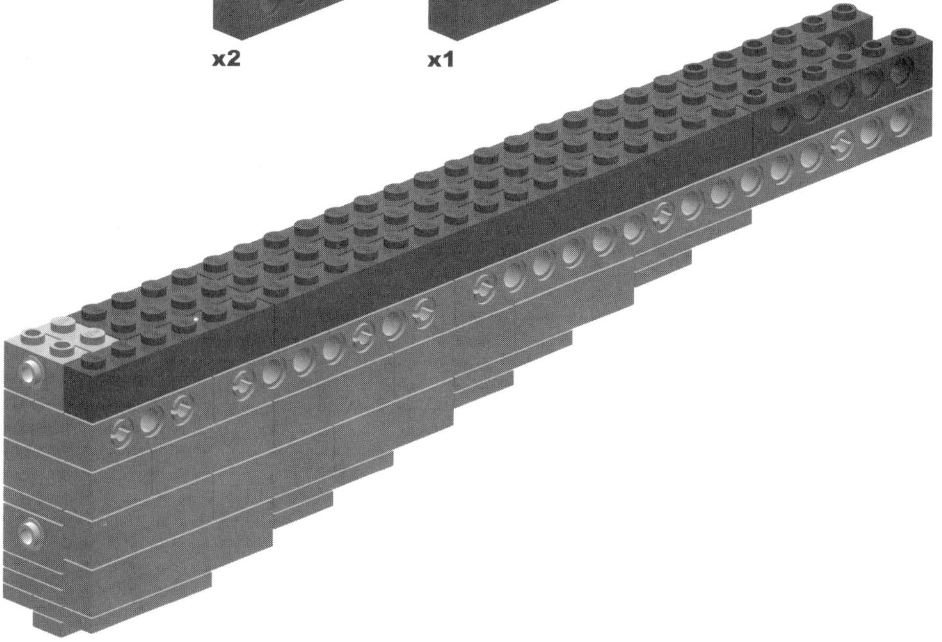

x1 x1

x3 x2 x1

19

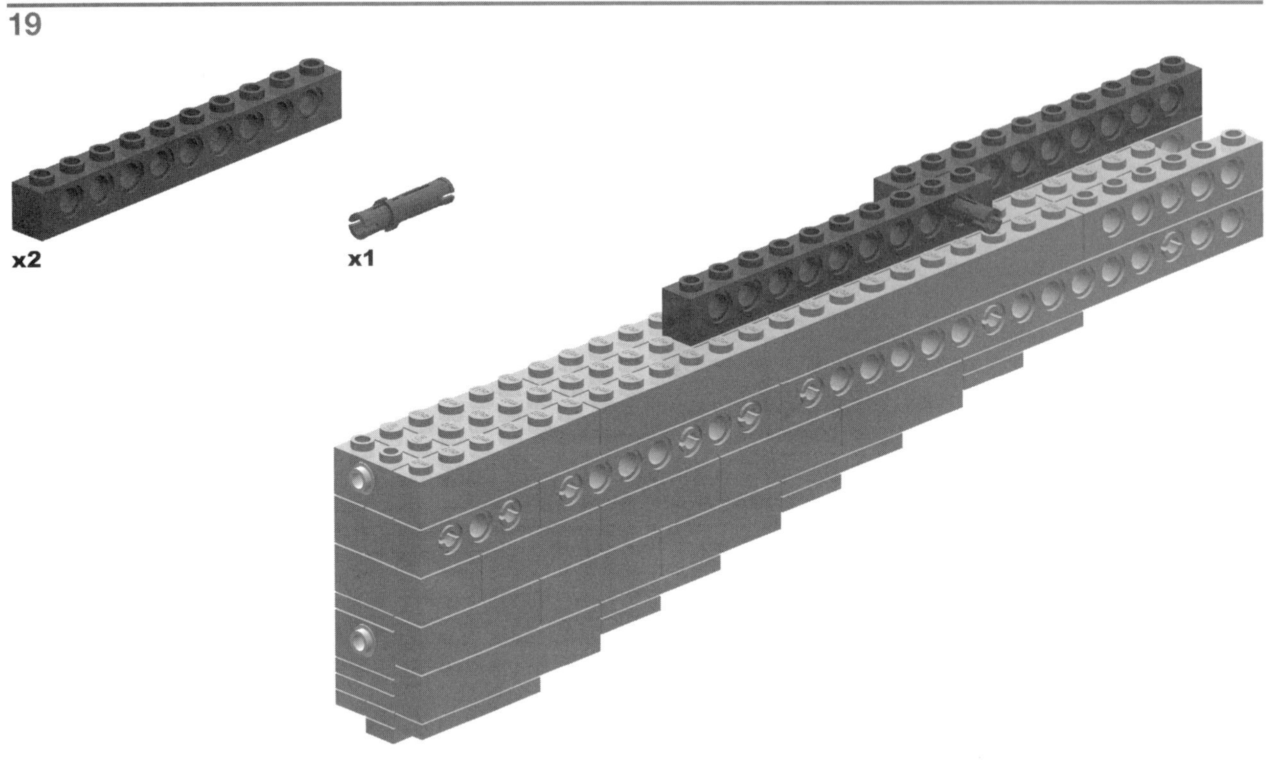

20

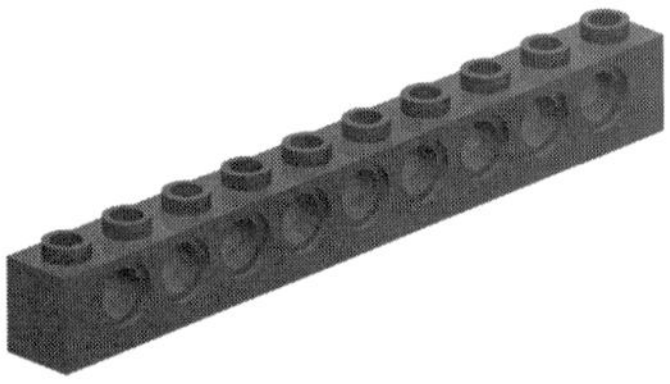

x1

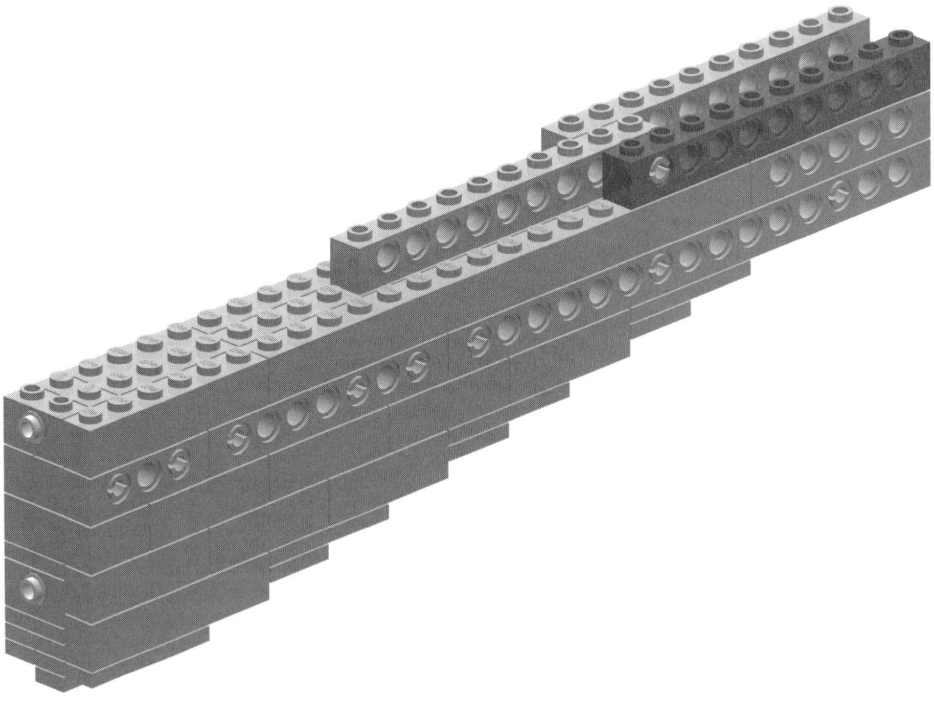

21

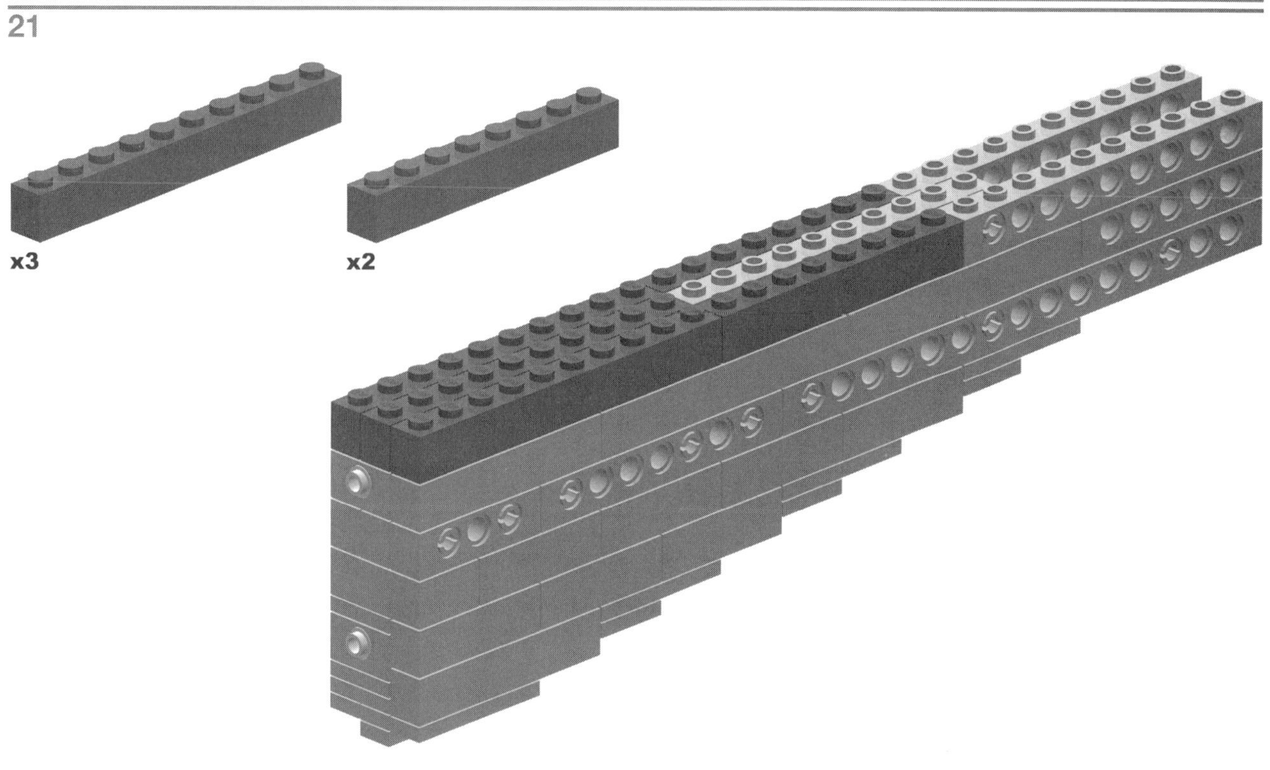

22

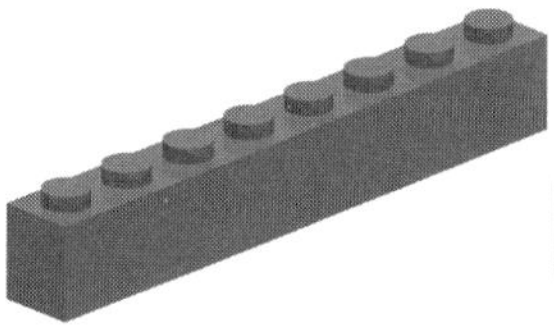

x2

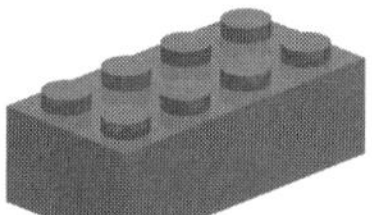

x4

23

x2

x1

x2

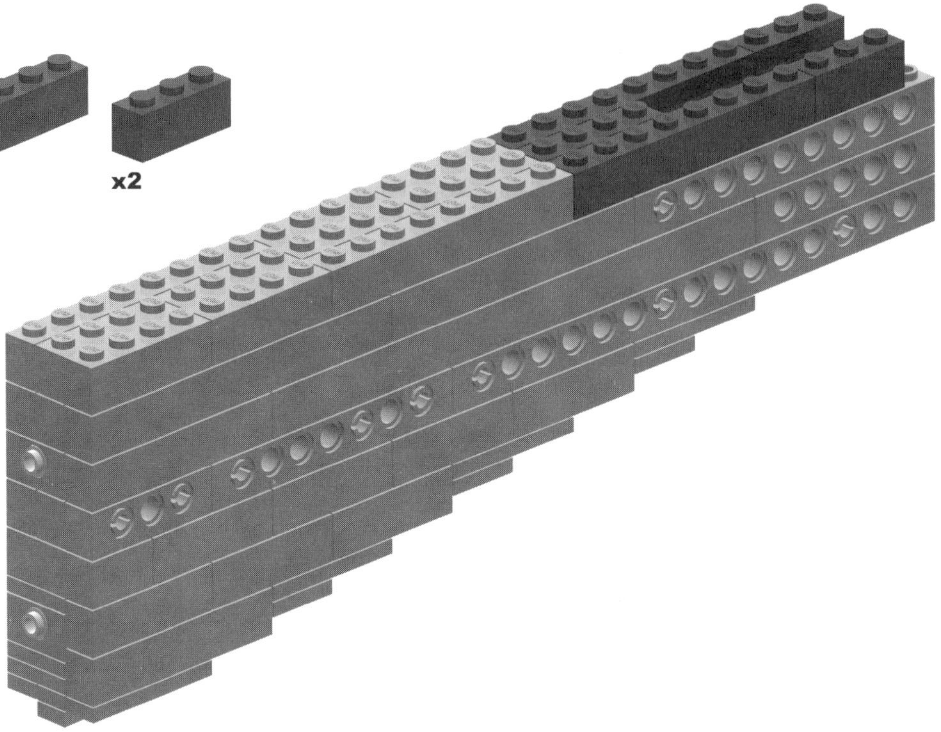

24

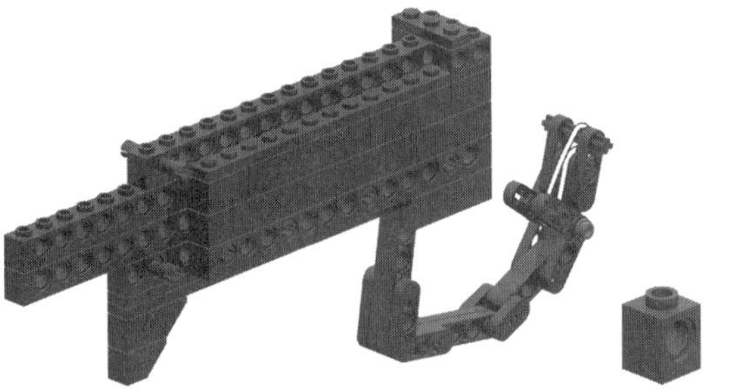

x1

Stock Grip

x2

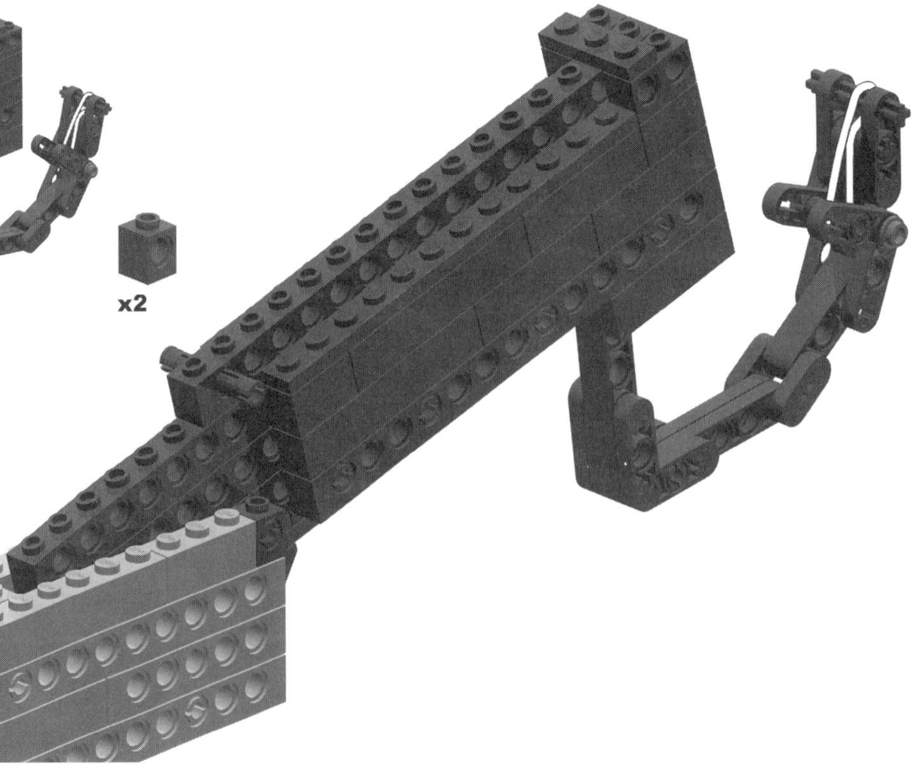

25

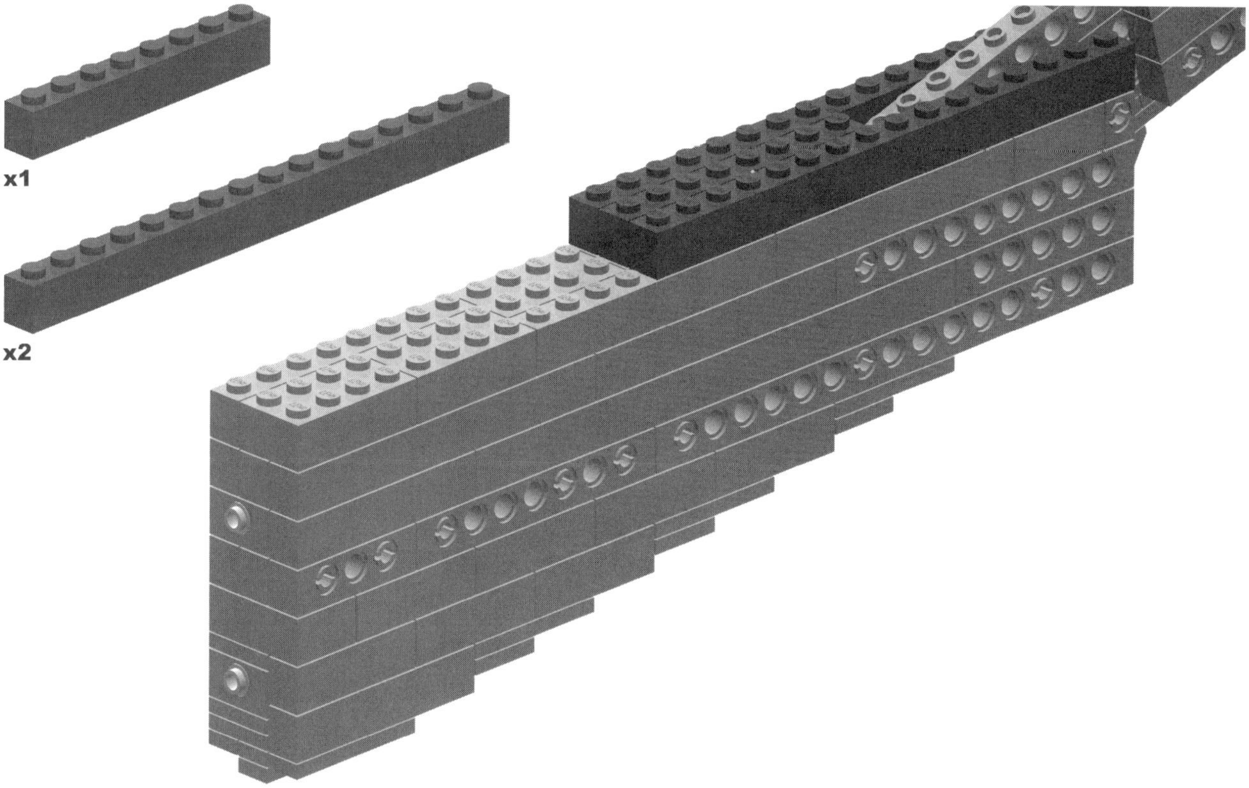

x1

x2

26

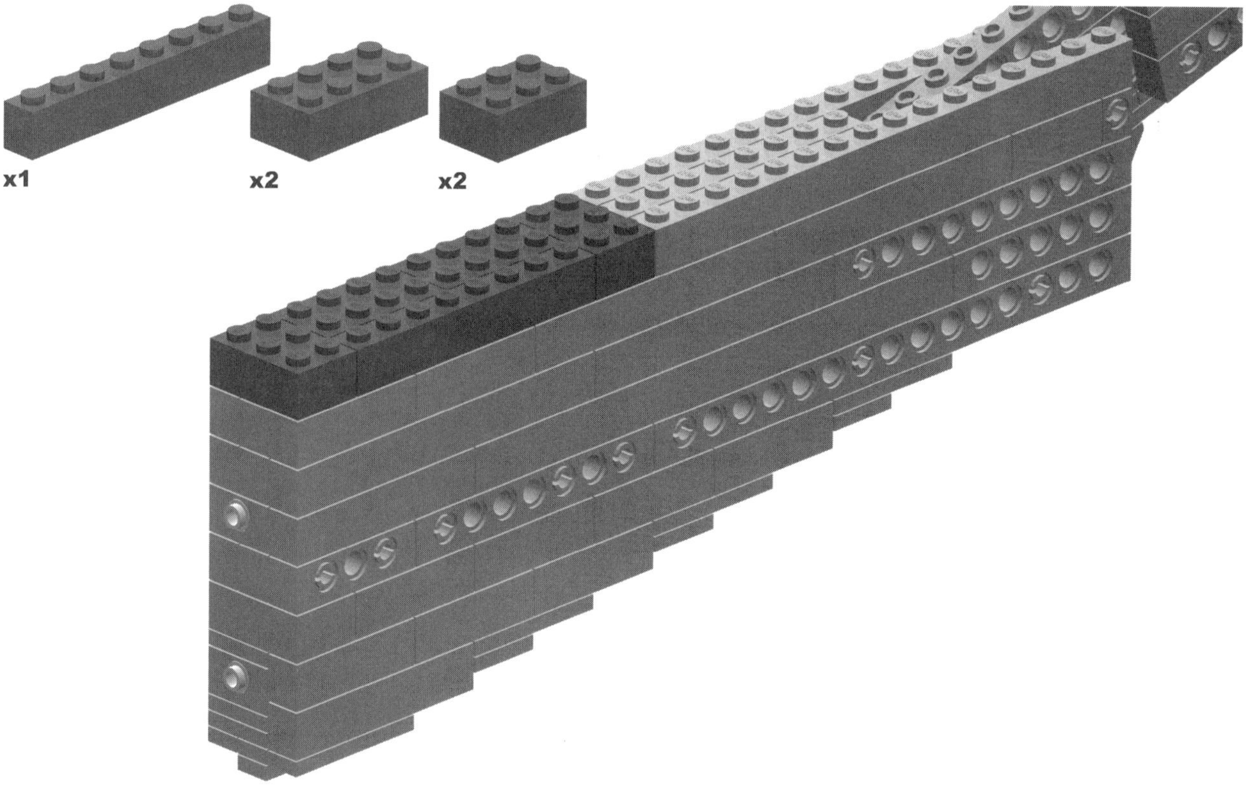

x1

x2

x2

27

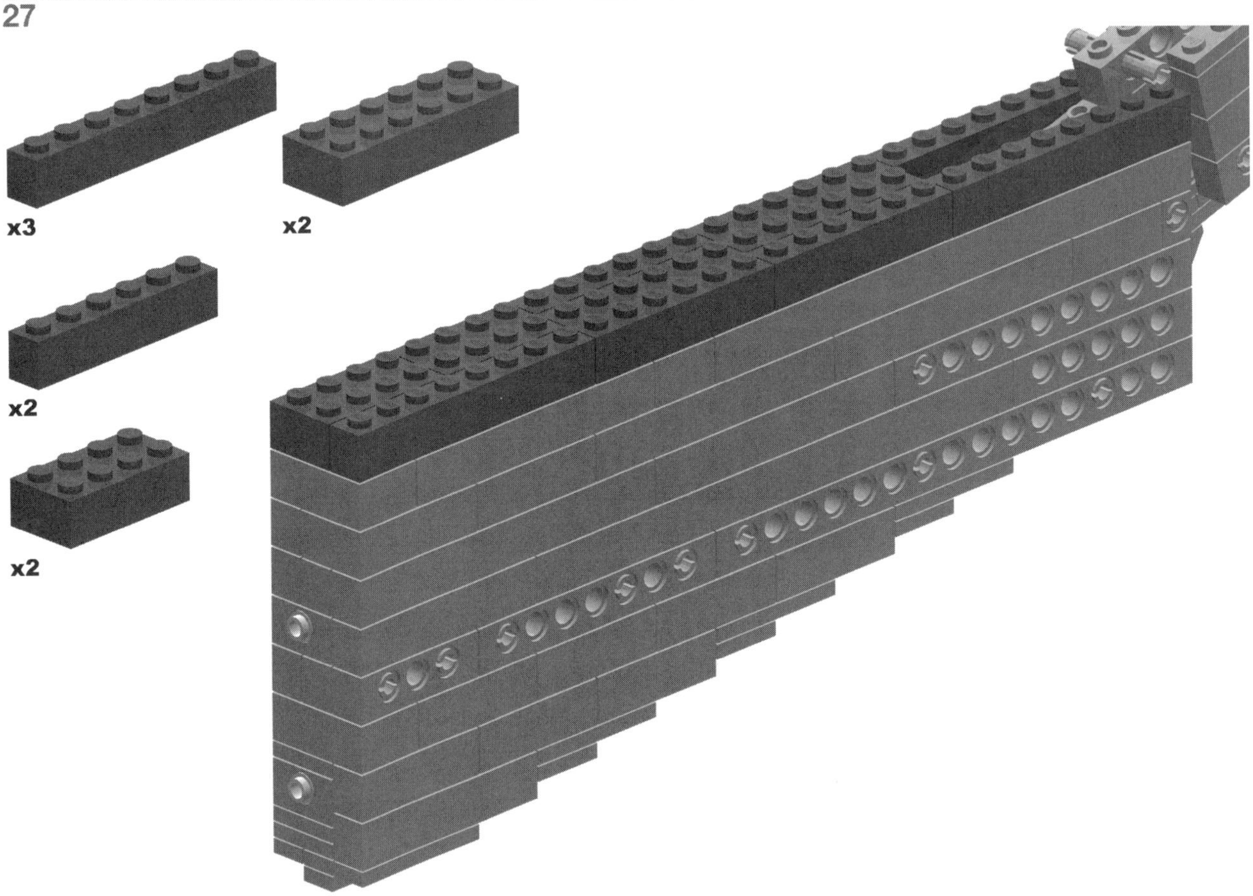

x3

x2

x2

x2

28

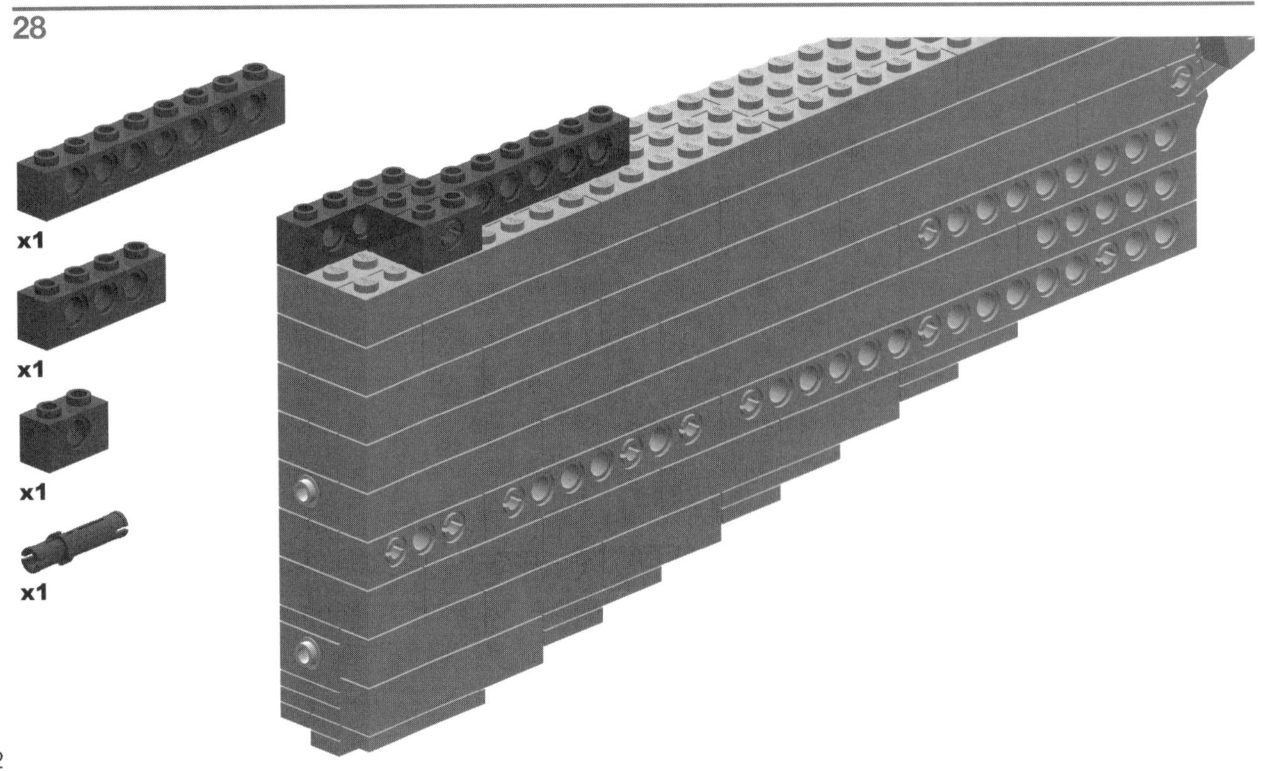

29

x1 x1 x1

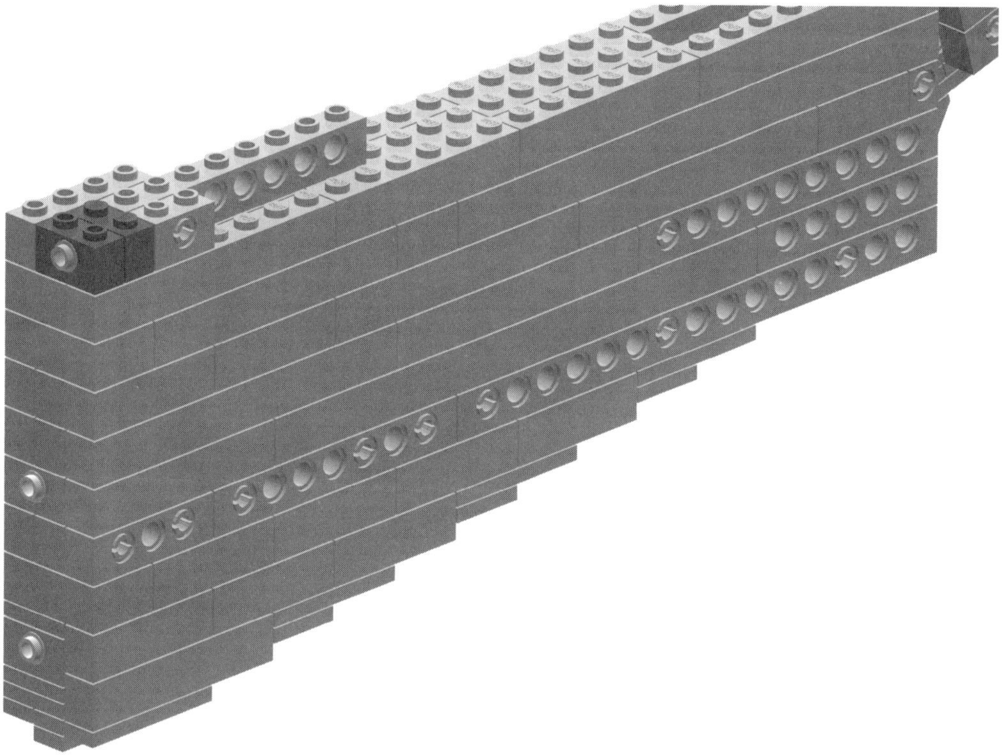

30

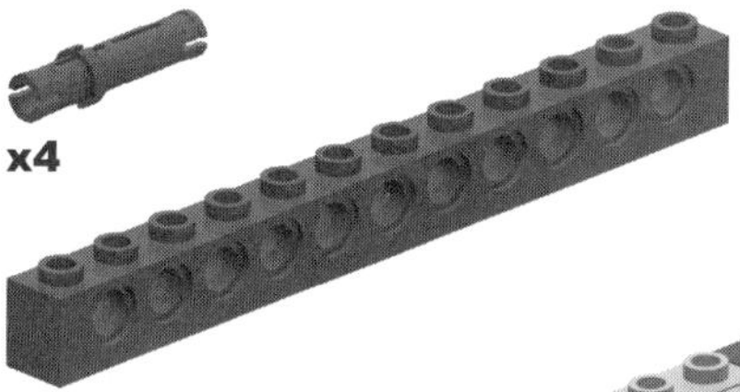

x4

x1

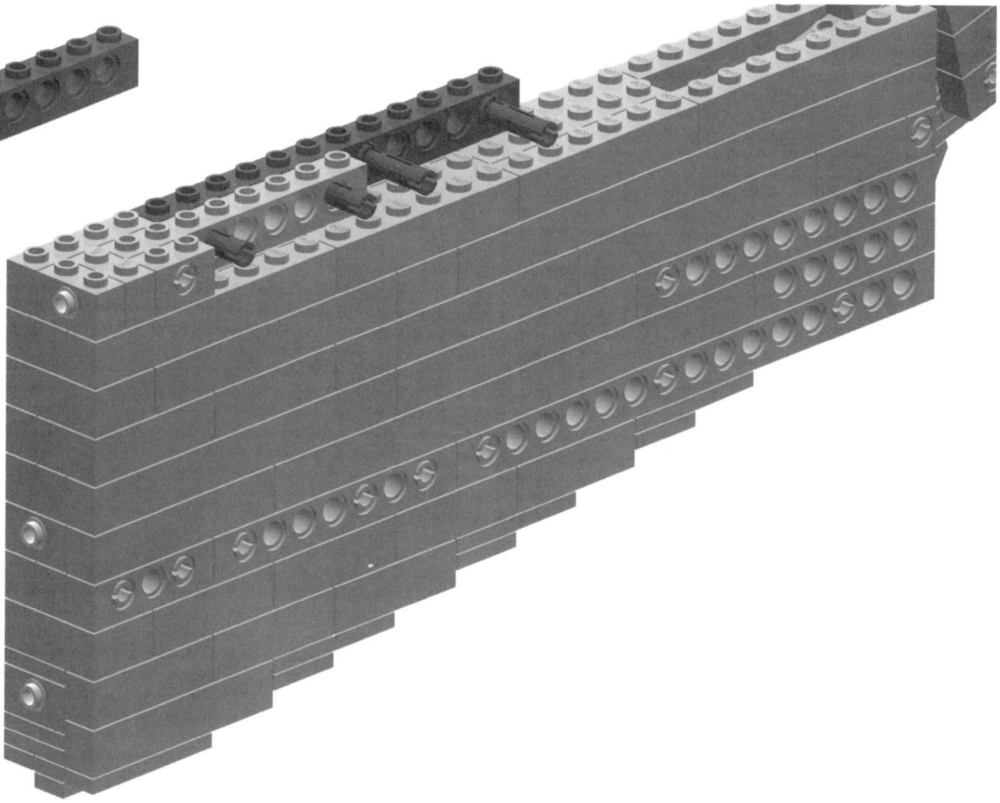

31

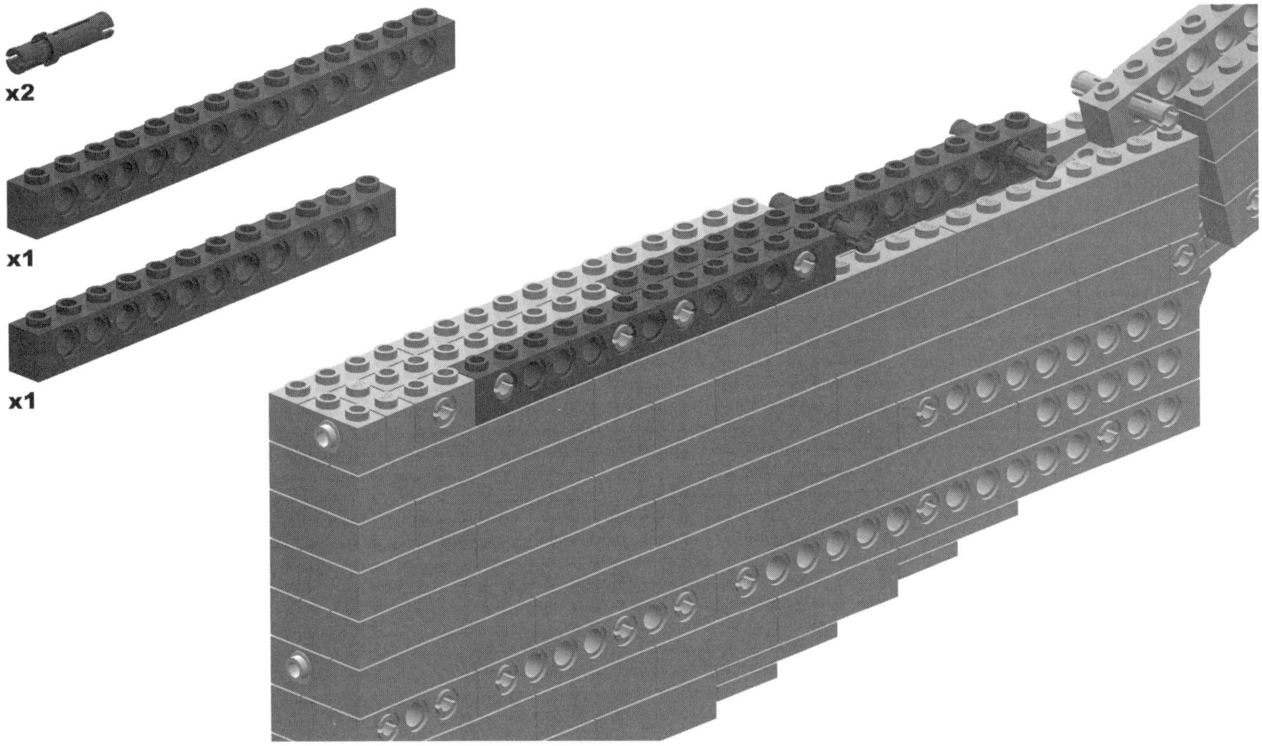

x2

x1

x1

32

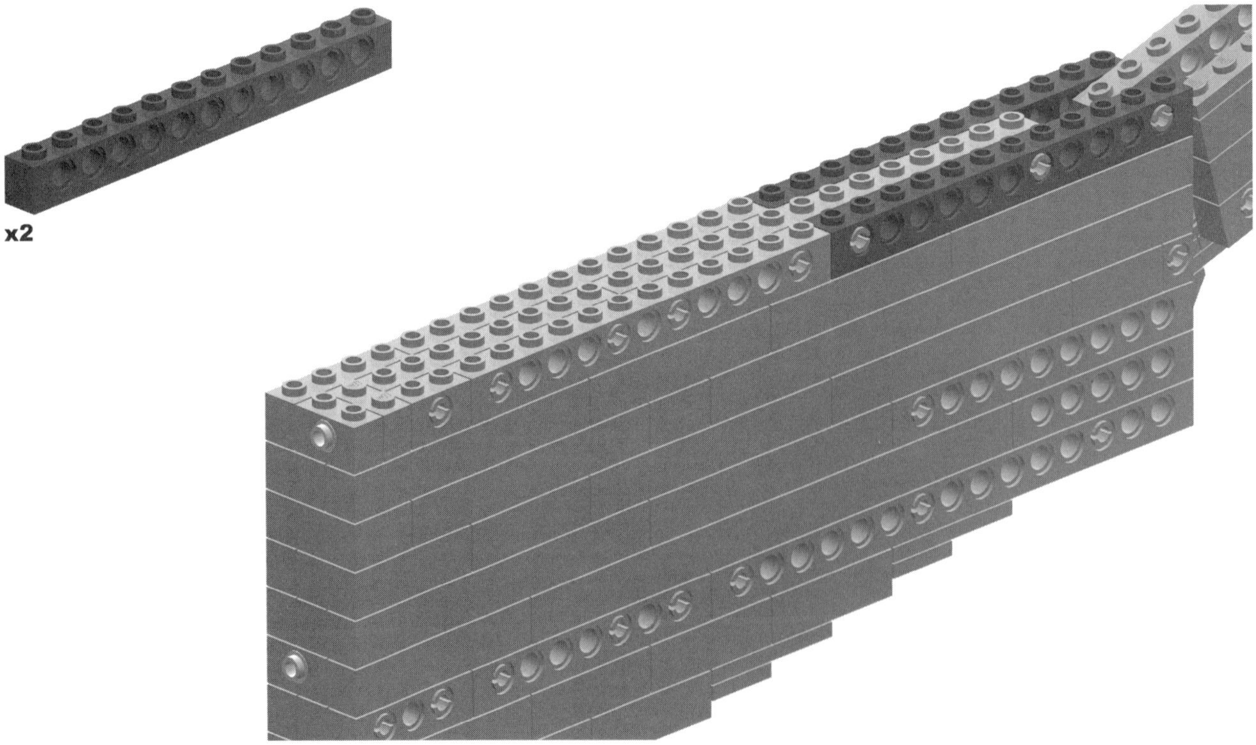

x2

33

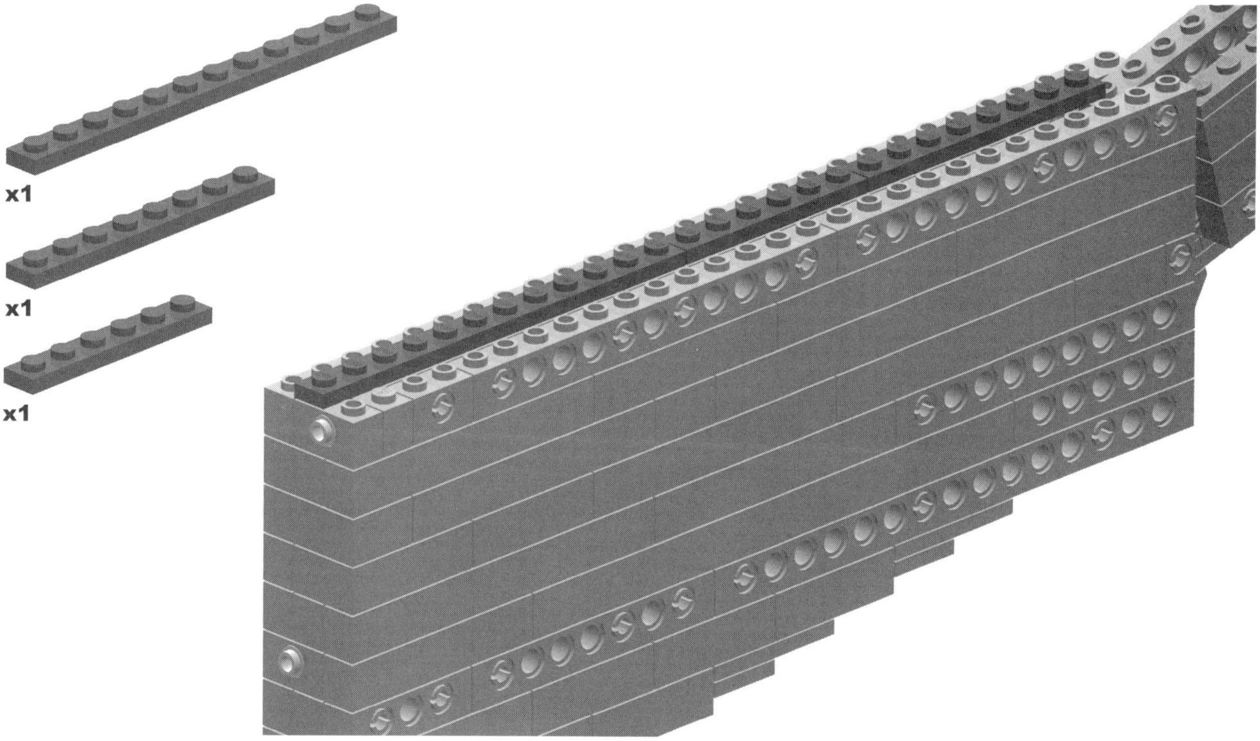

x1

x1

x1

34

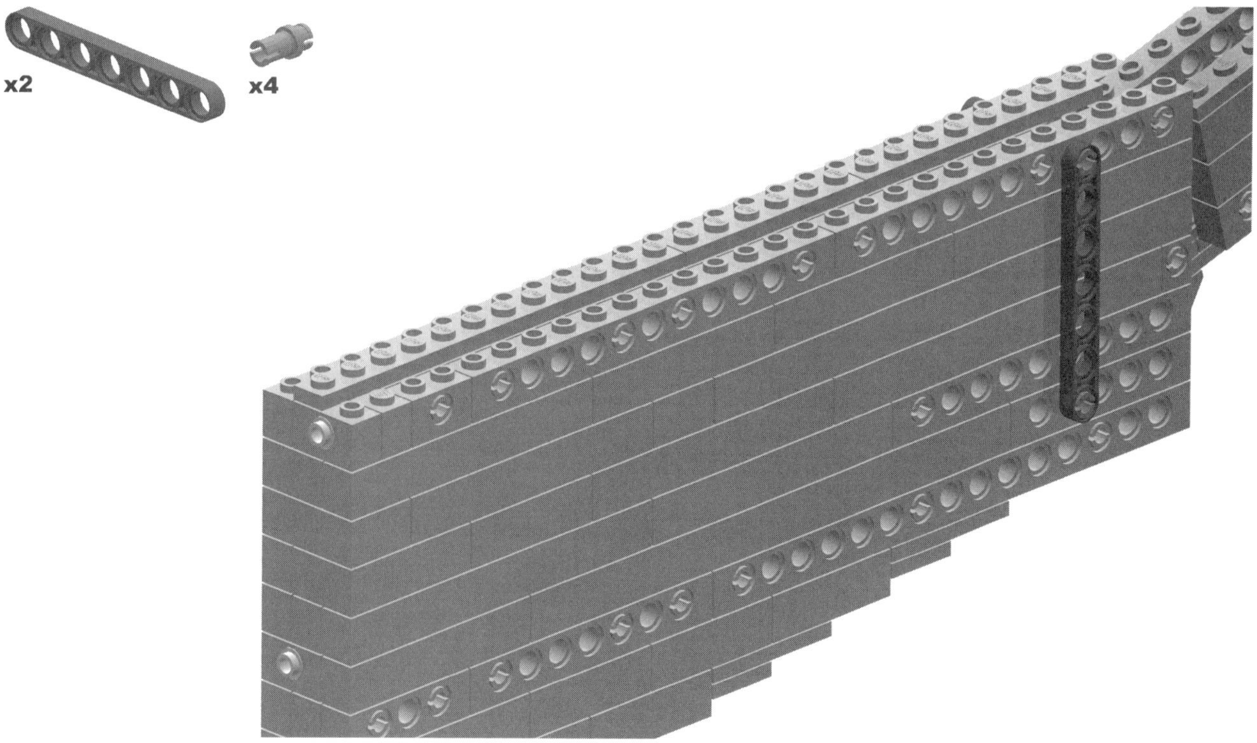

x2

x4

35

x2

x1

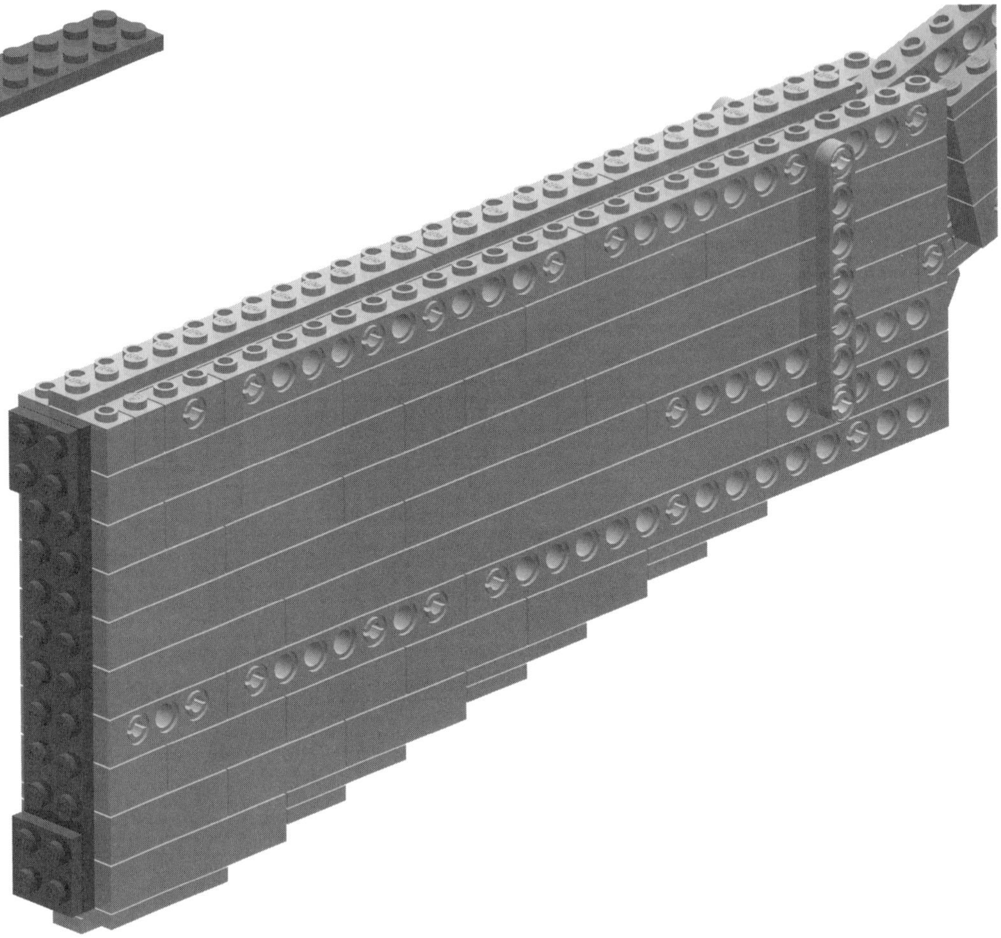

TRIGGER

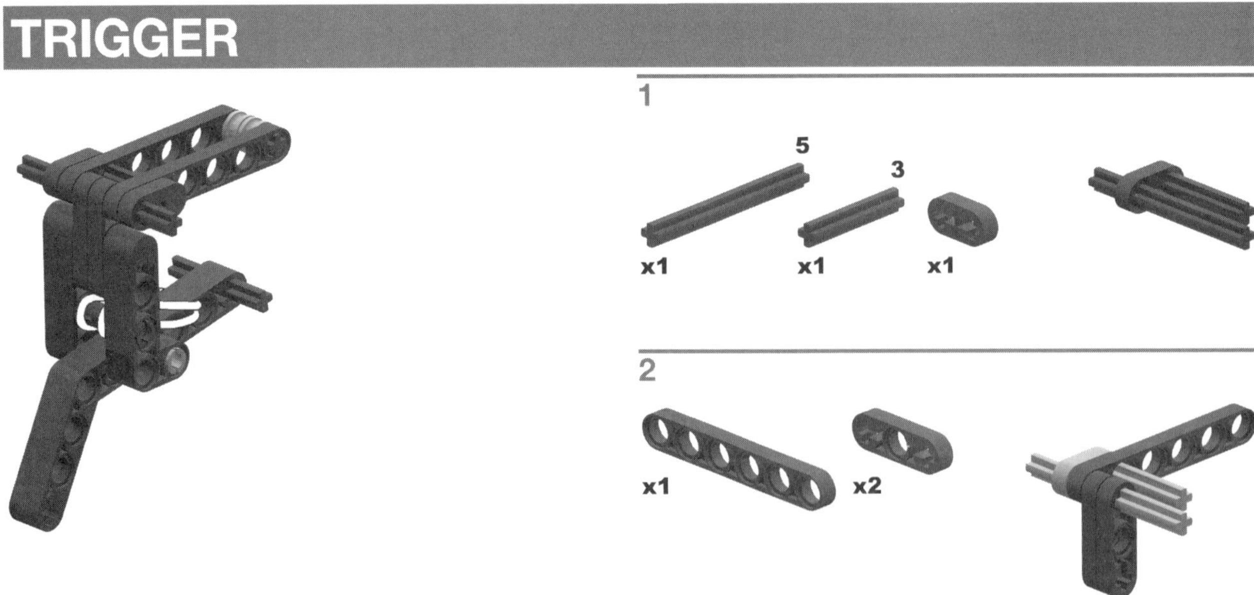

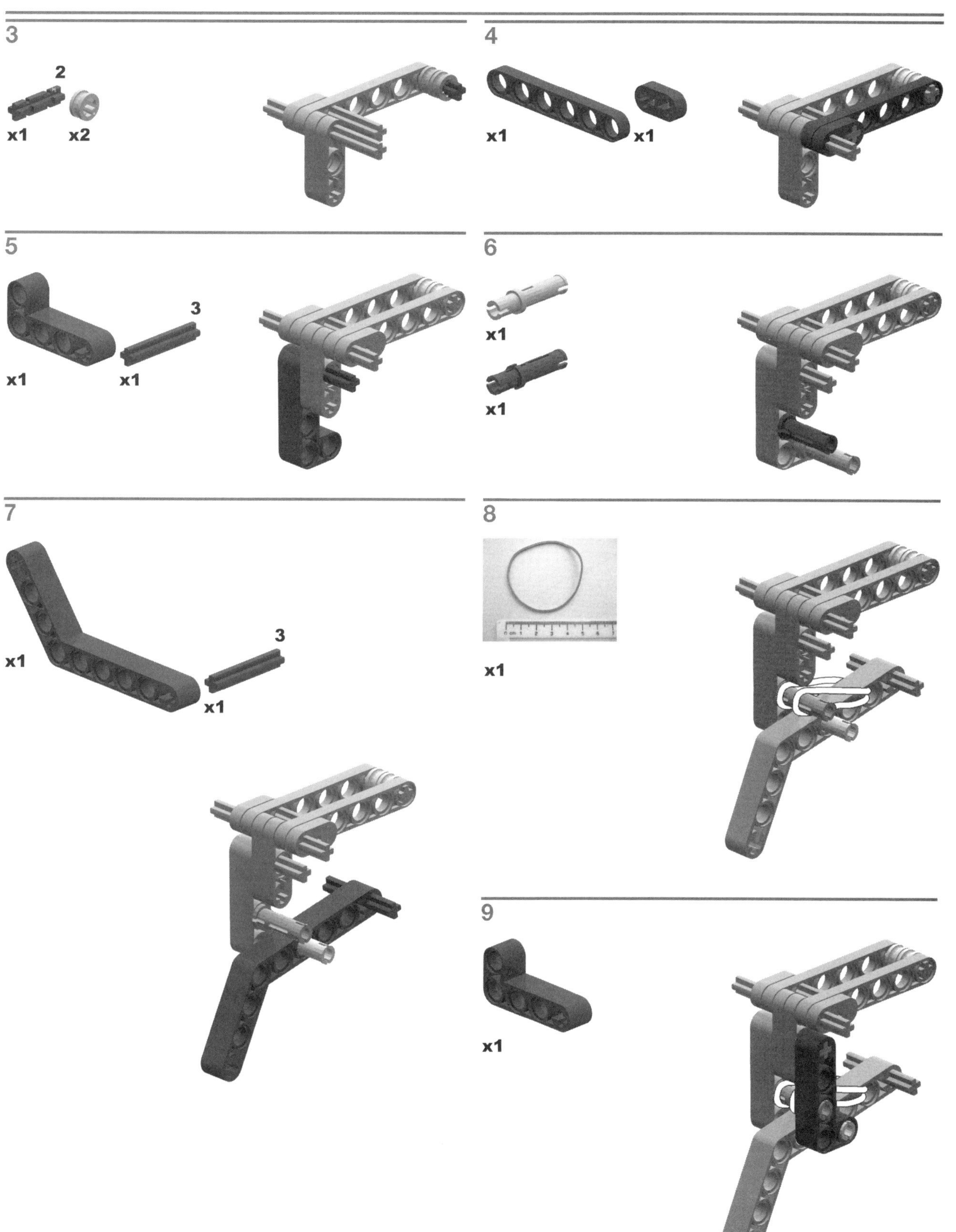
3
2
x1
x2
4
x1
x1
5
3
x1
x1
6
x1
x1
7
x1
3
x1
8
x1
9
x1

FRAME ROOF

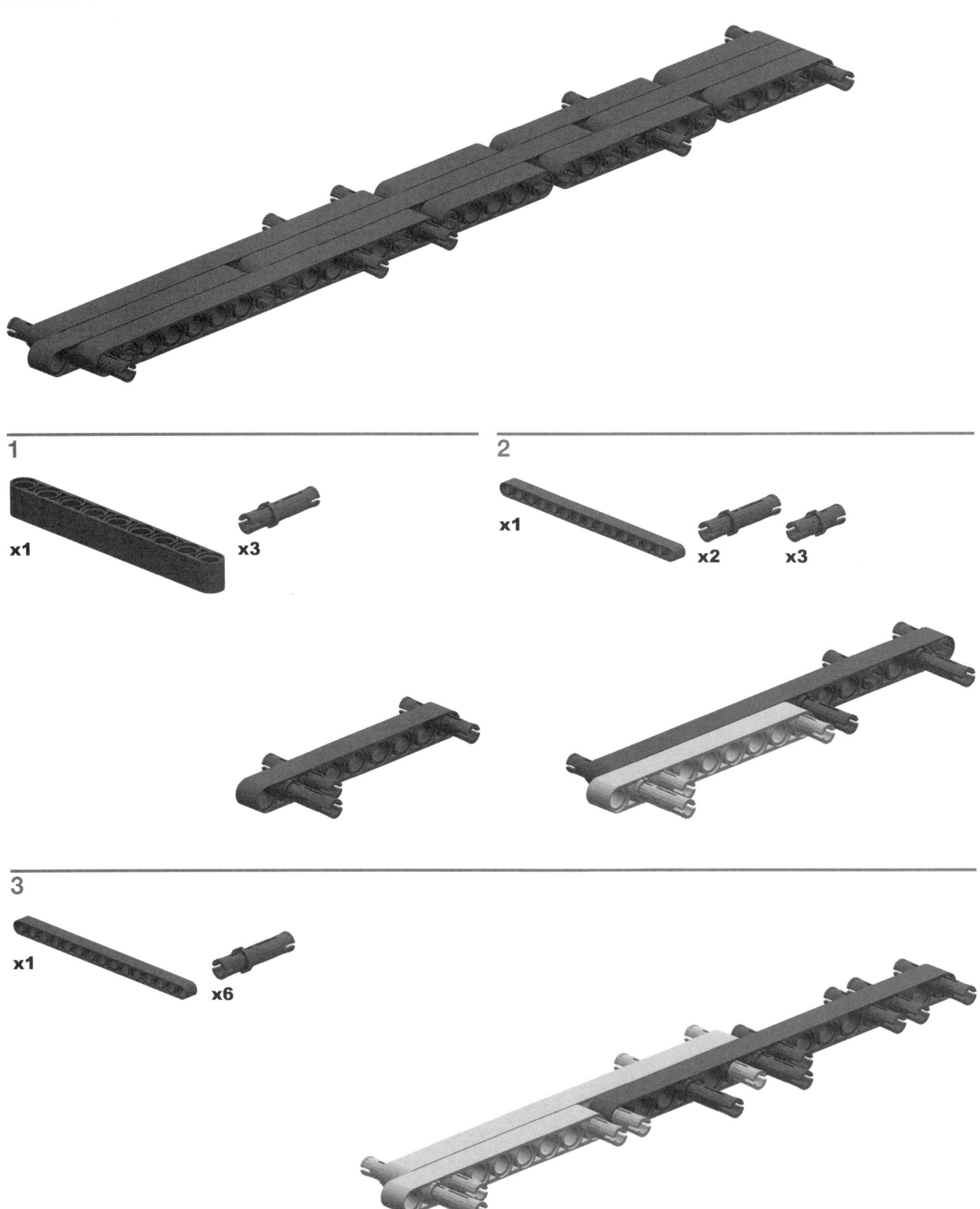

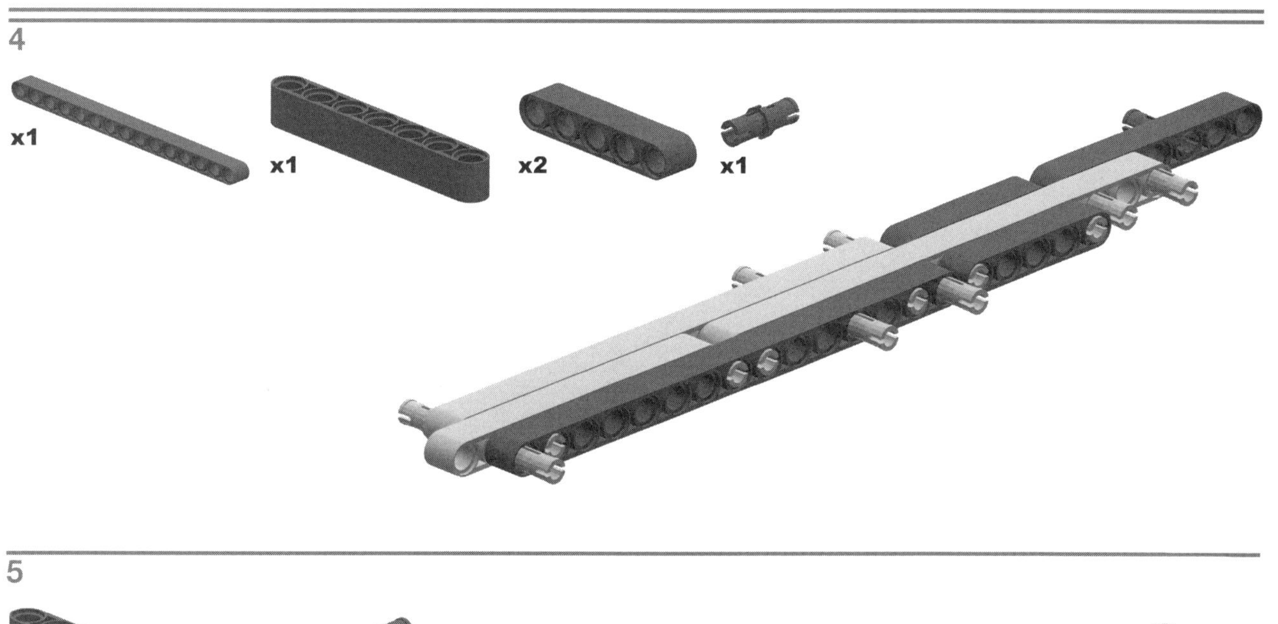
4
x1
x1
x2
x1

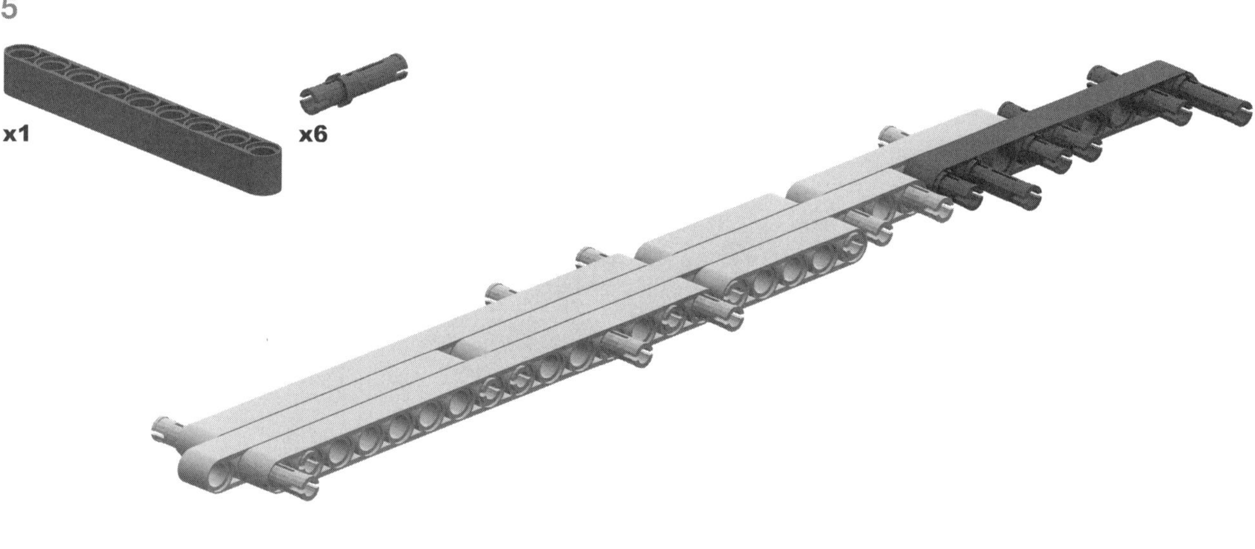
5
x1
x6

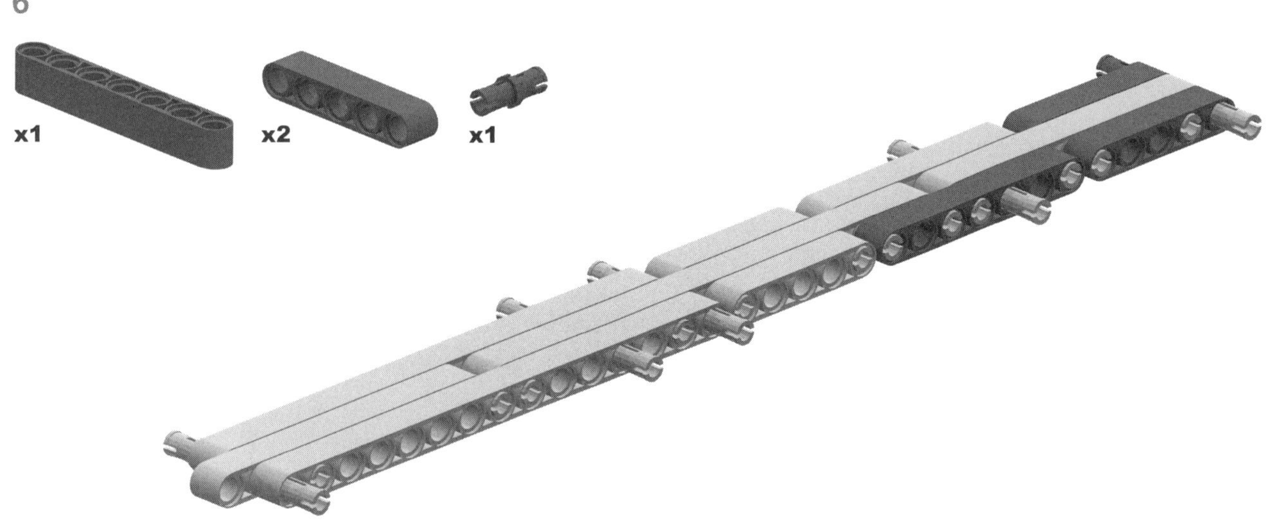
6
x1
x2
x1

RAMP

1

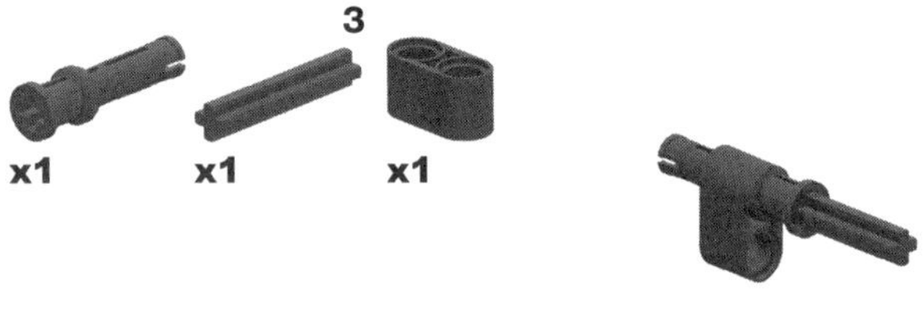

3

x1 x1 x1

2

3

x1 x2

3

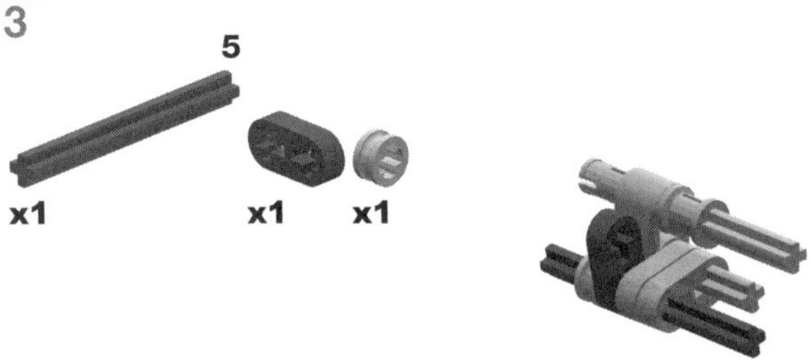

5

x1 x1 x1

4

2

x1

x1

5

x1 x1

6

x1

BARREL WALL LEFT

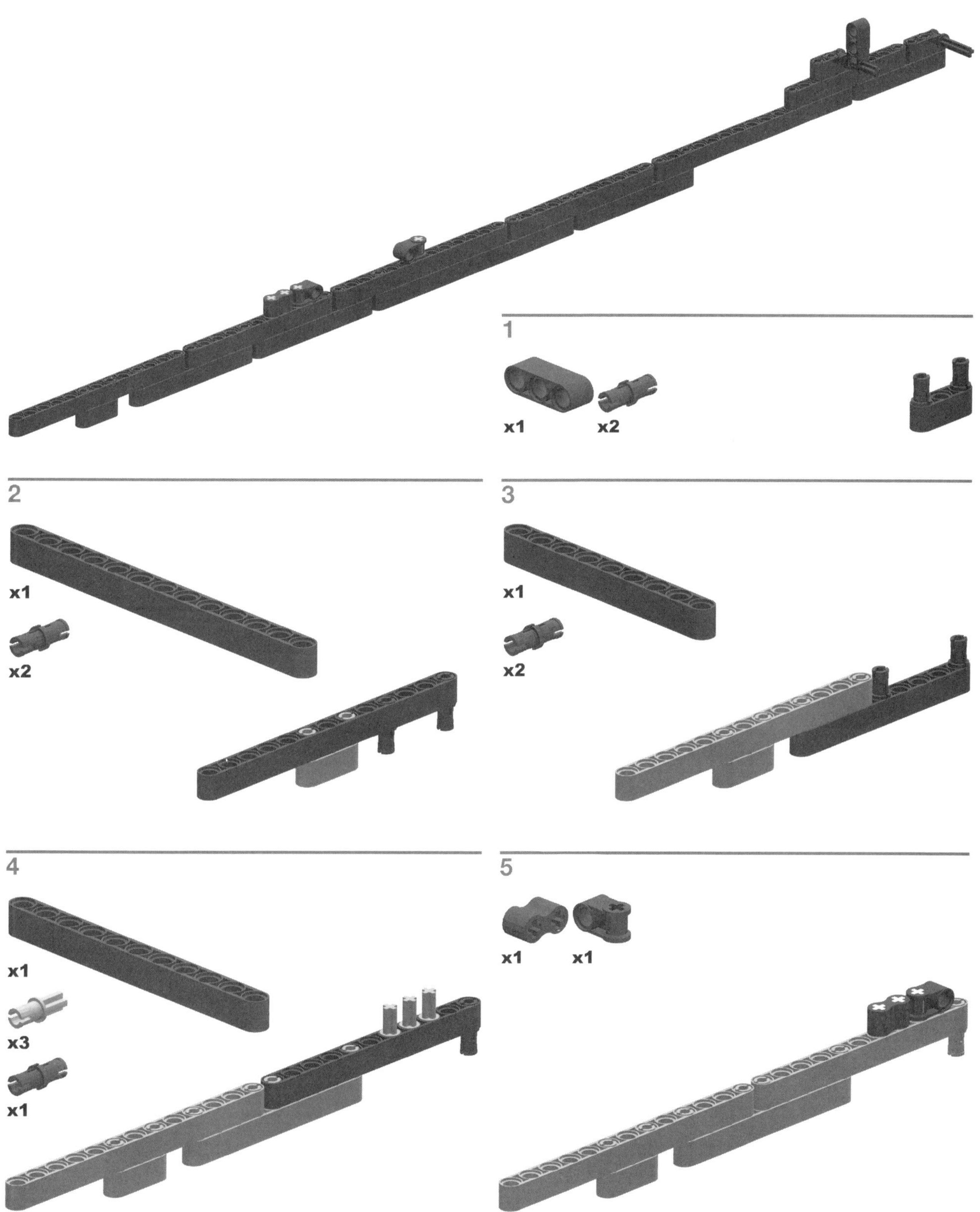

6

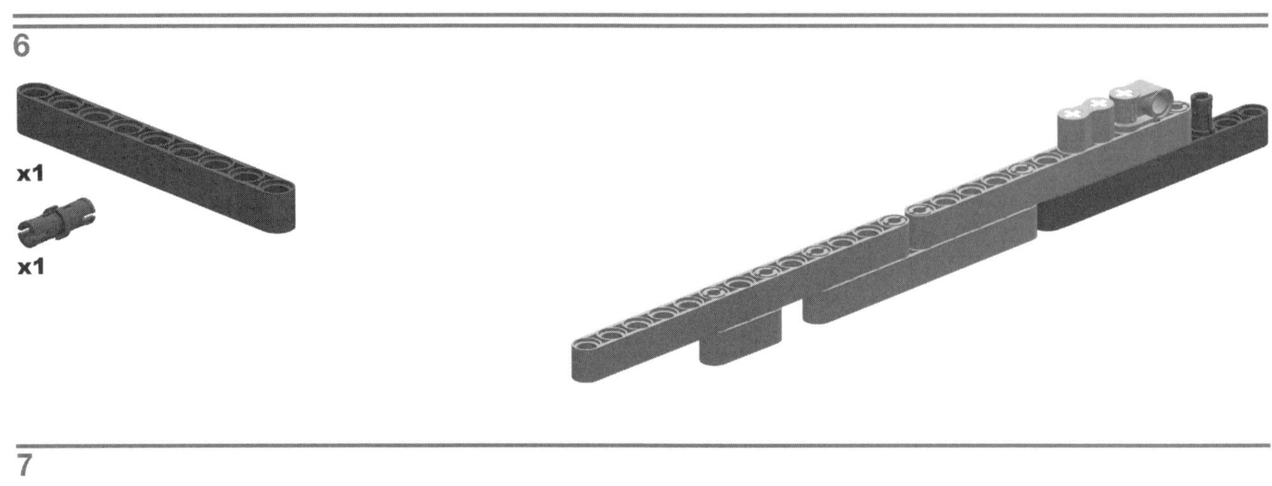

7

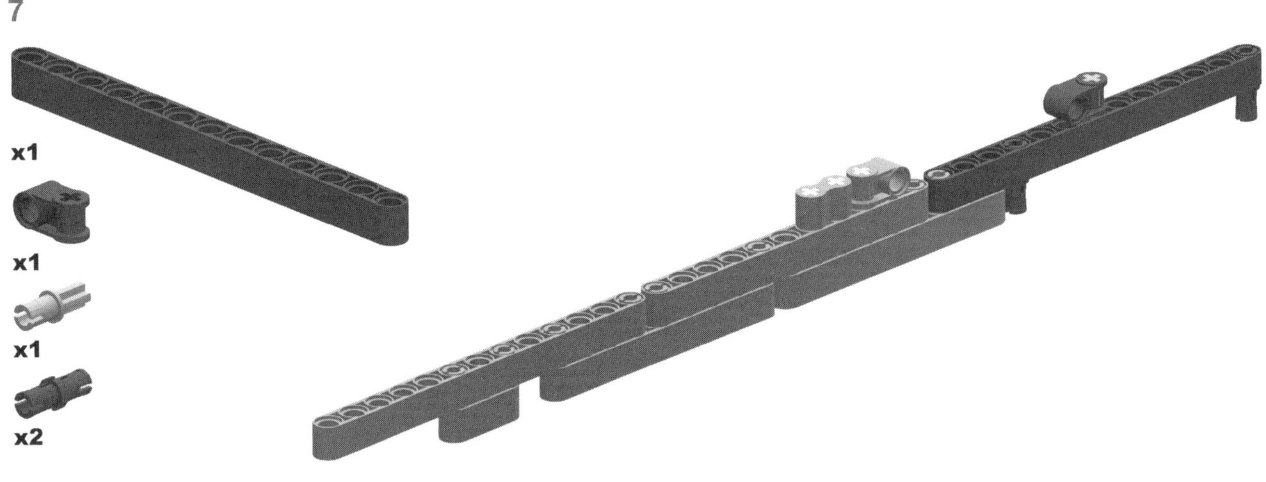

8

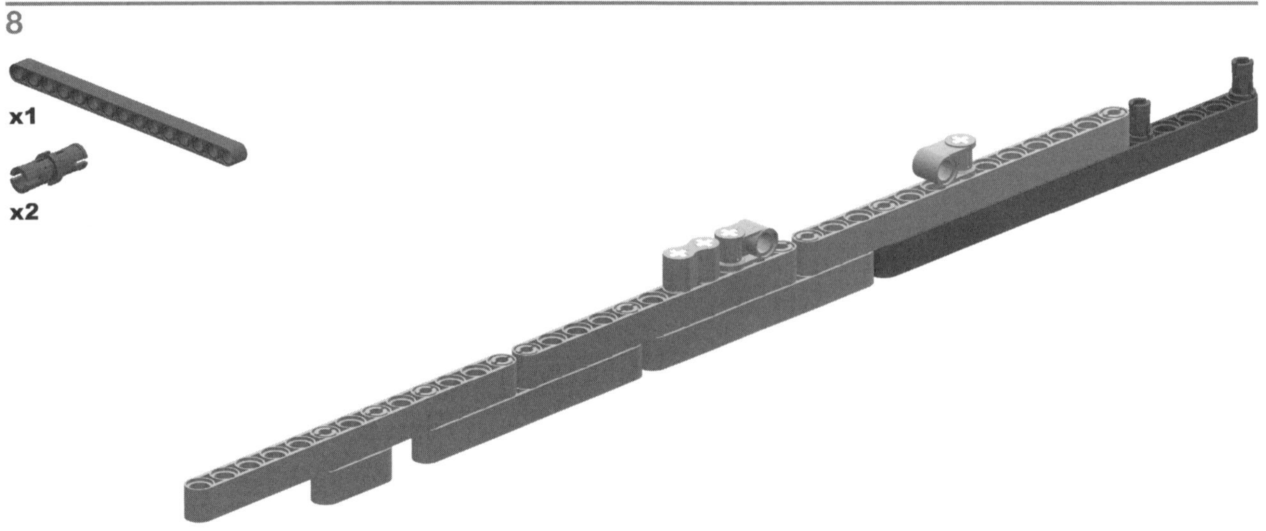

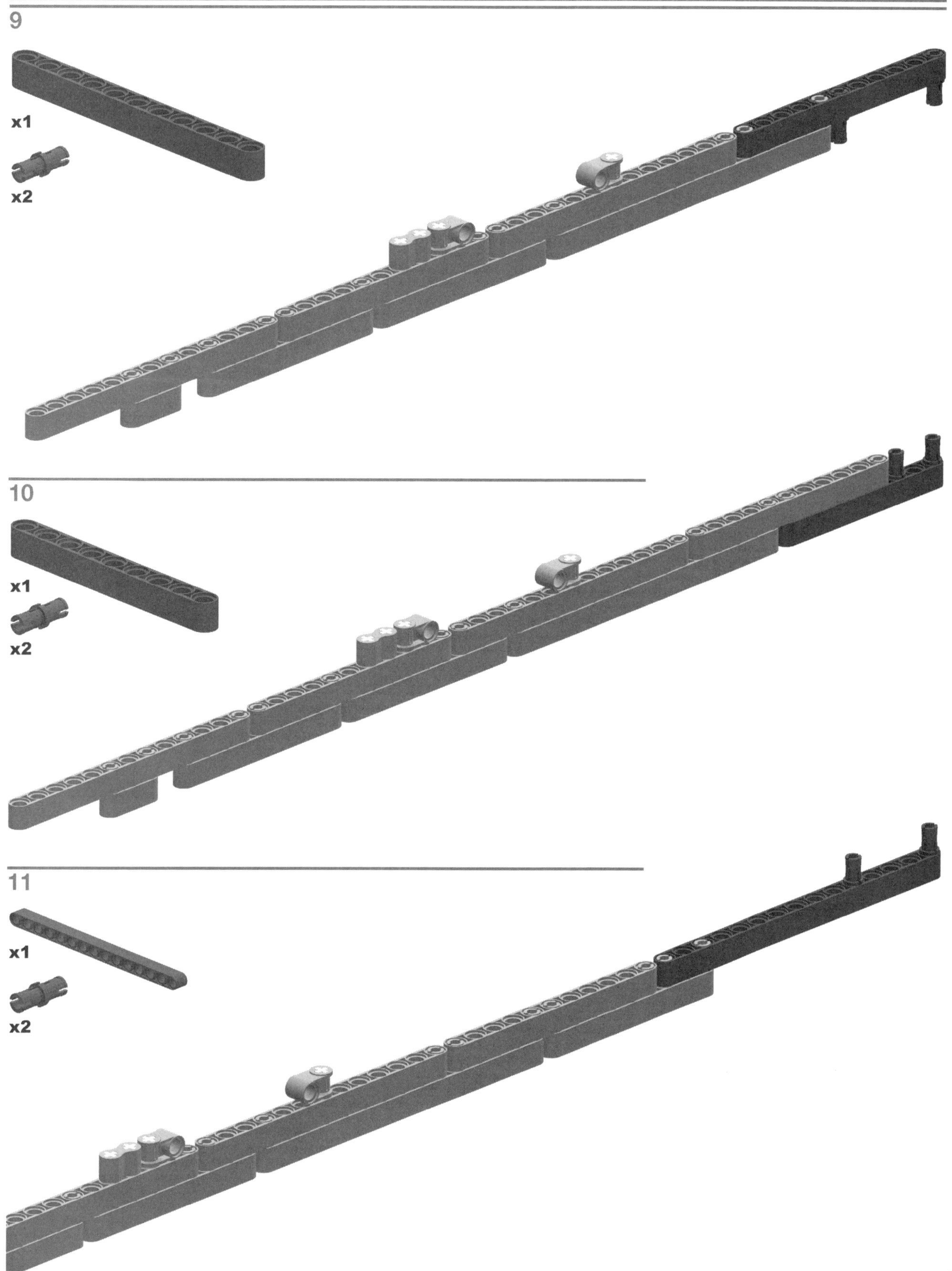
9
x1
x2
10
x1
x2
11
x1
x2

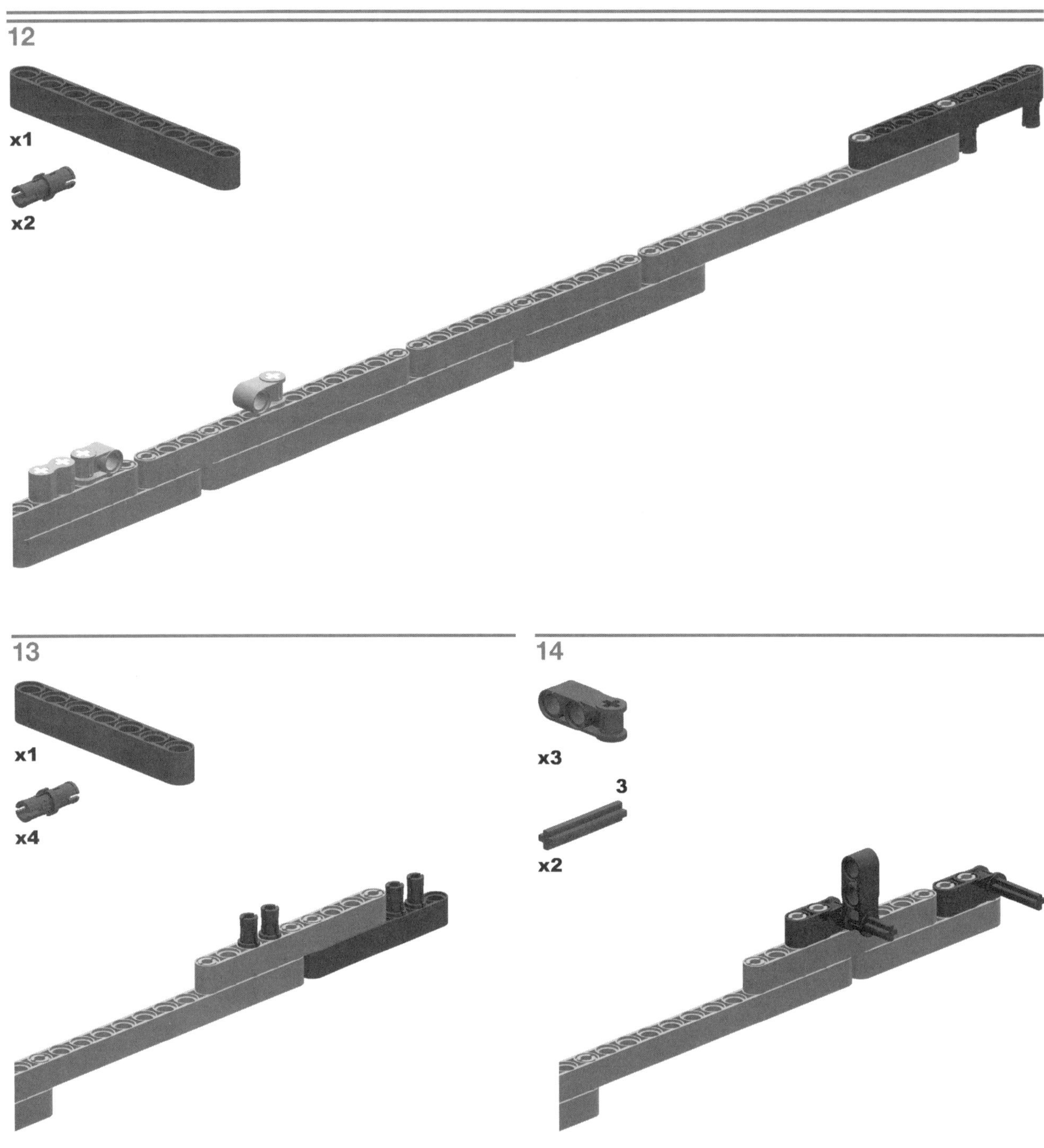
12
x1
x2
13
x1
x4
14
x3
3
x2

BARREL ROOF

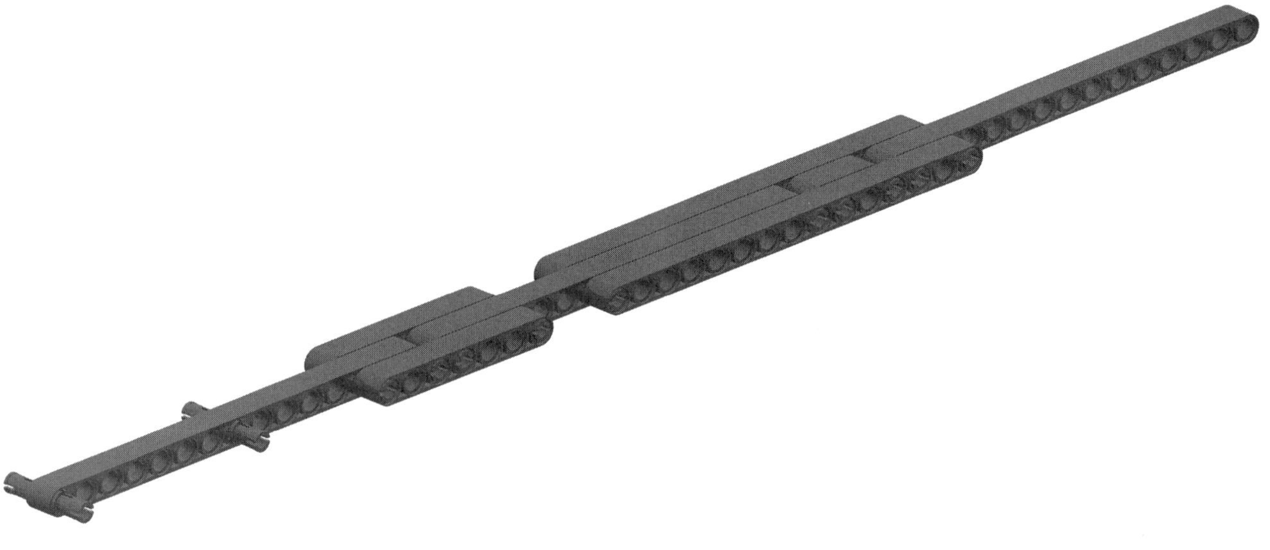

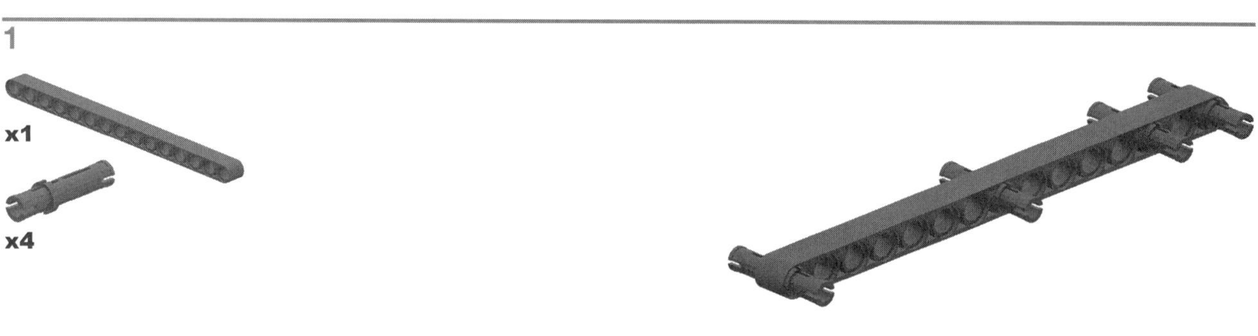

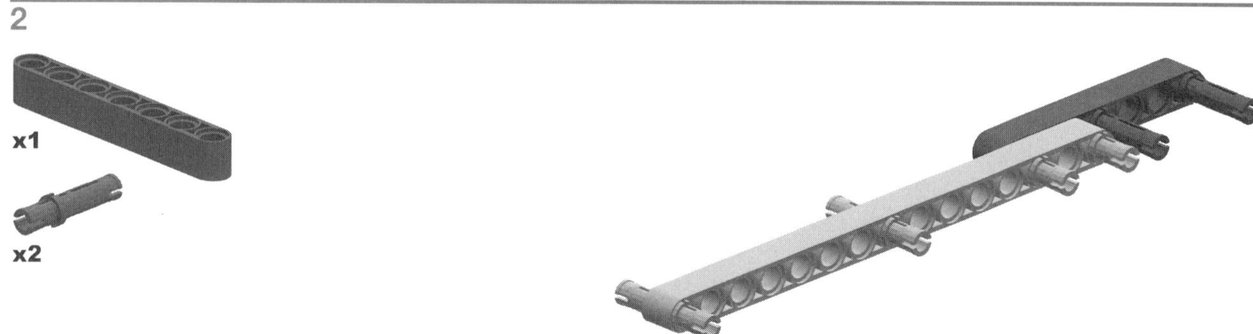

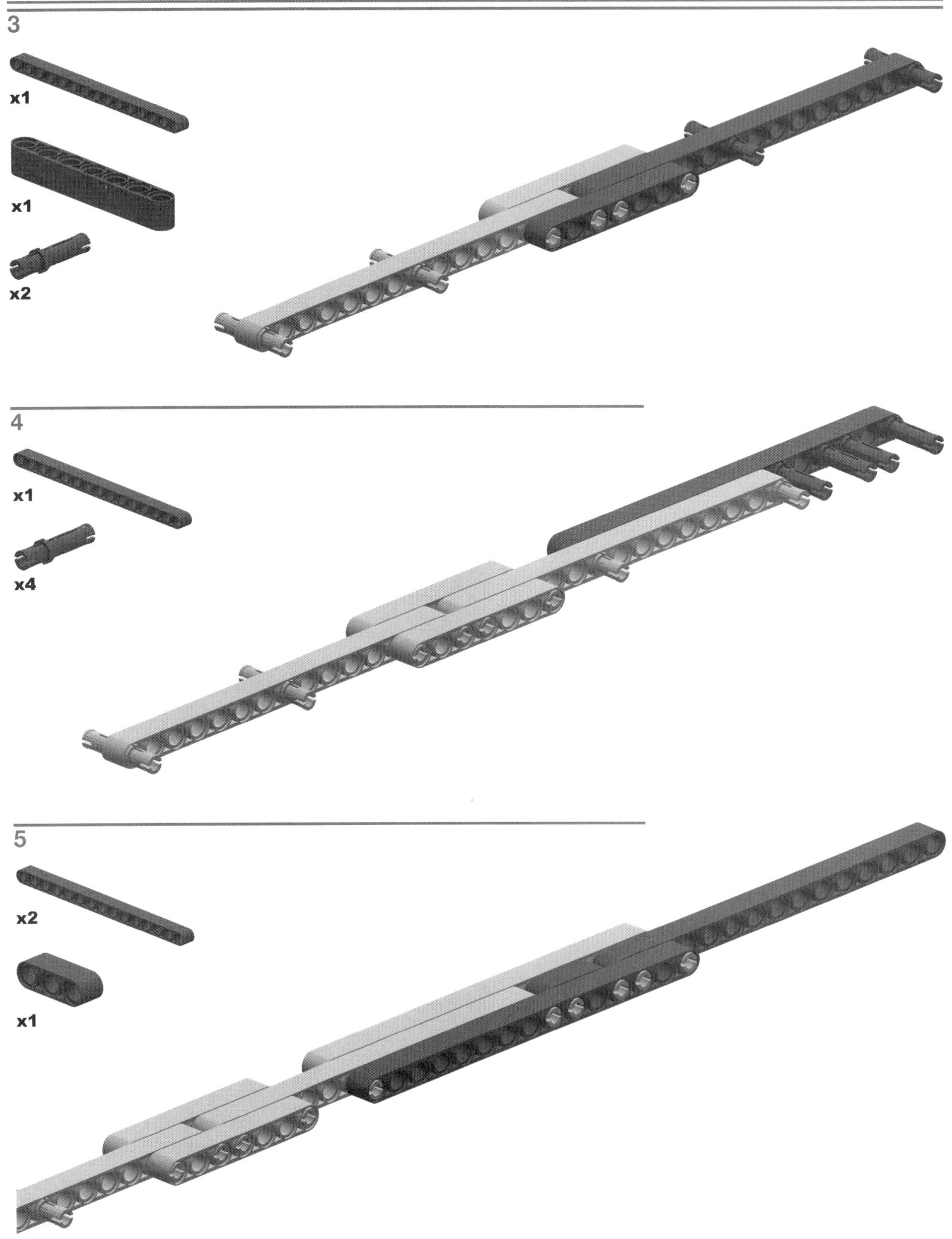

3
x1
x1
x2
4
x1
x4
5
x2
x1

BARREL WALL RIGHT

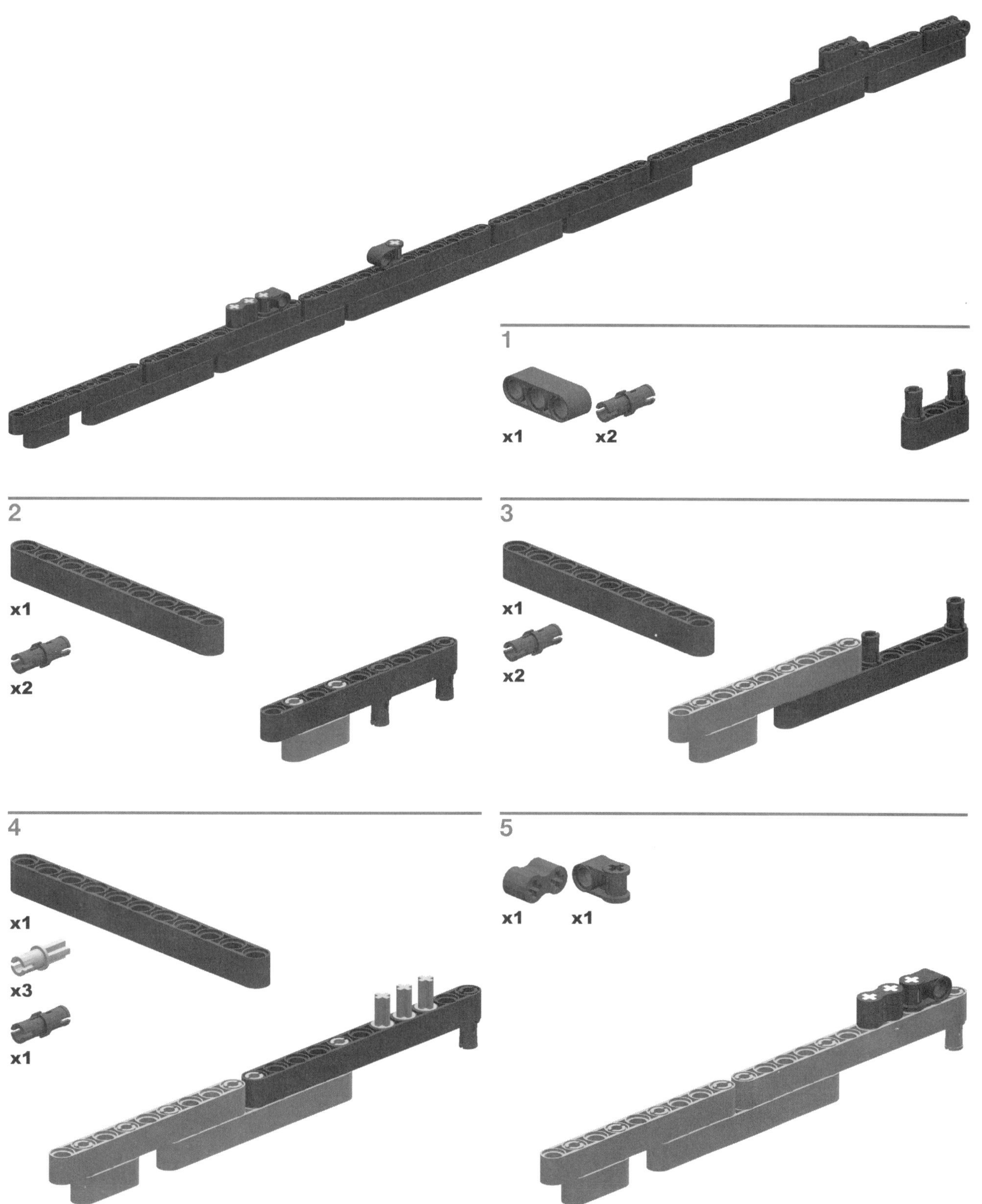

6

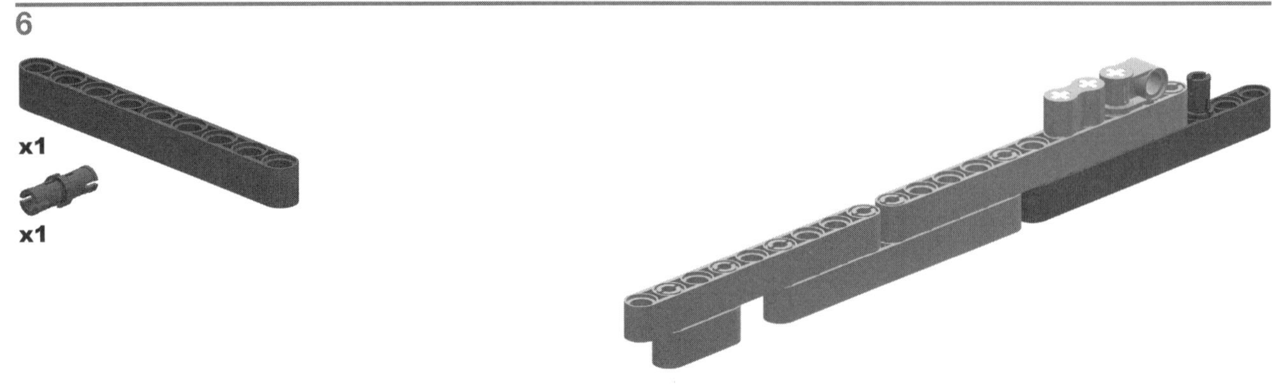

7

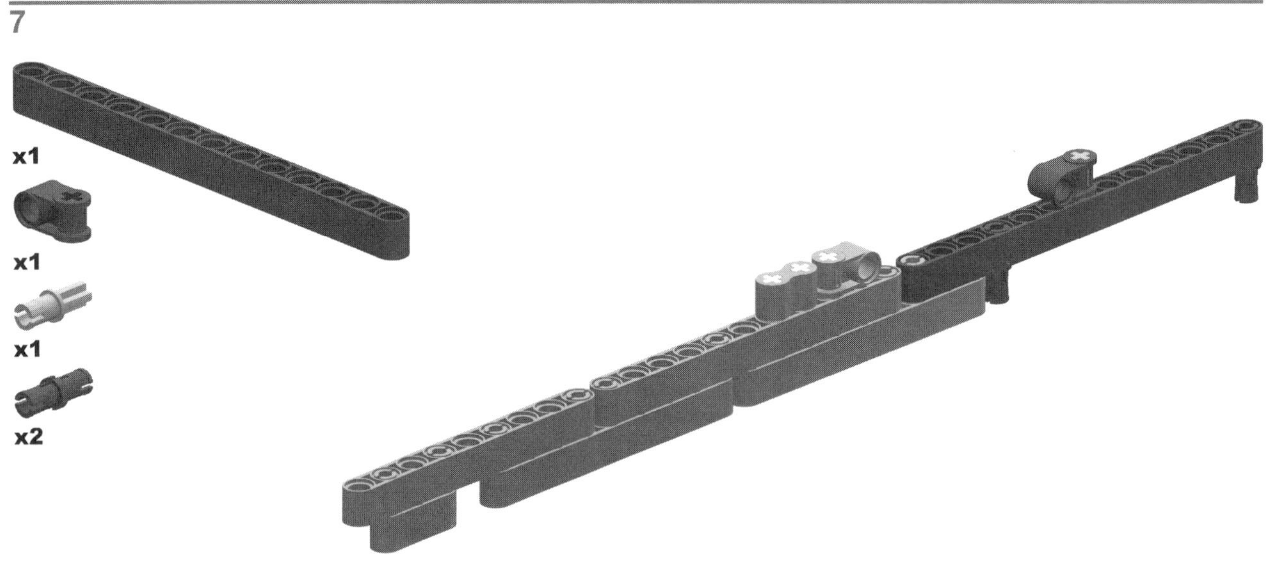

8

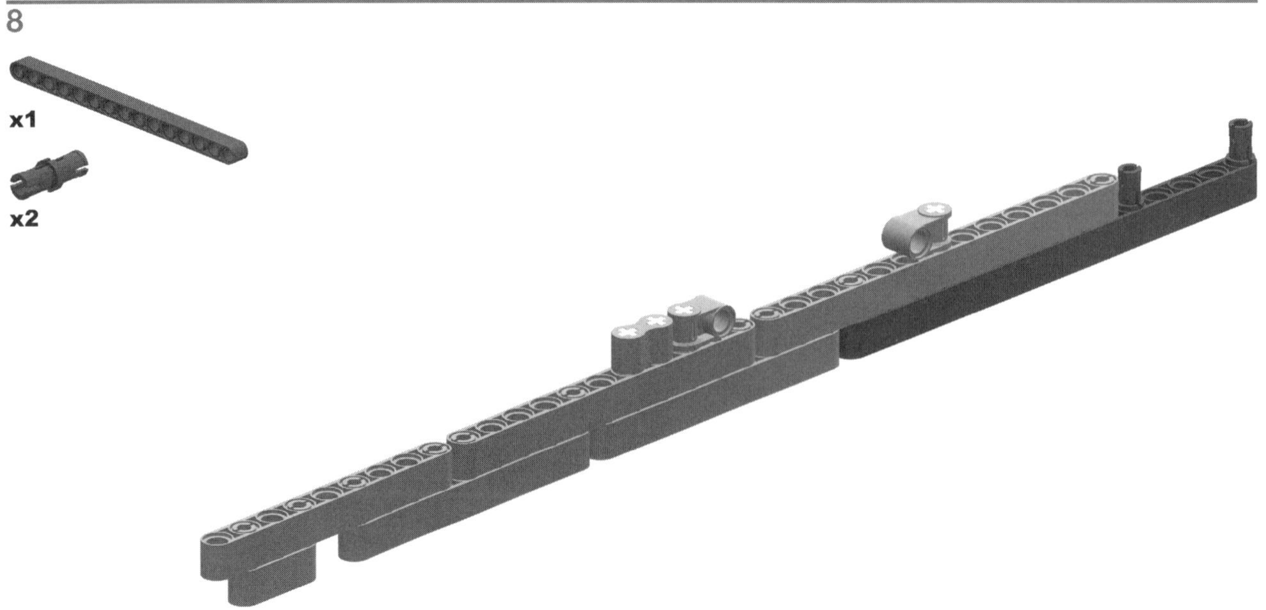

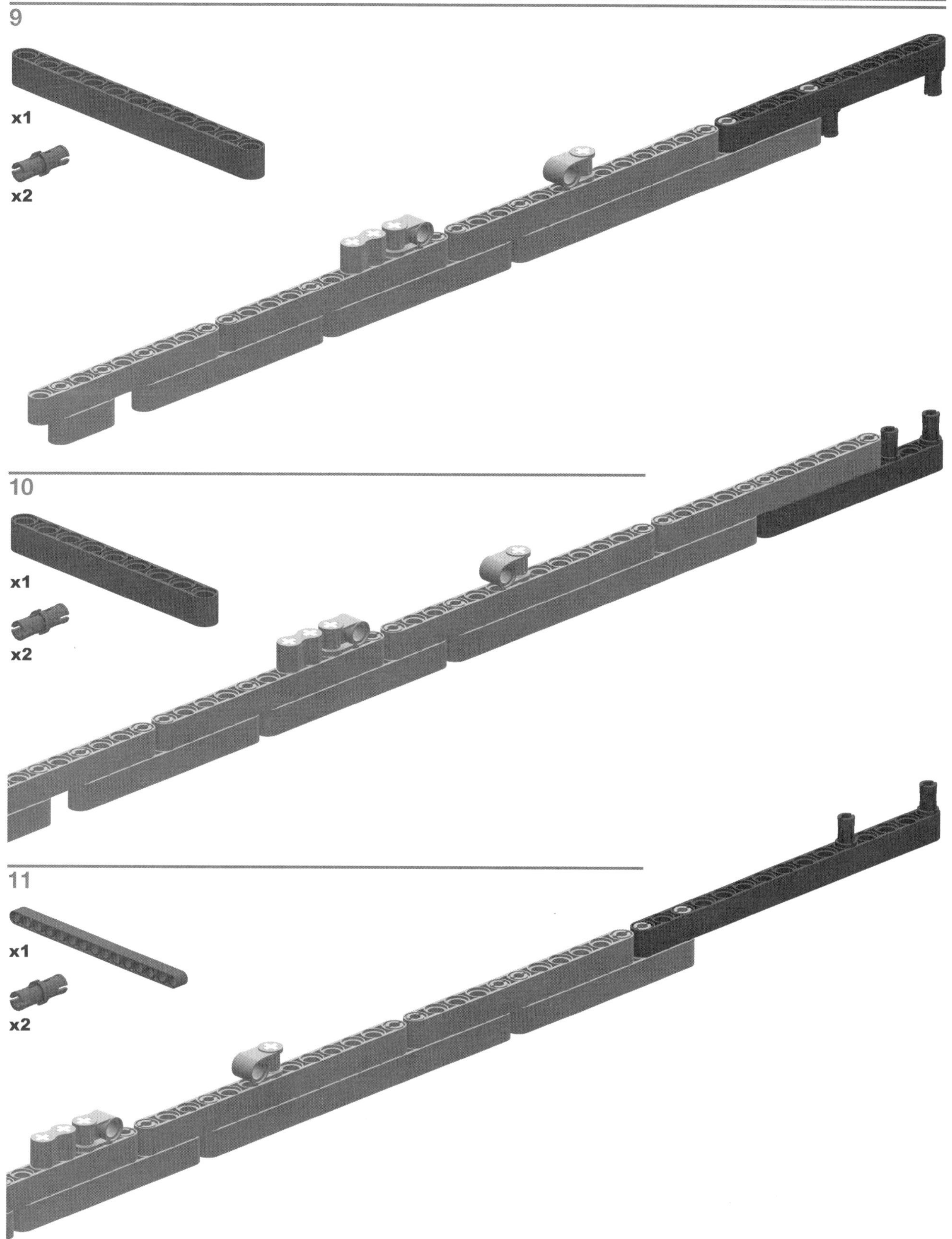
9
x1
x2
10
x1
x2
11
x1
x2

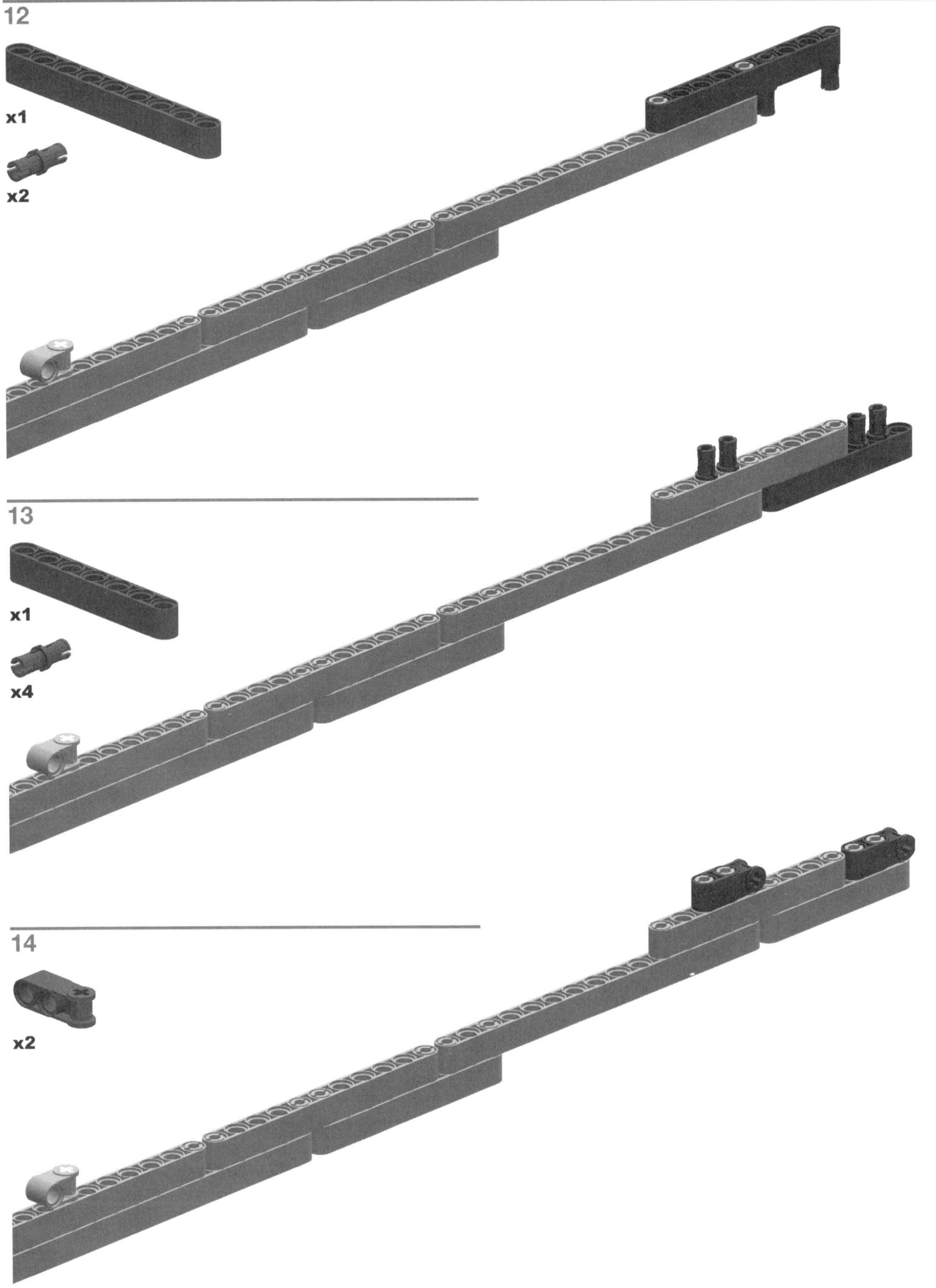
12
x1
x2
13
x1
x4
14
x2

BARREL BASE

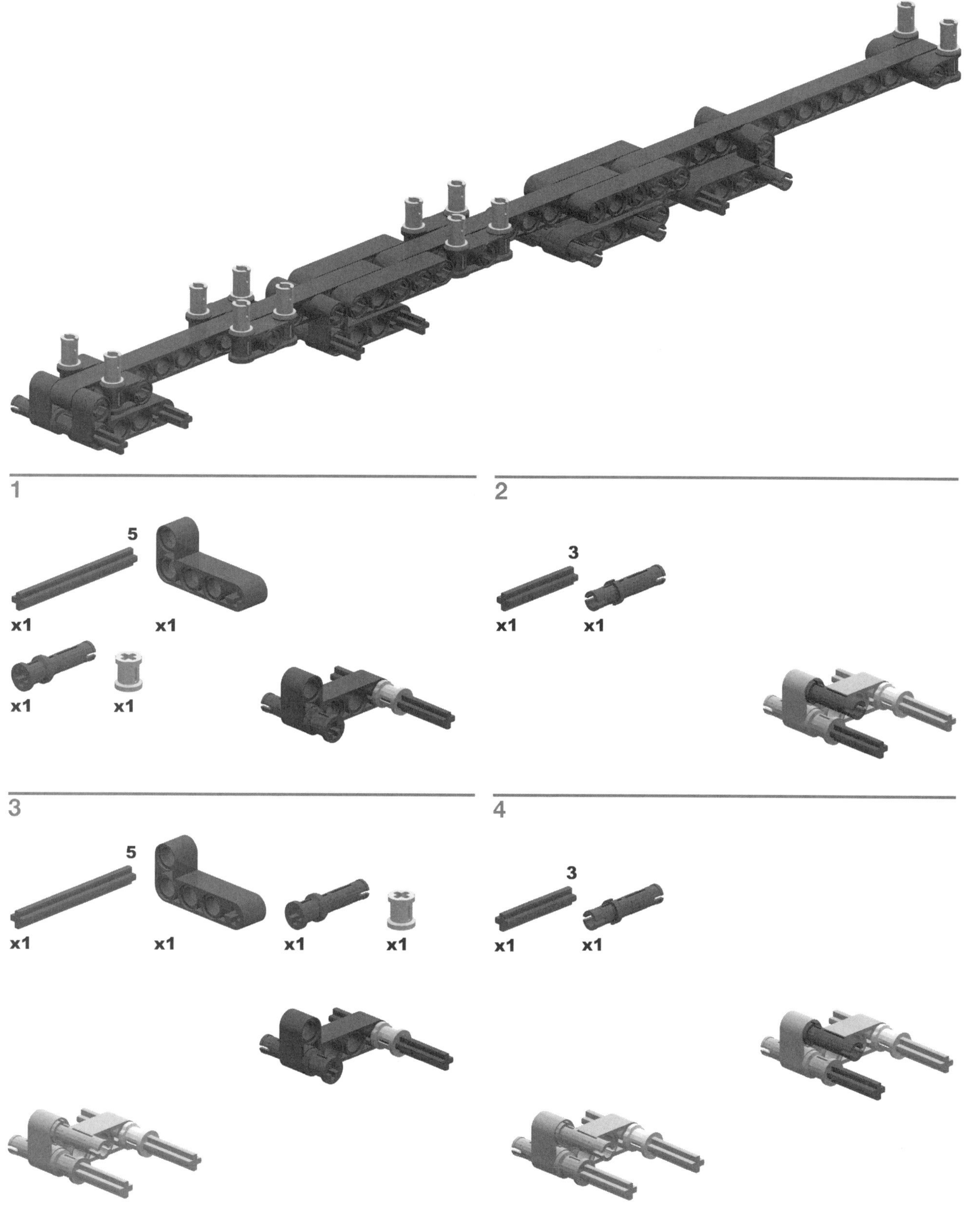

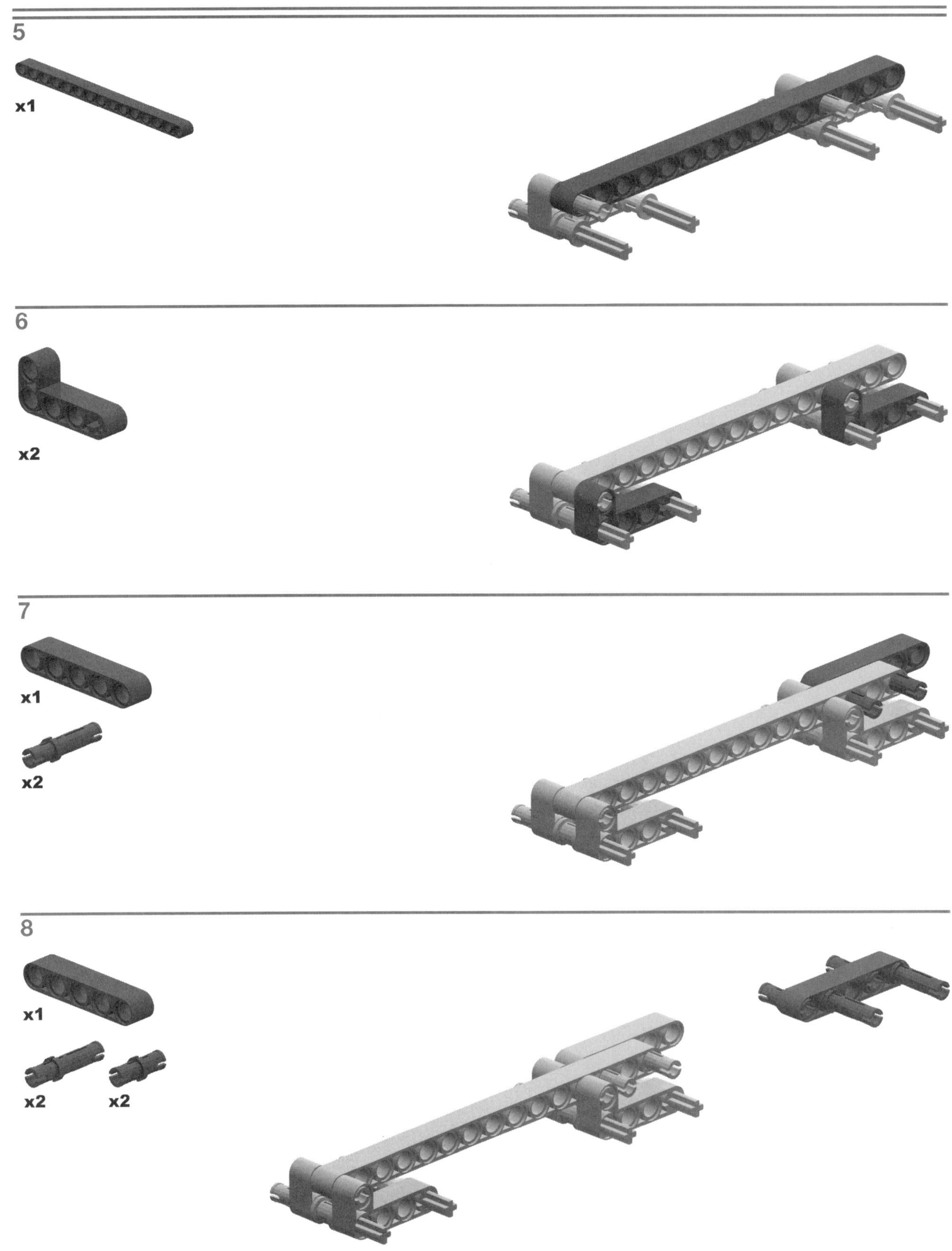
5
x1
6
x2
7
x1
x2
8
x1
x2
x2

9

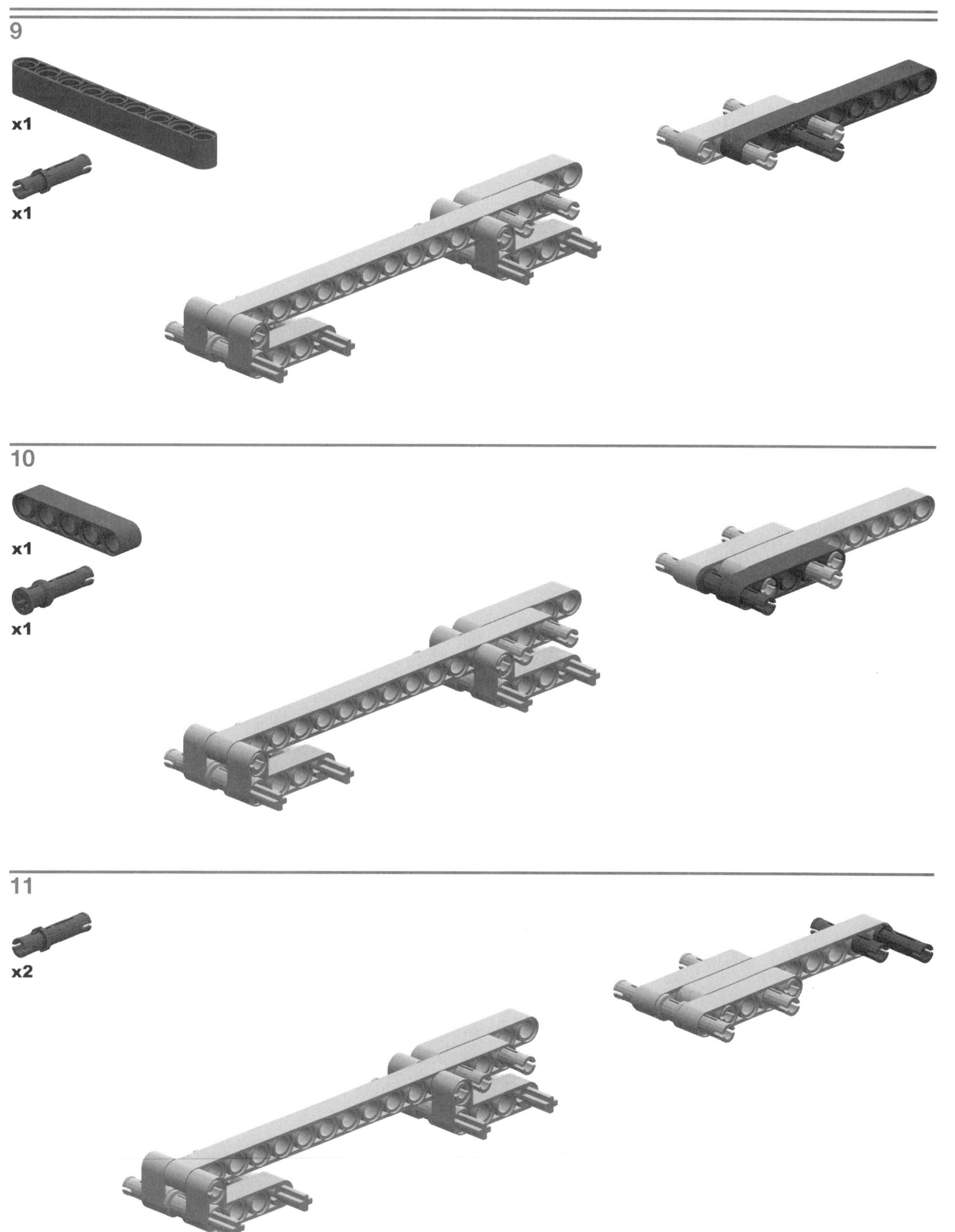

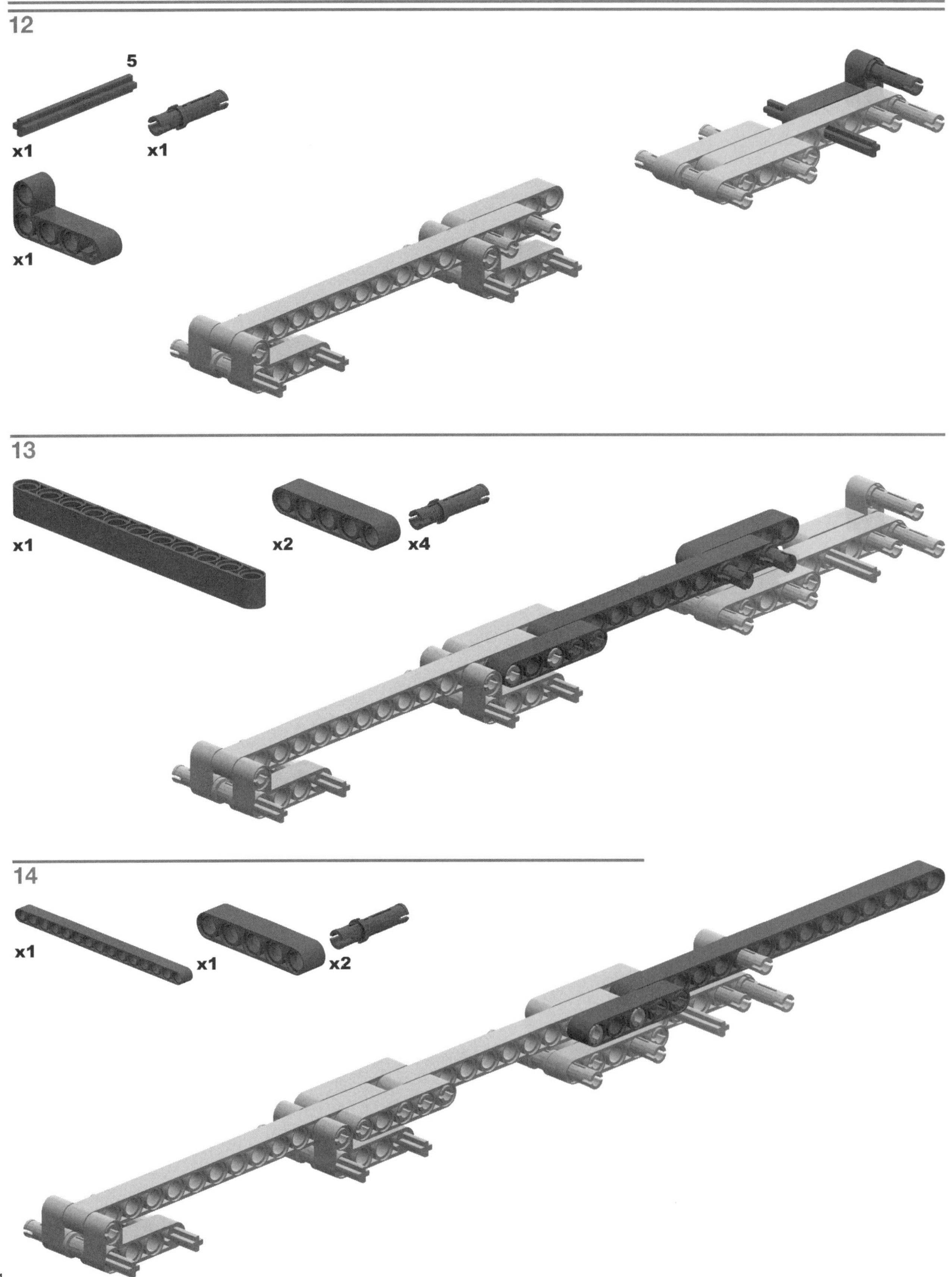
12
5
x1
x1
x1
13
x1
x2
x4
14
x1
x1
x2

15

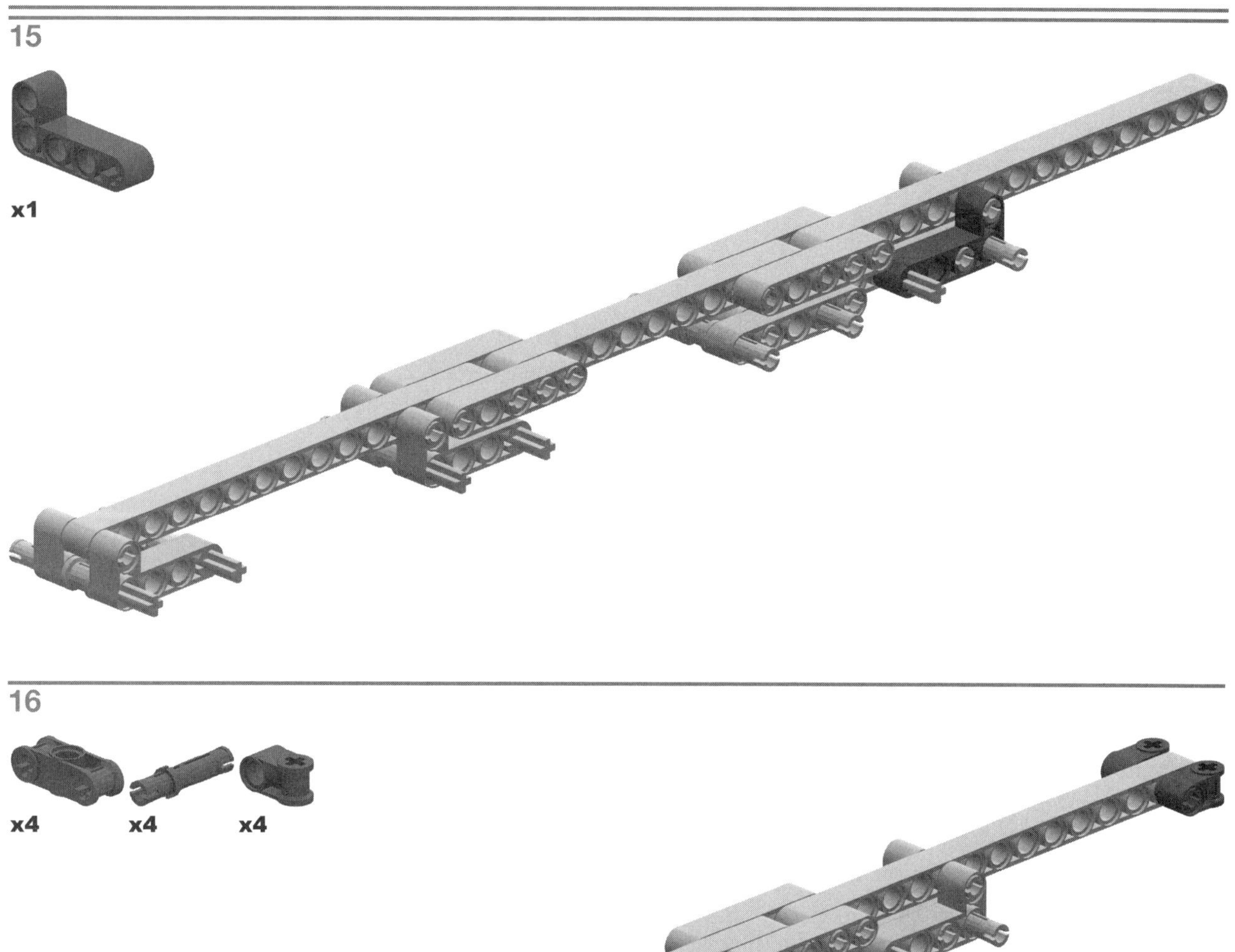

16

x4 x4 x4

17

x12

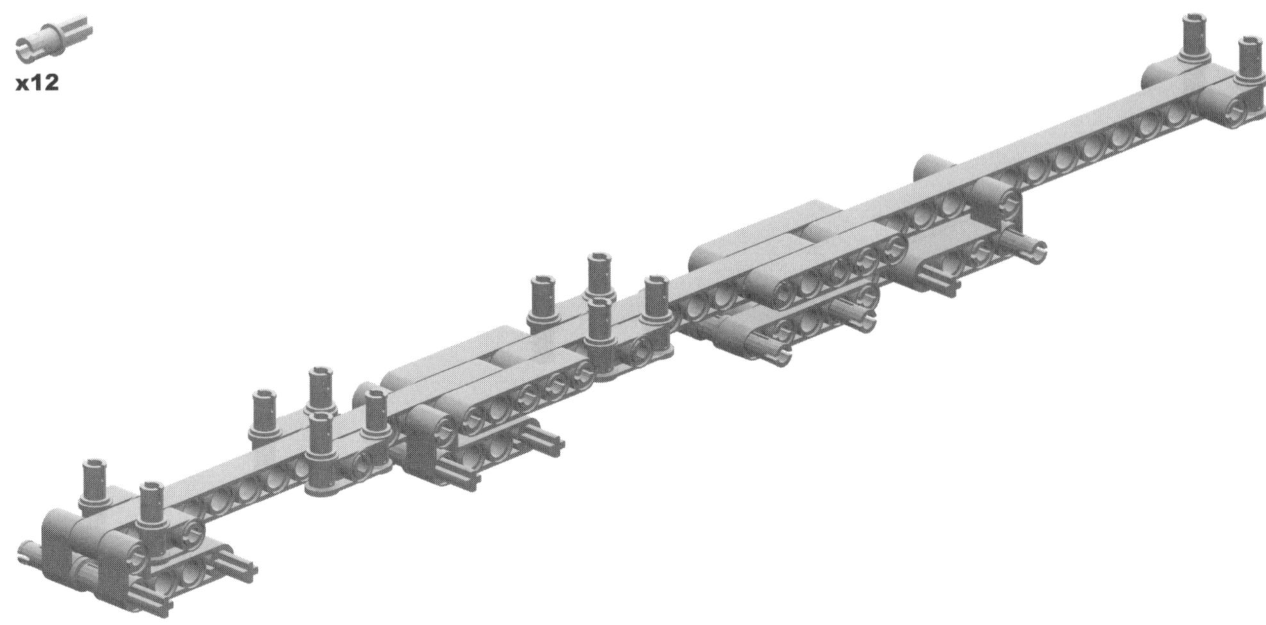

BARREL ASSEMBLY

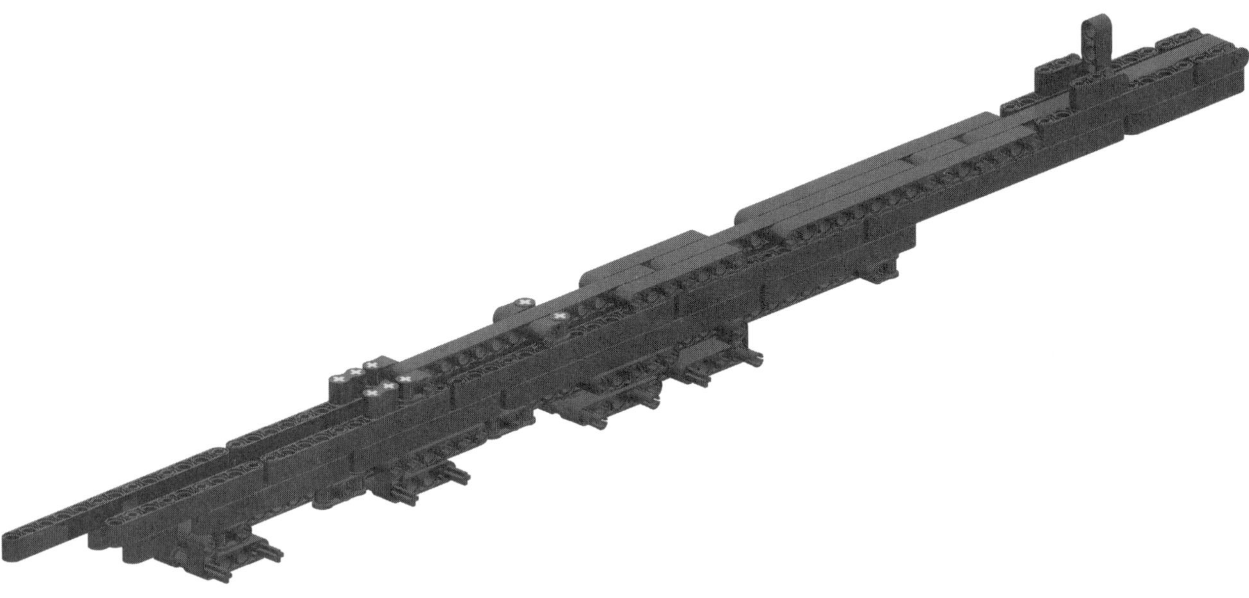

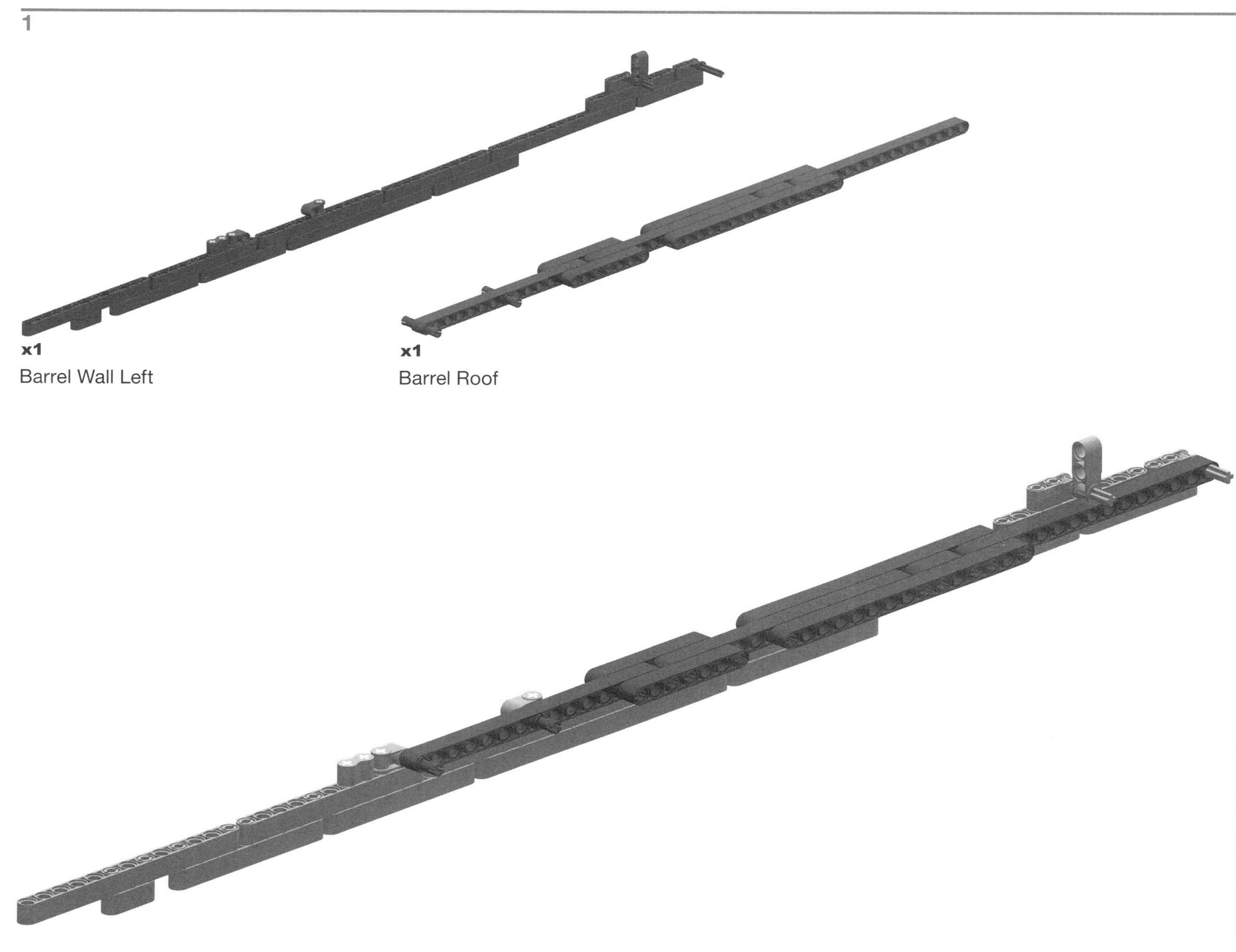
1
x1
Barrel Wall Left
x1
Barrel Roof

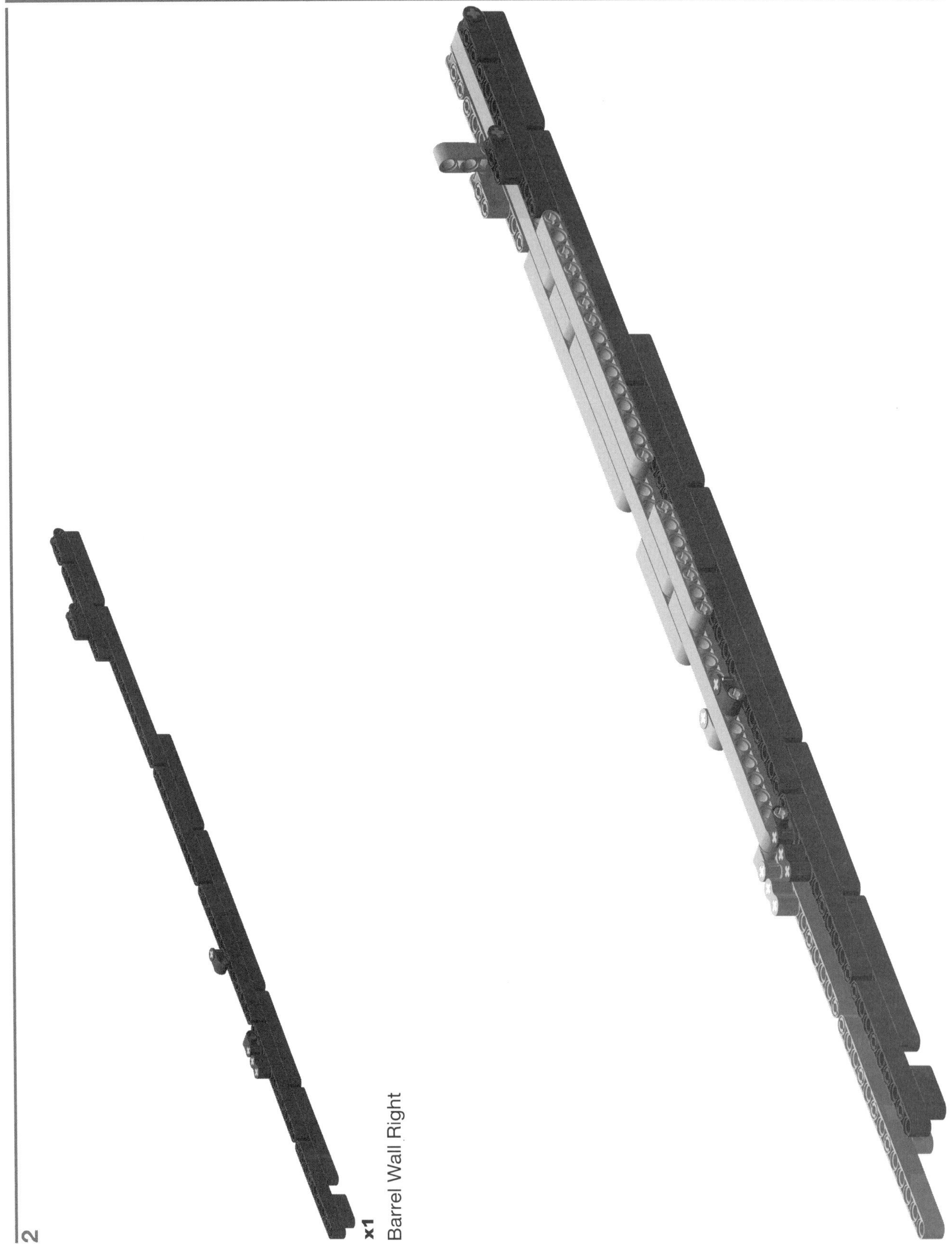
2
x1
Barrel Wall Right

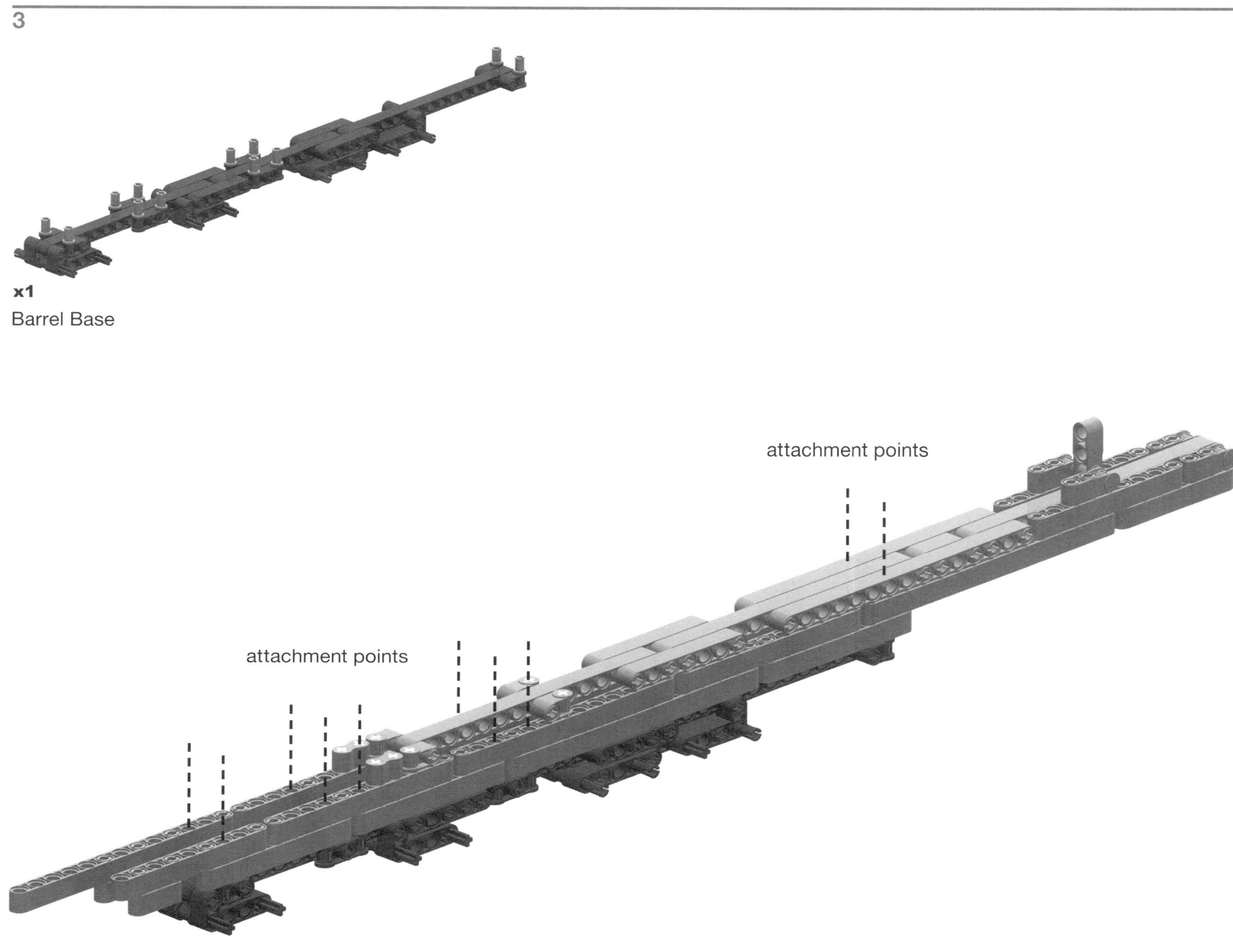
3
x1
Barrel Base
attachment points
attachment points

BOLT HANDLE

1

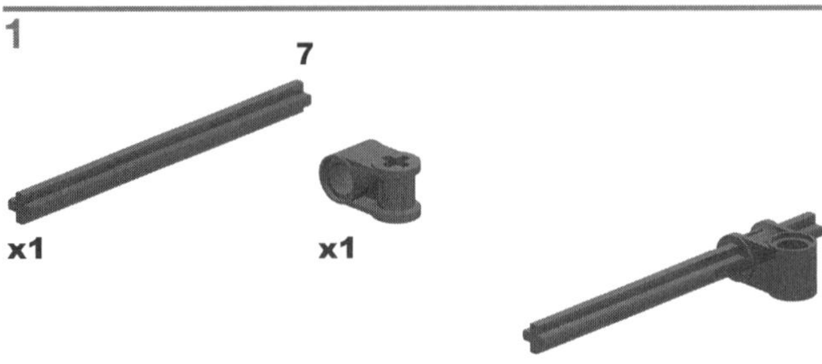

2

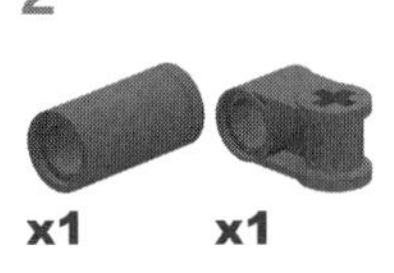

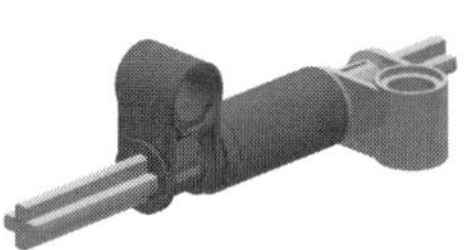

3

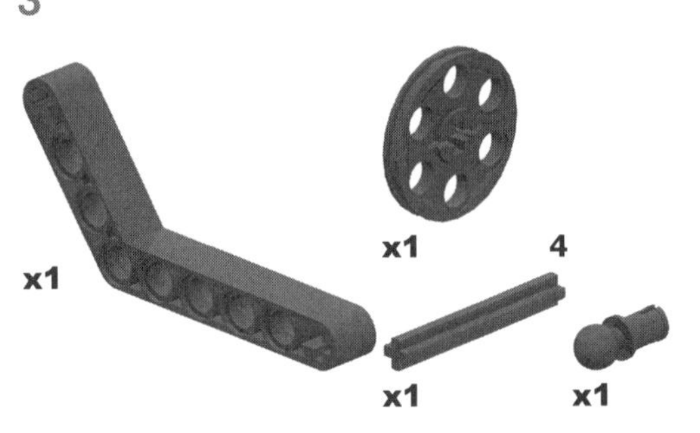

4

x4

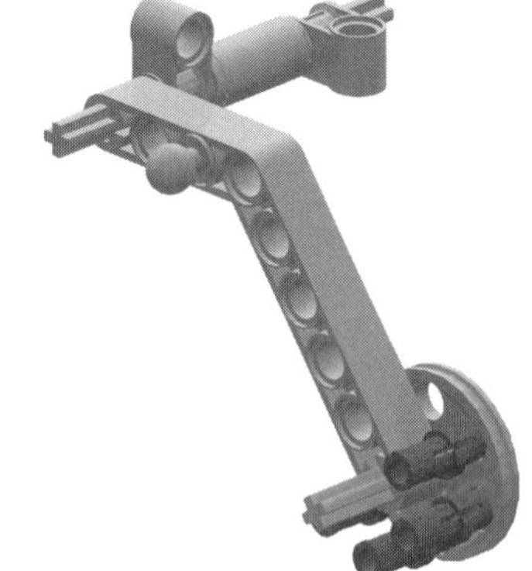

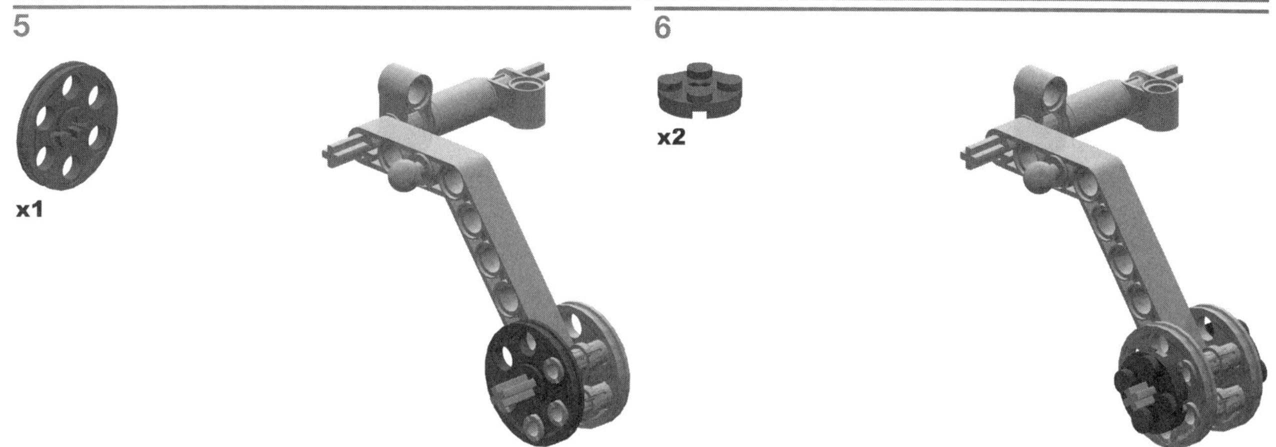

HAMMER

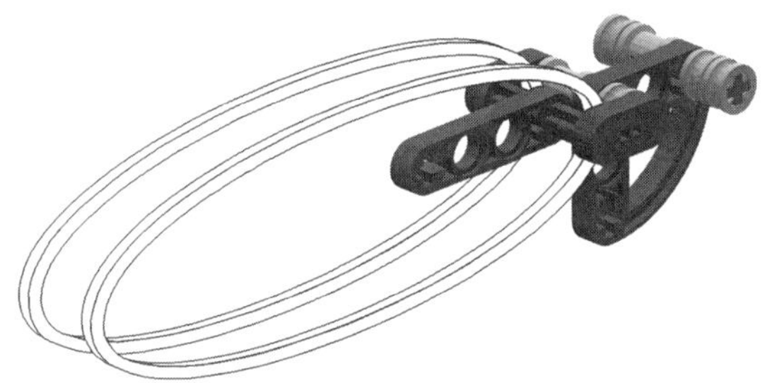

1

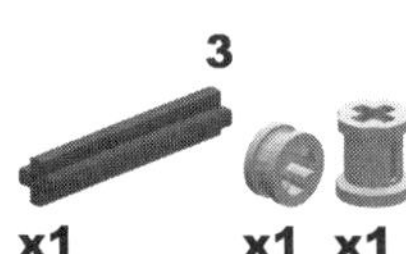

2

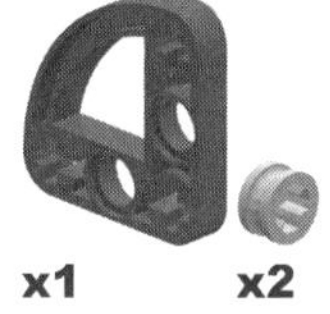

3

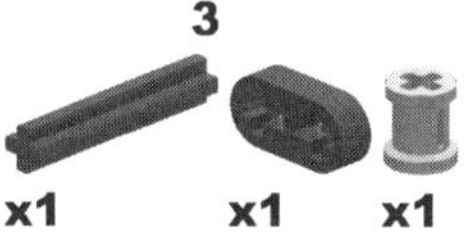

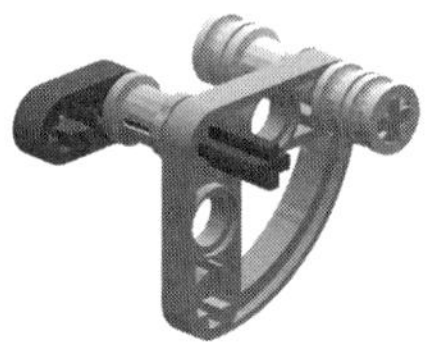

4

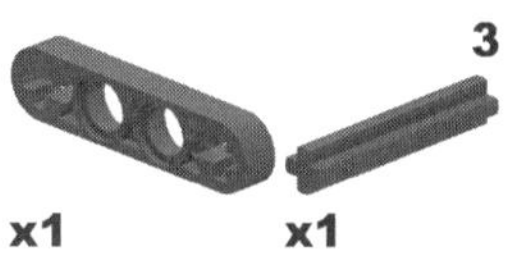

5

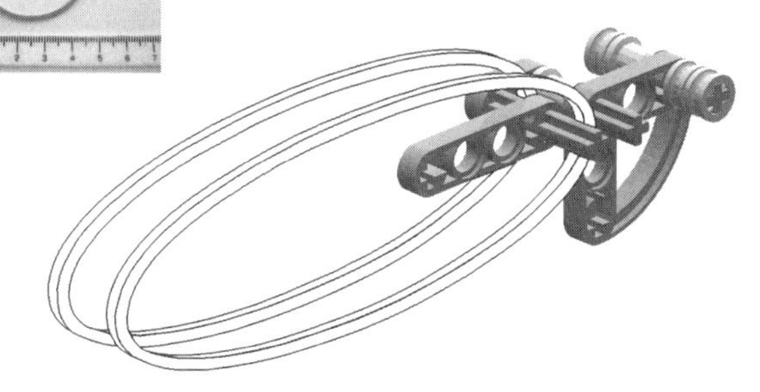

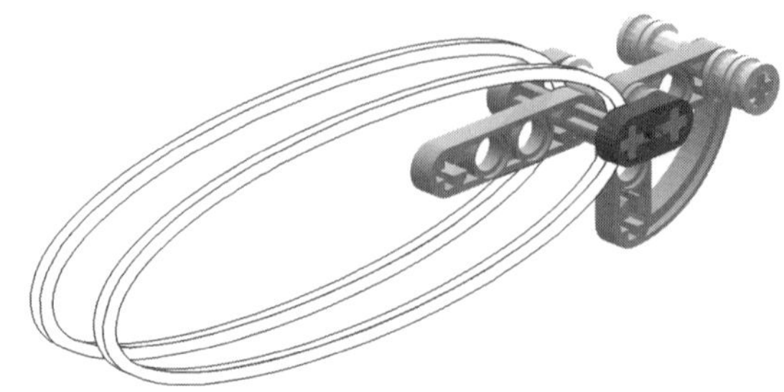

BOLT

1

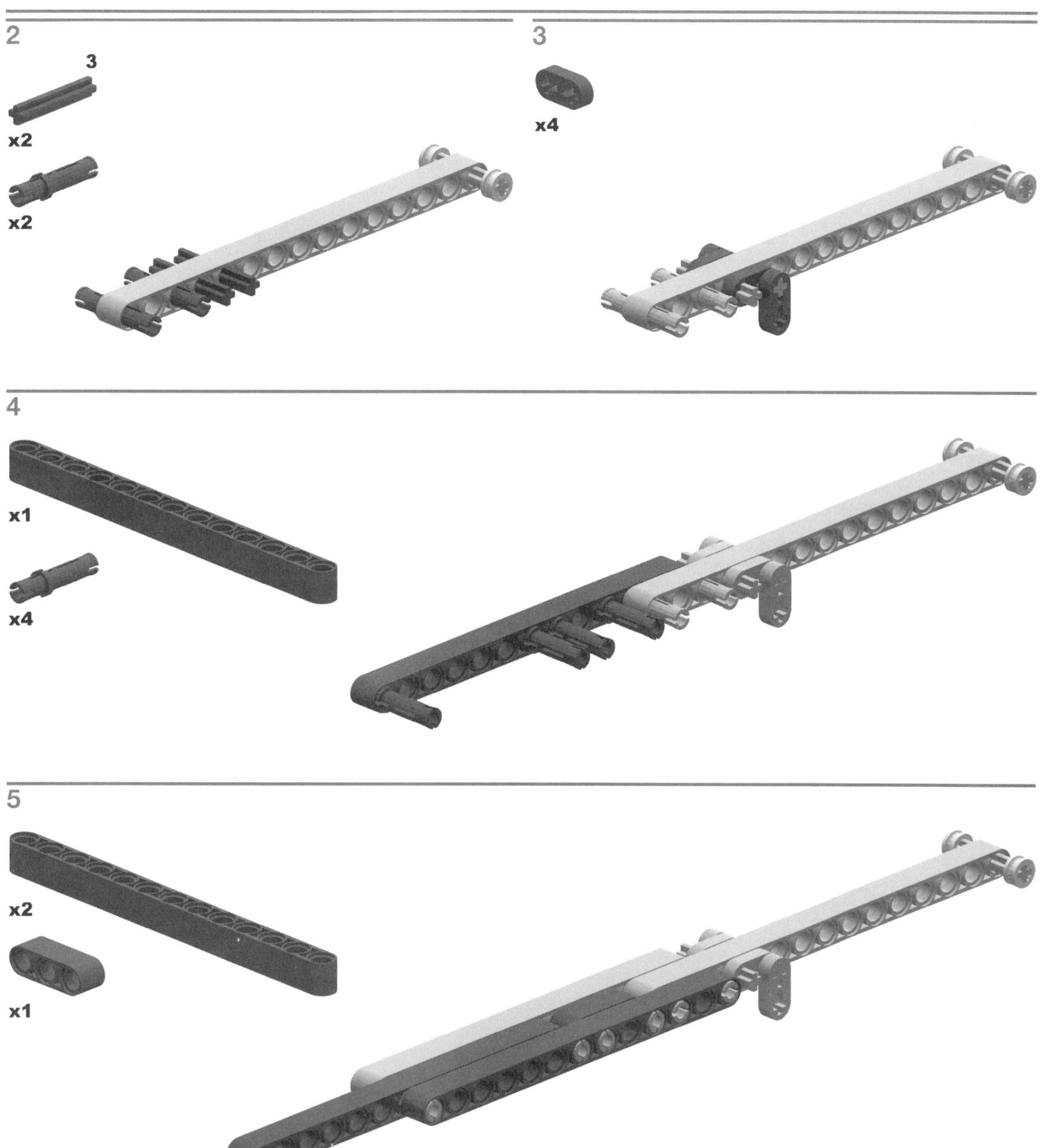
2
3
x2
x2
3
x4
4
x1
x4
5
x2
x1

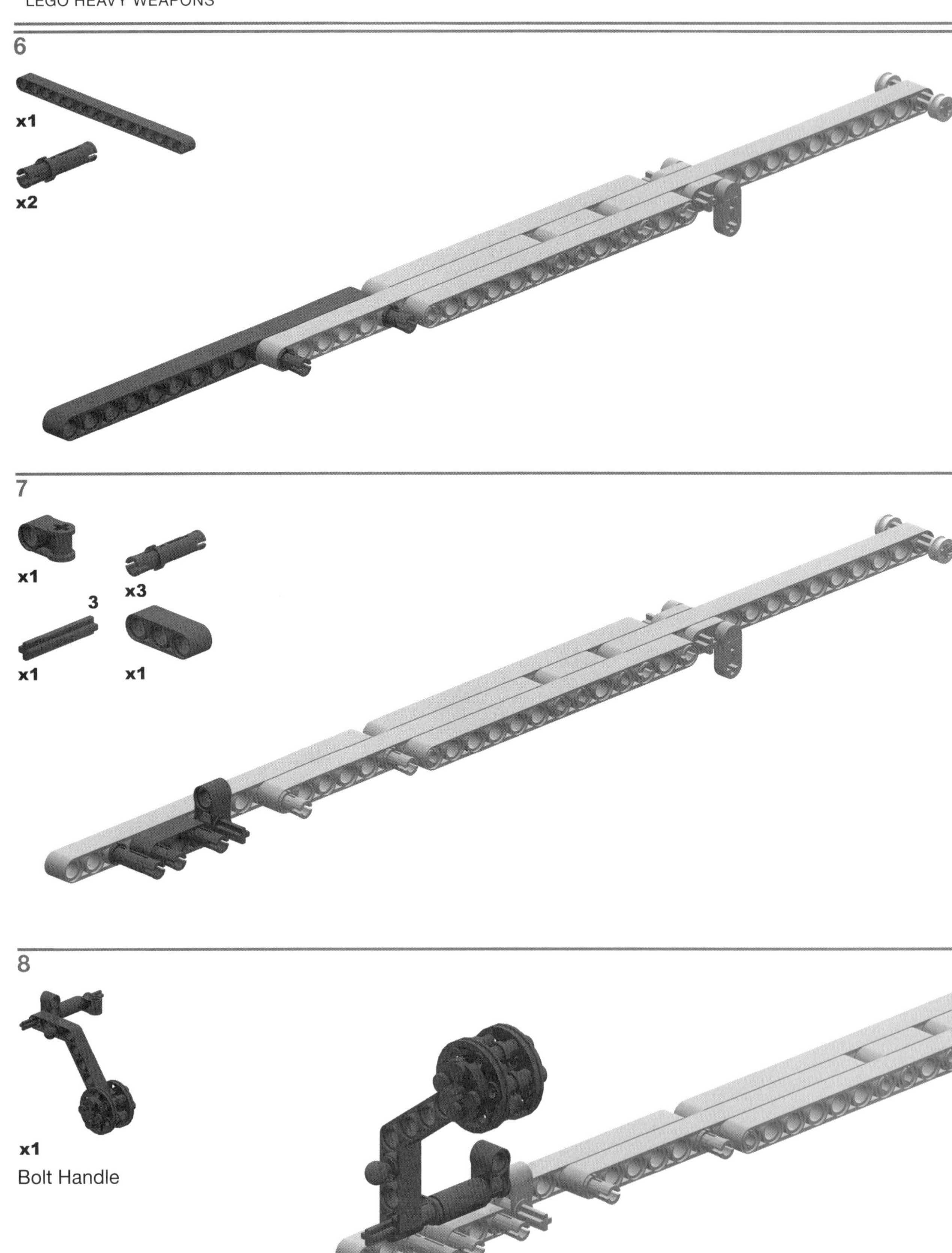
6
x1
x2
7
x1
x3
3
x1
x1
8
x1
Bolt Handle

9

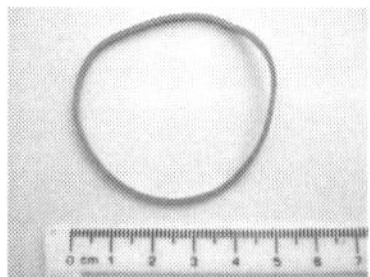

x1

Loop the rubber band around the towball pin, pull it through the bent liftarm, and loop the other end over the pin as shown. Make sure this band is relatively tight (loop it over itself if you need to), so that it flips the whole Bolt Handle down by itself, as shown. (It may be a bit loose at the moment, but you'll fix that in the next two steps.)

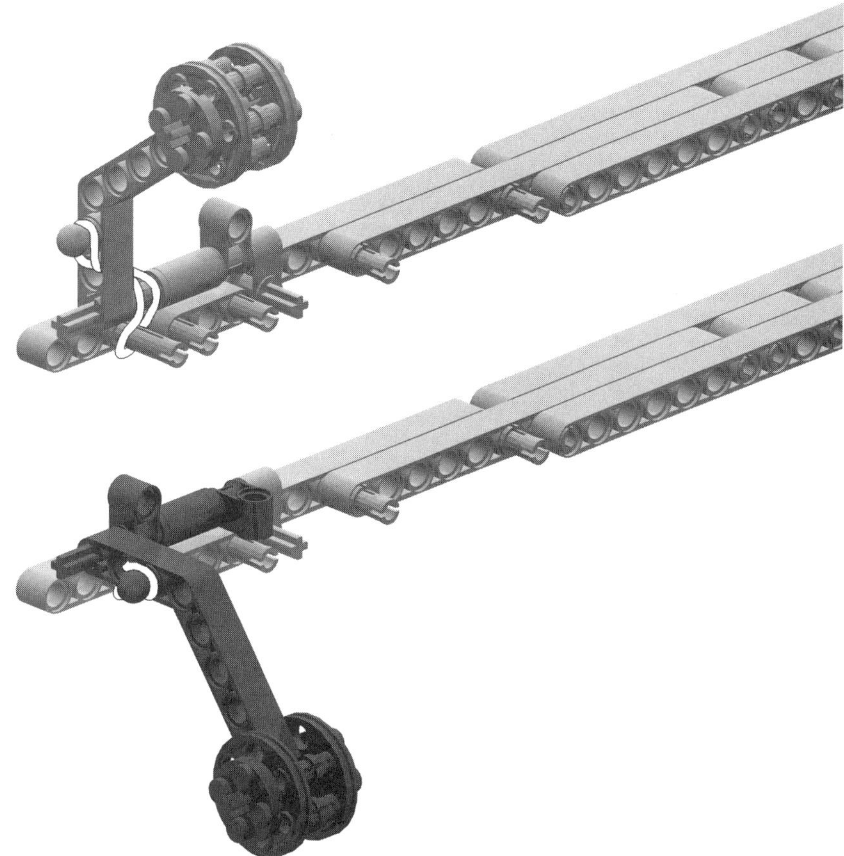

10

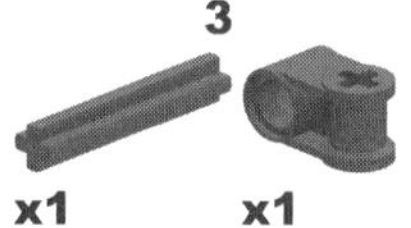

11

x1

12

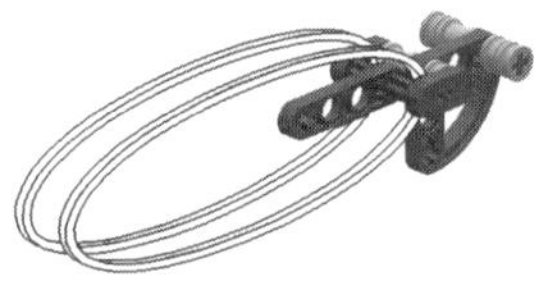

x1

Hammer

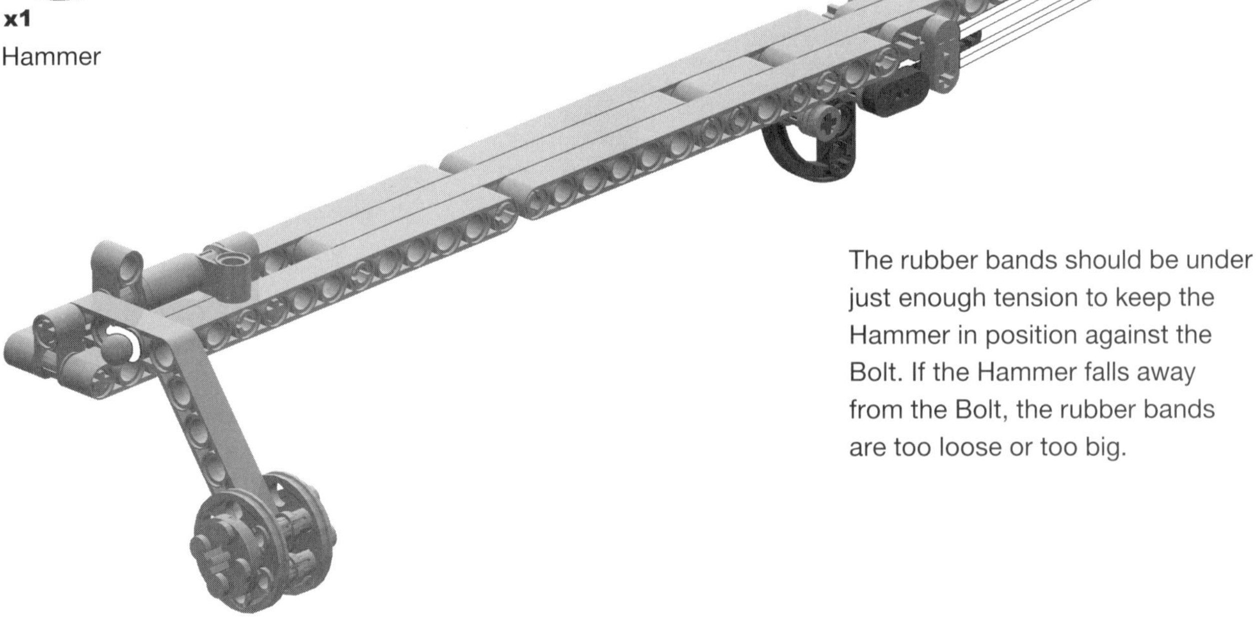

The rubber bands should be under just enough tension to keep the Hammer in position against the Bolt. If the Hammer falls away from the Bolt, the rubber bands are too loose or too big.

FRAME WALL RIGHT

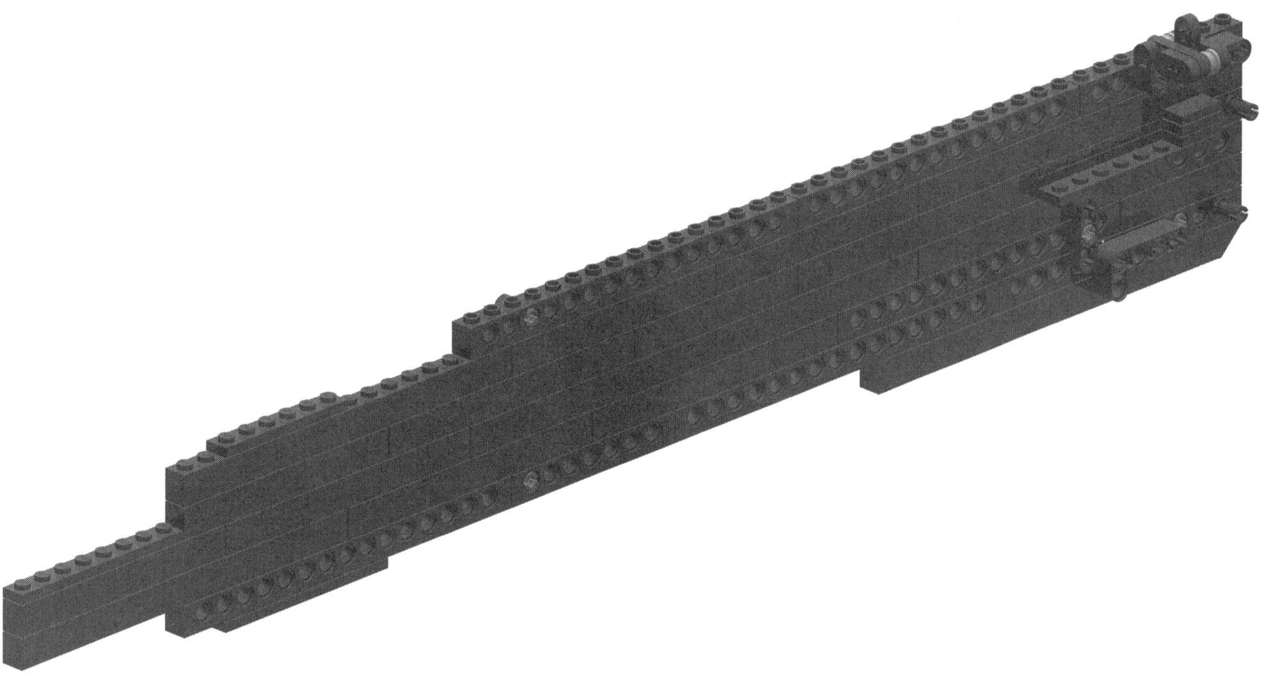

1

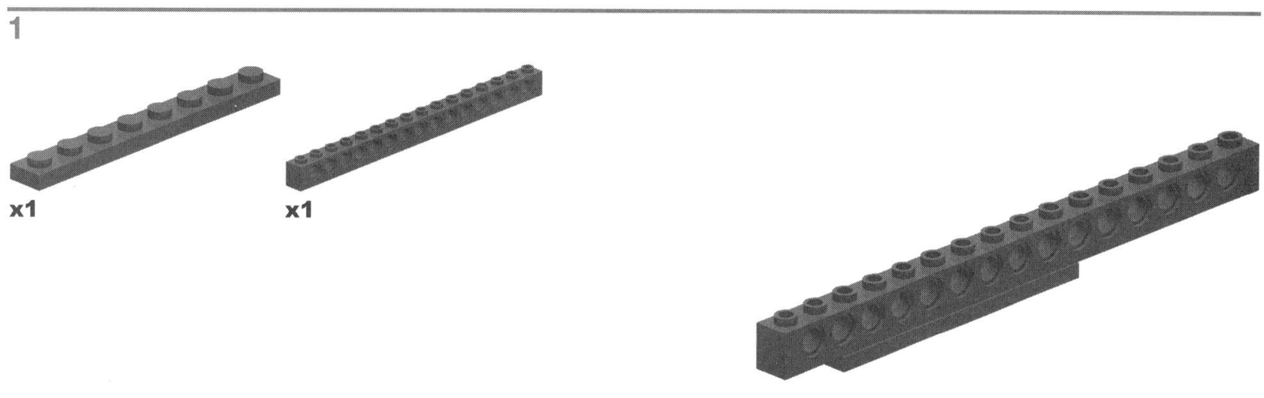

2

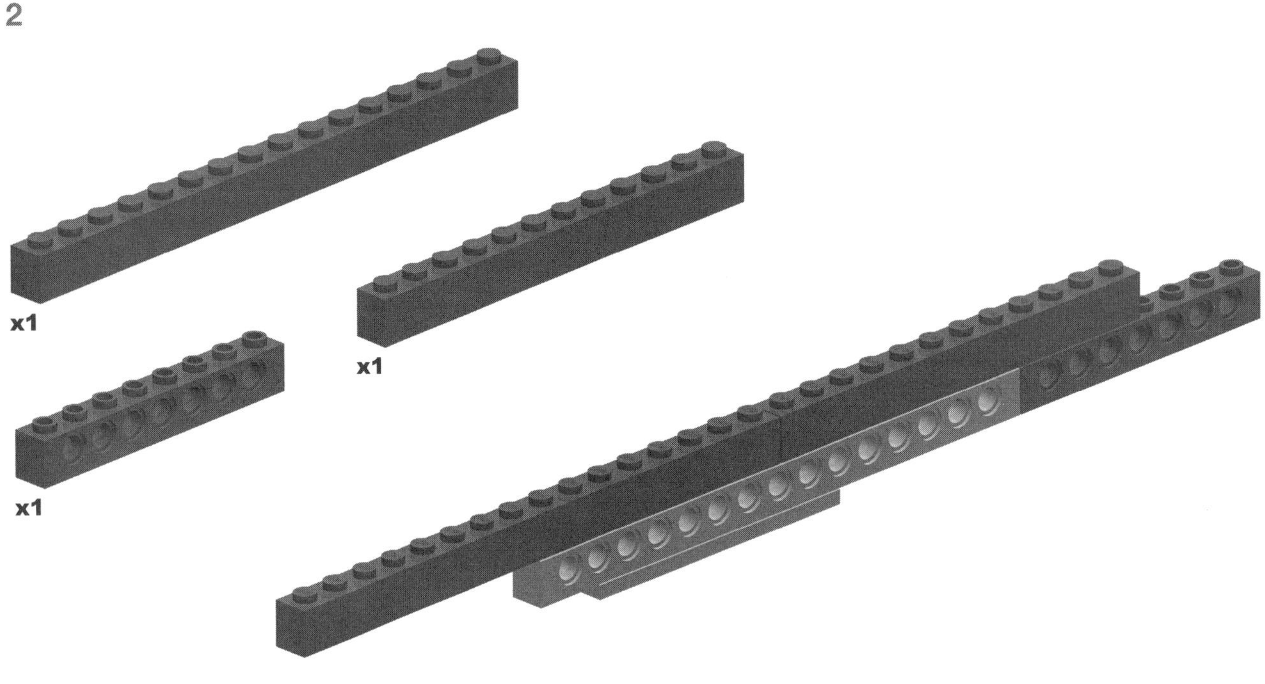

3

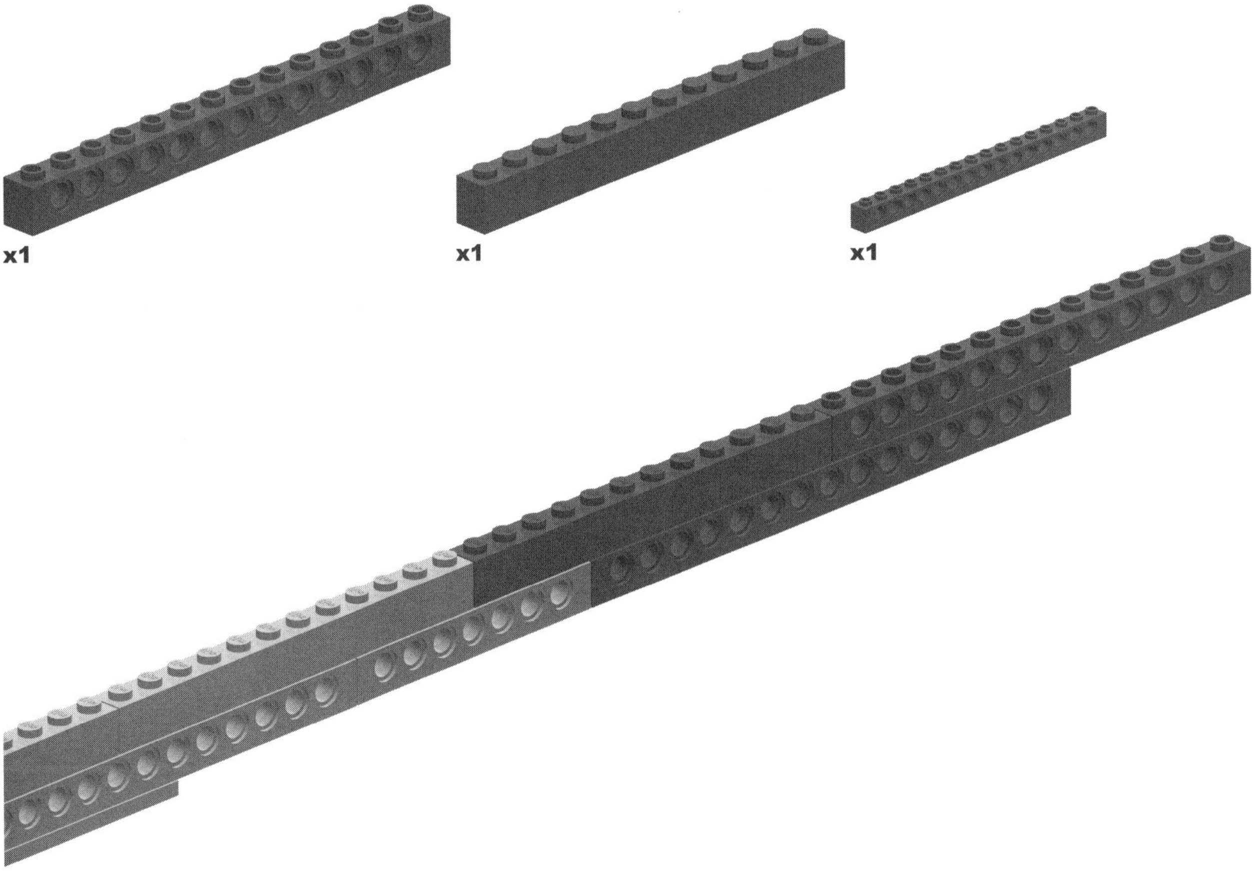

x1

x1

x1

4

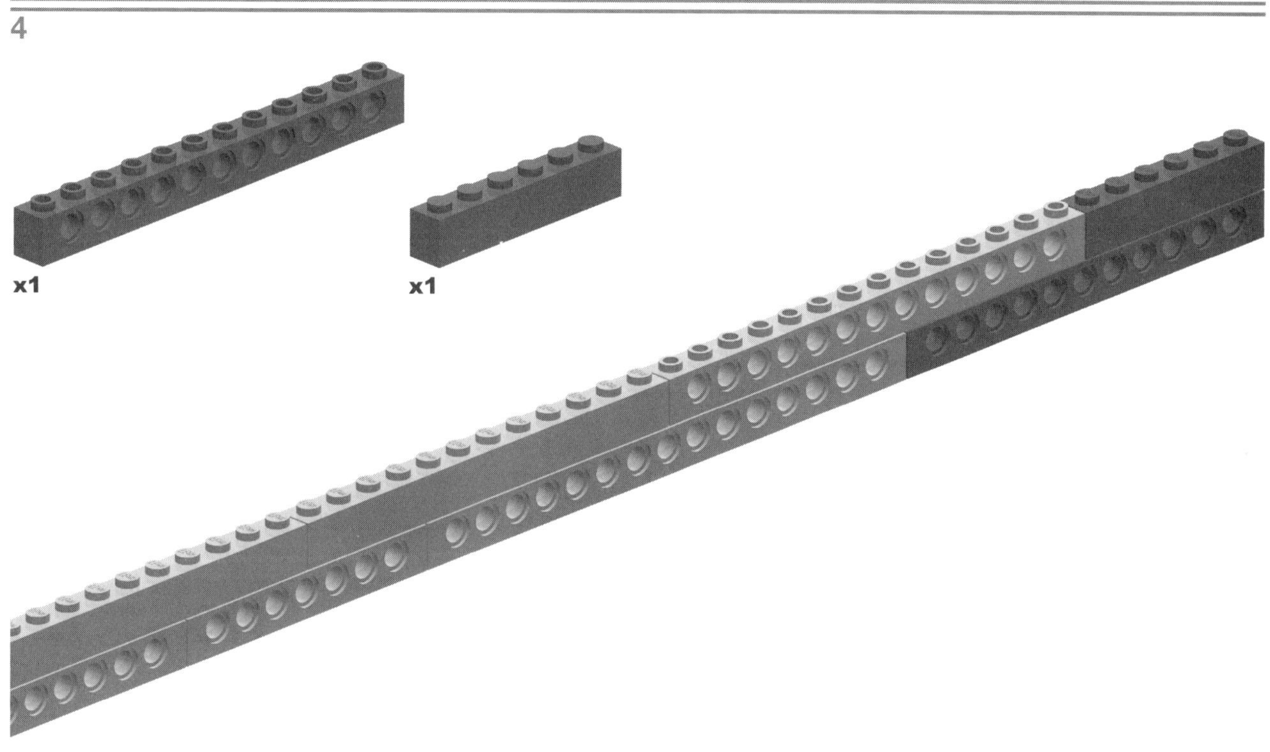

5

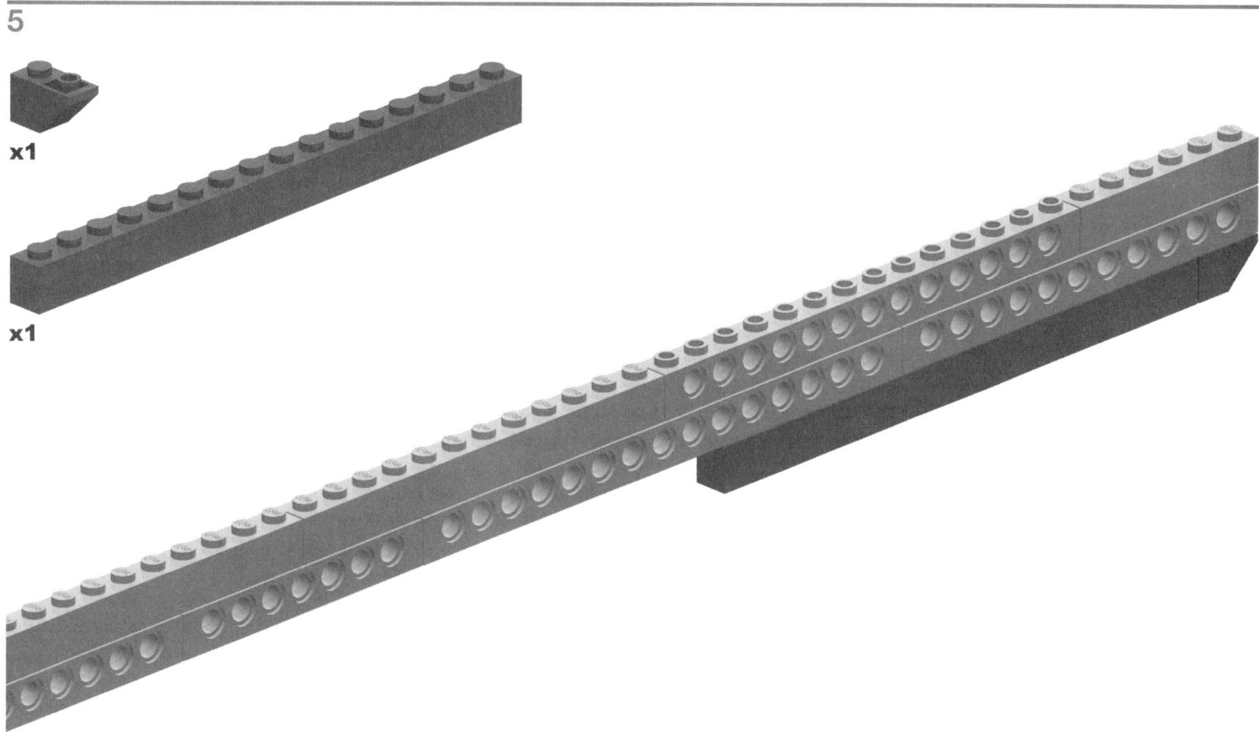

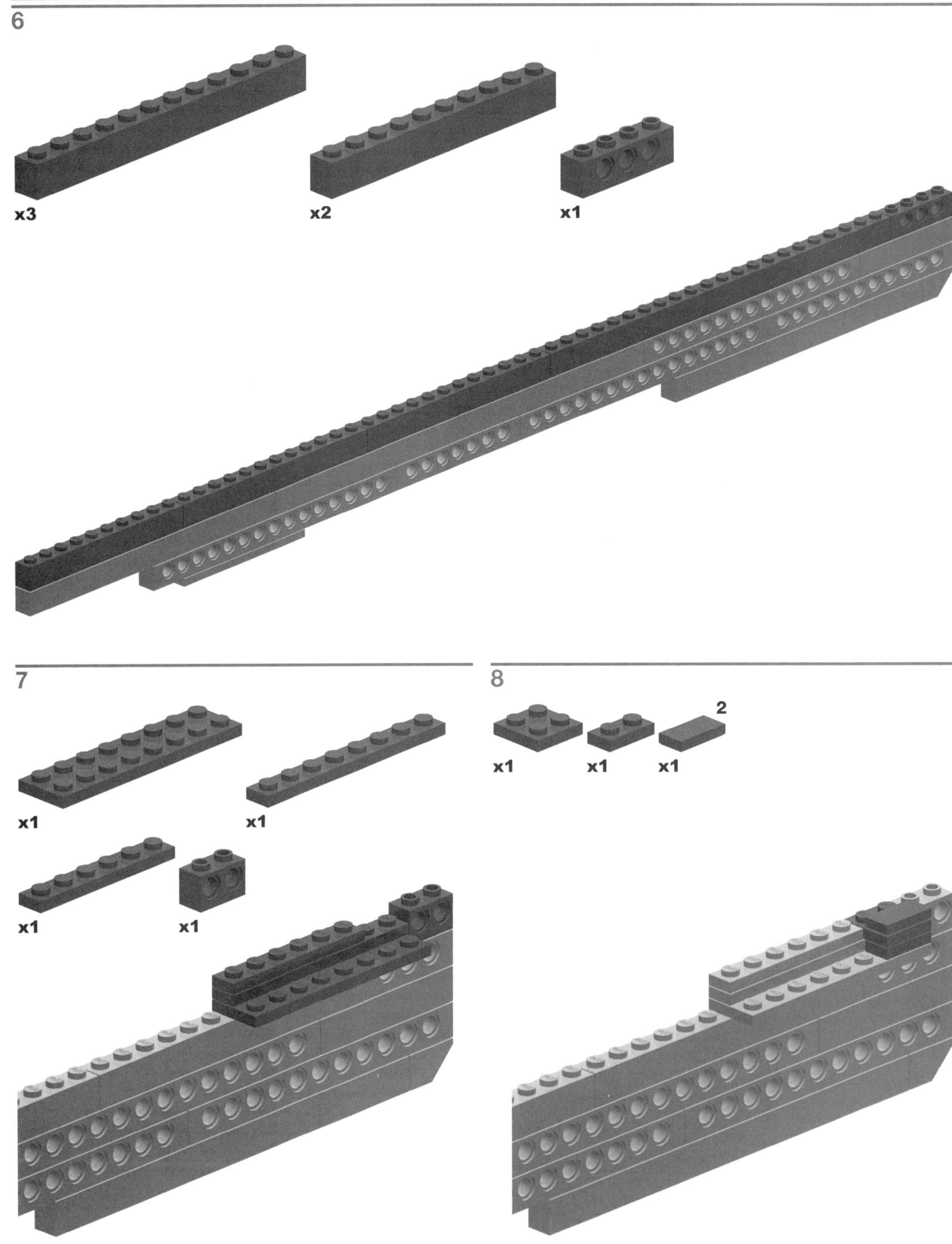
6
x3
x2
x1
7
x1
x1
x1
x1
8
2
x1
x1
x1

9

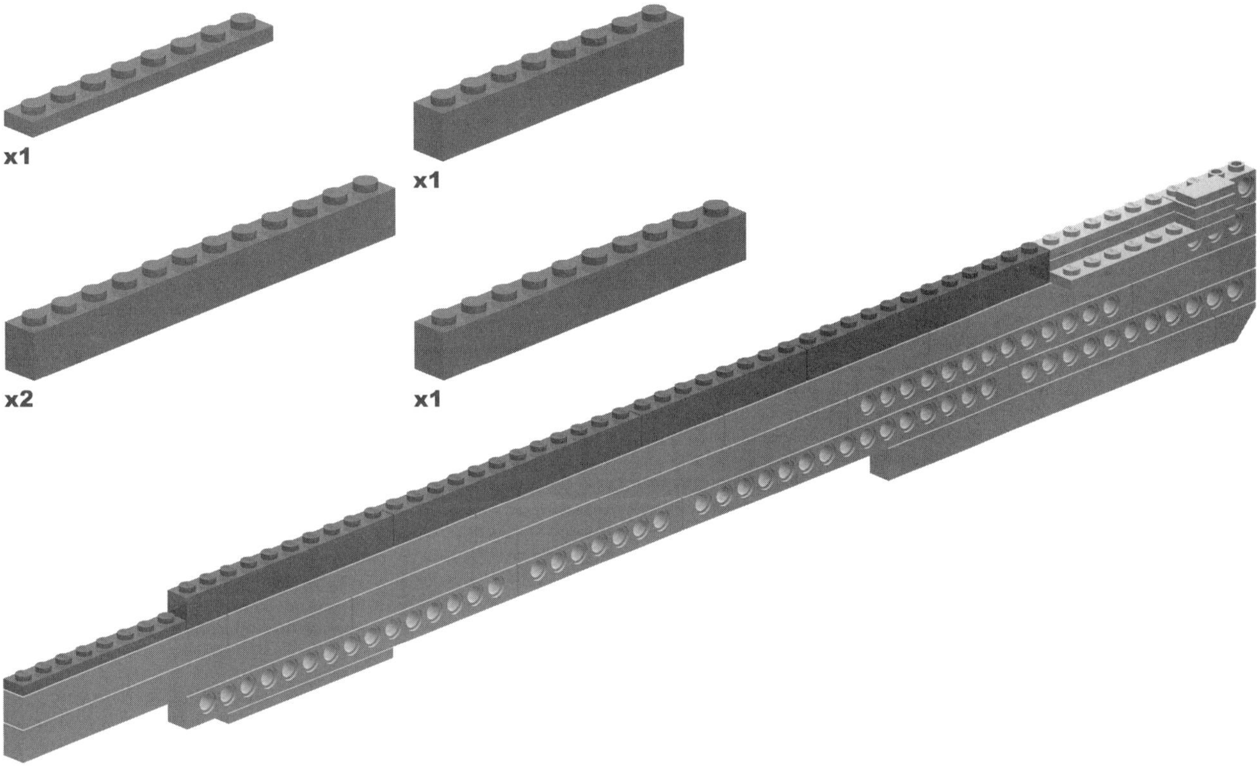

x1

x1

x2

x1

10

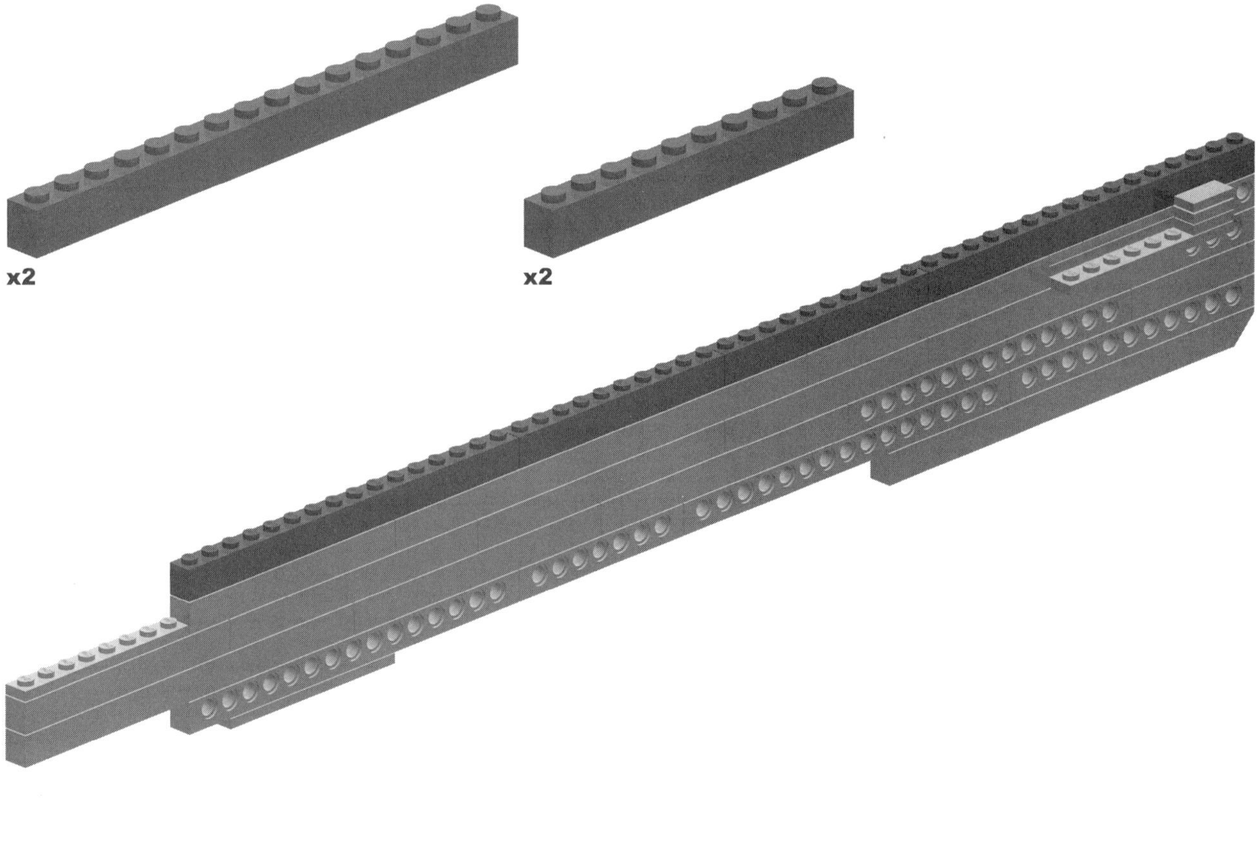

x2

x2

11

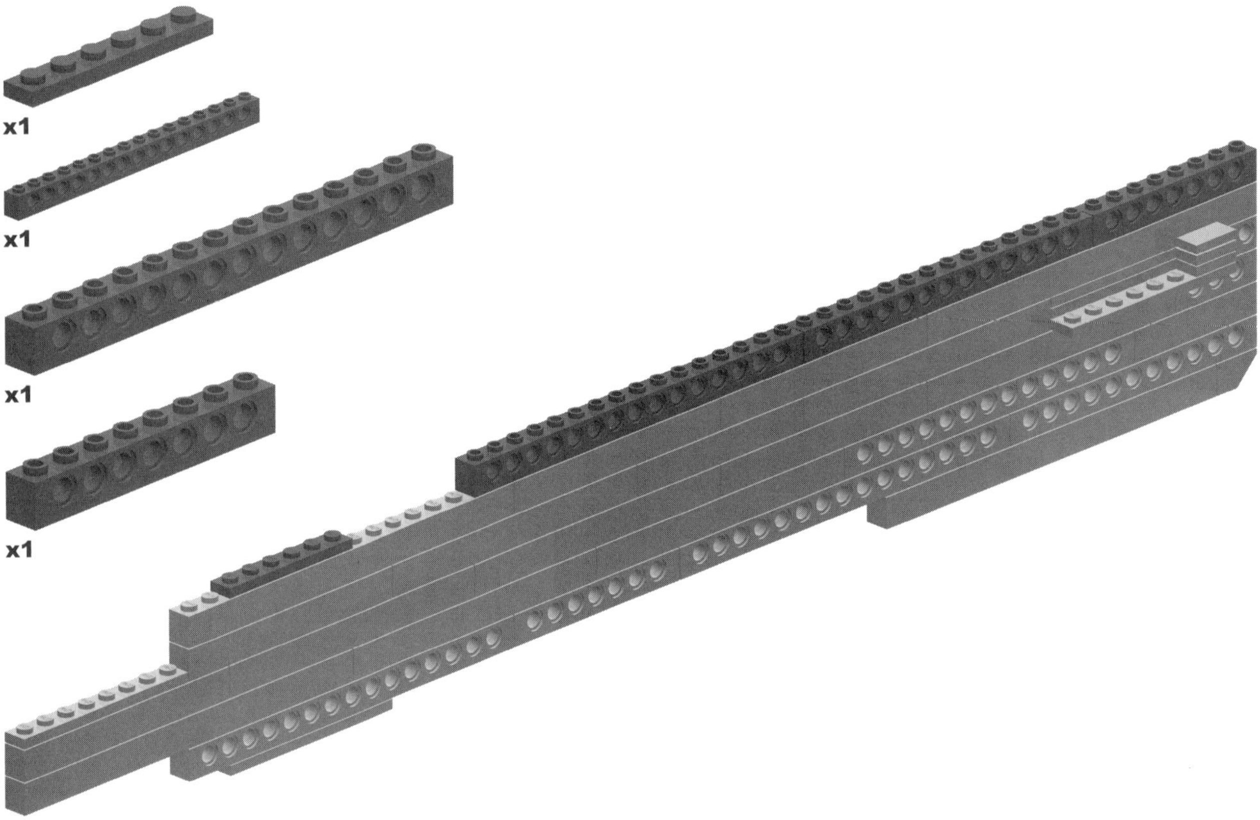

x1

x1

x1

x1

12

13

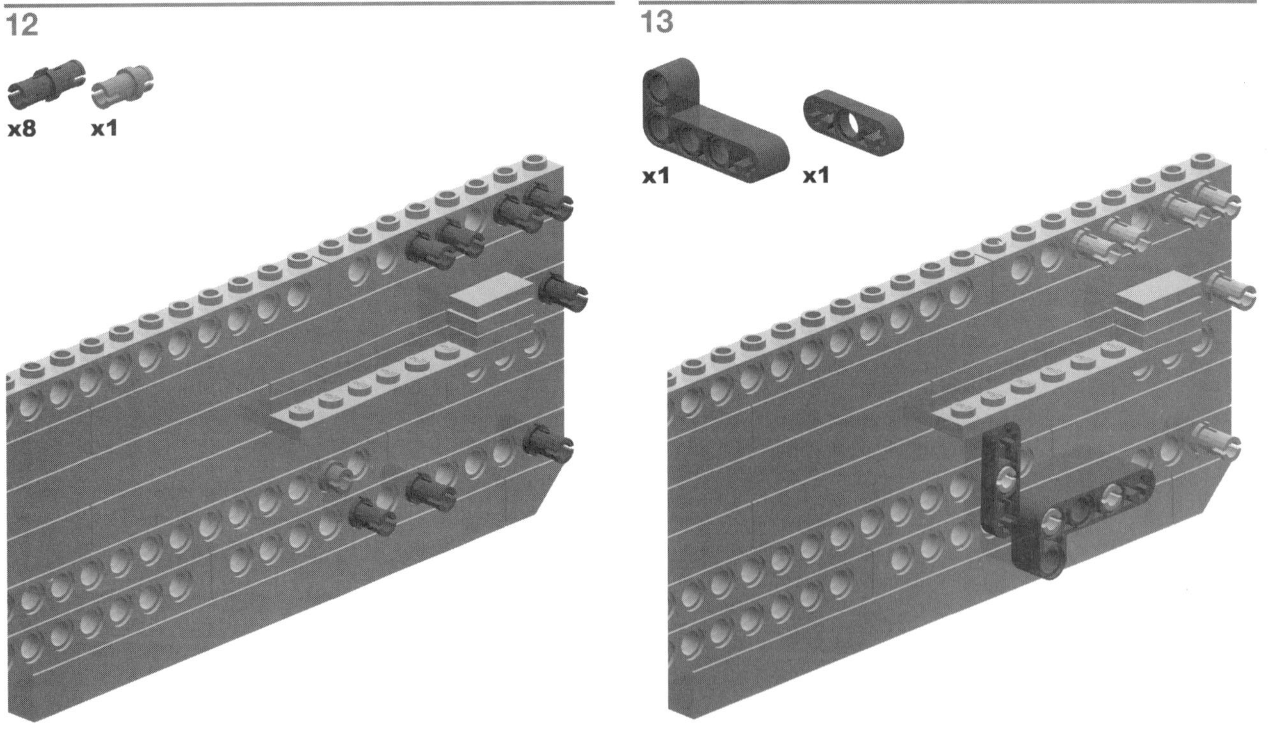

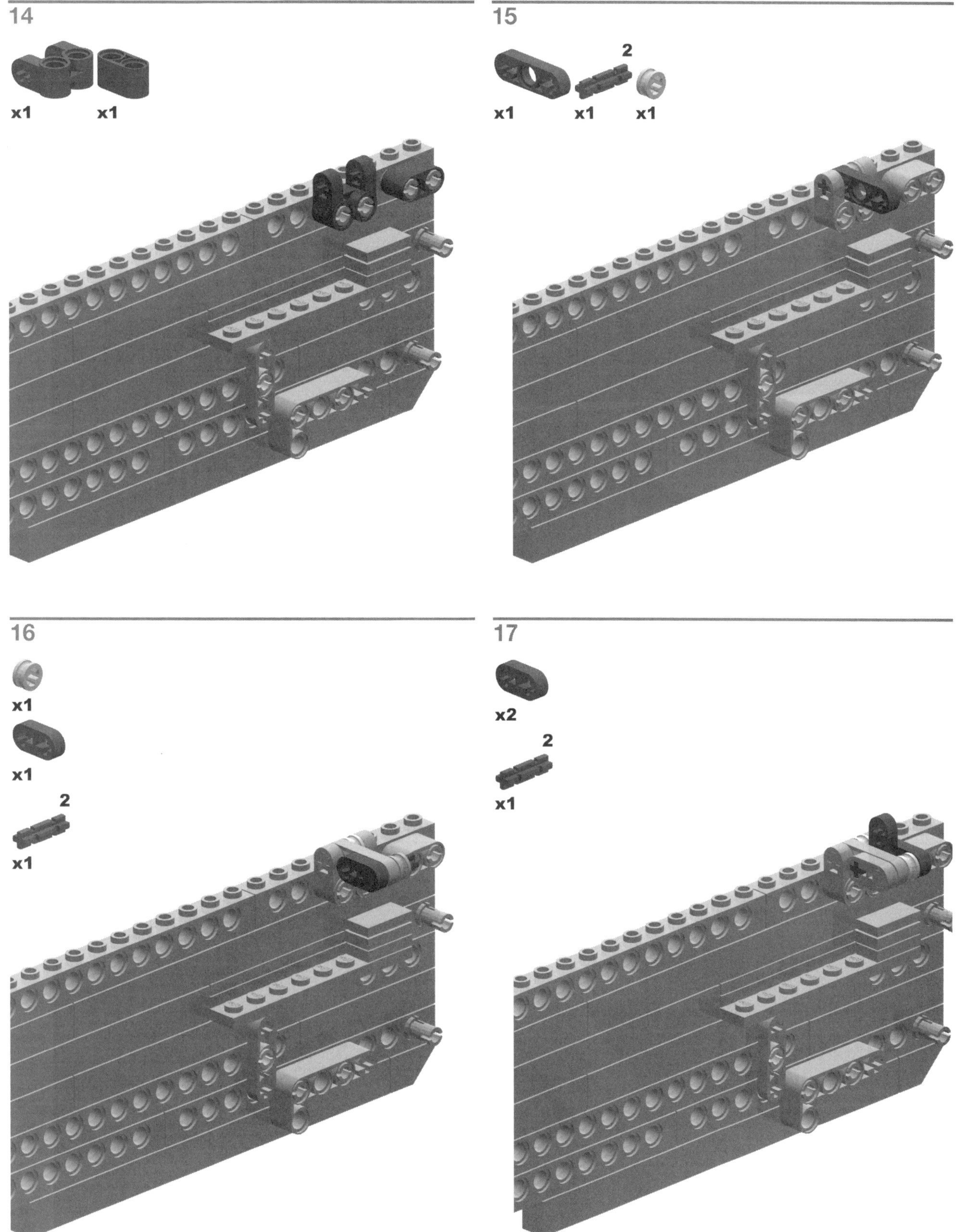
14
x1
x1
15
2
x1
x1
x1
16
x1
x1
2
x1
17
x2
2
x1

18

x2
x4

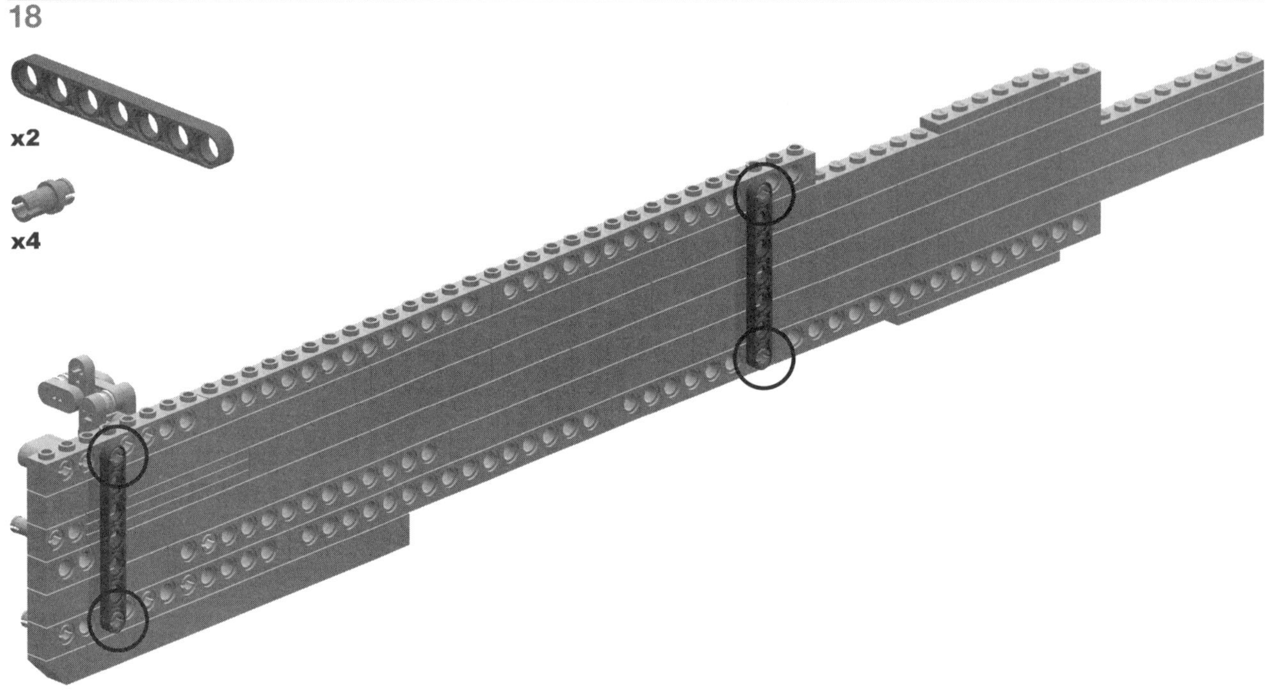

PLATE TOP FRONT

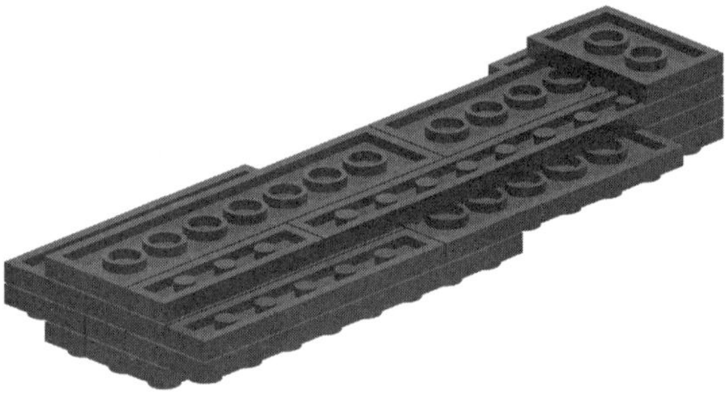

1

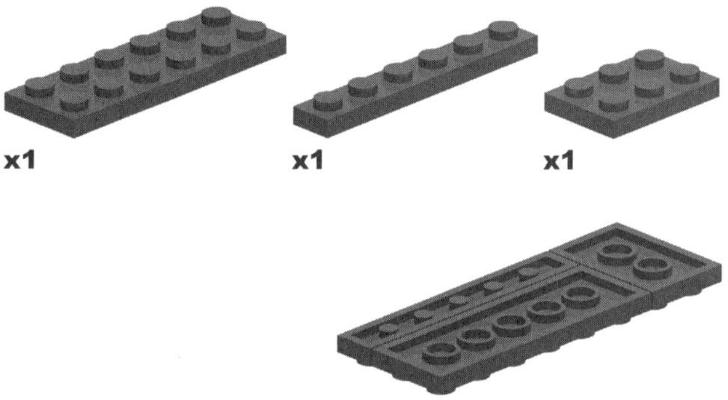

x1
x1
x1

2

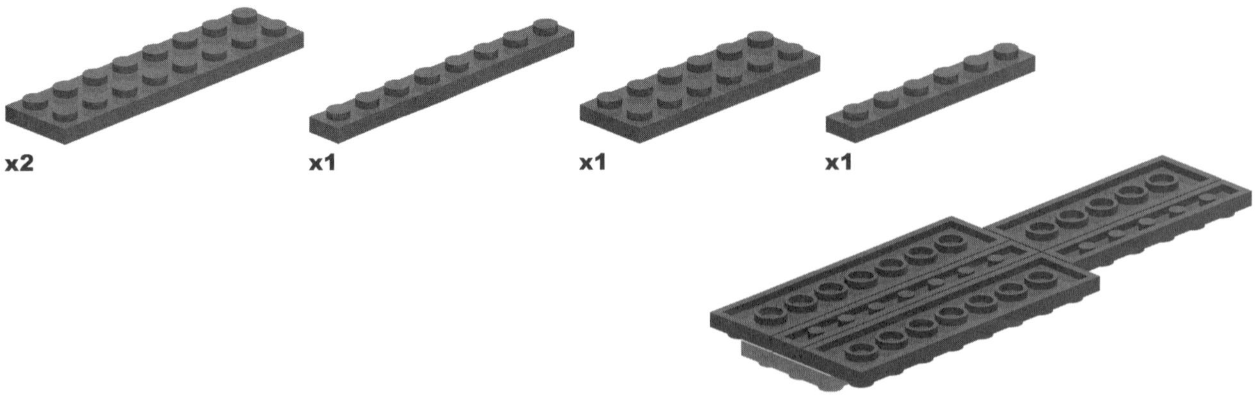

x2
x1
x1
x1

3

x2

x1

x1

4

x1

x1

x1

x1

5

x1

PLATE TOP BACK

1

x1

x1

2

x1

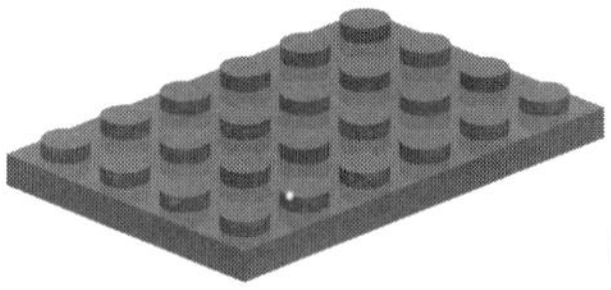

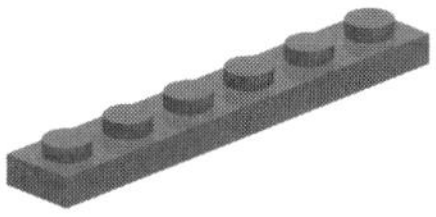

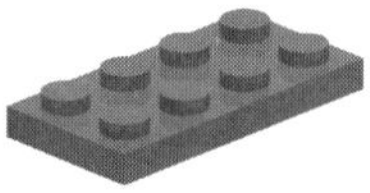

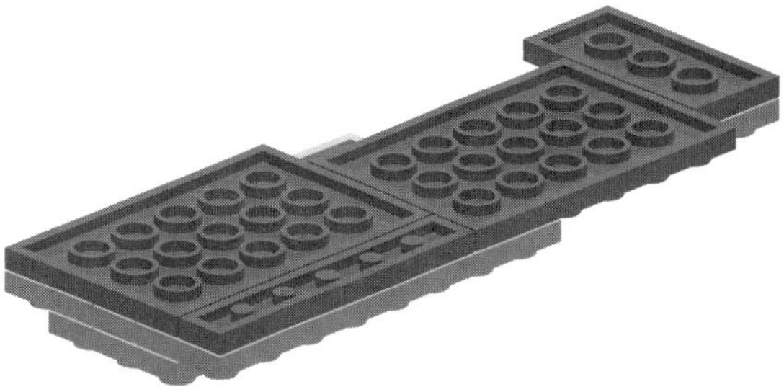

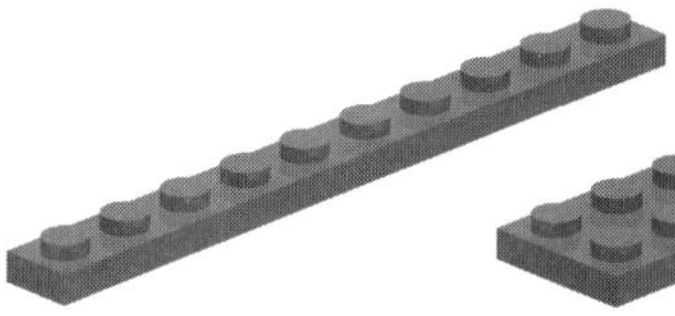

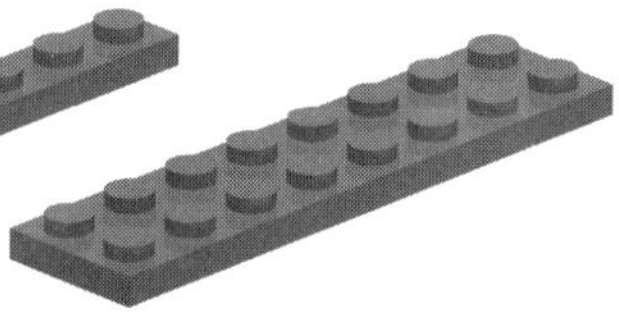

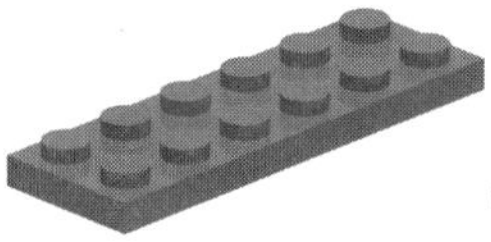

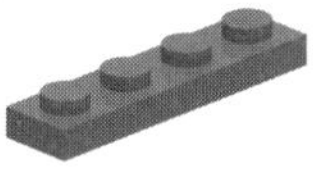

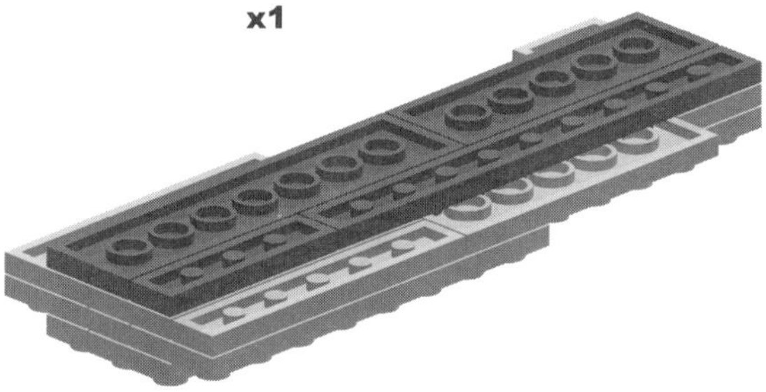

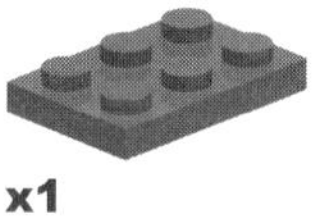

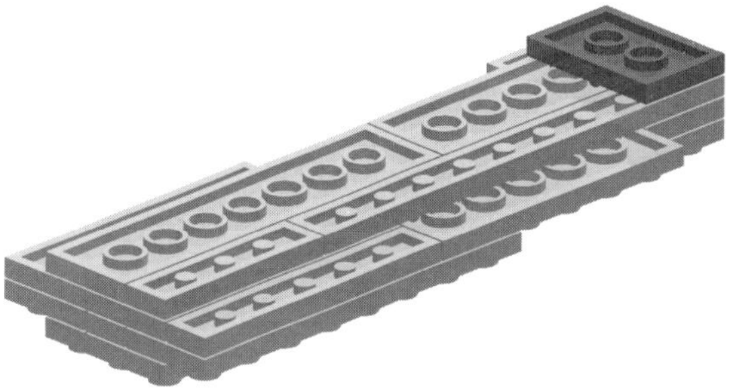

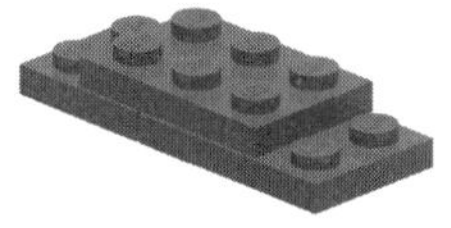

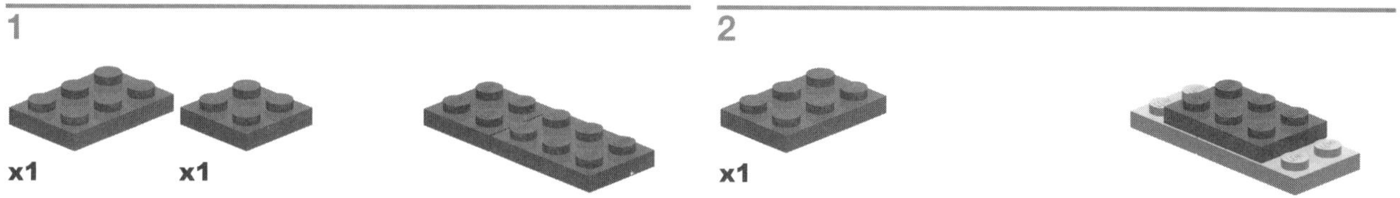

PLATE BOTTOM BACK

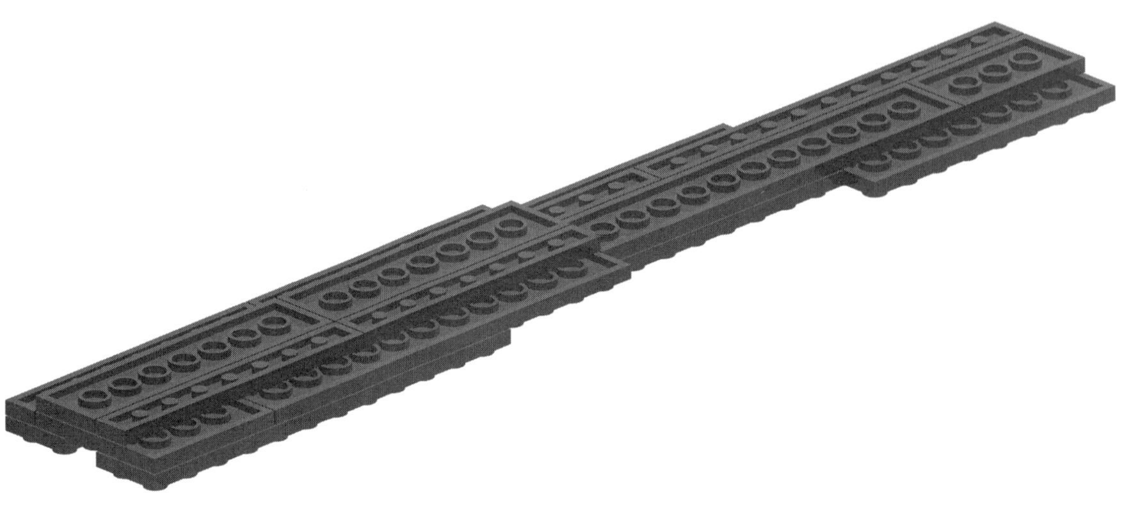

1

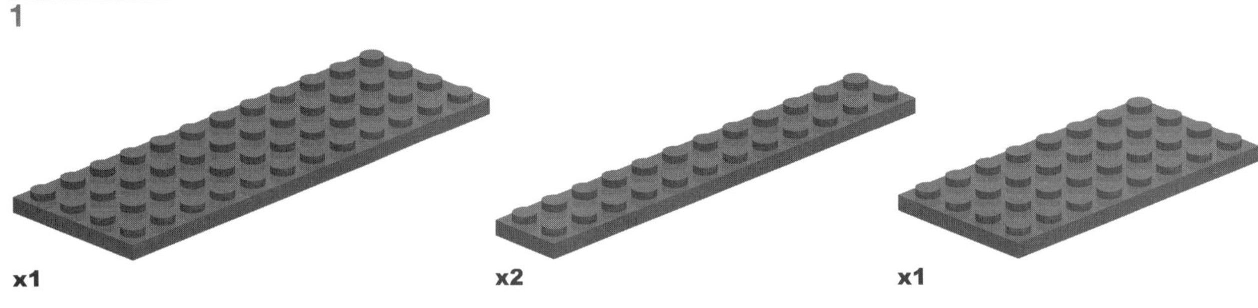

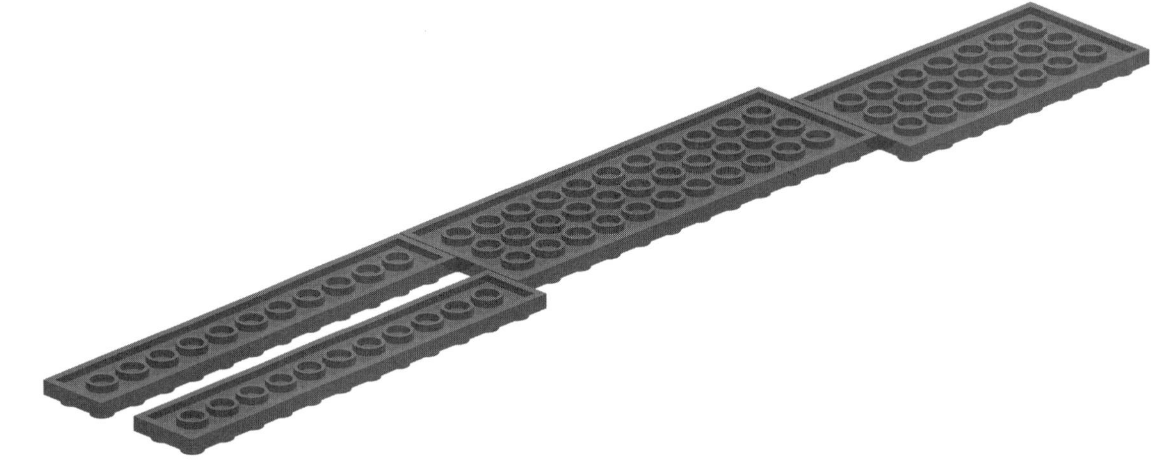

2

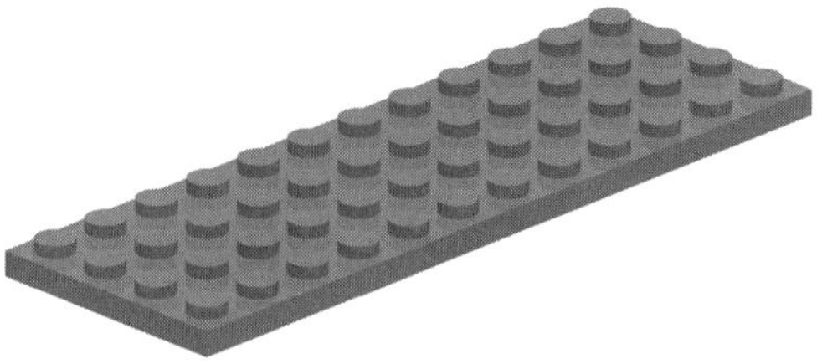

x1

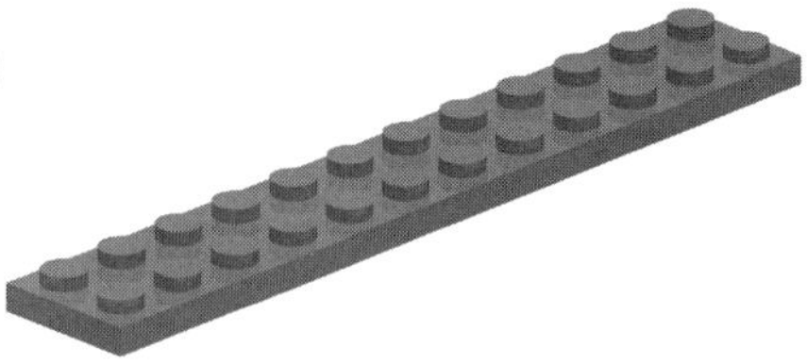

x1

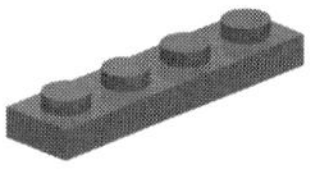

x1

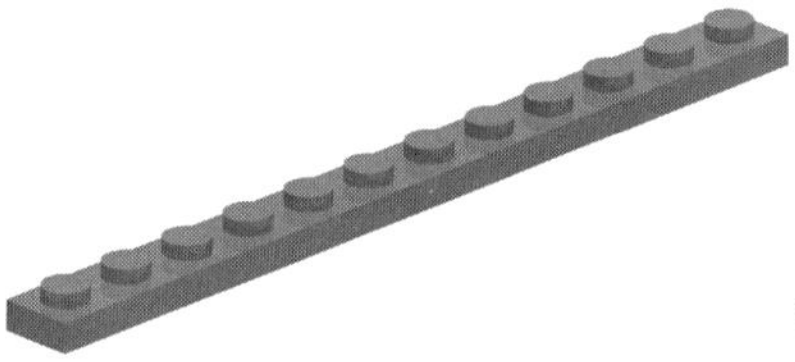

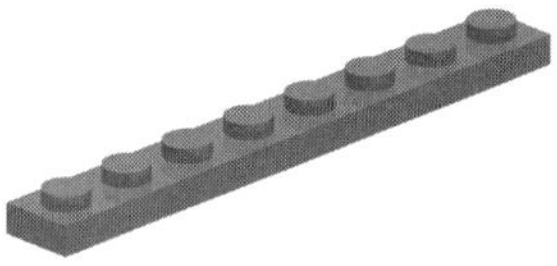

x2

x1

x1

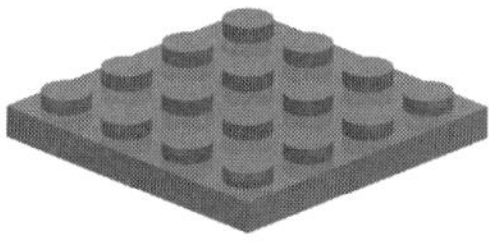

x1

3

x2

x2

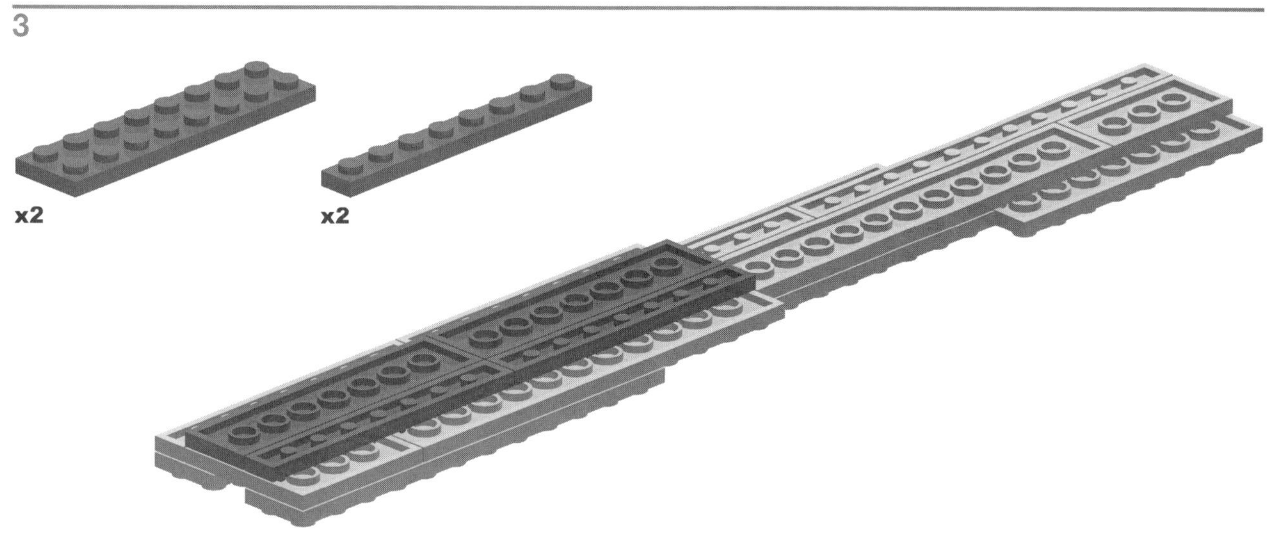

PLATE BOTTOM FRONT

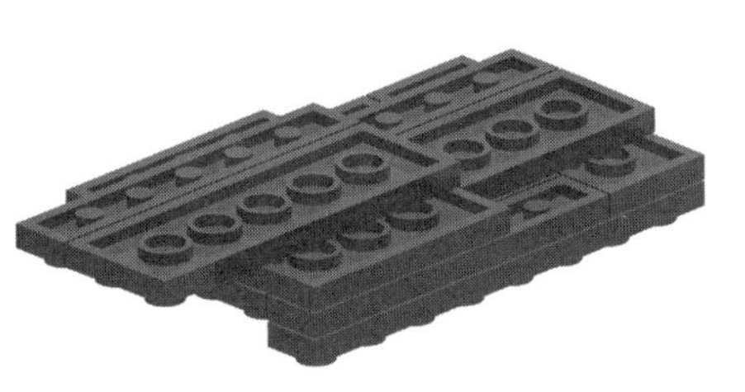

1

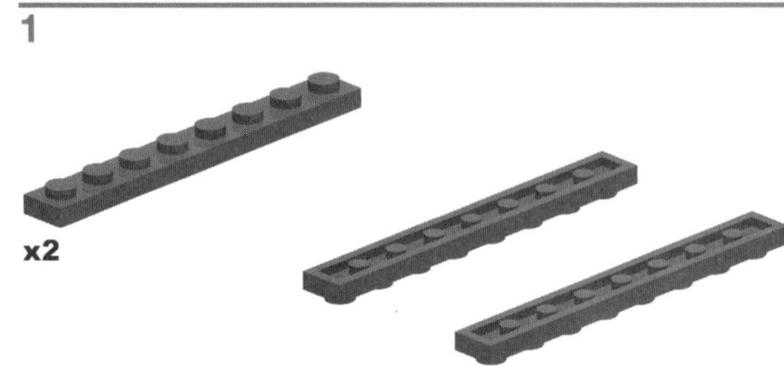

2

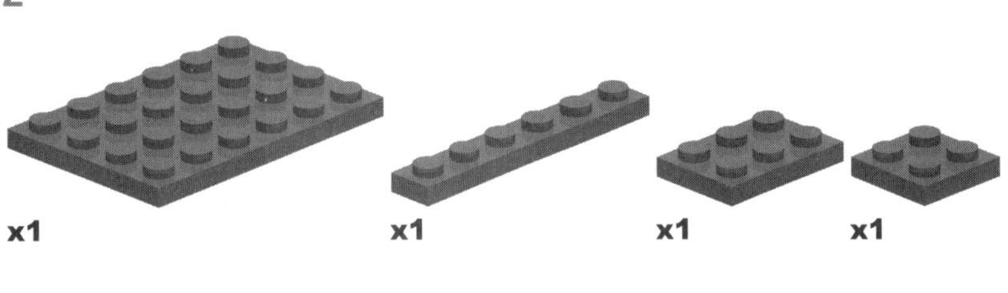

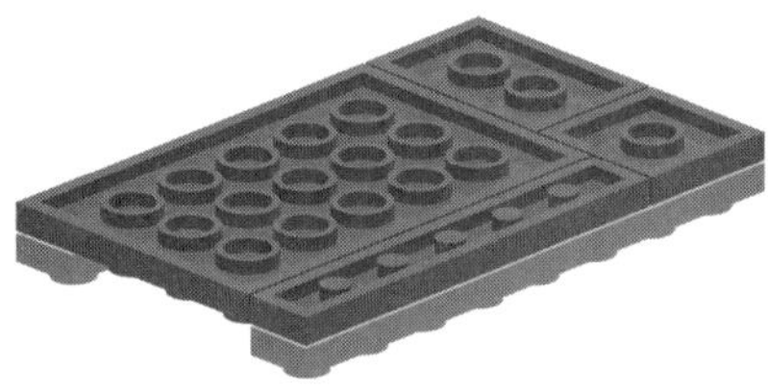

3

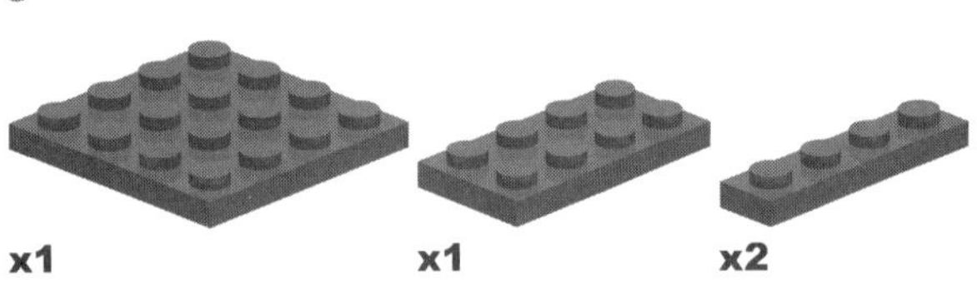

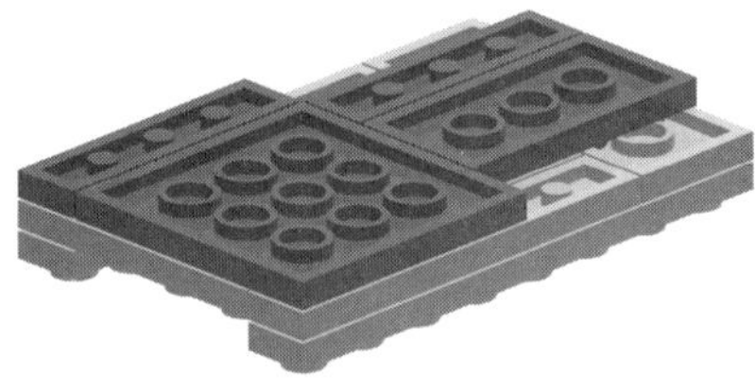

4

x1

x1

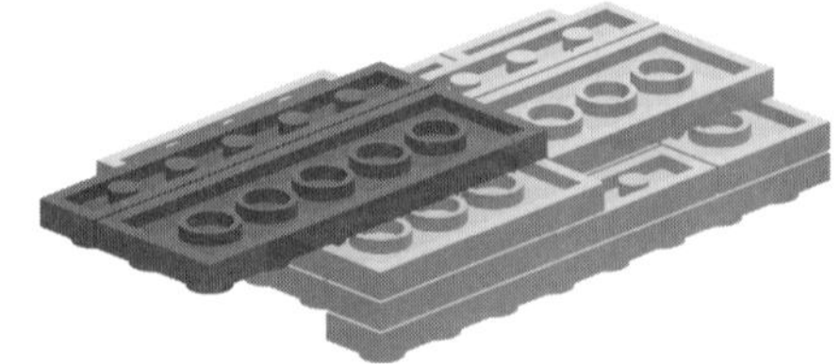

MAGAZINE FRONT

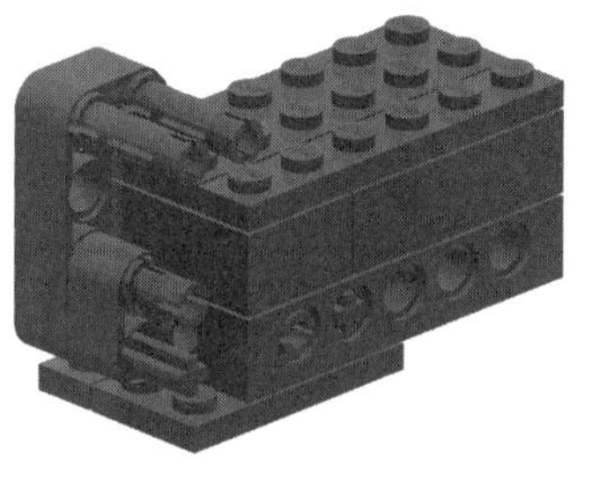

1

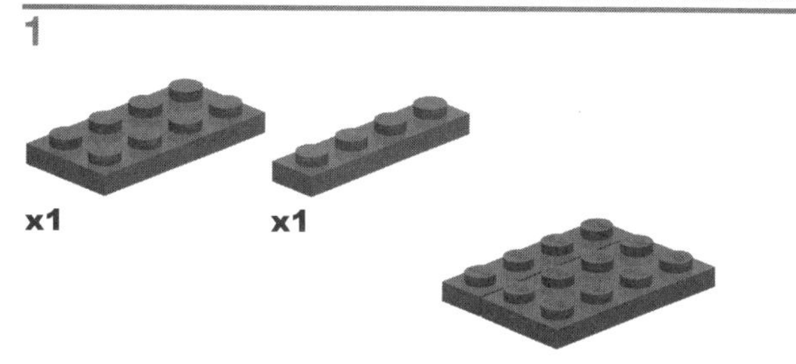

2

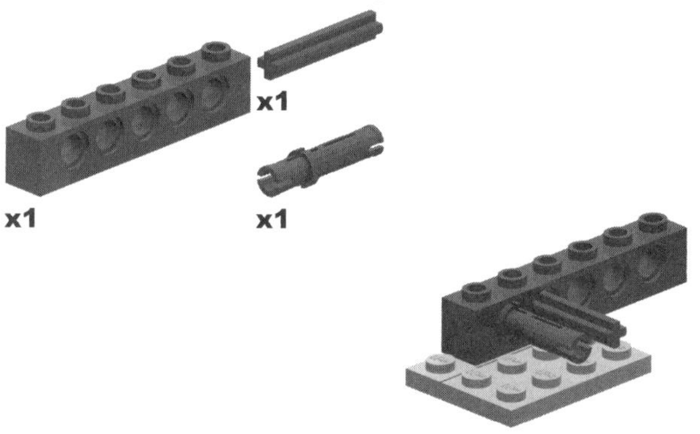

3

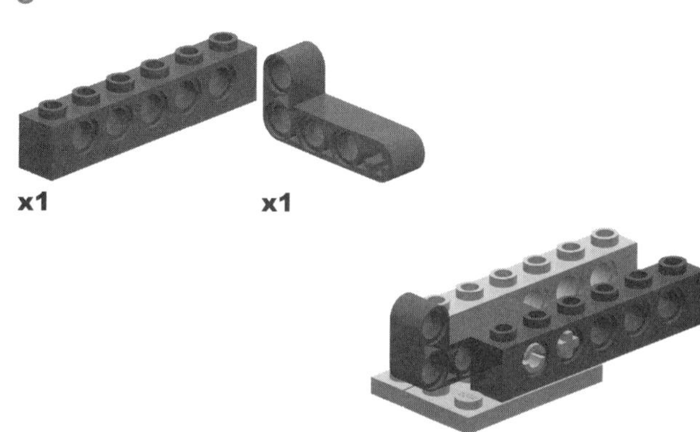

4

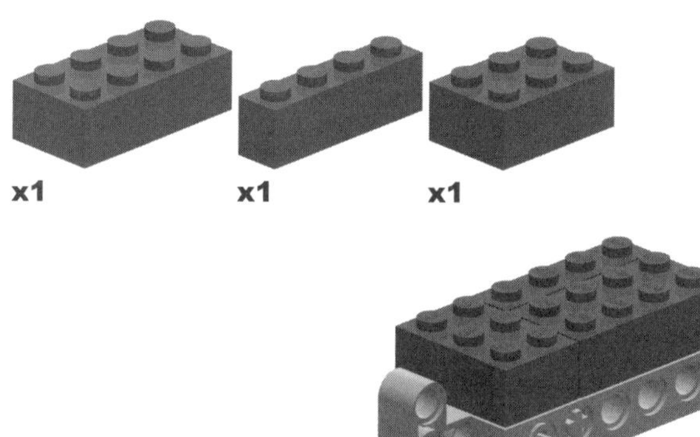

5

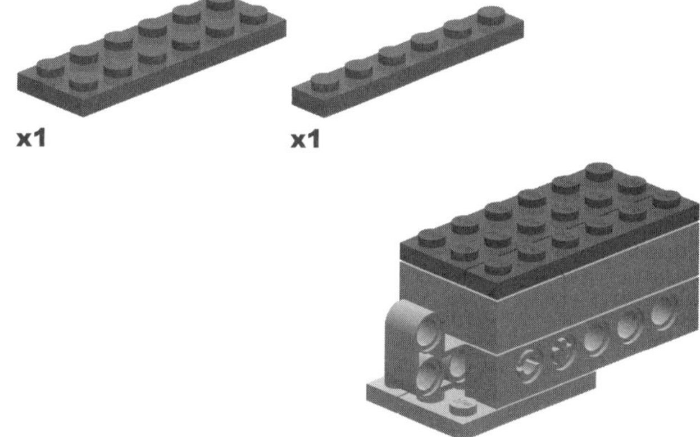

6

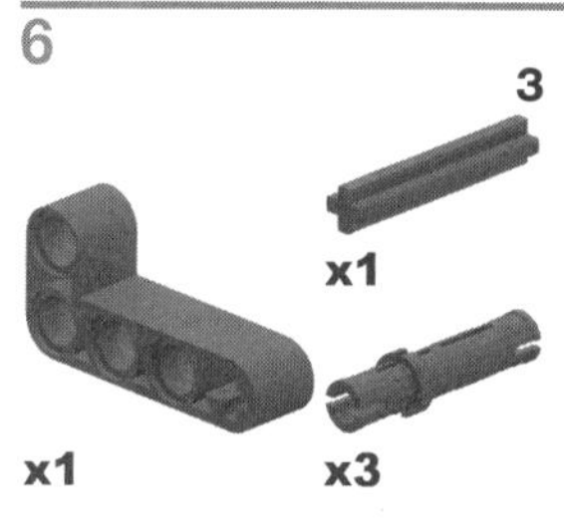

MAGAZINE SLIDE

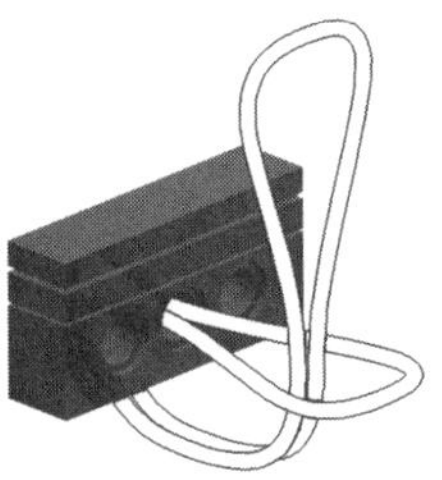

1

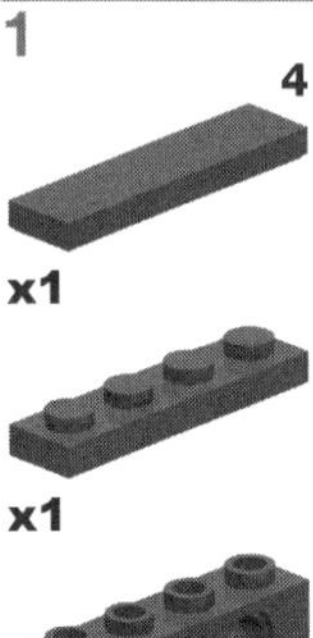

2

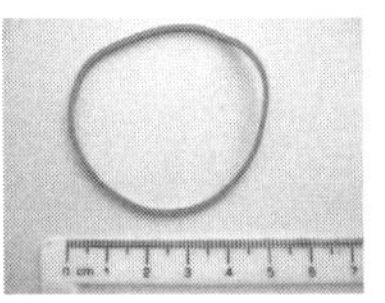

x1

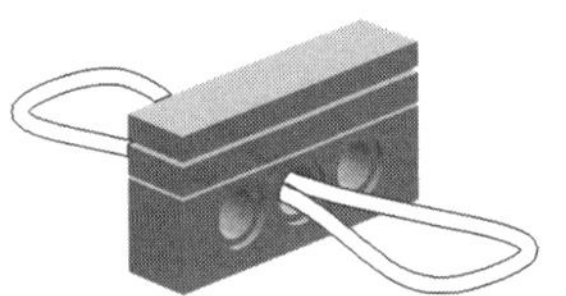

3

Pull one end of the rubber band under the brick and through the other end of the rubber band as shown.

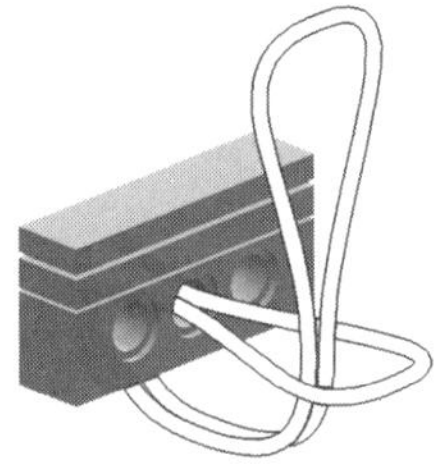

MAGAZINE ASSEMBLY

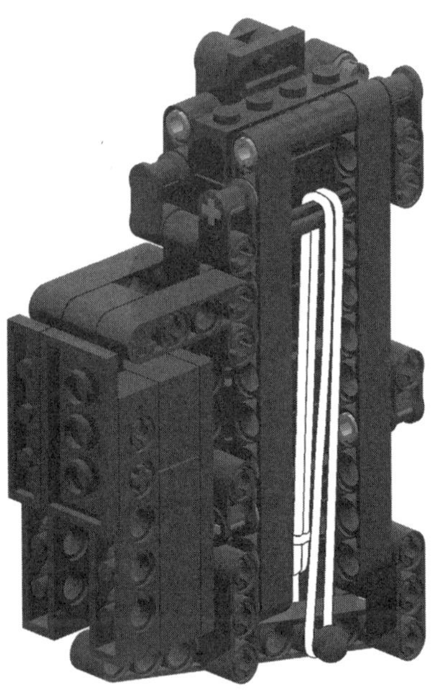

1

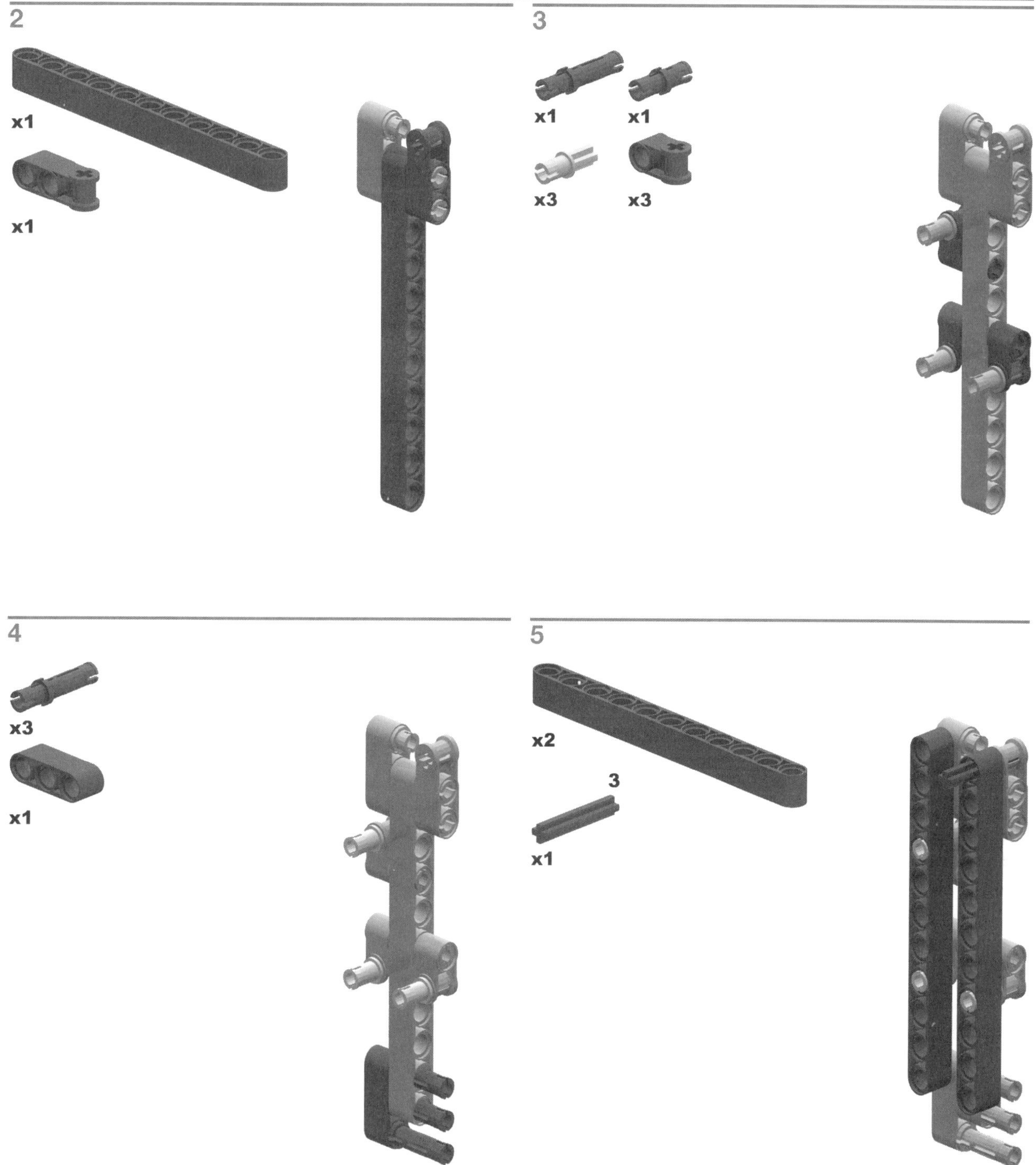
2
x1
x1
3
x1
x1
x3
x3
4
x3
x1
5
x2
3
x1

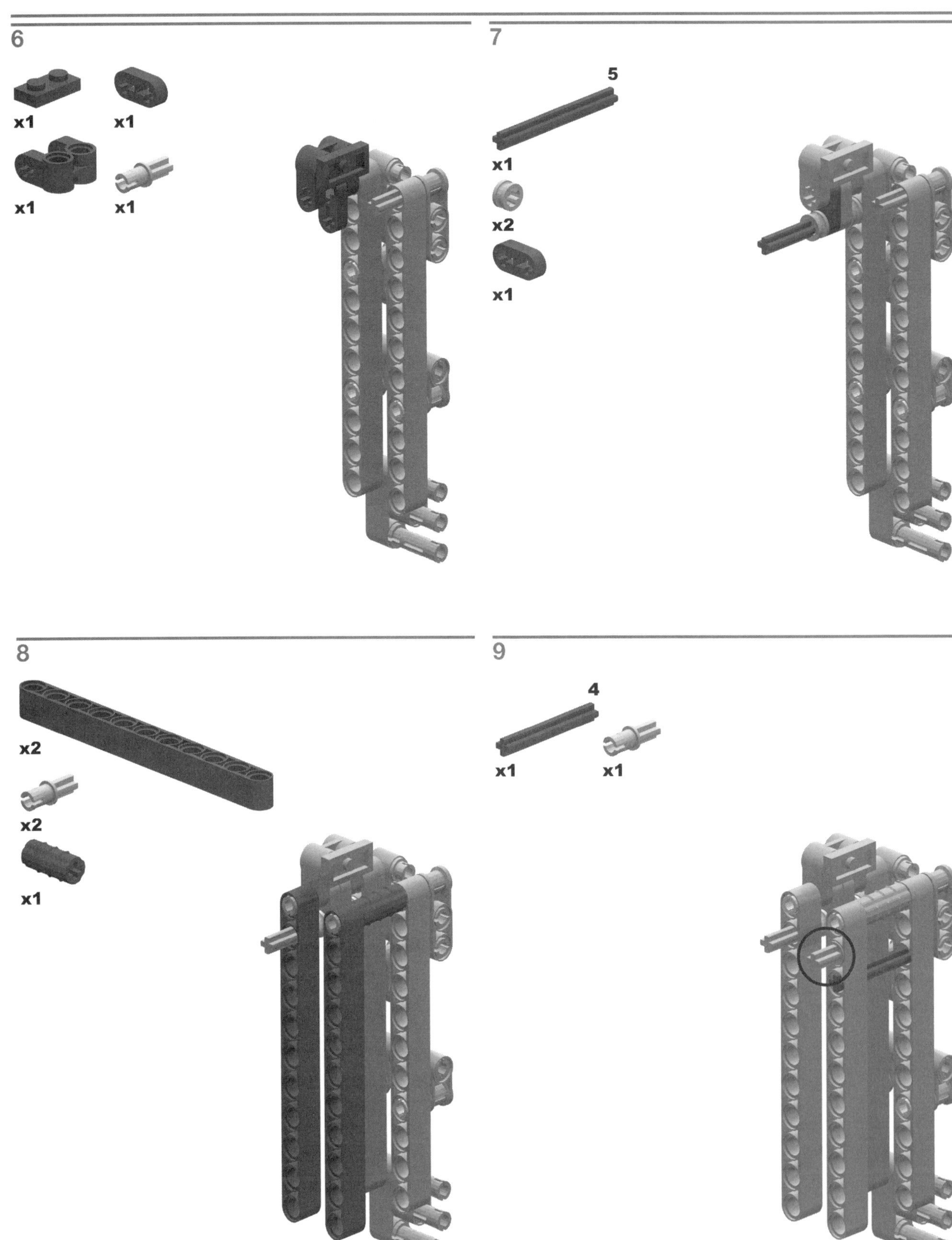
6
x1
x1
x1
x1
7
5
x1
x2
x1
8
x2
x2
x1
9
4
x1
x1

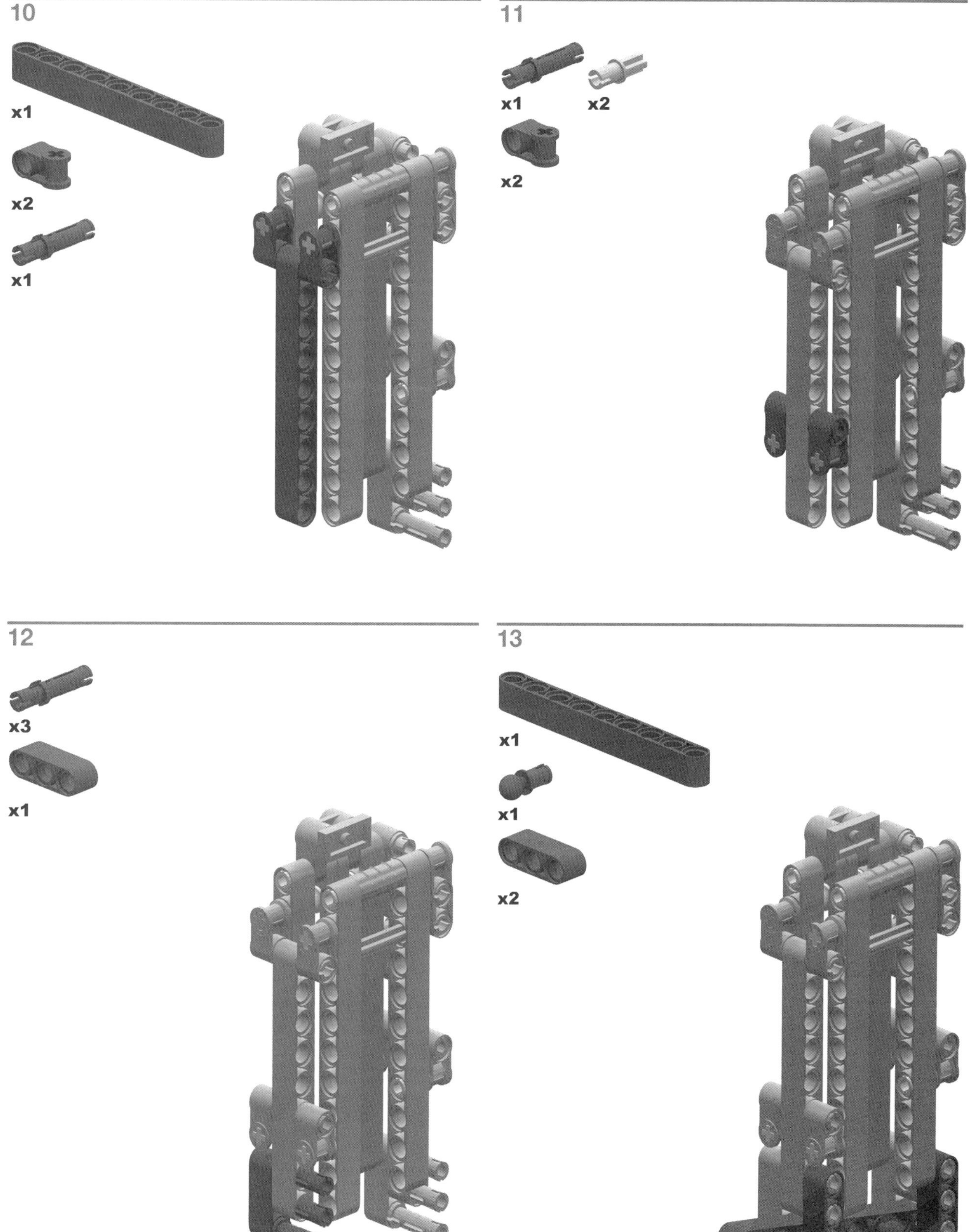
10
x1
x2
x1
11
x1
x2
x2
12
x3
x1
13
x1
x1
x2

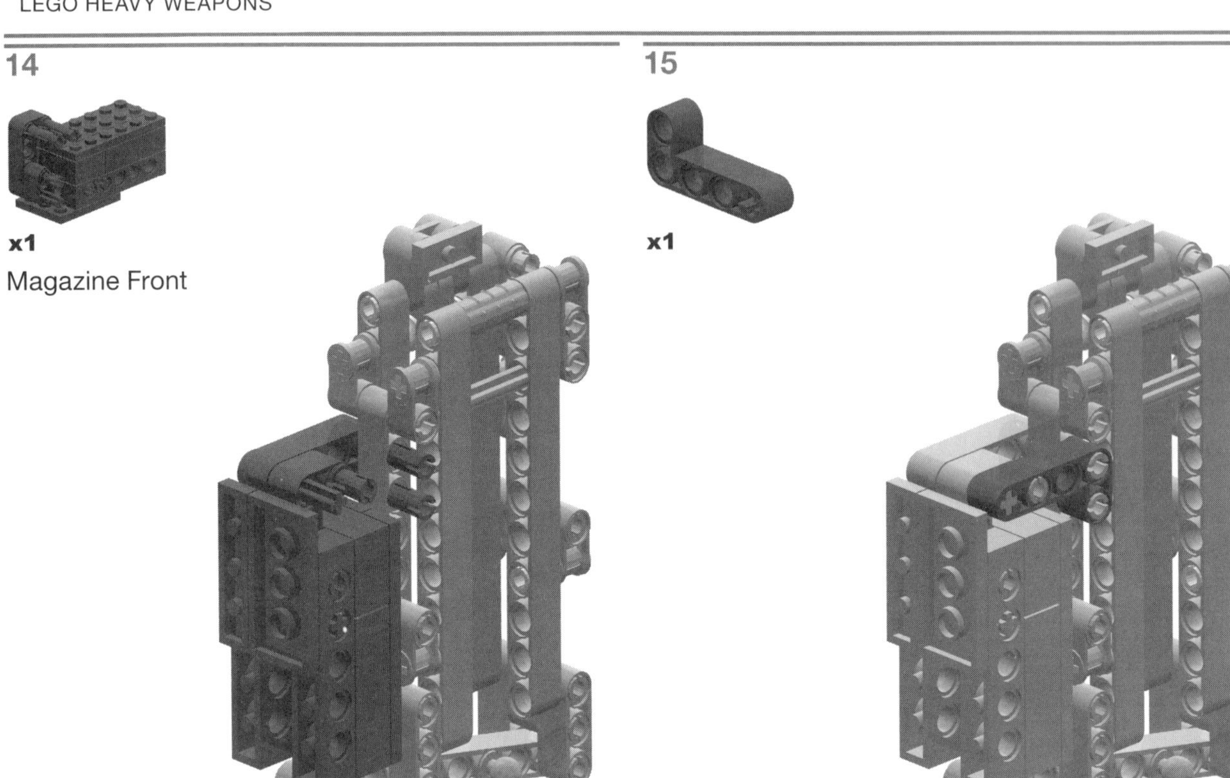

16

x6 x1

Magazine Slide

Insert the Magazine Slide into the hollow of the Magazine. Loop the rubber band over the 4-stud axle at the top, pull it down, and then slip it over the towball pin (added in step 13 on page 233). You may need to loop the band repeatedly over the towball pin for more pressure. Once you've added the Magazine Slide, load the 1×4 bricks one by one. Make sure to add them stud-to-stud and base-to-base so they don't accidentally snap together.

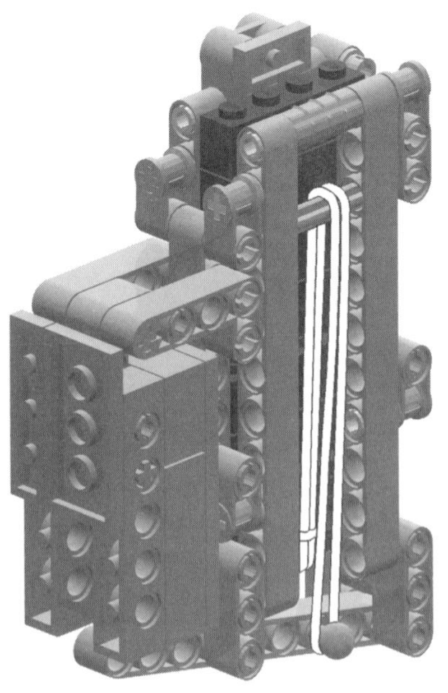

MAIN ASSEMBLY

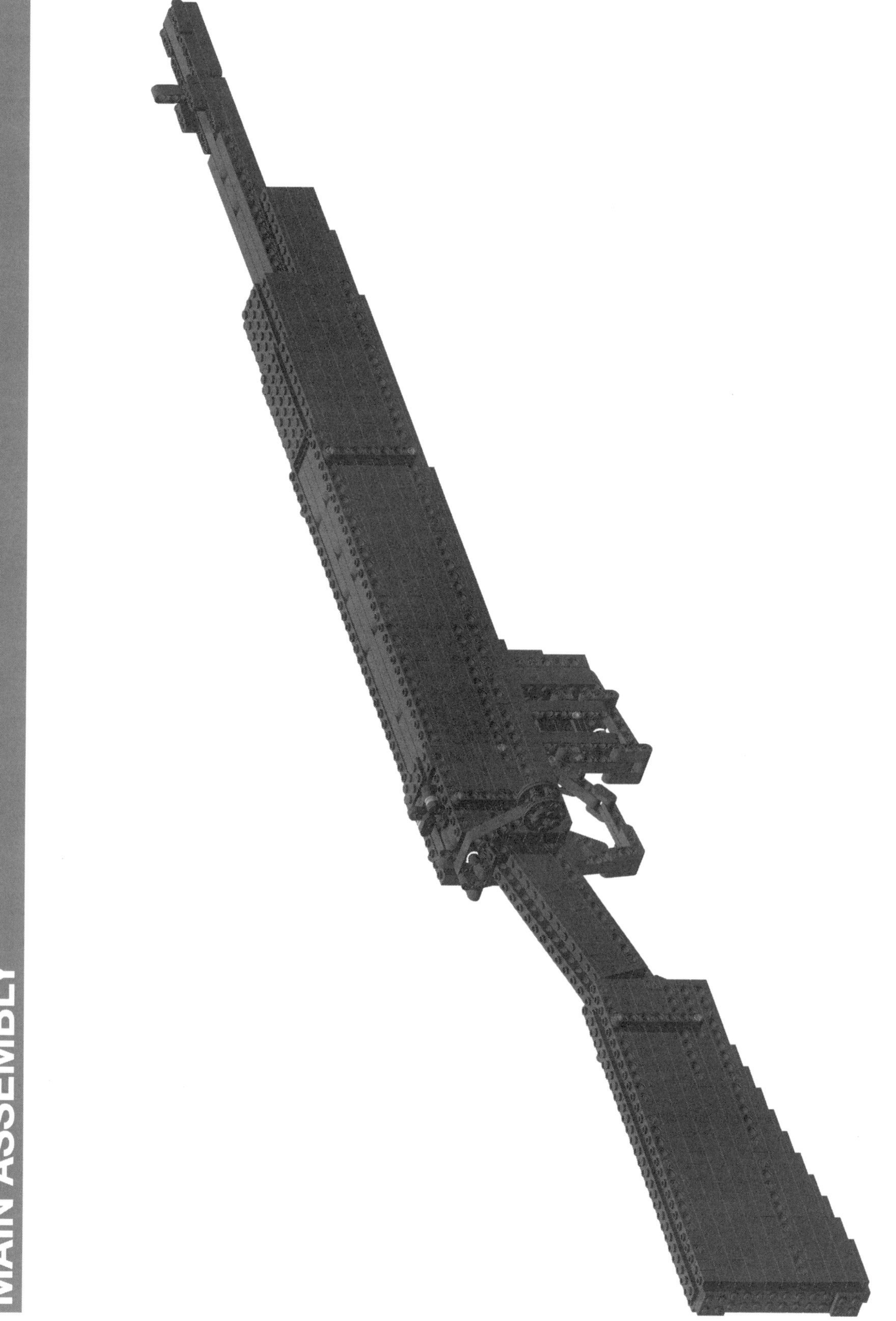

1

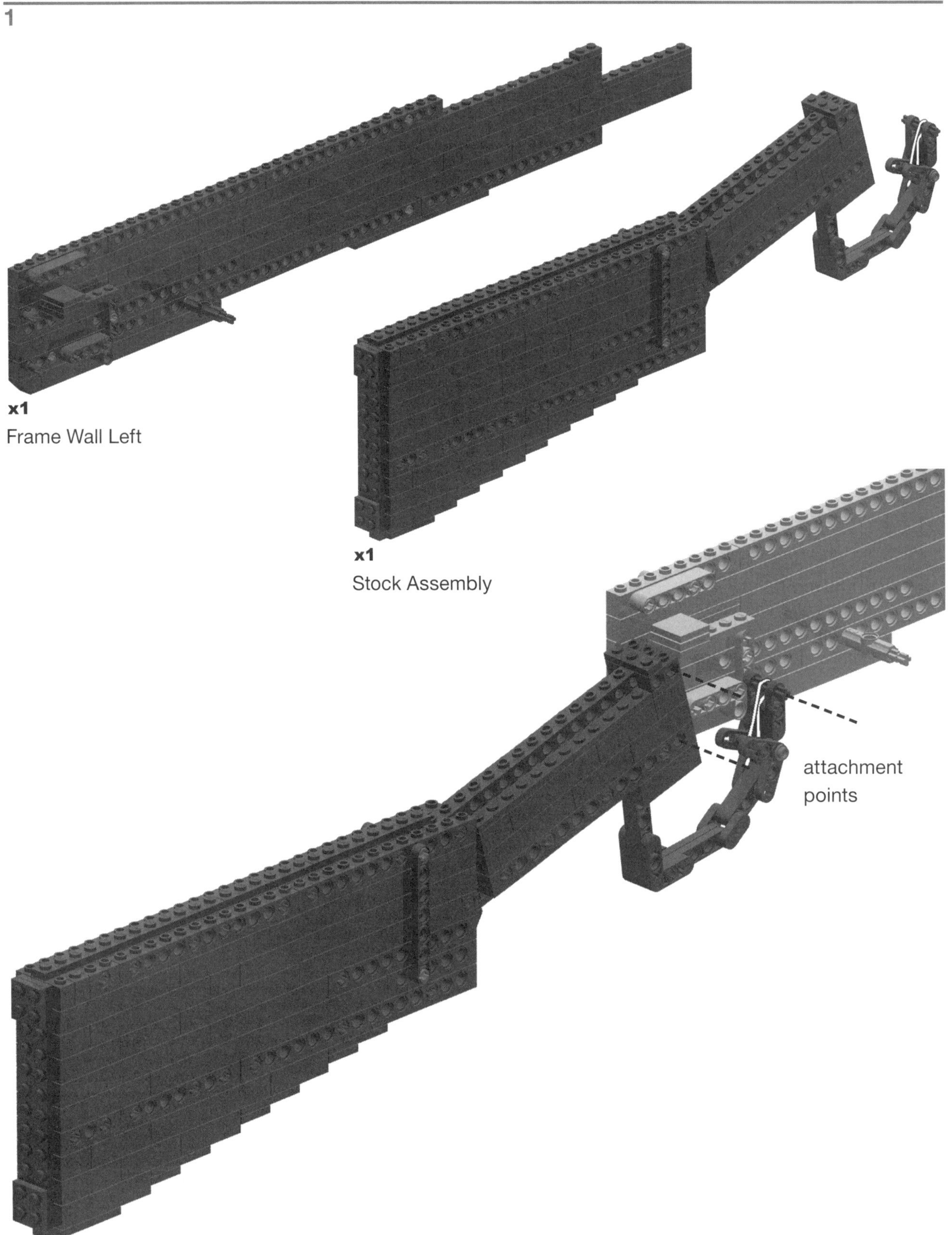

x1
Frame Wall Left

x1
Stock Assembly

2

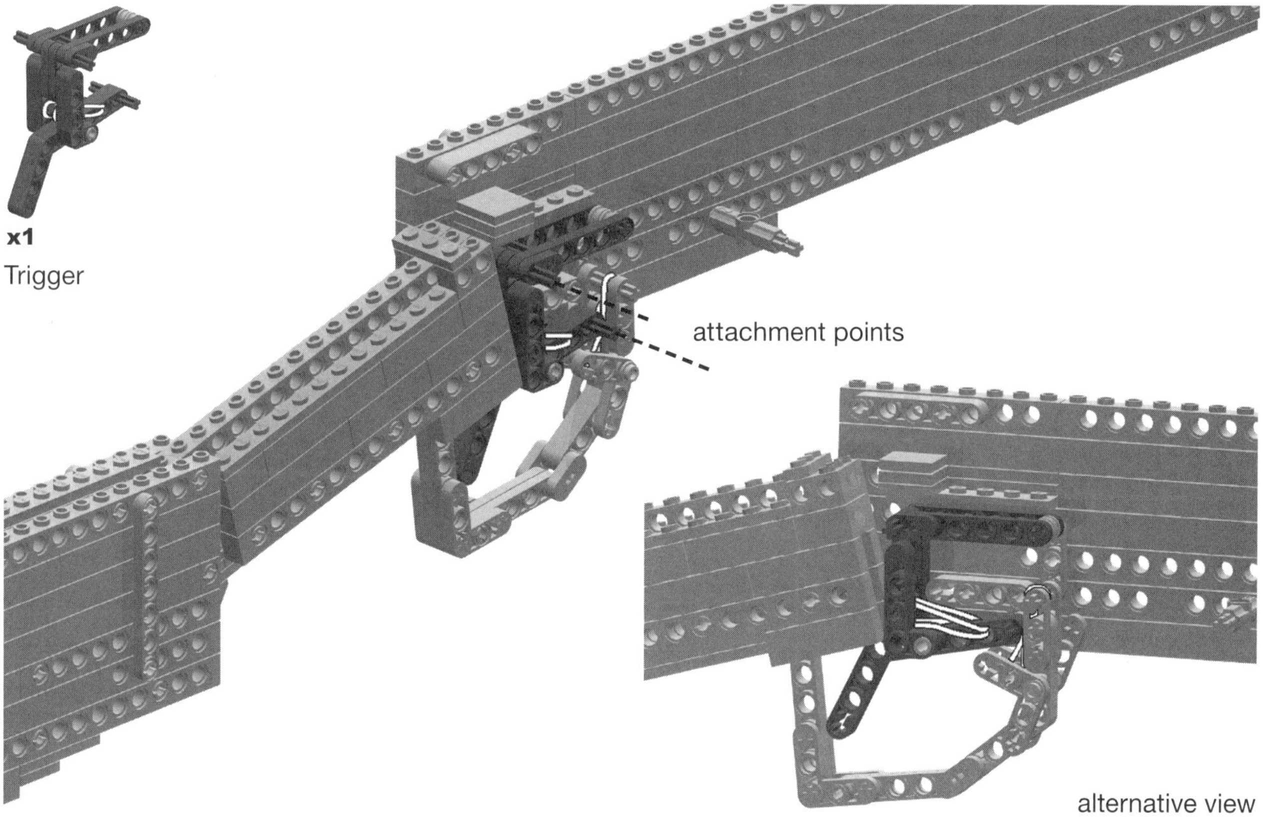

x1
Trigger

attachment points

alternative view

3

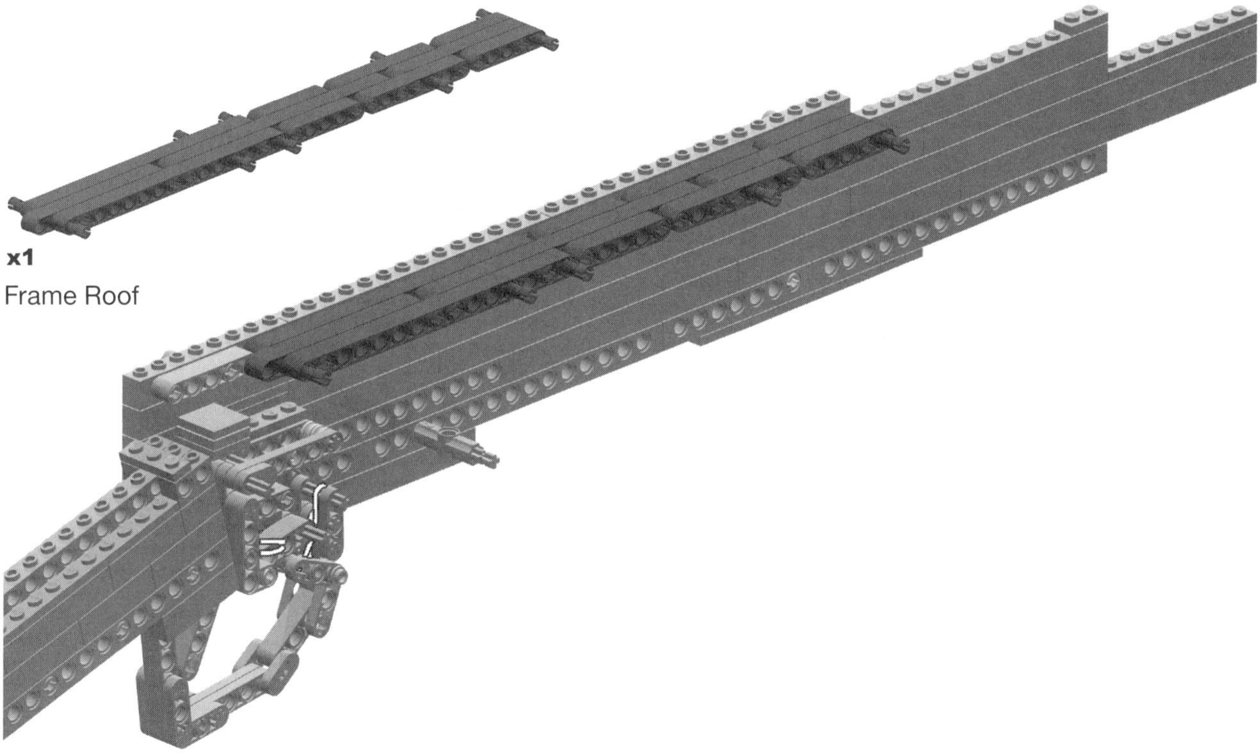

x1
Frame Roof

4

x1
Ramp

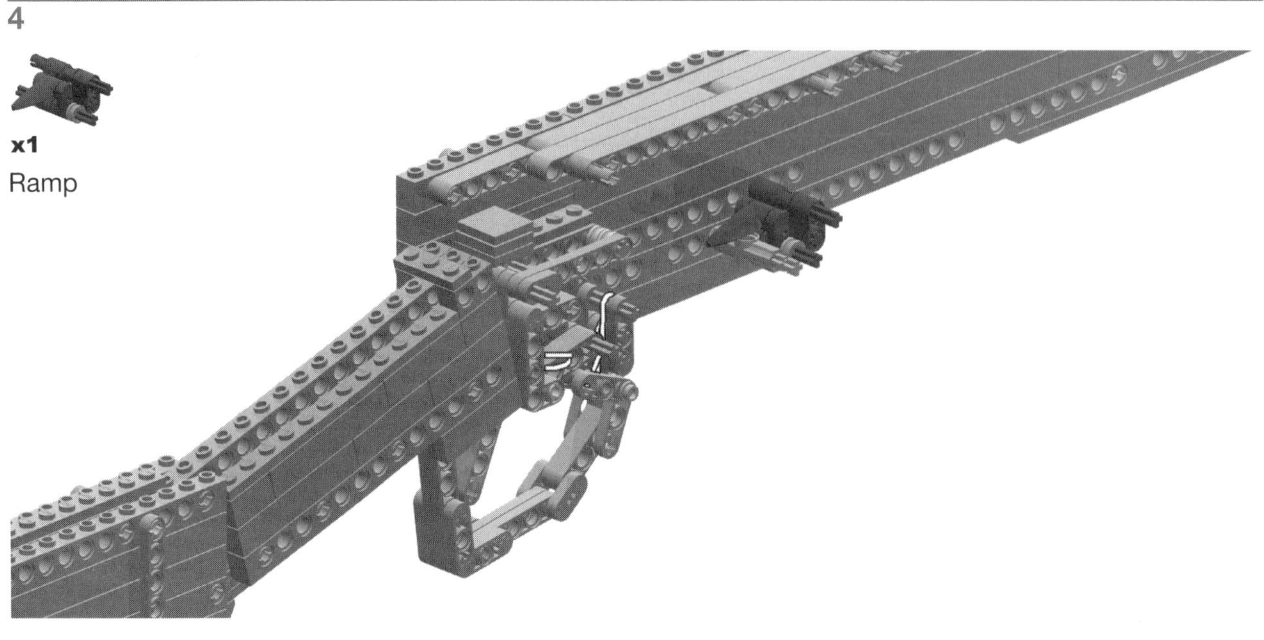

5

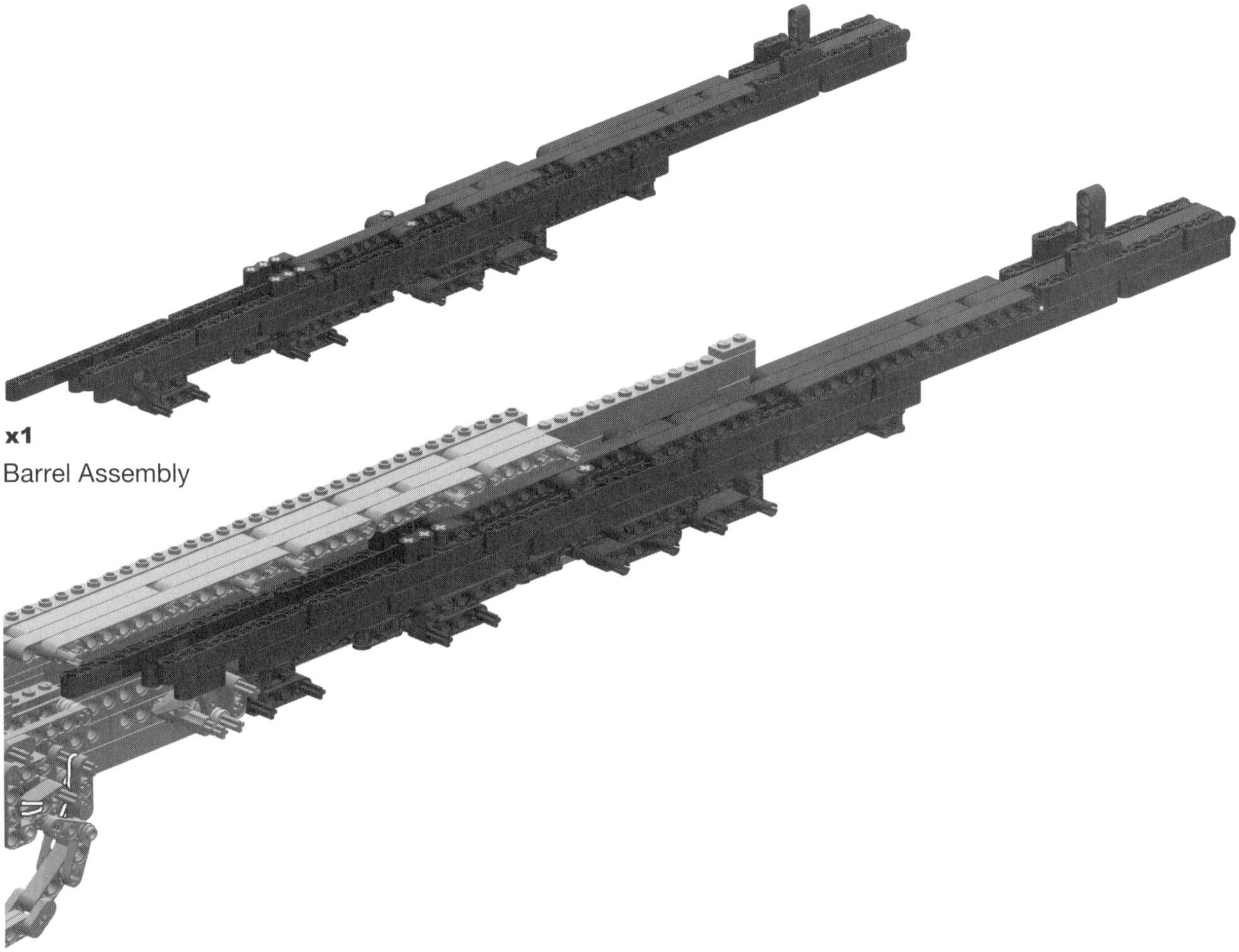

x1
Barrel Assembly

6

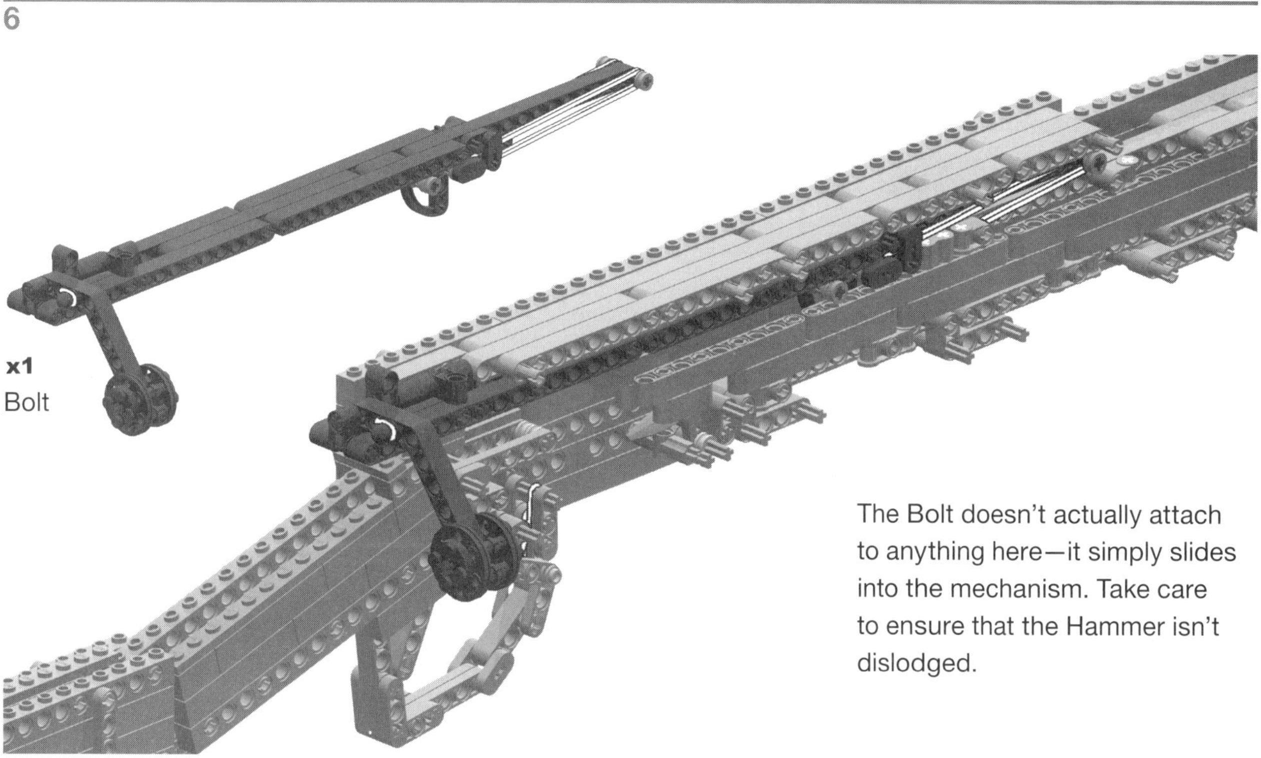

x1
Bolt

The Bolt doesn't actually attach to anything here—it simply slides into the mechanism. Take care to ensure that the Hammer isn't dislodged.

7

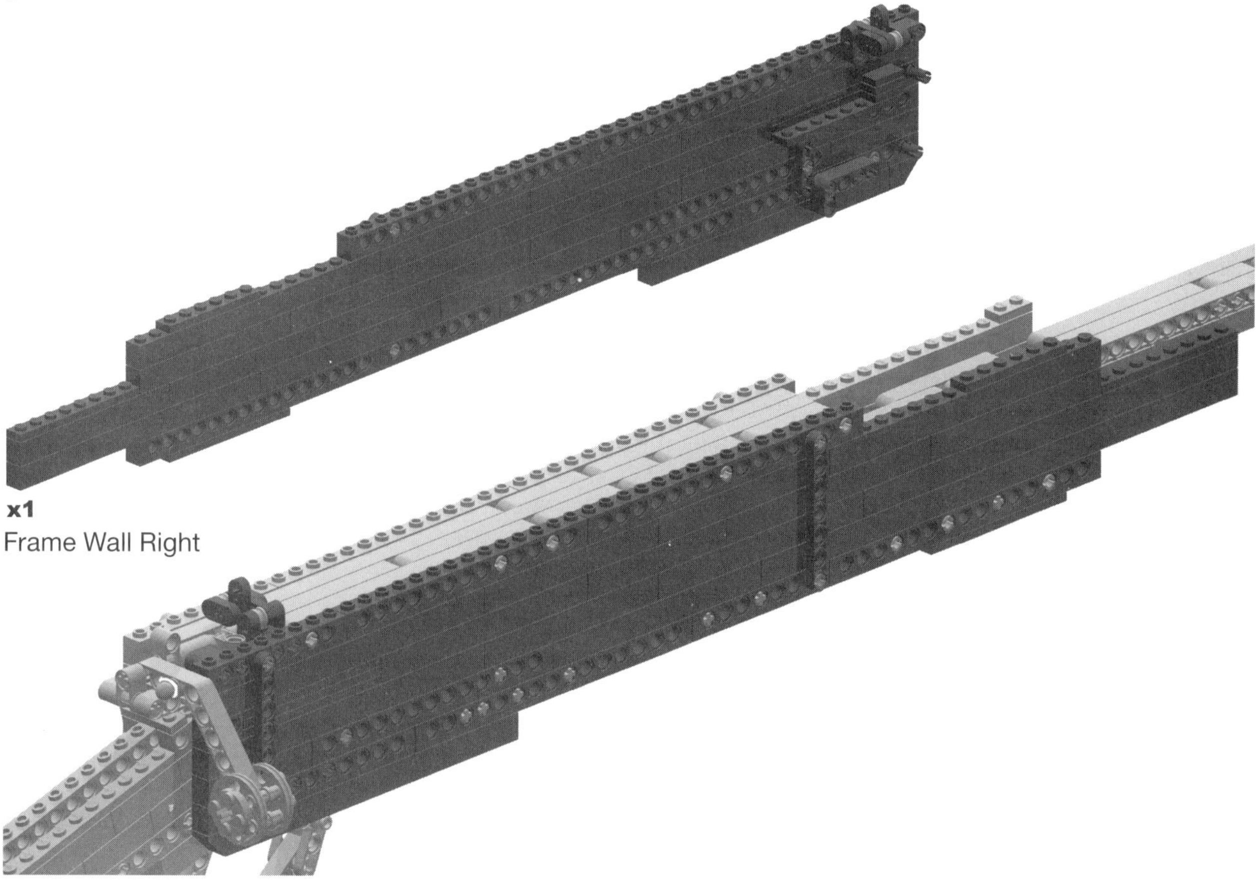

x1
Frame Wall Right

8

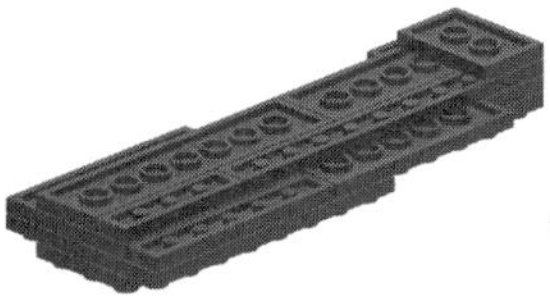

x1
Plate Top Front

x1
Plate Top Back

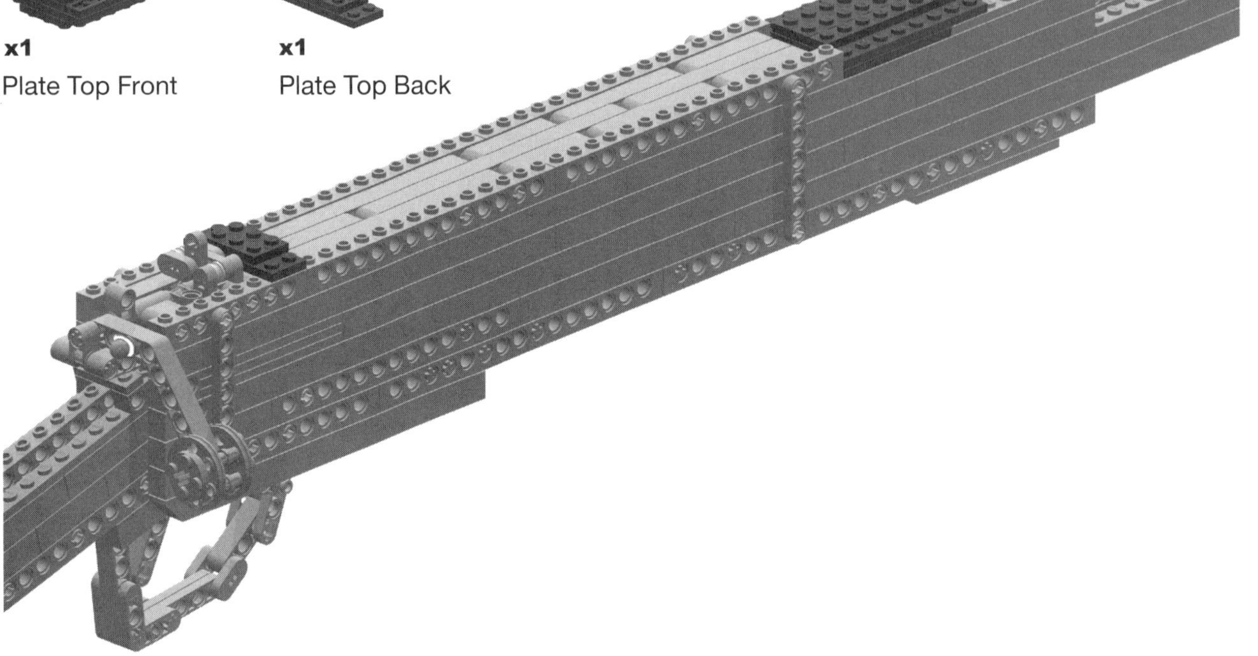

9

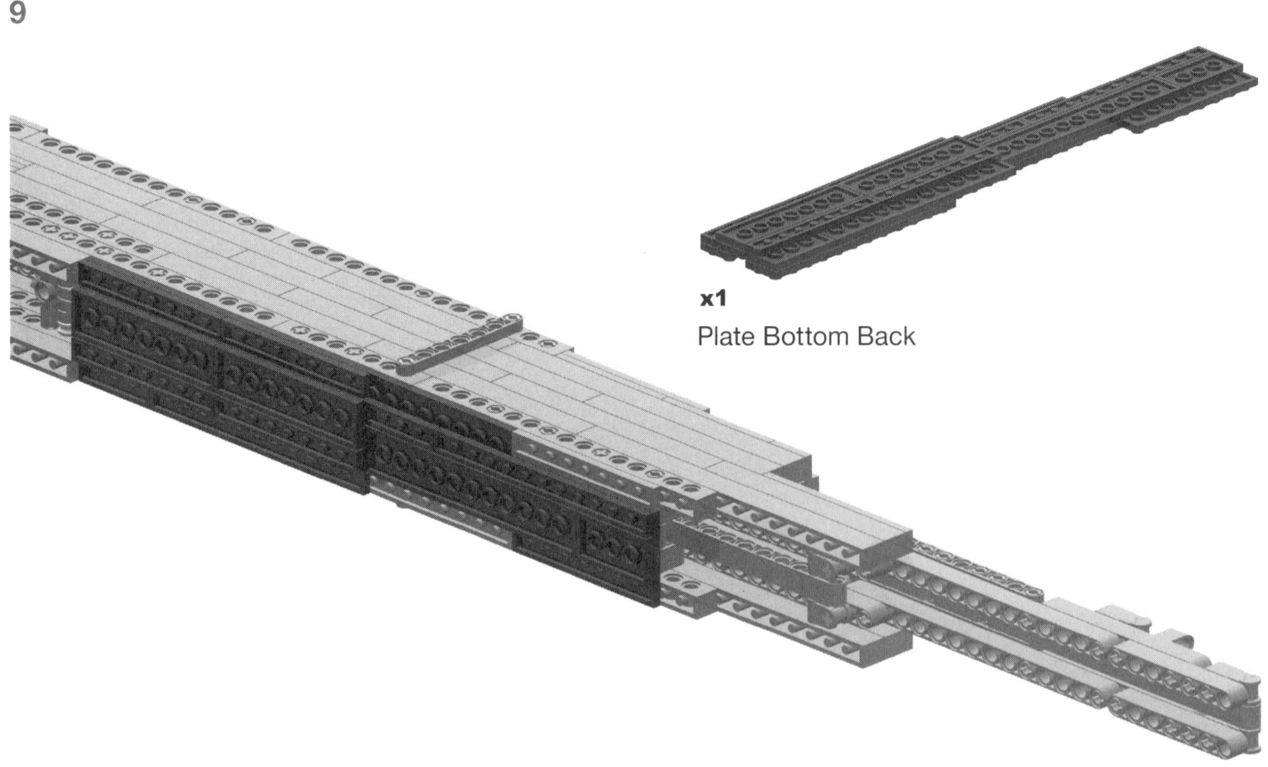

x1
Plate Bottom Back

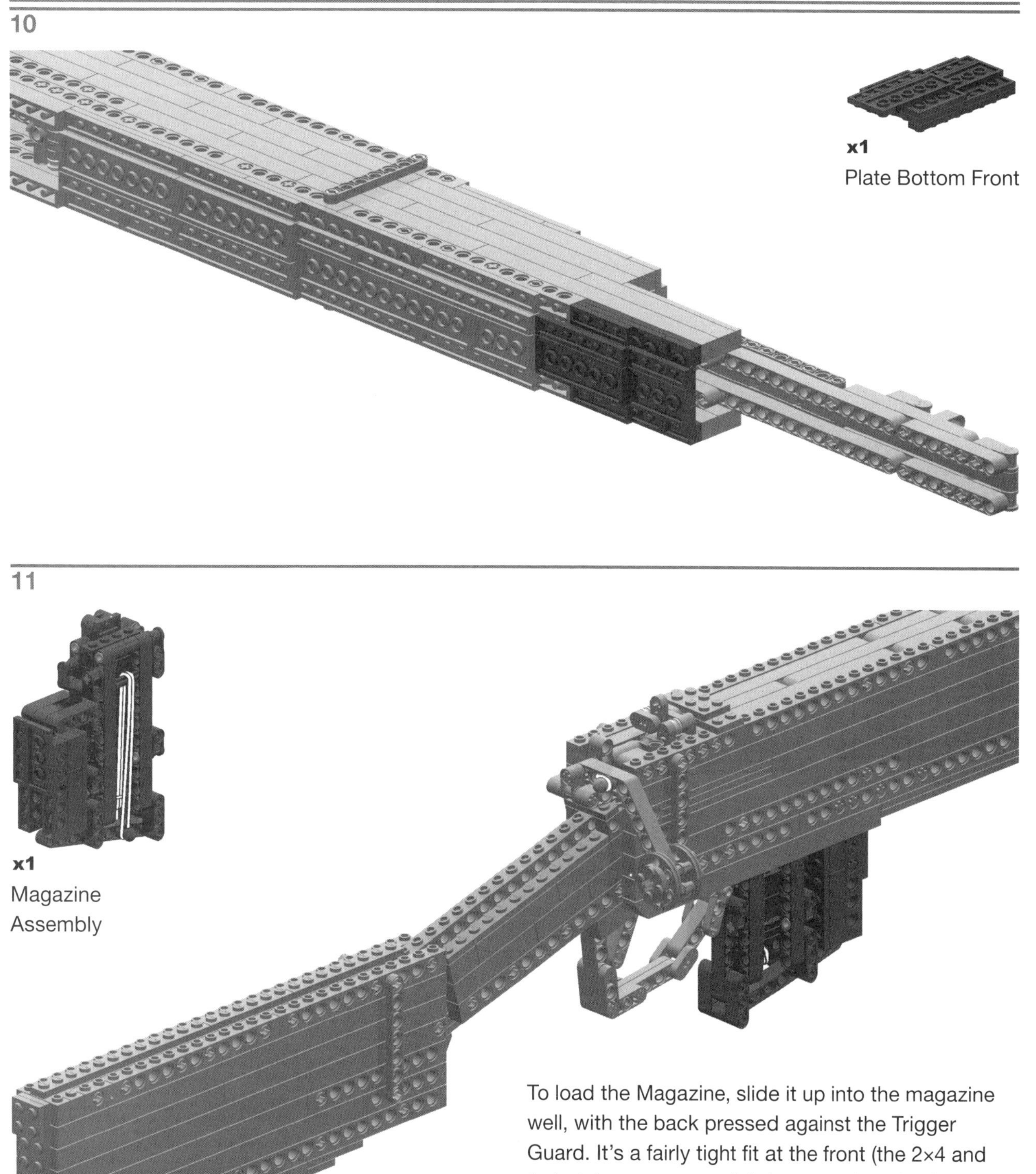

To load the Magazine, slide it up into the magazine well, with the back pressed against the Trigger Guard. It's a fairly tight fit at the front (the 2×4 and 1×4 plates are pressed right up against the front edge of the well), but this allows the Magazine to be properly secured in the gun. To remove, simply press the lower half of the magazine release forward (there's a lever on each side), so that it swivels away, letting you slide the Magazine out.

SPAS 12

LENGTH: *94 studs*
WIDTH: *9 studs*
HEIGHT: *26 studs*
PIECES: *1049*
MAGAZINE TYPE: *Tubular underbarrel magazine*
MAGAZINE CAPACITY: *Nine 1×4 bricks*

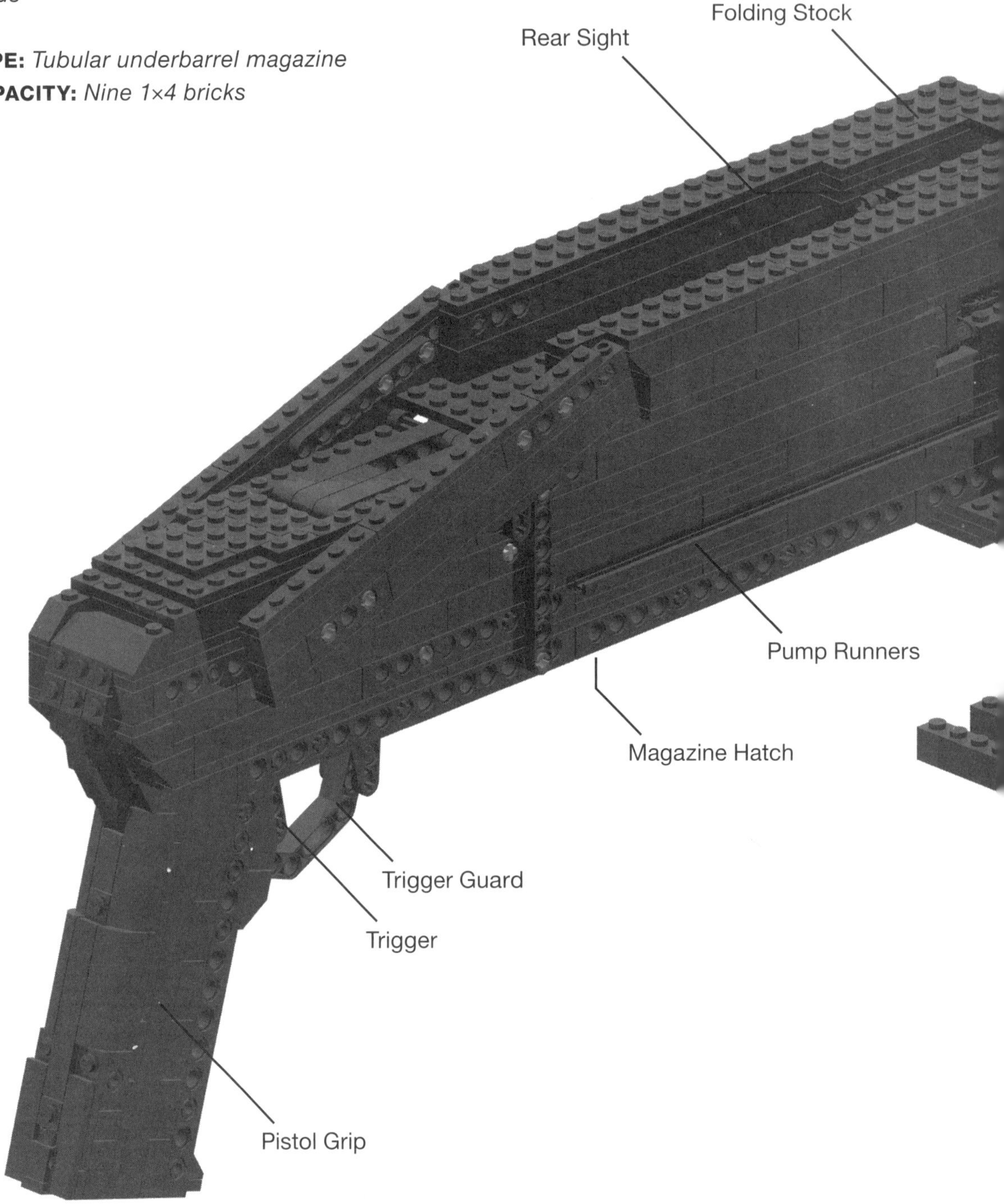

Rear Sight
Folding Stock
Pump Runners
Magazine Hatch
Trigger Guard
Trigger
Pistol Grip

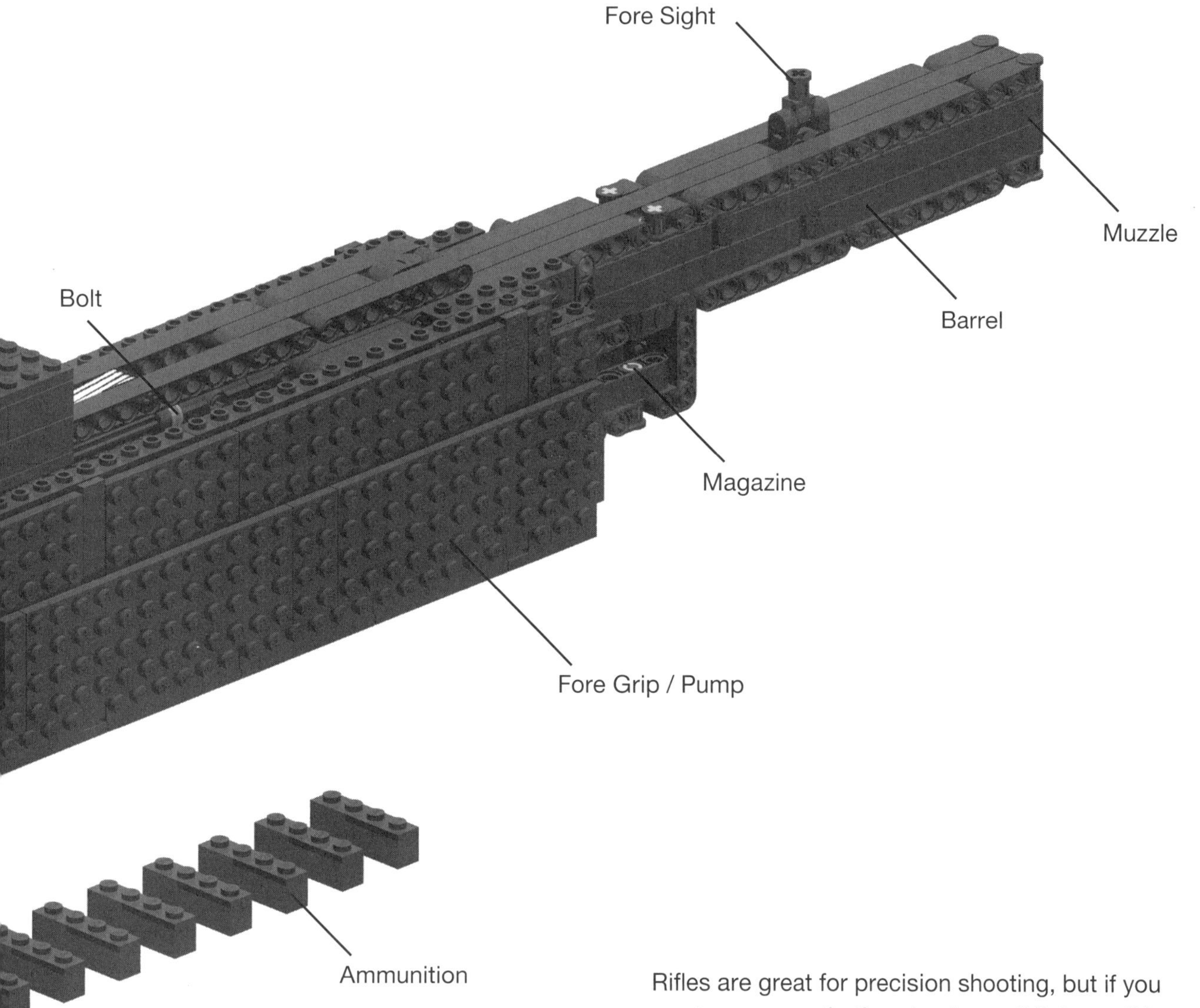

Rifles are great for precision shooting, but if you want a weapon that's going to annihilate anything and everything you point it at, the shotgun should be your weapon of choice.

Most shotguns were first designed with hunting and sport as their main focus. The SPAS 12 shotgun is unusual as it was designed for combat, not sport. Guns for combat situations have very different requirements than those for shooting sports. Such a gun needs a large magazine (no double-barreled shotguns here), a short reloading time, and a heat shield for protecting the shooter when the barrel heats up. And that's exactly what you get with the SPAS 12.

The designers at Franchi even added a nifty little switch that allows you to load a new cartridge straight into the chamber, bypassing the magazine. This enables the user to switch between all the different types of shot a shotgun can fire—from miniature grenades to "less-than-lethal" beanbag projectiles.

My LEGO SPAS 12 fires *slugs* (basically a large bullet)—in our case, a simple 1×4 brick. Loading a slug into a shotgun turns it into something like a small cannon. For design purposes, I had to go this route as I was never going to be able to create a shotgun-style loading mechanism with disintegrating projectiles. (If you do manage to create LEGO shot, be sure to let me know!)

DESIGN HISTORY

My first SPAS 12 model was the fourth gun I posted to the Internet, and to be perfectly honest, the firing mechanism was unreliable. After designing the Desert Eagle, I'd moved back to building with studless beams, and as a result, the SPAS 12 had a very skeletal look to it—not a great success. So nearly a year later, I tried building the gun again.

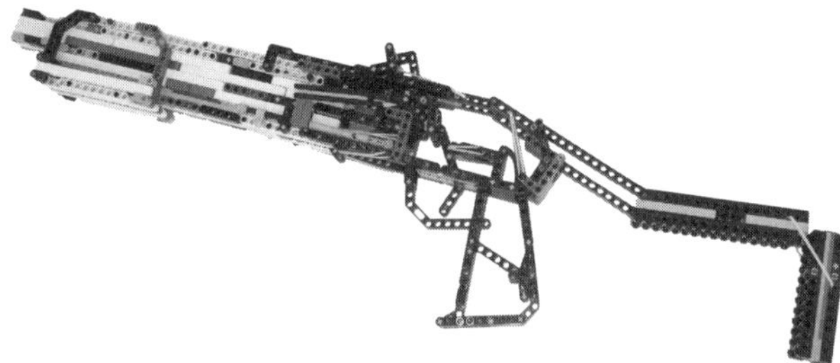

My first SPAS 12 was ugly, skeletal, and unreliable.

The second iteration of the SPAS 12 used the firing mechanism featured in my Lee Enfield and HK-416 models. In this design, the slug is chambered in the barrel and wedged behind a hammer, which is under tension from an elastic band. This is a great design for guns that are fed from box magazines, but I soon realized that I'd need to make some changes to the SPAS 12 in order for the underbarrel magazine to really work. The result was a mechanism that was possibly the most complex that I've ever made.

Finally, for this book, I needed a mechanism that was even more reliable. Although it's not as complex as it used to be, the SPAS 12 that you will build contains what is, without a doubt, the most intricate mechanism featured in this book.

With an extra year of weapon-building experience, my second version is an unmistakable improvement.

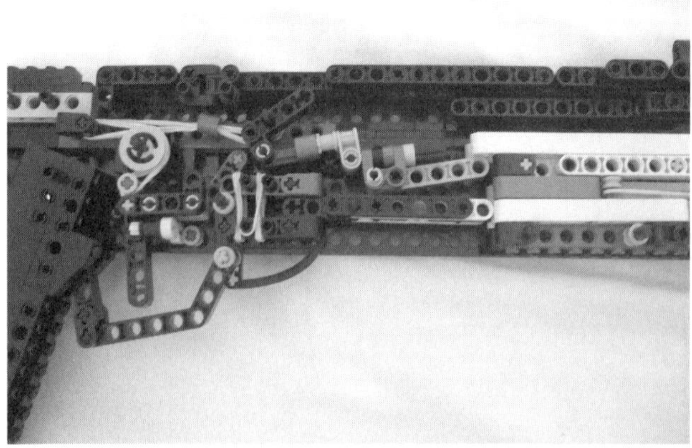

The firing mechanism of the second version is still my most complex ever, which came back to haunt me when I began modeling it in MLCad!

The firing mechanism wasn't the only part that changed. I made many cosmetic changes, most noticeably in the fore grip and the folding stock, which is now solely aesthetic. Losing the structural stock meant that all the pressure of cocking the gun was forced into the skin between the index finger and the thumb of the user's trigger hand. Combined with the square edges of the LEGO bricks, this made for a very uncomfortable shooting experience, so I also made the pistol grip more ergonomic.

The final result is the most brutal-looking and complex gun in this book. If I had to choose which of these guns to display on my wall, it'd be the SPAS 12, hands down.

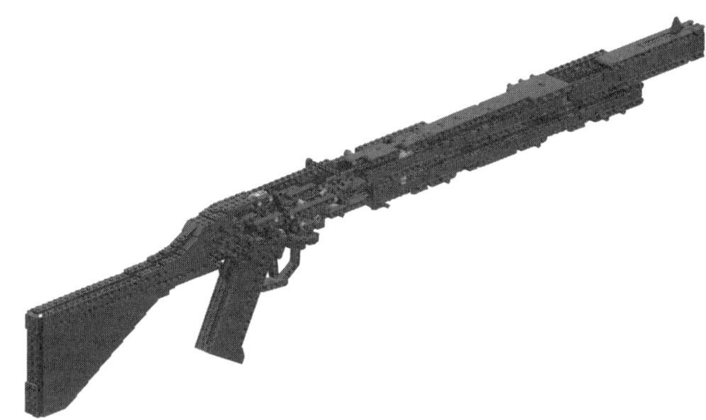

Note the fixed stock on this CAD model of the second version. I decided not to use it in favor of a smaller, folding stock, but if you want to give your shotgun a classic look, there's inspiration right there!

HOW IT WORKS

Always insert the bricks into the Magazine with the studs facing upward. When cocking the gun, gently pull the Fore Grip back until it feels like it's as far back as it'll go, and then pull it a bit more. After some initial resistance, you should hear and feel a few clicks as the mechanism sorts itself out. Then, push the Fore Grip forward to its original position (it's not spring loaded to return to the front). If you don't put in that extra pull to get that click, the gun will almost certainly jam. However, when you know what you're looking for it's actually a very easy mechanism to use.

1

When the Magazine is empty, the gun is not loaded.

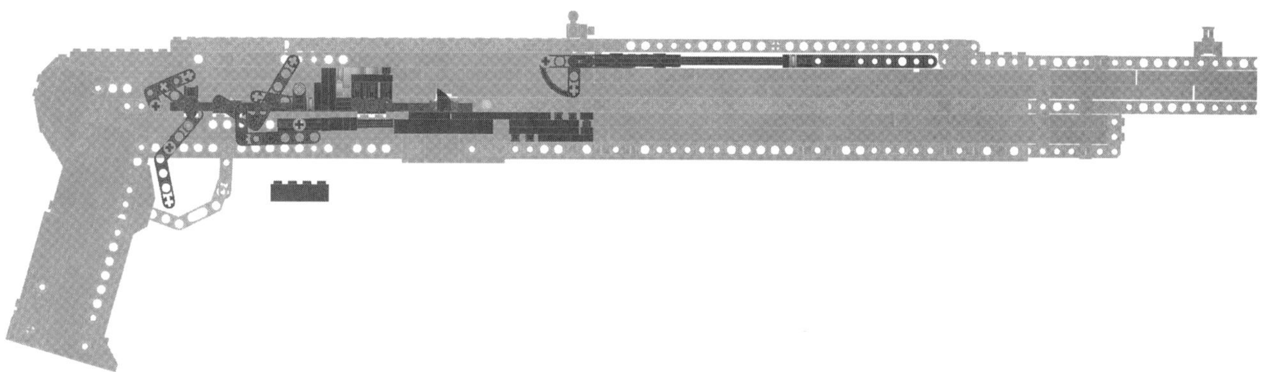

2

Load a slug (a 1×4 brick). The Magazine Hatch rotates out of the way, and the Magazine Slide is pushed out. Note how the studs of the slug slip between the 6-stud axles in the Magazine Hatch.

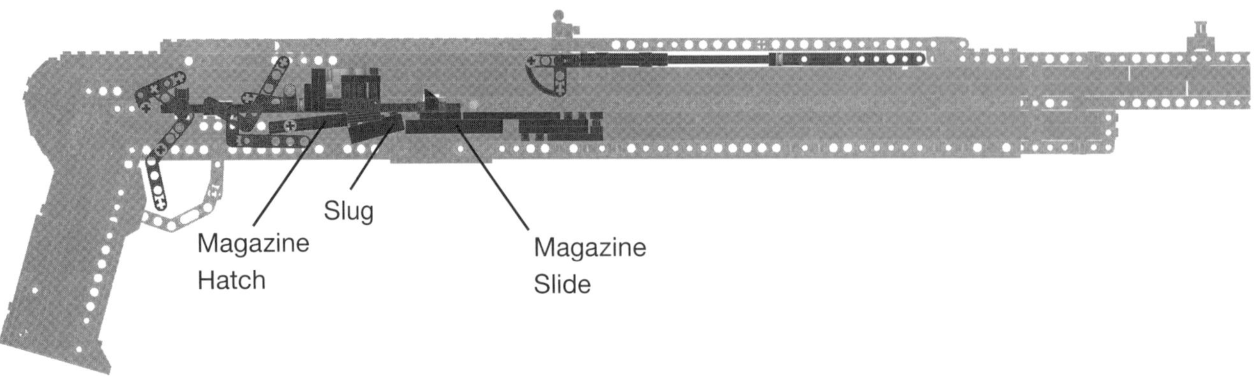

3

Once the slug is loaded, the Magazine Hatch moves back to its original position. The tension in the rubber band keeps the slug between the Magazine Slide and the Magazine Hatch.

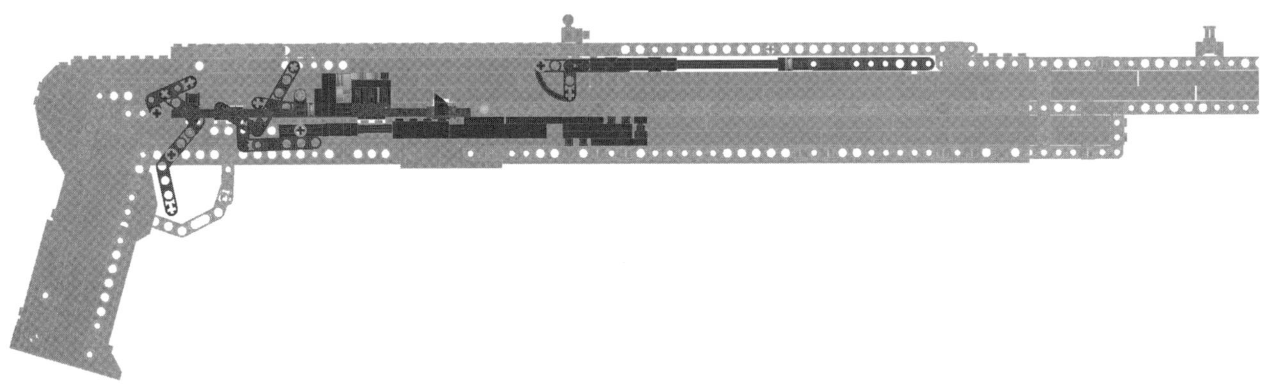

4

Pull the Fore Grip to begin cocking the weapon. The Bolt (attached to the Fore Grip) pushes the Hammer as it starts to move back.

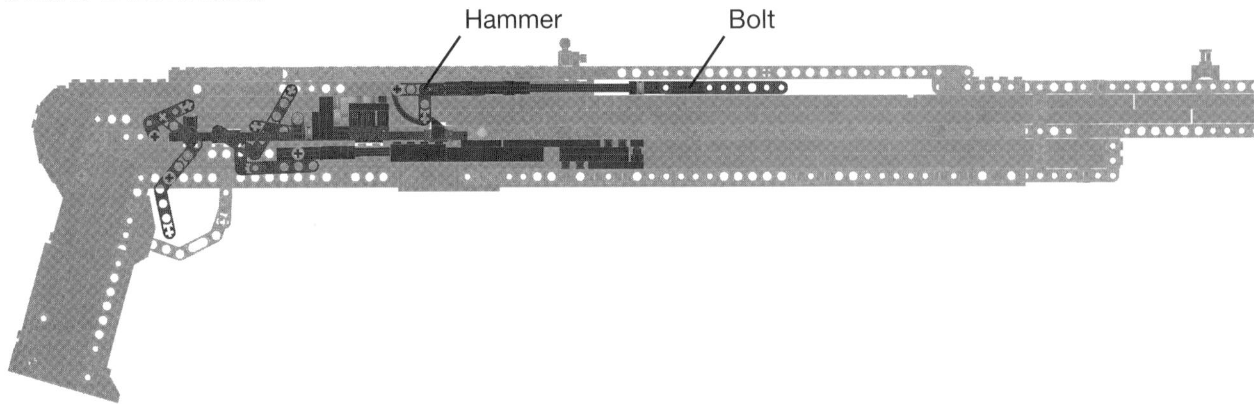

5

Continue to pull the Fore Grip back so that the Hammer pushes against the Chambering Slide, which pivots down and moves the Magazine Hatch out of the way. This allows the slug, under pressure from the Magazine Slide, to slide toward the Chambering Slide.

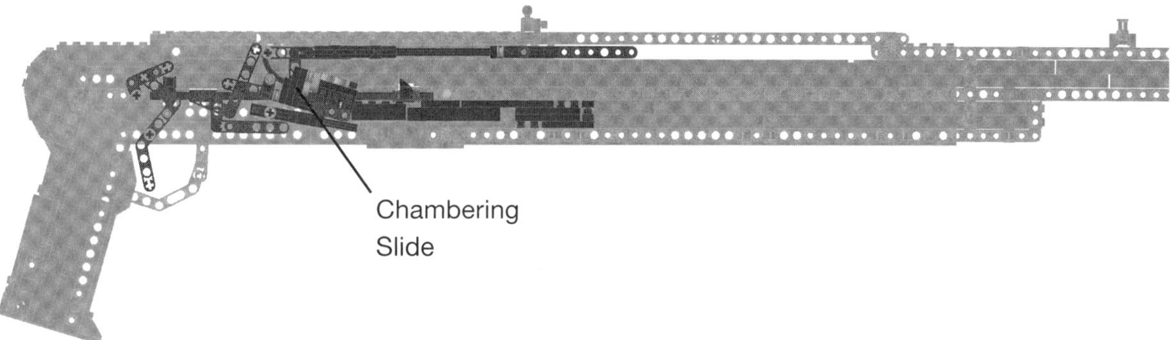

6

When the Fore Grip is pulled back all the way, the Chambering Slide is pushed even farther down and continues to move the Magazine Hatch out of the way. Now there is enough room for the slug (still under pressure from the Magazine Slide) to slide up into it.

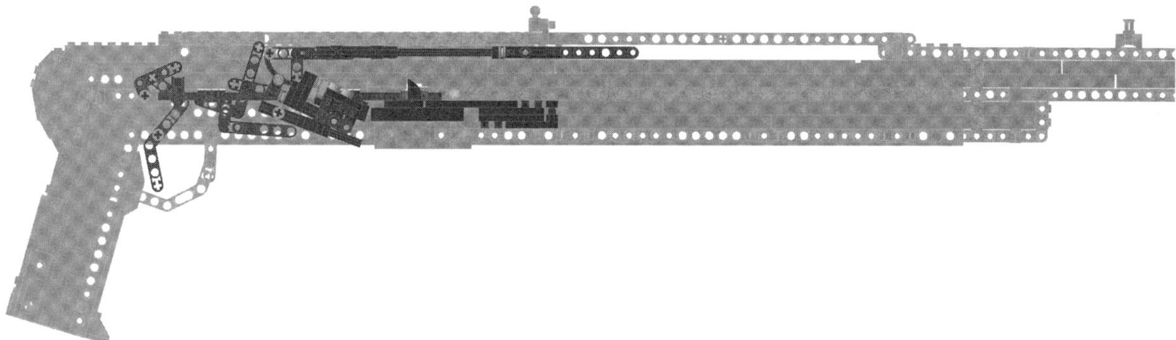

7

Begin sliding the Fore Grip (and the Bolt) back to its original position. Due to the lack of pressure from the Hammer, the Chambering Slide rotates back up, carrying the slug with it. The Magazine Slide returns to its original position, as the slug has completely left the magazine.

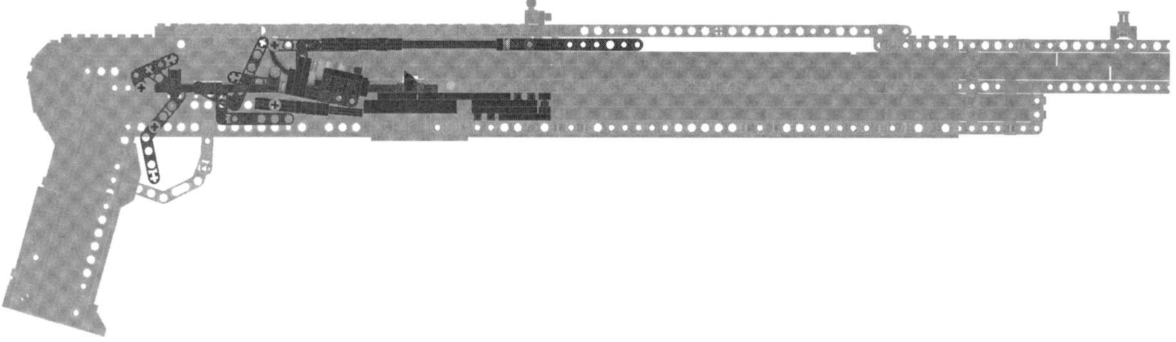

8

Now back in its original position, the Chambering Slide meets the Hammer, which just barely comes into contact with the slug hidden behind the Chambering Slide's wall. The Magazine Hatch returns to its original position as well.

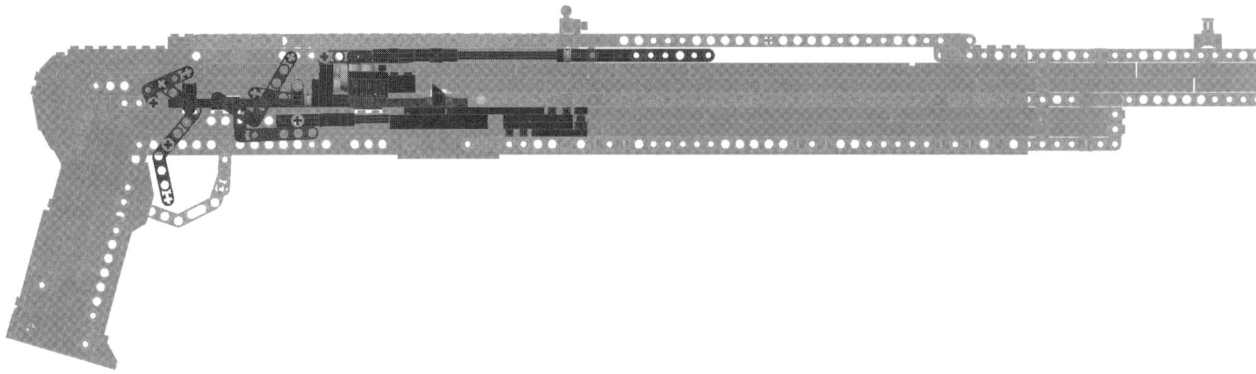

9

Once the Fore Grip is returned to the front of the weapon, the Bolt returns to its original position, but the Hammer is left behind, pressing against the back of the slug. The Trigger Rotator that protrudes into the barrel holds the slug back and keeps it from moving any farther forward.

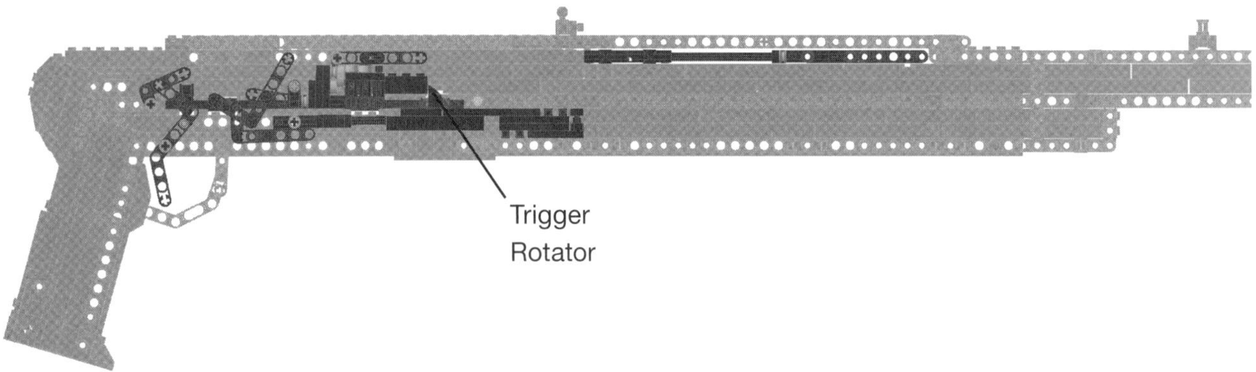

10

Pull the Trigger to rotate the Trigger Rotator and remove the protrusion in the barrel.

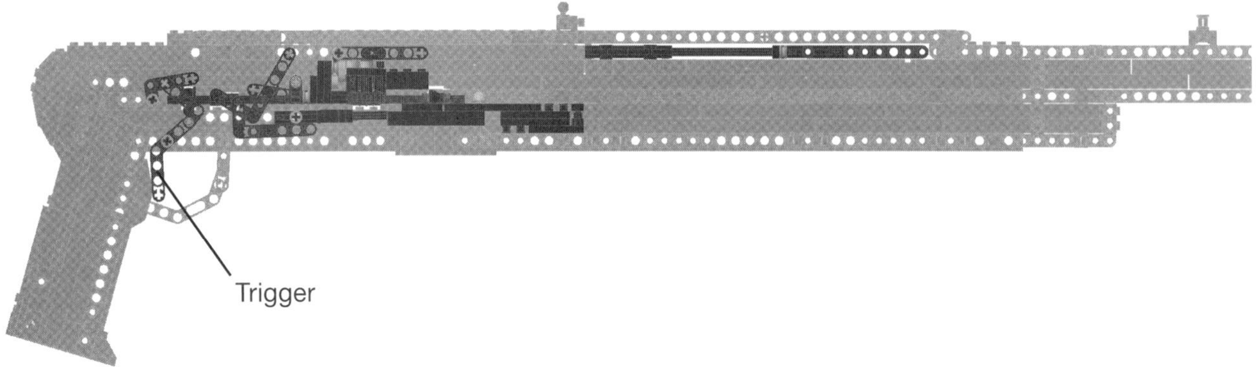

11

The Hammer immediately propels the slug down the barrel.

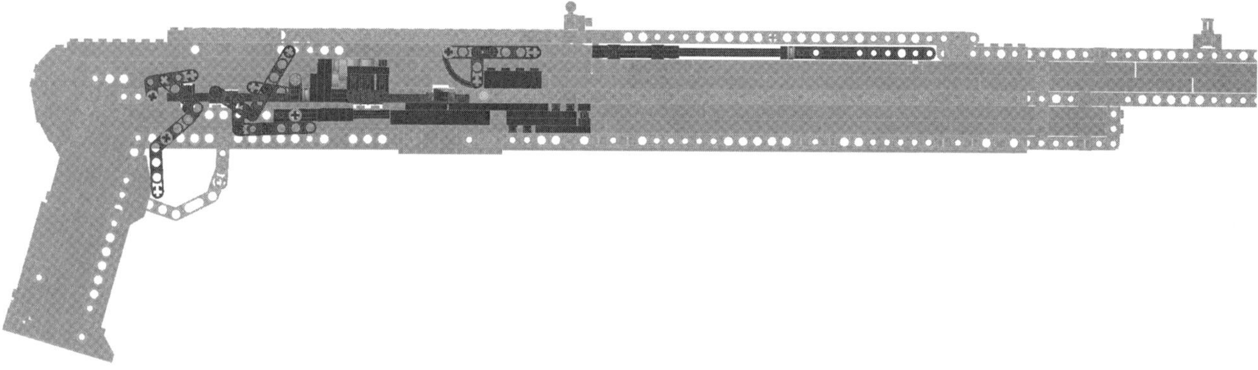

12

The Hammer comes to a stop when it reaches the Bolt. The slug continues down the barrel to exit the muzzle; that is, it is fired! Once the Trigger is released, both the Trigger and the Trigger Rotator will return to their original positions.

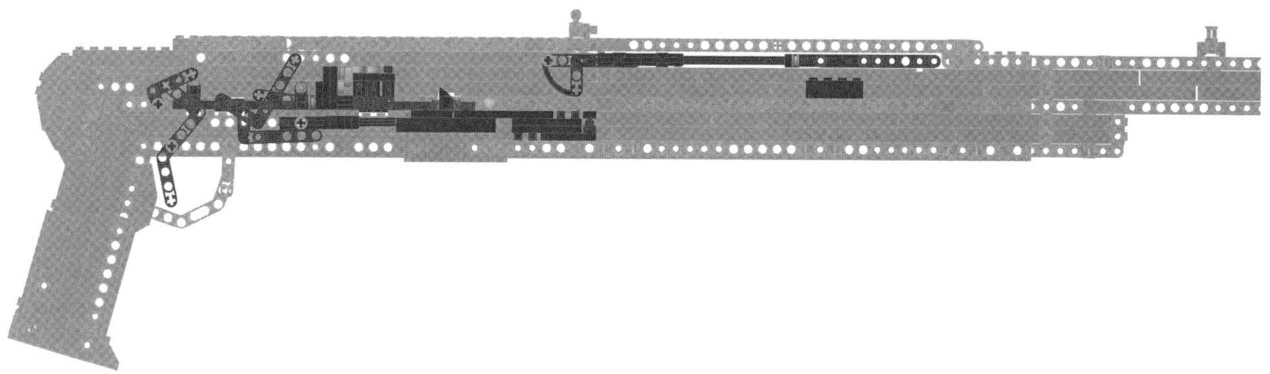

BILL OF MATERIALS

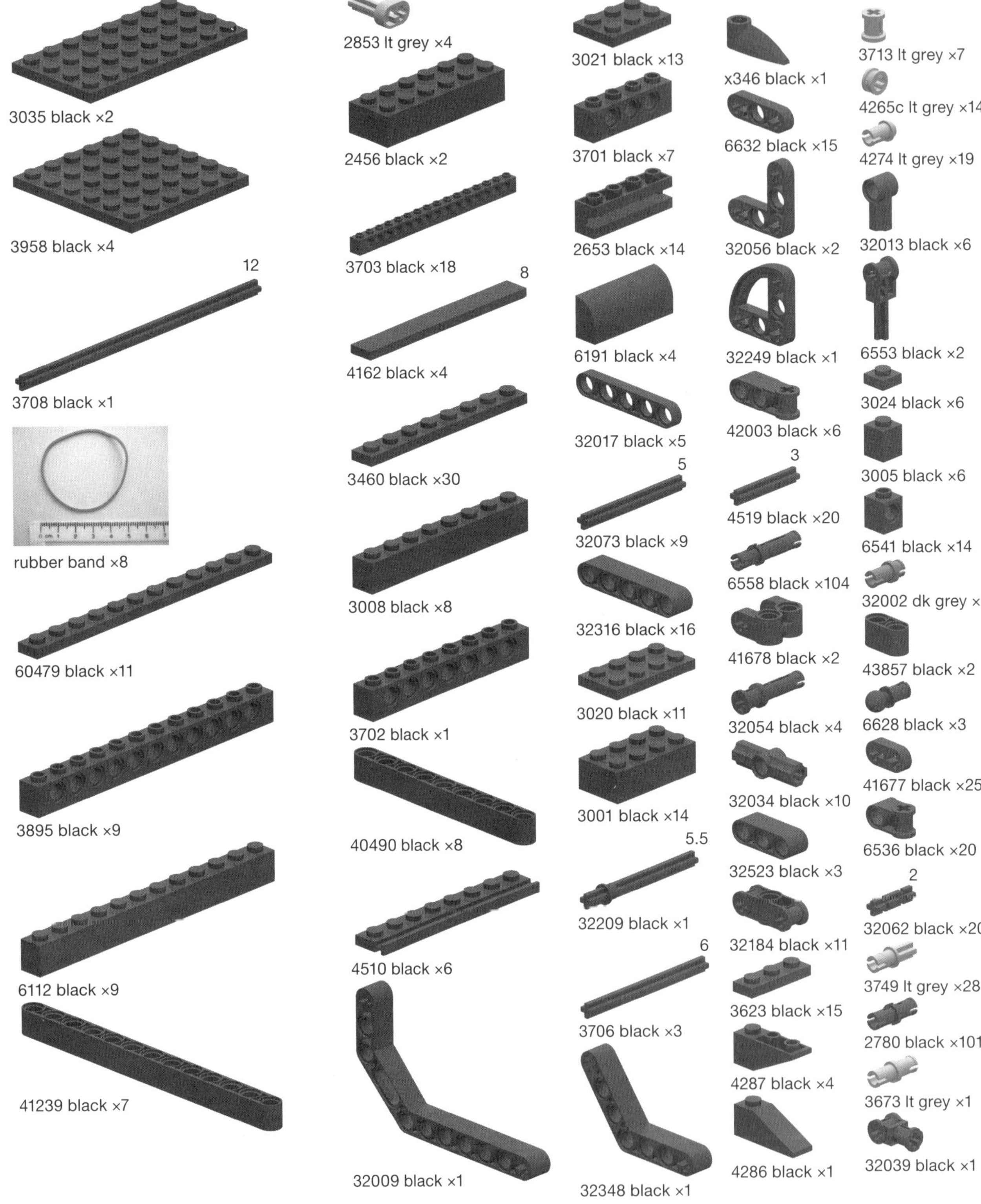

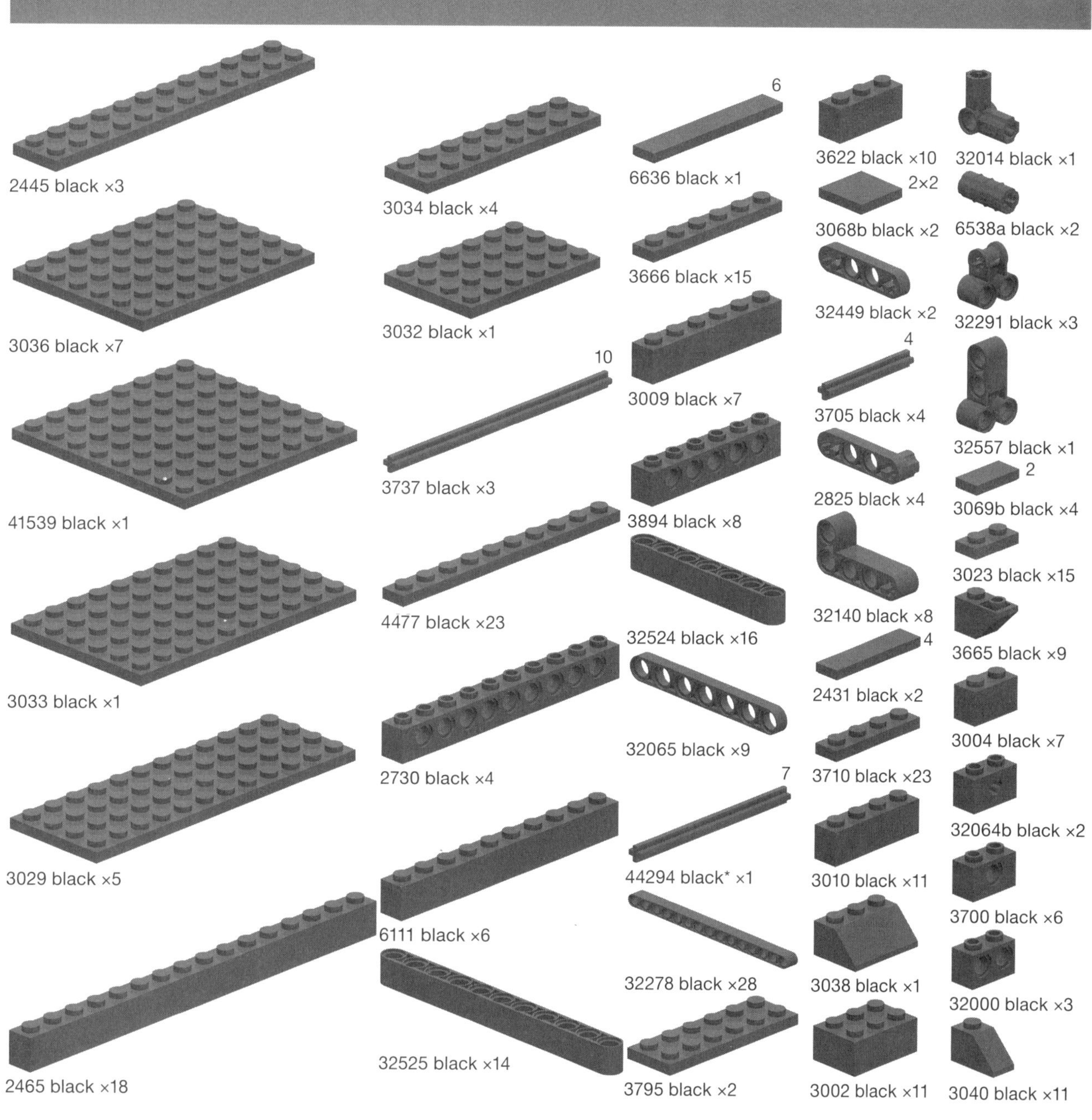

* Although this piece is available in black, you're far more likely to find it in light grey.

TRIGGER ROTATOR

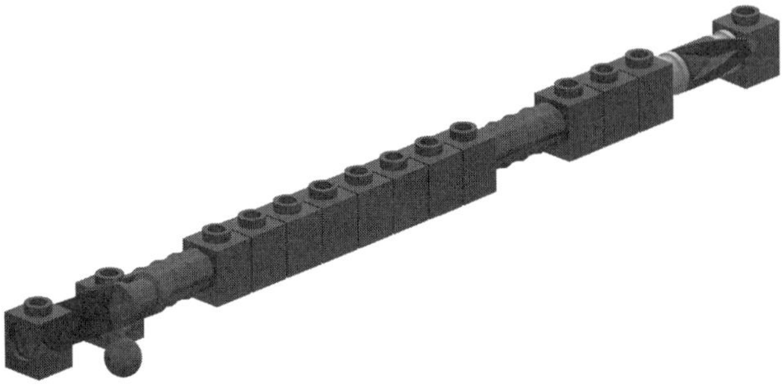

1

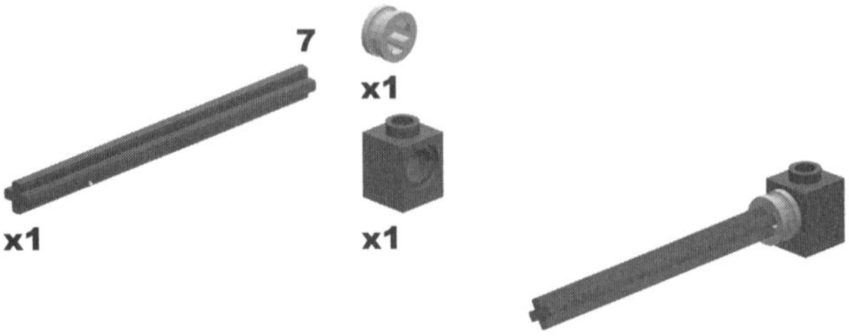

7 x1

x1 x1

2

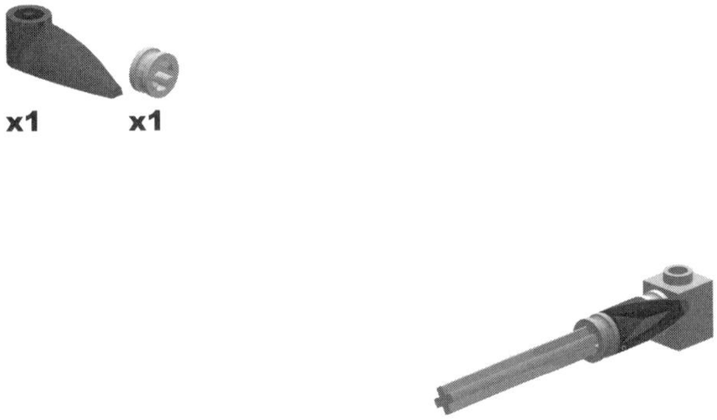

x1 x1

3

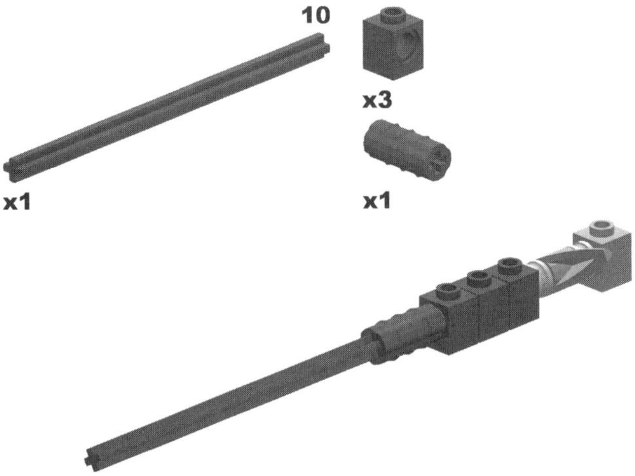

10 x3

x1 x1

4

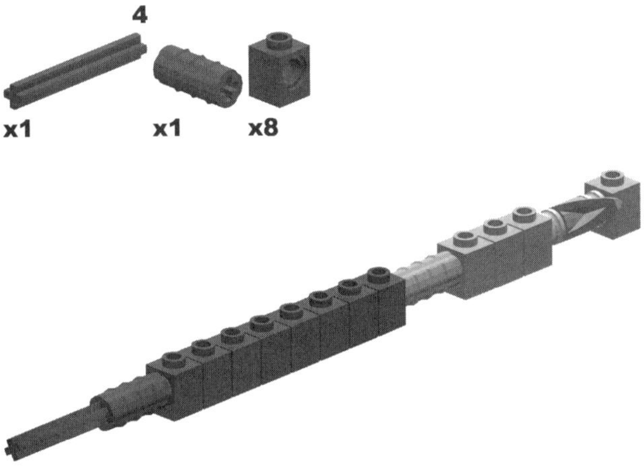

4

x1 x1 x8

5

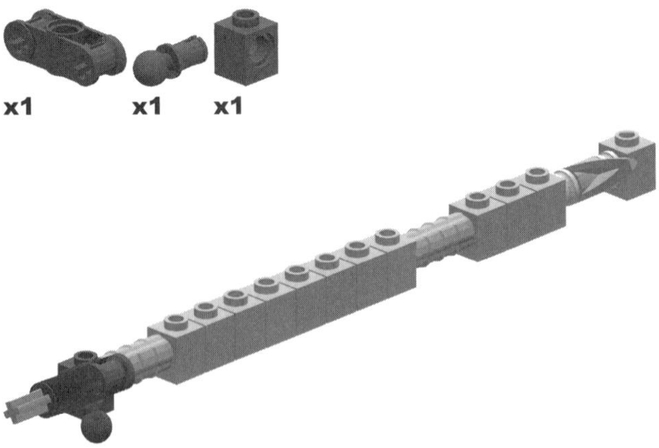

x1 x1 x1

6

x1

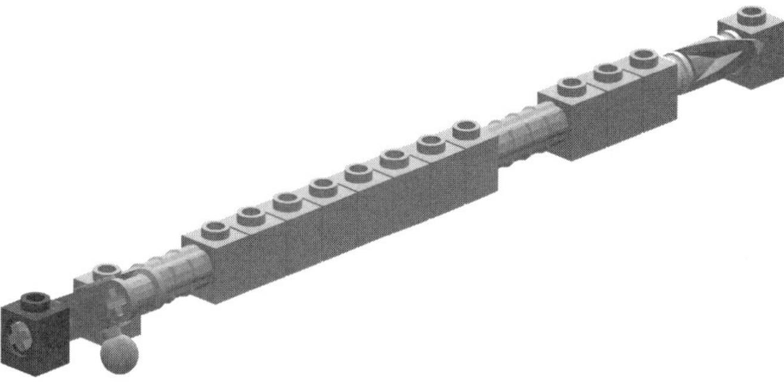

FRAME WALL LEFT

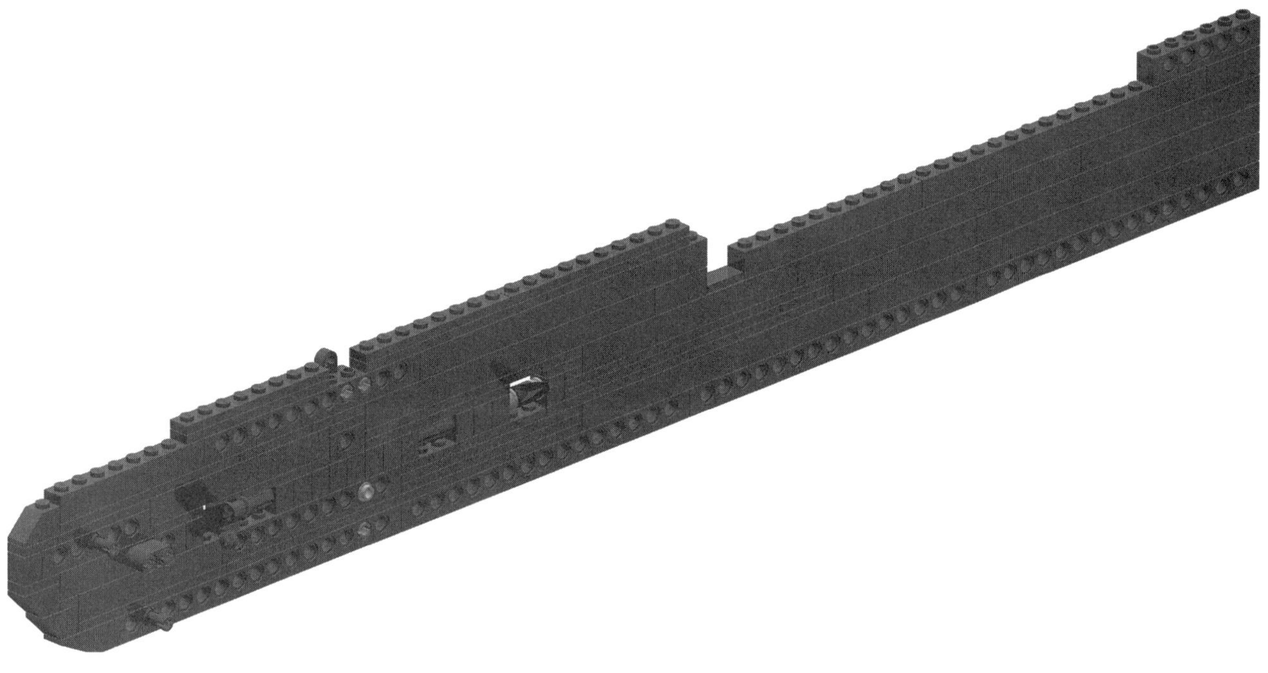

1

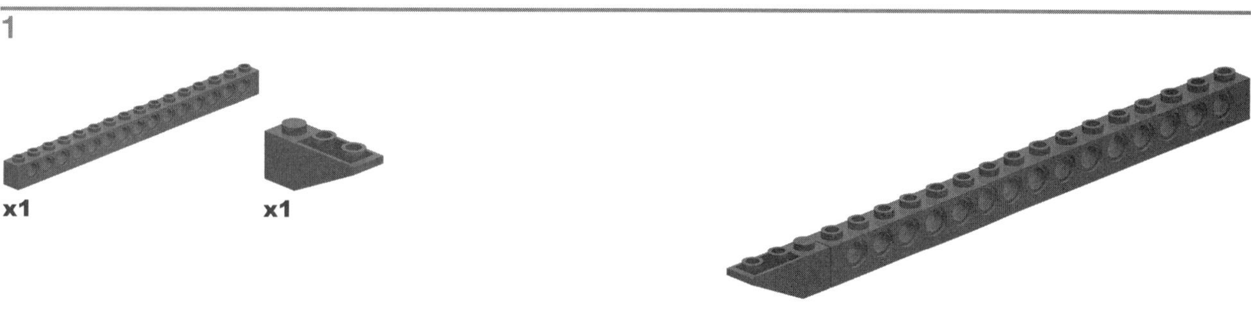

x1

x1

2

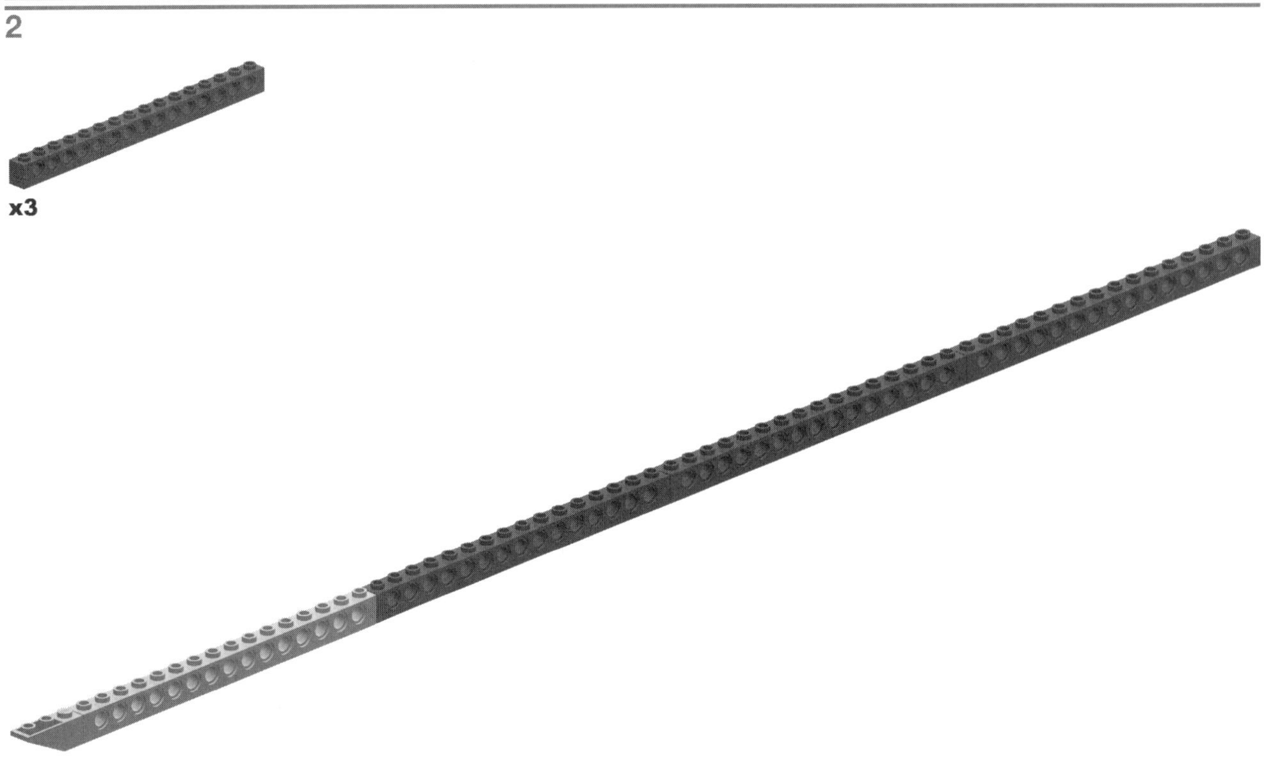

3

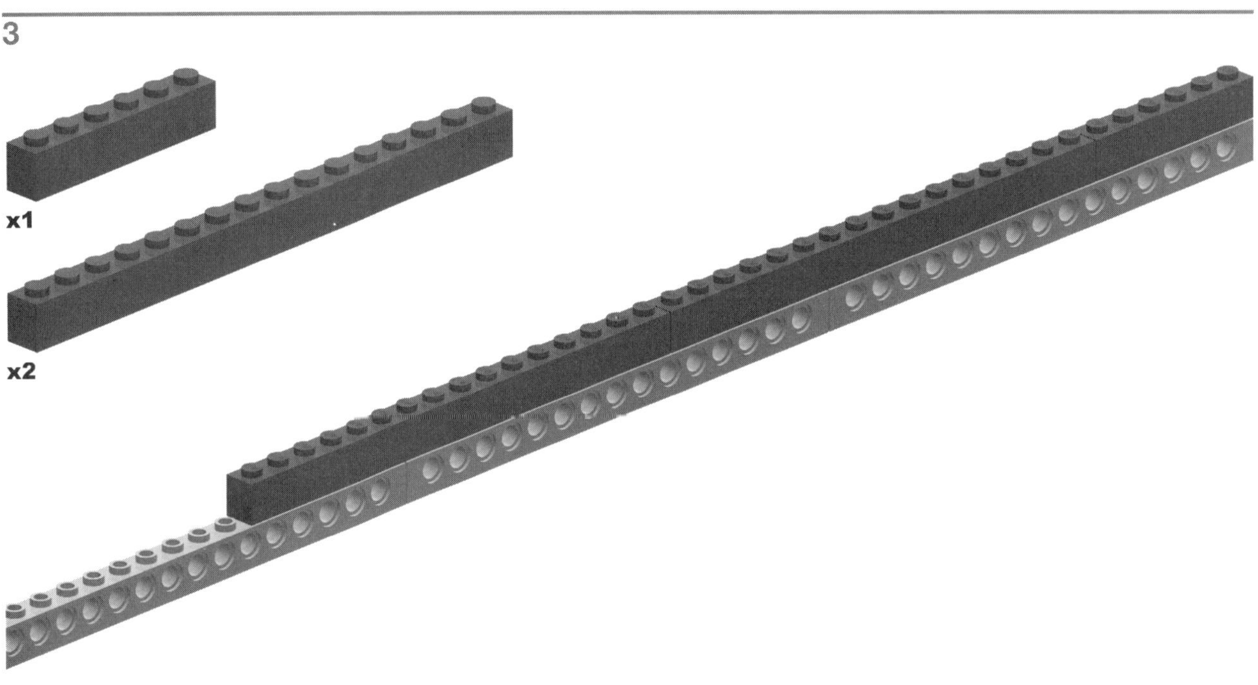

4

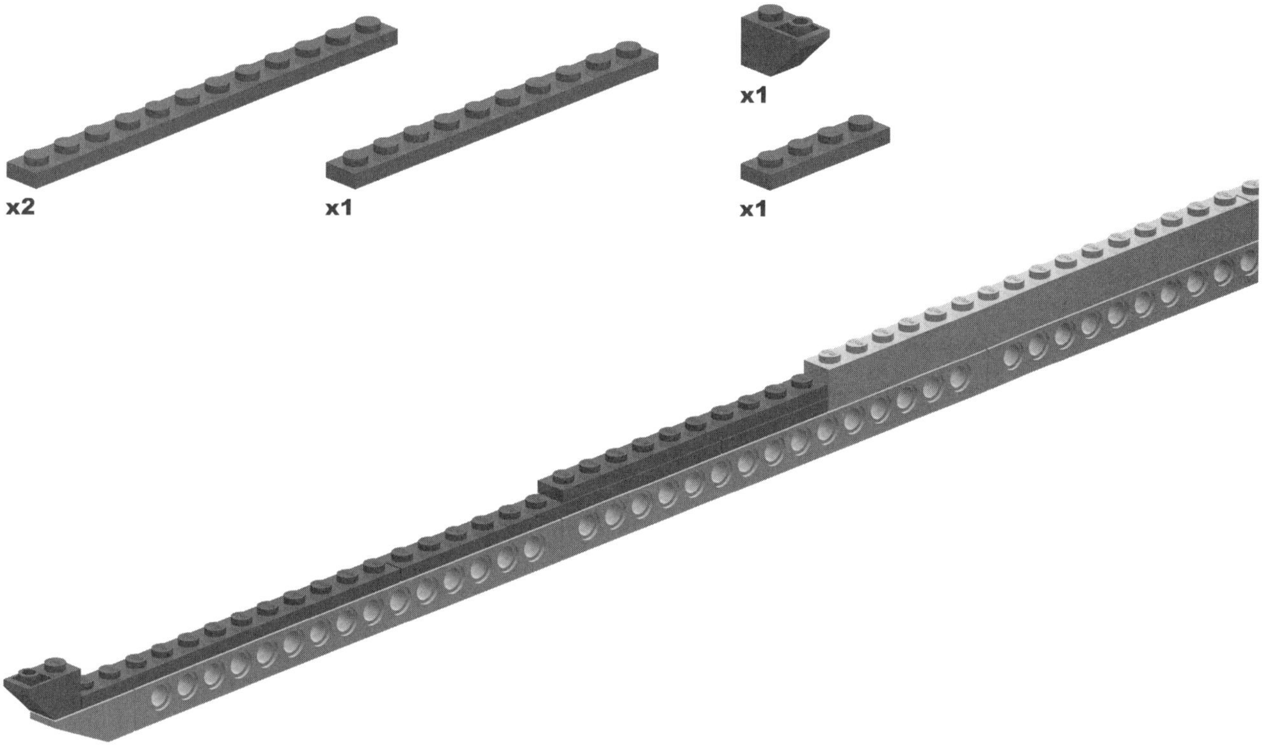

x2

x1

x1

x1

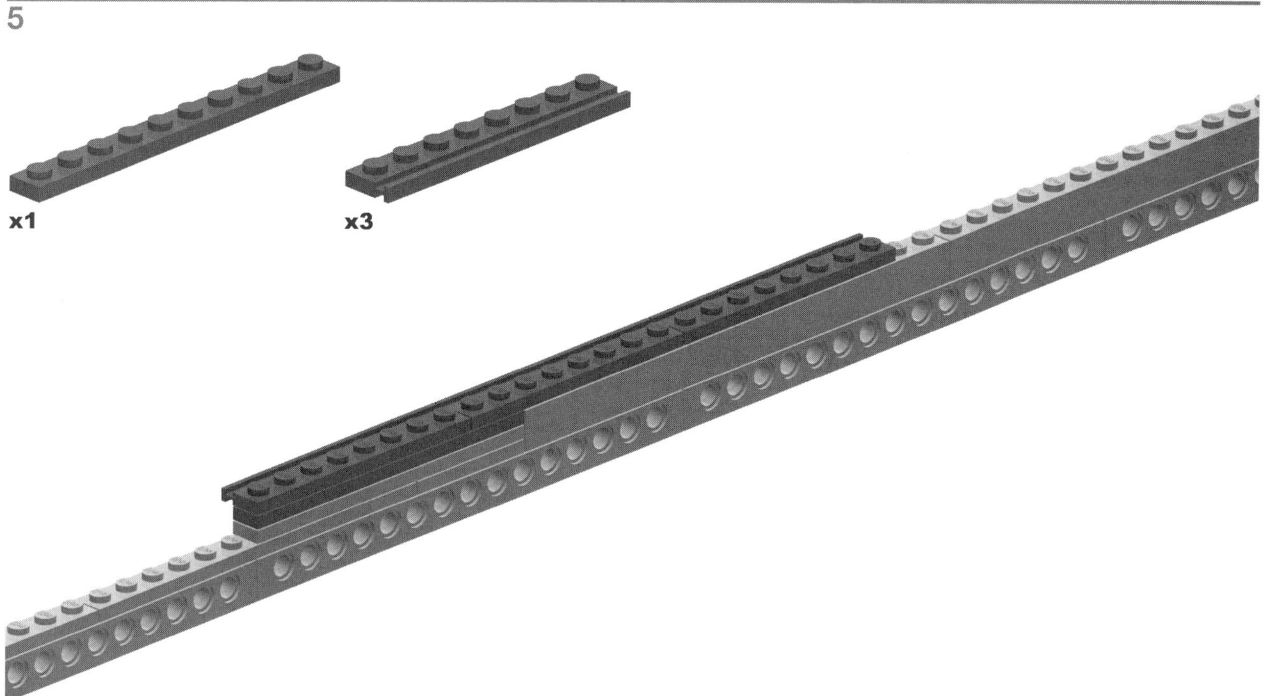

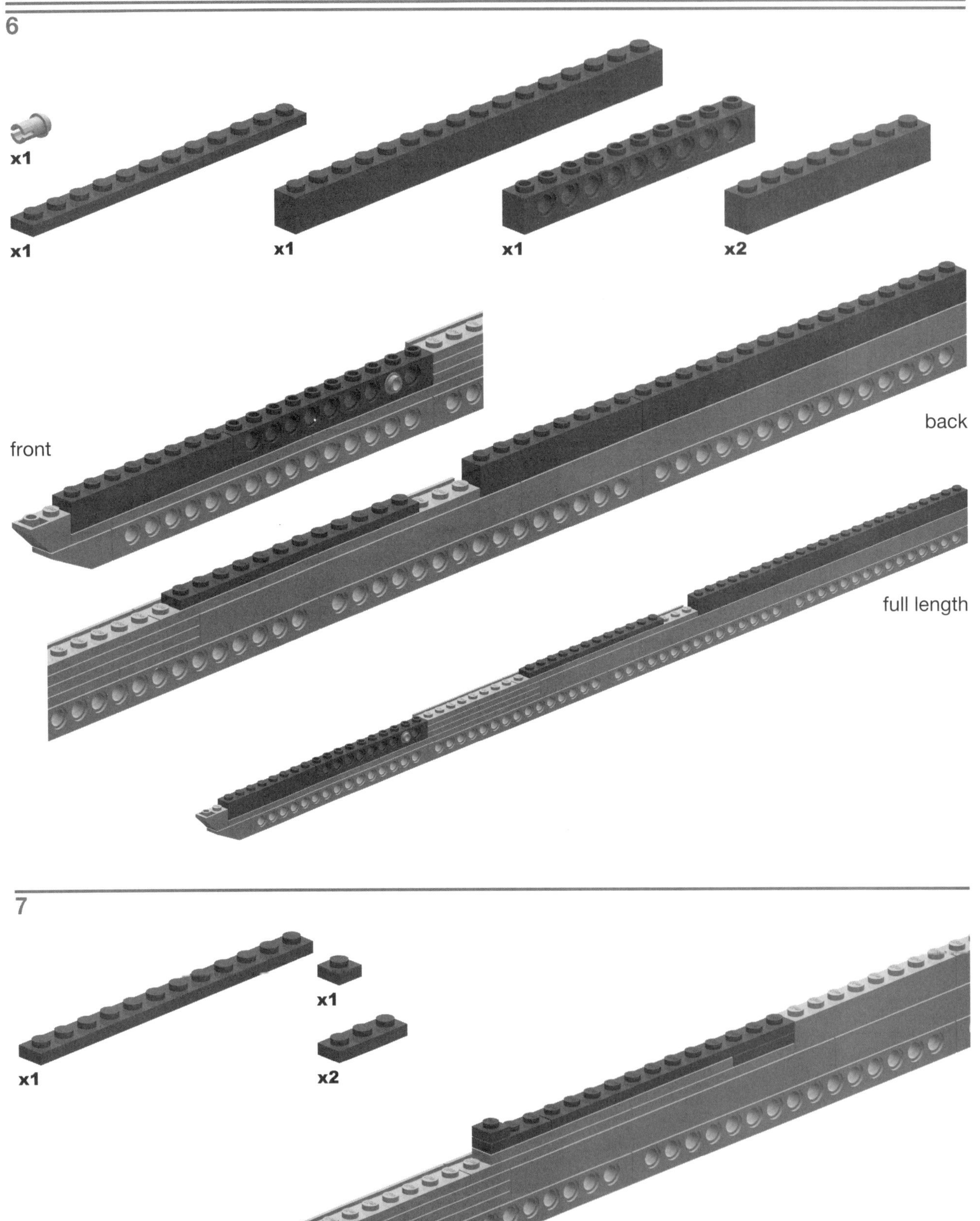
6
x1
x1
x1
x1
x2
front
back
full length
7
x1
x1
x2

8

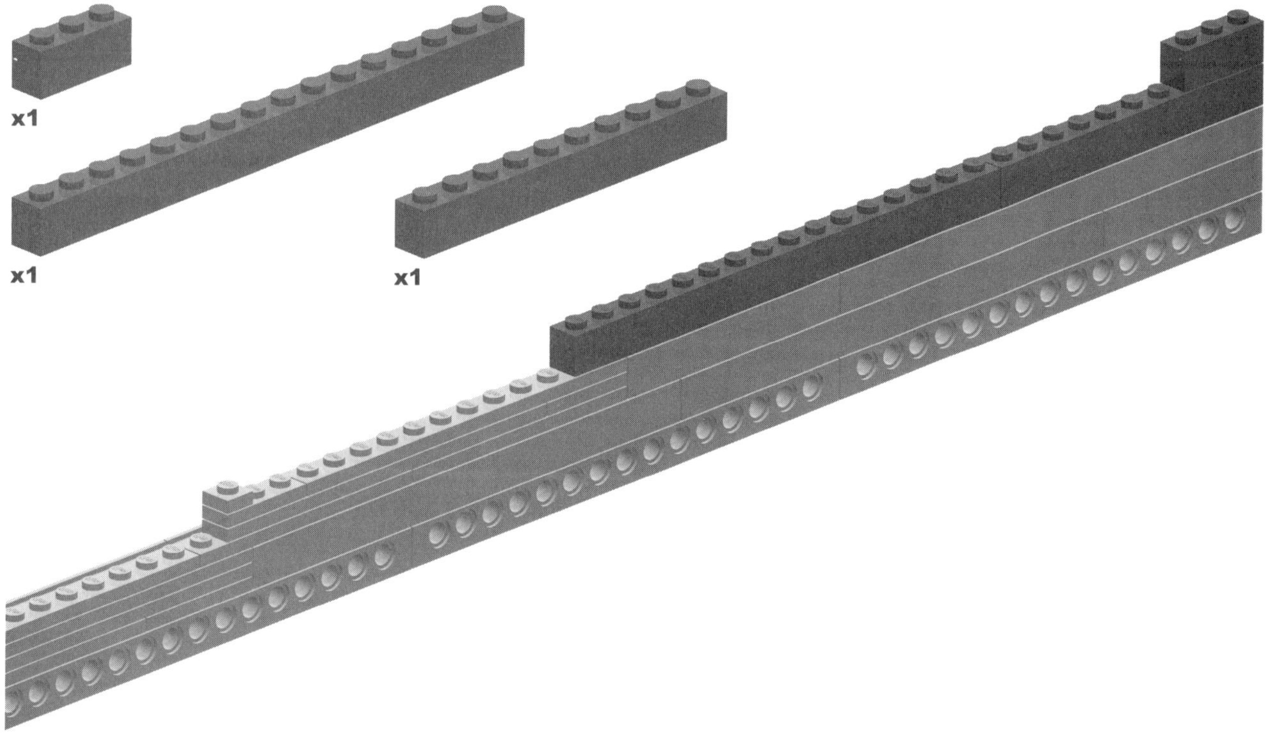

x1

x1

x1

9

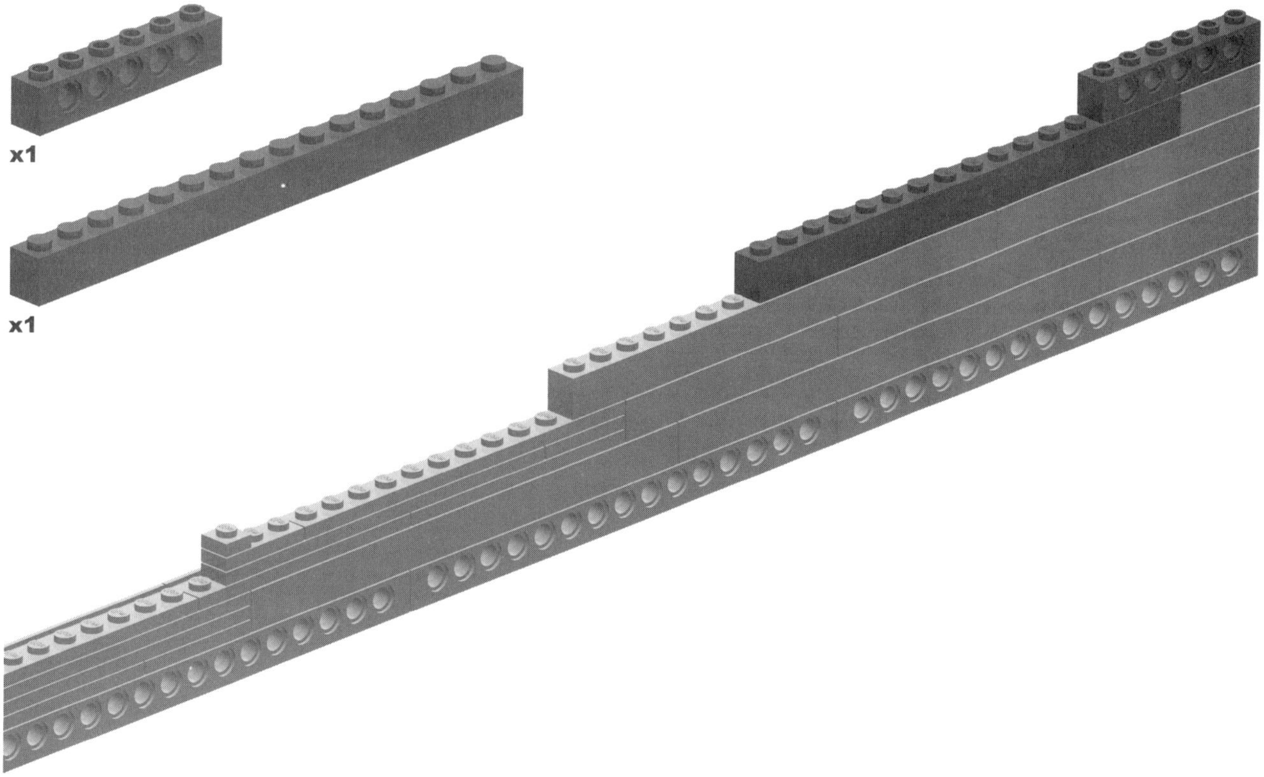

x1

x1

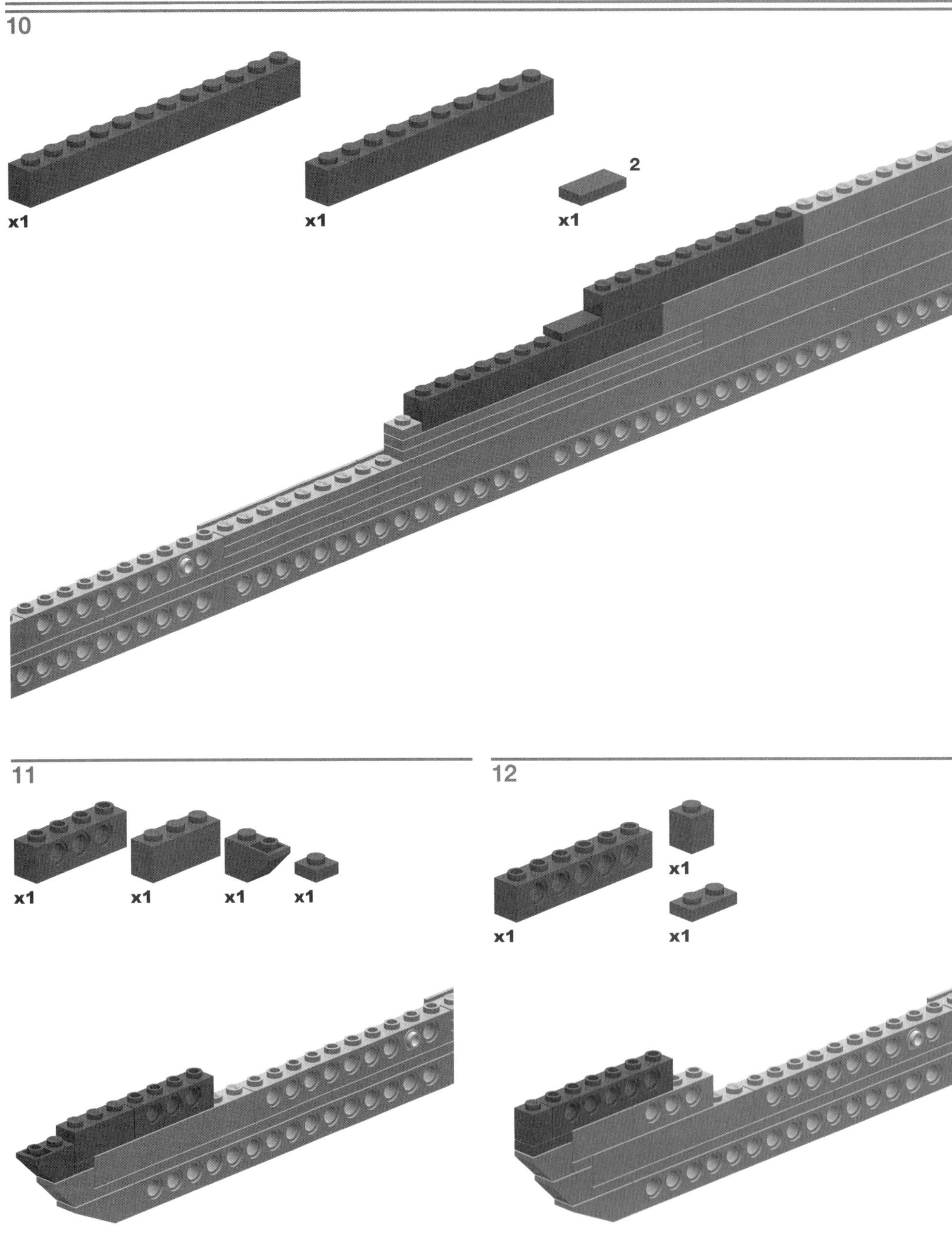
10
x1
x1
2
x1
11
x1
x1
x1
x1
12
x1
x1
x1
x1

13

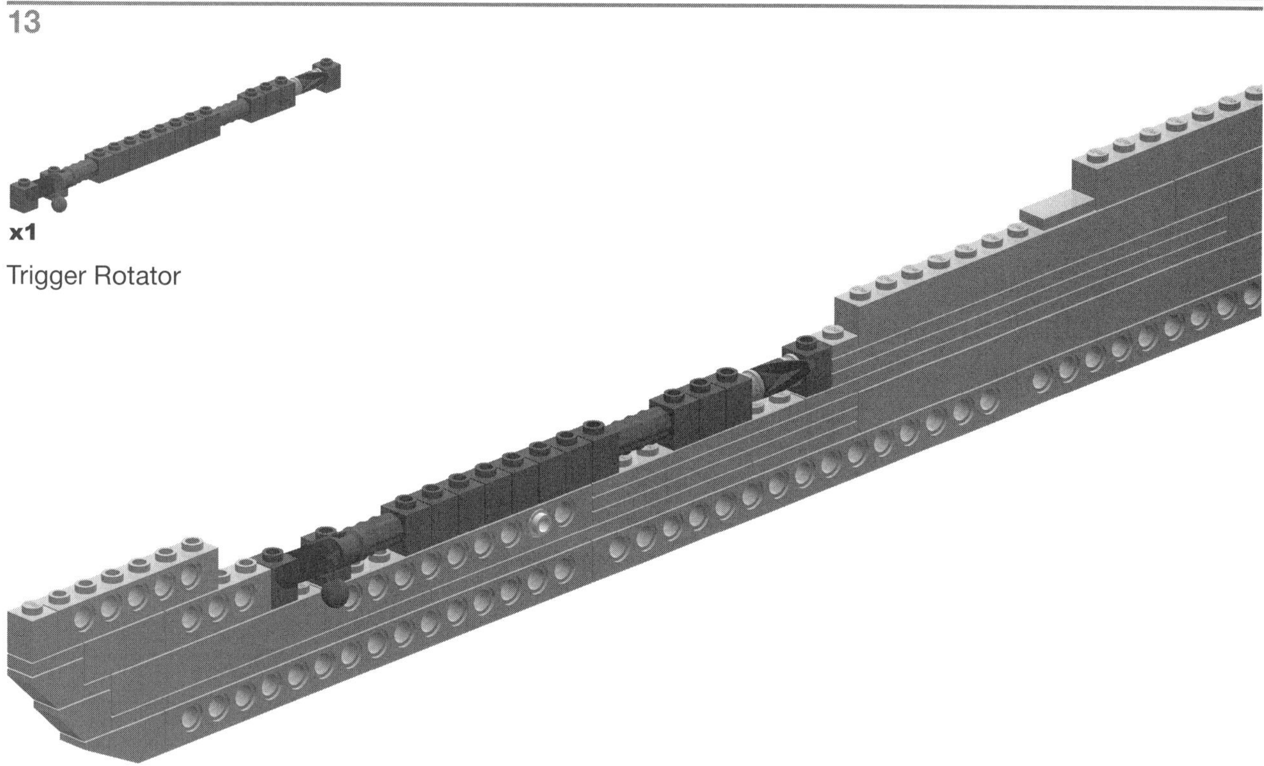

14

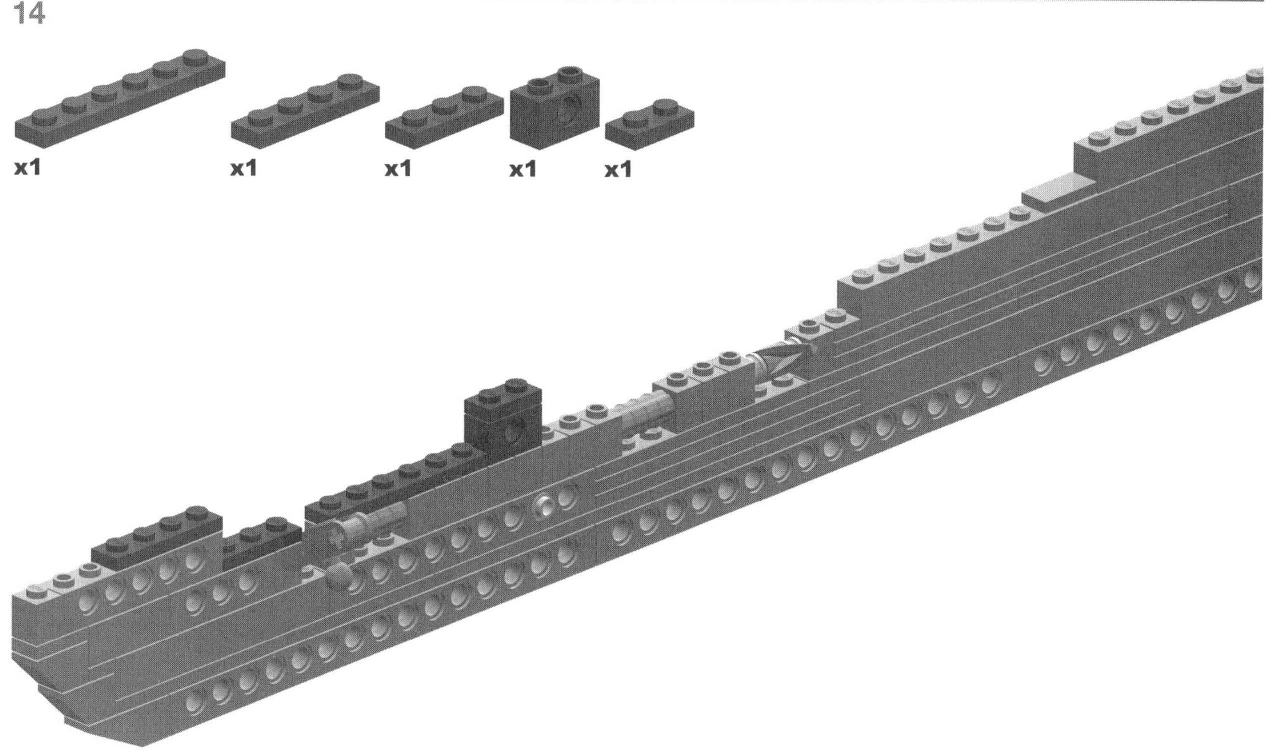

15

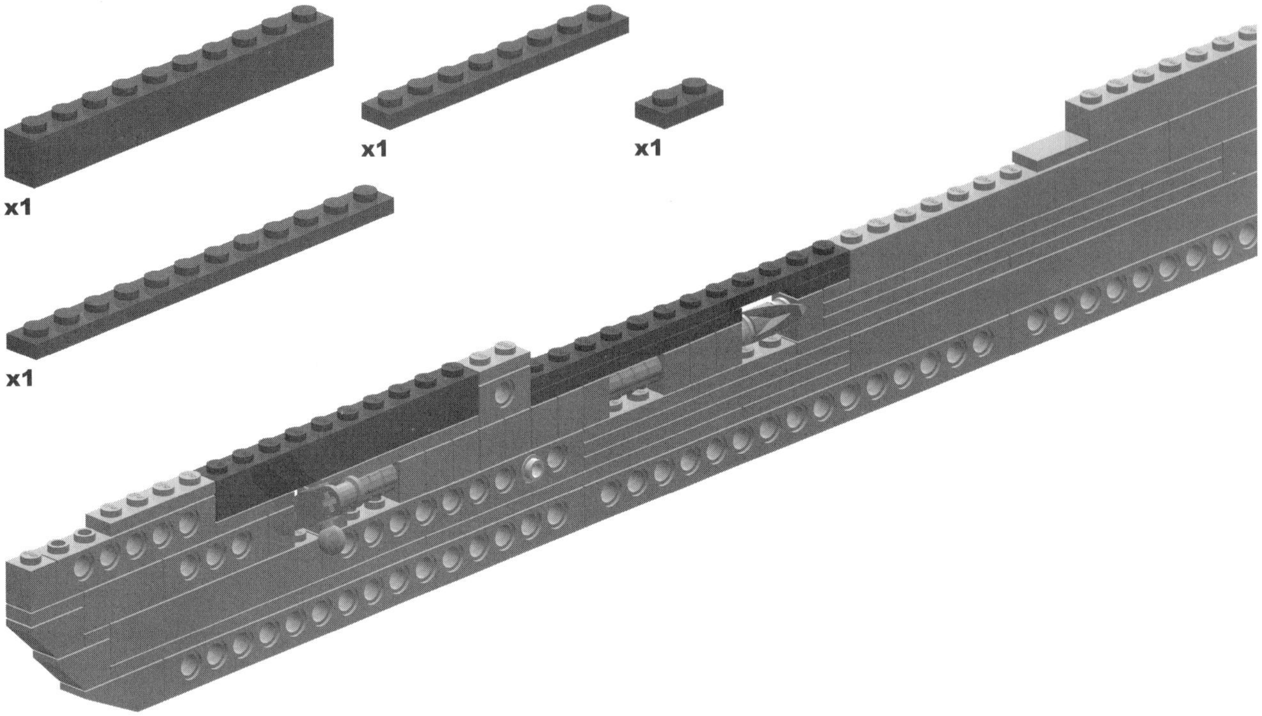

x1

x1

x1

x1

16

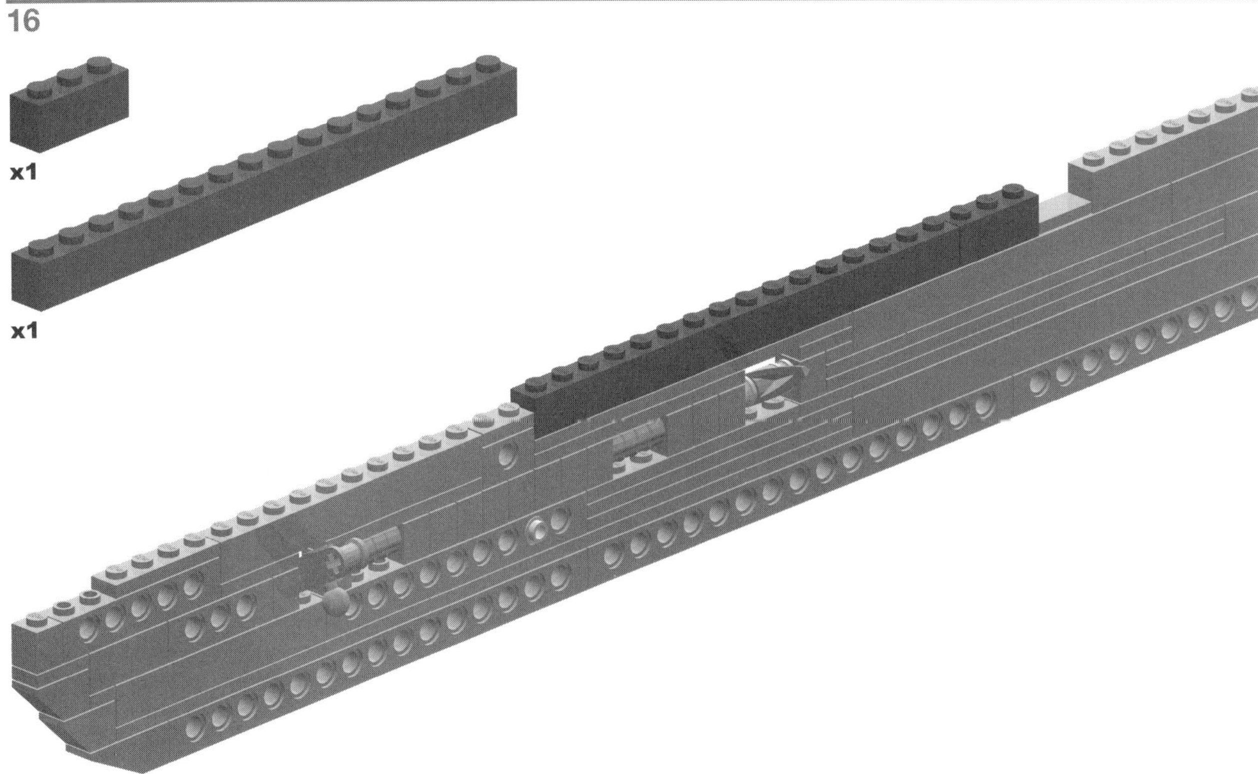

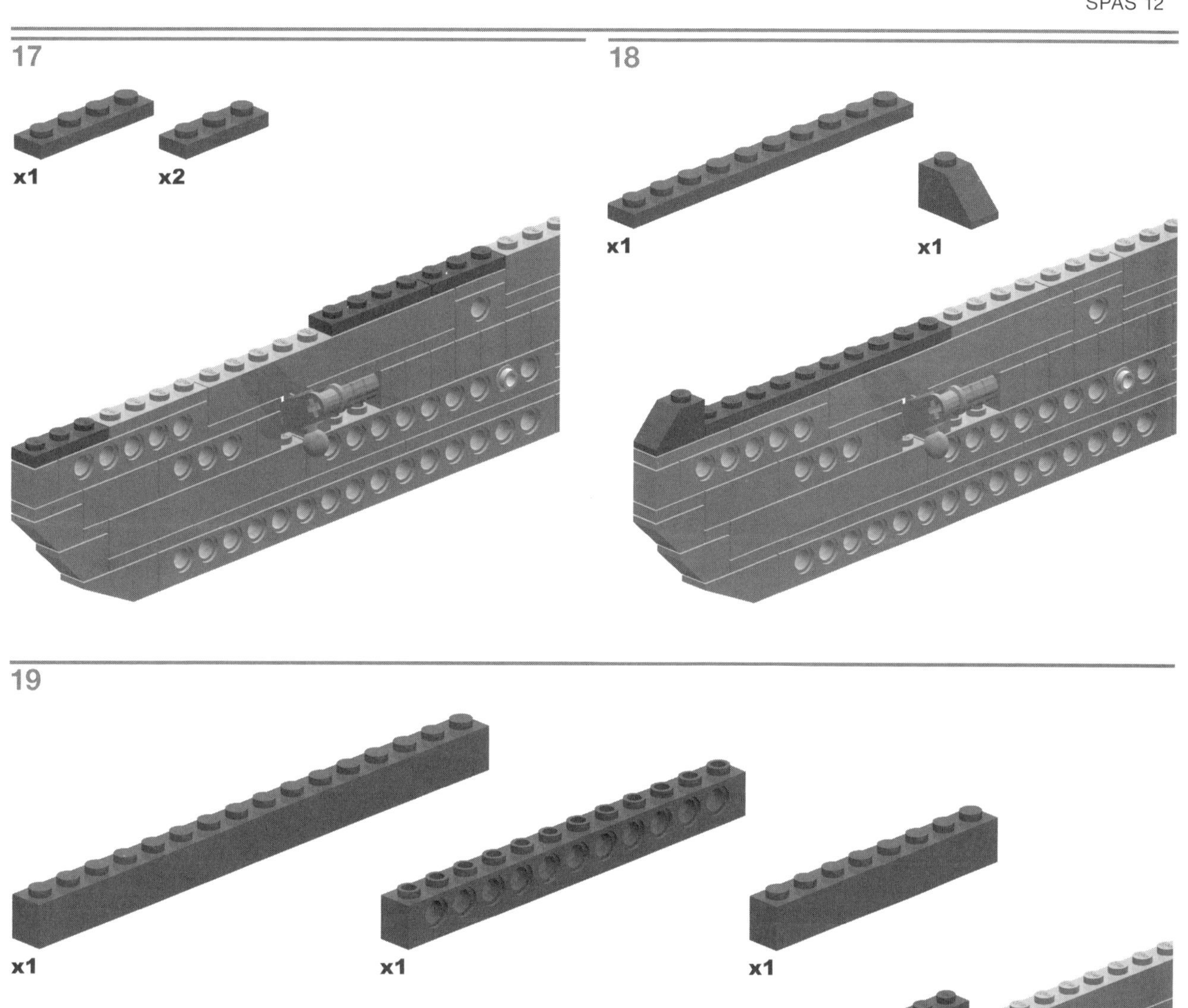
17
x1
x2
18
x1
x1
19
x1
x1
x1

20

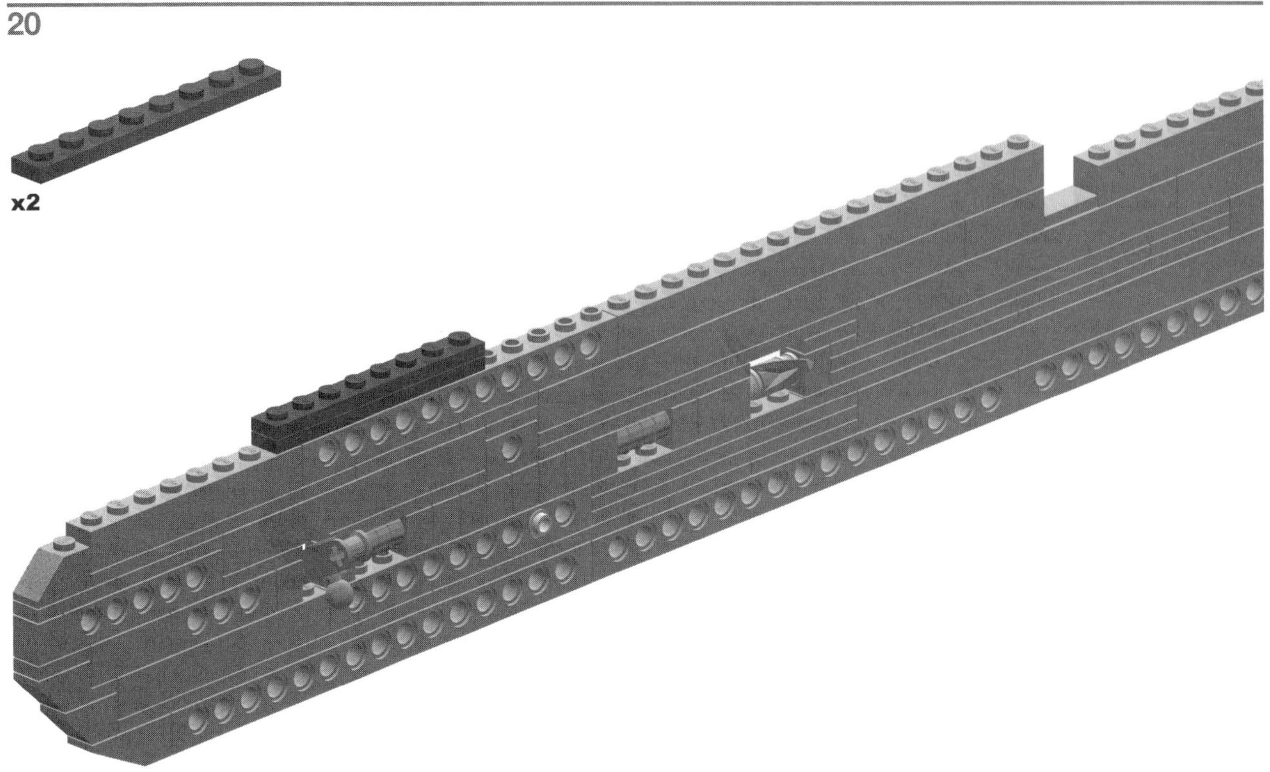

21

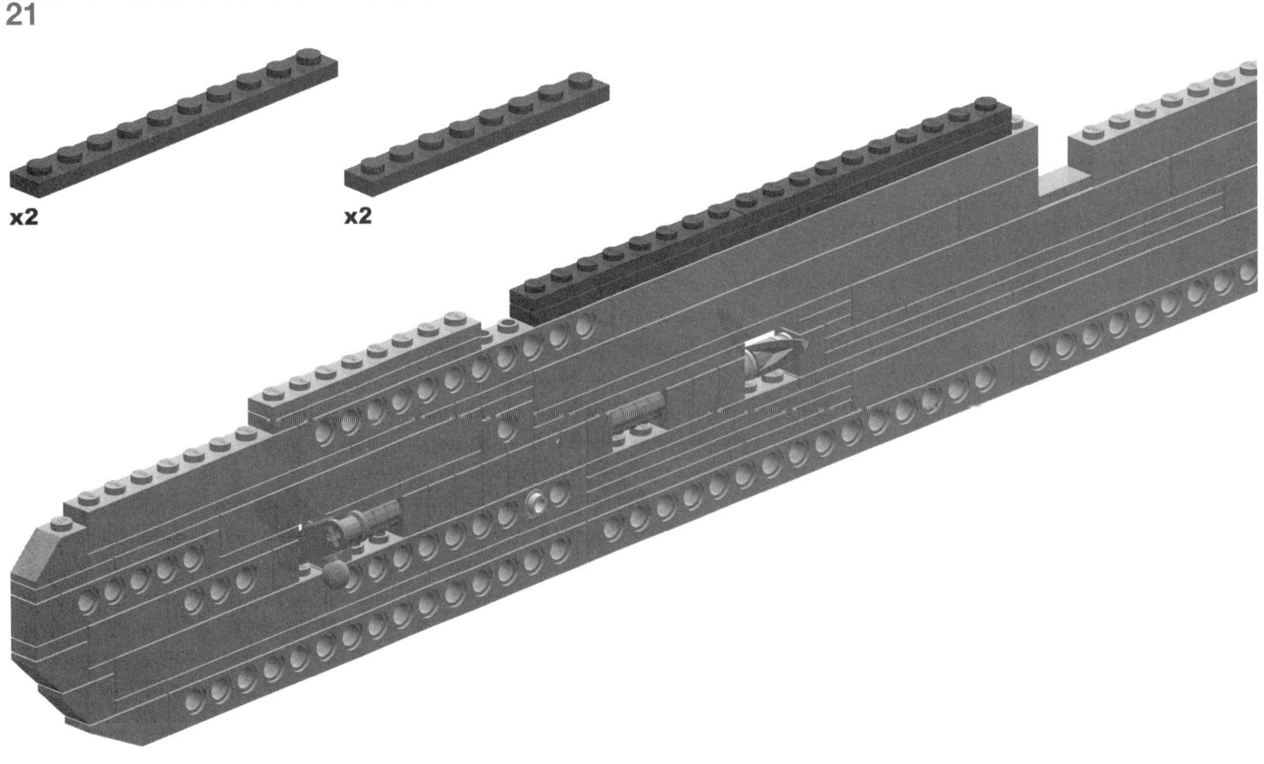

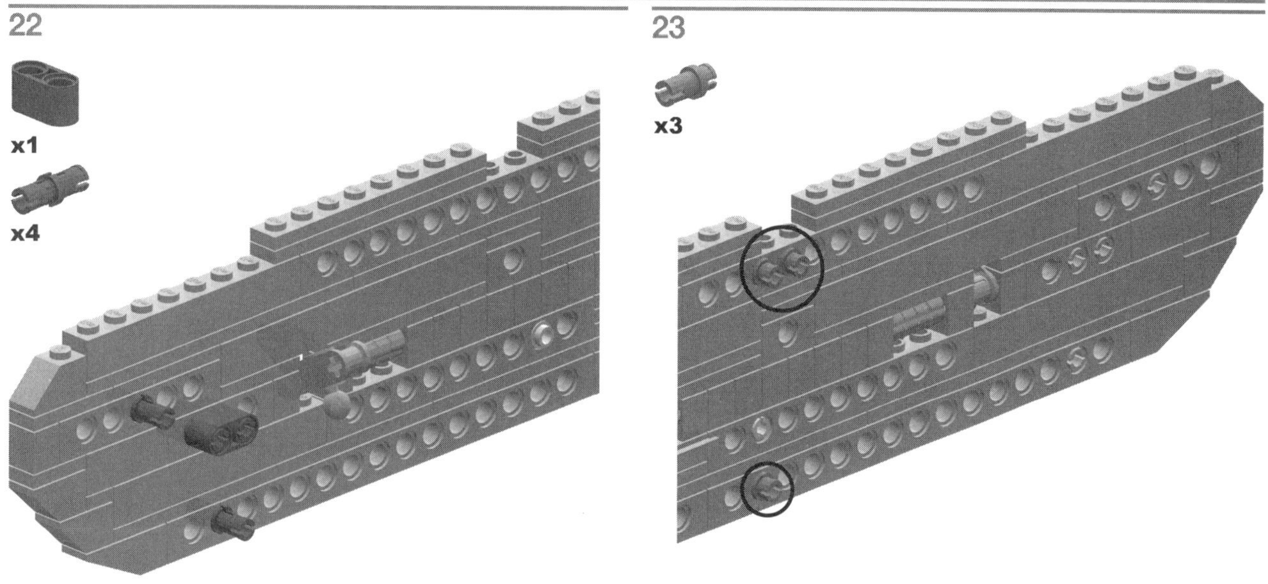

24

x1

x1

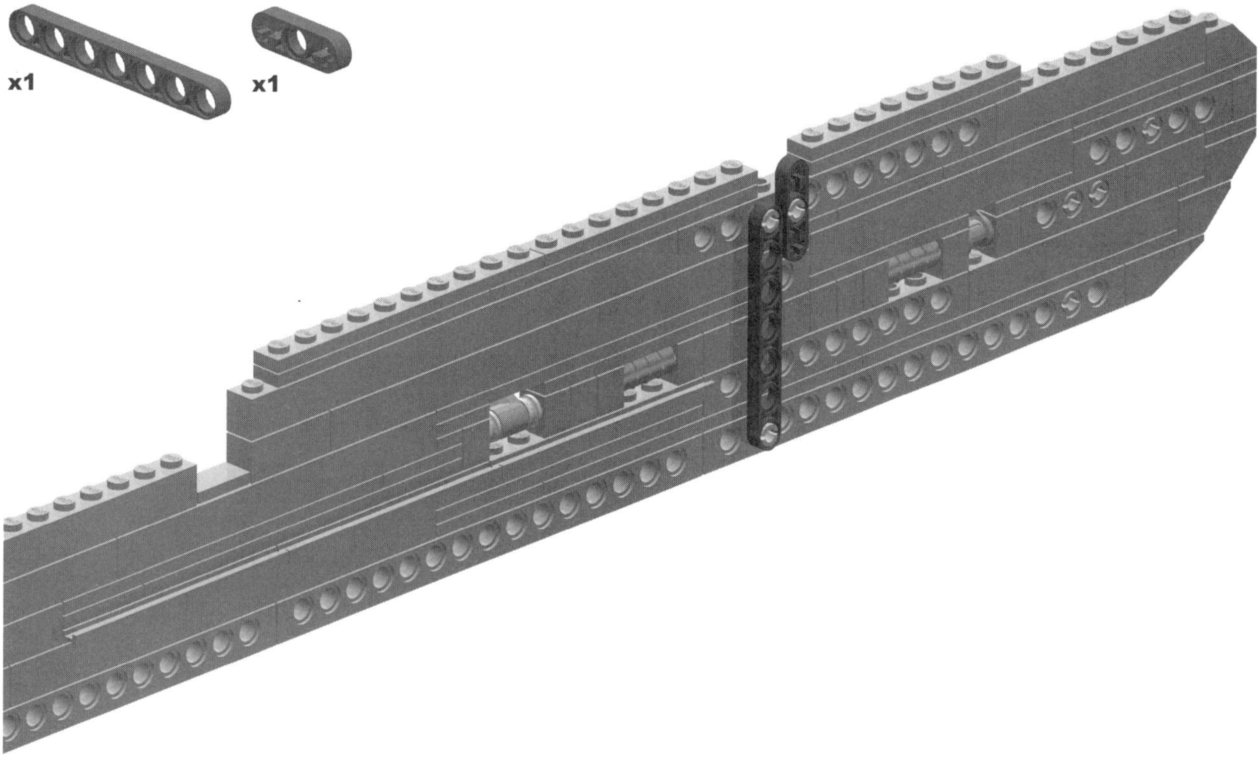

MAGAZINE HATCH

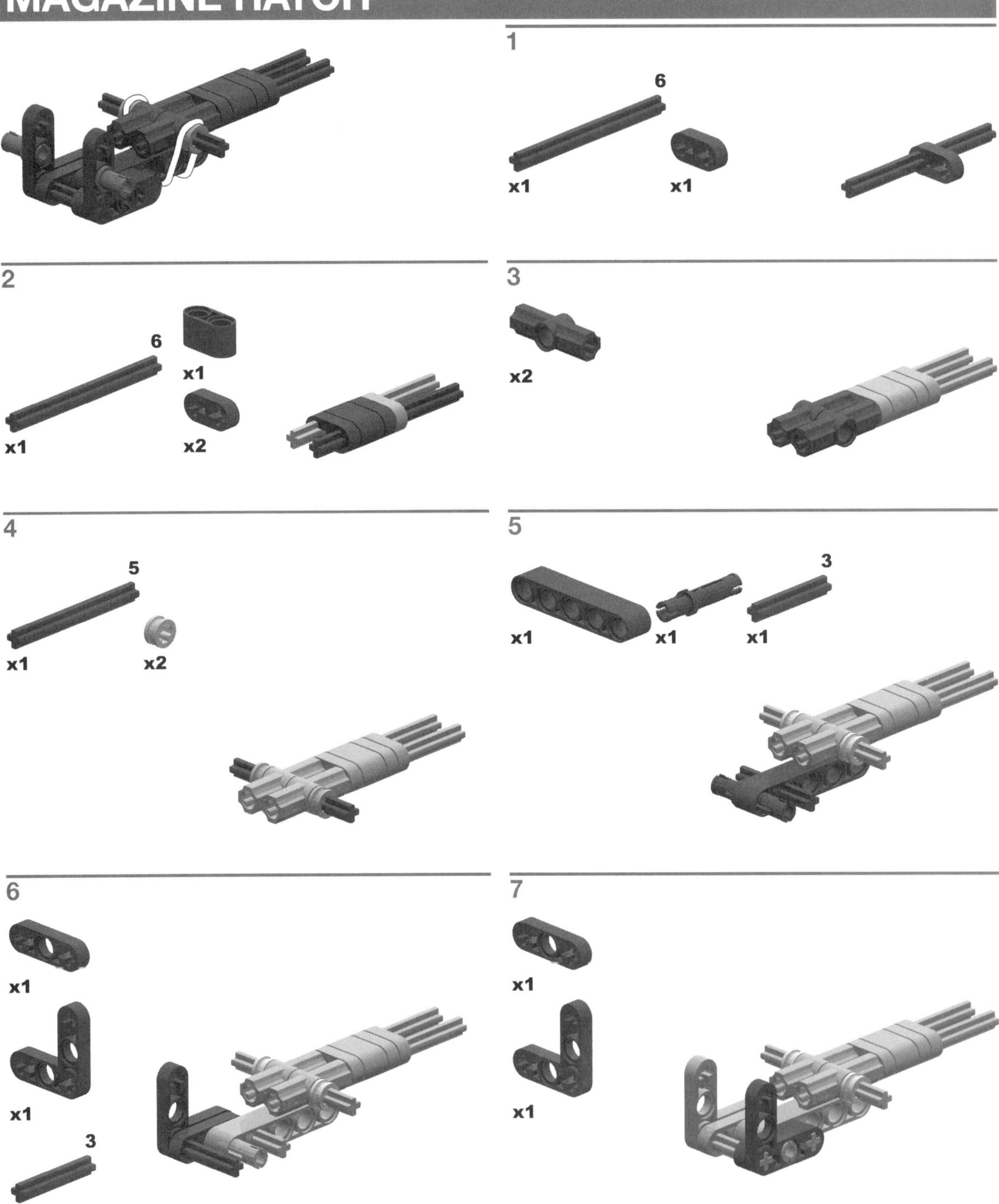

8

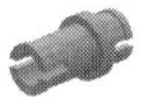

x2

9

x1

CHAMBERING SLIDE

1

x1 x1 x1 x1

2

x2 x1

3

x2 x1

4

x1

x1

5

x1 x2

x1 x2

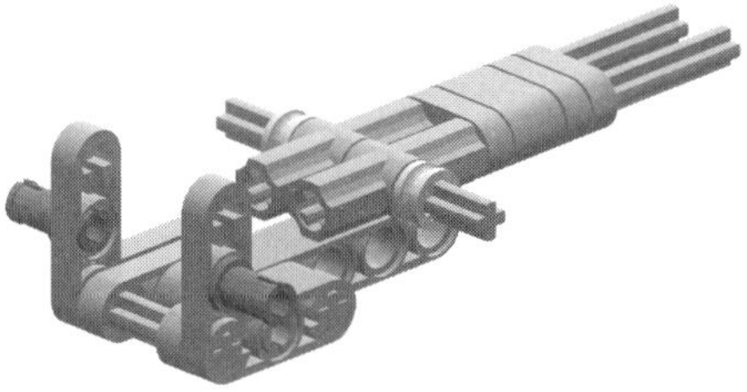

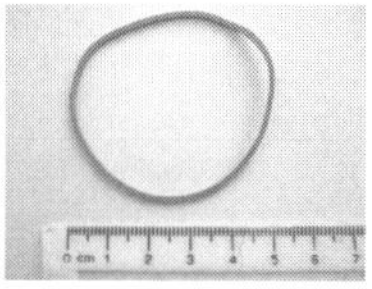

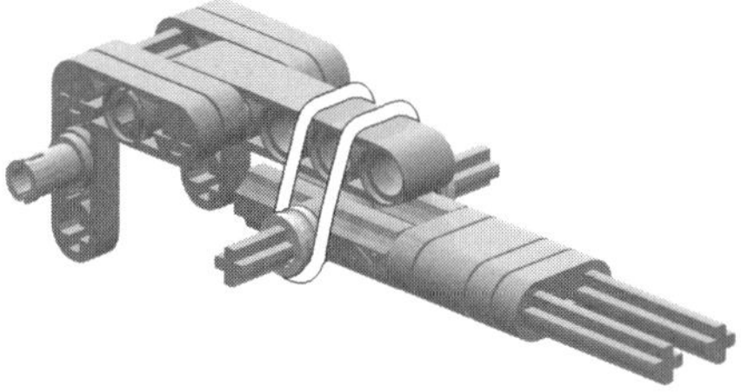

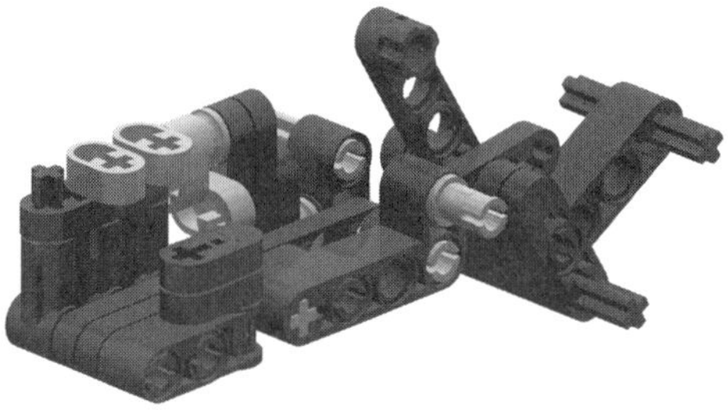

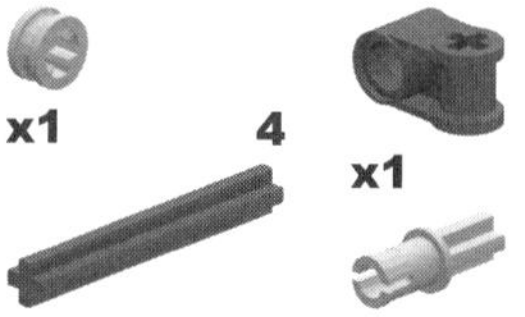

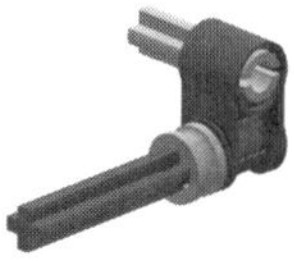

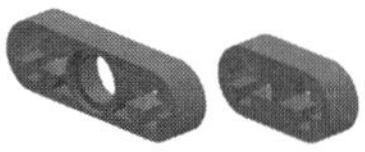

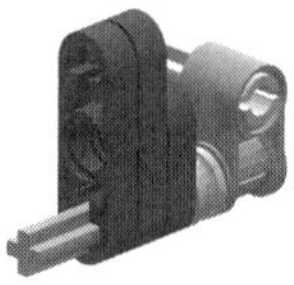

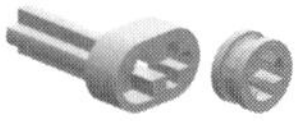

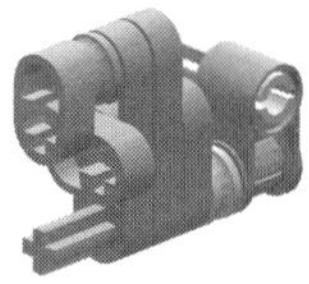

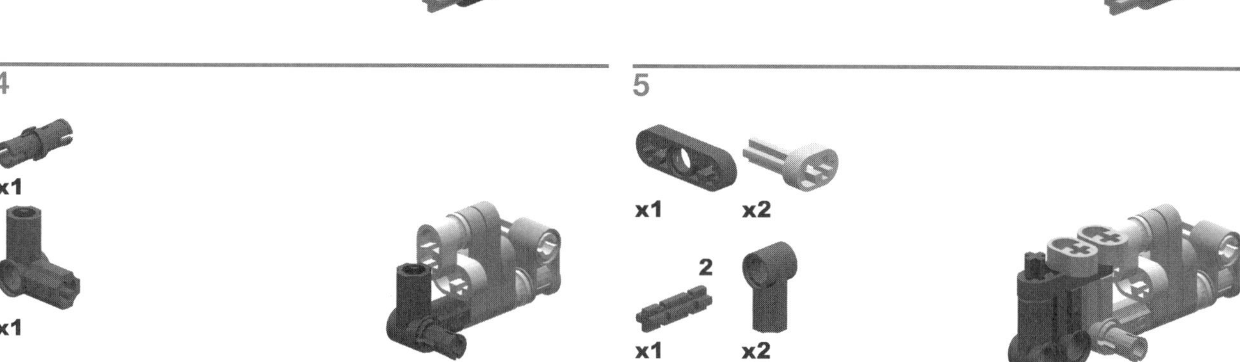

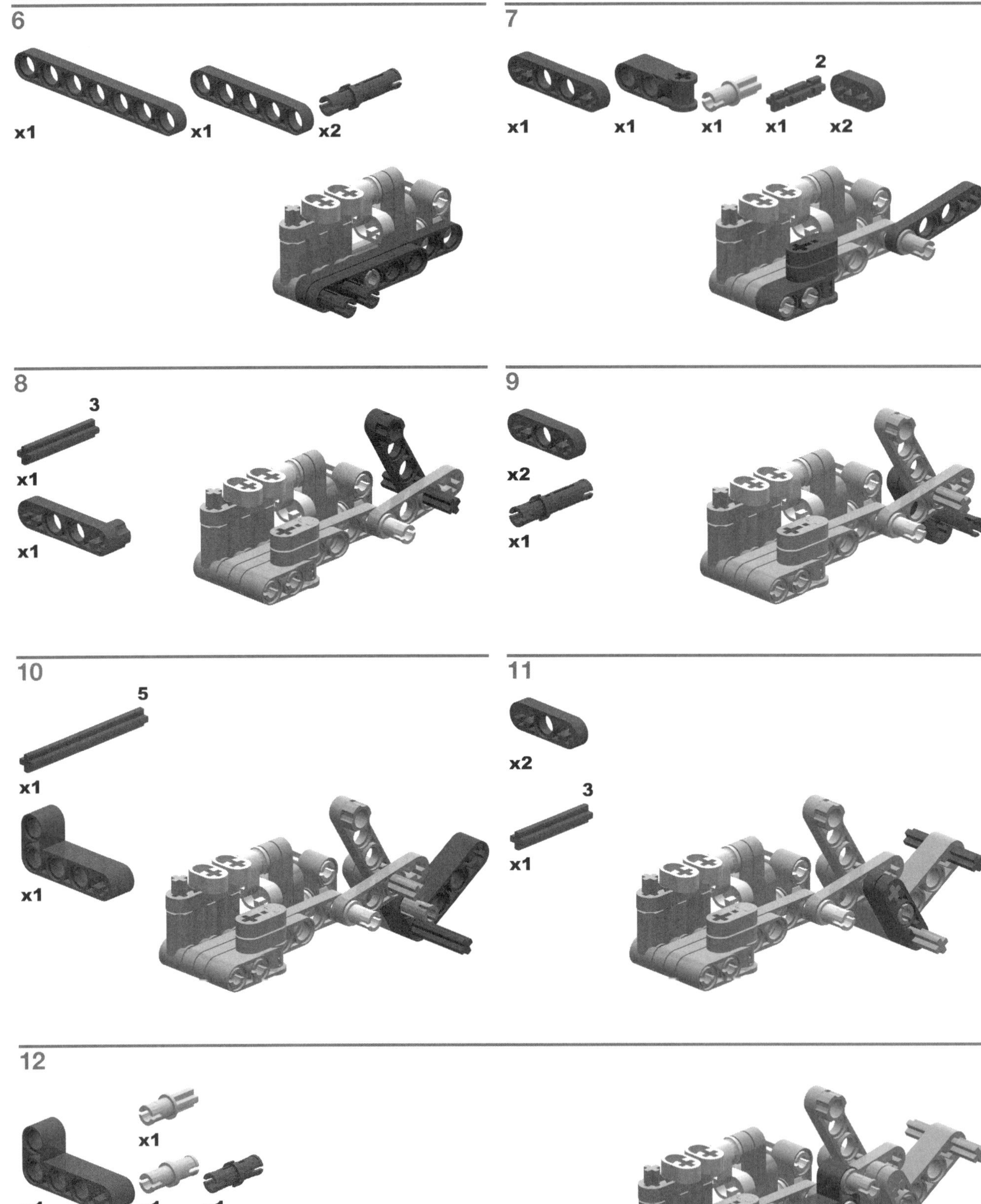
6
x1
x1
x2
7
2
x1
x1
x1
x1
x2
8
3
x1
x1
9
x2
x1
10
5
x1
x1
11
x2
3
x1
12
x1
x1
x1
x1

INTERNALS LOWER

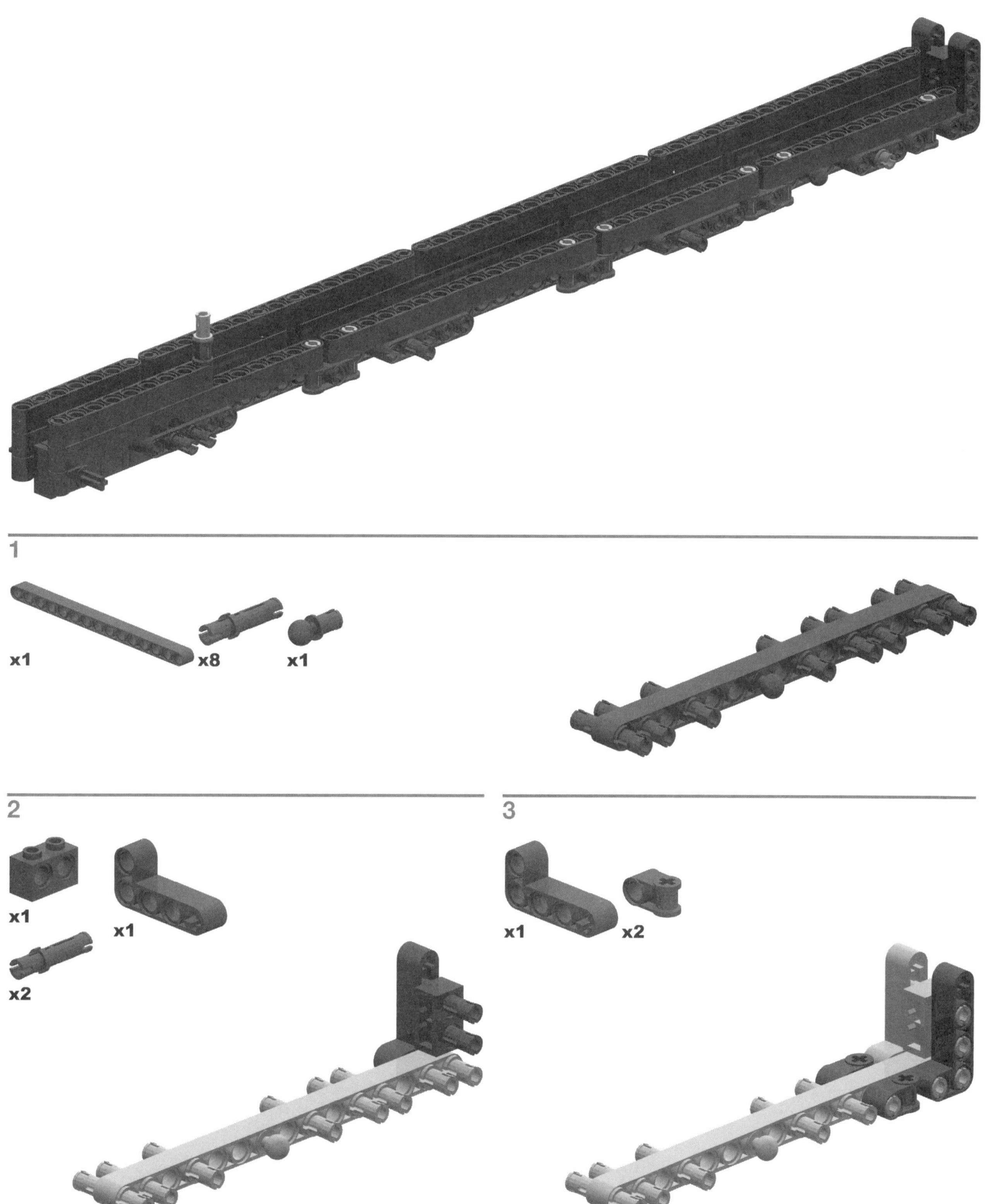

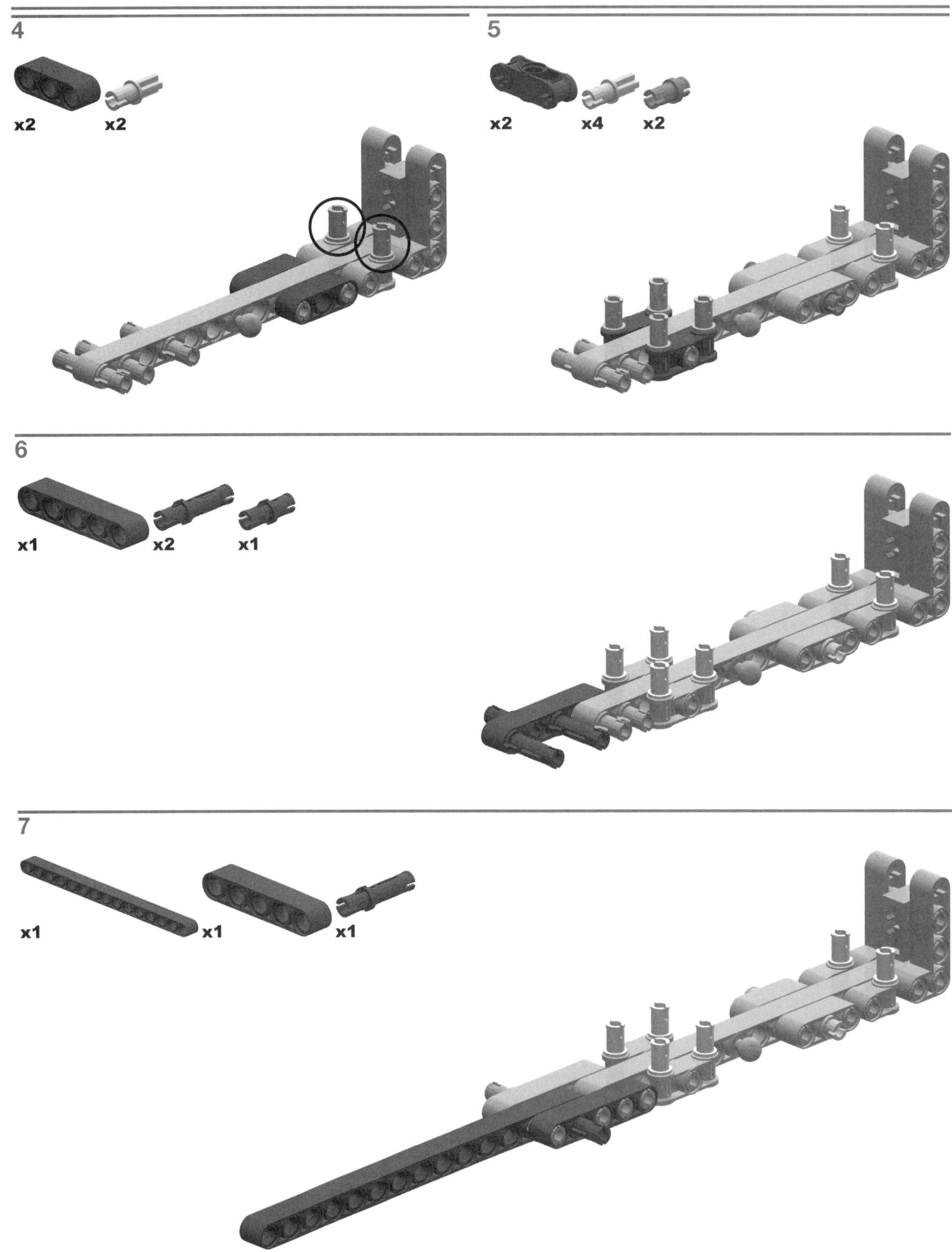
4
x2
x2
5
x2
x4
x2
6
x1
x2
x1
7
x1
x1
x1

8

x2

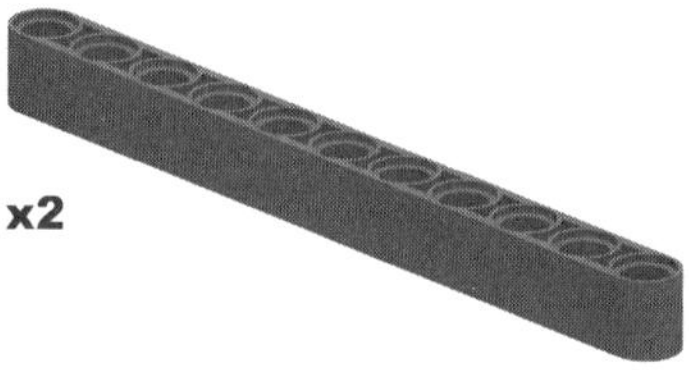

x2

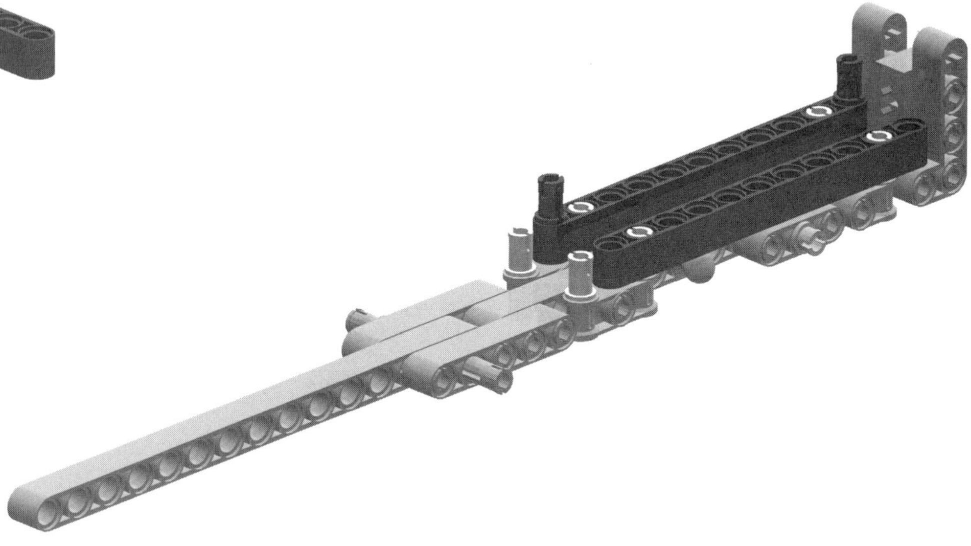

9

x2  x1 x4

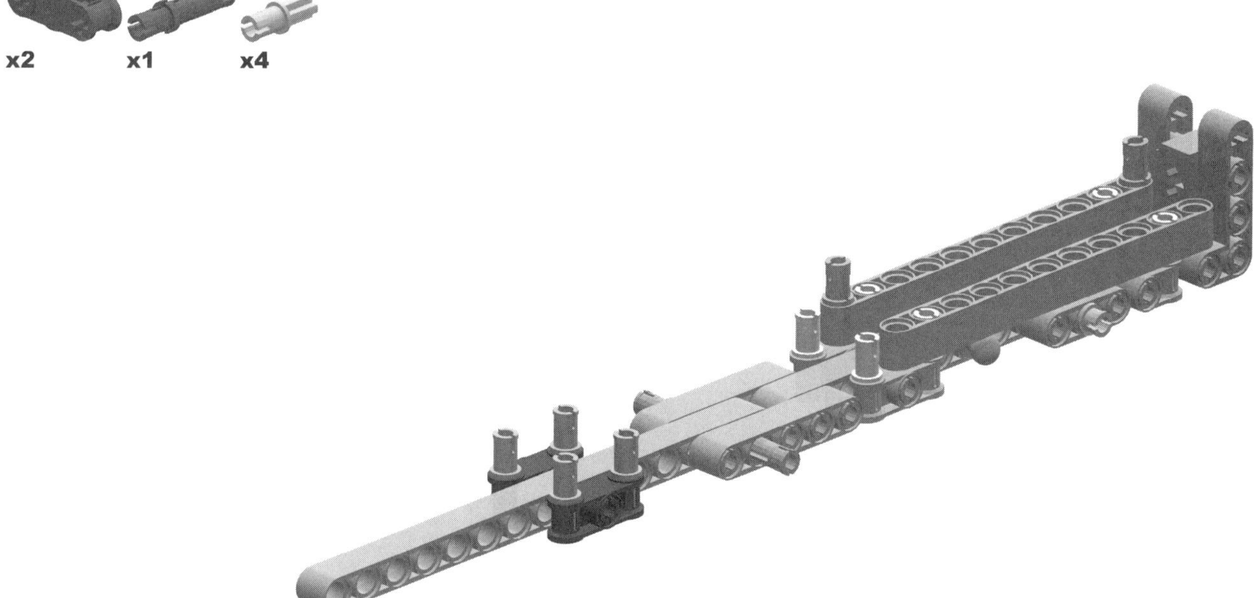

10

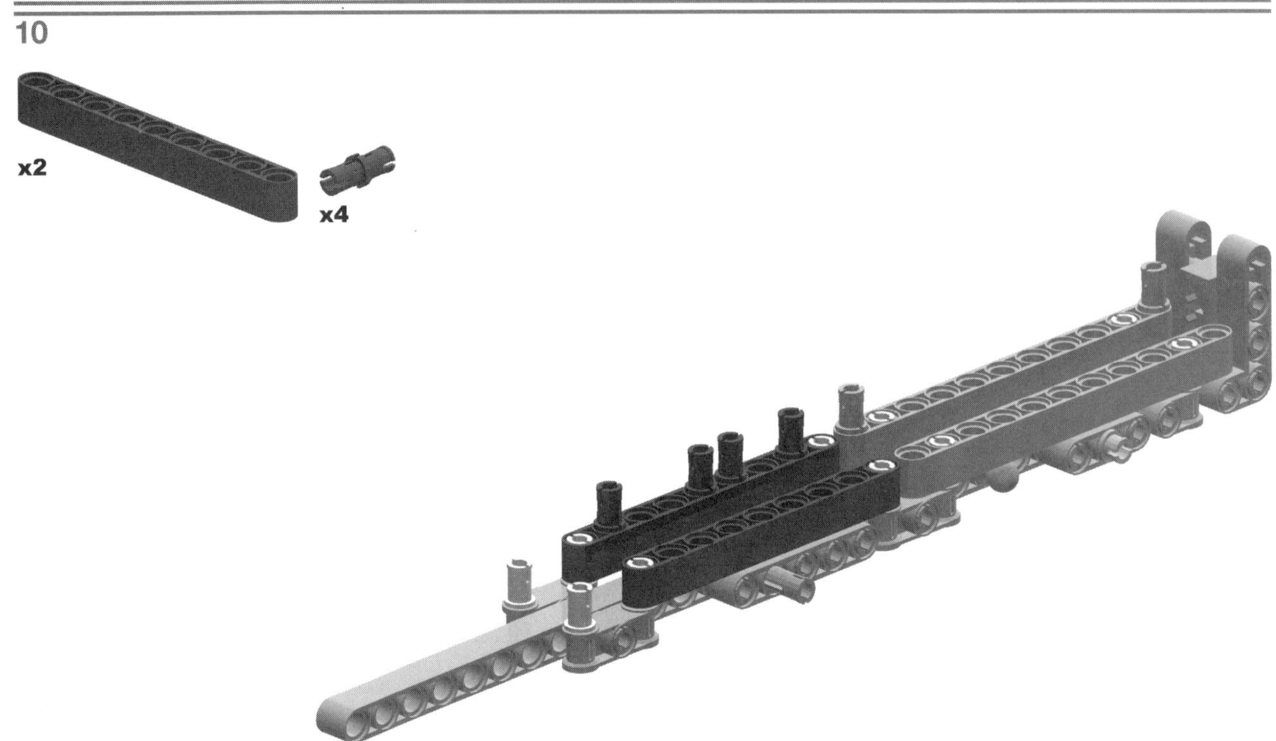

11

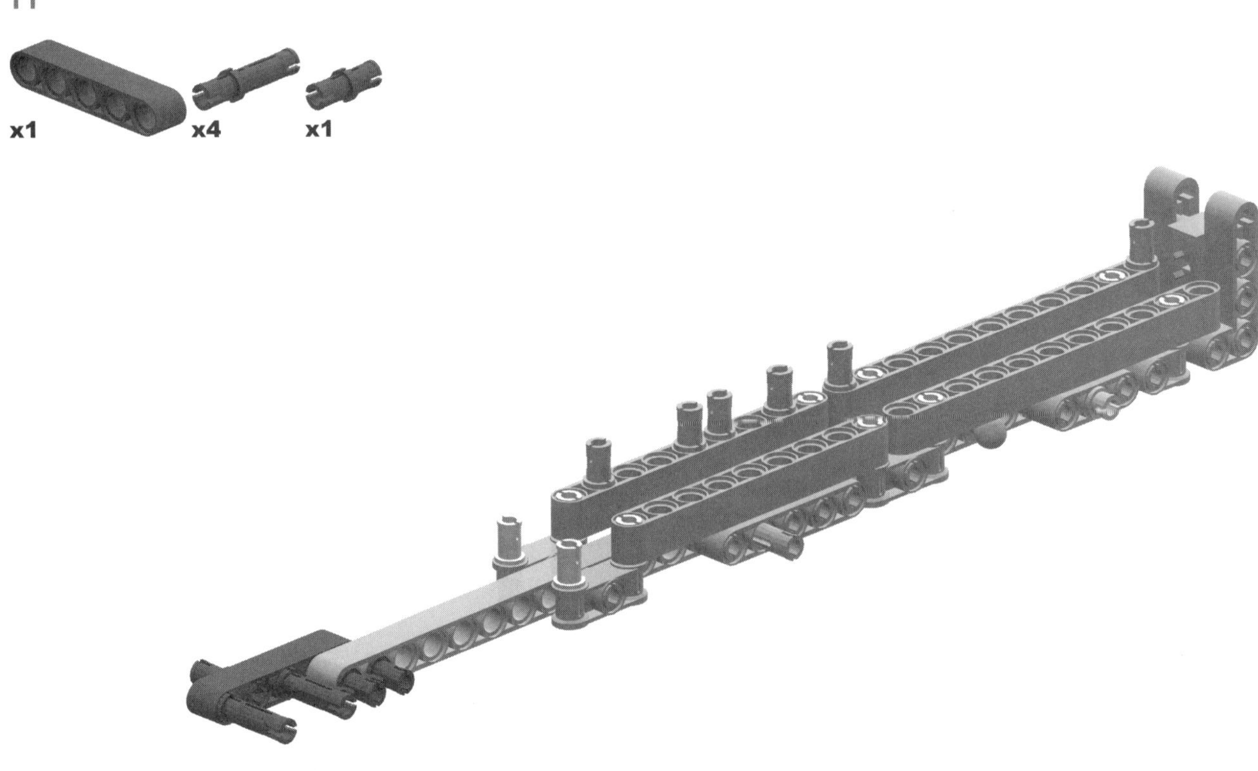

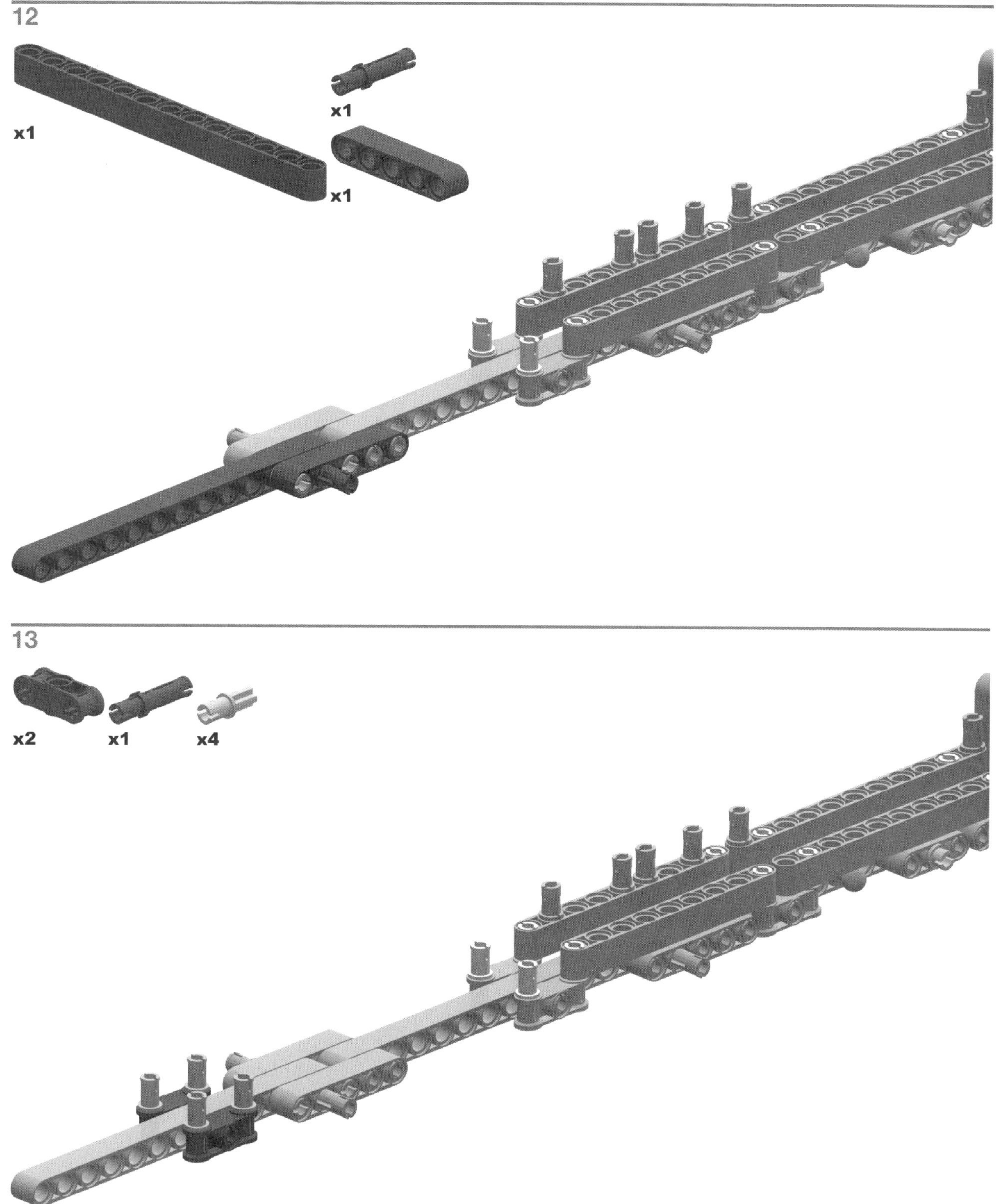
12
x1
x1
x1
13
x2
x1
x4

14

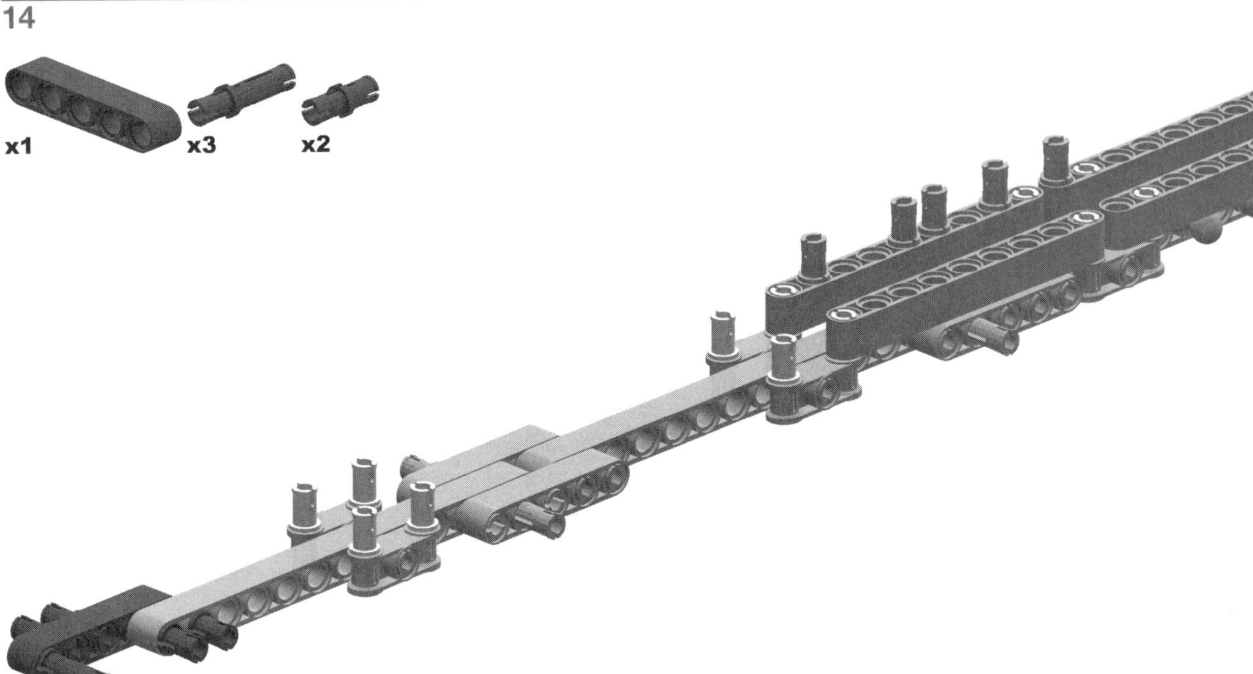

15

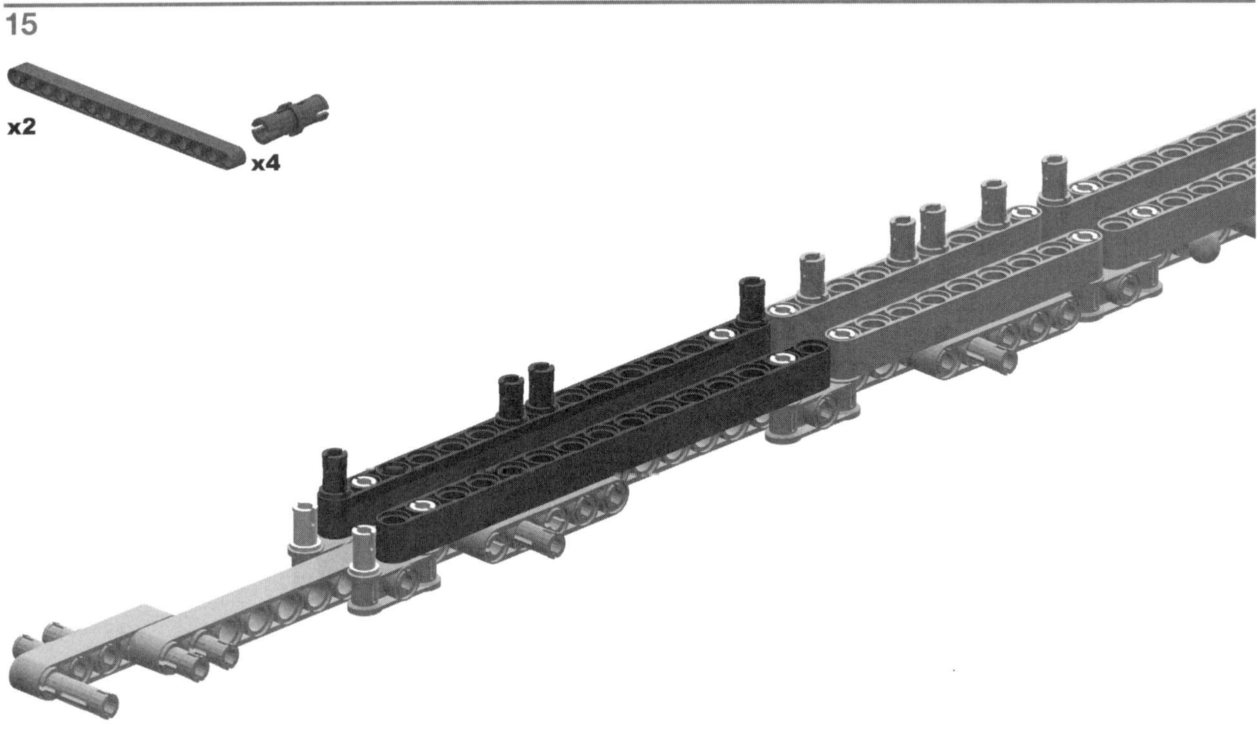

16

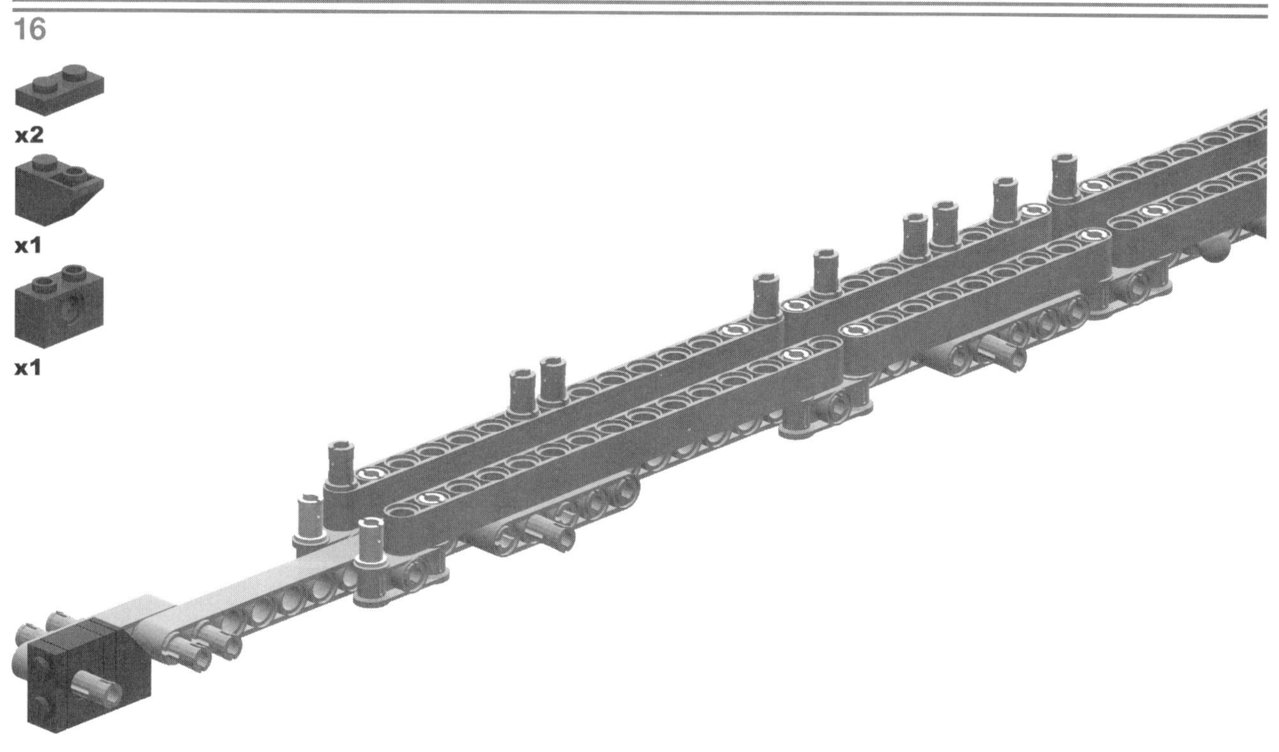

17

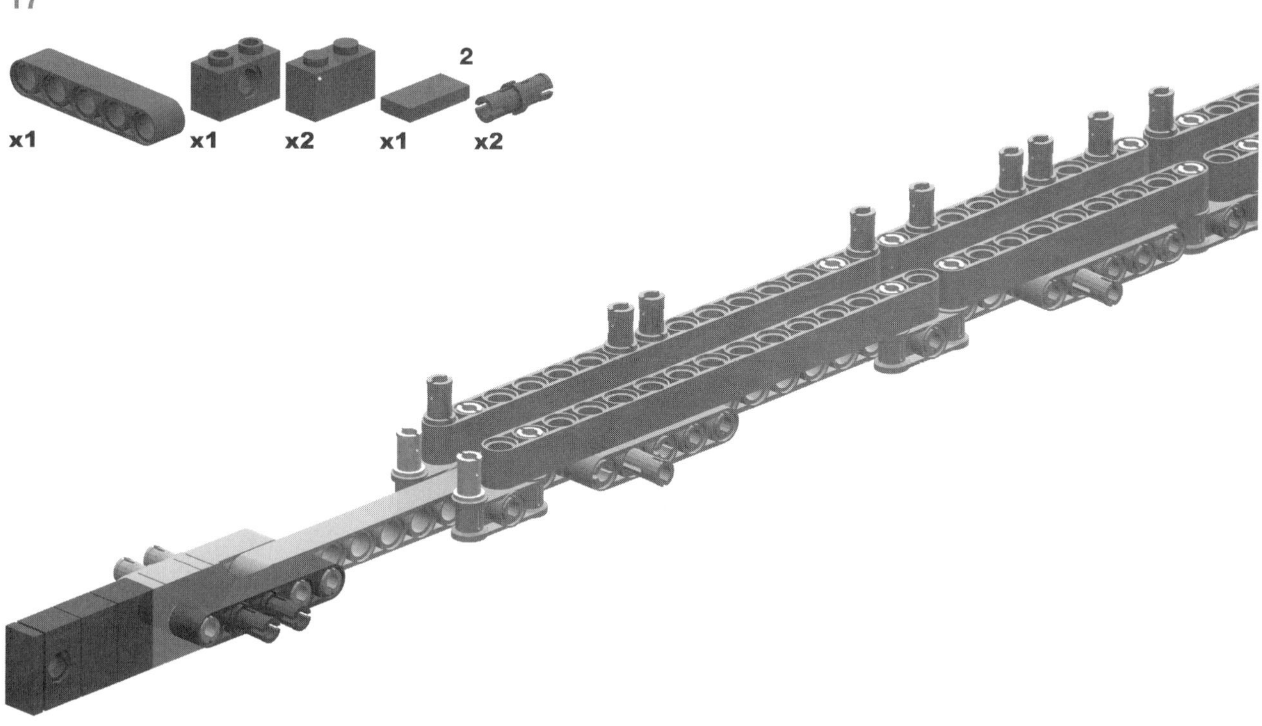

18

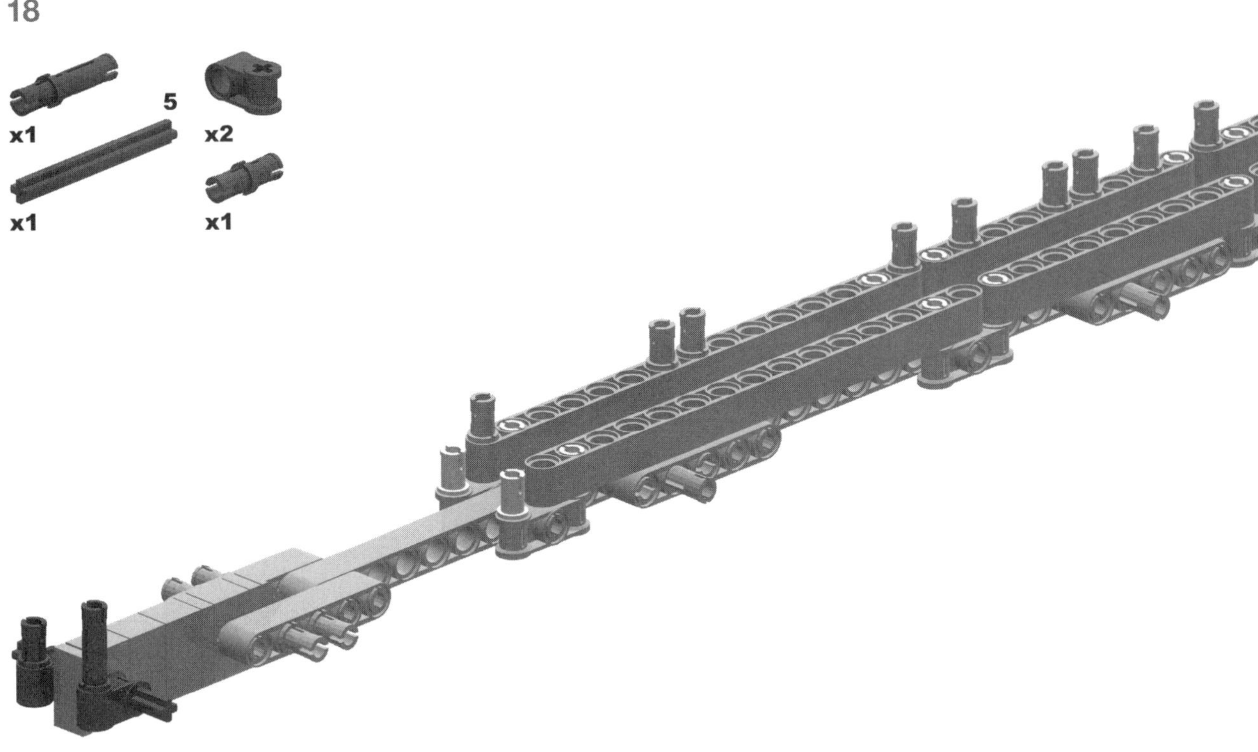

19

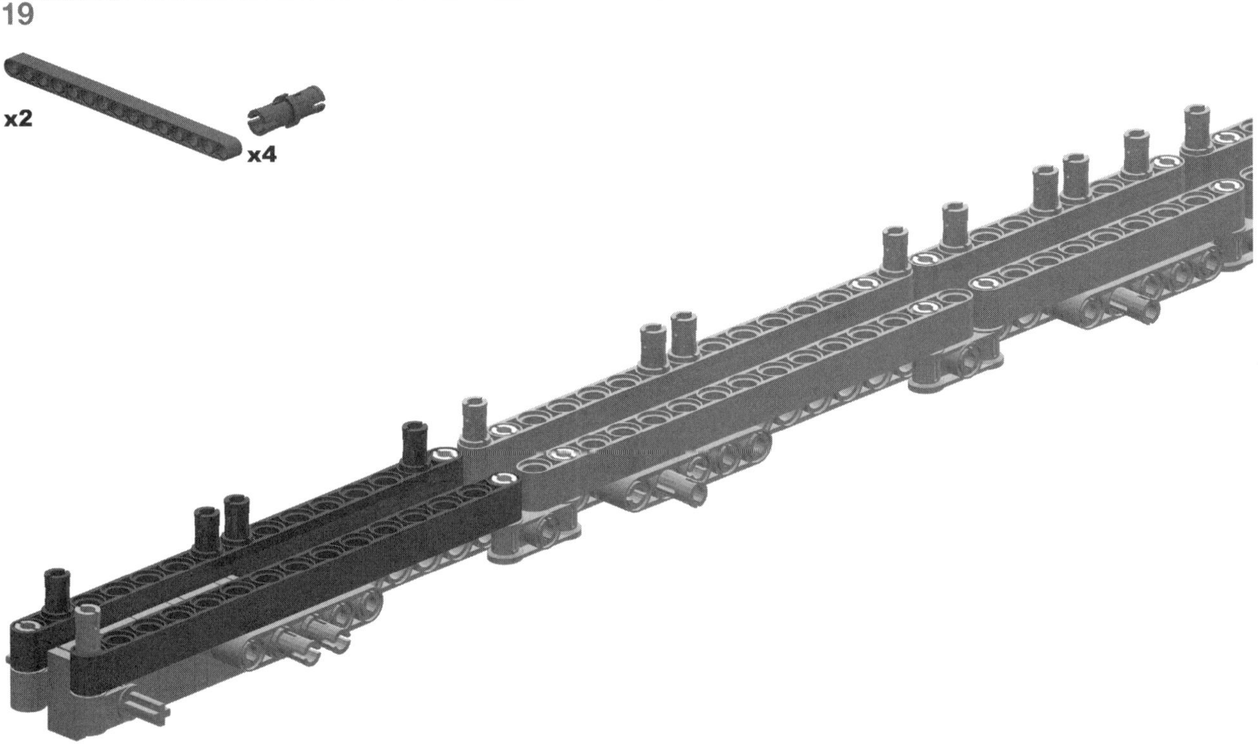

20

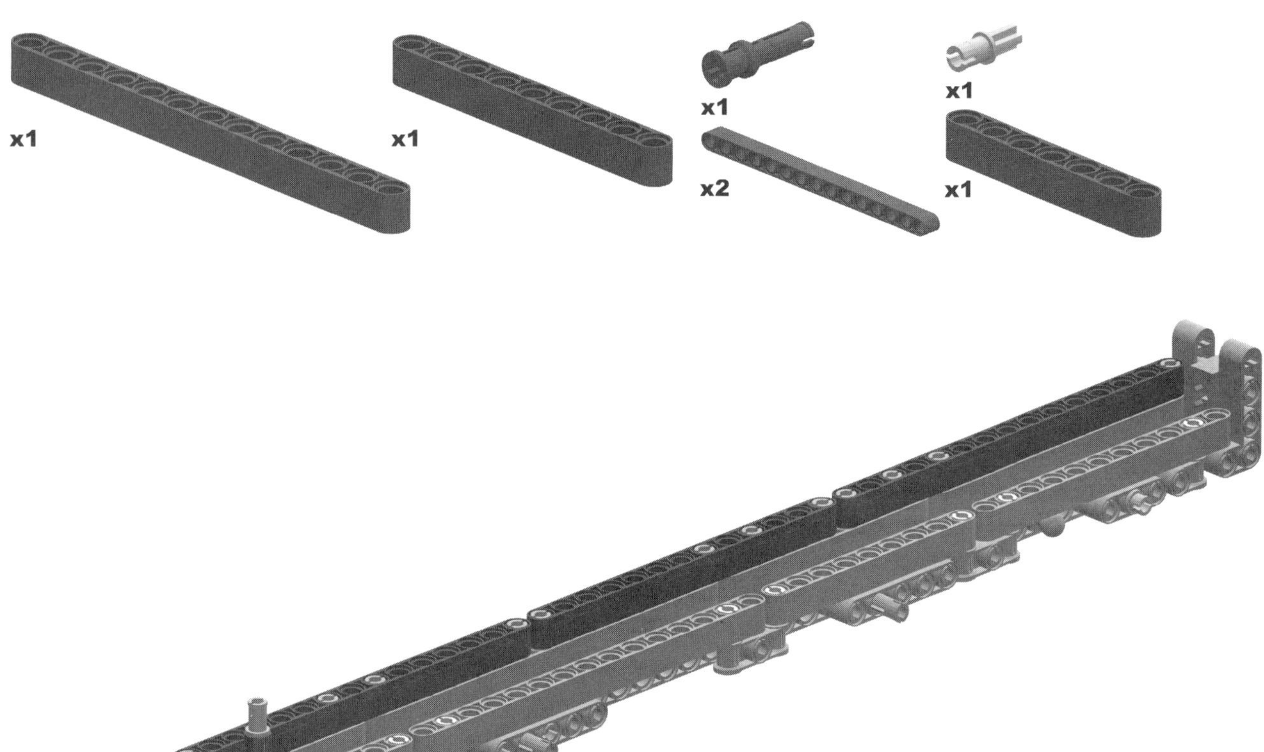

INTERNALS MAGAZINE SLIDE

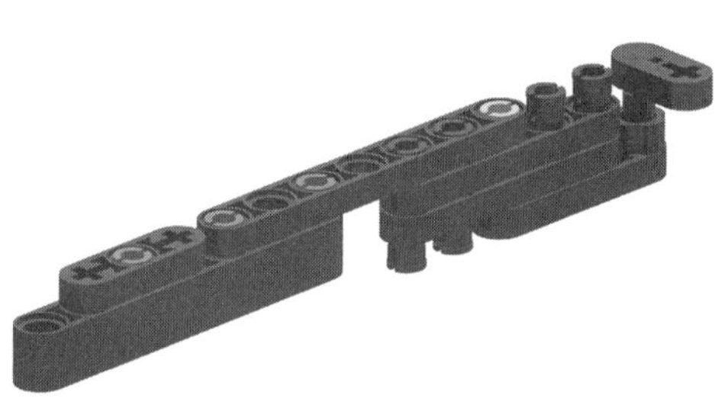

1

2

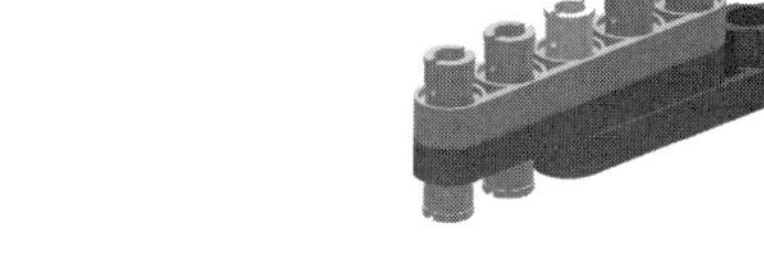

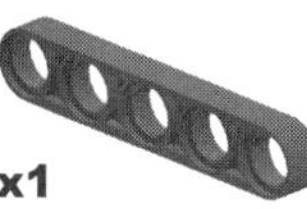

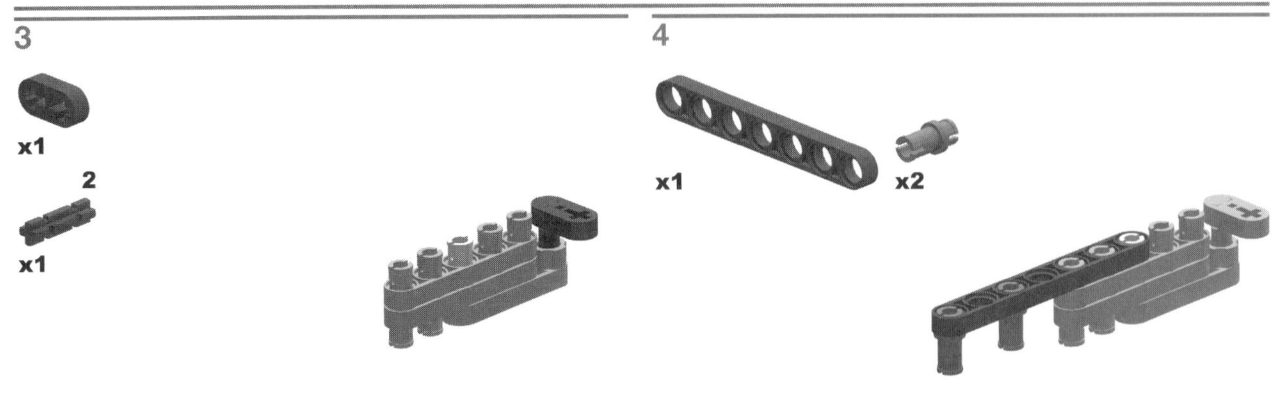

INTERNALS MIDDLE

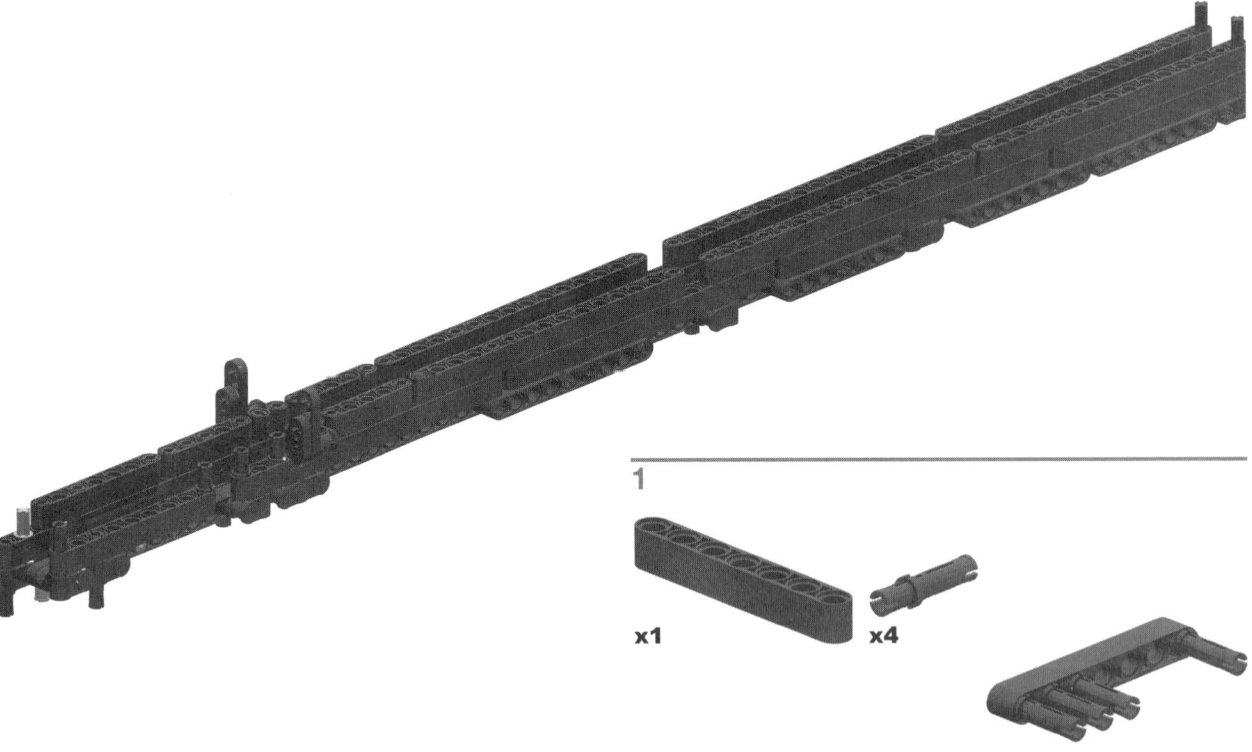

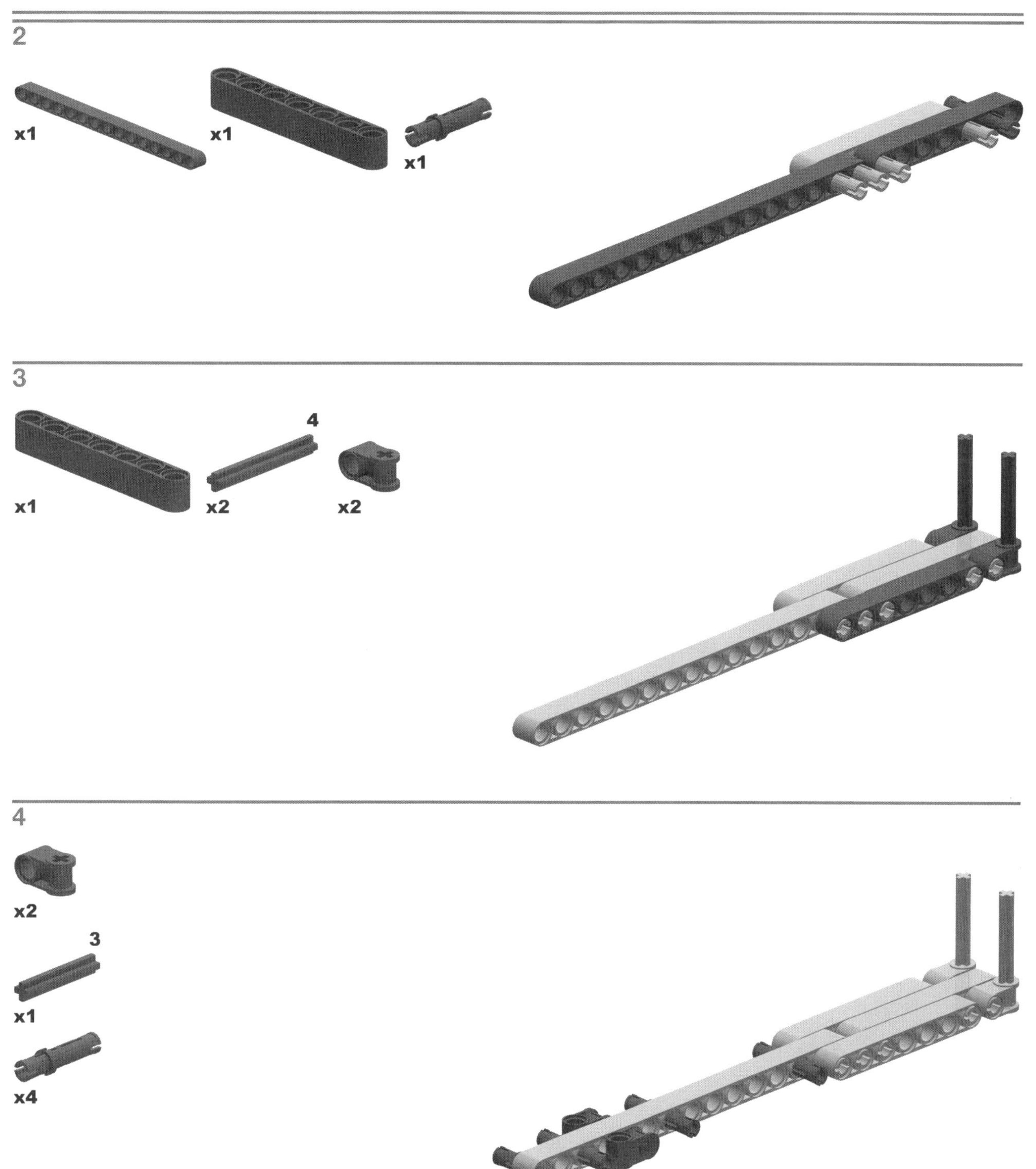
2
x1
x1
x1
3
4
x1
x2
x2
4
x2
3
x1
x4

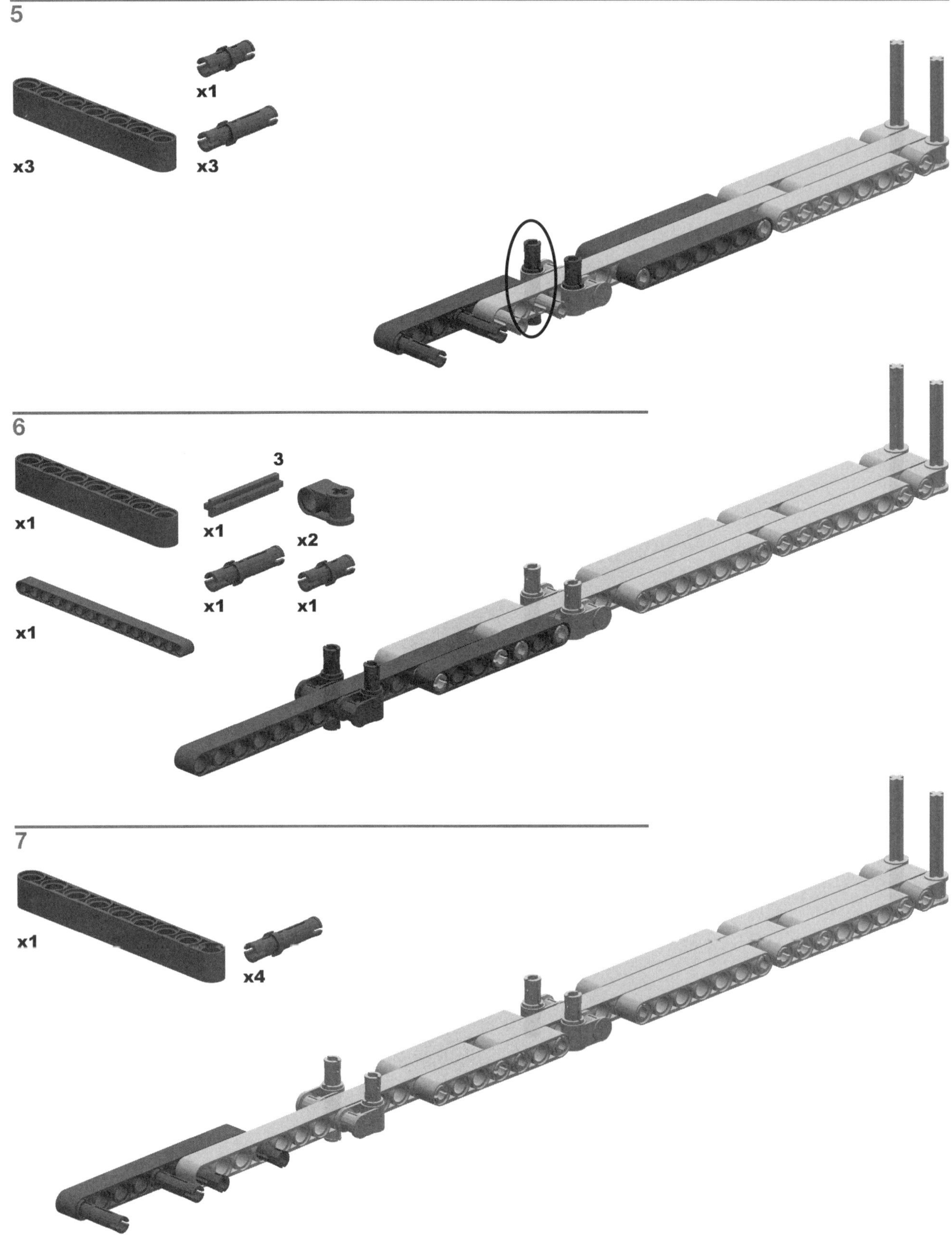
5
x1
x3
x3
6
3
x1
x1
x2
x1
x1
x1
7
x1
x4

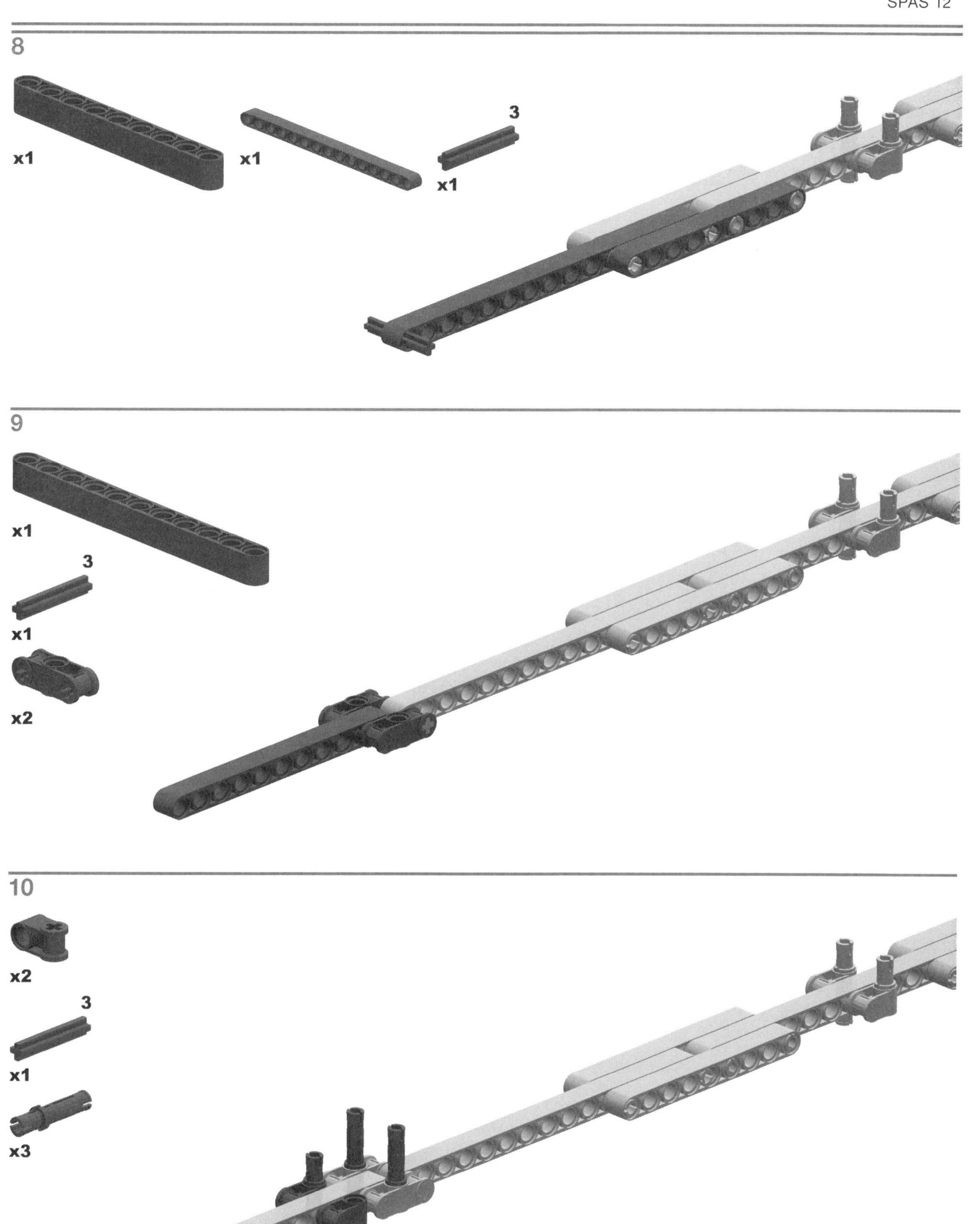
8
x1
x1
3
x1
9
x1
3
x1
x2
10
x2
3
x1
x3

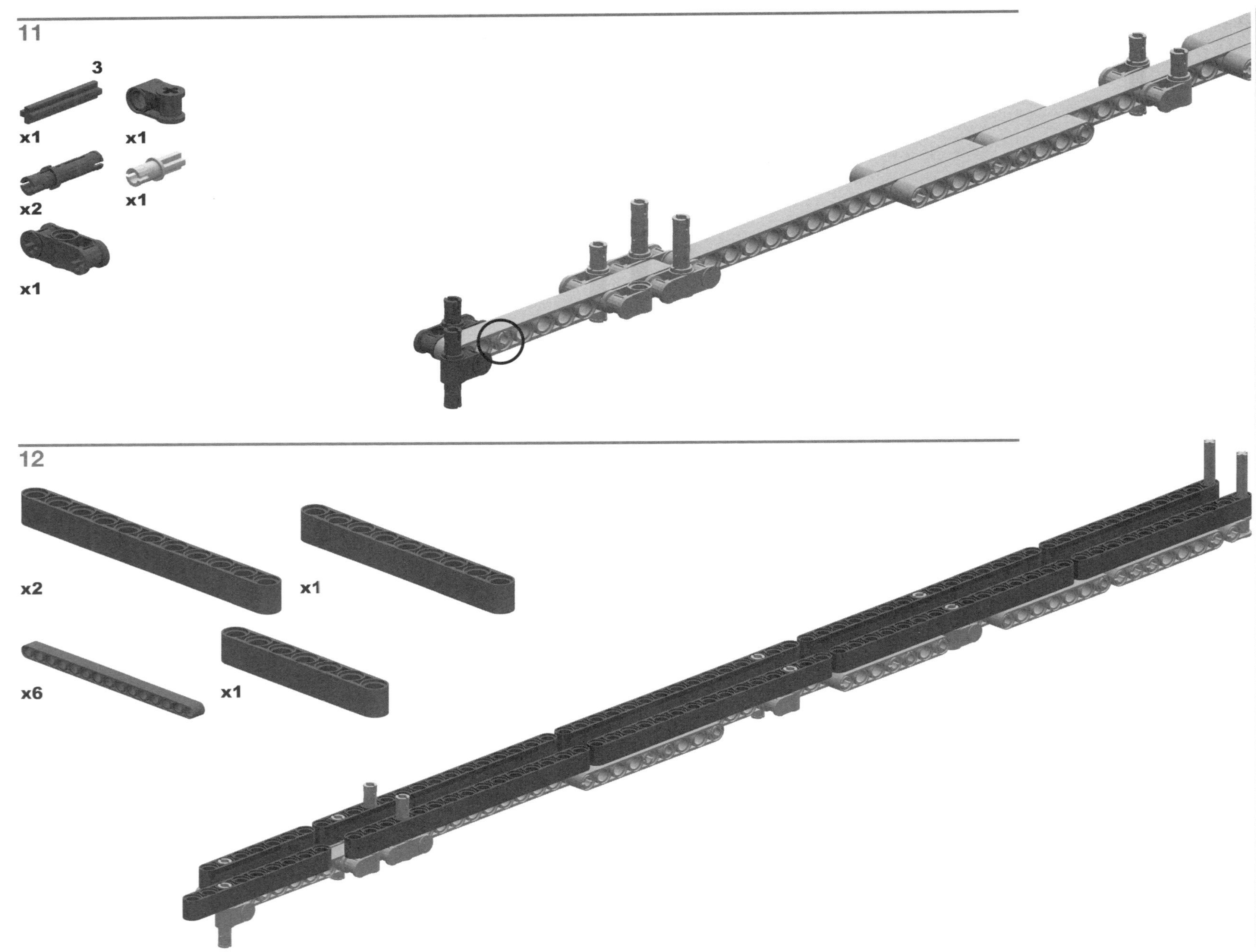
11
3
x1
x1
x2
x1
x1
12
x2
x1
x6
x1

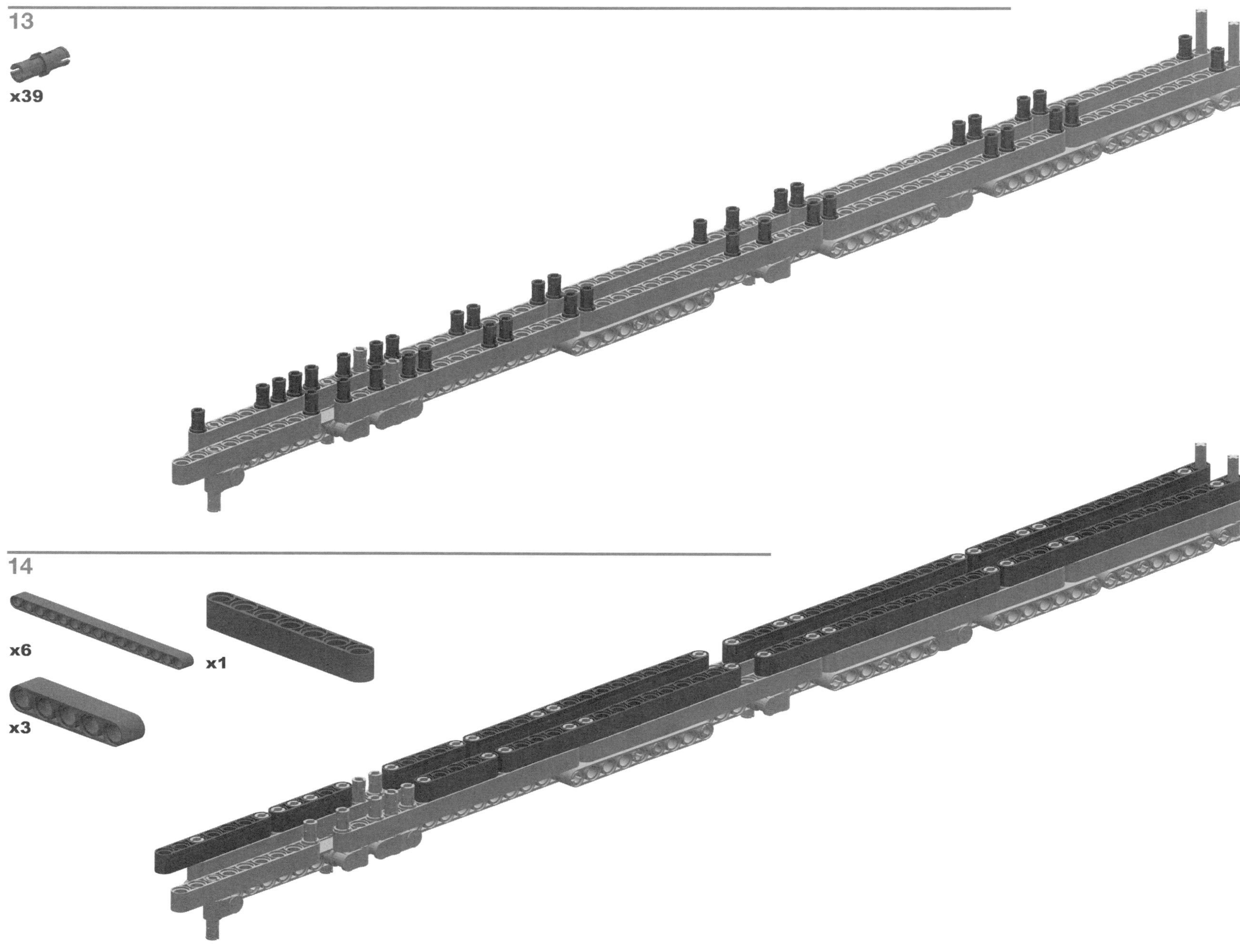
13
x39
14
x6
x1
x3

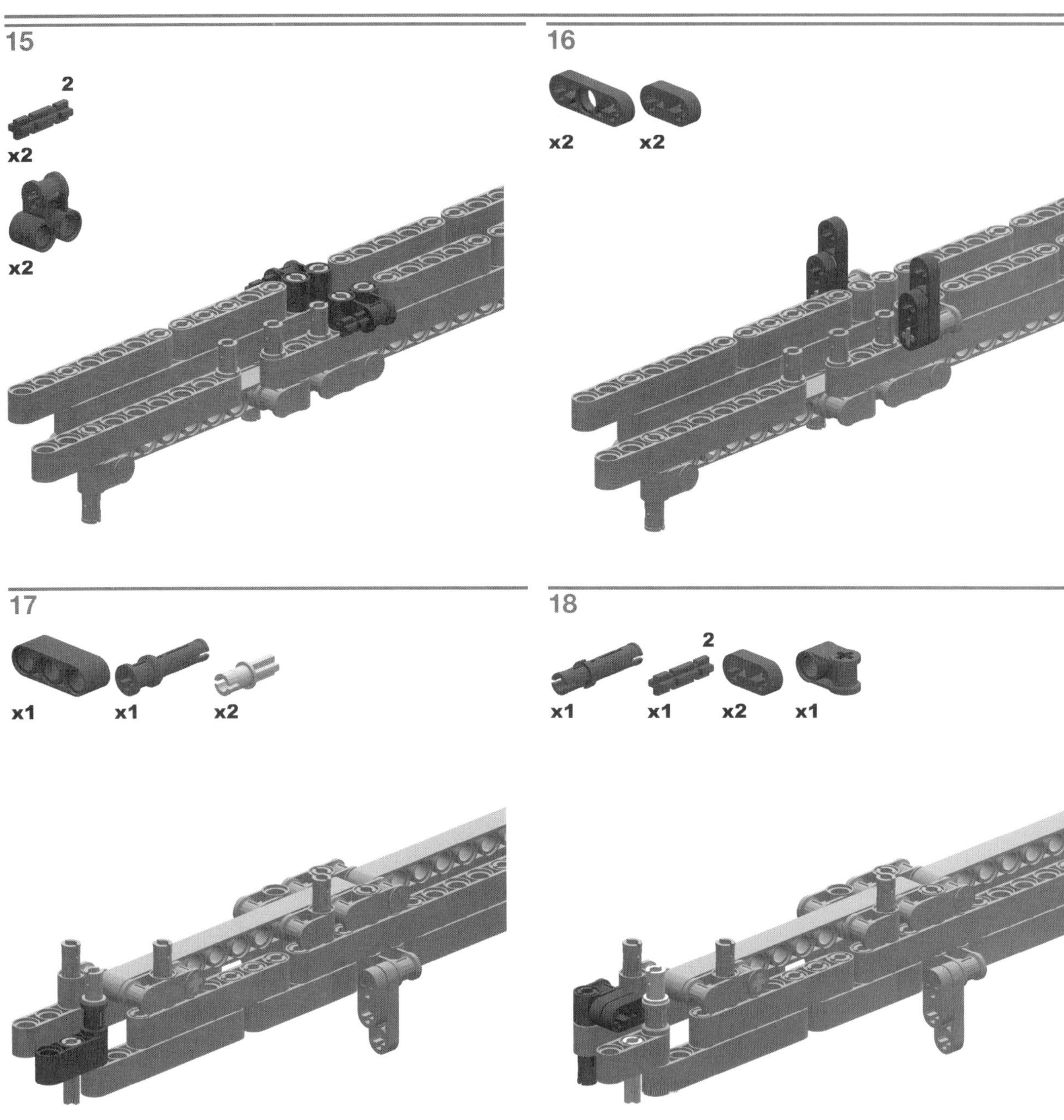
15
2
x2
x2
16
x2
x2
17
x1
x1
x2
18
2
x1
x1
x2
x1

19

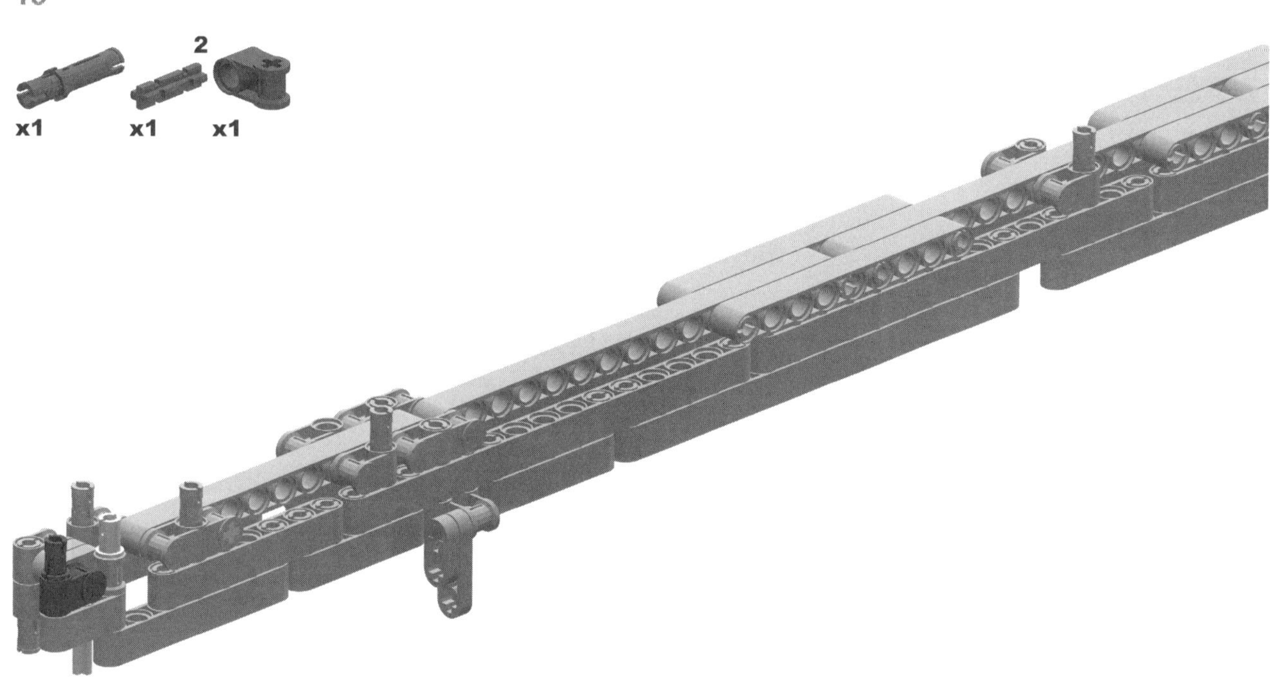

INTERNALS BOLT

1

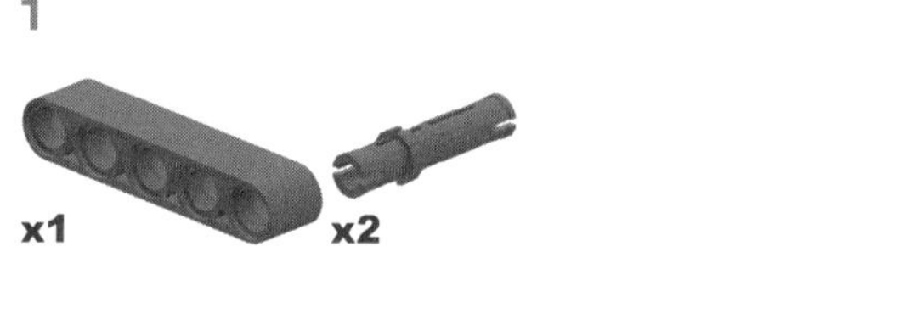

2

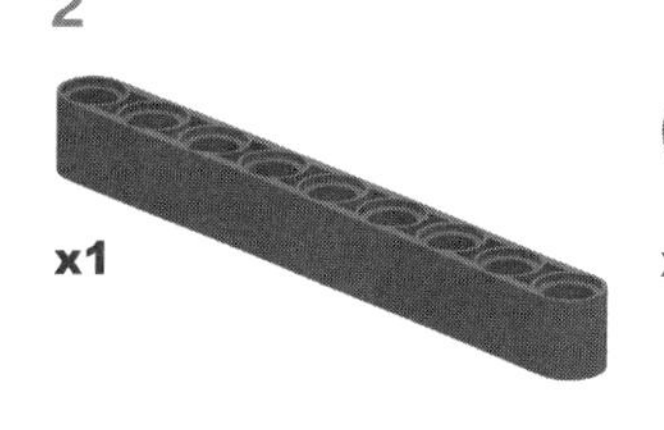

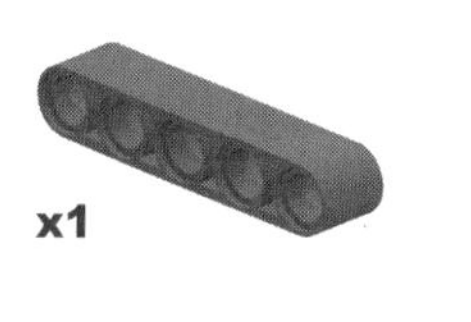

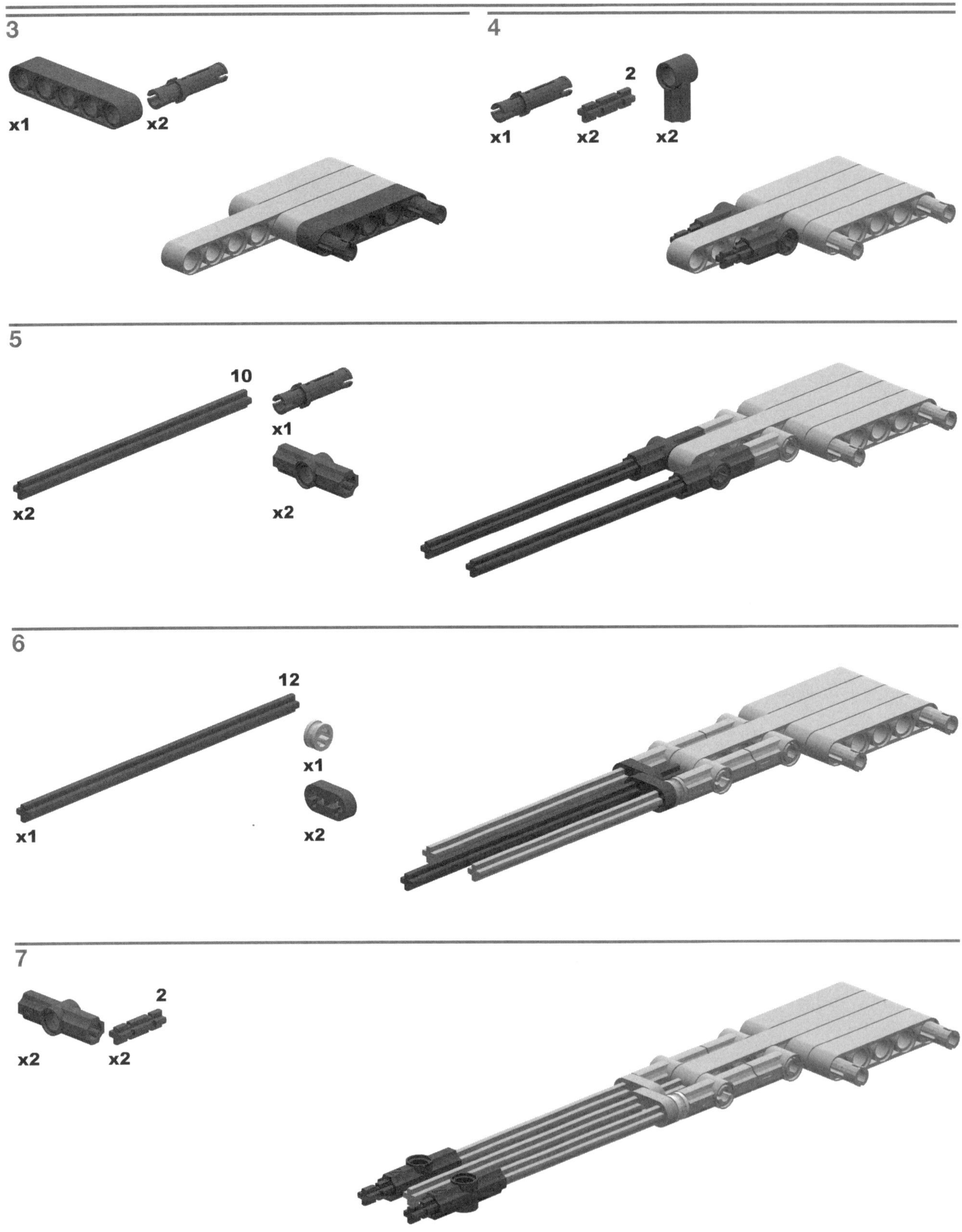
3
x1
x2
4
2
x1
x2
x2
5
10
x1
x2
x2
6
12
x1
x1
x2
7
2
x2
x2

8

x2

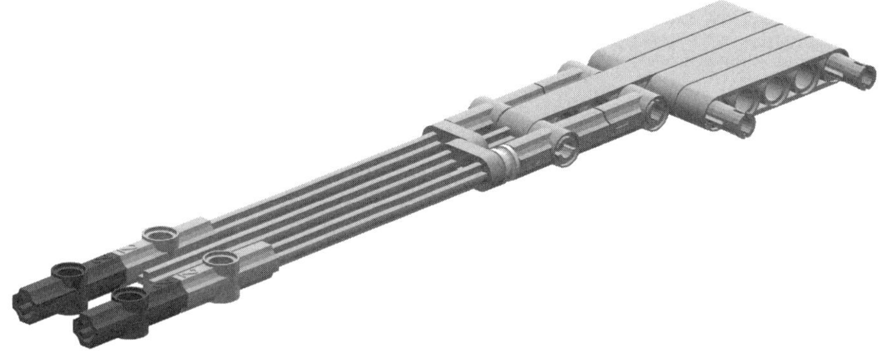

INTERNALS HAMMER

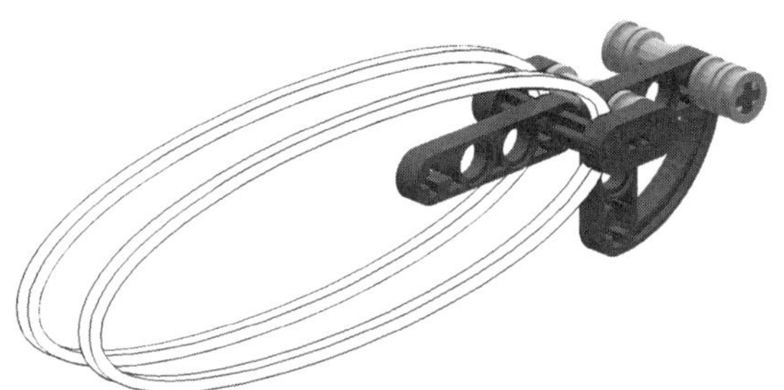

1

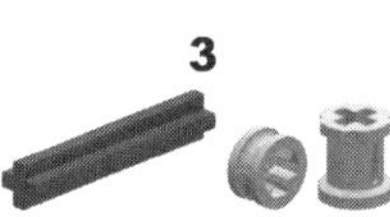

x1 x1 x1

2

x1 x2

3

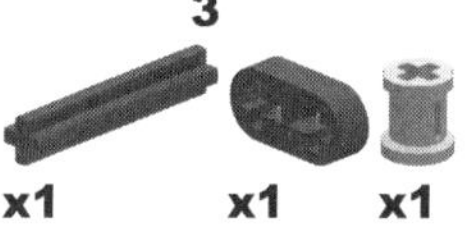

x1 x1 x1

4

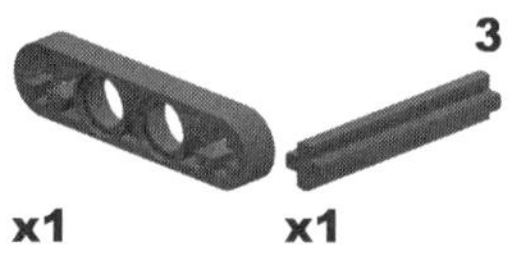

x1 x1

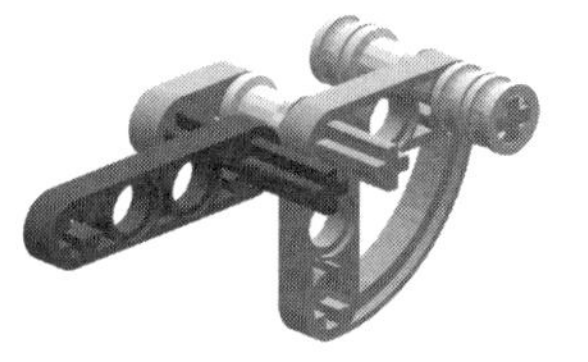

5

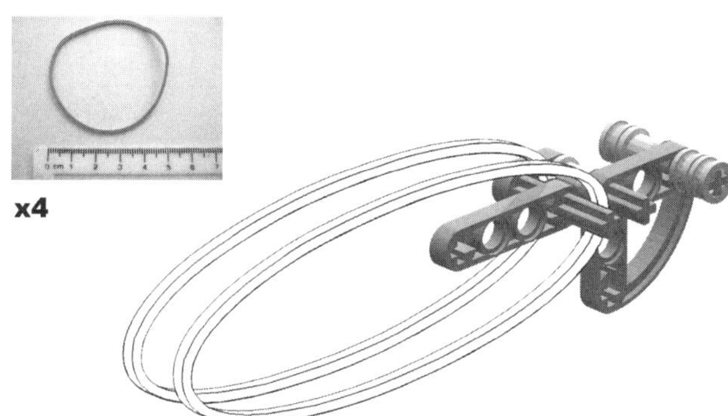

x4

6

x1 x1

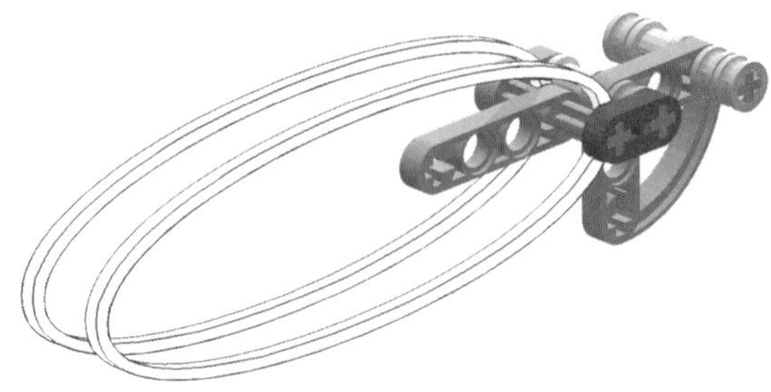

INTERNALS UPPER

1

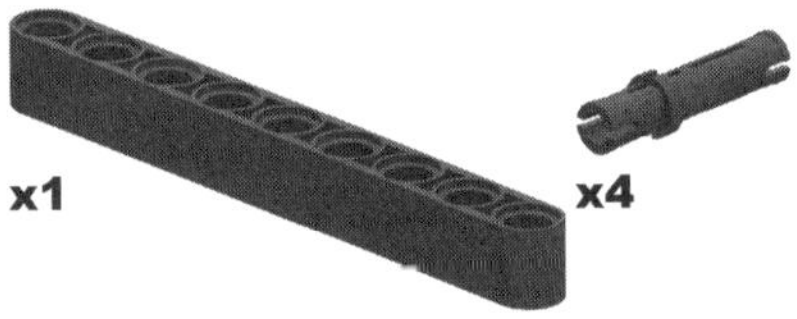

x1 x4

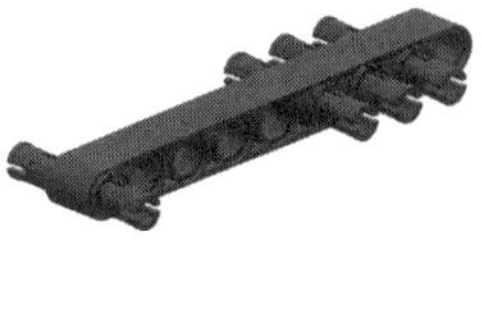

2

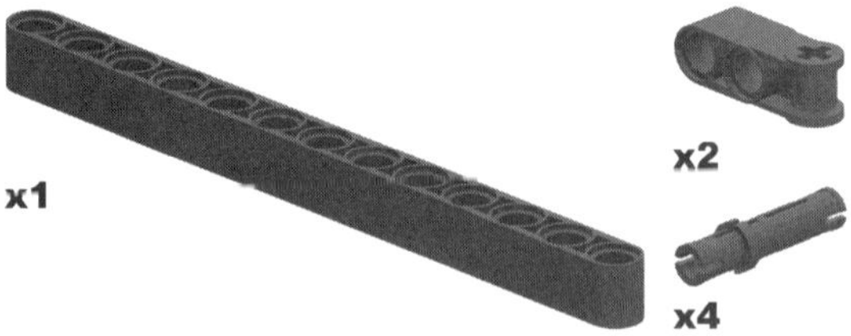

x1 x2 x4

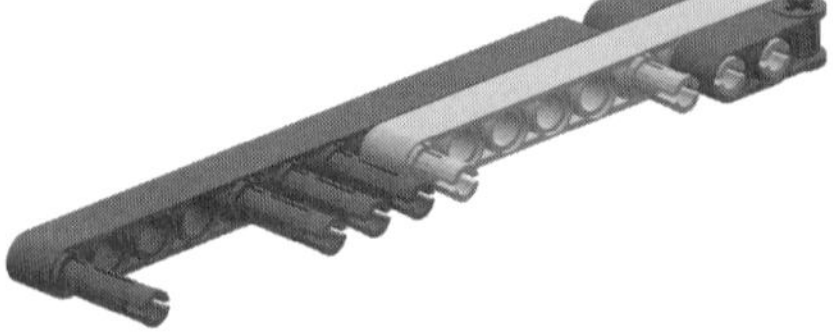

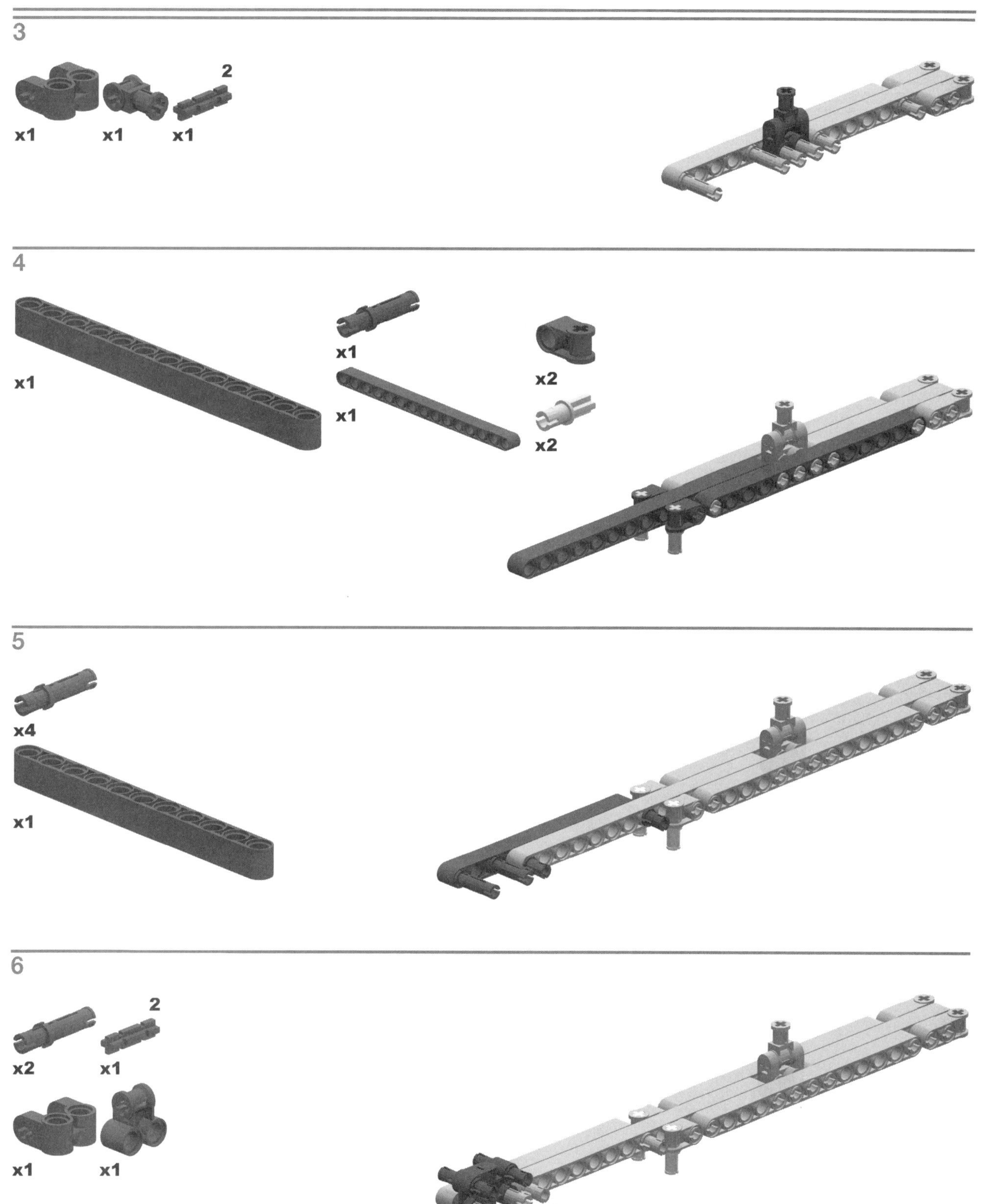
3
2
x1
x1
x1
4
x1
x1
x1
x2
x2
5
x4
x1
6
2
x2
x1
x1
x1

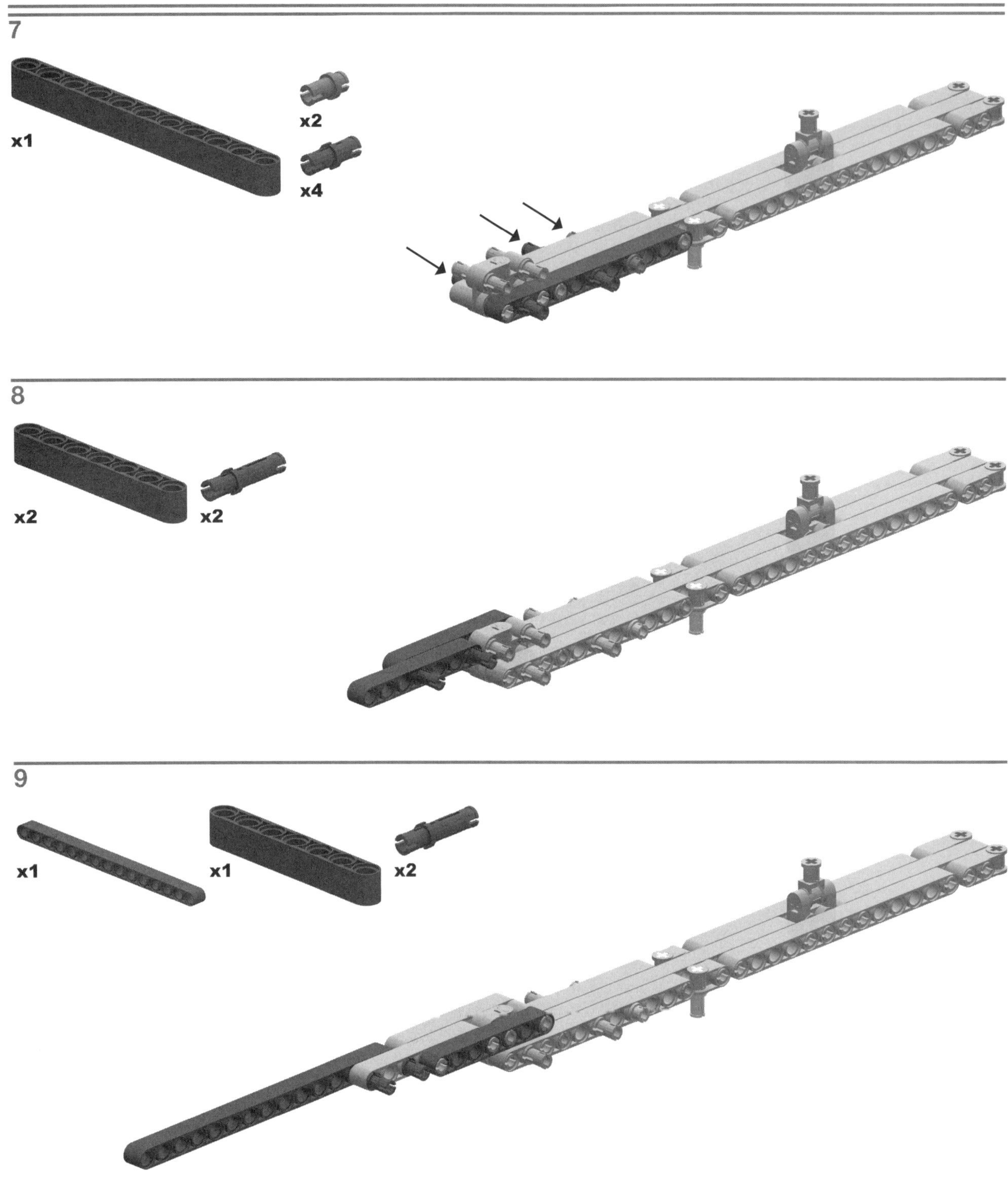
7
x1
x2
x4
8
x2
x2
9
x1
x1
x2

10

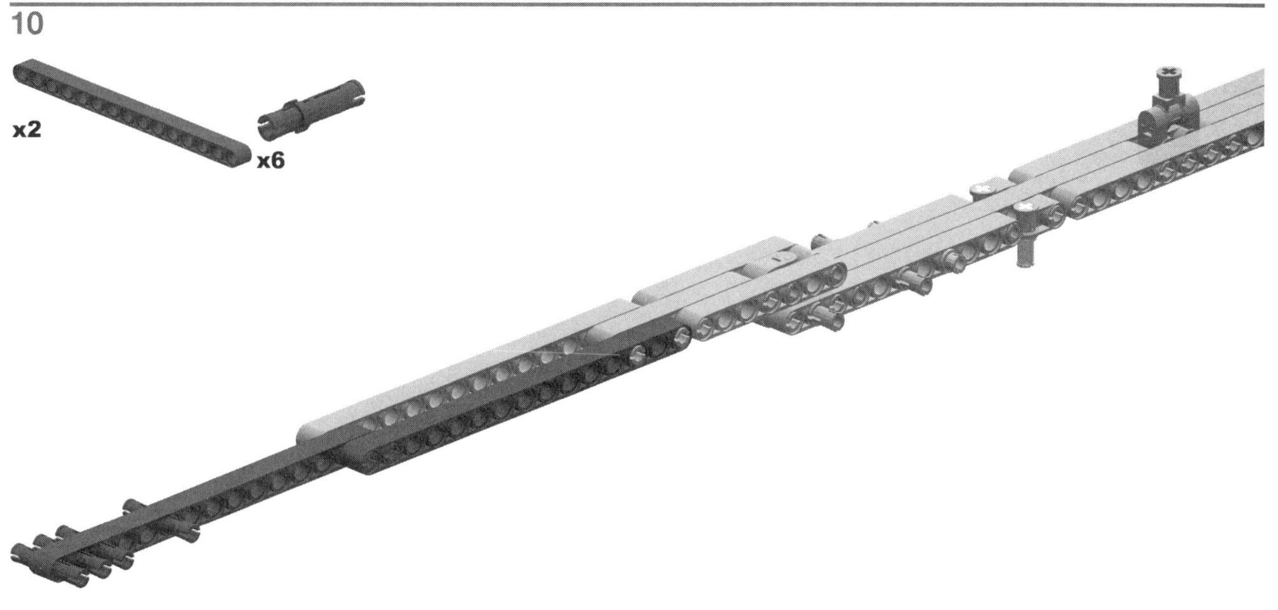

11

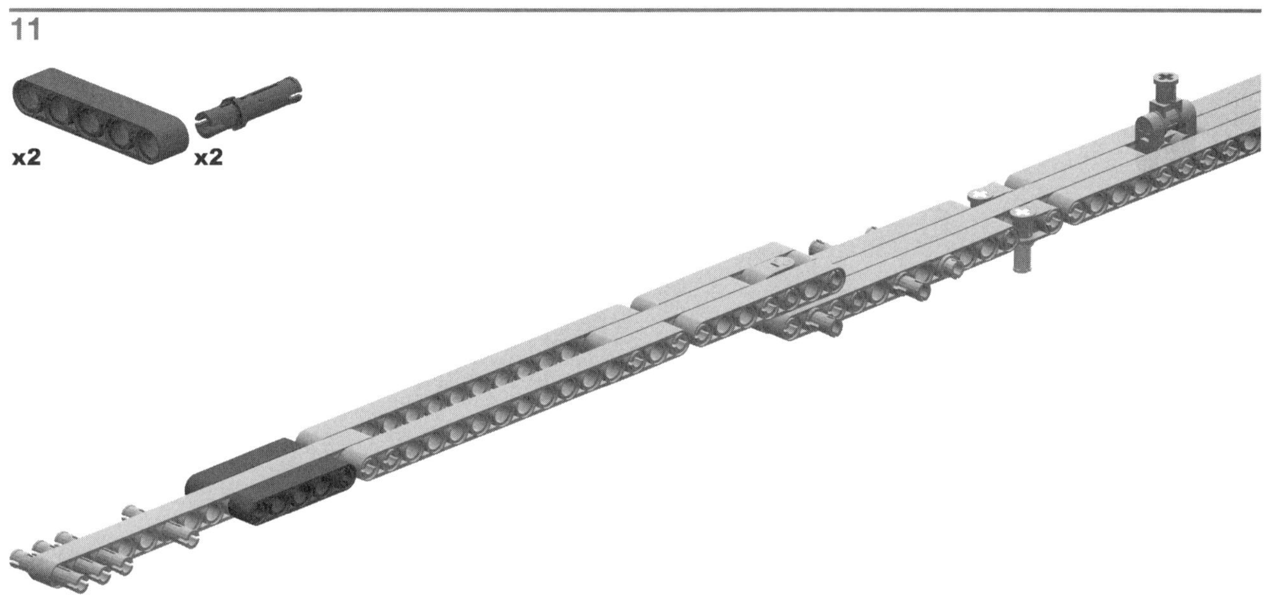

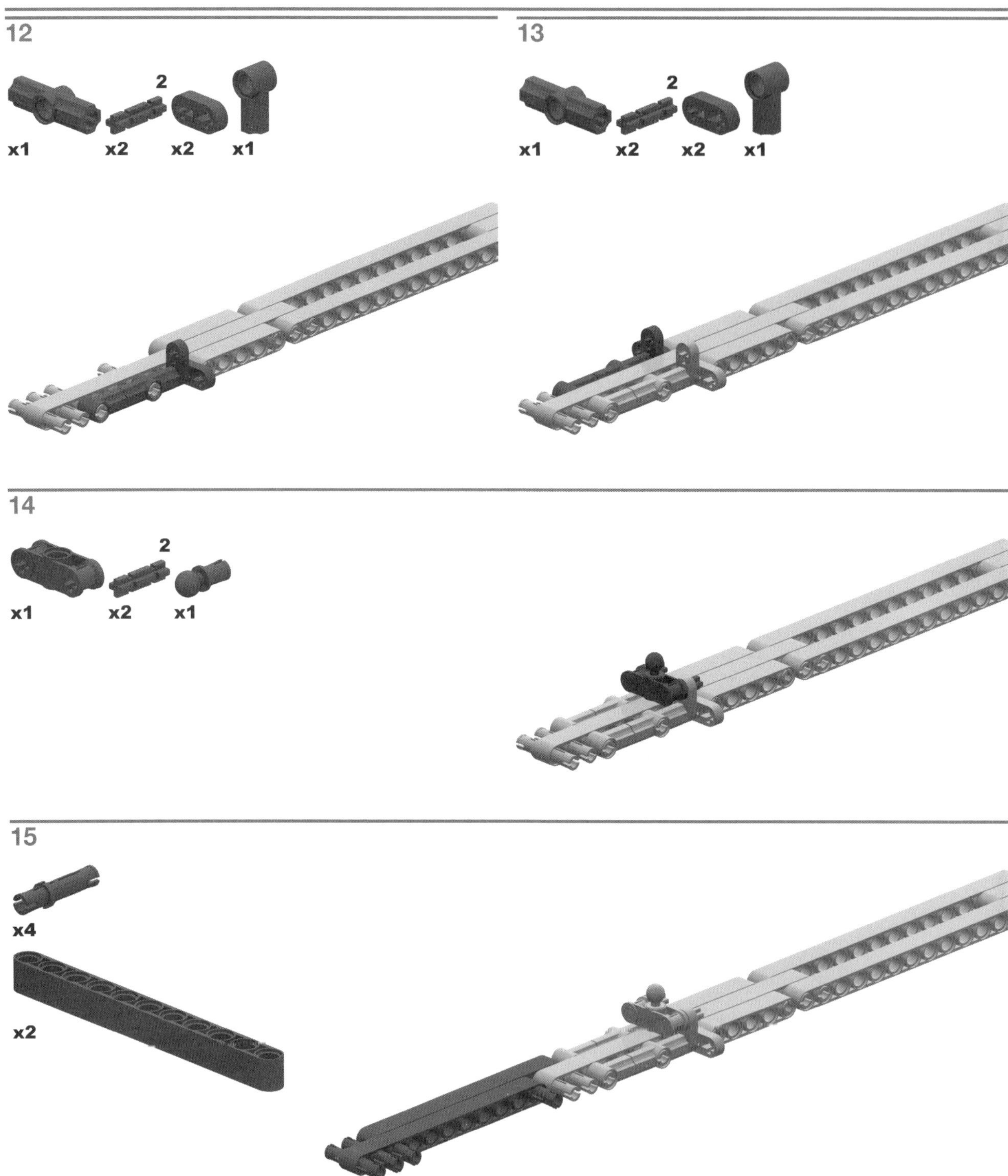
12
2
x1
x2
x2
x1
13
2
x1
x2
x2
x1
14
2
x1
x2
x1
15
x4
x2

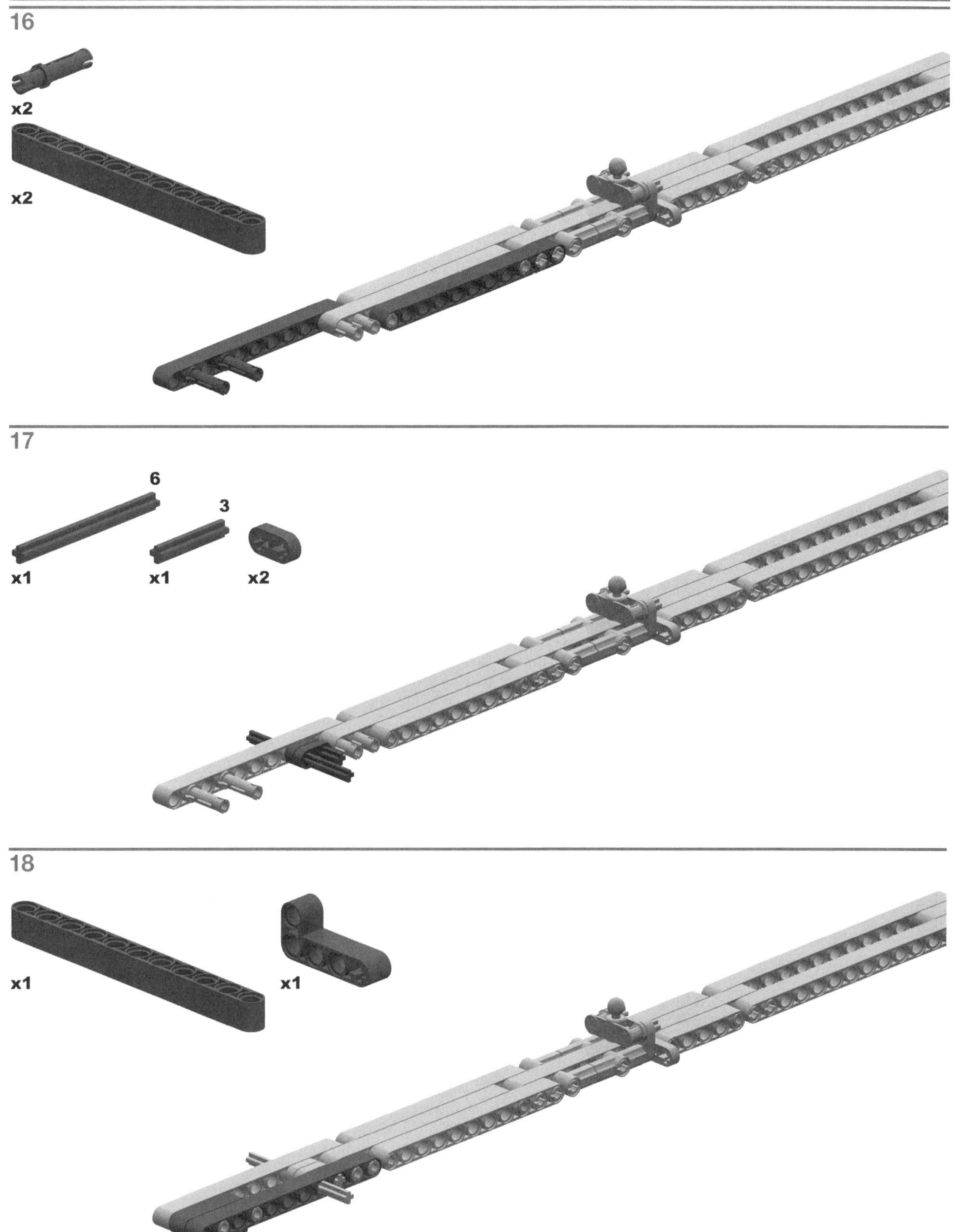
16
x2
x2
17
6
3
x1
x1
x2
18
x1
x1

19

20

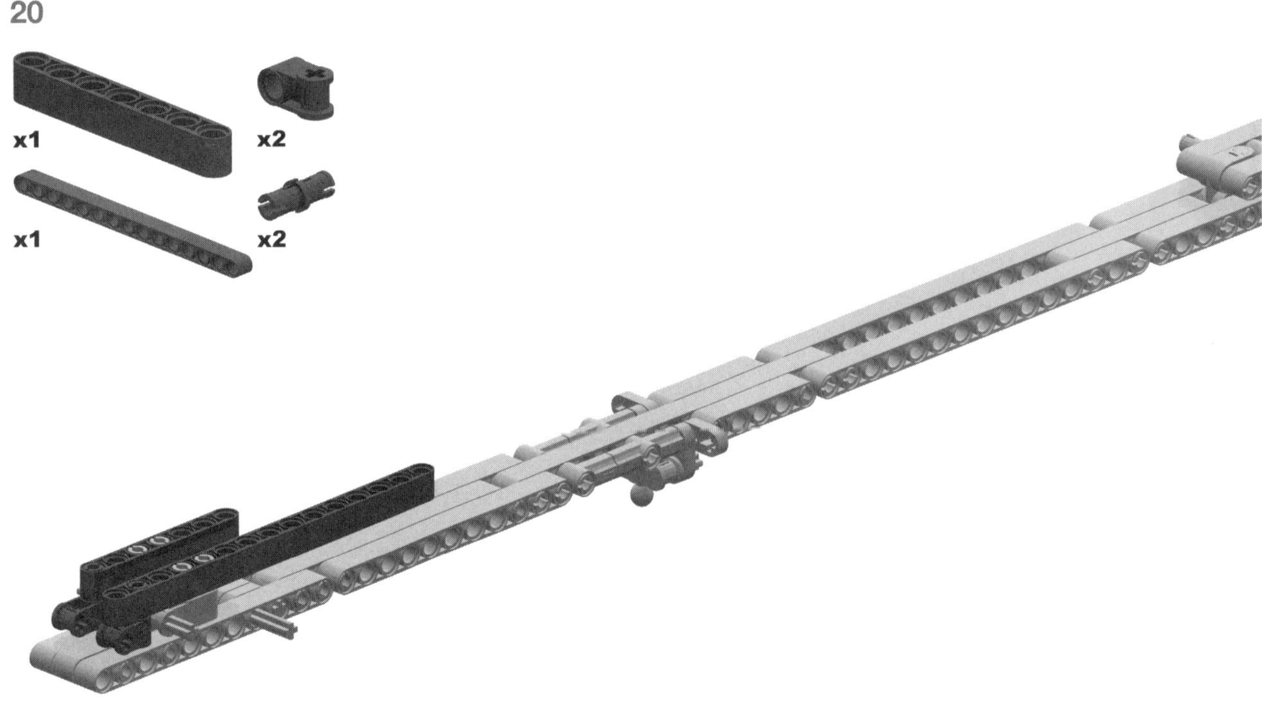

21

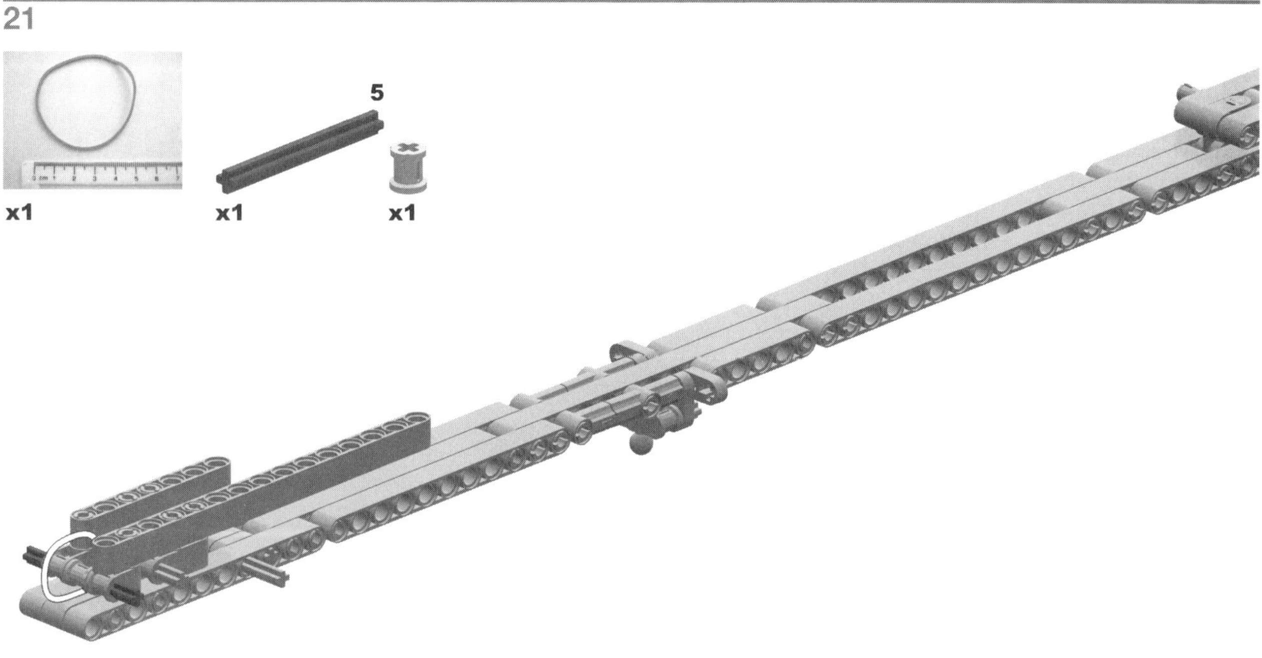

22

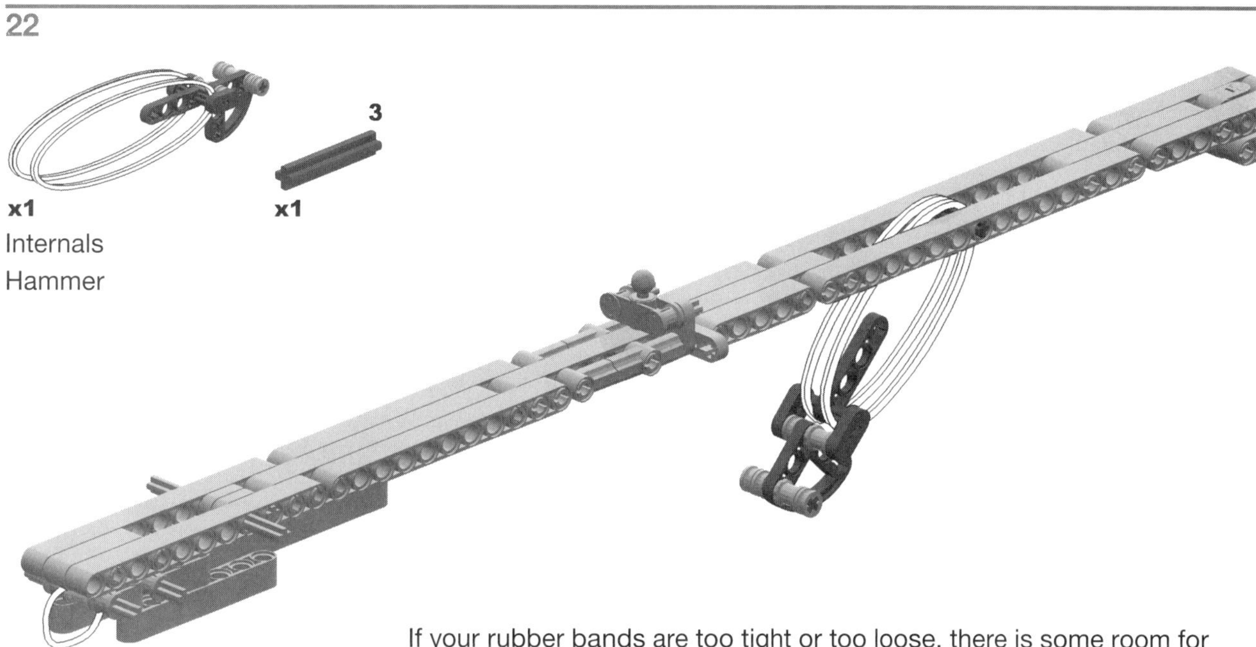

If your rubber bands are too tight or too loose, there is some room for adjustment. When you attach this module to the rest of the Internals (step 8 on page 298), position the 3-stud axle added here so that there is a decent amount of tension. I used four rubber bands, but depending on the type of rubber band you use, you may find it better to use two or six. For best results, use an even number of rubber bands, which will spread the force symmetrically over the two sides of the Hammer.

INTERNALS ASSEMBLY

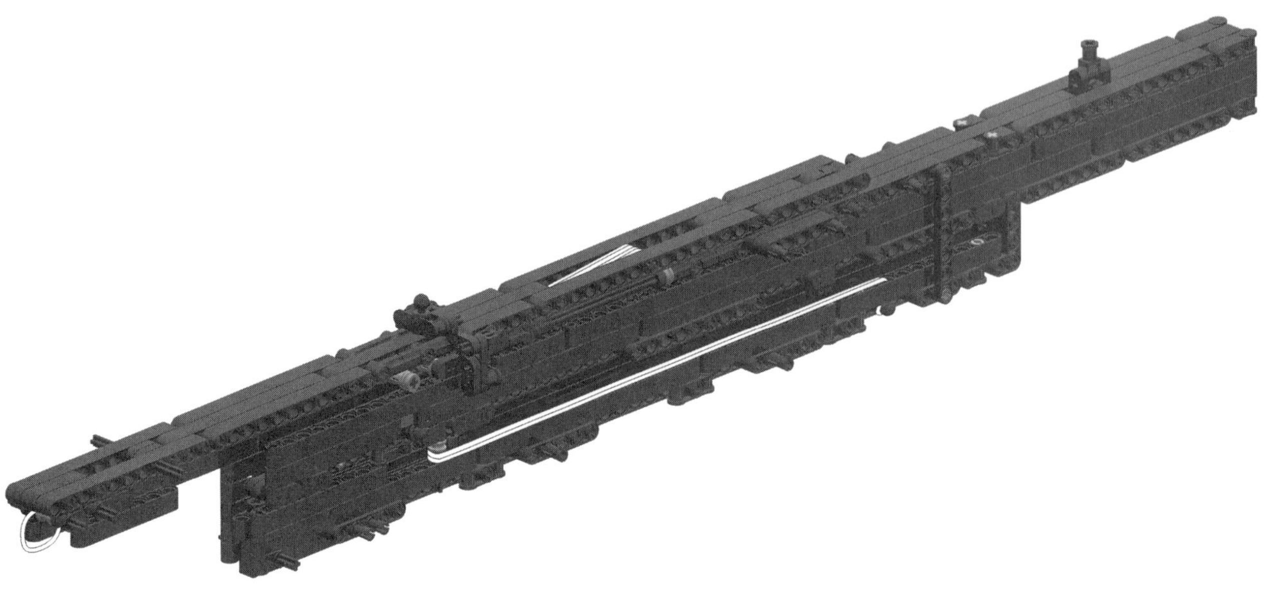

1

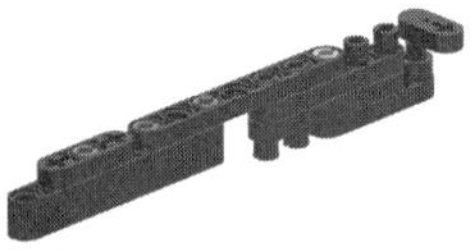

x1

Internals Magazine Slide

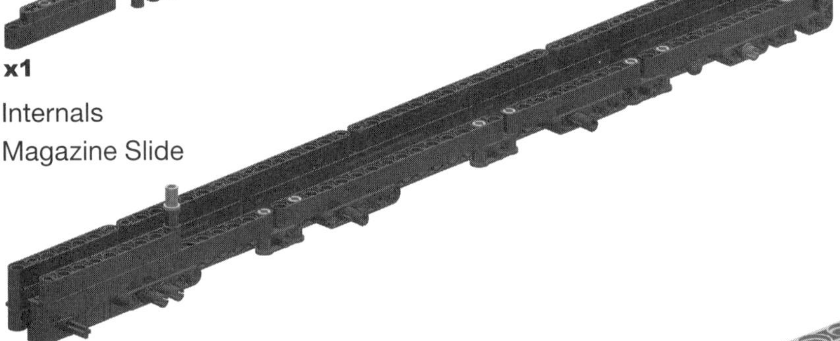

x1

Internals Lower

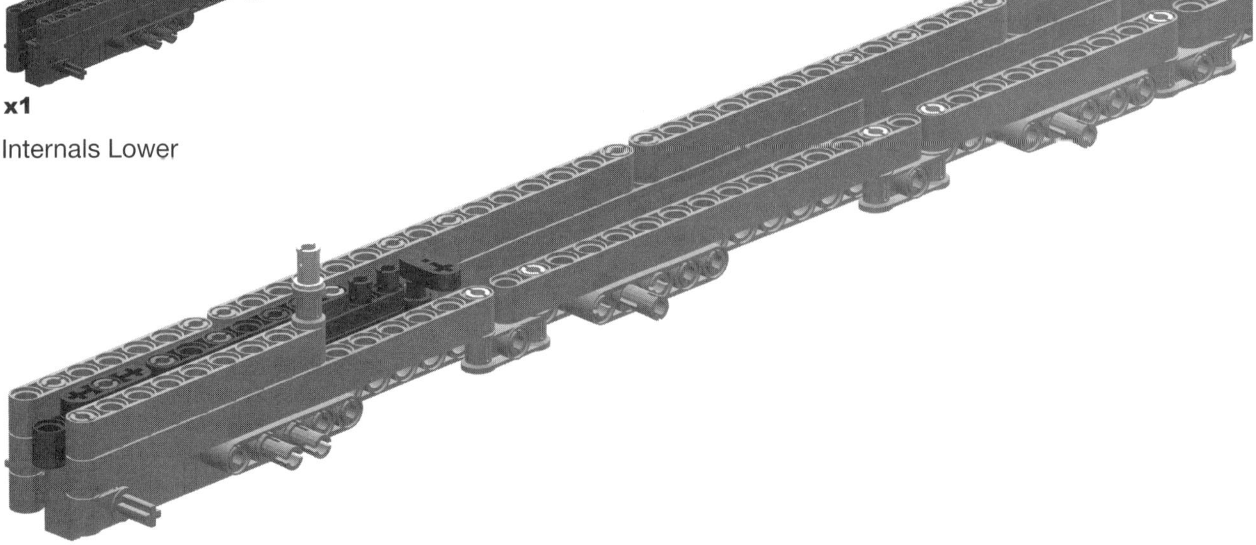

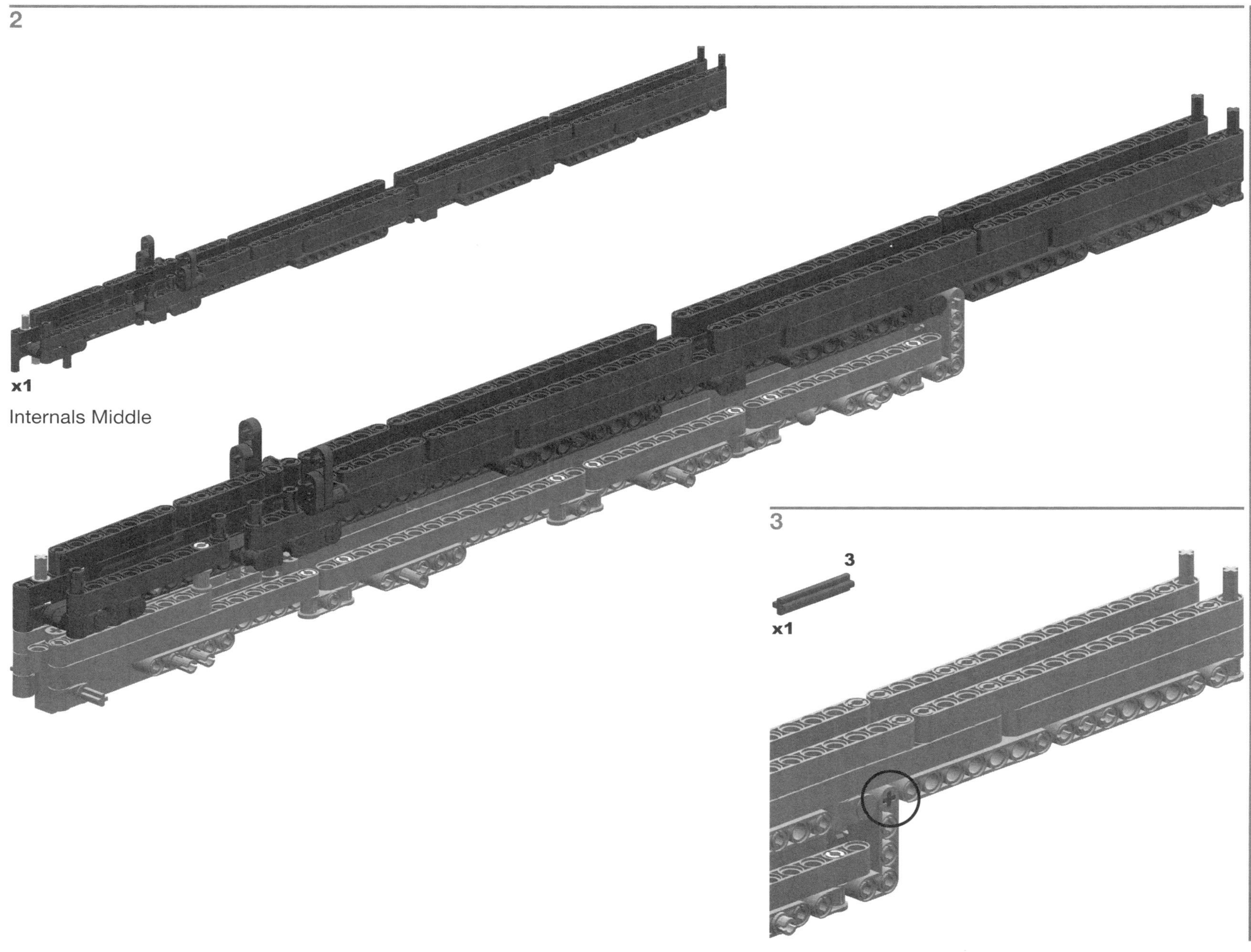
2
x1
Internals Middle
3
3
x1

4

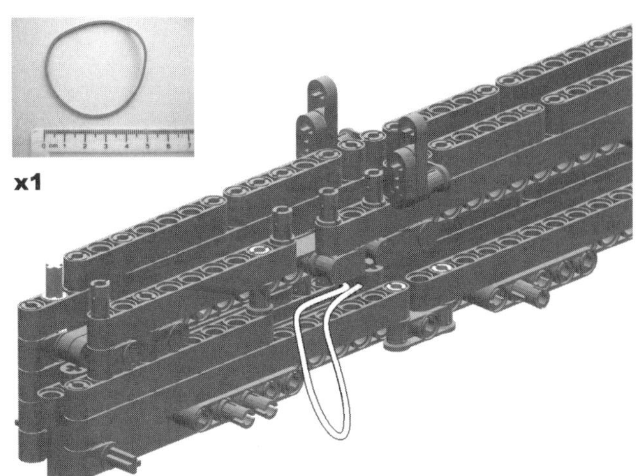

Here, the rubber band loops around the bare axle on the Magazine Slide. This can be quite fiddly. If you get really stuck, just undo the last few steps and put the rubber band on before you attach the Internals Middle (step 2 on page 295).

I used two rubber bands of the same type as those that I used for the Hammer, but I looped them together to make one rubber band that was twice as long. A longer rubber band will work much better here, since it stretches across a long distance and you want it to do so in a fairly linear way.

5

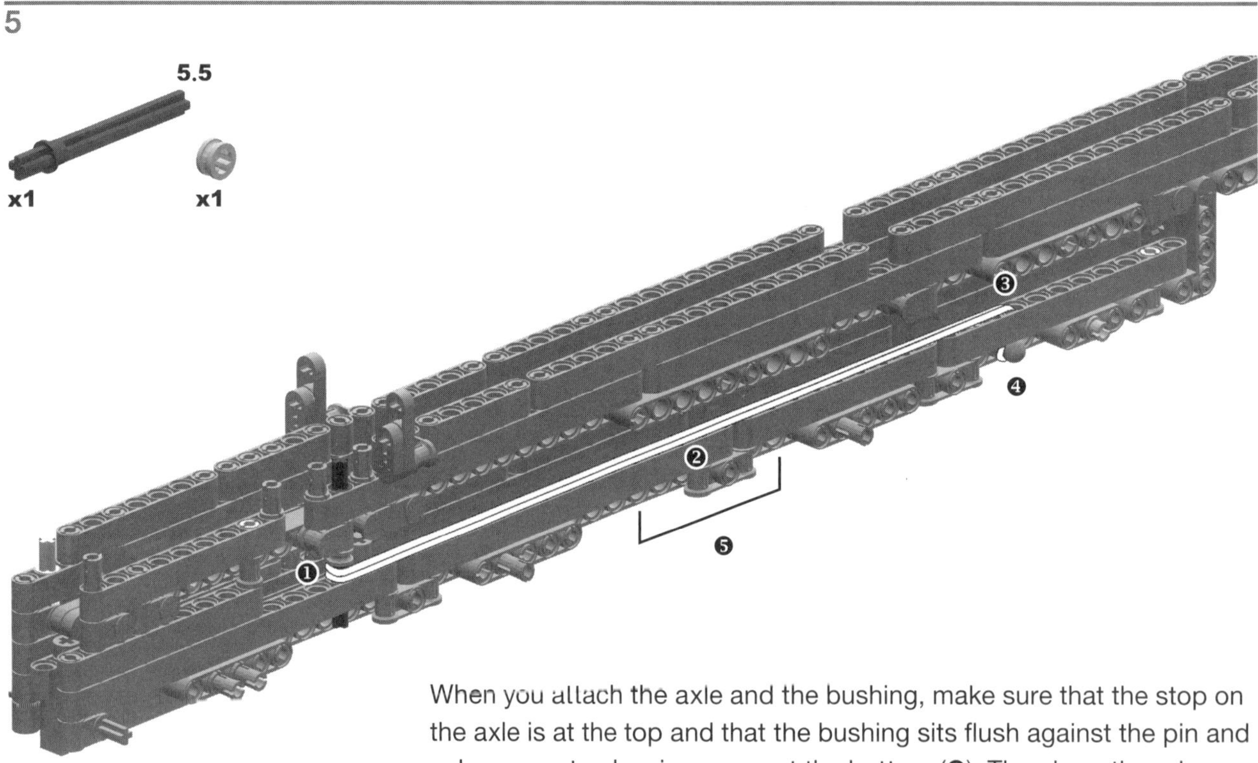

When you attach the axle and the bushing, make sure that the stop on the axle is at the top and that the bushing sits flush against the pin and axle connector, leaving a gap at the bottom (❶). Then loop the rubber band added in step 4 into this gap around the axle and toward the muzzle end of the magazine at ❷ so that the Magazine Slide is pulled toward the rear end. Pass the rubber band through the hole in the Technic beam at ❸ and loop it over the towball pin at ❹. You may need to experiment with different rubber band lengths or move the towball pin to a different hole in the lower beam at ❺ to give the rubber band a longer or shorter initial stretch. Just remember to keep everything out of the way of the Magazine Slide when you load it up!

6

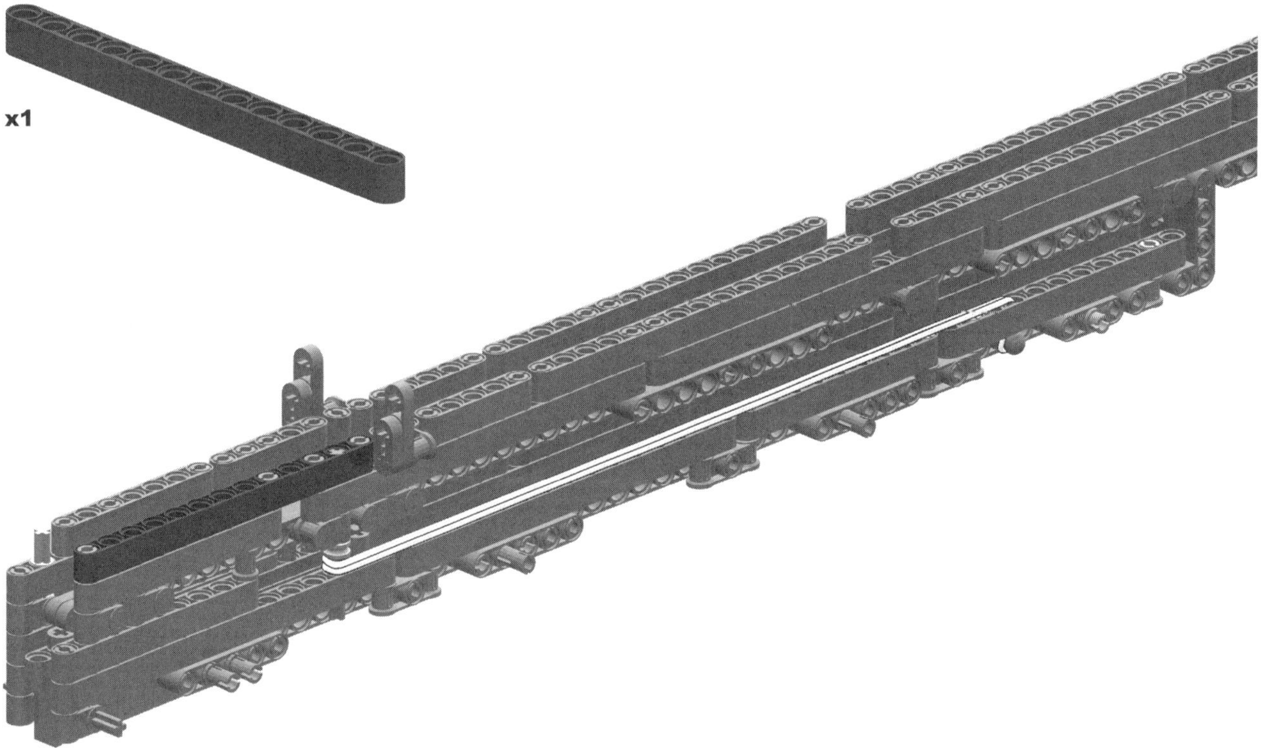

x1

7

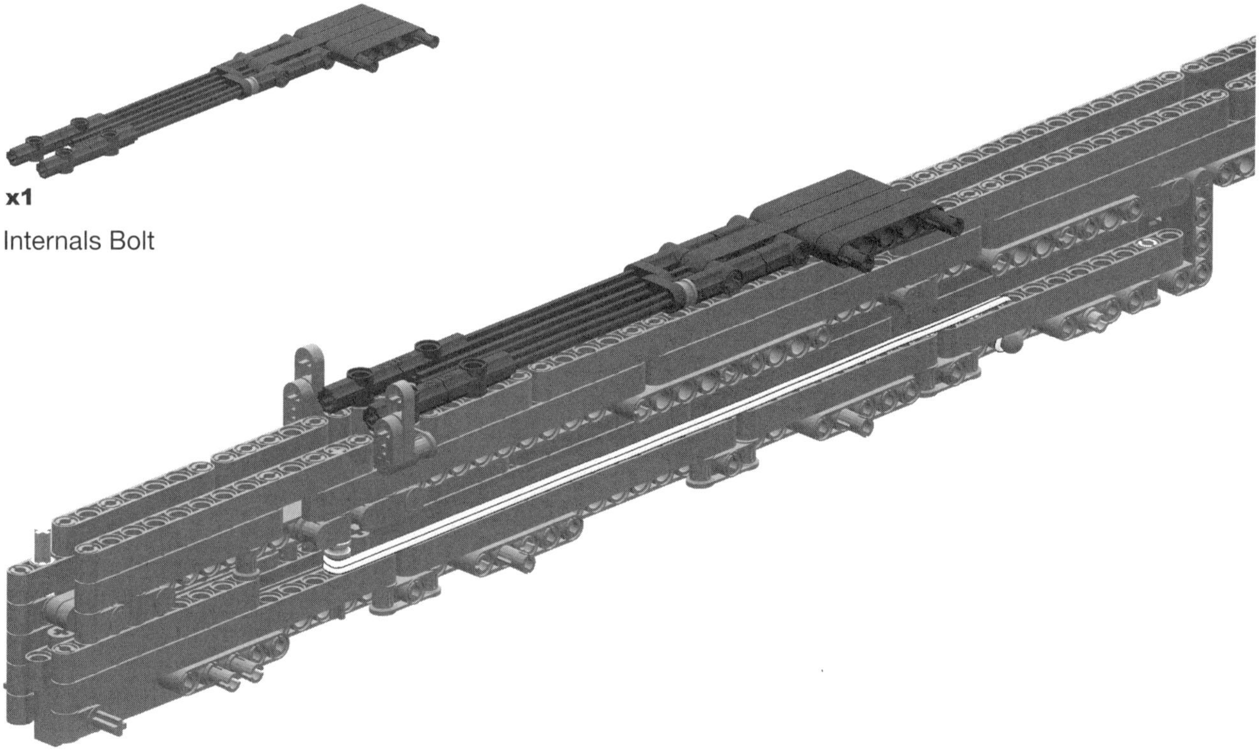

x1

Internals Bolt

8

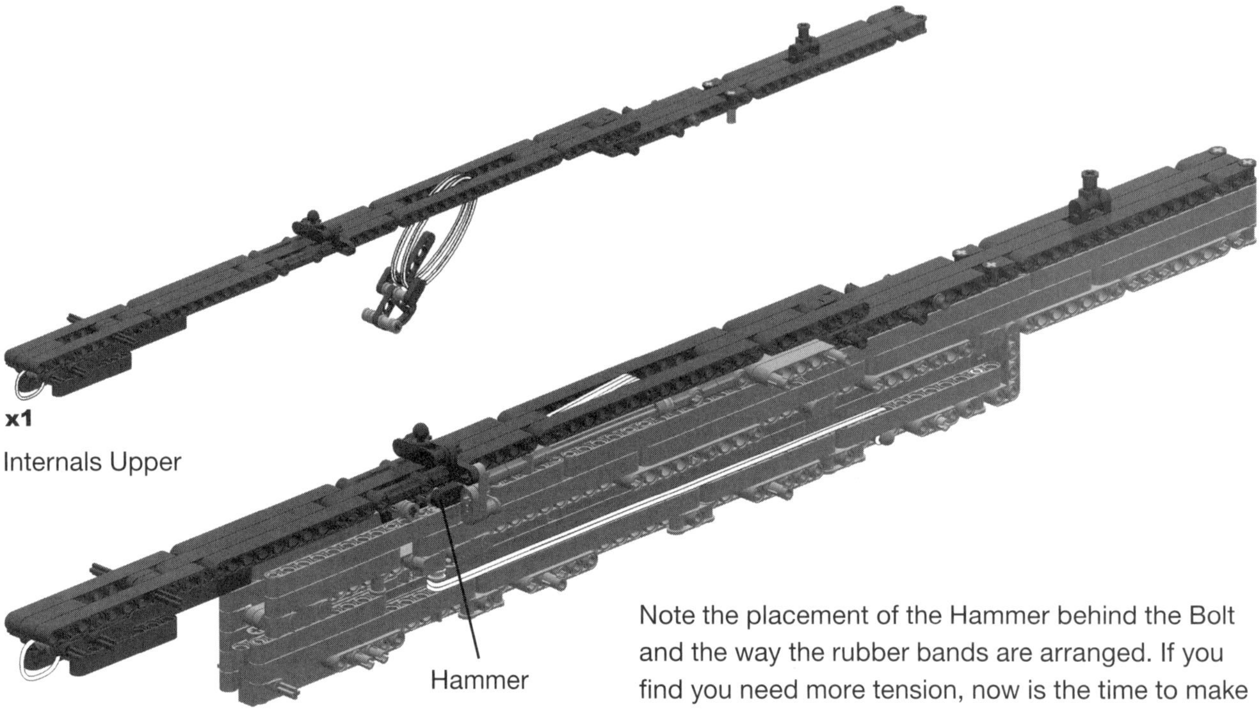

x1

Internals Upper

Hammer

Note the placement of the Hammer behind the Bolt and the way the rubber bands are arranged. If you find you need more tension, now is the time to make your adjustments: Add more rubber bands (but I wouldn't use more than six) or move the 3-stud axle (added in step 22 on page 293) a bit farther toward the muzzle end.

9

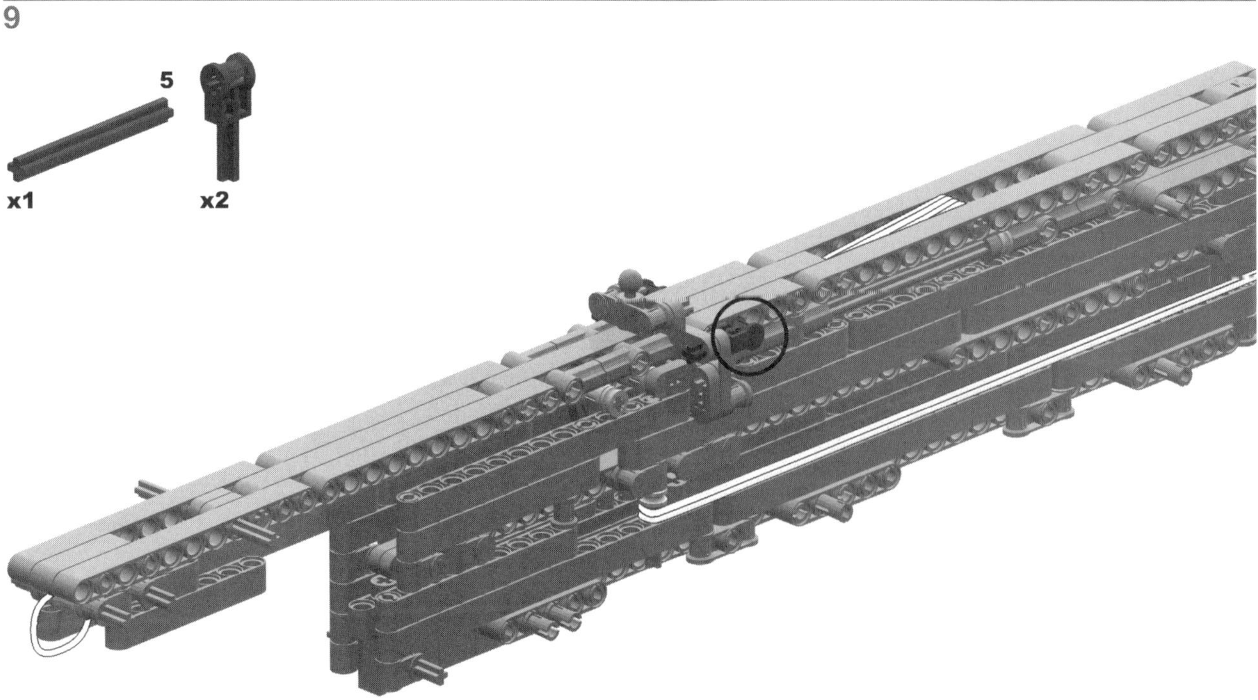

10

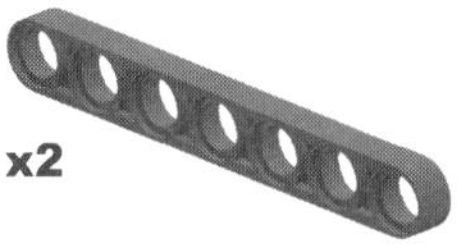

x2

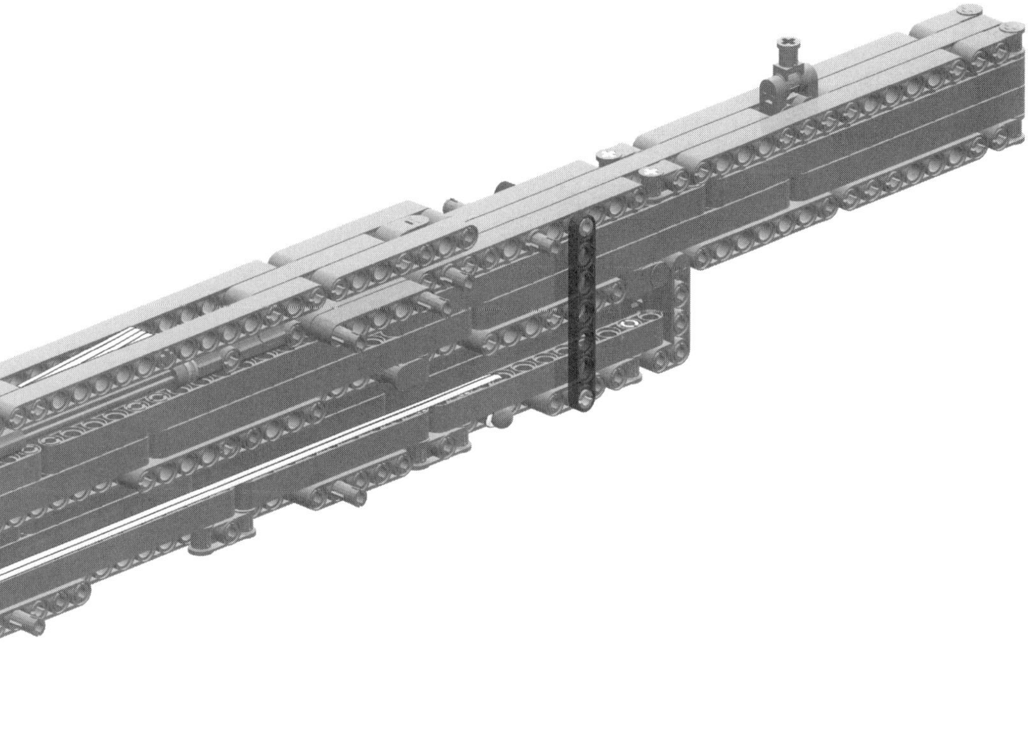

TRIGGER

1

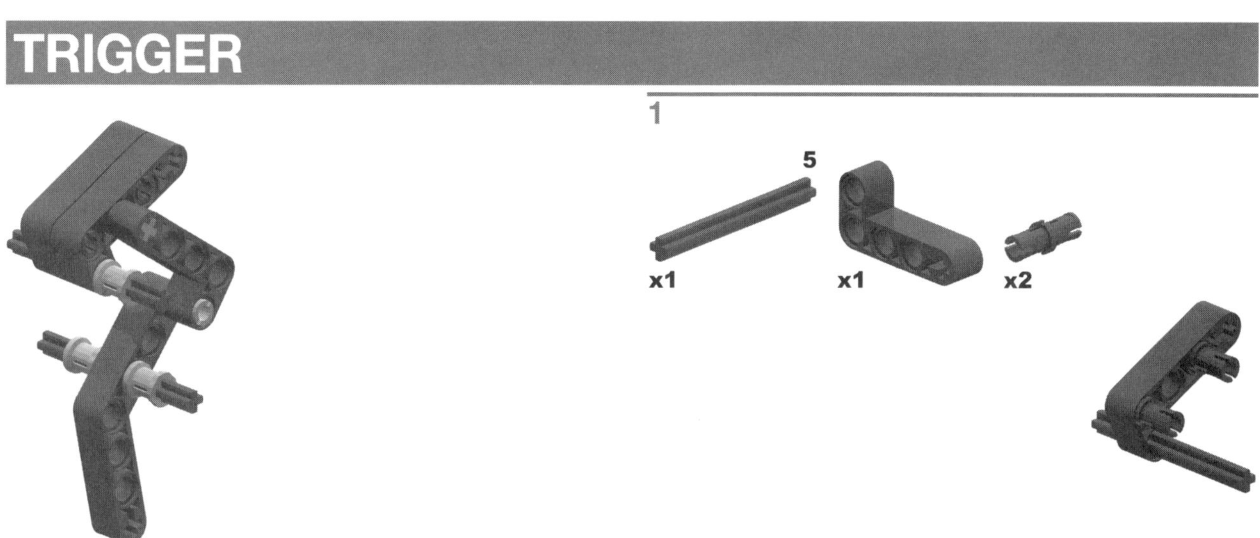

2

x1
x1
x1

3

5
x1
x1

4

x1
x1
x1

5

x1

PISTOL GRIP TOP

1

x1
x1

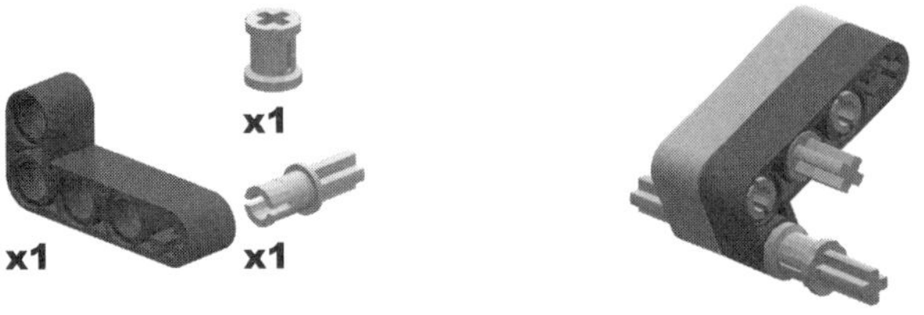

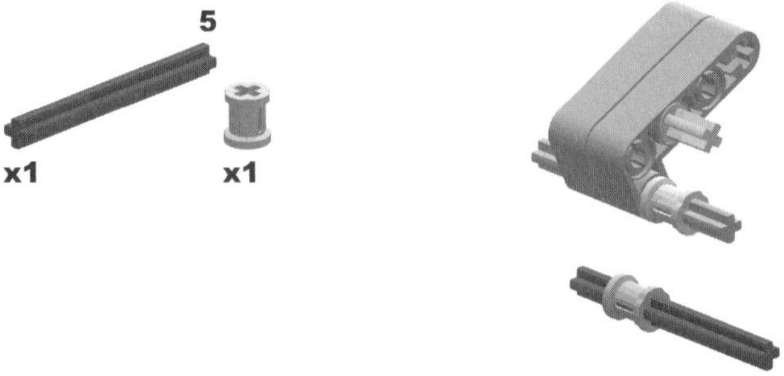

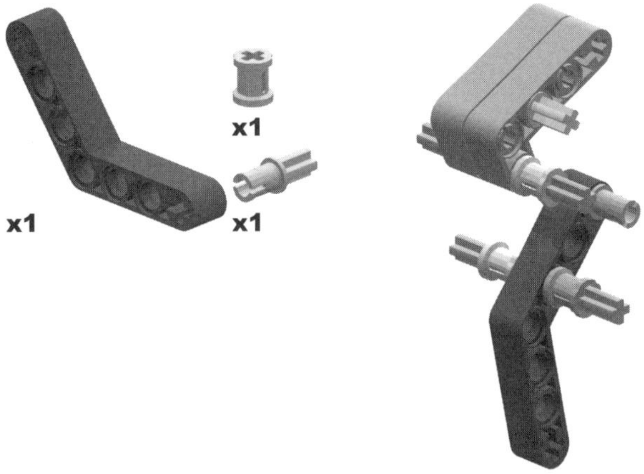

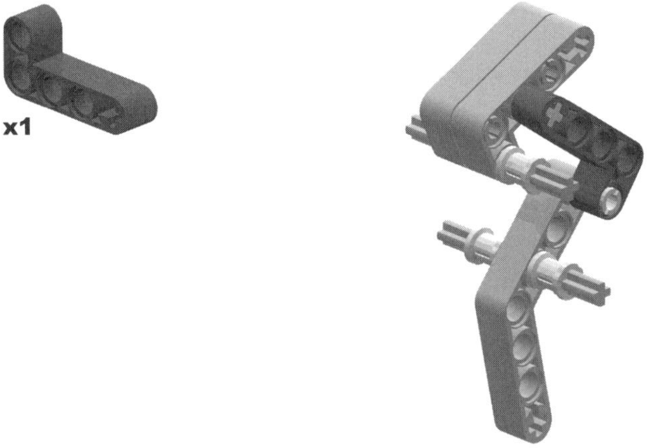

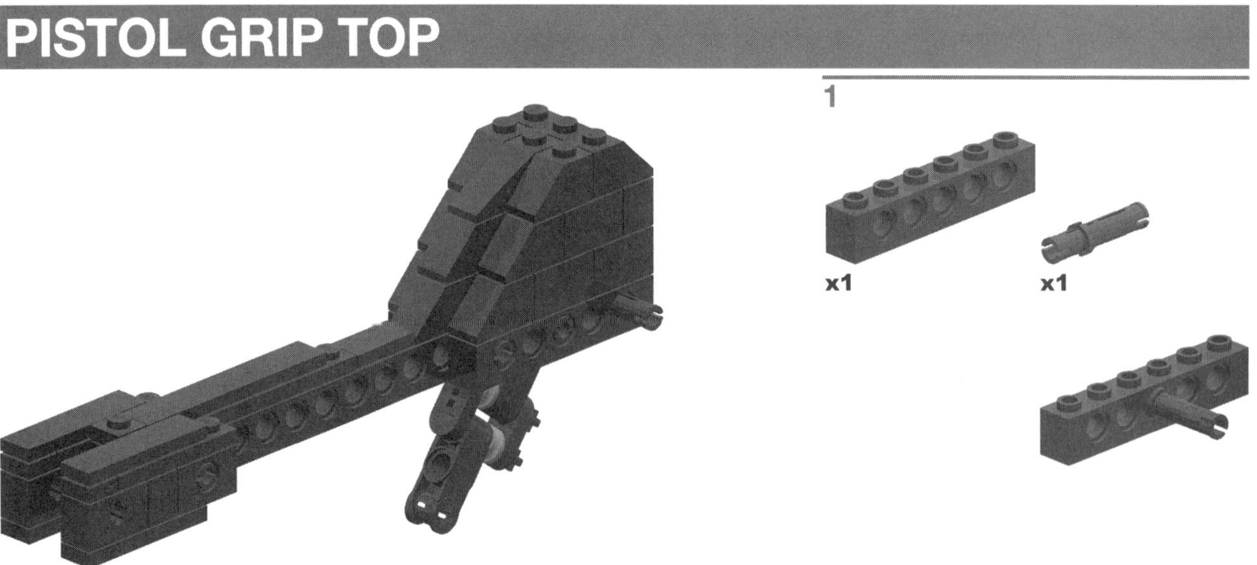

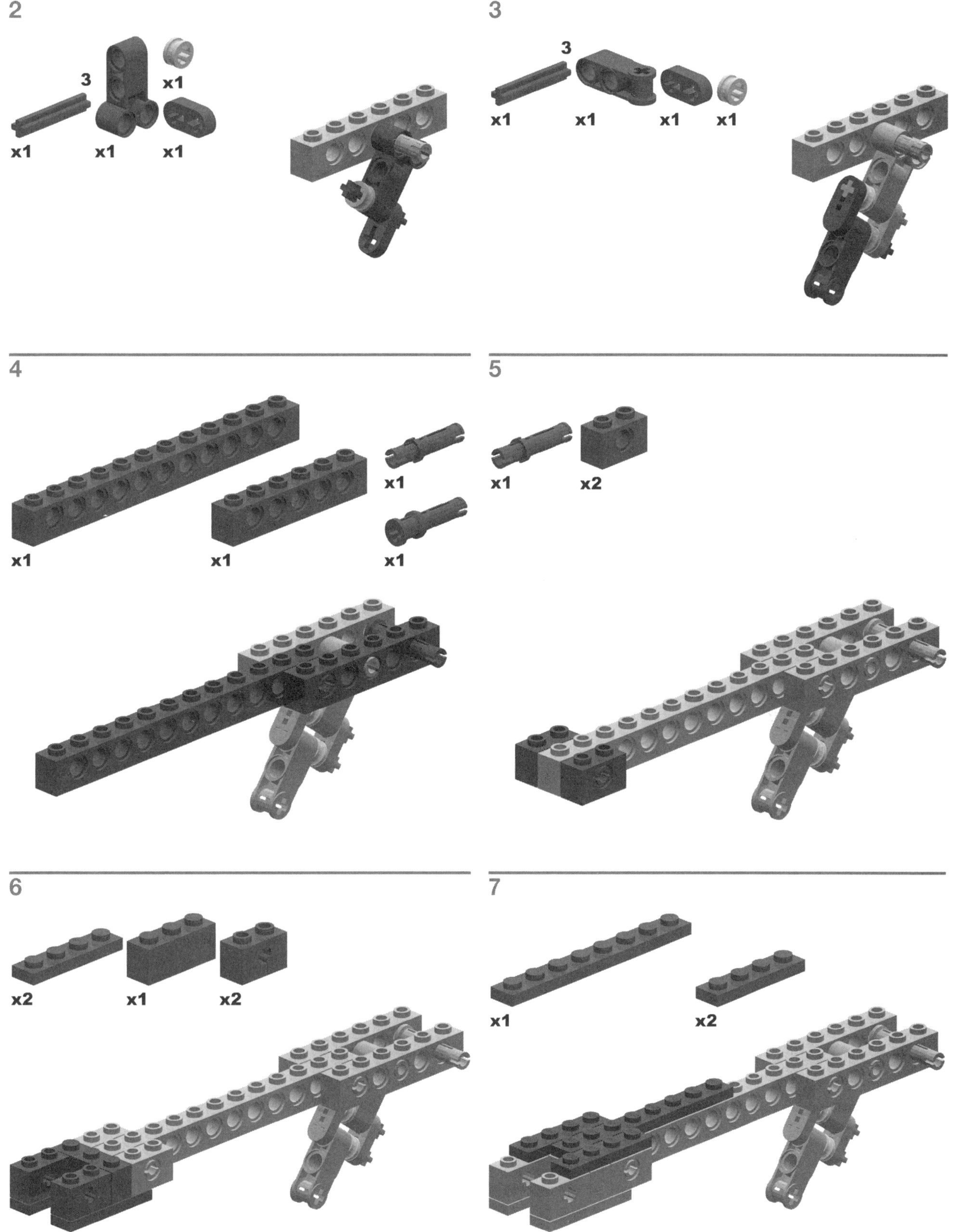
2
3
x1
x1
x1
x1
3
x1
x1
x1
x1
4
x1
x1
x1
x1
5
x1
x2
6
x2
x1
x2
7
x1
x2

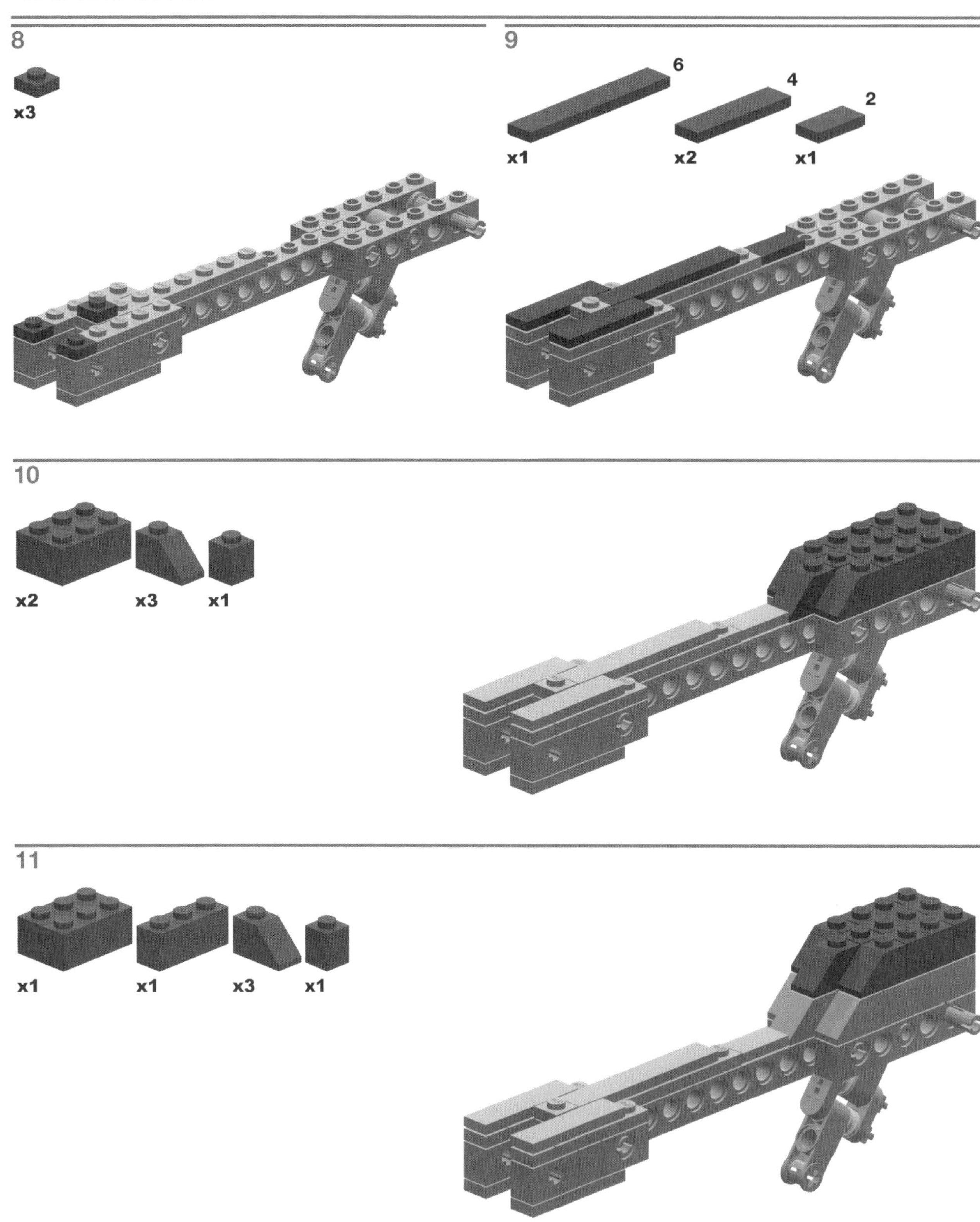
8
x3
9
6
4
2
x1
x2
x1
10
x2
x3
x1
11
x1
x1
x3
x1

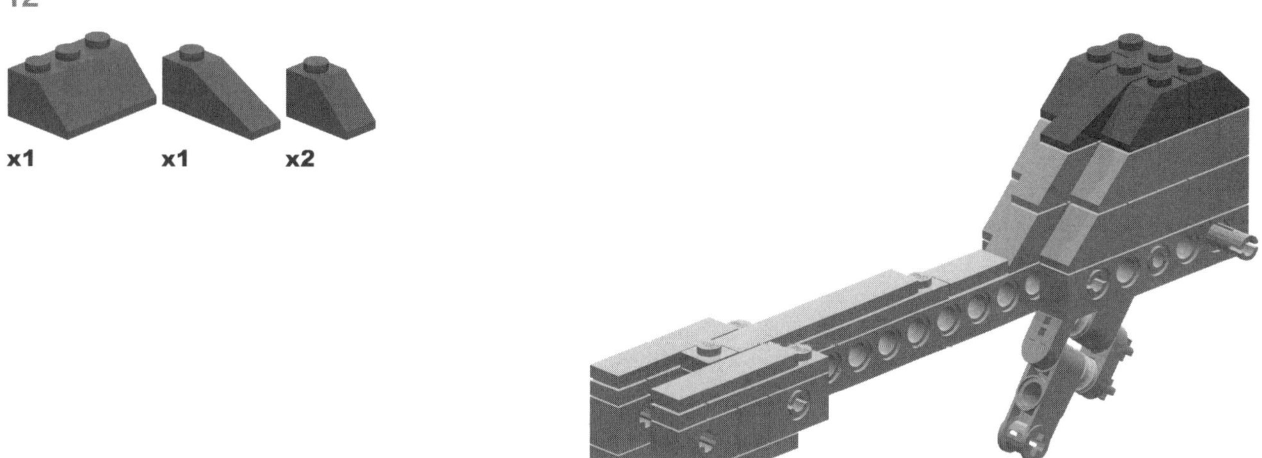

PISTOL GRIP ASSEMBLY

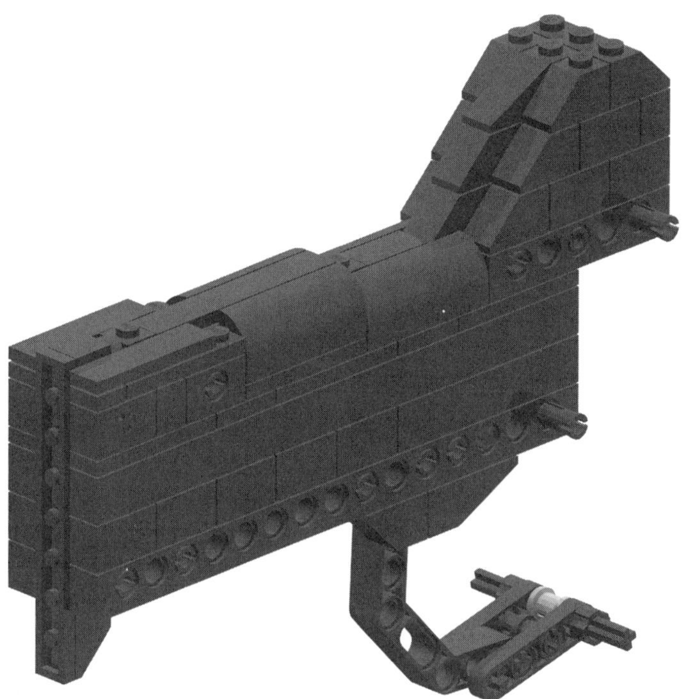

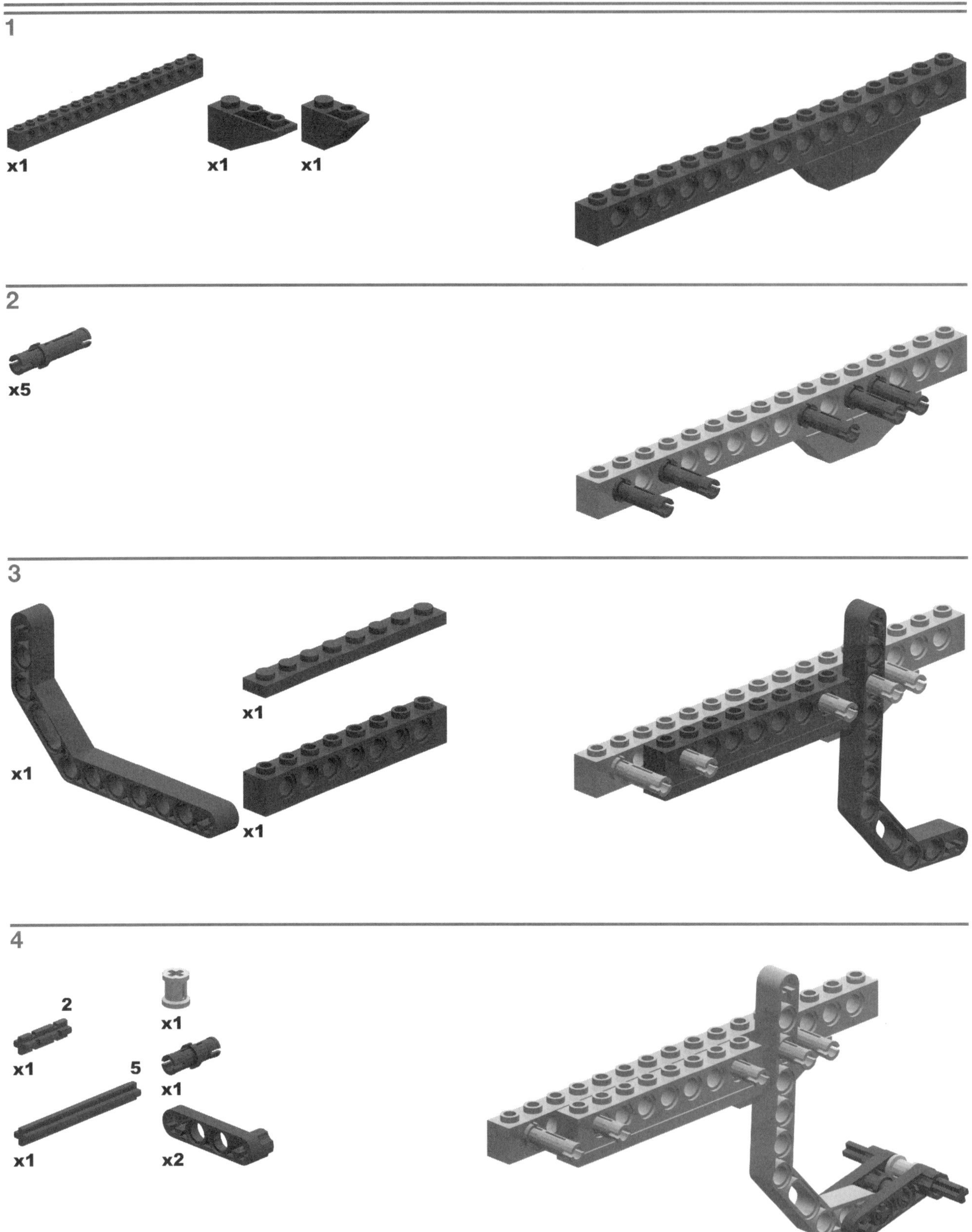
1
x1
x1
x1
2
x5
3
x1
x1
x1
4
2
x1
5
x1
x1
x1
x1
x2

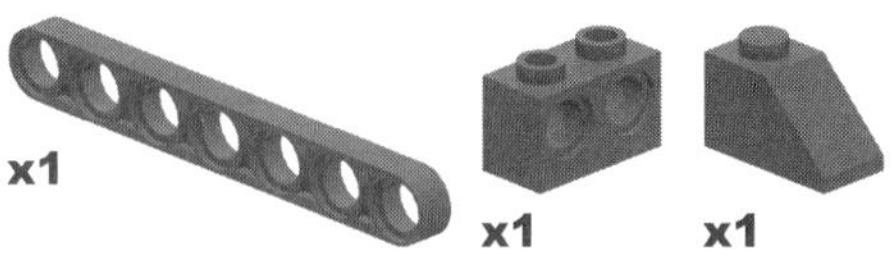
x1
x1
x1

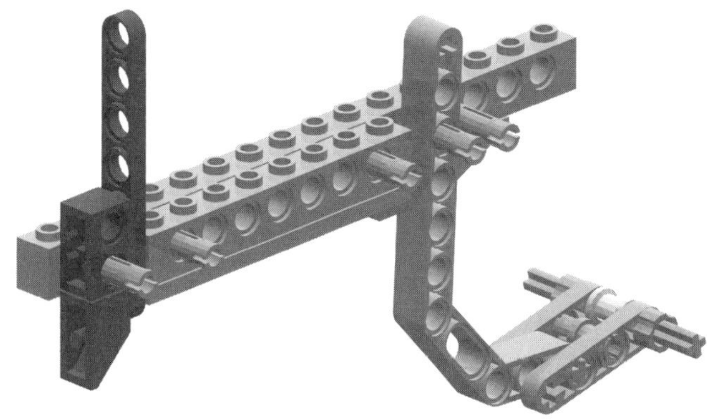

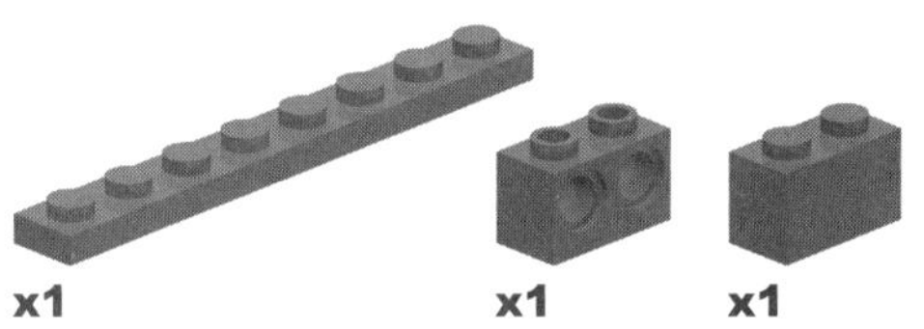
x1
x1
x1

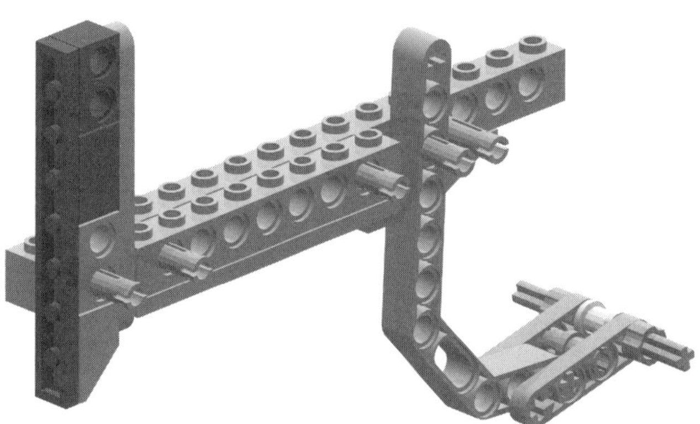

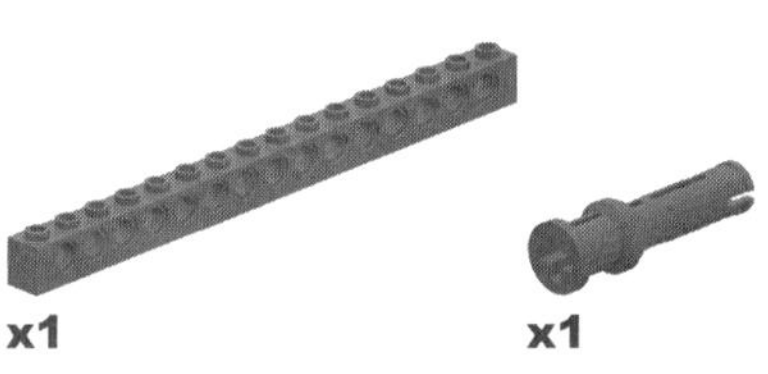
x1
x1

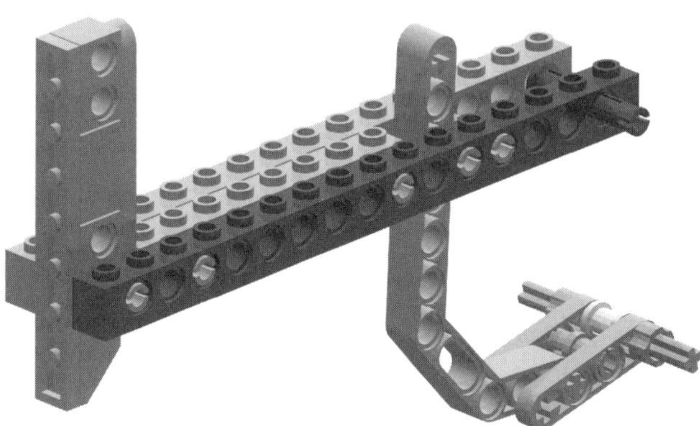

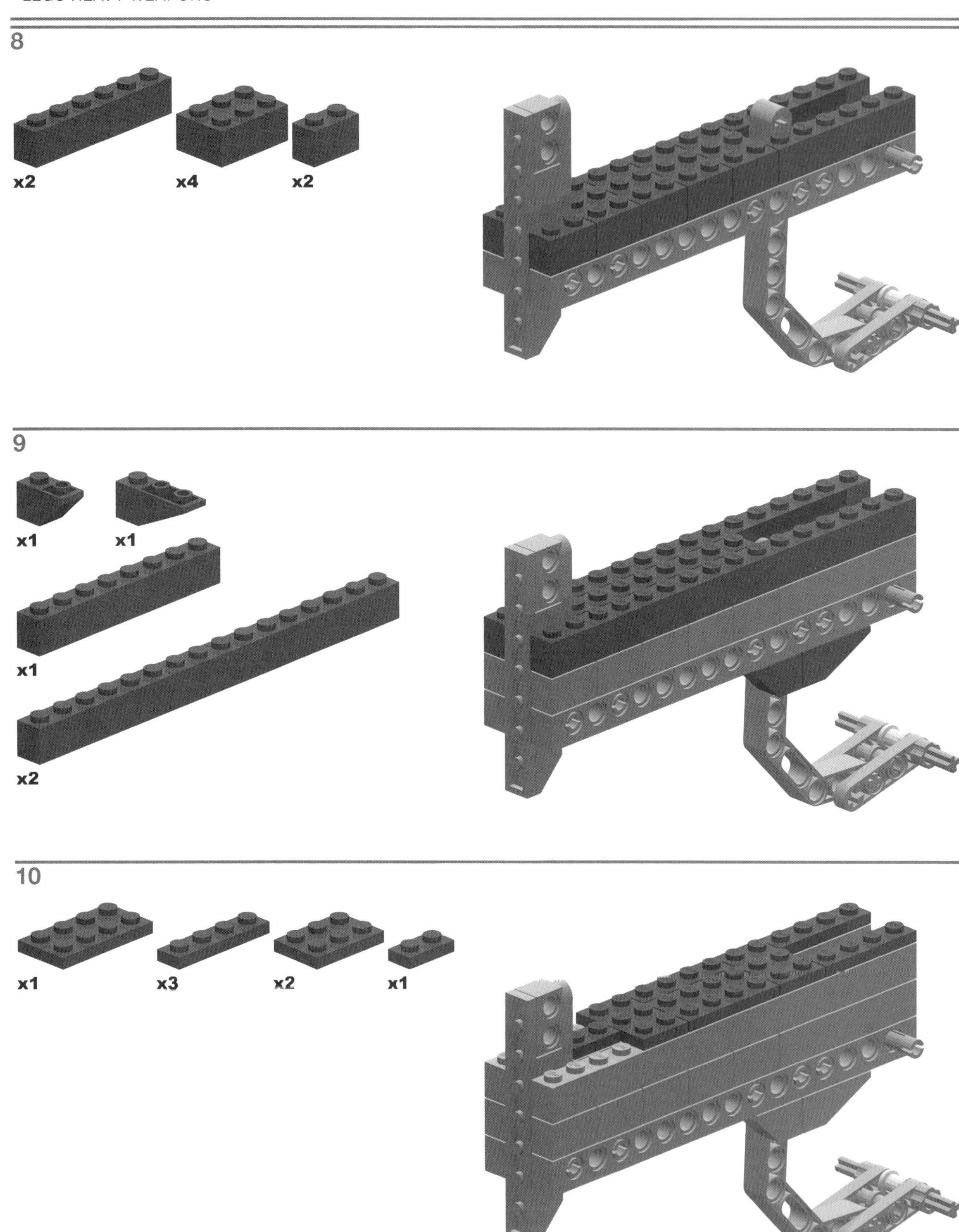
8
x2
x4
x2
9
x1
x1
x1
x2
10
x1
x3
x2
x1

11

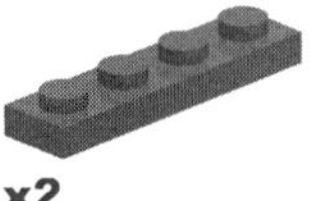

x2

x4

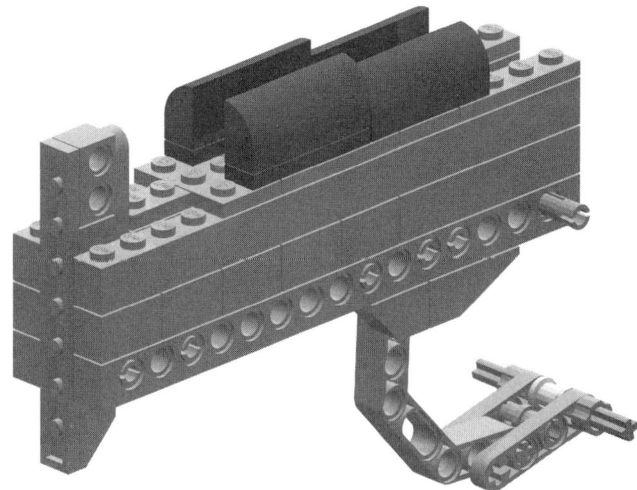

12

x1

Pistol Grip Top

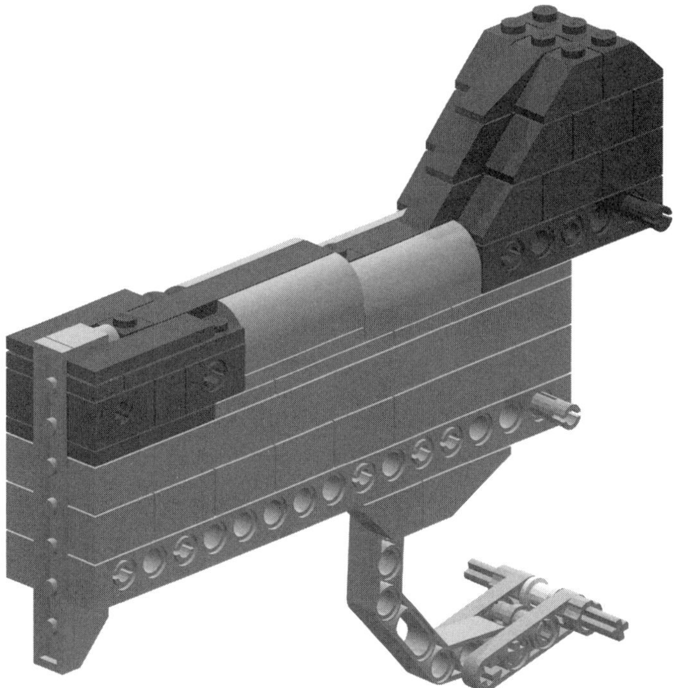

13

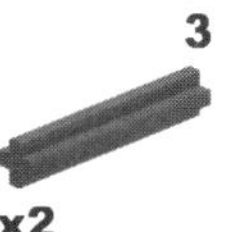

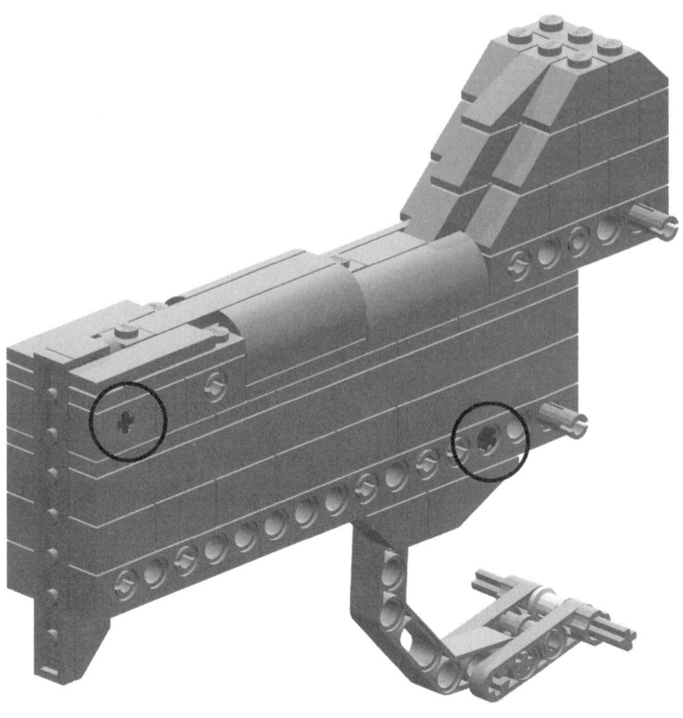

FRAME WALL RIGHT

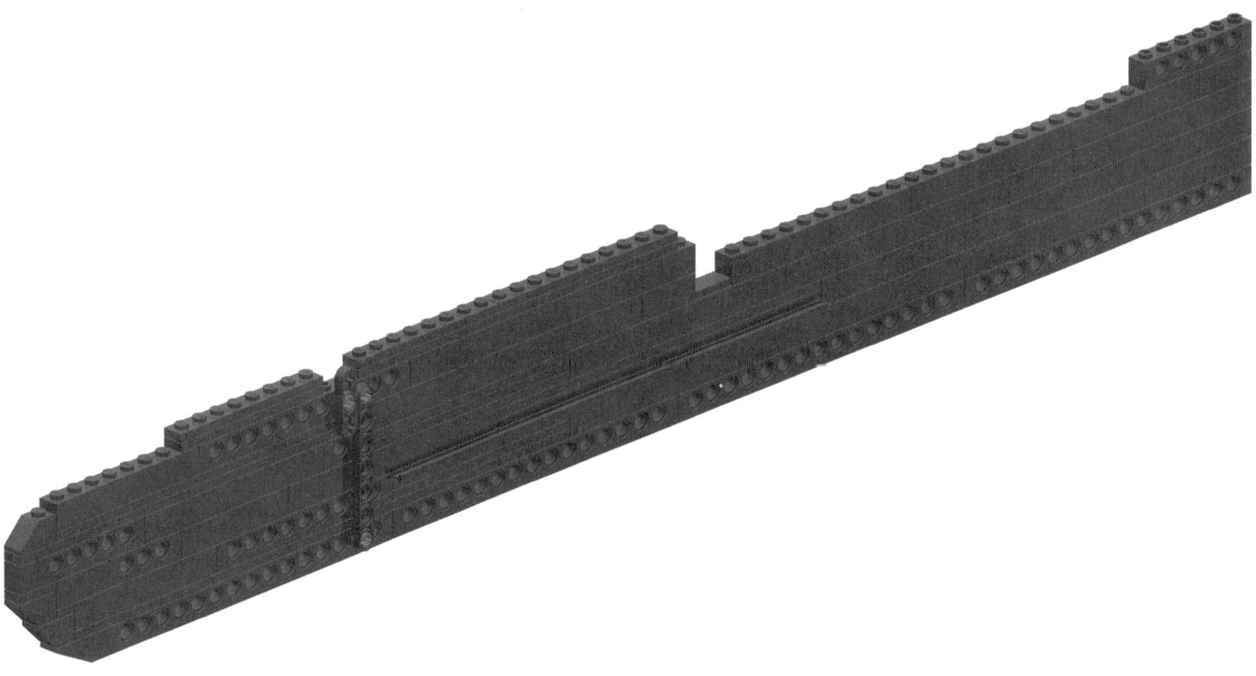

1

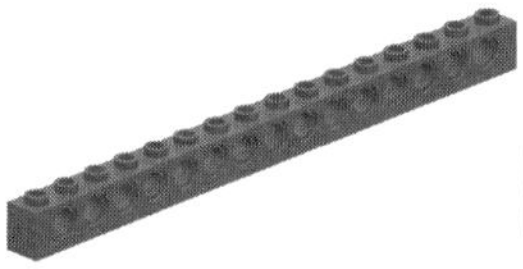

x1  x1

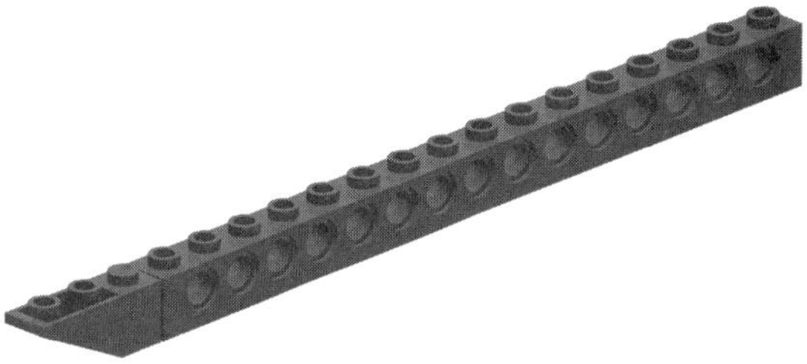

2

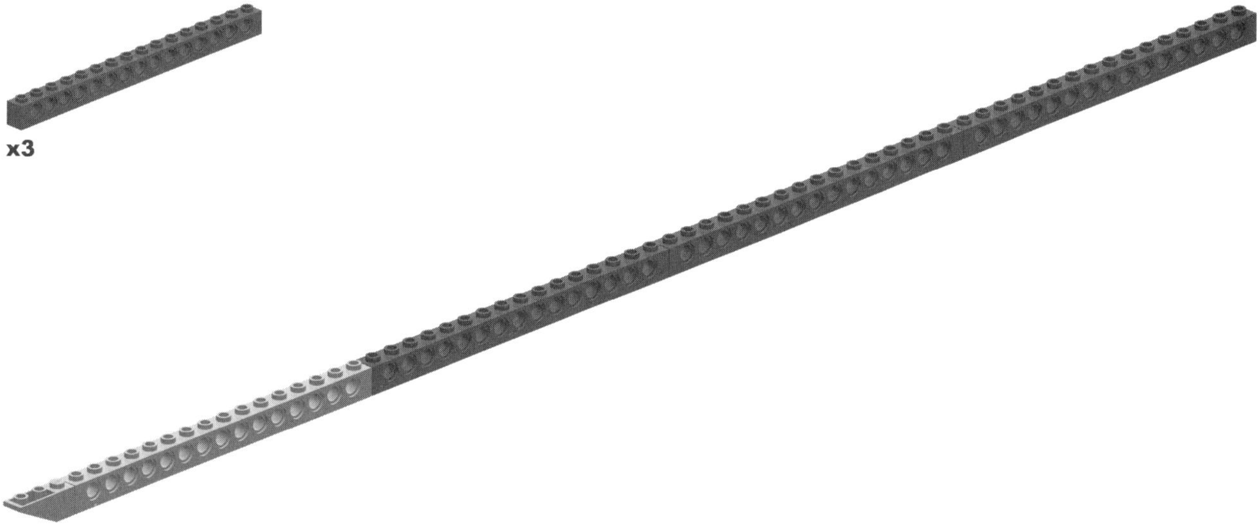

x3

3

x1

x2

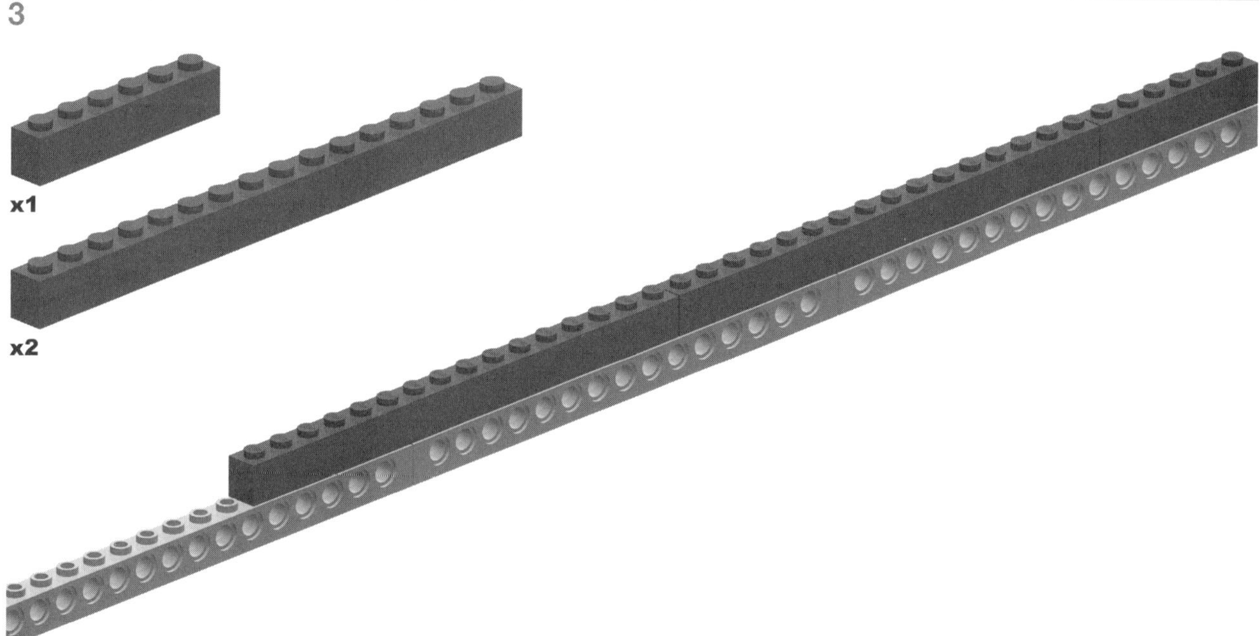

4

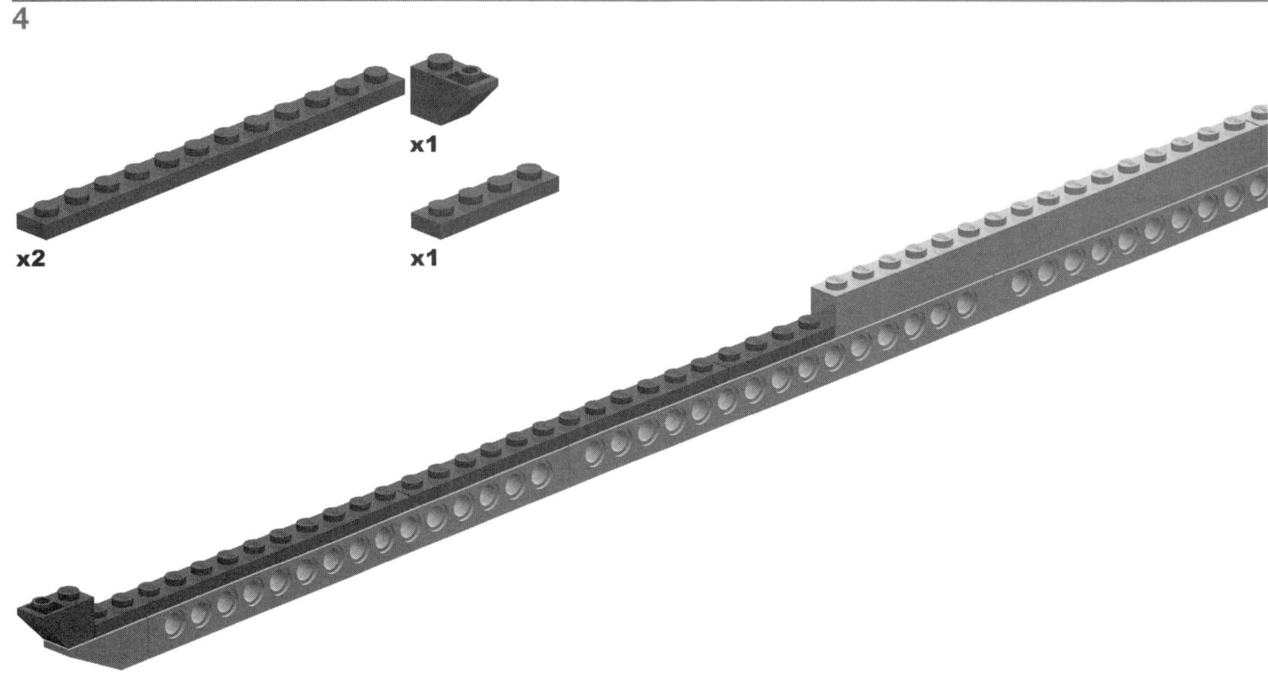

5

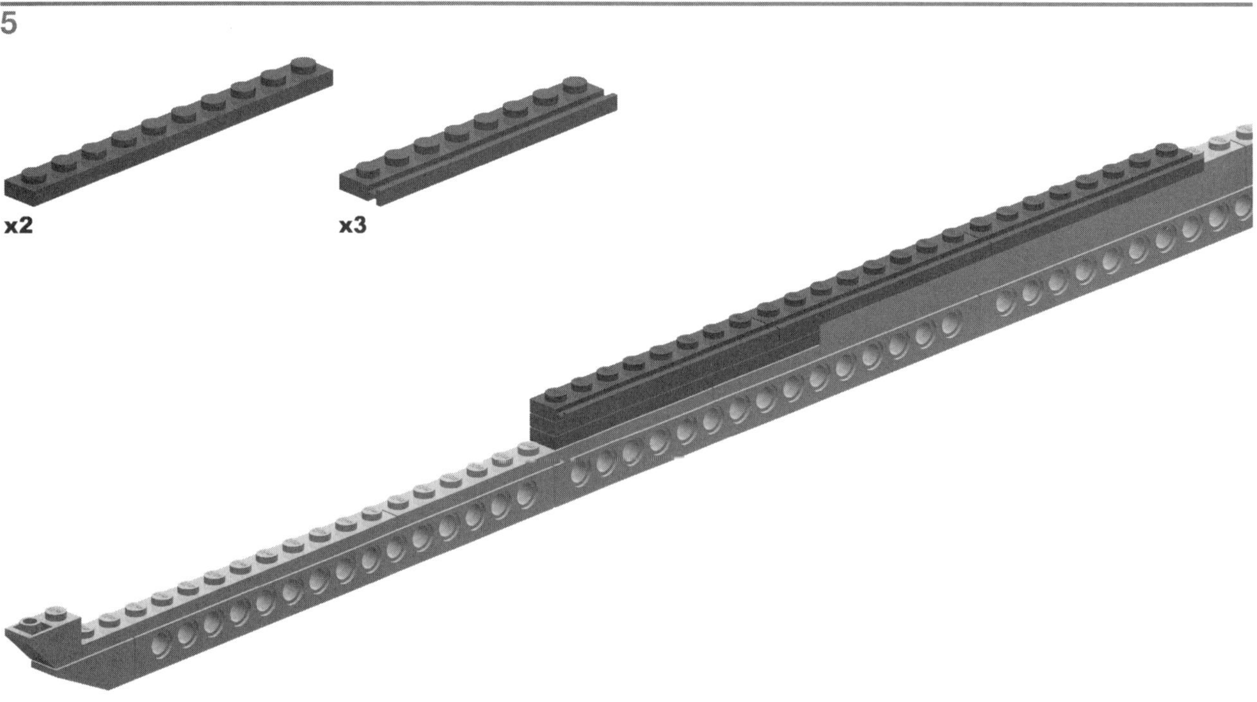

6

x2
x1
x1
x1
x2

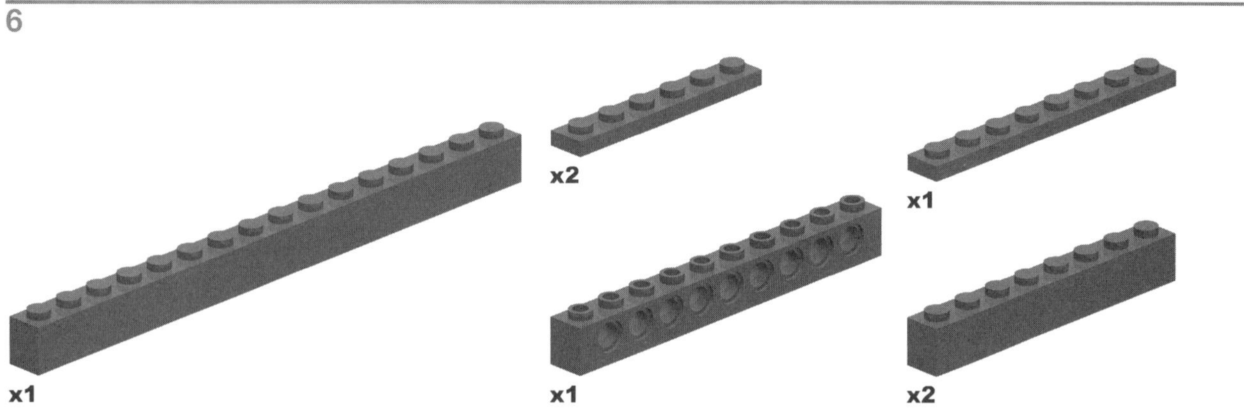

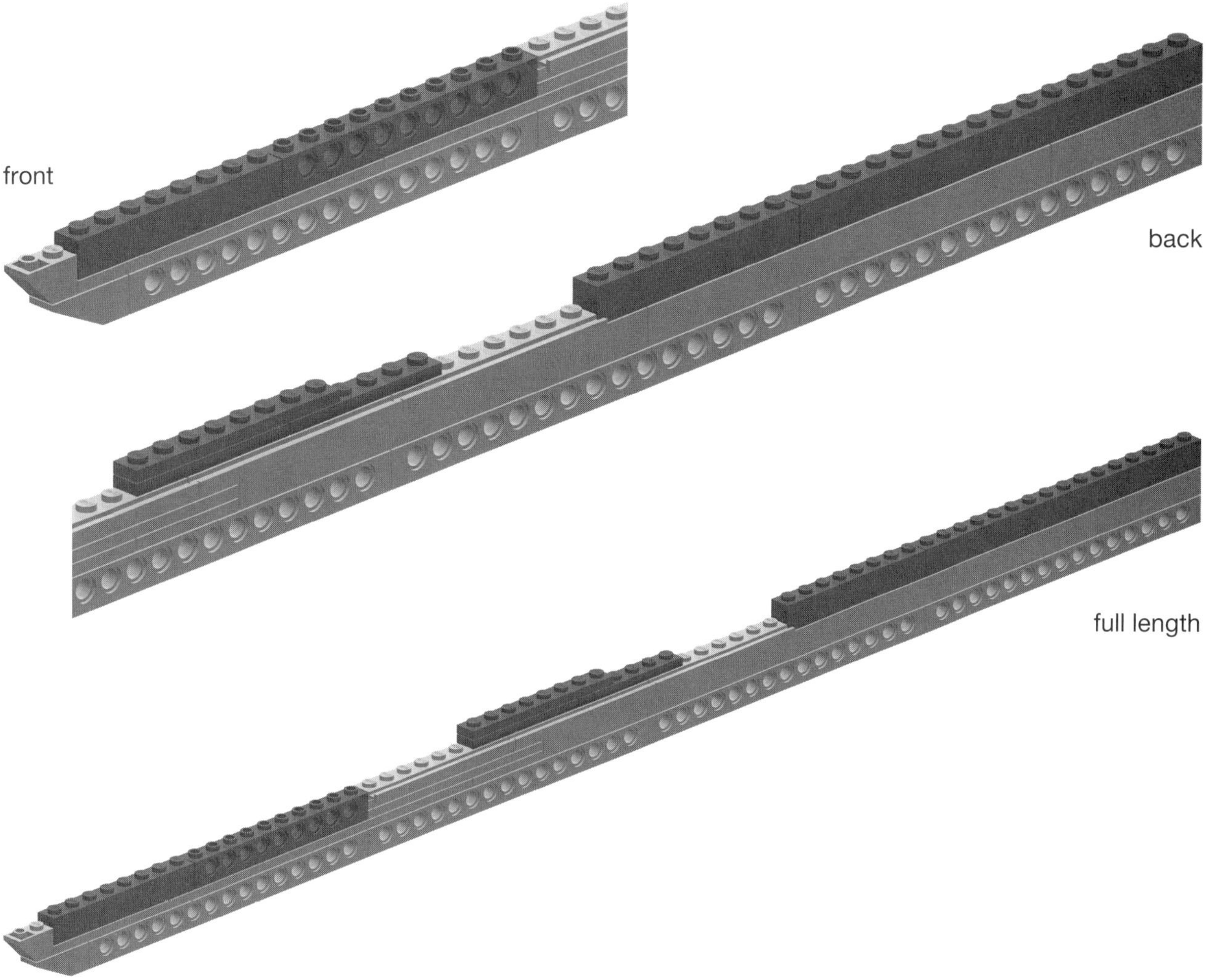

front
back
full length

7

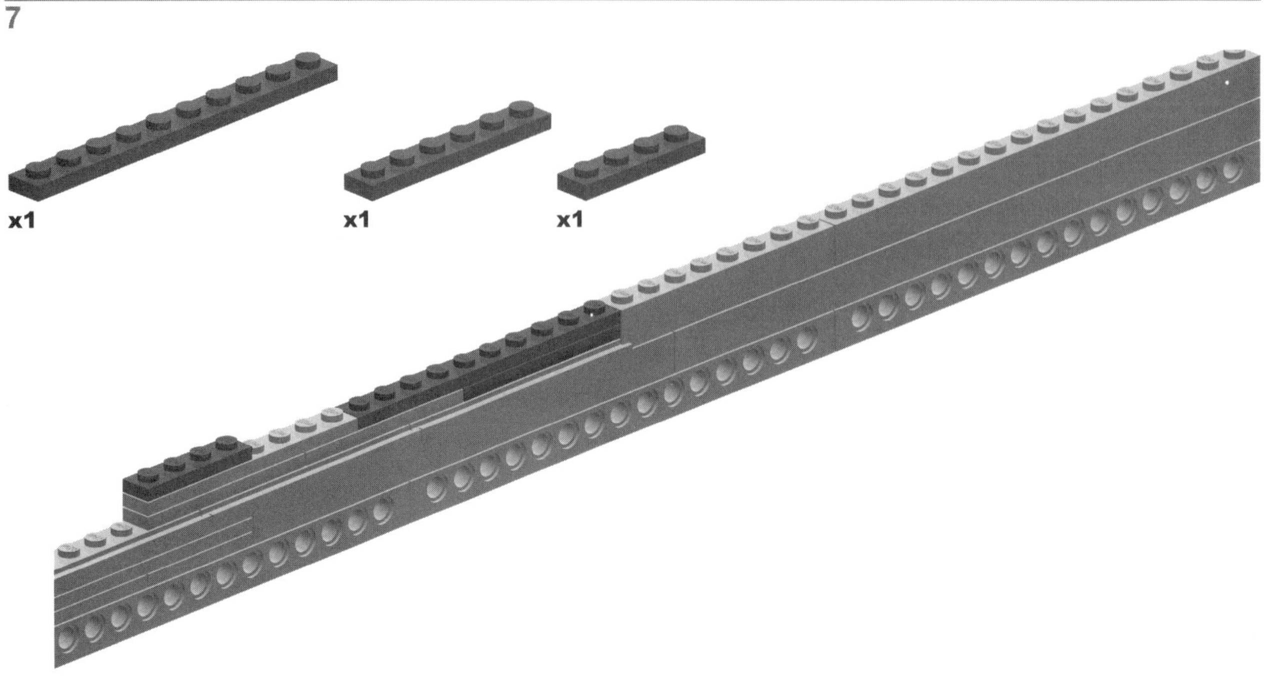

8

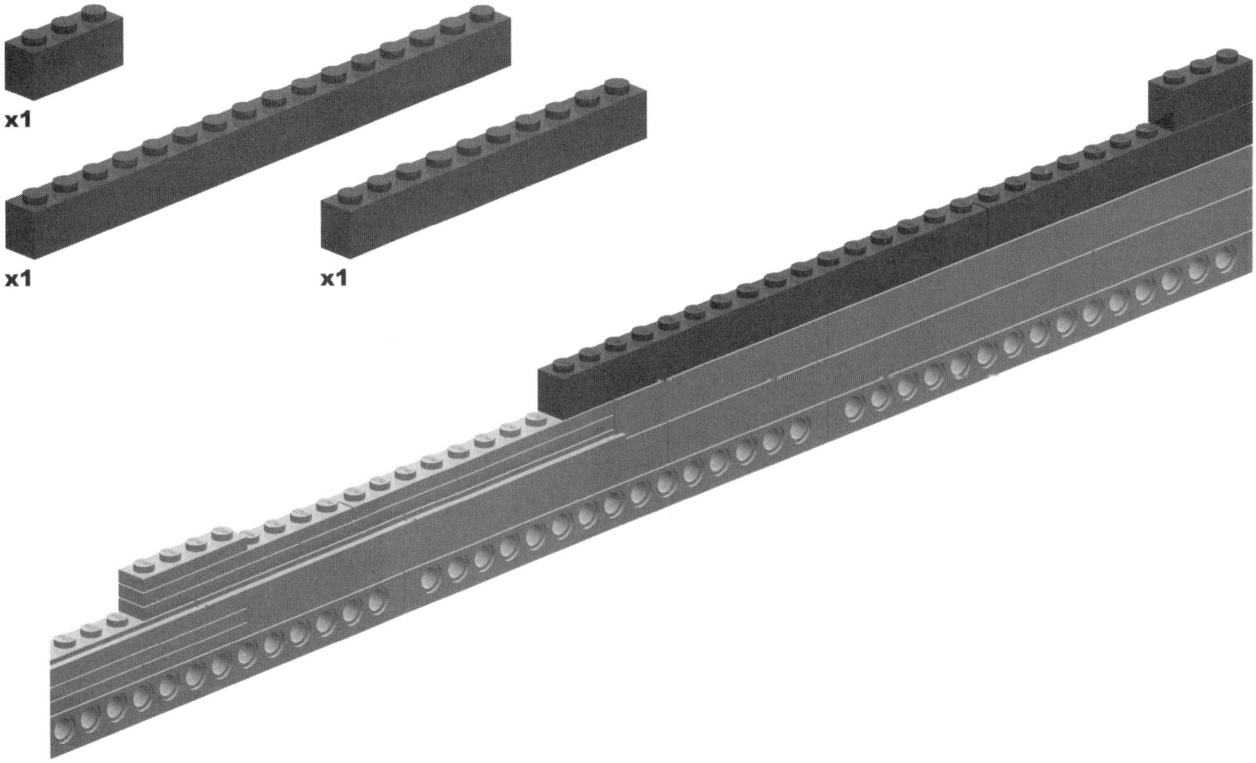

x1

x1

x1

9

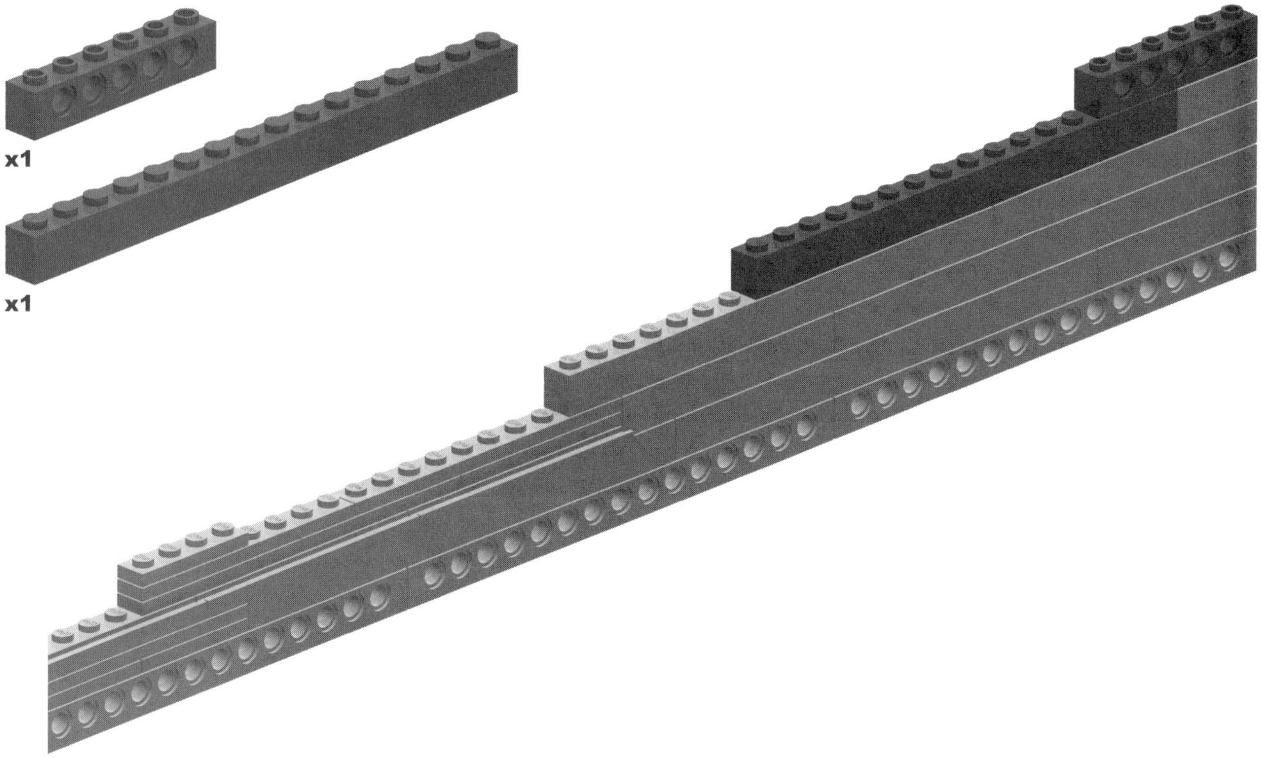

x1

x1

10

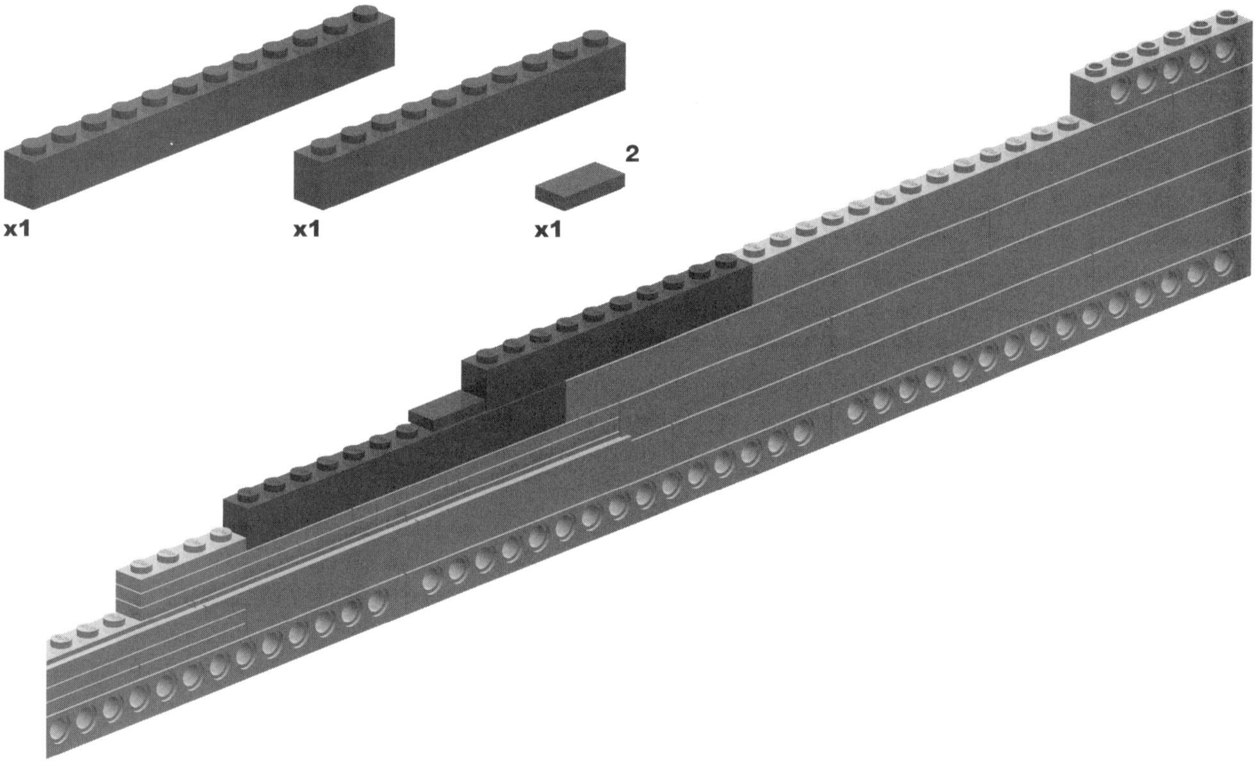

x1

x1

2

x1

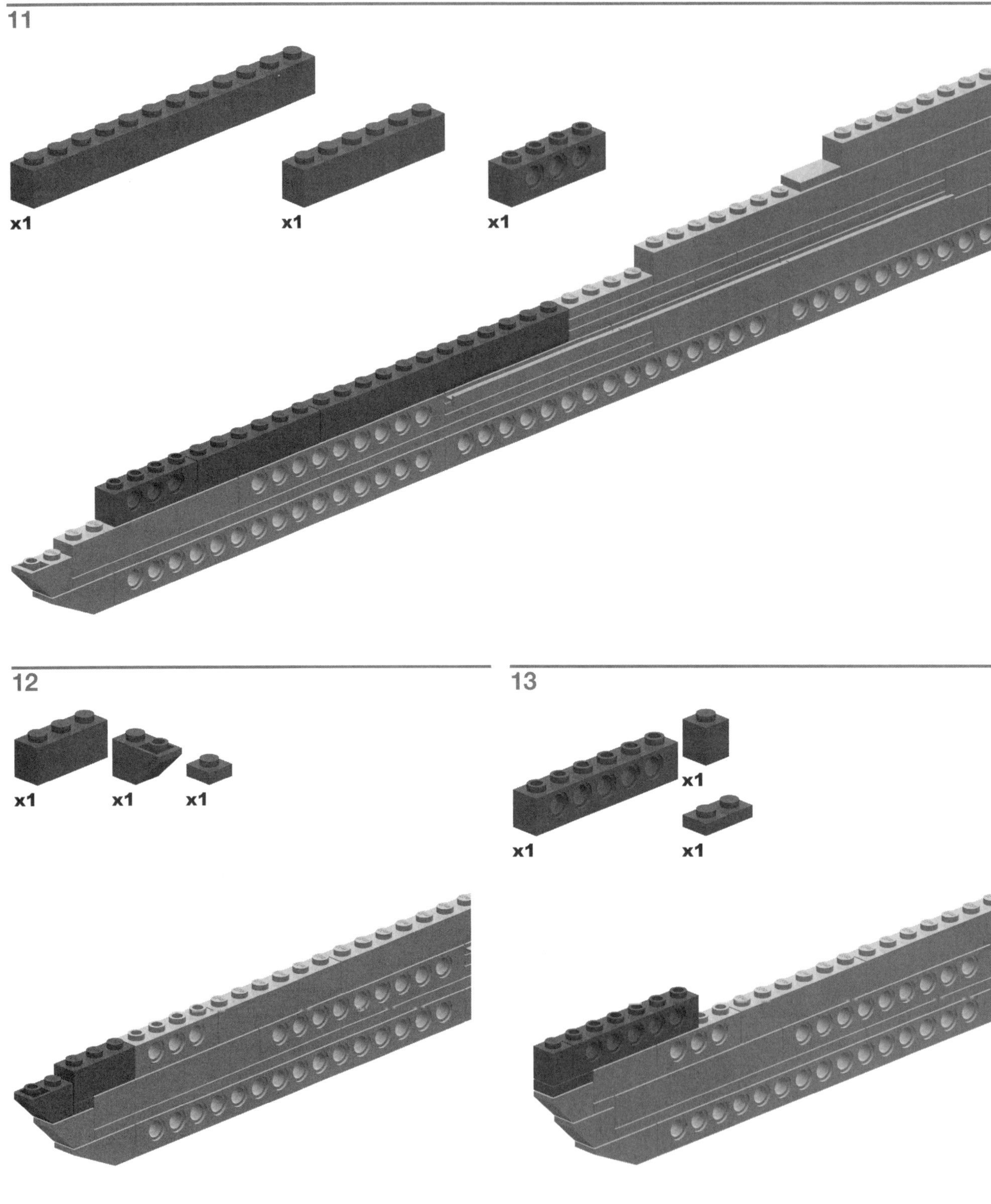
11
x1
x1
x1
12
x1
x1
x1
13
x1
x1
x1
x1

14

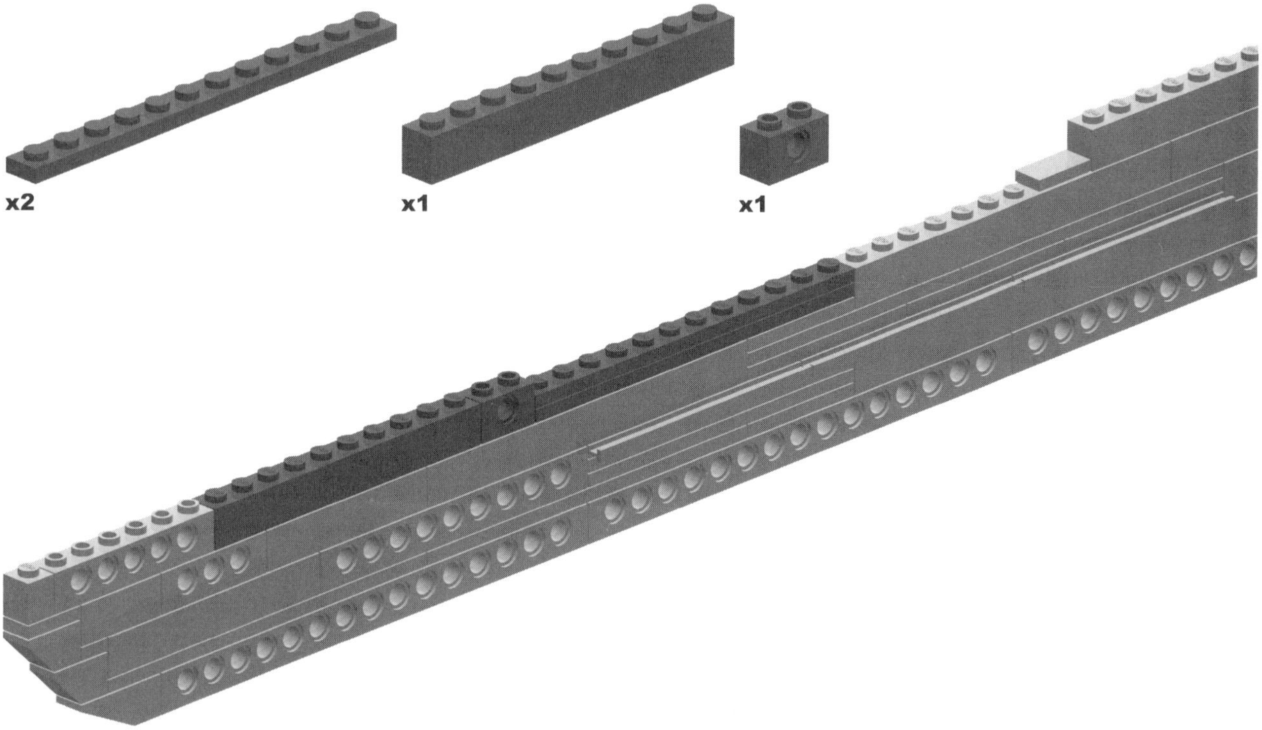

x2

x1

x1

15

x1

x1

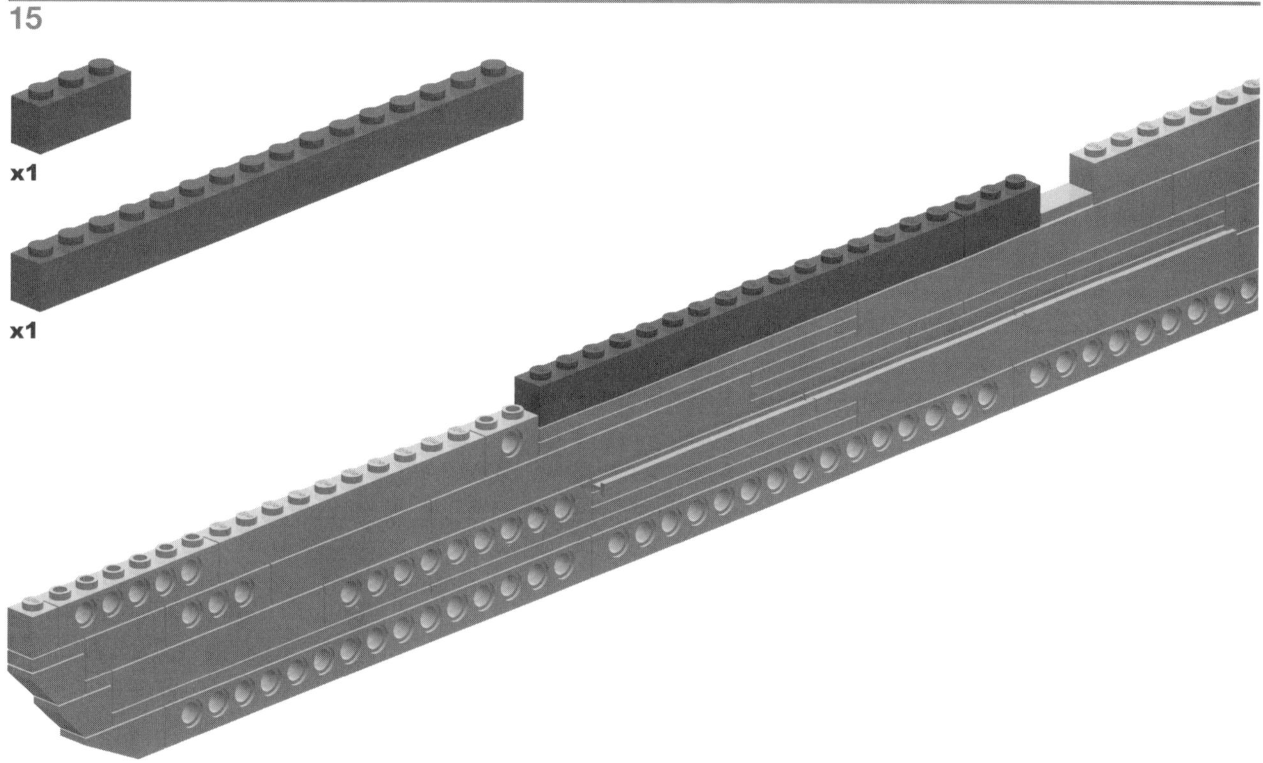

16

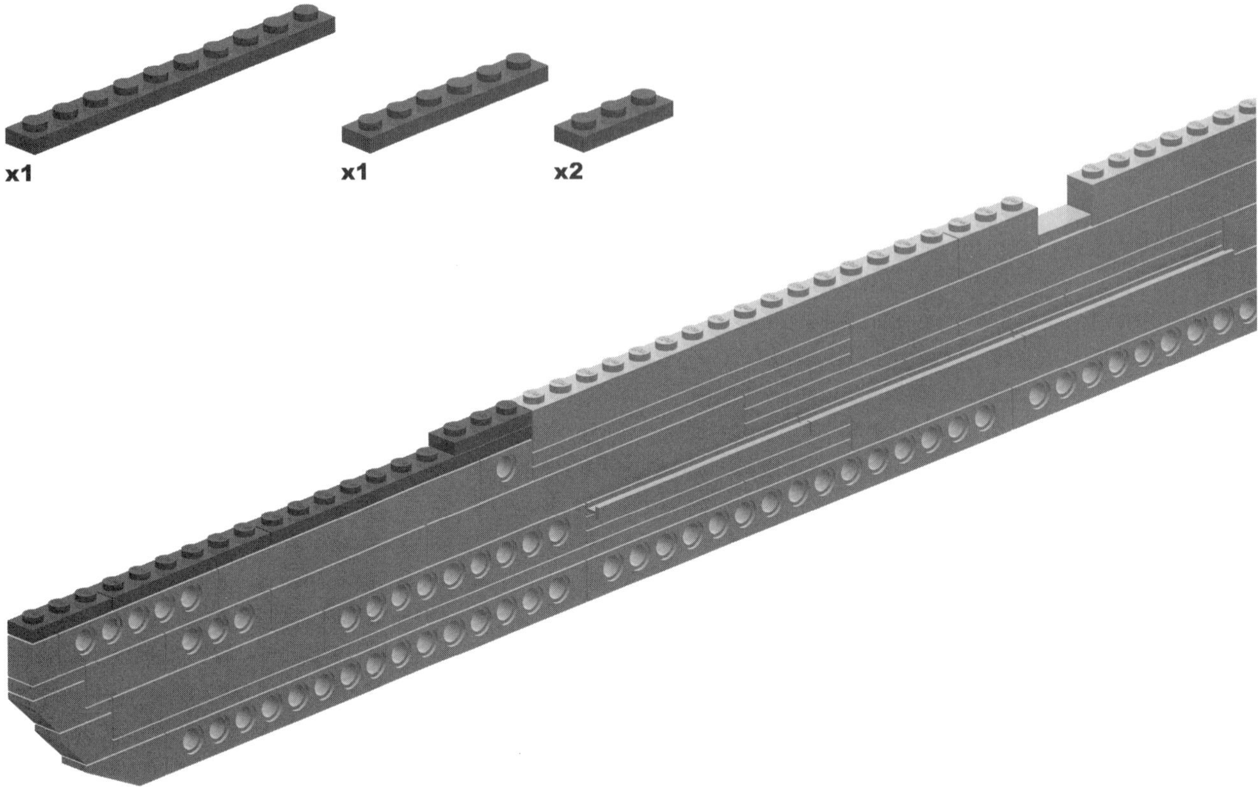

x1

x1

x2

17

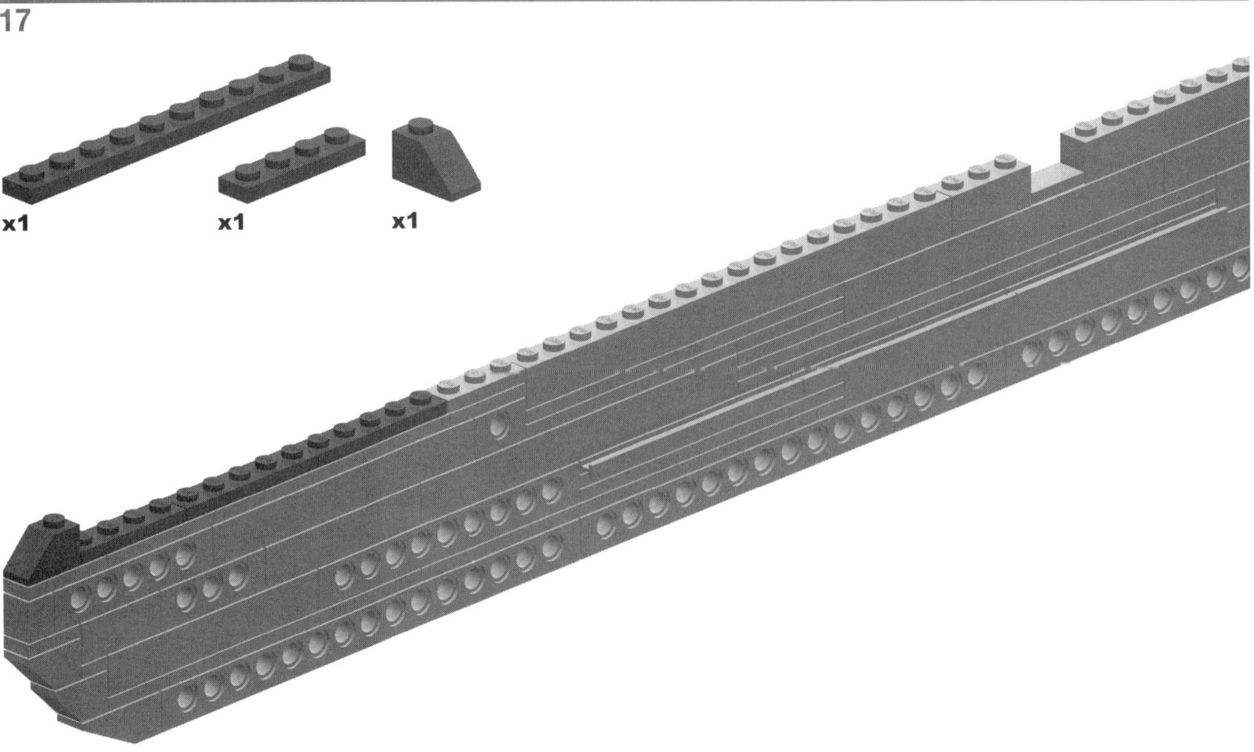

18

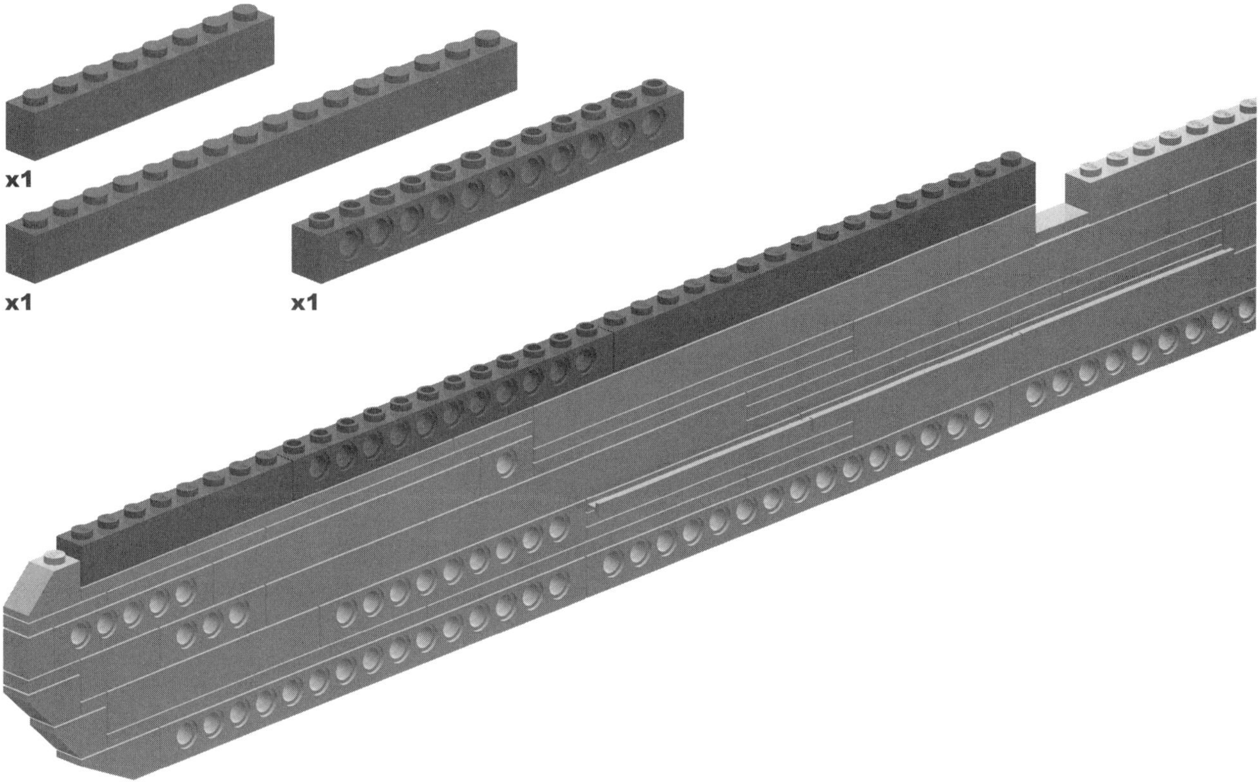

x1

x1

x1

19

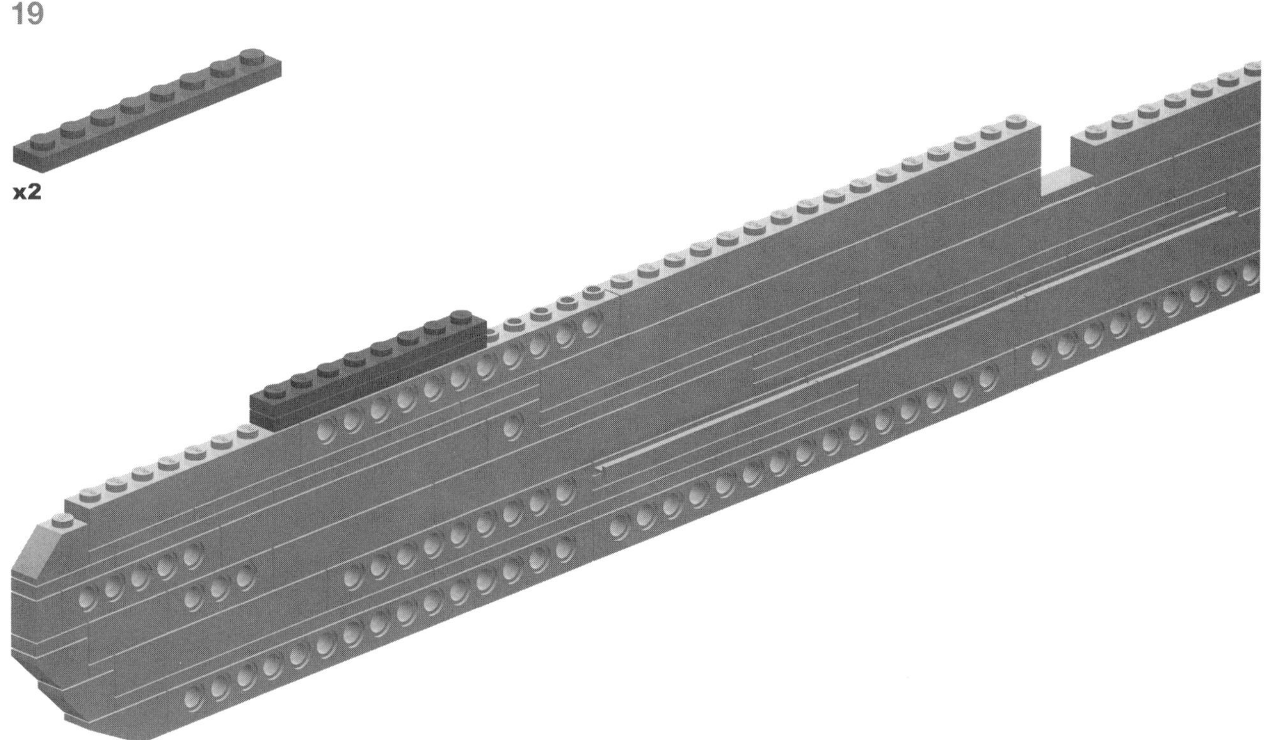

20

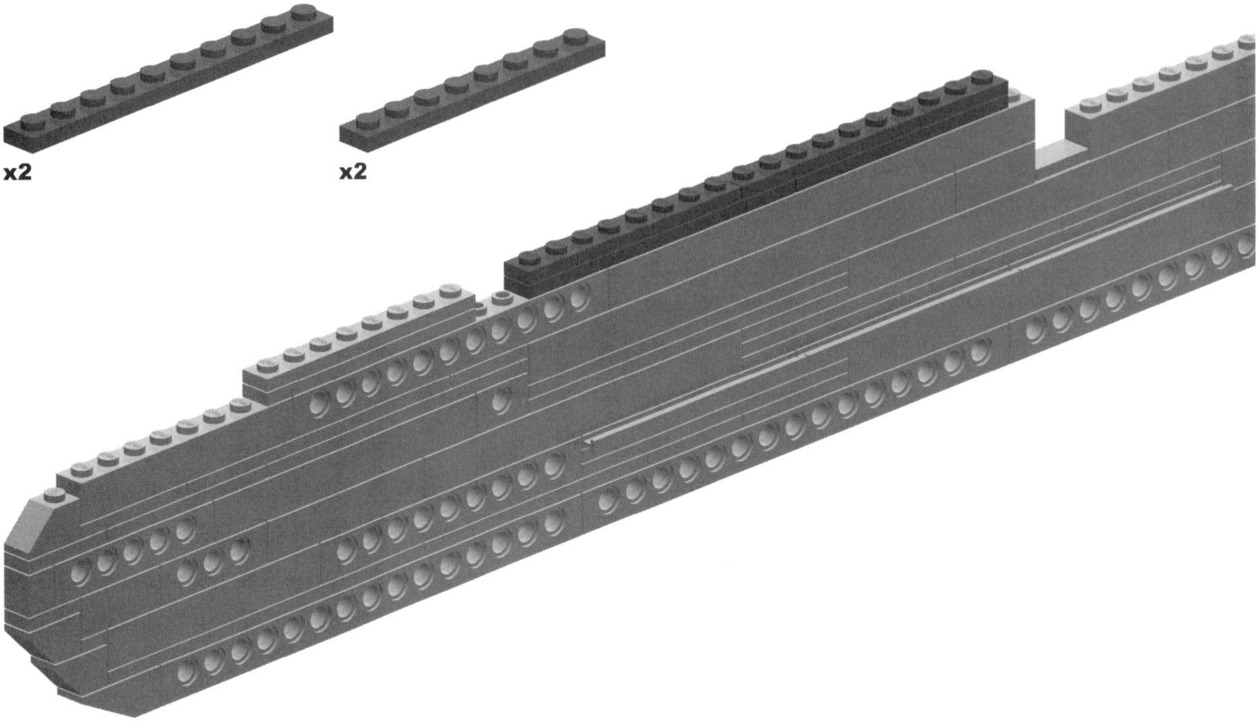

x2

x2

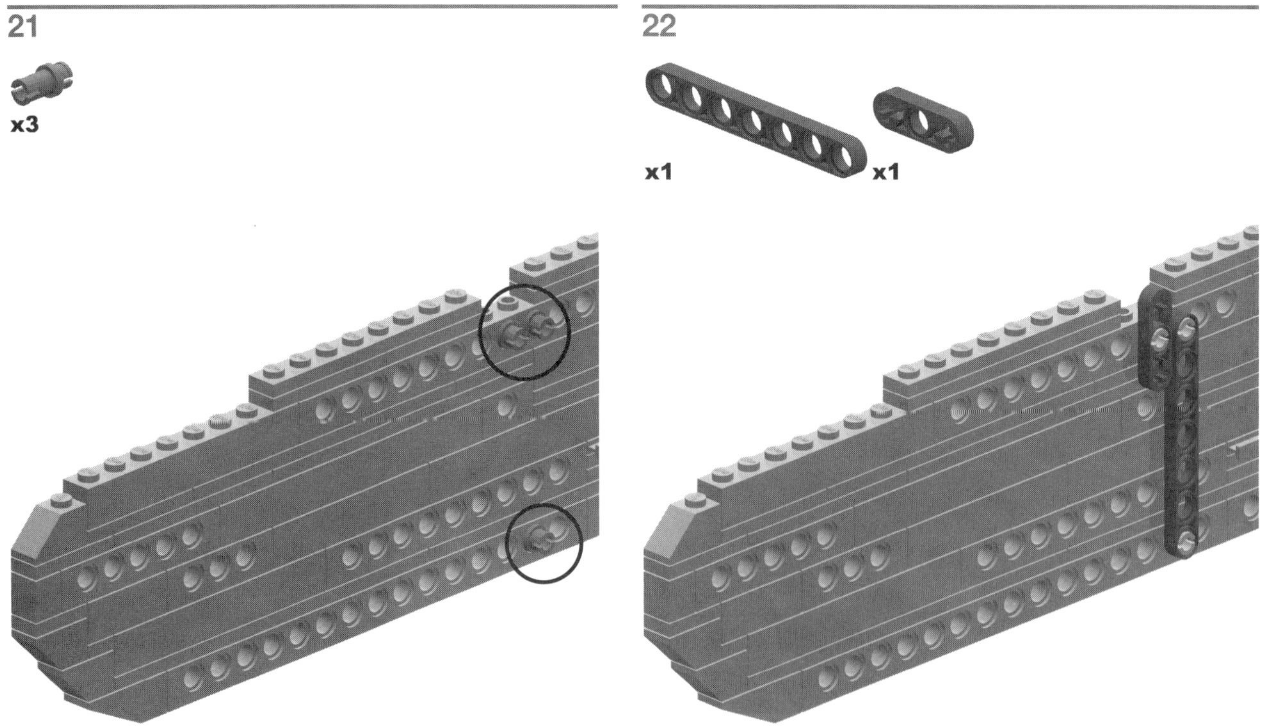

ROOF PLATE

1

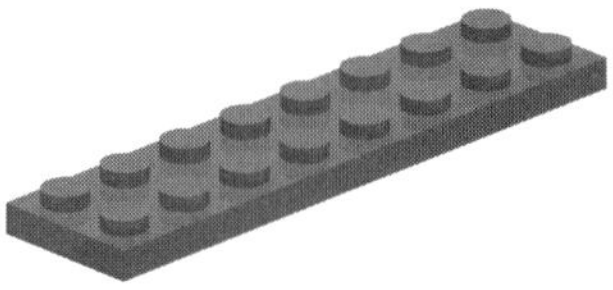

x1

x1

2

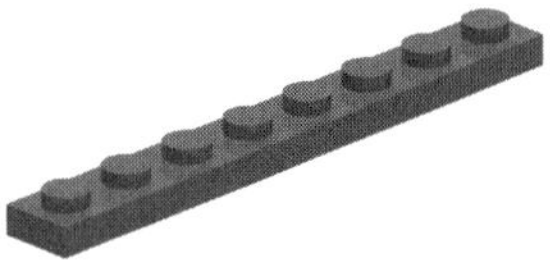

x1

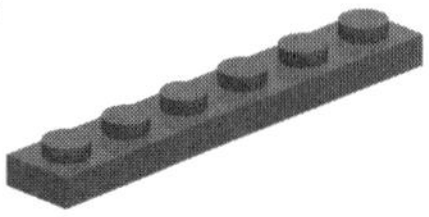

x1

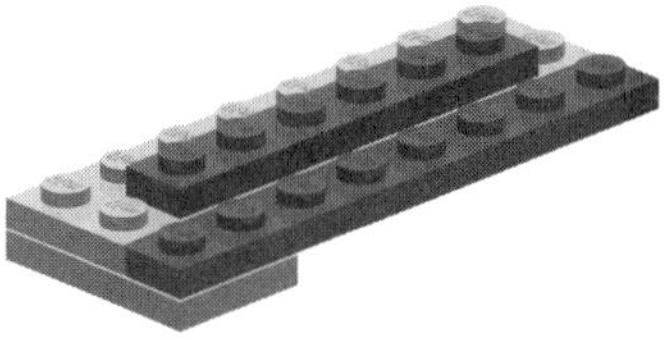

3

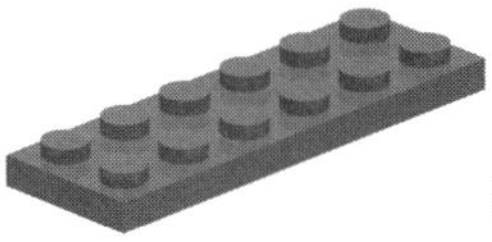

x2

x1

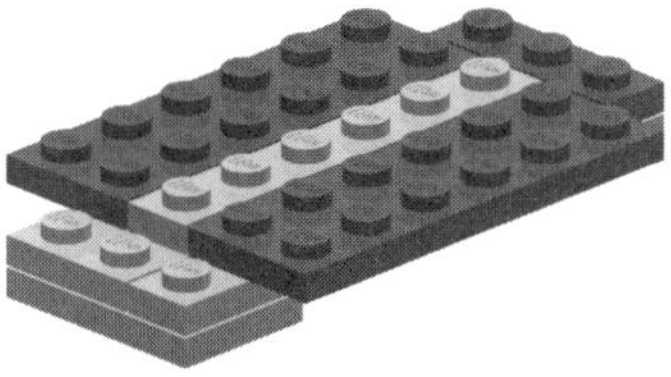

4

x3

x2

FORE GRIP LEFT

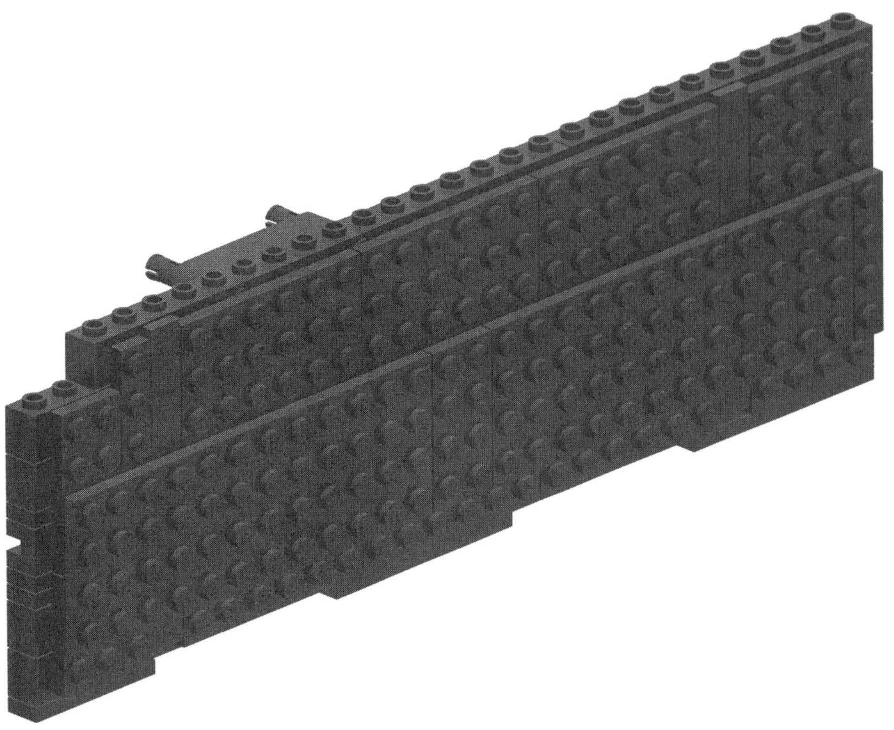

1

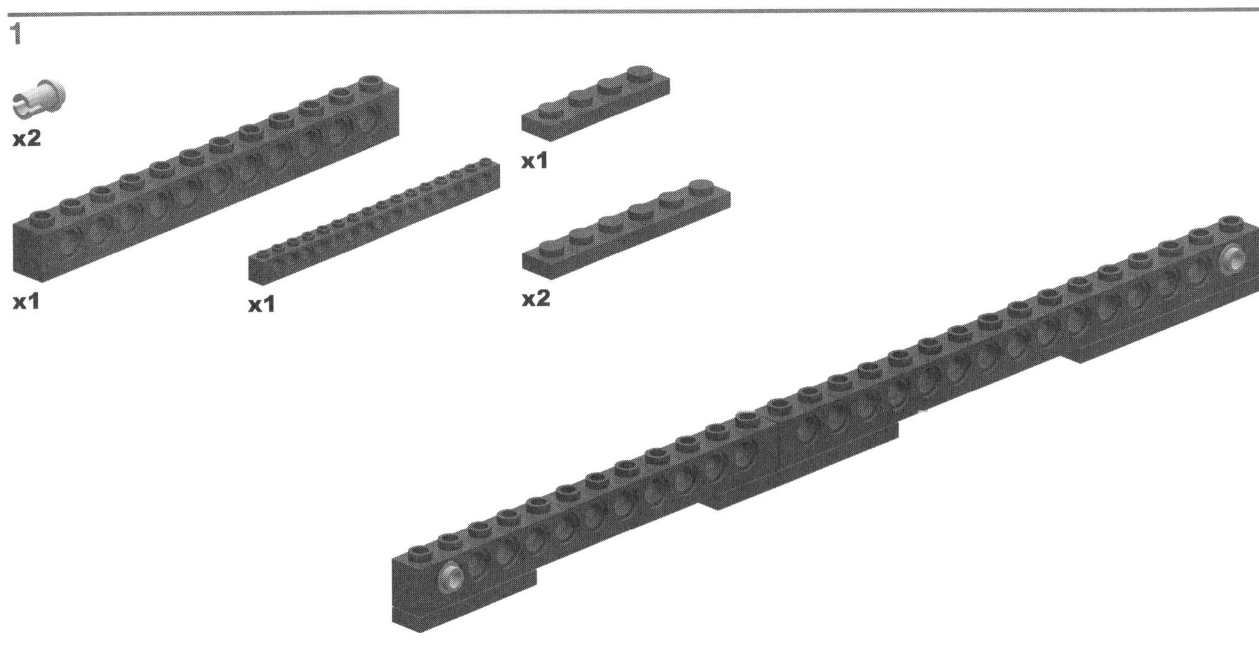

2

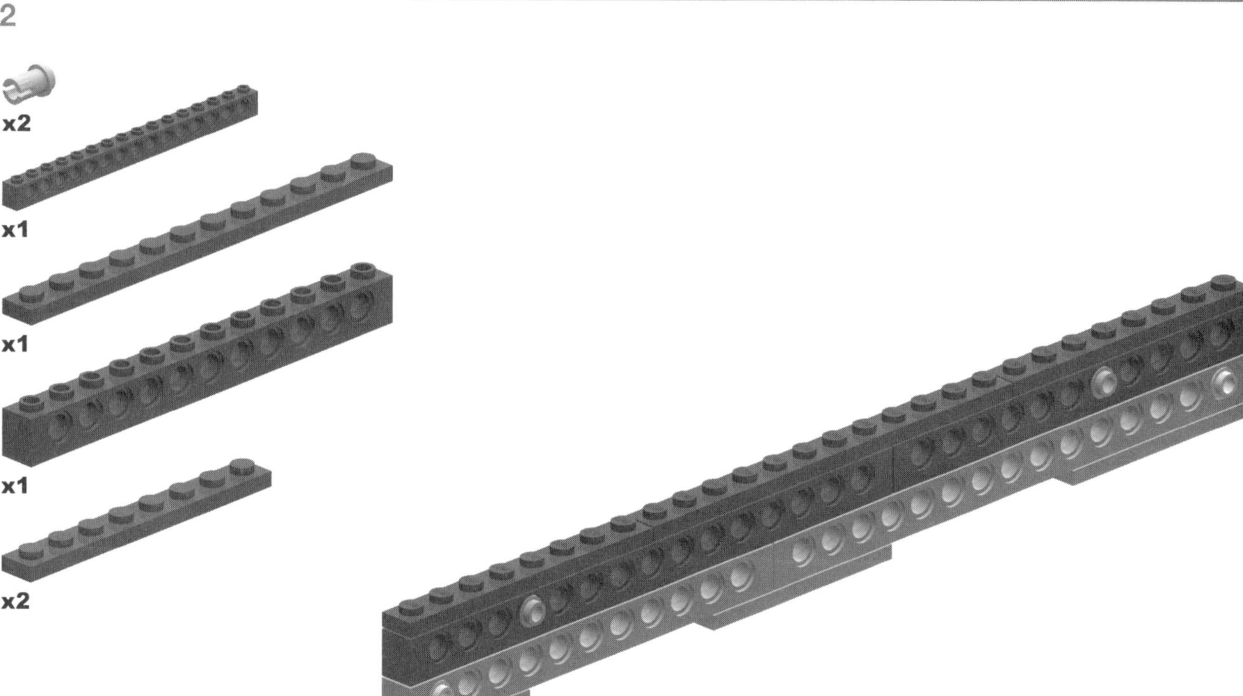

3

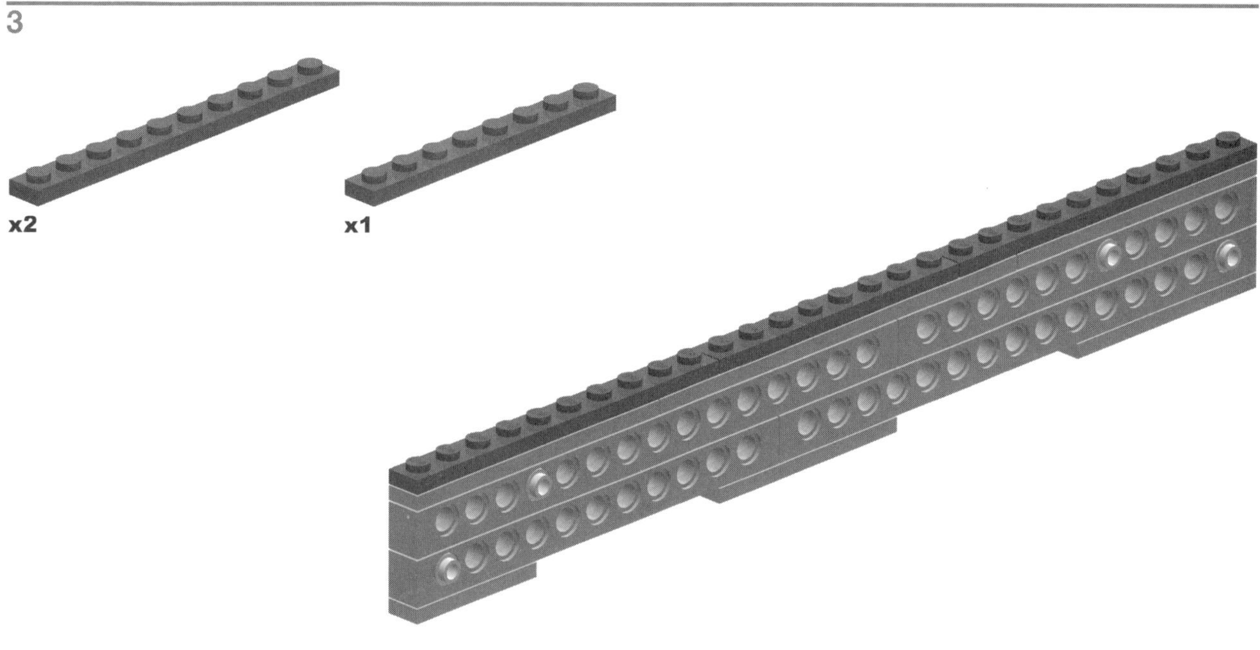

4

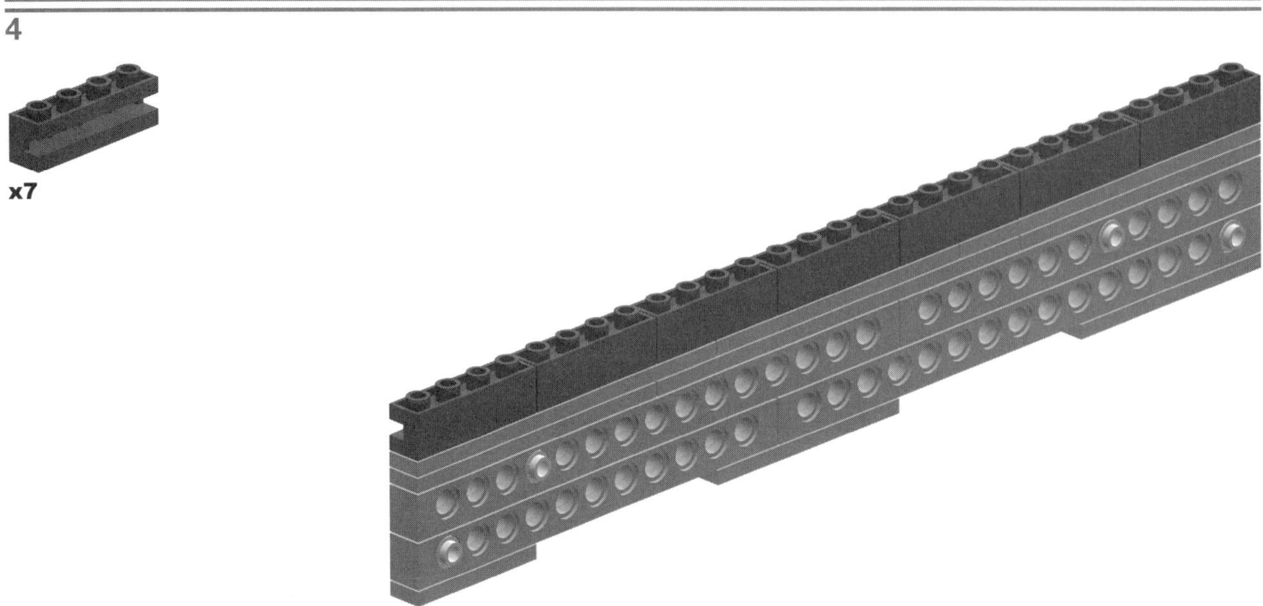

5

x1

x1

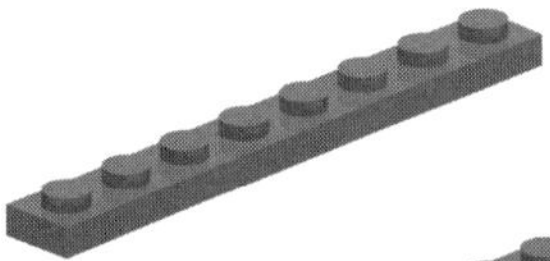

x1

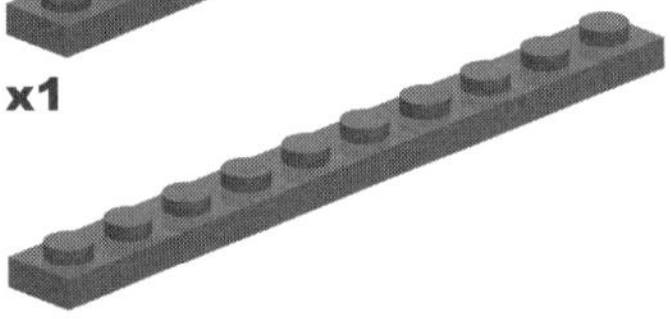

x2

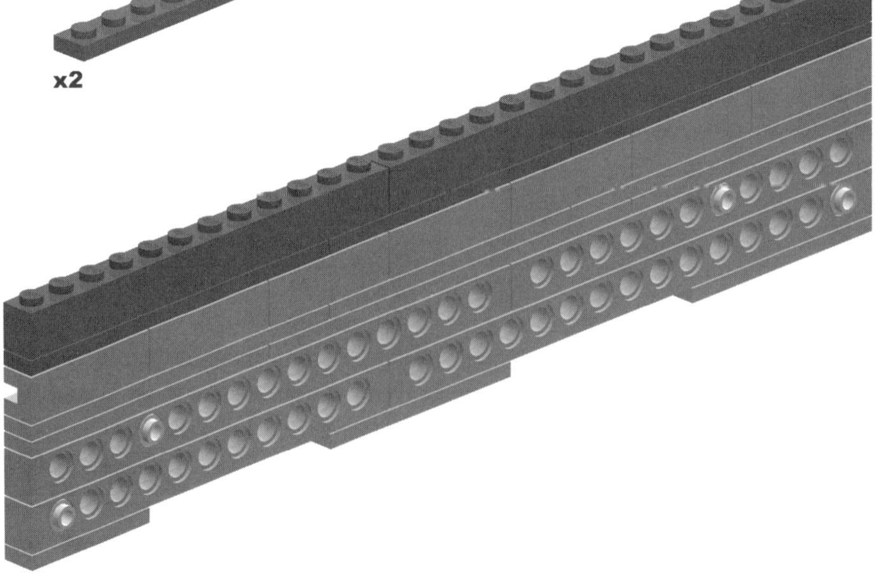

6

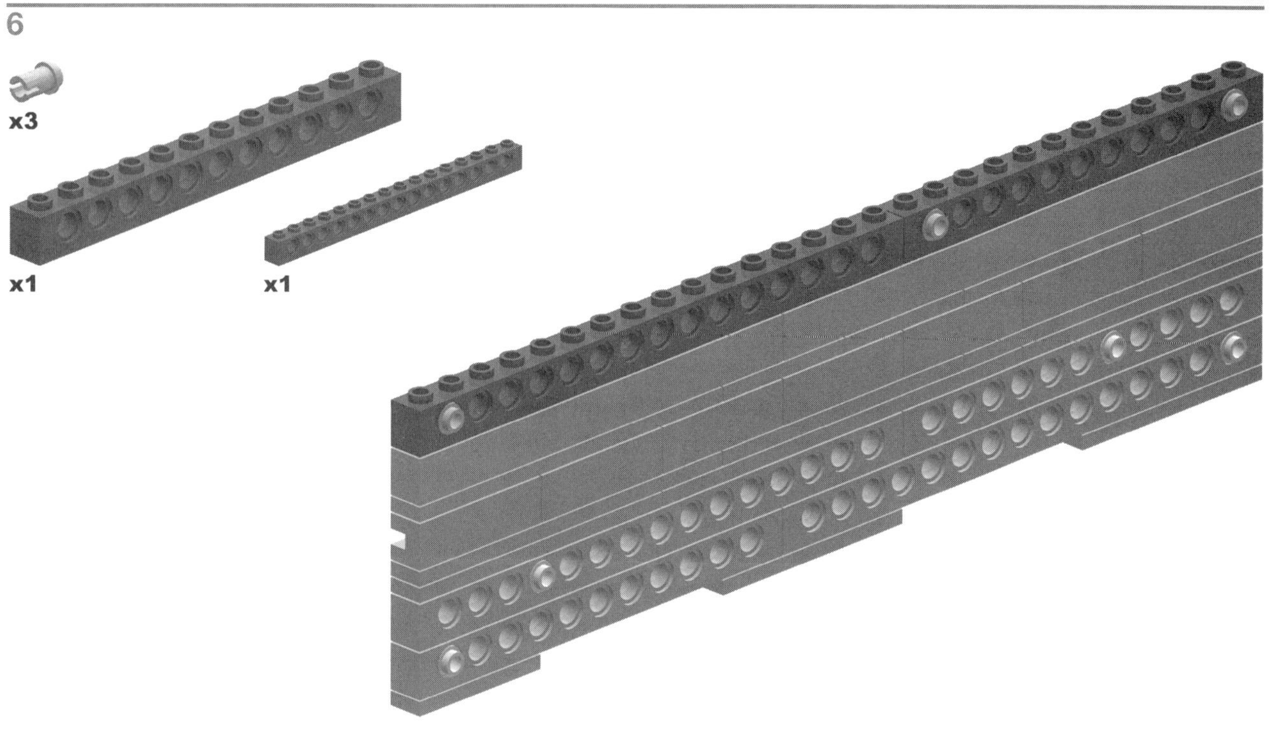

7

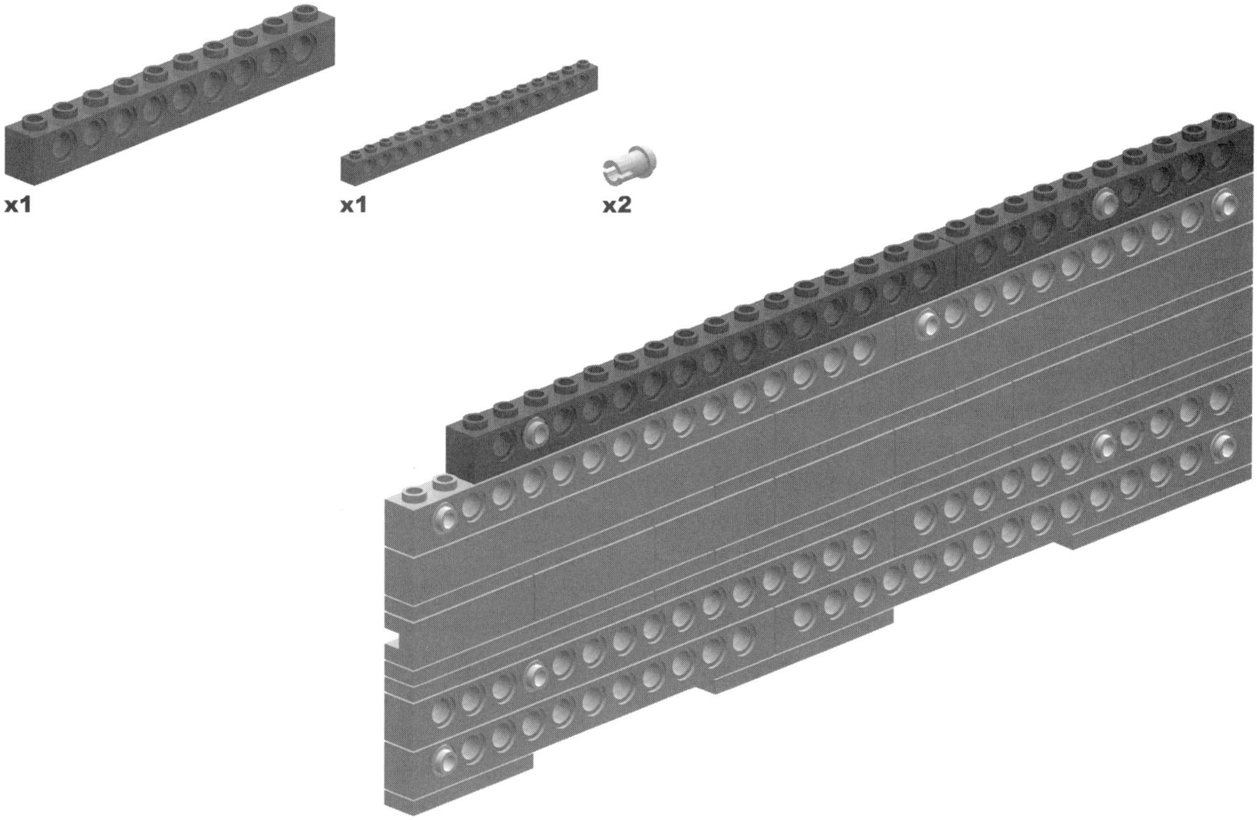

x1

x1

x2

8

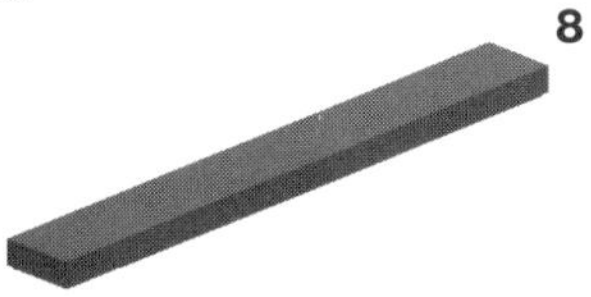

8

x2

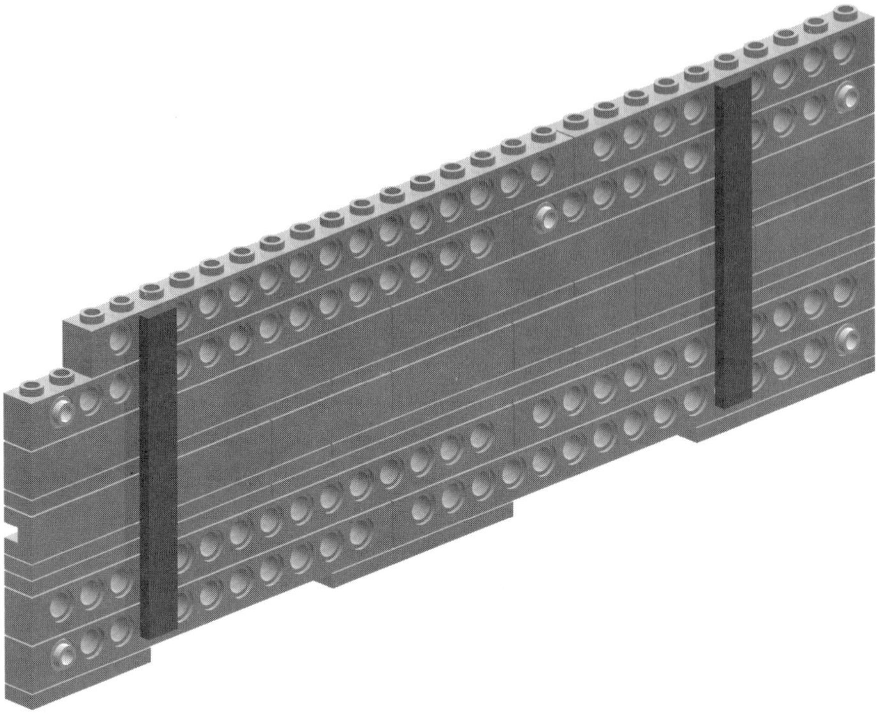

9

x1

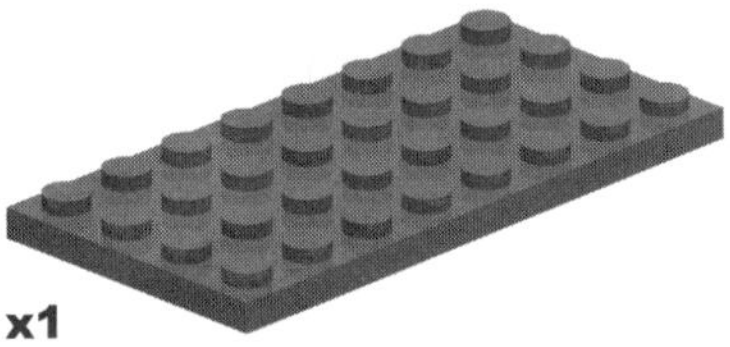

x1

x1

x1

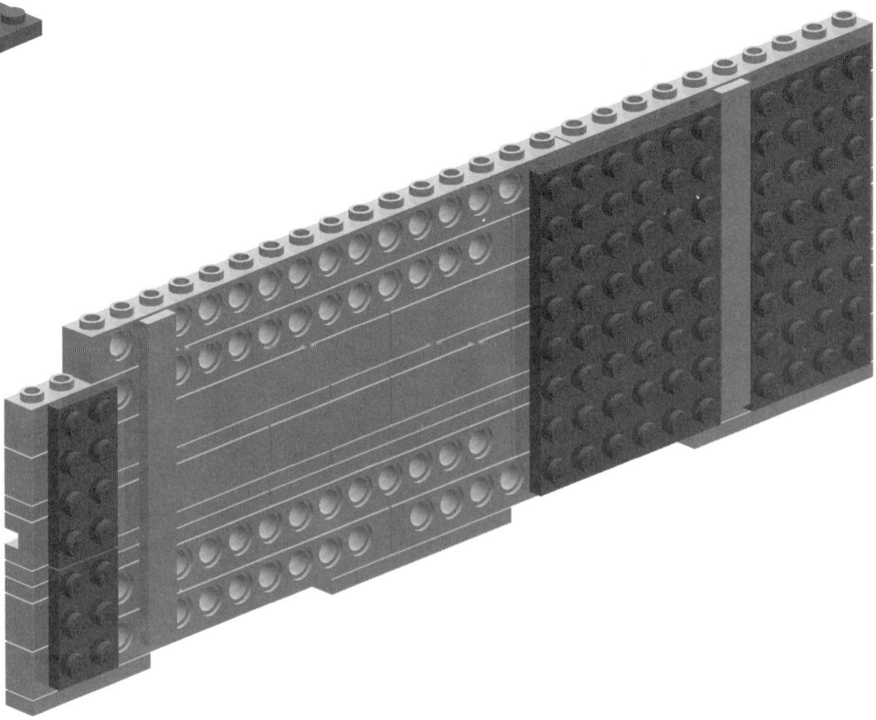

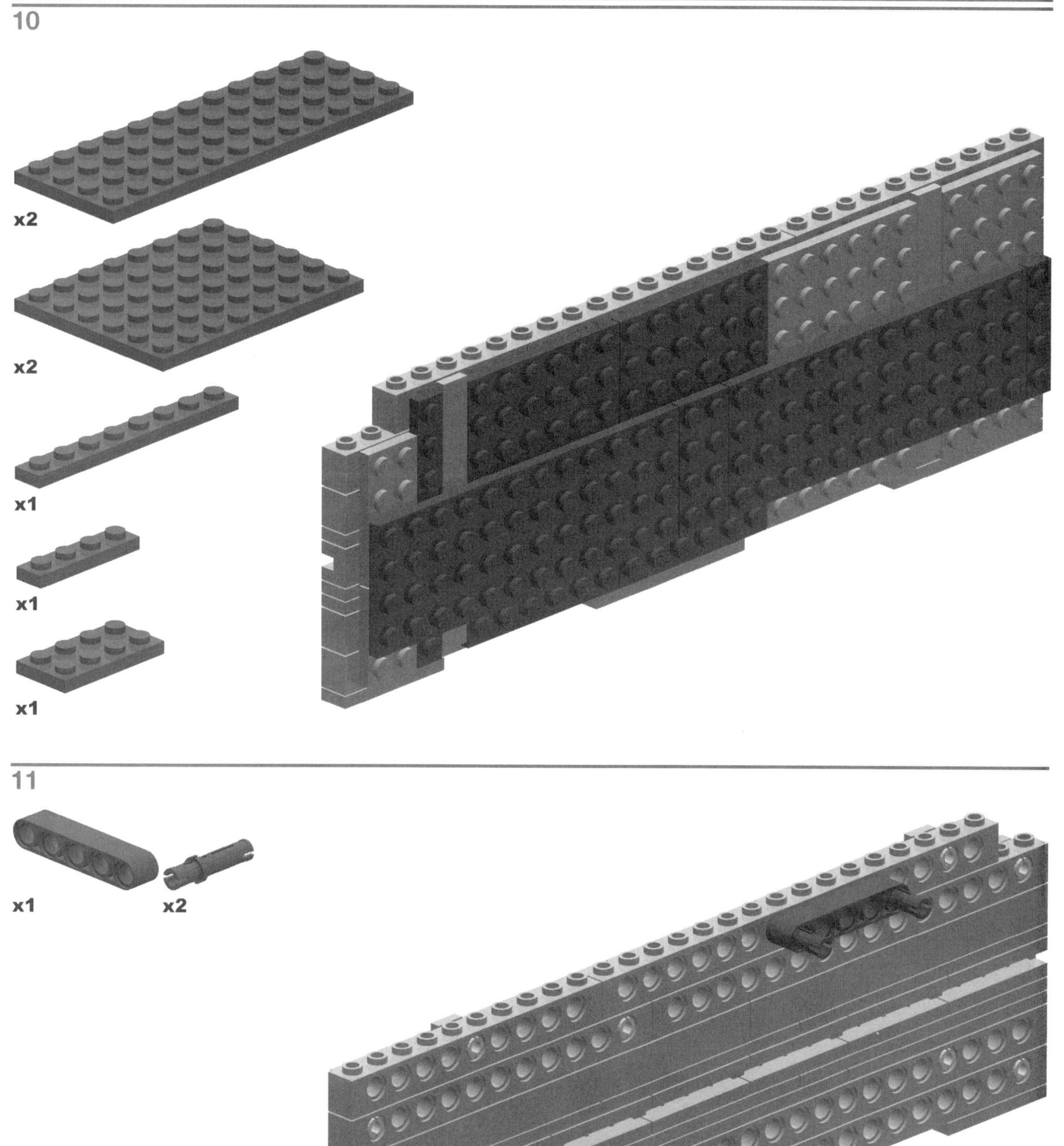
10
x2
x2
x1
x1
x1
11
x1
x2

12

x4

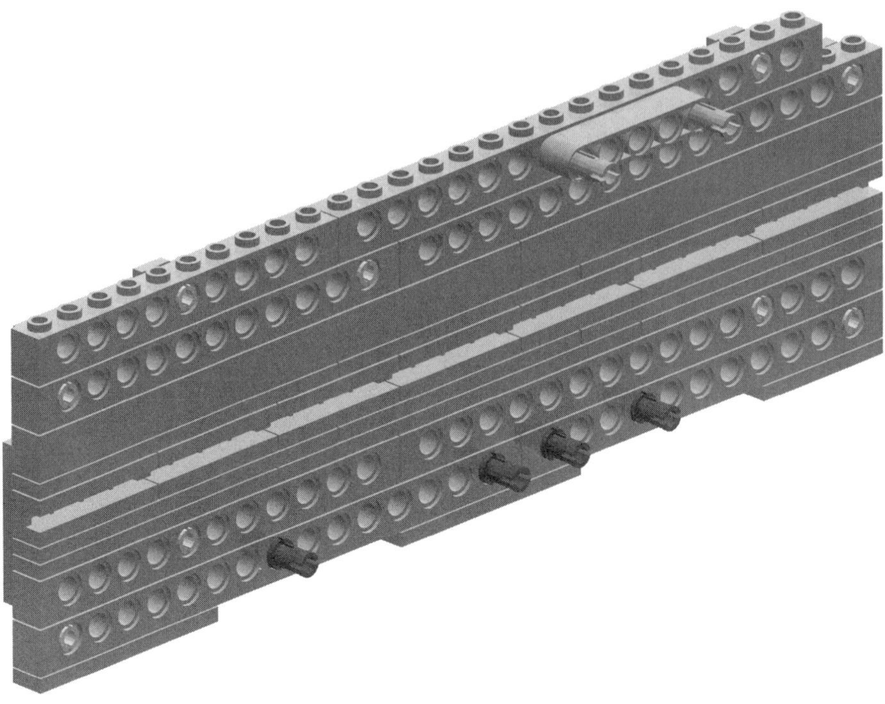

13

x3

x1

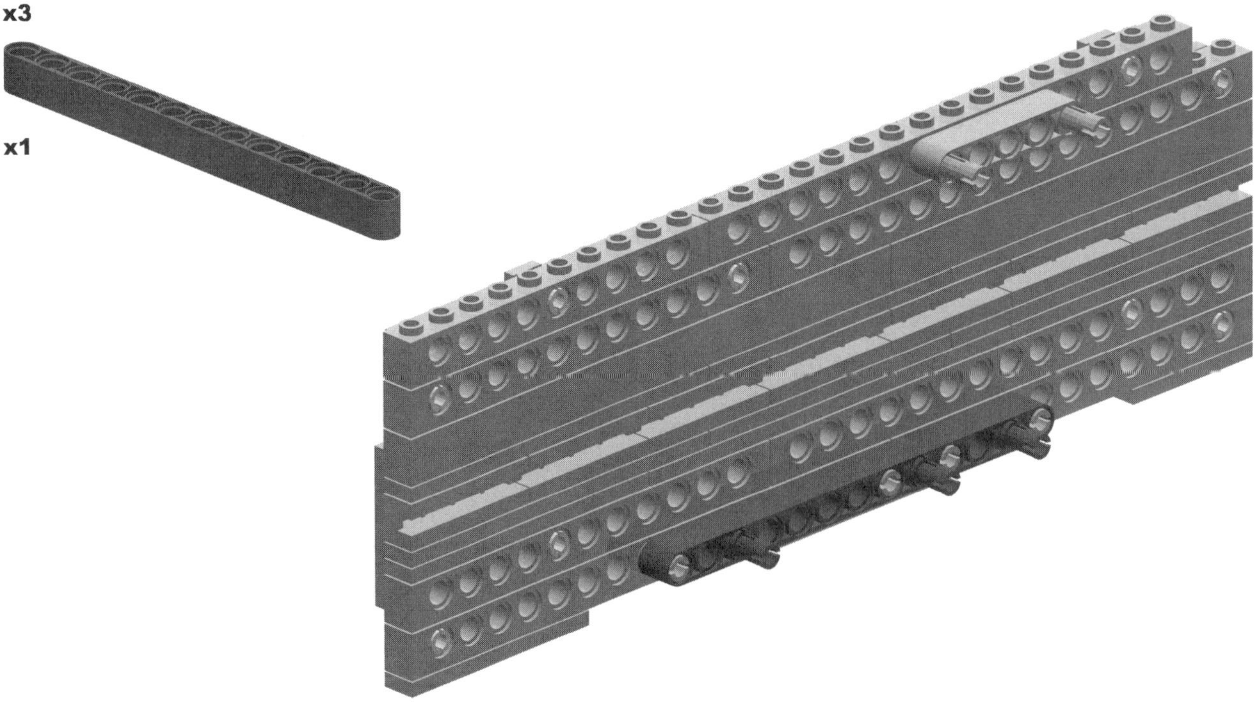

14

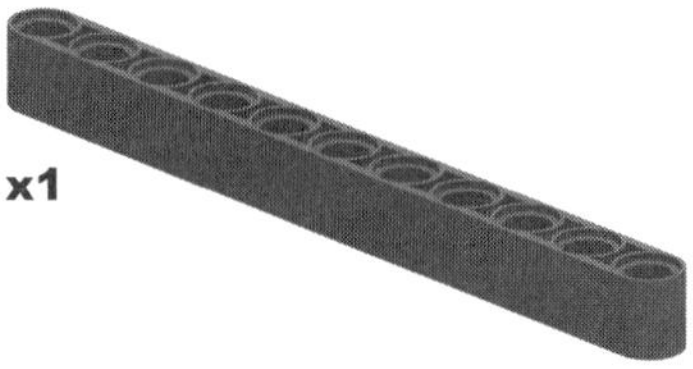

x1

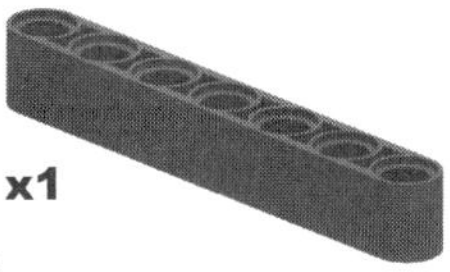

x1

x3

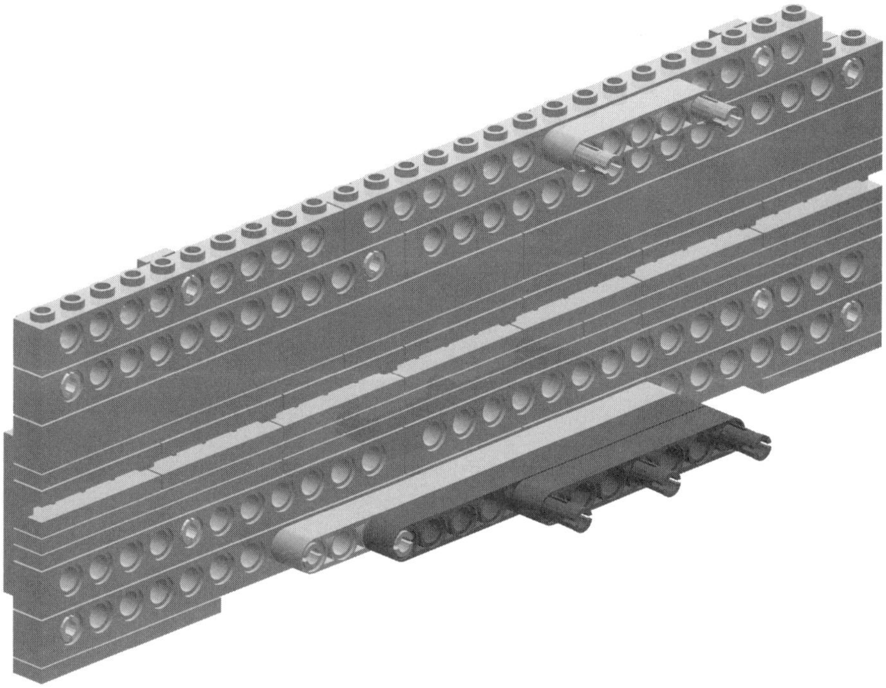

15

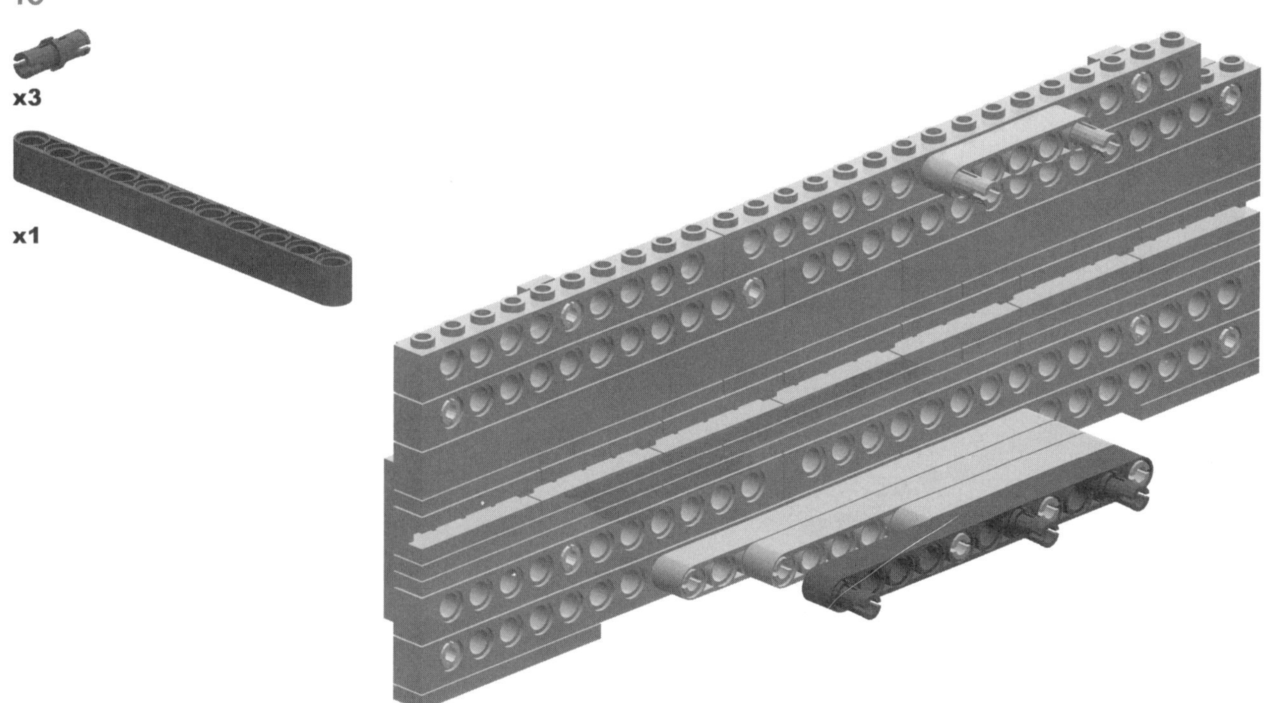

16

x4

x1

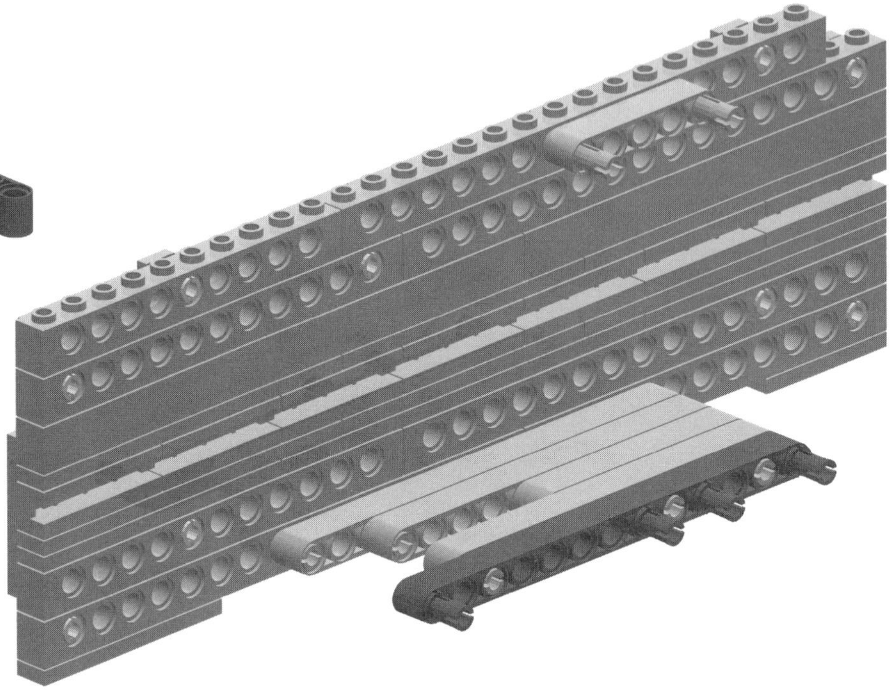

FORE GRIP RIGHT

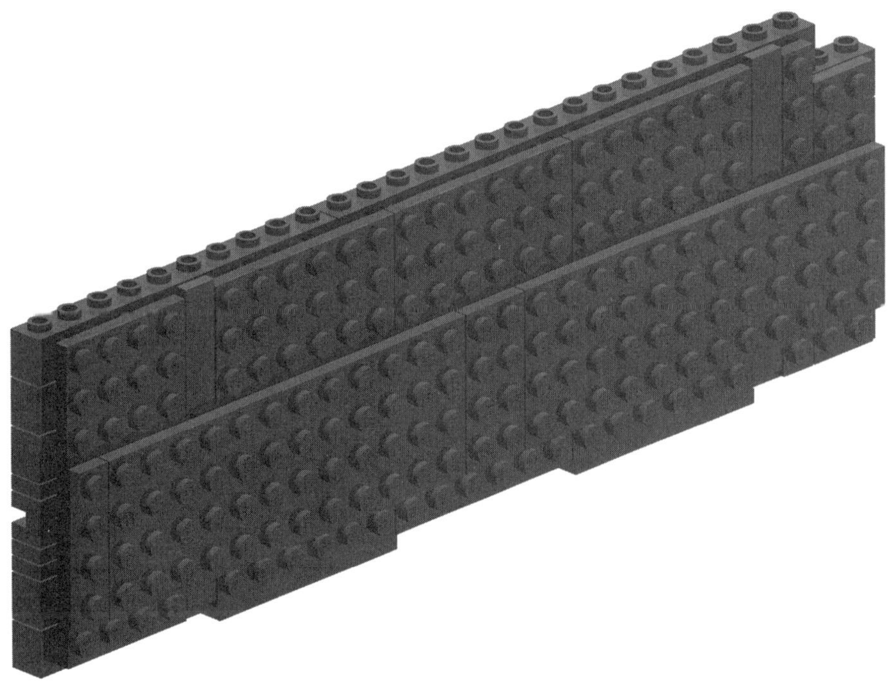

1

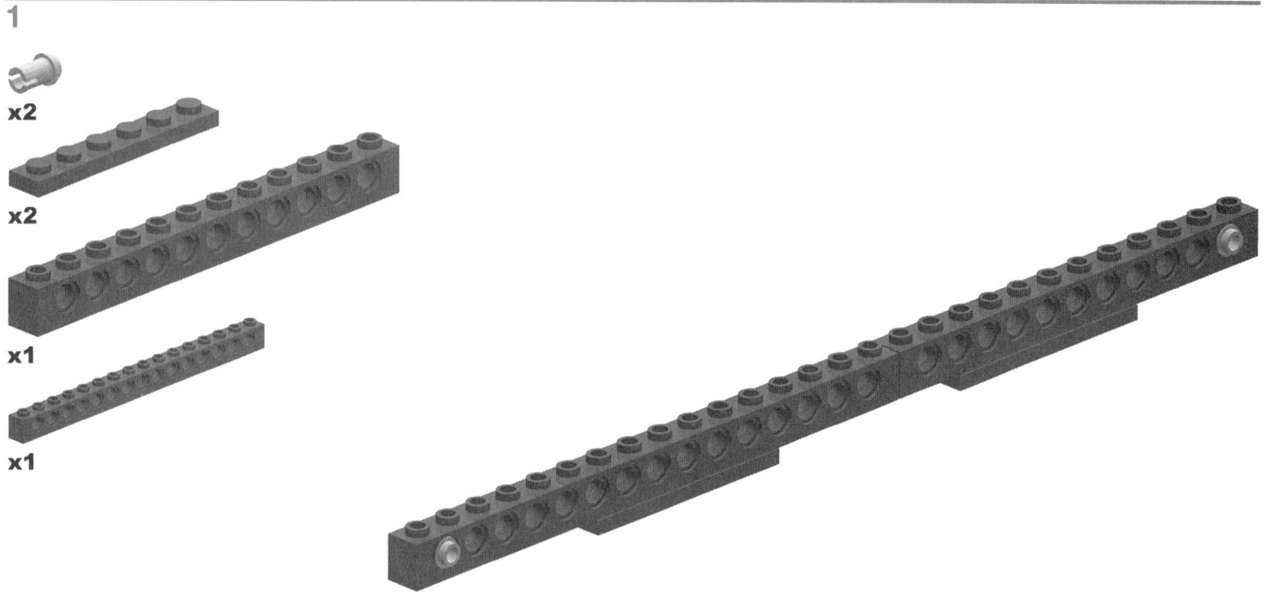

2

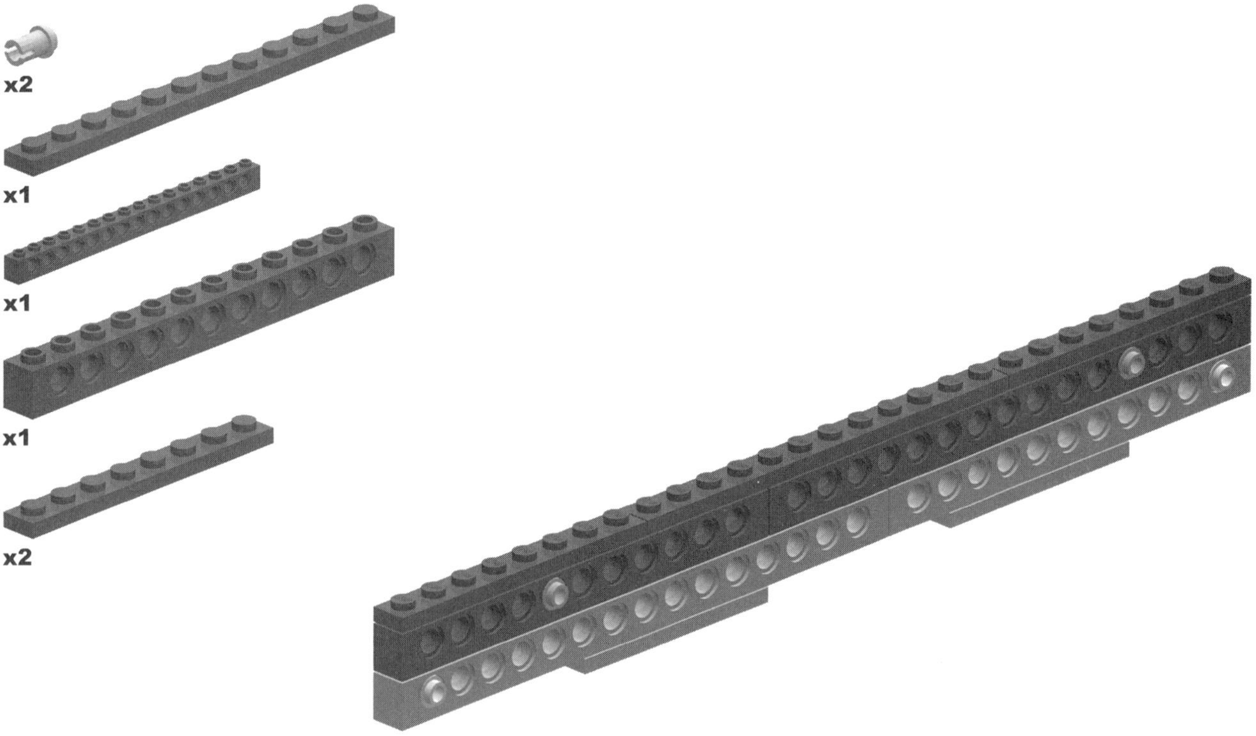

x2

x1

x1

x1

x2

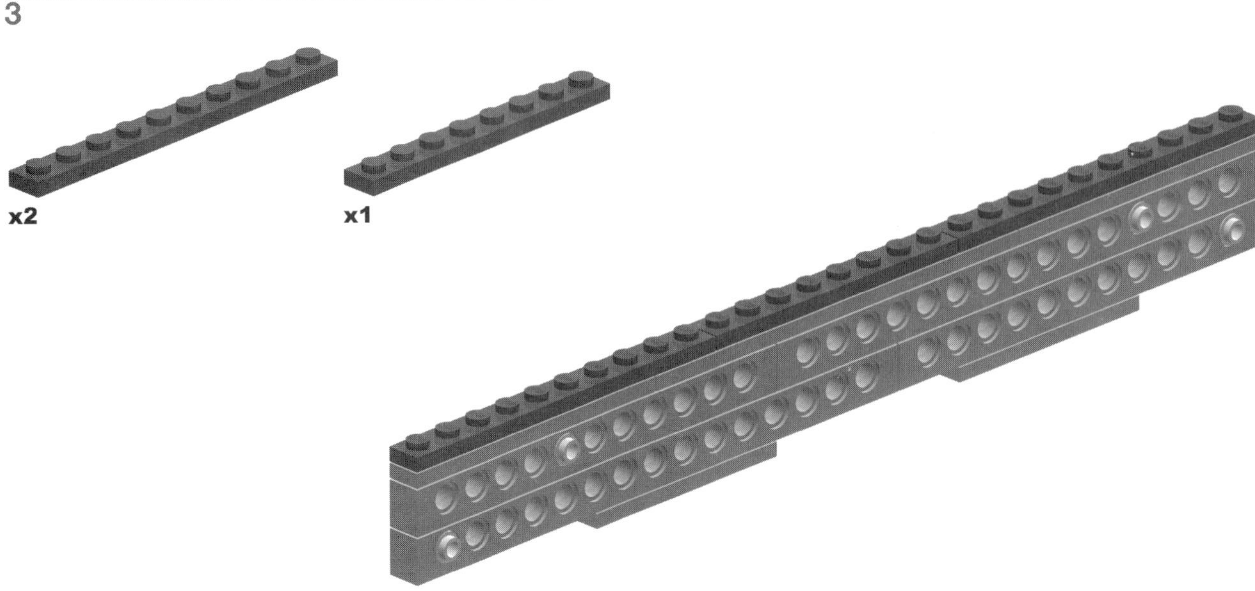
3
x2
x1

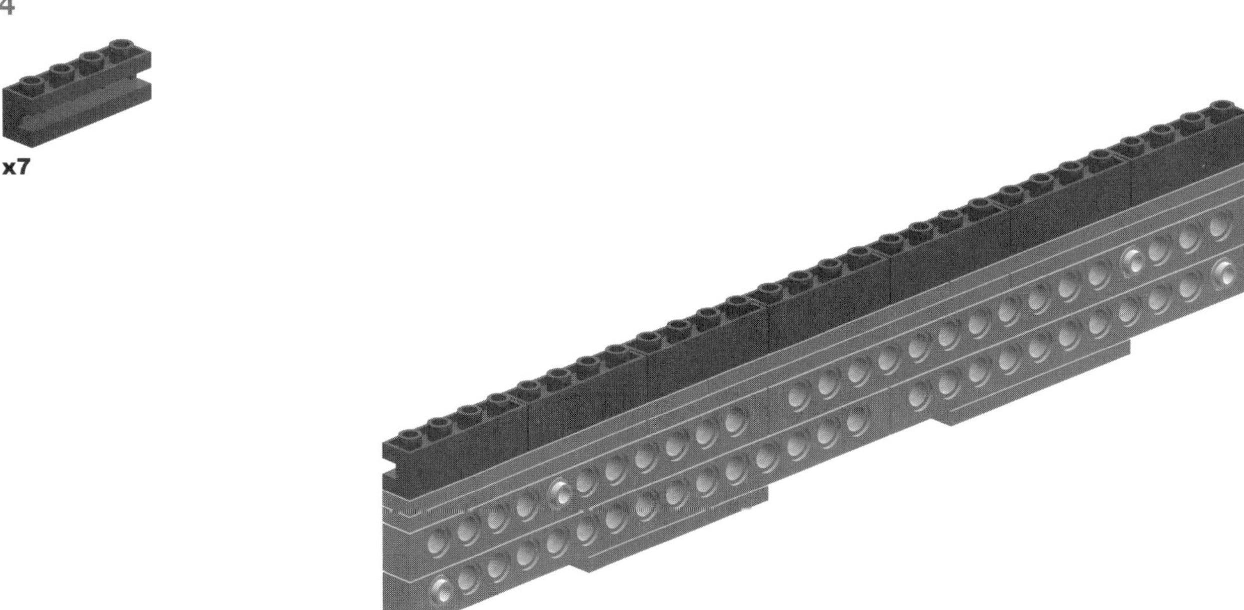
4
x7

5

x1

x1

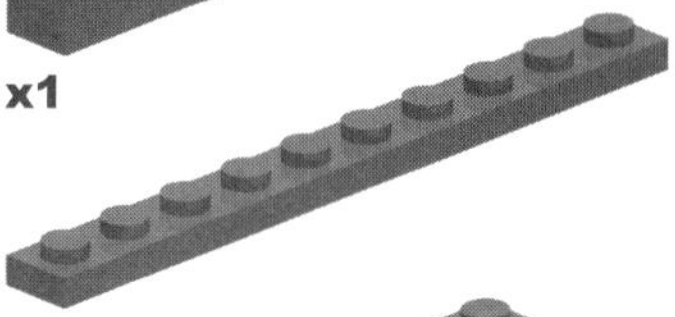

x2

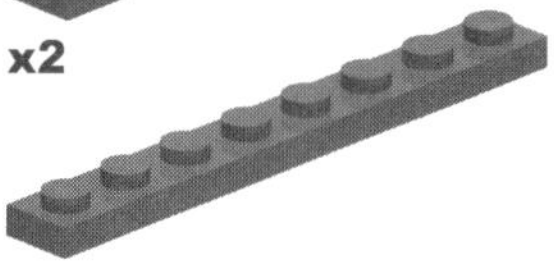

x1

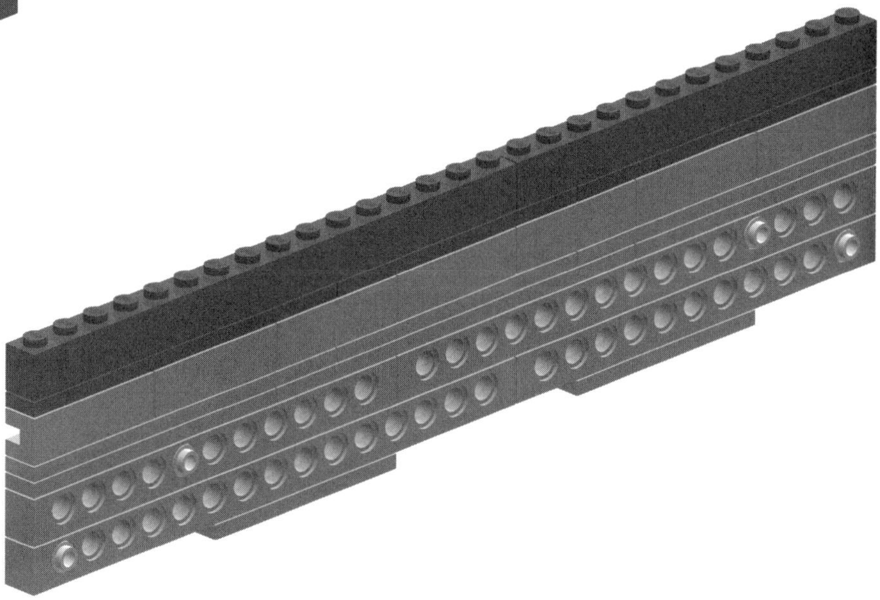

6

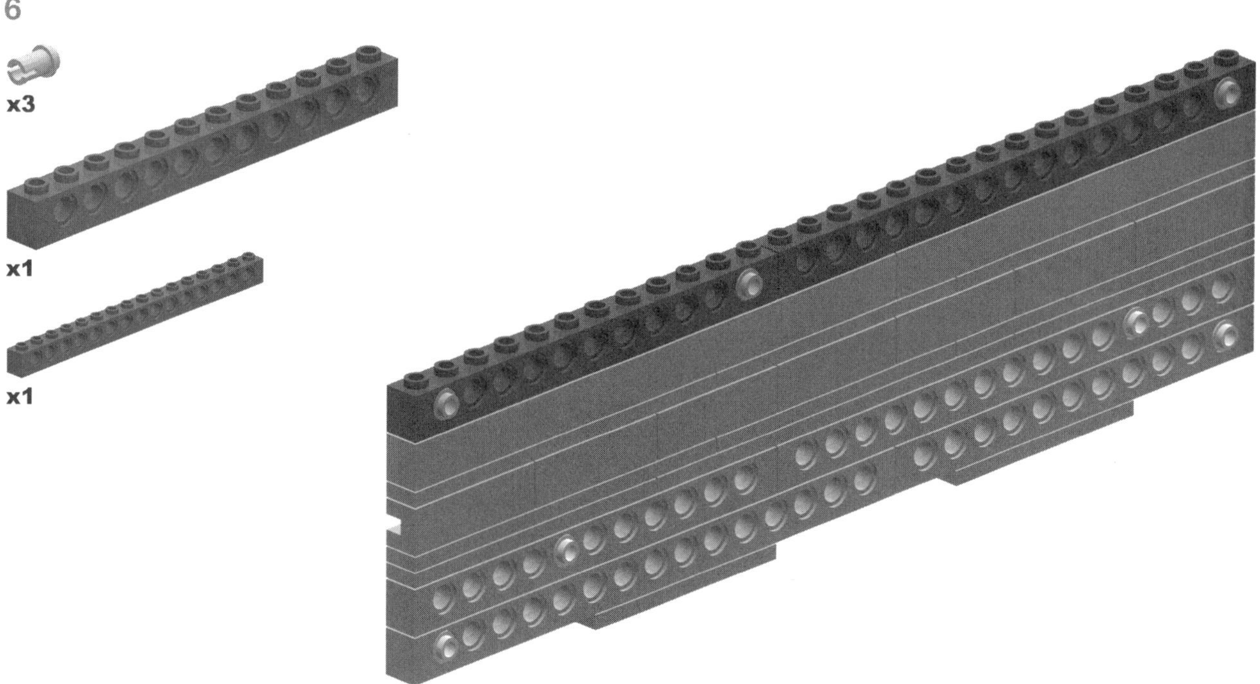

7

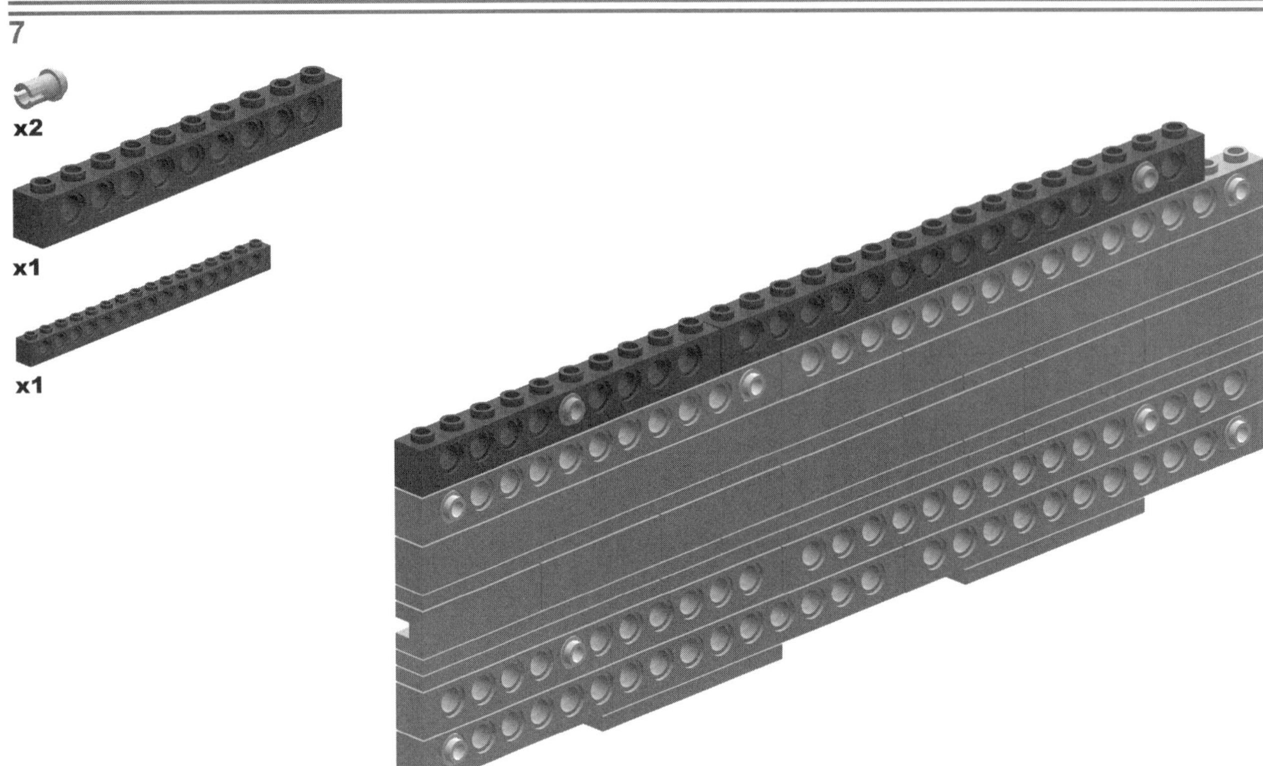

8

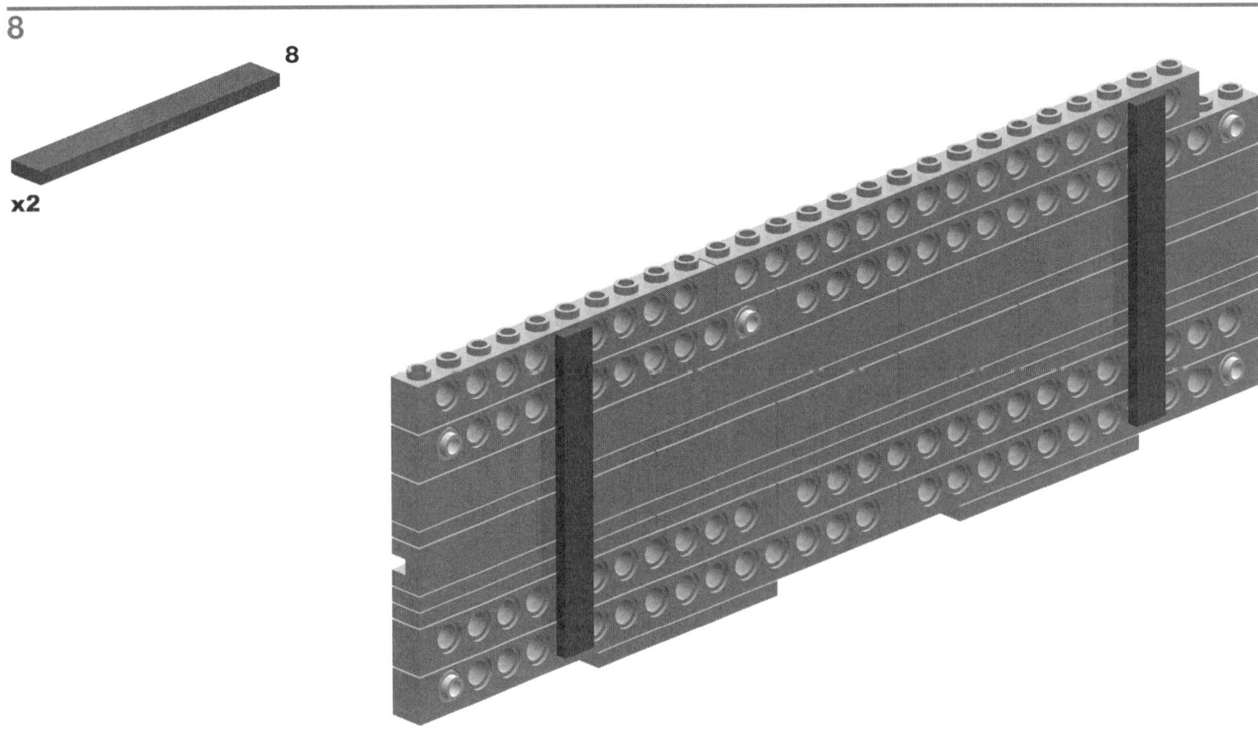

9

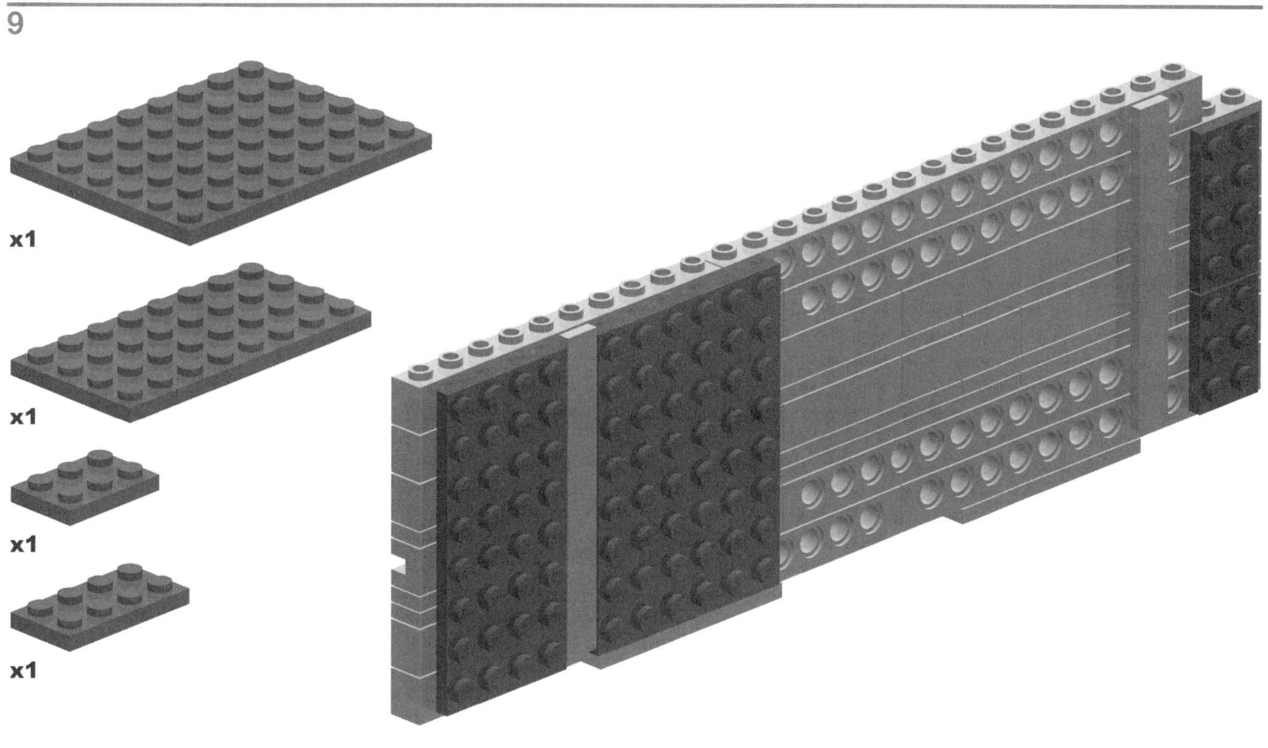

10

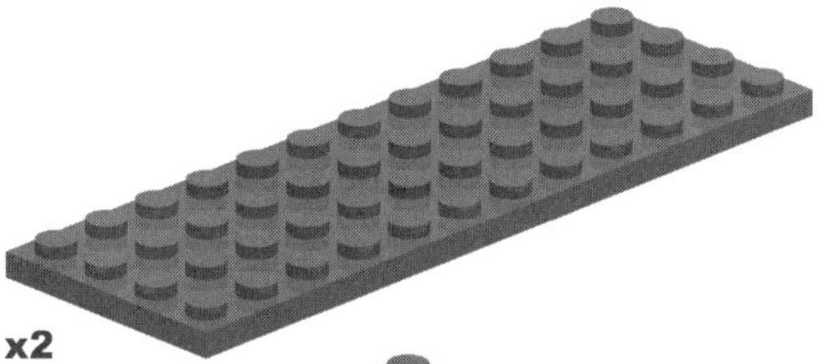

x2

x2

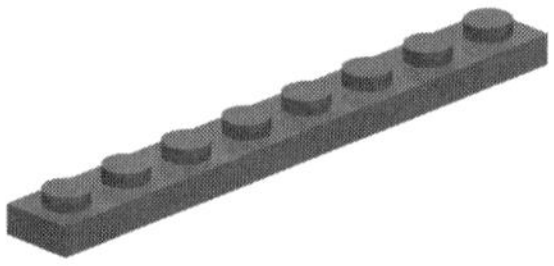

x1

x1

x1

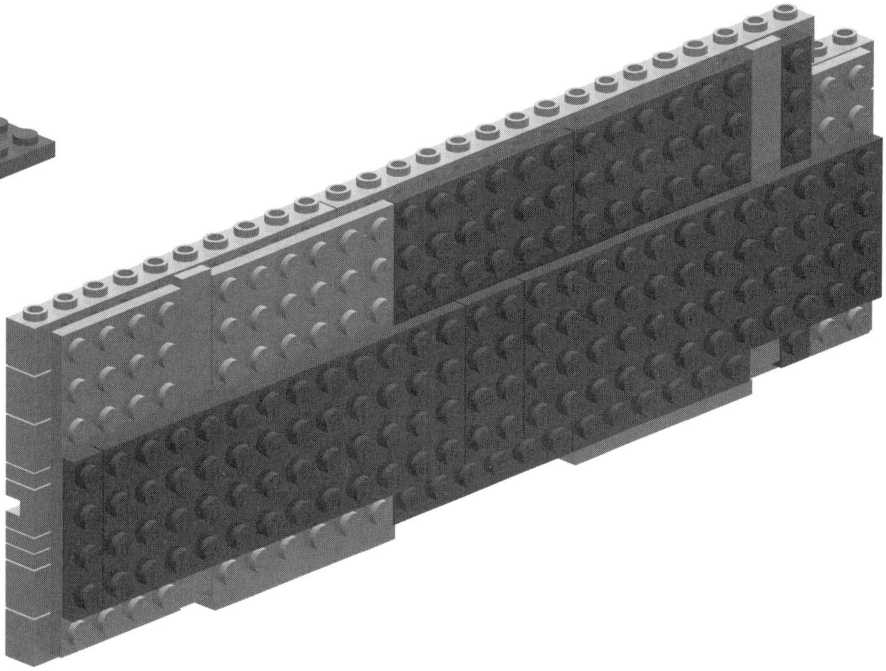

FORE GRIP PLATE

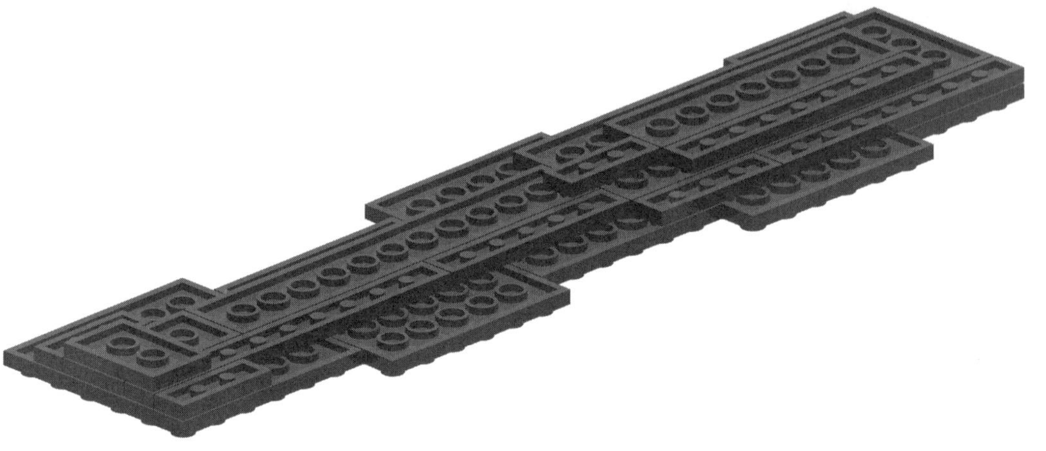

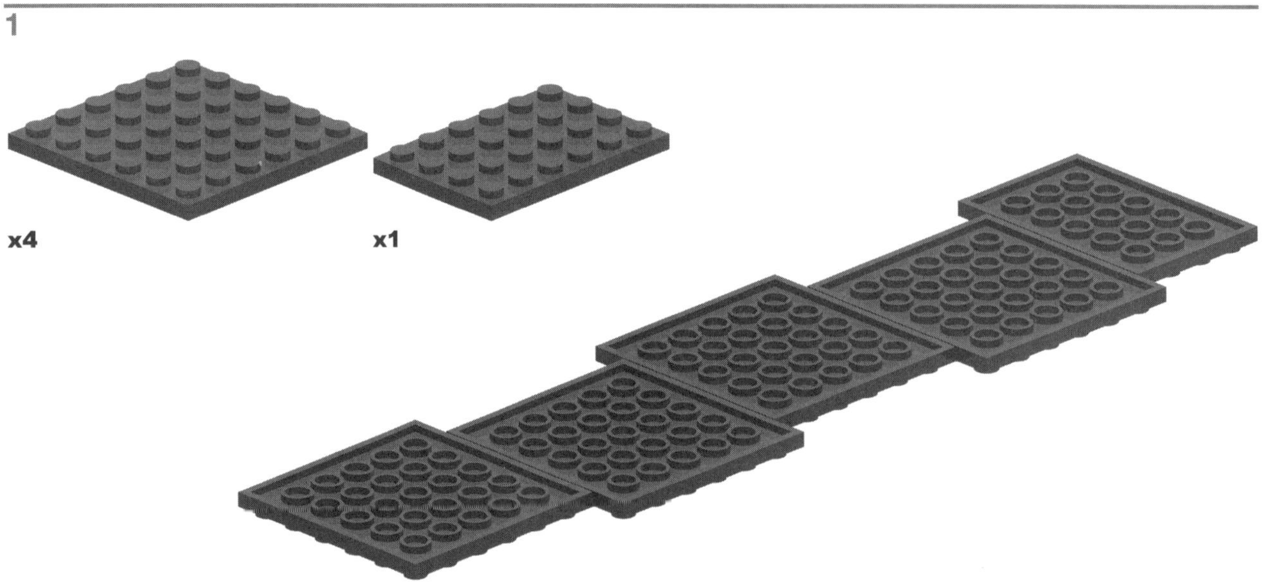

2

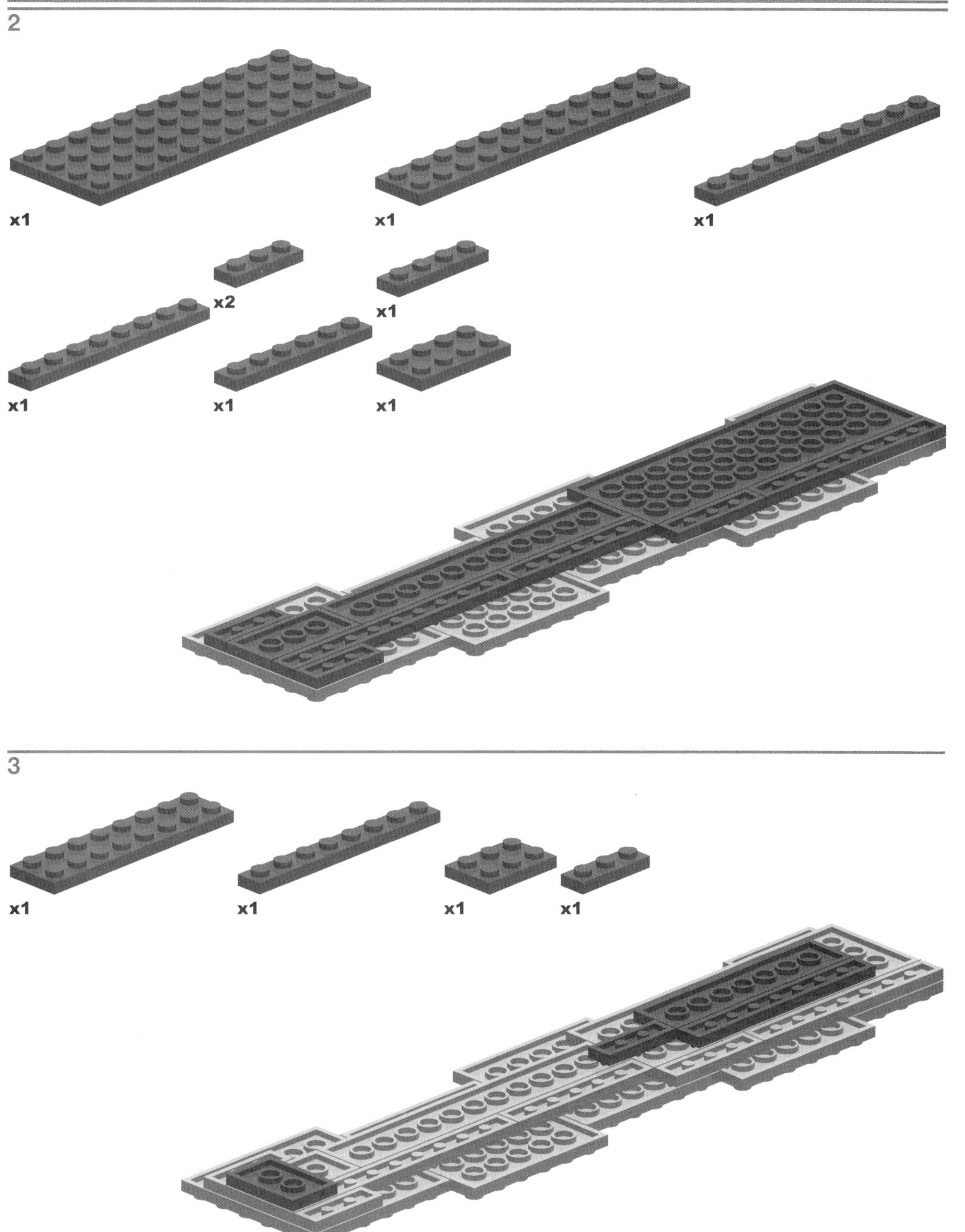

FOLDING STOCK

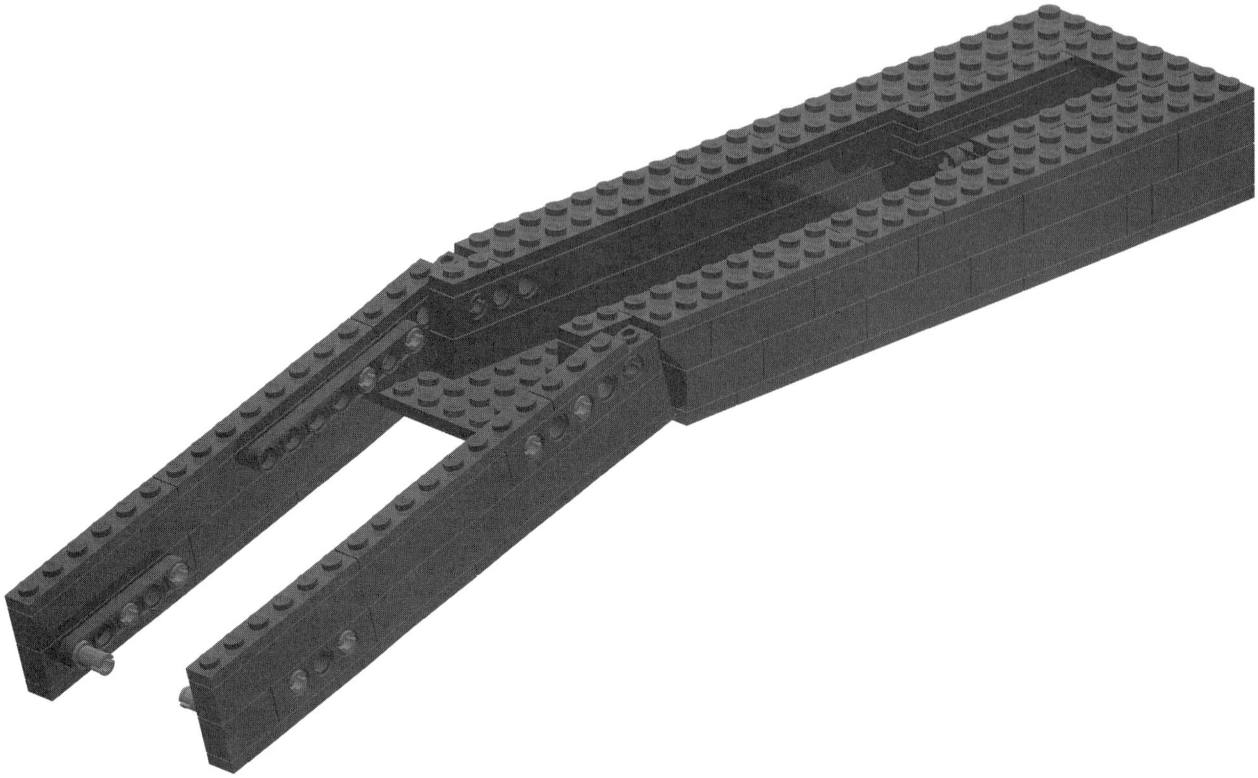

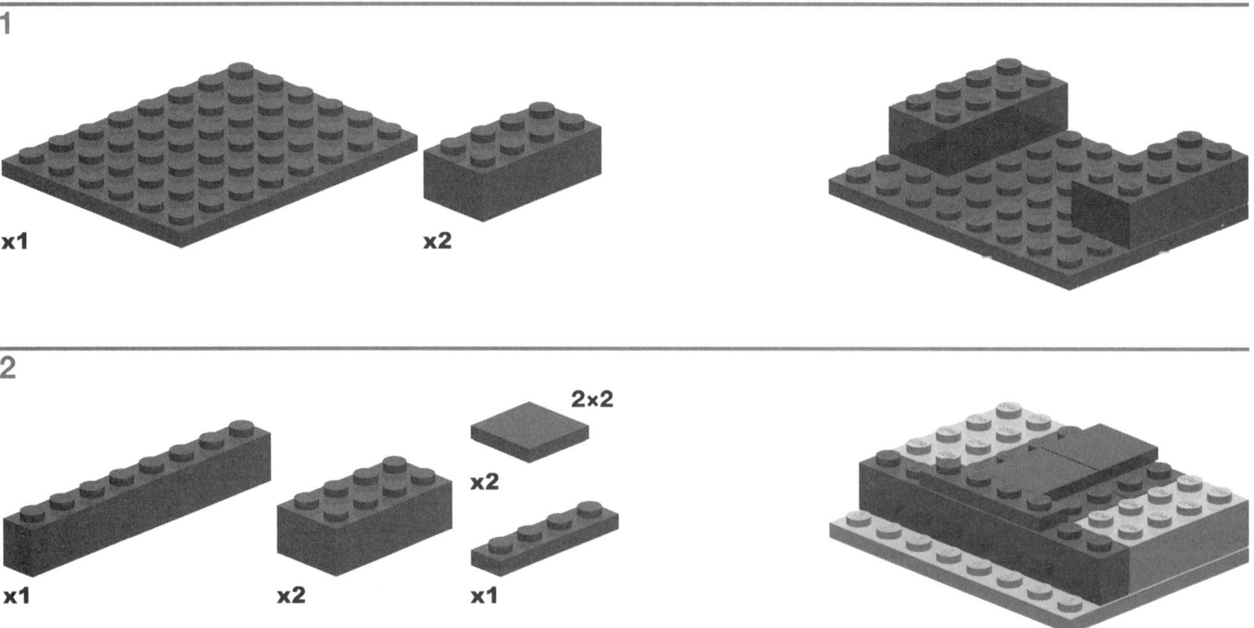

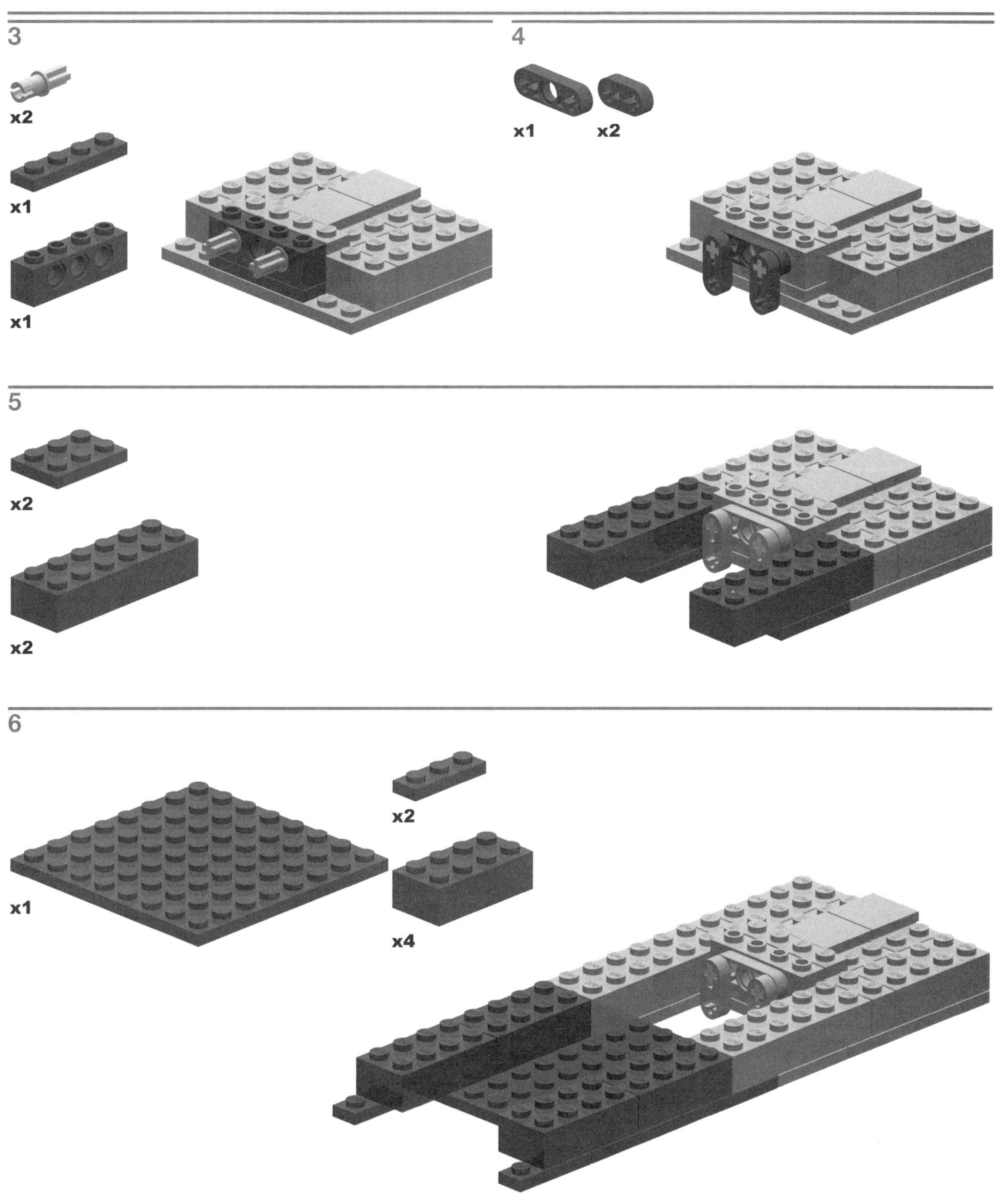
3
x2
x1
x1
4
x1
x2
5
x2
x2
6
x2
x1
x4

7

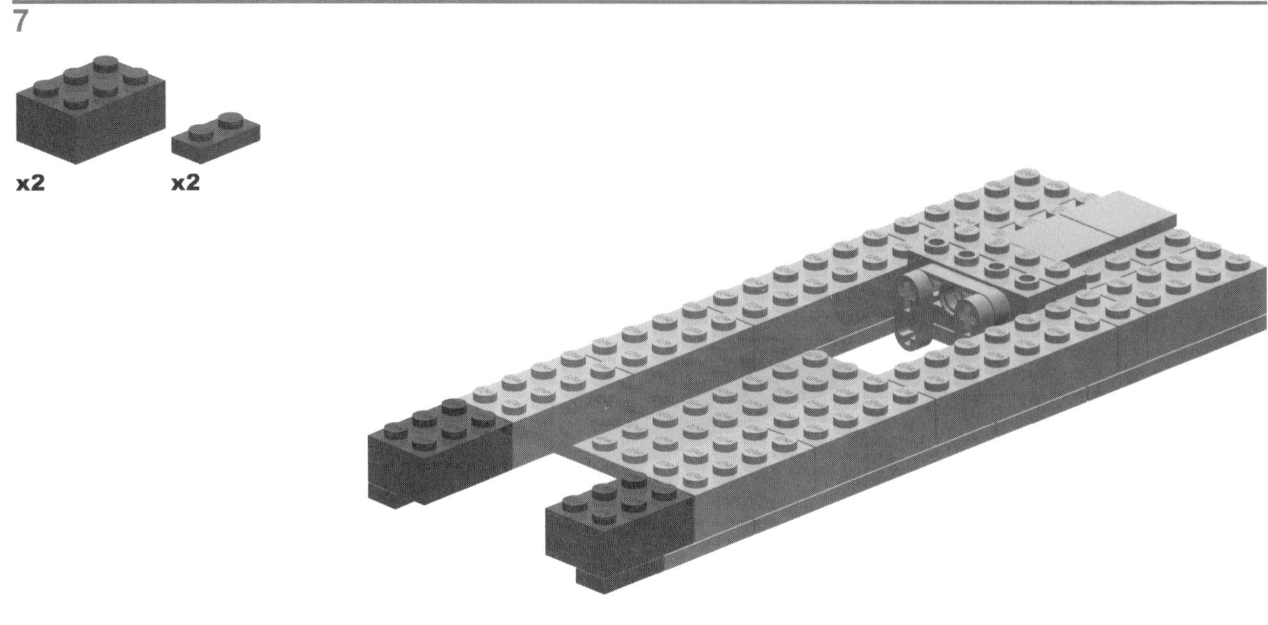

8

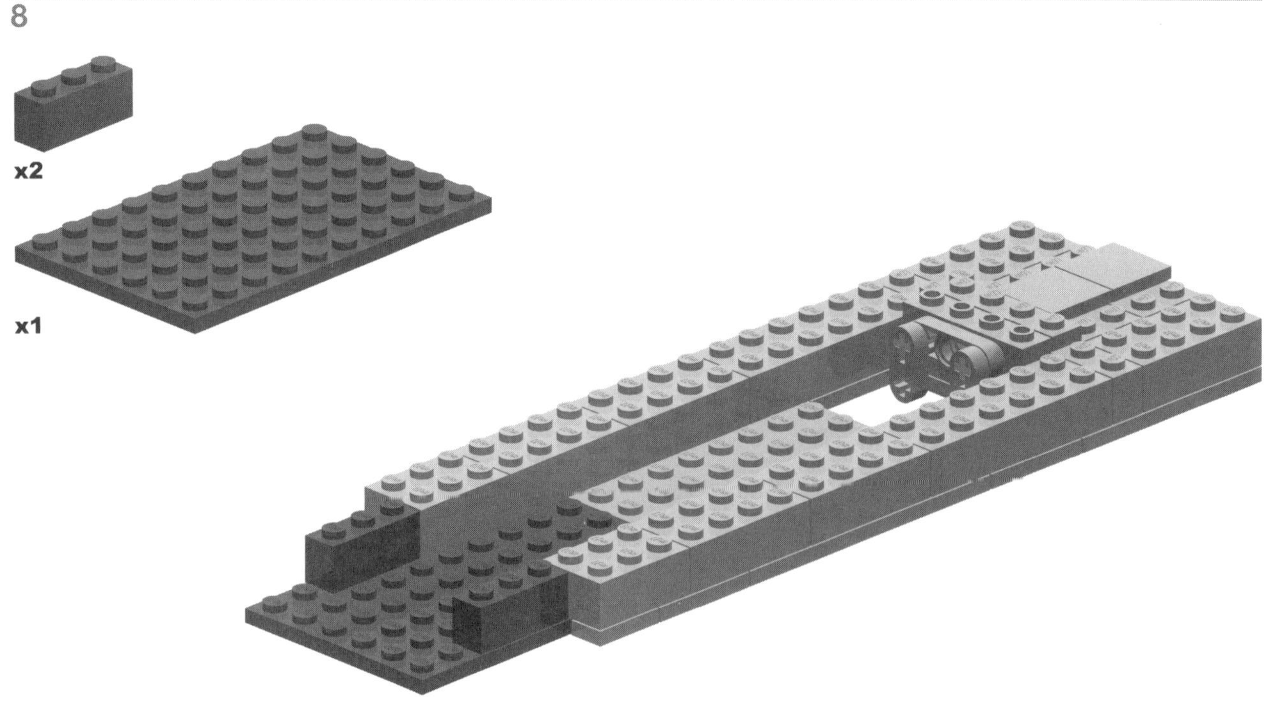

9

x2

x2

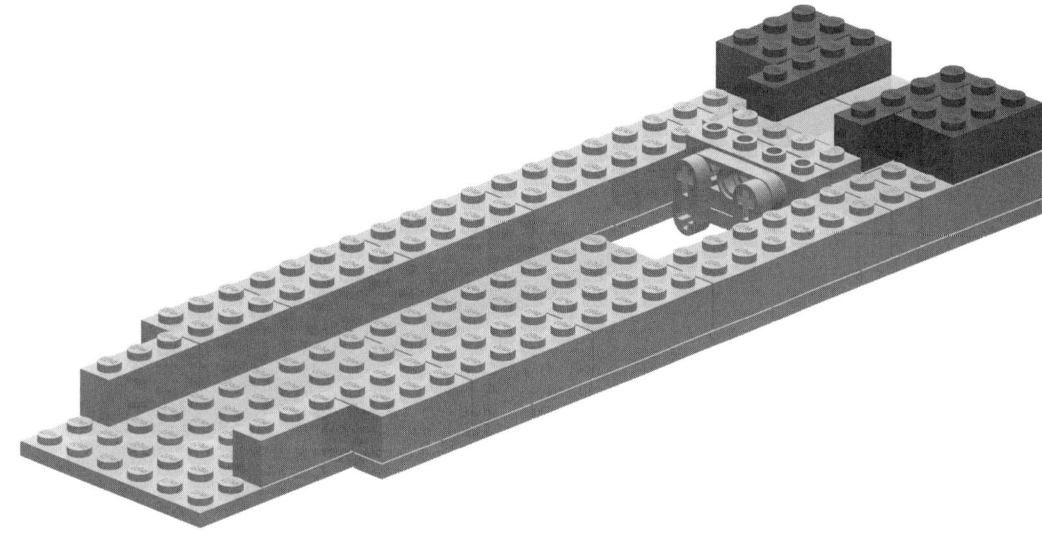

10

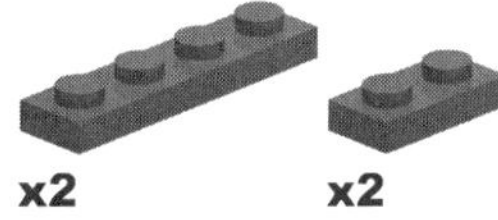

x2 **x2**

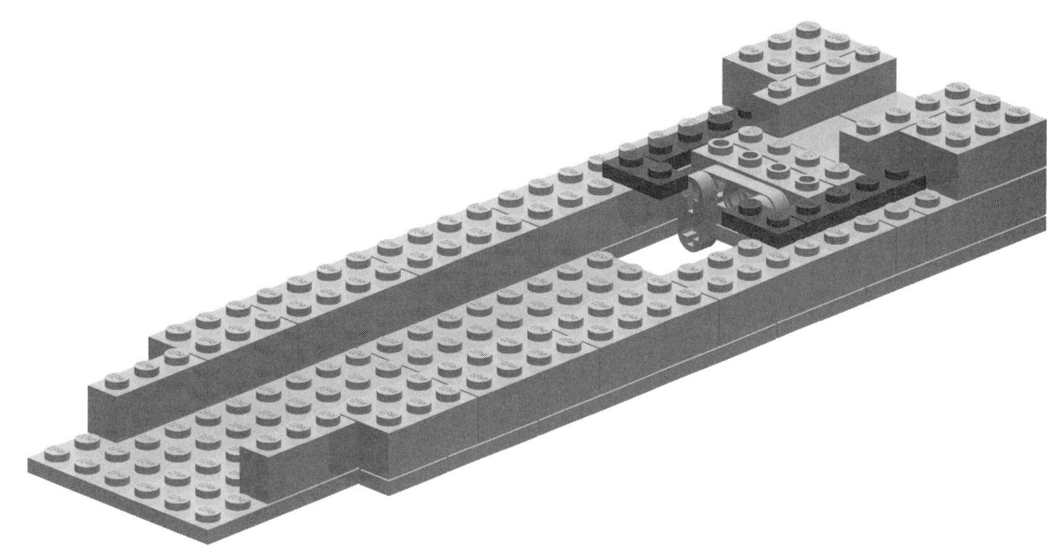

11

x4

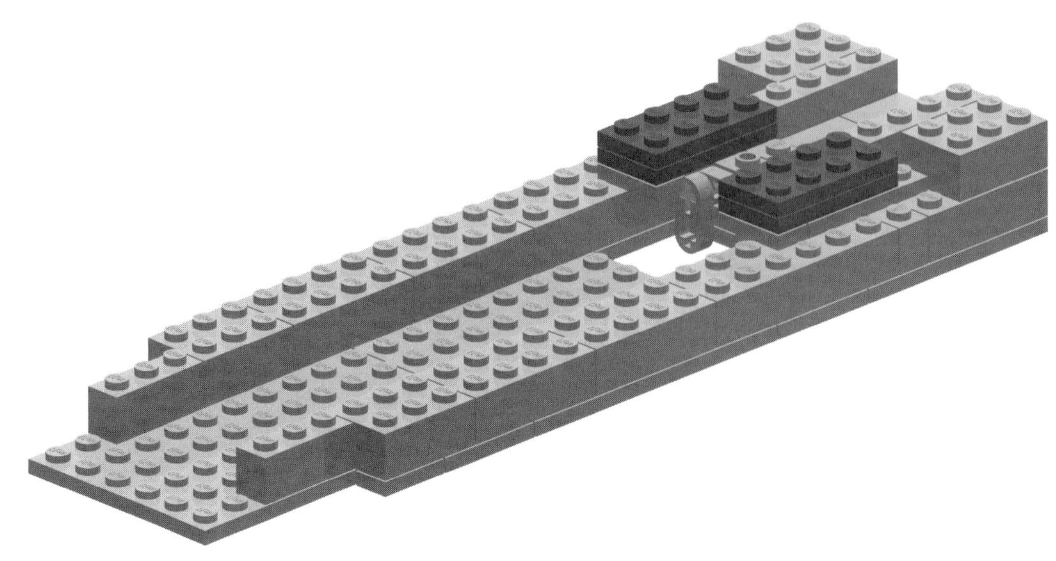

12

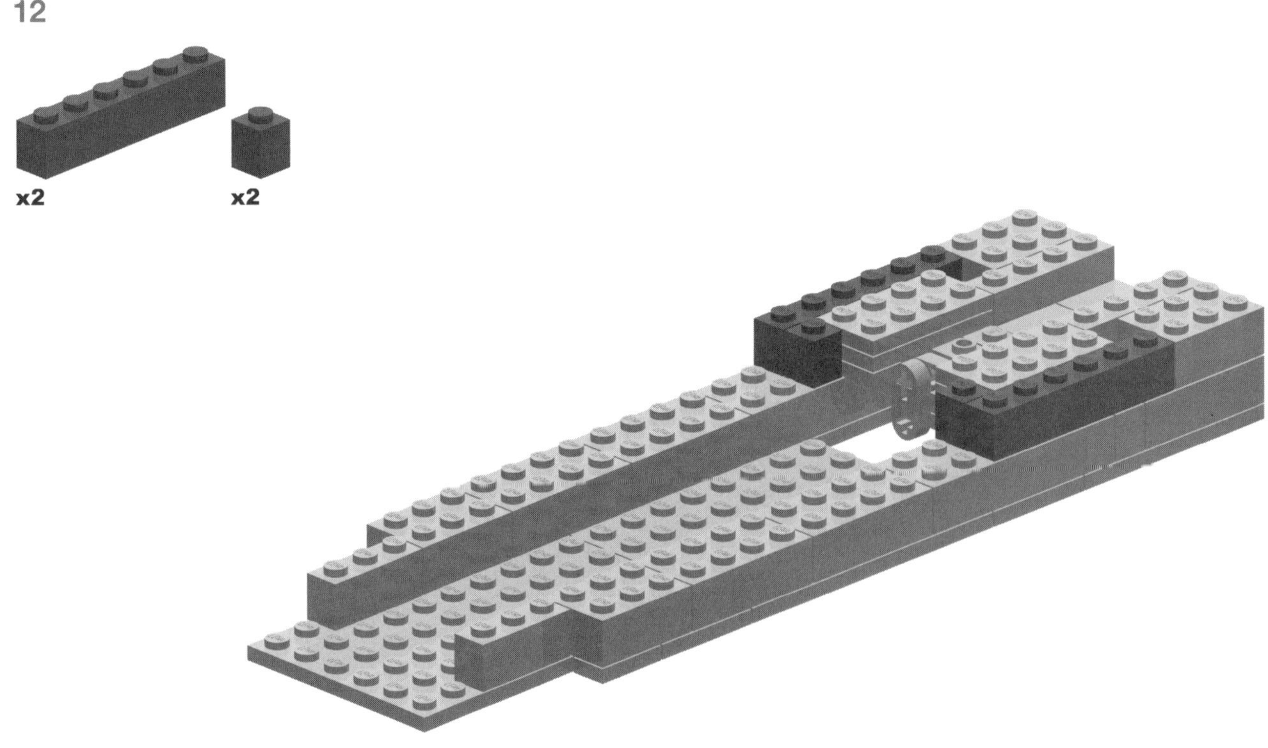

x6

x2 **x2**

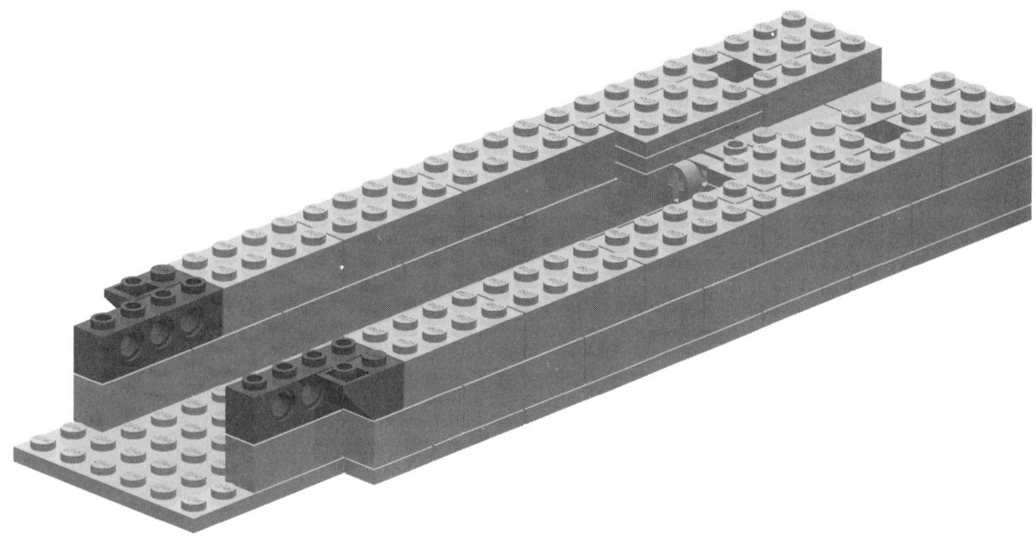

15

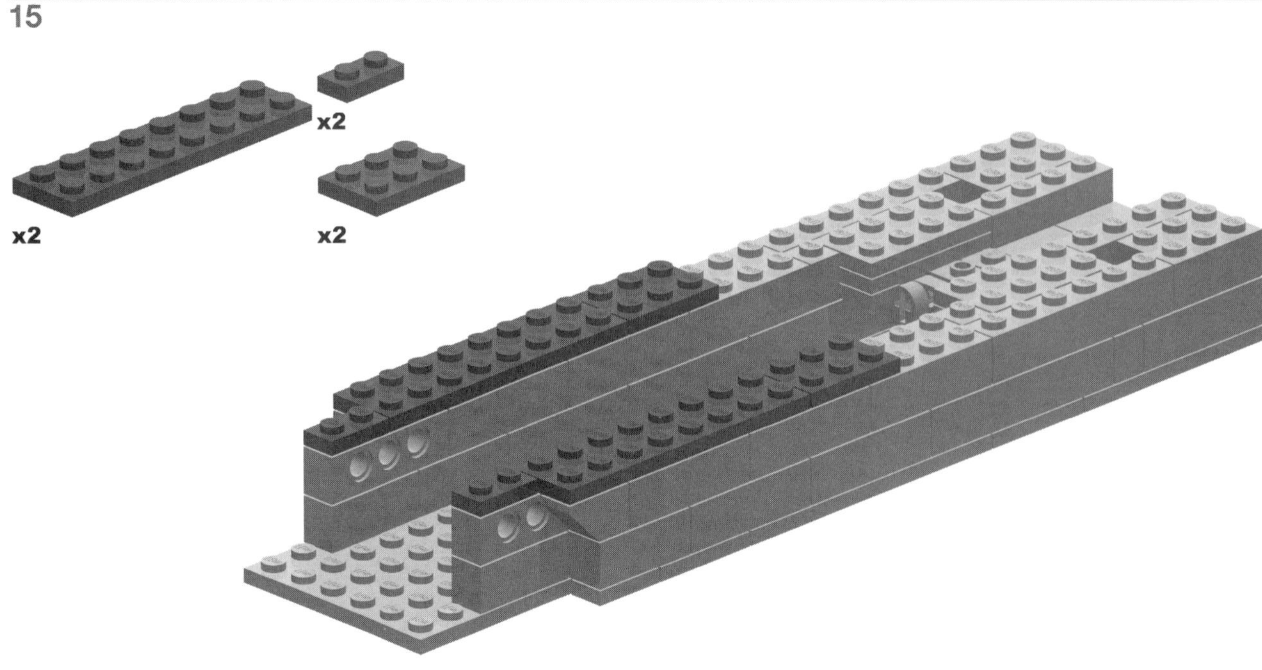

16

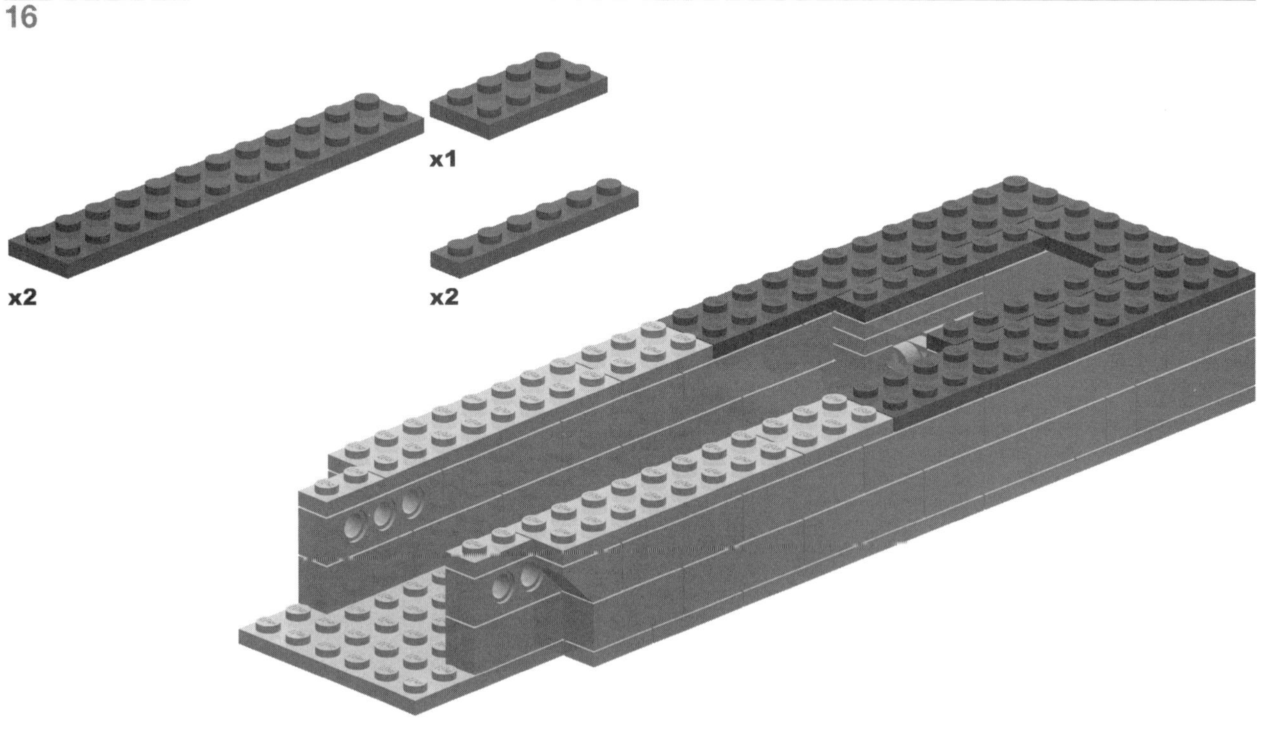

17

x2

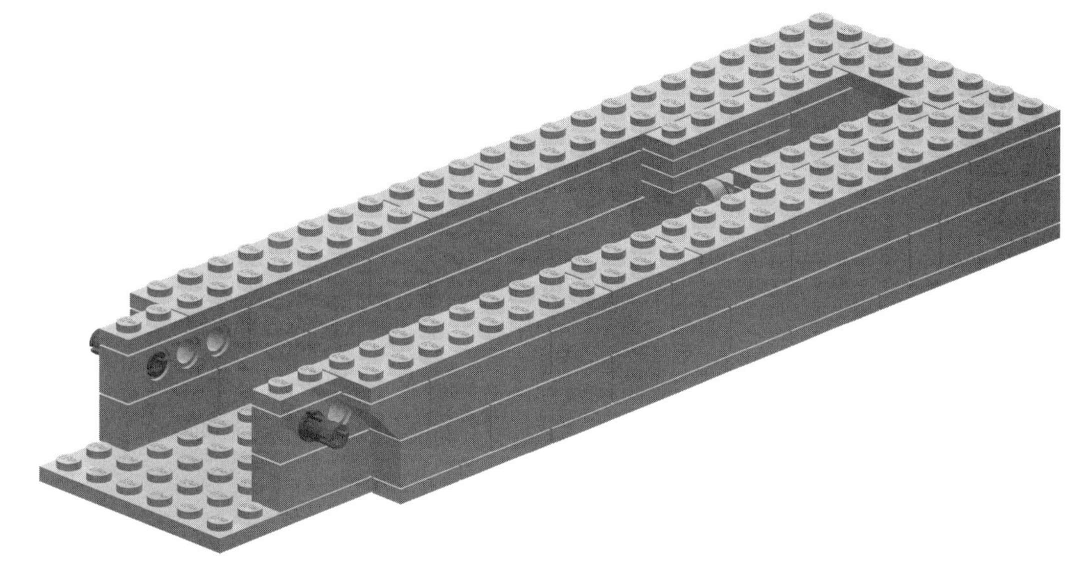

18

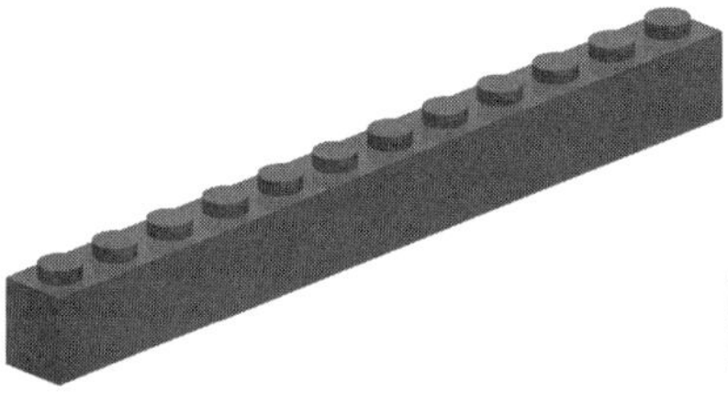

x2

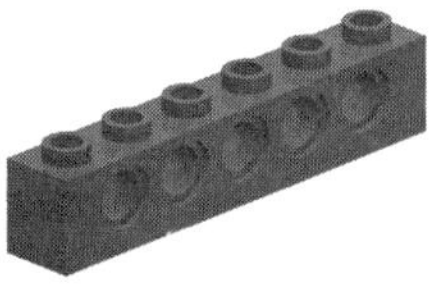

x2

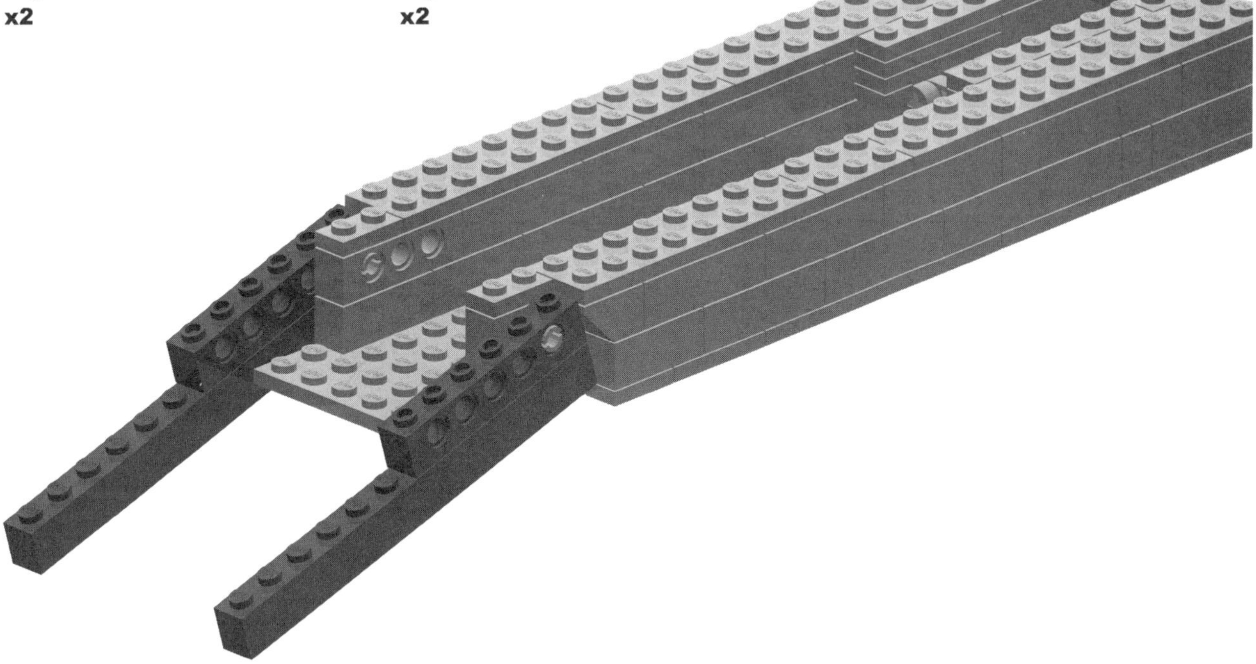

19

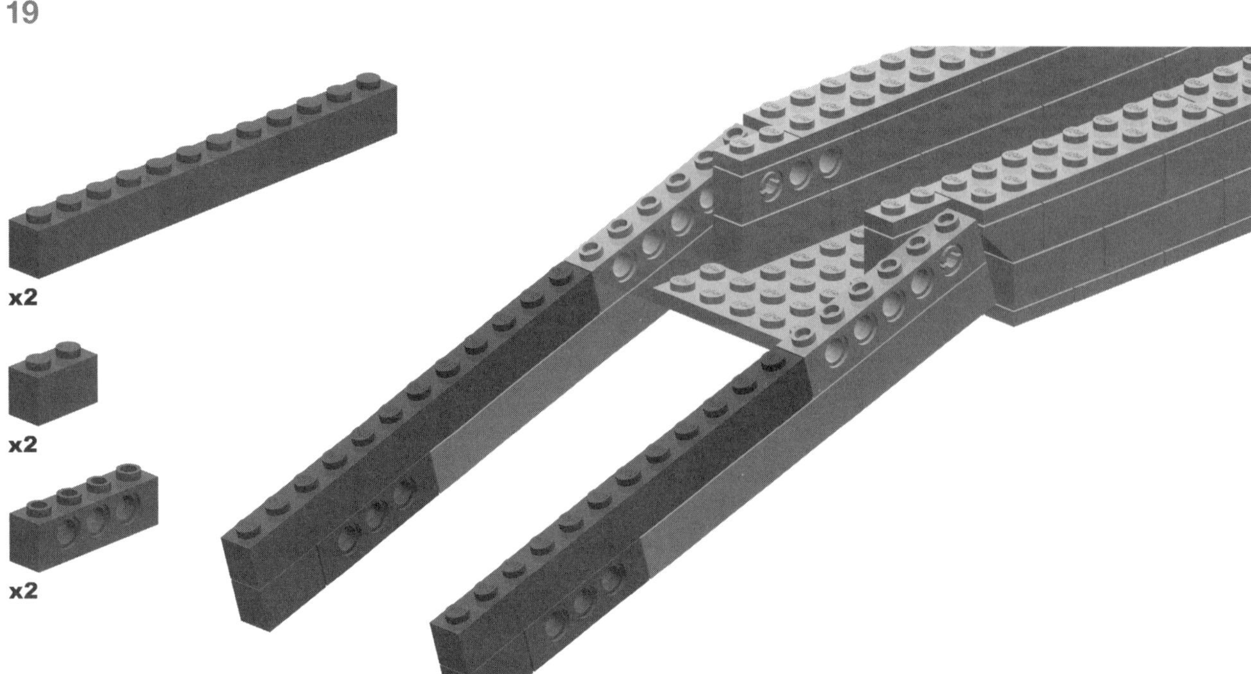

20

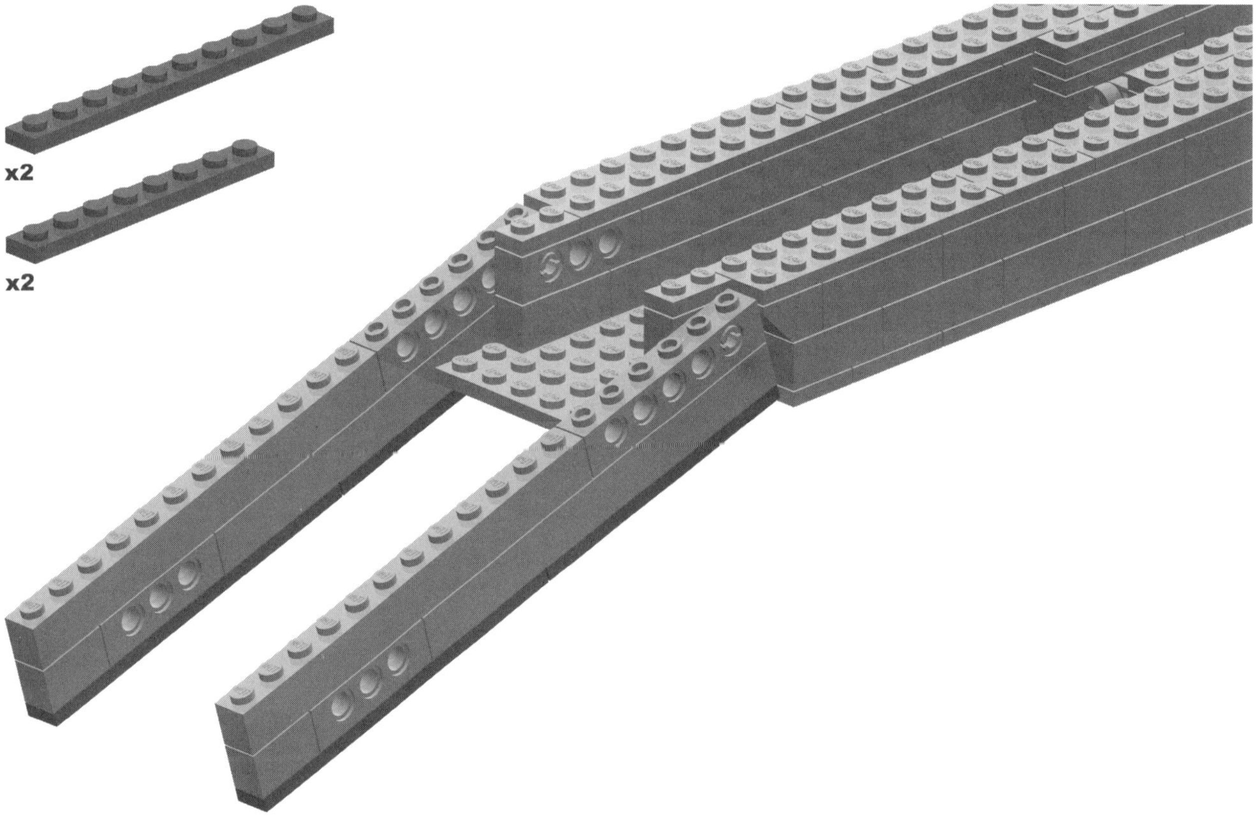

x2

x2

21

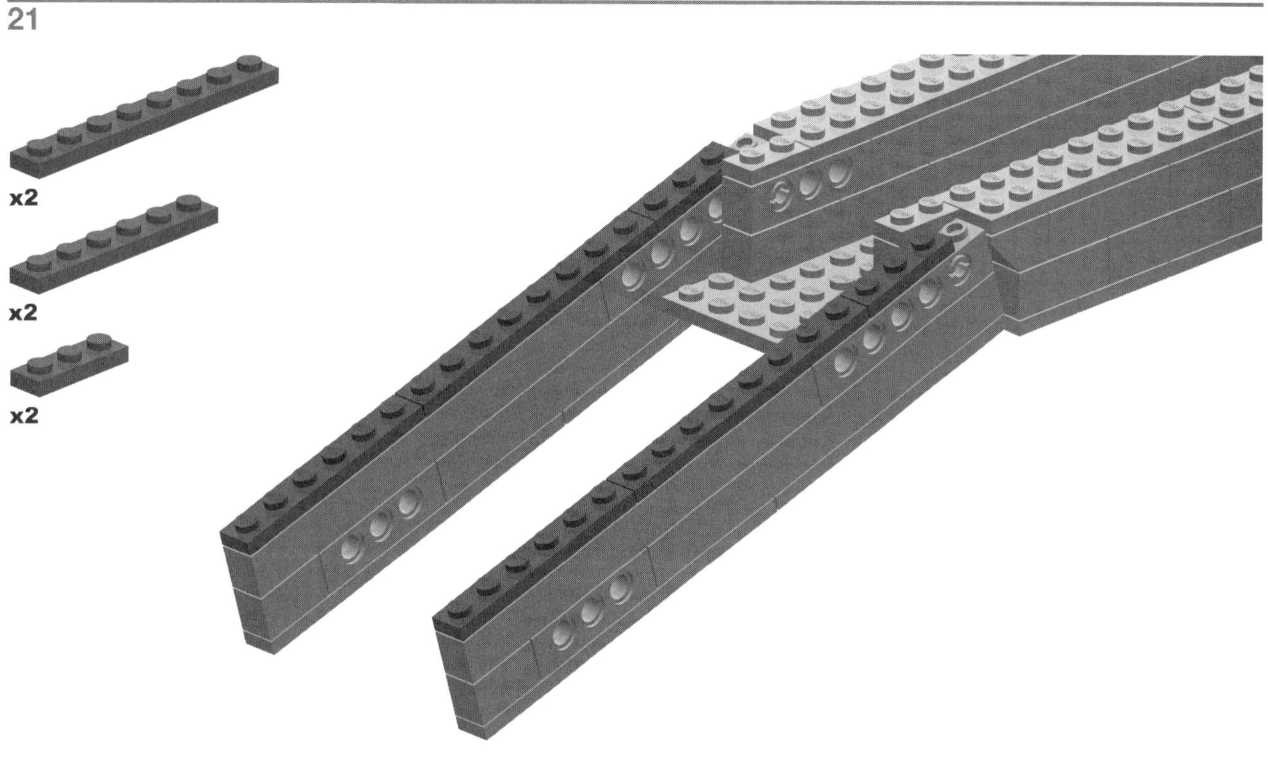

22

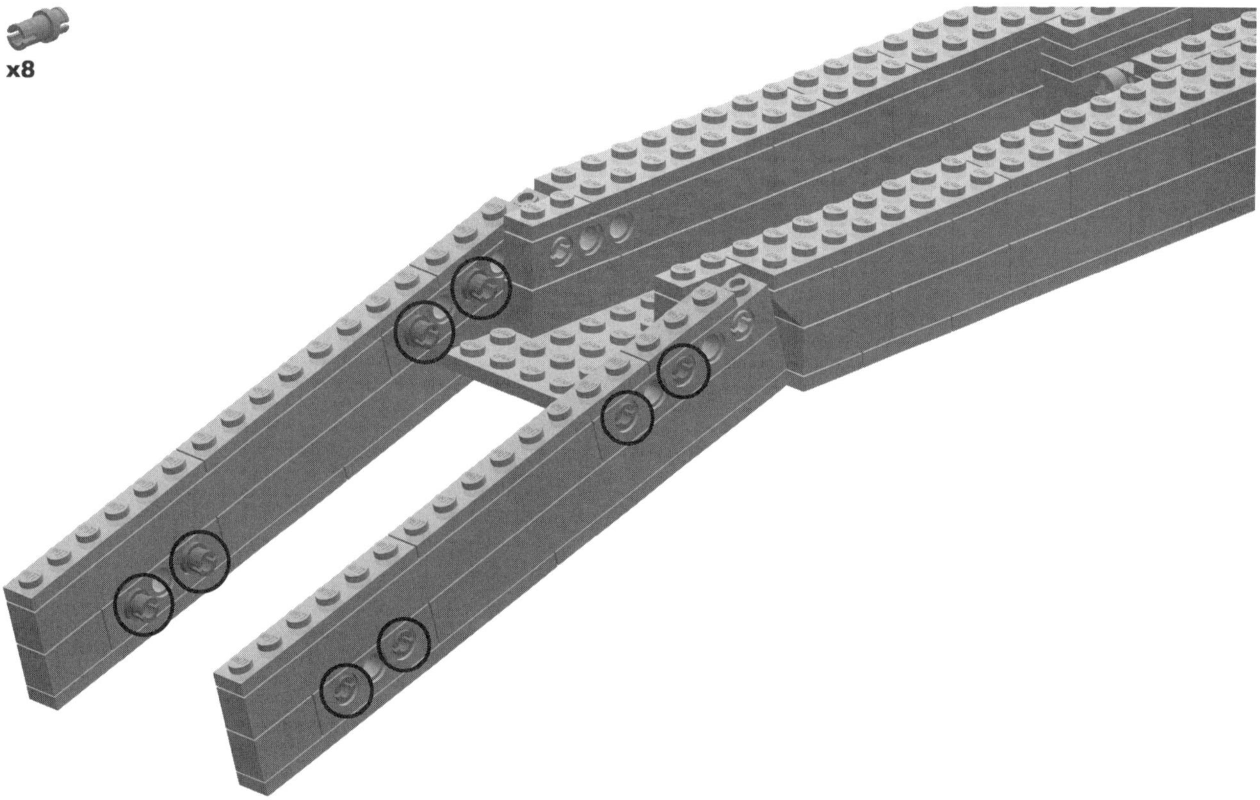

x8

23

MAIN ASSEMBLY

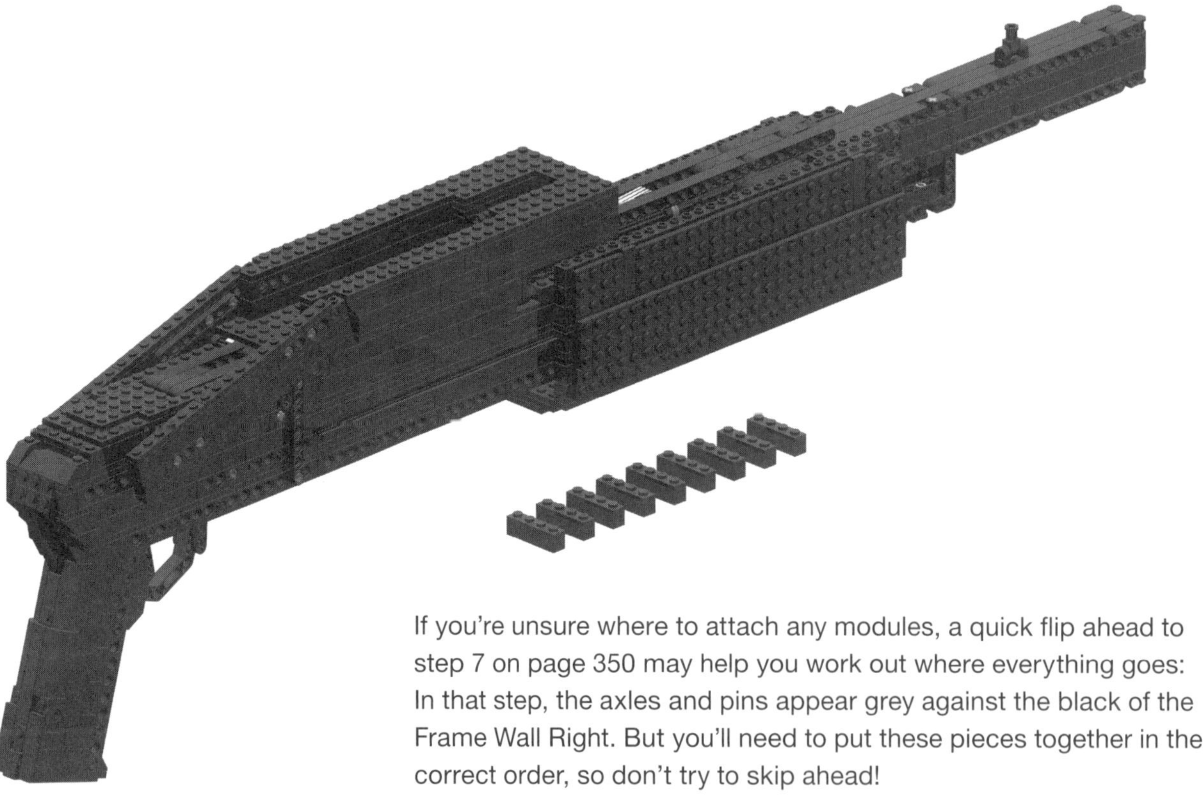

If you're unsure where to attach any modules, a quick flip ahead to step 7 on page 350 may help you work out where everything goes: In that step, the axles and pins appear grey against the black of the Frame Wall Right. But you'll need to put these pieces together in the correct order, so don't try to skip ahead!

1

attachment points

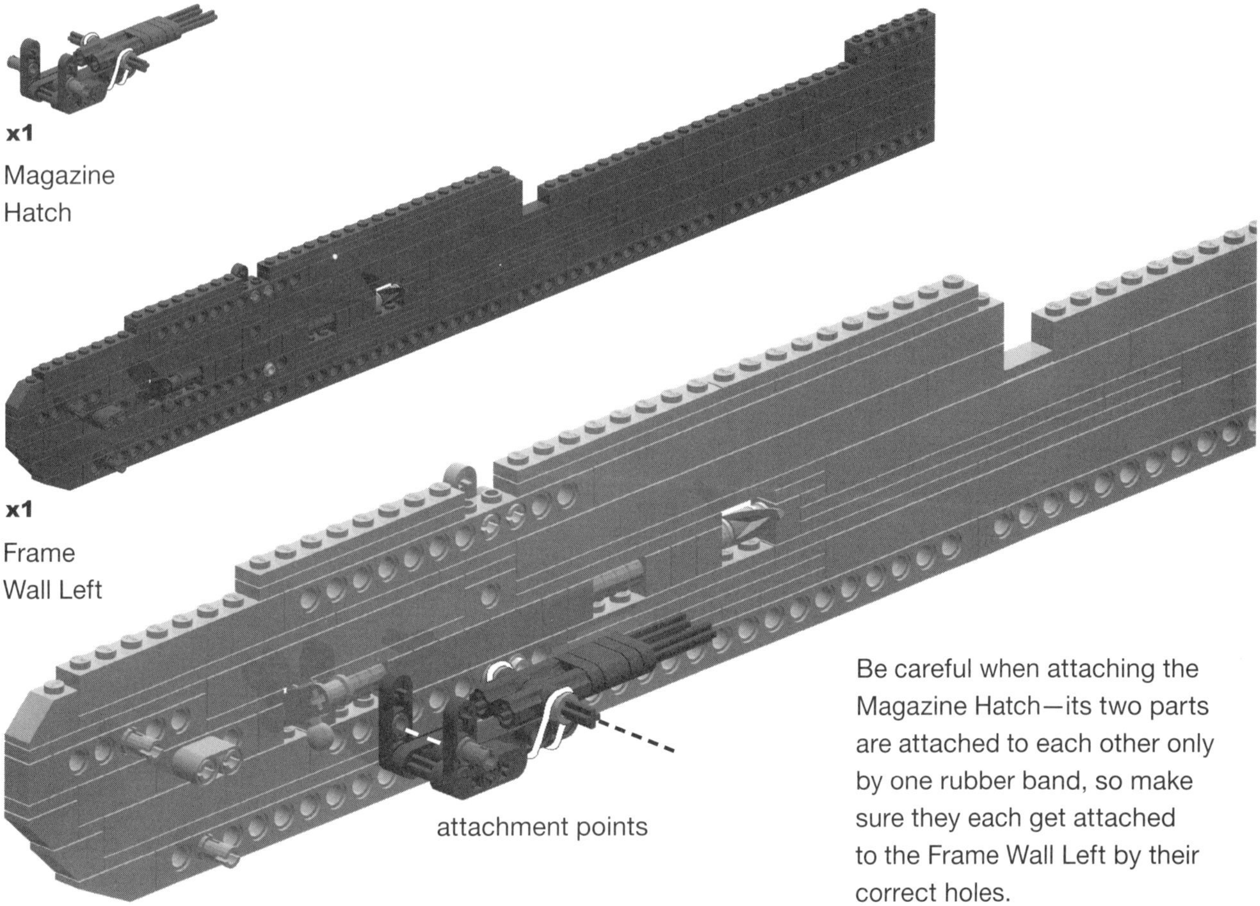

x1

Magazine Hatch

x1

Frame Wall Left

Be careful when attaching the Magazine Hatch—its two parts are attached to each other only by one rubber band, so make sure they each get attached to the Frame Wall Left by their correct holes.

2

attachment points

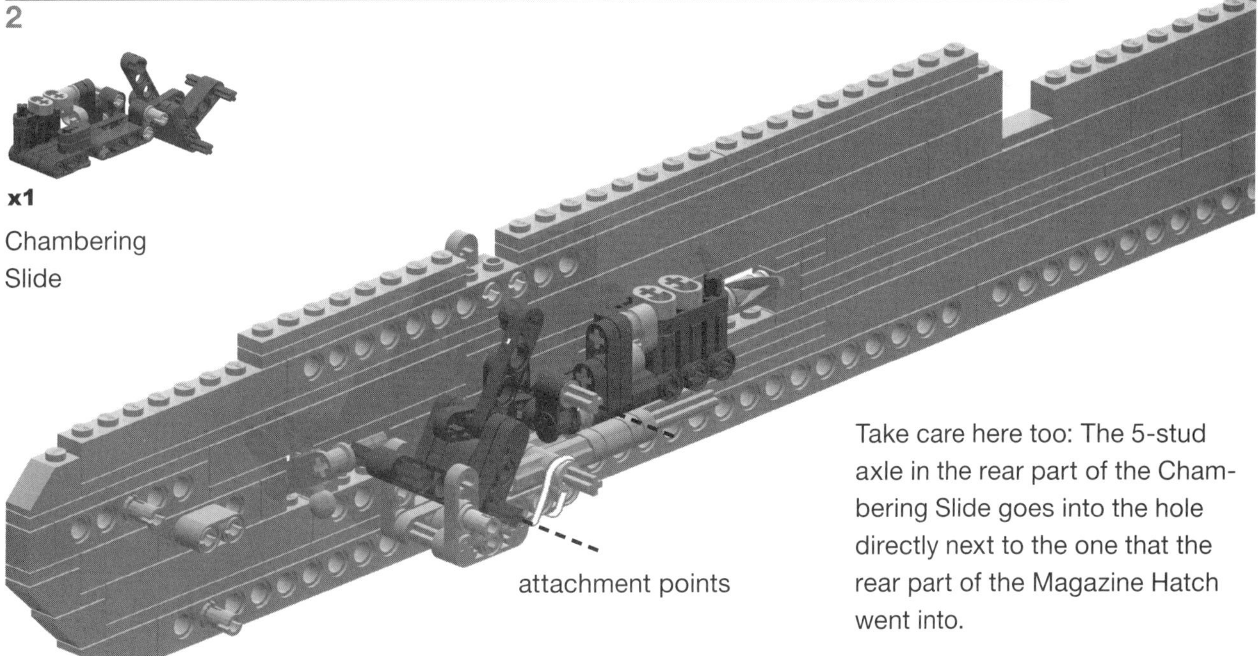

x1

Chambering Slide

Take care here too: The 5-stud axle in the rear part of the Chambering Slide goes into the hole directly next to the one that the rear part of the Magazine Hatch went into.

3

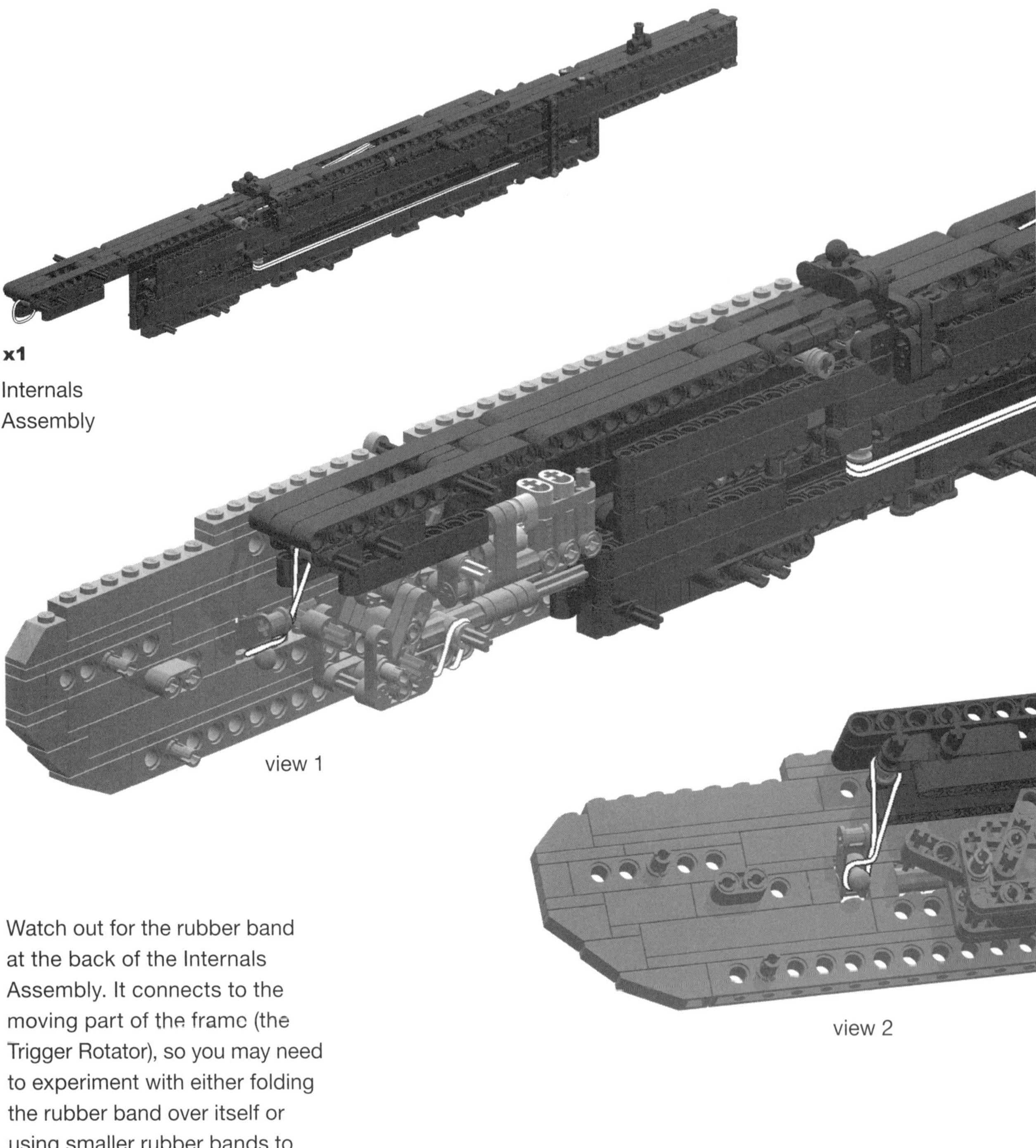

Watch out for the rubber band at the back of the Internals Assembly. It connects to the moving part of the frame (the Trigger Rotator), so you may need to experiment with either folding the rubber band over itself or using smaller rubber bands to get the right amount of tension.

4

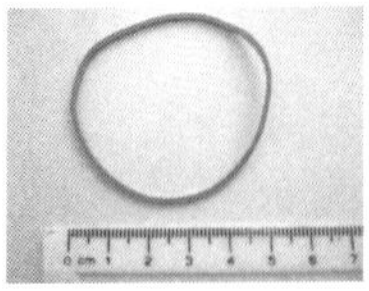

x1

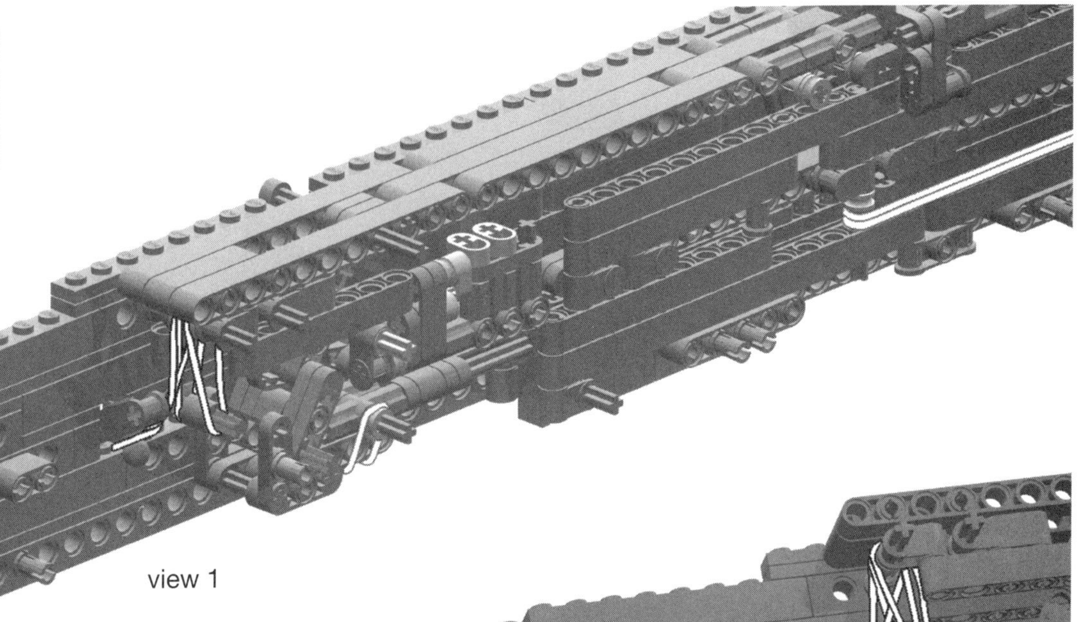

view 1

This rubber band attaches to the Internals Assembly at the same place as the one in the previous step, but its other end hooks over the 3-stud axle on the end of the Chambering Slide, as shown. As usual, some experimentation may be needed to get the correct amount of tension—this rubber band needs quite a lot of it! I managed by folding it over itself a few times.

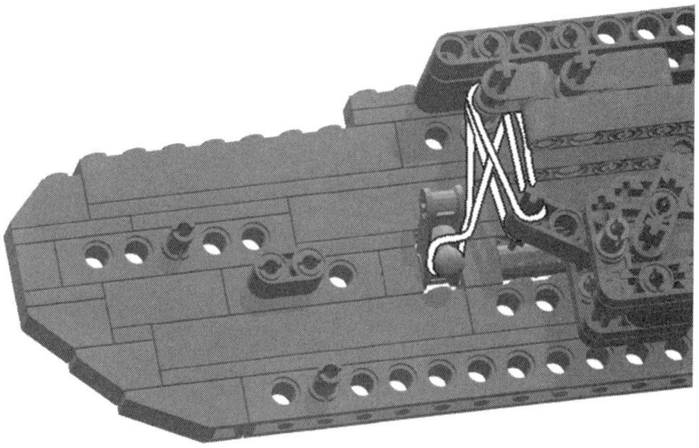

view 2

5

x1

Trigger

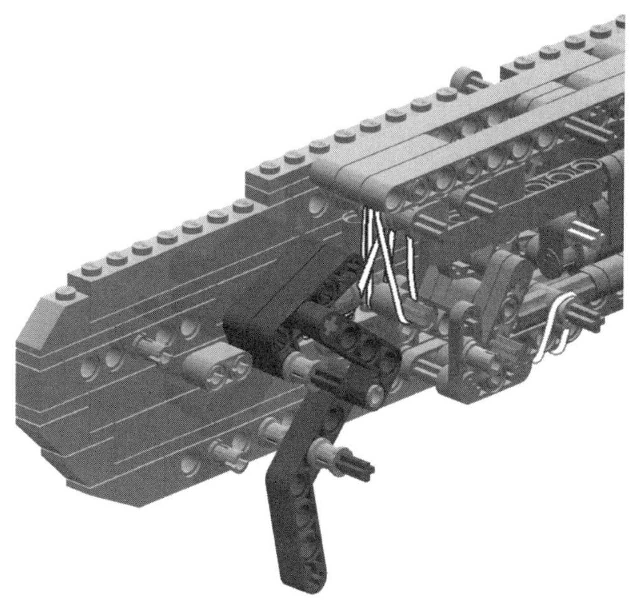

A pull of the Trigger (the part protruding from the bottom of the frame) should rotate the Trigger Rotator, and the rubber band attached in step 3 on page 348 should pull it back into place once the Trigger is released.

6

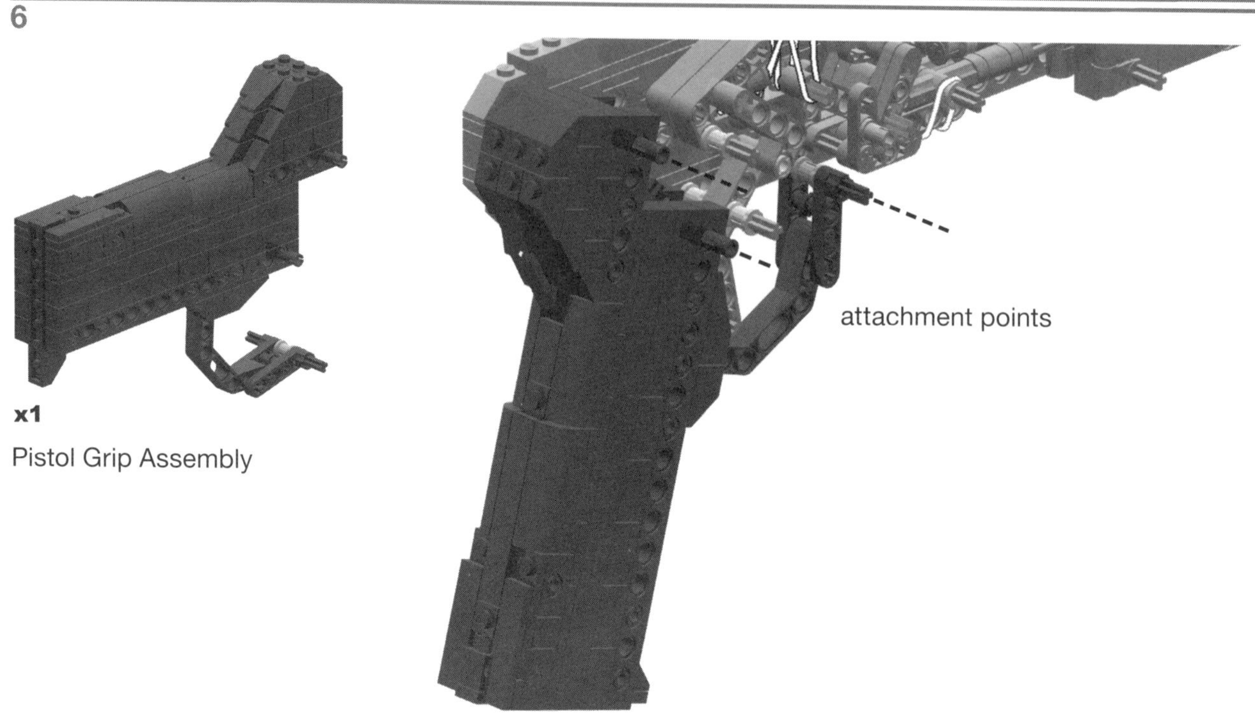

x1

Pistol Grip Assembly

7

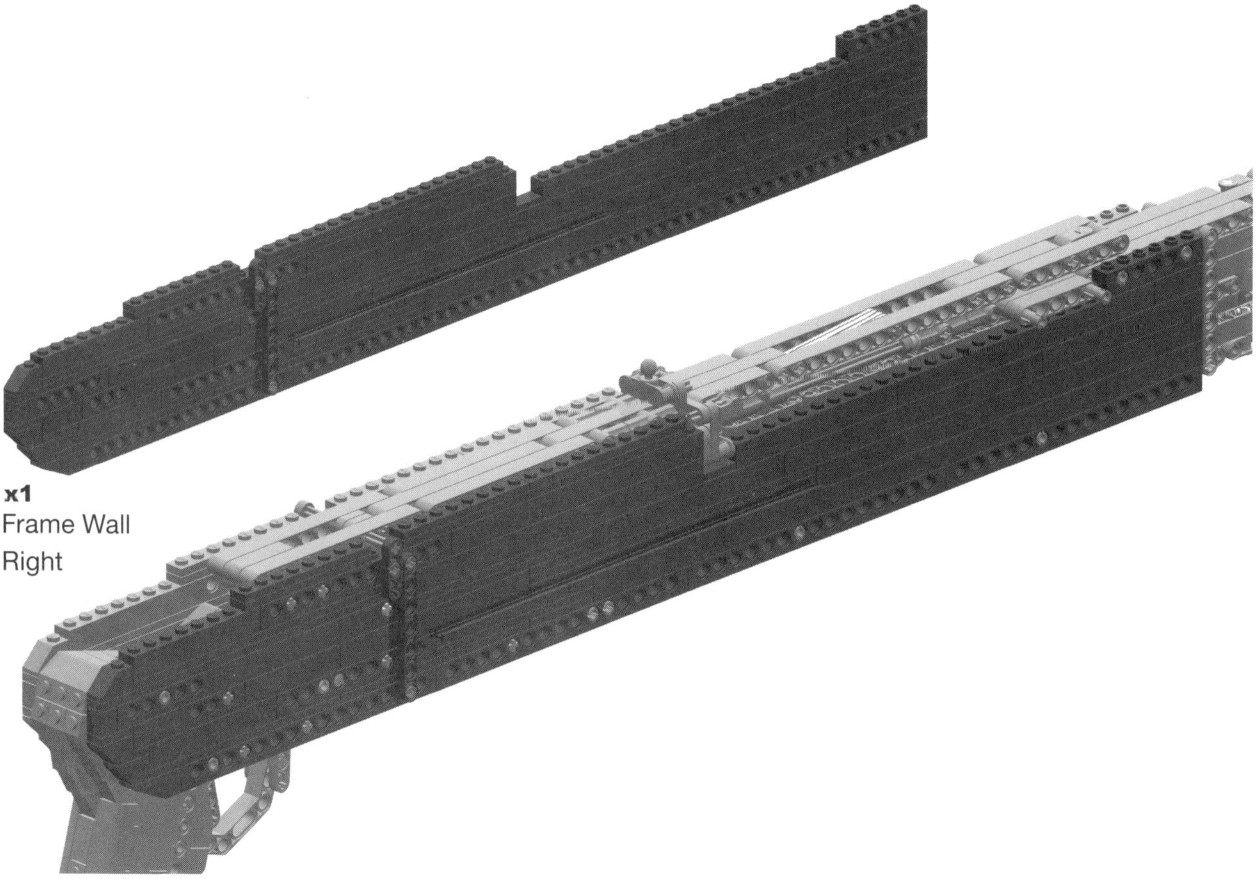

x1

Frame Wall
Right

8

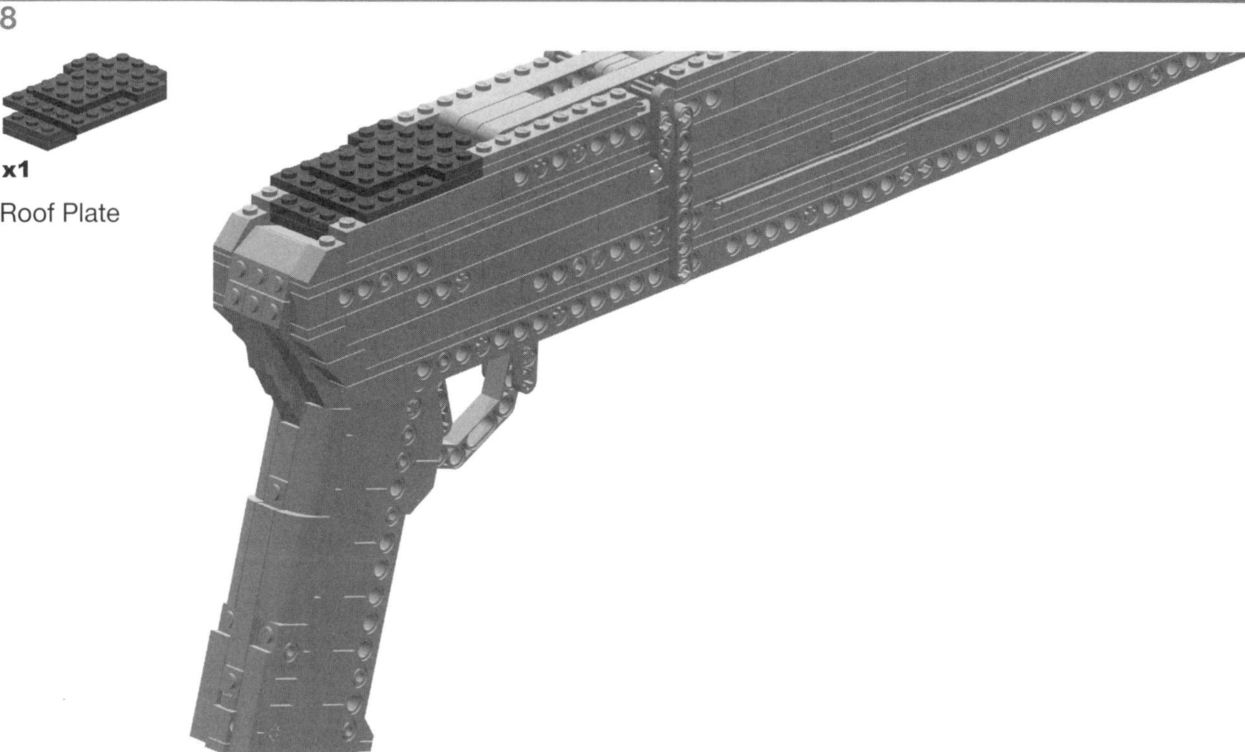

x1

Roof Plate

9

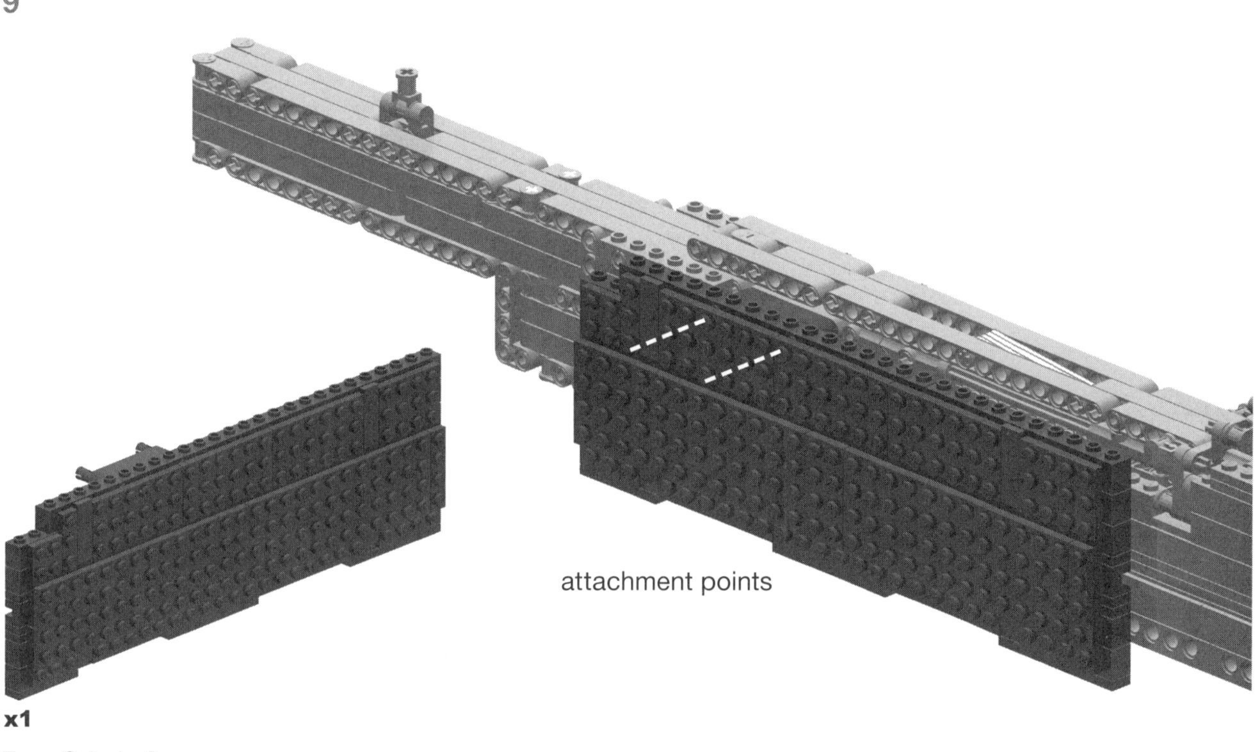

x1

Fore Grip Left

10

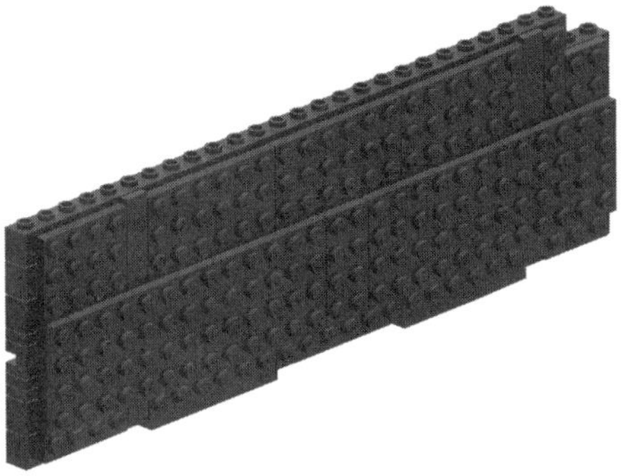

x1

Fore Grip Right

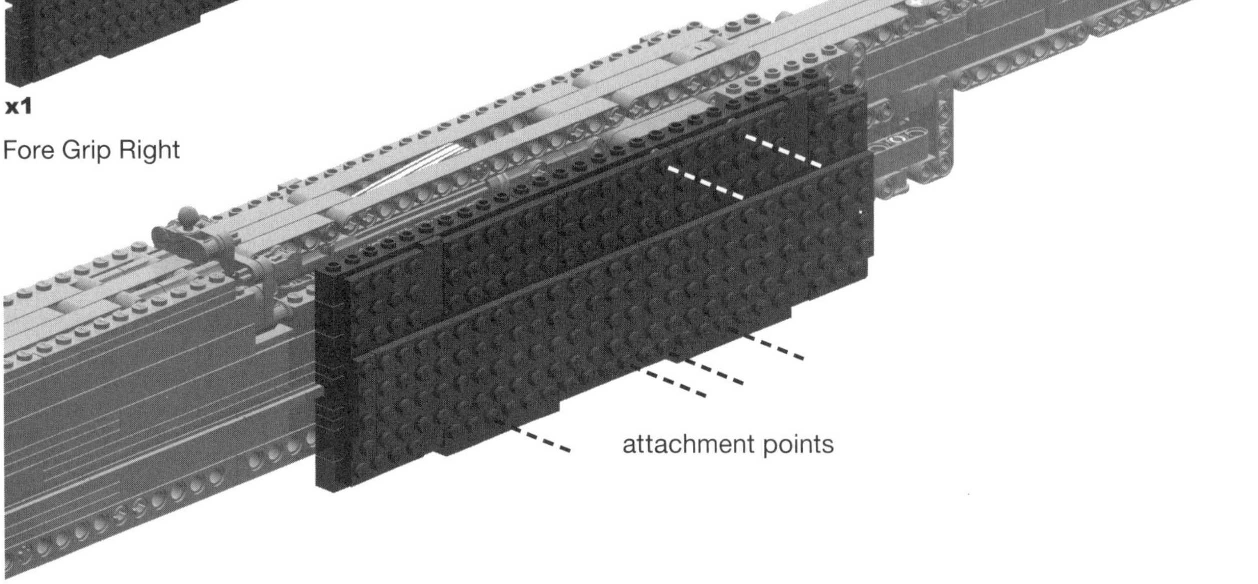

attachment points

11

x1

Fore Grip Plate

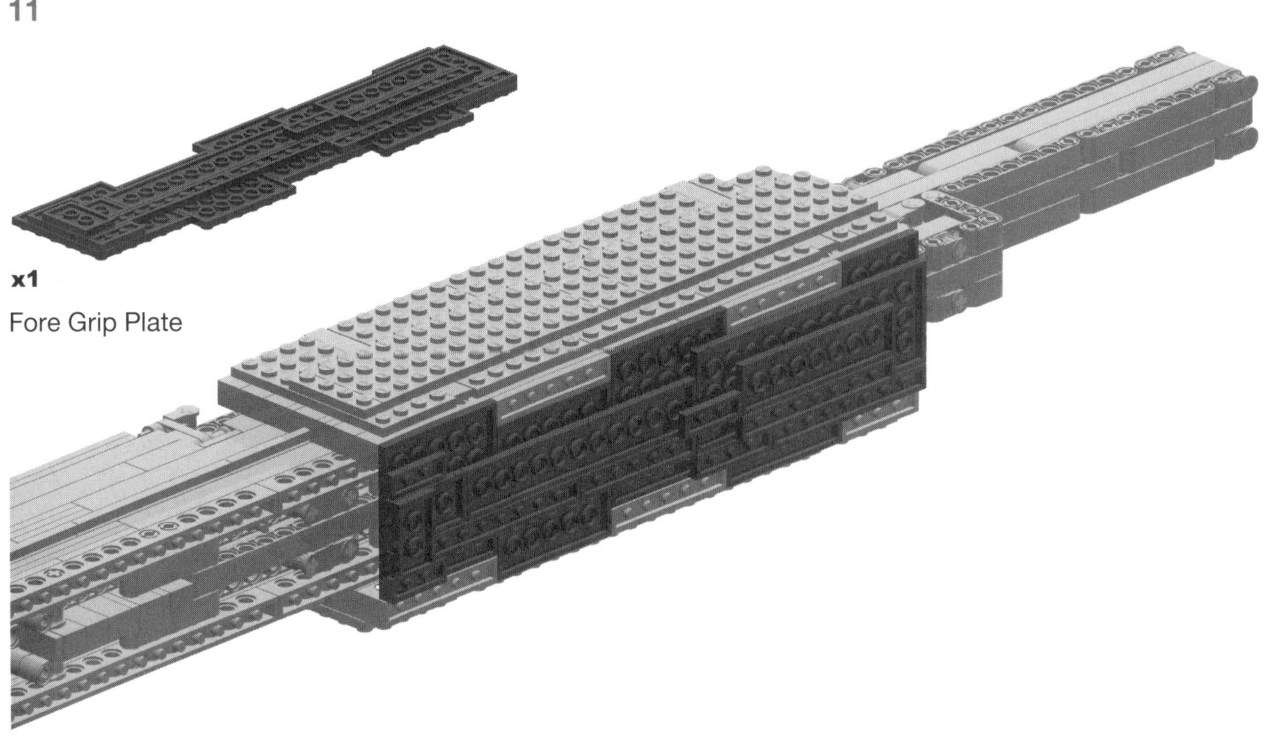

12

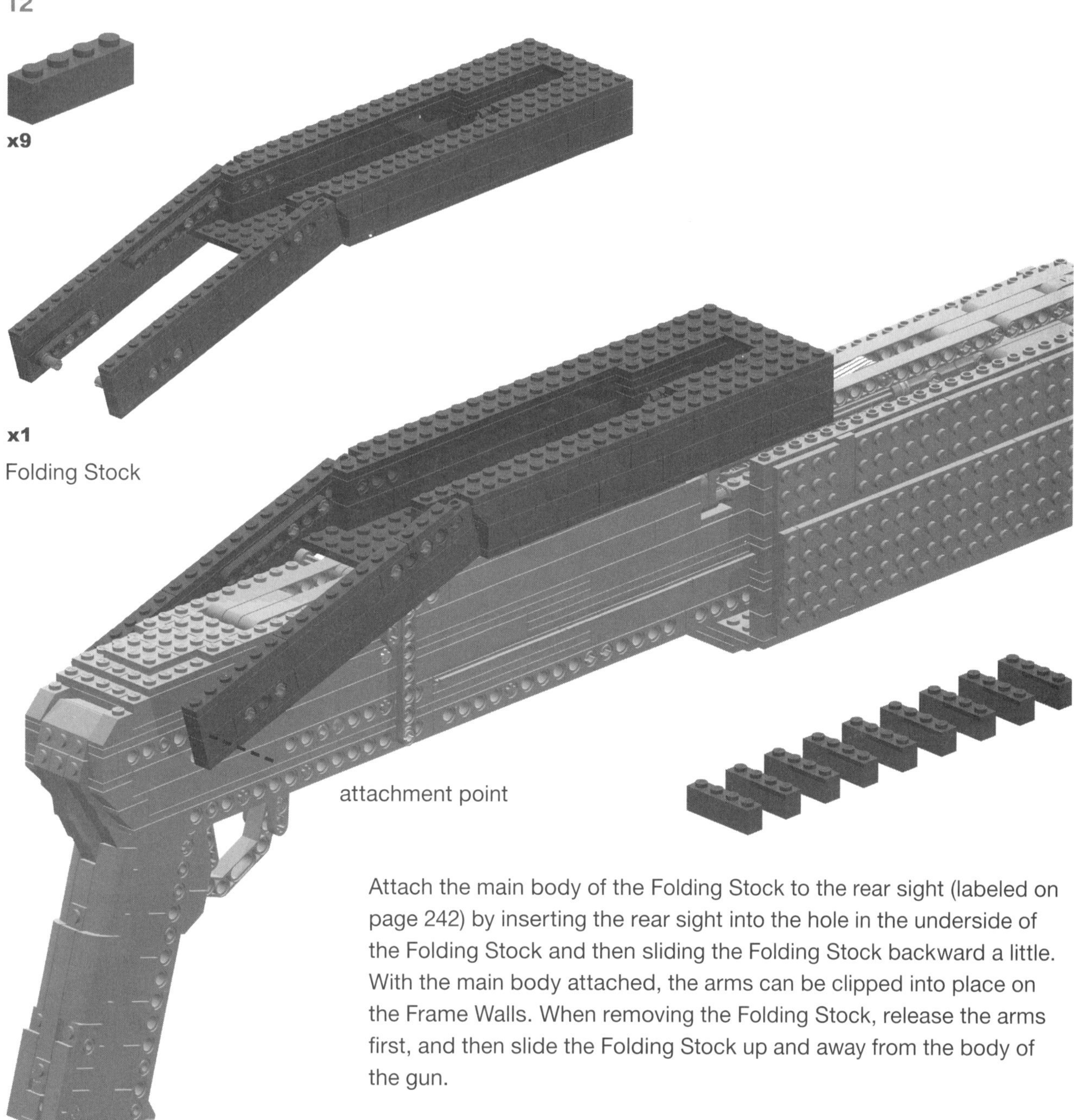

Attach the main body of the Folding Stock to the rear sight (labeled on page 242) by inserting the rear sight into the hole in the underside of the Folding Stock and then sliding the Folding Stock backward a little. With the main body attached, the arms can be clipped into place on the Frame Walls. When removing the Folding Stock, release the arms first, and then slide the Folding Stock up and away from the body of the gun.

When loading the gun, remember to insert the bricks into the Magazine Hatch with *studs facing upward*.

WARNING: *The stock is for aesthetic purposes only, as the LEGO construction would be far too flimsy to withstand the forces needed when cocking the gun. As a result, it can't be used as a normal stock; it's either folded away or not attached at all. When you cock the gun, you'll need to keep pressure on the Pistol Grip—hence its curved rear edges.*

LEGO Heavy Weapons is set in Helvetica Neue. The book was printed and bound at Edwards Brothers Malloy in Ann Arbor, Michigan. The paper is 60# Spring Forge Smooth, which is certified by the Sustainable Forestry Initiative (SFI). The book uses a RepKover binding, which allows it to lie flat when open.

UPDATES

Visit *http://nostarch.com/legoheavyweapons* for updates, errata, and other information.